The European Economy

The global context

Christopher M. Dent

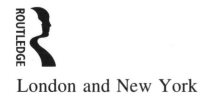

London and New York

First published 1997
by Routledge
11 New Fetter Lane, London EC4P 4EE

Simultaneously published in the USA and Canada
by Routledge
29 West 35th Street, New York, NY 10001

© 1997 Christopher M. Dent

Typeset in Times by
J&L Composition Ltd, Filey, North Yorkshire

Printed and bound in Great Britain by
TJ Press (Padstow) Ltd, Padstow, Cornwall

British Library Cataloguing in Publication Data

A catalogue record for this book is available from the
British Library

Library of Congress Cataloging in Publication Data

Dent, Christopher M.
    The European economy: the global context/Christopher M. Dent.
        p. cm.
    Includes bibliographical references and index.
    1. Europe—Economic conditions. 2. Regionalism—Europe.
    3. Europe—Economic integration. 4. Europe—Commerce.
    5. Technological innovations—Economic aspects—Europe.
    6. Economic forecasting—Europe. I. Title.
    HC240.D453 1997   96–19787
    330.94—dc20

ISBN 0–415–13487–0
        0–415–13488–9 (pbk)

The European Economy

The shape of the world economy is changing. Globalisation and regionalism have led to the development of powerful but interdependent economic blocs. Much economic potential has shifted from the Atlantic to the Pacific area. In view of this *The European Economy: The Global Context* argues that economists need a broader, worldwide base of information if these processes and their effect on Europe are to be fully understood. Topics discussed include:

- Europe's experience of the growing trend of regionalism
- the single market
- plans for economic union
- EU enlargement
- Europe's Triad rivals
- EU external trade and trade relations
- technology and innovation
- foreign direct investment
- human capital issues
- environmental issues

This fresh approach highlights the issues which will challenge European countries into the twenty-first century.

Christopher M. Dent is Senior Lecturer in Economics at the University of Lincolnshire and Humberside.

To Ruth

Contents

Figures

Tables

Boxes

Preface

The idea for this book has been primarily driven by a belief that most current student texts on the European economy have up to now adopted a somewhat introspective approach. In a world economy that is more and more characterised by its global as well as regional interdependence, such an approach could become increasingly untenable. Europe will continue to play an important part in the economic events and developments of the twenty-first century, being both a large constituent part of the world economy and highly integrated into it. The European Union is responsible for over a quarter of total world output and is the largest global trader and investor. Thus it has an enormous influence over the destiny of other countries and regions, especially where the links of interdependence are strongest. Conversely, external forces have played an ever more important part in the development of the European economy itself.

Hence, it has been the main aim of this book to contextualise the European economy within the frame of the growing internationalisation and globalisation of economic activity. In attempting to achieve this I have covered most of the established themes normally found in more conventional texts (e.g. core aspects of European integration and policy). Thus, a parallel aim has been to provide readers with the usual wide grasp of the issues that concern the 'internal' dimension of European economy as well as the 'external'. Indeed, it will be shown that current overlapping forces at work within the European and wider world economy mean that we cannot talk about one without considering the other. This text will therefore have strong appeal both to those studying or teaching conventional type courses on the European economy and to those with a more global orientation.

Chapter 1 explores the nature of the European challenge that lies ahead and introduces some of the key themes that run through the text. The next three chapters analyse the different processes of European integration while providing a global perspective on them. Theoretical, historical and global views on regional integration are covered in Chapter 2. The more advanced stages of European integration are the subject of Chapter 3, namely the single European market (SEM) and the EU's intended plans for economic and monetary union (EMU). On the theme of EU enlargement, Chapter 4 discusses the prospects for widening the EU and the associated ramifications for third countries and regions.

Chapters 5 to 8 consider the wider global context of the European economy. The tripolar or triadic structure of the world economy is the subject of Chapter 5 in which Europe's traditional and newly emergent rivals are examined in close detail. Chapter 6 makes an extensive study of the EU's external trade order. A theoretical and historical analysis of the internationalisation and globalisation is made in Chapter 7, providing a key reference for other chapters and introduction for the chapter that follows. The most dynamic aspect of globalisation – foreign direct investment (FDI) – is investigated in Chapter 8, paying particular attention to Europe's role as host and source of FDI.

In the book's last three chapters, generic topics have been chosen which relate to key challenges facing the European economy. Chapter 9 is concerned with those which lie in the field of technology and innovation, noting many of the fundamental changes to which European organisations have had to adapt. In addition, Europe's own technological performance over recent years is evaluated while also highlighting those high-tech sectors where it must develop a stronger competitive position. Four different aspects of the European economy's human dimension are considered in Chapter 10: unemployment and employment, education and training, the impact of demographic change and social policy issues. The environment is the theme of Chapter 11 in which the ultimate global challenge to Europe and, of course, to other countries and regions, is discussed.

Within most chapters, text boxes have been used to provide overviews of related themes and thus enhance the reader's understanding of the issues covered.

At this point, I would like to clarify certain terms of reference that run through the text. The 'Commission' refers to the European Commission of the European Communities to give it its full title, while 'the Community' has been deployed to signify the European Union, or EU, during its historic precursial guises (i.e. the EEC and EC). Some readers may be confused by the use of the EU as a term that is almost interchangeable with Europe itself. This at times appears out of convenience but also owing to the coalescent function served by the EU on behalf of the European continent. While, admittedly, the EU member states do not yet constitute even half of the European landmass, around 80 to 90 per cent of the European economy's GDP can be attributed to the EU. Moreover, this figure can be expected to rise with the possible accession of new countries into membership by the turn of the century.

Finally, I should like to thank a number of people for the support they have given me while writing this book. I owe a great deal to the staff of my university library, especially Alison and Helen, who have had to deal with a number of my obscure requests and time-consuming tasks. The same must also be said of Freda and Eric 'next door' at Hull's European Documentation Centre. Thanks too to my colleague Pam Barnes for her advice on certain aspects of Chapter 11. I am very much in gratitude to Anna Oakshot at the EBRD who performed the very kind task of faxing through parts of a document that proved key to Chapters 4 and 8. I would also like to extend my gratitude to the Routledge team: Alison Kirk, Kate Smith, Anne Owen and Mo James, and to the copy editor Penny Allport.

Of course, the rigours entailed in an endeavour of this nature are not entirely borne by the one who receives any of the recognition that is forthcoming. I would therefore like to thank my family for their love and support, and in particular my wife who, above all else, has had to cope with an inordinate share of the domestic division of labour over the past year or so.

Cottingham
March 1996

Abbreviations

ACP	Africa Caribbean Pacific
ADD	Anti-dumping duty
AFTA	ASEAN Free Trade Area
APEC	Asia–Pacific Economic Co-operation forum
ASEAN	Association of South-East Asian Nations
CAP	Common Agricultural Policy
CCP	Common Commercial Policy
CEC	Commission of the European Communities
CEDEFOP	Centre for the Development of Vocational Training
CEE	Central and Eastern Europe
CEFTA	Central European Free Trade Area
CET	Common external tariff
CFSP	Common Foreign and Security Policy
CIS	Commonwealth of Independent States
CMEA	Council for Mutual Economic Assistance
CP	Contracting party
CUSFTA	Canada–United States Free Trade Agreement
CVD	Countervailing duty
DG	Directorate-General (of the CEC)
EAEC	East Asian Economic Caucus
EAP	Environmental Action Programme
EBRD	European Bank for Reconstruction and Development
EC	European Community
ECB	European Central Bank
ECIP	European Community Investment Partners
ECSC	European Coal and Steel Community
ECU	European Currency Unit
EDF	European Development Fund
EEA	European Economic Area
EEC	European Economic Community
EFTA	European Free Trade Area
EIA	Environmental Impact Assessment
EIB	European Investment Bank

EMEA	Euro-Mediterranean Economic Area
EMI	European Monetary Institute
EMP	Euro-Med Partnership
EMS	European Monetary System
EMU	Economic and Monetary Union
EPRG	Ethnocentrism–Polycentrism–Regiocentrism–Geocentrism
EPU	Economic and Political Union
ERM	Exchange Rate Mechanism
ESCB	European System of Central Banks
ESF	European Social Fund
E&T	Education and Training
EU	European Union
EWC	European Works Council
FDI	Foreign Direct Investment
FPI	Foreign Portfolio Investment
FTA	Free Trade Area
FTAA	Free Trade Area of the Americas
GATS	General Agreement on Trade in Services
GATT	General Agreement on Tariffs and Trade
GCC	Gulf Co-operation Council
GDP	Gross domestic product
GNP	Gross national product
GPA	Government Procurement Agreement
GSP	Generalised System of Preferences
HEI	Higher Education Institution
IBRD	International Bank for Reconstruction and Development (World Bank)
IGC	Inter-Governmental Conference
ILO	International Labour Organisation
IMF	International Monetary Fund
ISC	International Scientific Co-operation
ITTO	International Tropical Timber Organisation
JESSI	Joint European Sub-micron Silicon Initiative
LDC	Less Developed Country
LLDC	Least Developed Country
M&A	Mergers and Acquisitions
MEA	Multilateral Environmental Agreement
MFA	Multi-Fibre Agreement
MFN	Most Favoured Nation
MITI	Ministry of Industry and International Trade
MNE	Multinational Enterprise
MPD	Modulated Preferential Duty
NAFTA	North American Free Trade Area
NCPI	New Commercial Policy Instrument
NIC	Newly Industrialising Country

NIDL	New International Division of Labour
NTA	New Trans-Atlantic Agenda
NTB	Non-tariff barrier
OCA	Optimum Currency Area
ODA	Official Development Assistance
OECD	Organisation for Economic Co-operation and Development
OEEC	Organisation for European Economic Co-operation
OLI	Ownership–Locational–Internalisation
OMA	Orderly marketing agreement
OPEC	Organisation of Petroleum Exporting Countries
PAFTA	Pacific Free Trade Area
QMV	Qualified majority voting
QRs	Quantitative Restrictions
R&D	Research and Development
RIA	Regional Integration Arrangement
RSE	Research scientists and engineers
SBCD	Second Banking Co-ordination Directive
SEA	Single European Act
SEM	Single European Market
S&T	Science and Technology
STD	Science and Technology for Development
TAD	Trans-Atlantic Declaration
TAFTA	Trans-Atlantic Free Trade Area
TENs	Trans-European Networks
TQM	Total quality management
TREMs	Trade-related environmental measures
TRIMs	Trade-related investment measures
TRIPs	Trade-related intellectual property rights
UN	United Nations
UNCED	United Nations Conference on the Environment and Development
UNCTAD	United Nations Conference on Trade and Development
US	United States
USTR	United States Trade Representative
VER	Voluntary export restraint
WTO	World Trade Organisation

1 Global and regional interdependence
The context of the European challenge

INTRODUCTION

In recent years, the world economy has experienced a series of fundamental changes that has recast the underlying relationships on which it functions. The two principal dynamic forces that have driven this change are regionalism and increasing tendencies towards globalisation. Regionalism involves nation-states forming closer integrational links between them to varying levels of sophistication. These have been mostly formalised through regional integration arrangements (RIAs) or have evolved 'naturally' or informally through a private sector led rise in intra-regional trade, investment and financial flows. Regional co-operation is seen by some as another strand of regionalism which can consist of measures to link up infrastructures, improve the management of common resources or have more overtly political objectives than economic ones.

Globalisation is more difficult to define but can be thought of as the highest form of internationalised economic activity. This has chiefly entailed a deepening and widening of corporate integration both within and between the operations of multinational enterprises (MNEs). Both these trends combined have produced an ever elaborate network of relationships that has simultaneously blurred the demarcations of national borders and the internationalised firm's true identity and origins. Consequently, these developments and continuing reactions to them have created an increasingly interdependent world economy.

Europe has been a major participant in these formative processes. The European Union (EU), which represents fifteen of some of the world's richest nations, is the most advanced RIA that has yet emerged. The EU has also made substantial endeavours both to assist the regional integration of other nations and develop its own inter-regional links with them. European MNEs are among the largest foreign traders and investors whose corporate presence has been well established in every global region. The size of the European market and progressive European integration has itself induced foreign multinationals to locate there in growing numbers.

In trying to comprehend the position of the European economy within the framework of global and regional interdependence an equally critical examination of its contextual features needs to be considered. These comprise of trends and developments that, in unison with regionalism and globalisation, have affected the structural characteristics of the world economy and the conventional wisdom on which new modes of economic activity have been predicated. Hence, they are also reflective of the fundamental changes that have been engendered by the two dynamic forces. Such features and the challenges that lie therein include:

- The triad structure of world economic superpowers: consisting of the EU, the USA and Japan which together still dominate world trade and investment flows and constitute the major poles of economic wealth. The gravitational pull of these powers has resulted in stronger regionalism, for example, EU enlargements, the North American Free Trade Agreement (NAFTA) and the Asia–Pacific Economic Co-operation (APEC) forum. The Europe–Japan/East Asia link in triadic relationships remains, though, by far the weakest.
- The rise of the 'new competition': a number of developing economies, most notably from East Asia, have acquired newly industrialising country (NIC) status in post-war years. For some time they have undermined the competitive advantage of many European producers in labour-intensive, low-tech industries. However, many NICs have now begun to compete in higher value-added sectors spurred on by regional developments, the enabling role played by globalisation and a more integral multilateral trading system.
- The advent of new techno-industrial paradigms: the growth industries of the future appear to rest on the core technology clusters that have formed around information technologies, biotechnologies and new material sciences. The microchip revolution has brought about radical changes to how industrial activity is organised and co-ordinated, both in the workplace and on a cross-border basis. A wider socio-economic impact is also associated with the emergence of the information society.
- The improved management of knowledge and human resources: as a consequence of the above, companies, governments and other organisations have had to adopt a new approach to managing knowledge and human resources. The imperative to develop effective capabilities in knowledge-intensive industries and other activities requires a higher priority to be given to education and training.
- Establishing more sustainable patterns of economic development: the planet has had to bear severe ecological pressures that have originated from an accumulation of environmental malpractices. Most current scientific studies suggest that new patterns of development are necessary to avert global ecological collapse. European and other industrial nations have up to now been largely responsible for these pressures,

though developing countries are becoming increasingly answerable on a global scale. This is particularly pronounced where past established patterns have been emulated and growth rates are high.
- The market-oriented pluralist democracy as the leading credible model of economic development: this has led from the large-scale retreat of communism, most notably in Central and Eastern Europe (CEE), and the general implementation of more market friendly policies and practices across countries of diverse economic backgrounds.

In this opening chapter, we shall examine the nature of the European response, both actual and potential, to these challenges. Owing to the coalescent function performed by the EU and its dominance of the European economy, it will take the centre stage of our analysis. We will show that heightening global and regional interdependence and their contextual features has revealed the greater necessity for both:

- improving competitiveness against traditional and new rivals;
- extending or creating collaborative relations with accordant regional or national partners.

Although tensions may arise in balancing these two objectives, we shall also demonstrate that the latter has taken on a primary strategic role in helping to secure the former while consolidating European interests in a broader sense. Thus, a major theme emphasised in our analysis will be the strategic determinants that continue to underlie those actions taken by European business leaders and policy-makers alike in their efforts to meet those challenges.

THE TWIN FORCES OF REGIONALISM AND GLOBALISATION

The growth of regionalism

The development of stronger regional links between proximate countries will, of course, engender a higher degree of interdependence between them. They have also lent to global interdependence where RIAs have nurtured collaborative relations with others. Even among those states which have recently acquired independent status a concurrent aspiration to be part of regionalist initiatives can be noted. For example, the Baltic states and Slovenia have all expressed a wish to join the new Central European Free Trade Area (CEFTA). Institutionalised regionalism between participating members is most likely to commence with the objective of installing a free trade area, whereby tariffs are eliminated between them but each country retains the ability to set its own tariff rates on external imports. These, however, are harmonised within a customs union with the introduction of a common external tariff. Common or internal markets and monetary unions are respectively more progressive forms of RIAs which commit members both to remove further impediments to factor movements and converge their sets of regulations, standards and policies.

The economic attraction of joining such an arrangement lies in the static and dynamic gains that are internally generated and shared. Generally speaking, these include the wider scope for efficiency gains, market opportunities and the acquisition of key strategic assets. Implementing a successful RIA will depend on accommodating its members' strengths and weaknesses. The presence of significant incompatibilities can lead to the arrangement having to embrace a 'variable geometry' approach whereby different integrational schedules and agendas are set within the group. As the 1990s have progressed, this has become more and more relevant and applicable to the EU's plans for future economic and monetary union (EMU).

The RIA is largely a post-war phenomenon and throughout this period Europe has provided the template for most other aspiring regional groupings. The inauguration of the single European market (SEM) programme, the devising of plans for EMU and the international stature of the EU have made it not only the predominant RIA in Europe but also within the world. Regional agreements have become very popular among nation-states, particularly in very recent years with 33 of the total 108 RIAs that have been notified to the General Agreement on Tariffs and Trade (GATT) Secretariat since 1948 being signed in the early 1990s (see Figure 2.4, p. 47).

While an RIA can be mainly understood in terms of an internally focused, organisational body of countries its external impact and dimension is of great consequence. This can be most clearly illustrated by briefly charting the progress of the EU since its conception in the 1950s. Even the earliest stages of regionalism could be interpreted as a strategic reaction to the shift in geo-political power that had relatively disadvantaged the international position of Western Europe. This shift was gradually redressed by combining a wider range of activities and attracting new members to its core. The urgency of completing market integration and to realise the benefits it afforded was further underlined by the rise of new sources of competition, first from Japan and later on from the NICs. Fears of the SEM programme creating a 'Fortress Europe' in which the market it created was guarded by high protectionist walls and access granted through reciprocity agreements were subsequently articulated by outsiders. As it transpired these fears have been largely unfounded, as we shall discuss in later chapters, although certain defensive mechanisms have been installed.

The most important global effect of RIAs concerns the breaking down of the world economy into separate and sometimes overlapping regional blocs and the implications conveyed for the multilateral trade order. Those analysts who are opposed to the proliferation of regional agreements argue that both sets of relations cannot co-exist owing to the inherent tensions that lie between them. This is based on the belief that regional groups tend to protect their own internally liberalised markets by deploying high tariffs against third country imports.

A corollary of this is replacement of rule-based international relations, upon which multilateralism depends to function effectively, with power-based relations which ultimately endangers it. Moreover, welfare losses can arise through trade diversion (see Chapter 2) which would have been avoided if regional trade concessions were converted at a multilateral level. It is further argued that the stability of the world trade system is placed at greater risk by RIAs as they act as a safe haven to which its members tactically retreat when faith in multilateralism has been effectively undermined (Bhagwati 1990, 1992).

Conversely, the case for compatibility between formalised regionalism and multilateralism is founded on the notion that RIAs have provided the essential building blocks with which global free trade can be constructed (Lawrence 1991). However, this rests on the assumption that internal liberalisation is matched by equivalent actions in any external regimes. Expectations of such behaviour originate from the hypothesis that what is preached at home will be practised elsewhere. For instance, the liberal mindedness inculcated from the installation of the SEM programme is thought to have had a positive influence upon the Uruguay Round of GATT talks with which it coincided (Woolcock 1993). Where regional integration has been accomplished by the maintenance of liberal external regimes then this has been favourably termed 'open regionalism'. This objective has even been recently endorsed by the World Trade Organisation (WTO 1995).

The active participation of open-minded RIAs in multilateral negotiations can also simplify them by the fact that fewer contracting parties are now involved. This was shown at the Uruguay Round when the European Commission acted as the interlocutor on behalf of the EU member states. Some regional arrangements may have also introduced liberalisation measures in advance of those that are moderated at a multilateral level in the future. The convergence of the EU's policy rules on foreign investment and competition could provide the WTO with advantageous starting-points in these respective fields if competence is to be granted over them in the future.

The formation of regional agreements has surfaced in all global regions and only countries with the most autarkic inclinations have remained non-signatories to them (see Table 1.1). Their strength relies on the economic capability and relations that exist between member states, in addition to a common political will. Consequently, the most developed forms of regionalism and those that demonstrate the highest potential are located in relatively prosperous global regions. Hence, the triadic structure of the world economy and the regional links that have been built around it are seen by some as mutually reinforcing to each other.

Table 1.1 Major regional integration arrangements (actual and planned)

RIA	Members	Main features
European Union (EU)	Austria, Belgium, Denmark, Finland, France, Germany, Greece, Ireland, Italy, Luxembourg, Netherlands, Portugal, Spain, Sweden, UK.	Common market more or less complete by the end of 1992. Plans to establish EMU between at least some members by 1999 are still intact but have been beset by both political and economic circumspection. A future enlargement into central and eastern Europe has also been scheduled. Currently the world's largest trading bloc and unified market.
European Free Trade Area (EFTA)	Iceland, Liechtenstein, Norway, Switzerland.	Established in 1960 as a looser regional arrangement to the EU's precursor, EFTA has experienced a gradual haemorrhage of its members to the former. This has recently culminated in the accession of three of its largest members to the EU in 1995. The European Economic Area enables the EFTA states to participate in most aspects of the SEM programme.
North American Free Trade Agreement (NAFTA)	Canada, USA, Mexico.	Signed in 1993 with a commitment to inaugurate a free trade area within 15 years. Some policy convergence in areas such as foreign investment, public procurement, the environment and labour standards.
Free Trade Area of the Americas (FTAA)	34 countries from the American continent (Cuba not a member).	The December 1994 summit laid out draft plans to install a free trade area across the continent by 2005.
Mercosur	Argentina, Brazil, Paraguay, Uruguay.	The most significant regional agreement to have emerged in Latin America. First conceived in 1991 with the Southern Cone Common Market set up by 1995. This, though, is more approximate to a customs union with a near complete common external tariff and some macro-economic policy co-ordination.

Association of South East Asian Nations (ASEAN)	Brunei, Indonesia, Malaysia, Philippines, Singapore, Thailand, Vietnam.	Formed in 1967 but whose initial objectives were more political than economic. Since 1977 a preferential trade agreement has covered an increasing number of sectors. In 1995, the idea of creating a free trade area (AFTA) by 2003 was accepted.
Asia–Pacific Economic Co-operation forum (APEC)	ASEAN, Australia, Chile, China, Hong Kong, Japan, NAFTA, New Zealand, Papua New Guinea, South Korea, Taiwan.	First formed in 1989 but took until its 1993 summit to make any progress towards any reciprocated trade concessions of note. An ambitious future agenda was set at the 1994 summit with intentions to establish a gradualised free trade area by 2020. Raised doubt over such plans concern the diversity of member countries and a number of serious internal disputes that continue to persist.

In East Asia, where institutionalised regionalism has remained weak, a more informal path to regional integration has occurred through the dynamic expansion of its economy. North American countries currently participate in their own specific RIA and two other overlapping arrangements, thus raising the degree of complexity with respect to regional and global interdependence. The variable geometry that is also evident could be the cause of considerable inconsistencies, arising from potentially conflicting integrational policies and political–economic objectives.

The Pacific Free Trade Area envisaged by the APEC forum and the possibility of a future transatlantic counterpart would leave only the European–East Asian arrangement to complete a triadic framework of trade liberalisation. A scenario of this kind cannot be ruled out for the same reason that it cannot be held as credible. Future plans to establish deeper regional integrational links in all parts of the Triad are dependent on a series of imponderable factors. These become more significant both in relation to the ambitiousness of those plans and the long-range schedules that are trajected for them. The member states of the EU have recently encountered this with the Maastricht Treaty's programme for economic and monetary union.

Moves towards globalisation

For most of history the internationalisation of economic activity has been typified by the exporting and importing of products between countries. The post-war acceleration of trade intensified this trend; more importantly newer kinds of international exchange began to alter the complexion of the world economy and internationalisation itself. Foreign direct investment (FDI), whereby multinationals have sought to establish both control and ownership of assets that exist beyond the home country of origin, is the most notable of these. Indeed, this is what essentially defines an MNE. The dispersion of a company's operations across national borders has made it more difficult to determine its own nationality while also threading the links of global interdependence between countries by integrating them into the systems of international production.

In more recent times, this have been achieved through complex integration strategies where the firm has often resembled more a network than a hierarchy, facilitated by international subcontracting, licensing agreements, strategic alliances and other forms of corporate linkage. The integrity of the firm has remained simultaneously intact while it orchestrates these network relationships from a centralised or decentralised command structure.

The latter of these – international strategic alliances – entail firms collaborating together at differing levels of commitment in activities that are designed to render mutual benefits, and hence are orchestrated jointly. They are not a new phenomenon (Kindleberger 1988), but their increased frequency and centrality to the core strategies of many companies make them particularly relevant when understanding MNE behaviour. Multiple participants may be involved in such co-operative ventures from various locations and tend to arise in industries with high entry costs, scale economies and rapidly changing technologies. In many ways they reflect interdependent reactions to compete within oligopolistic market structures with the added significance of the international or global level at which they are pitched. Pressures to collaborate in order to compete are partially founded on the more risk averse strategy this composes.

The multinational enterprise is essentially the product of modern times. Revolutionary technological advances in communications, transport and production have enabled firms to co-ordinate and configurate their actions across different international locations, partly through being able to adapt to the prevailing factoral and market conditions encountered. The cost competitiveness of producing standardised products and the convergence of international consumption patterns have also proved lucrative. Moreover, expansion into a more global competitive environment has been made possible through the MNE's utilisation of certain advantages (Dunning 1983, 1988). These fall into three generic categories:

1 Ownership-specific: these may be derived from the company's size (e.g. economies of scale and scope) and the ownership of intangible assets (e.g. proprietary technologies, skills, knowledge).
2 Location-specific: examples can range from the ability to obtain inputs of a higher quality, lower price or general strategic value; conducive

government policies and infrastructural factors; the spatial distribution of markets.

3 Internalisation: internalised transactions within the firm have at times proven more attractive than external market transactions for factor inputs, final products and technological exchange and transfer. The effective use of market power and differentiation policies further enables MNEs to internalise benefits and gives incentive to integrate production and service facilities internationally.

A successful exploitation of these advantages by multinational firms has incurred radical structural changes on the world economy, especially when the corporate strategies deployed have progressed past the 'stand alone' and 'simple integration' stages (see Figure 1.1 and Table 1.2). More 'complex integration' strategies have redefined the manner in which international production is managed and organised by 'turning their geographically dispersed affiliates and fragmented production systems into regionally or globally integrated production and distribution networks' (UN 1994a: 138). As a result of this exploitation and the subsequent changes for which they have been responsible, the MNE has come to

Table 1.2 The strategies and structures of multinational enterprises

Strategy	*Intra-firm linkages*	*Foreign affiliate type*	*Degree of integration*	*Environment*
Stand-alone (e.g. multi-domestic).	Ownership, technology, finance; mostly uni-directional.	Miniature replica of the parent firm.	Weak.	Host country accessible to foreign direct investment; trade barriers; costly communications and transportation.
Simple integration (e.g. outsourcing).	Ownership, technology, markets, finance, other inputs; mostly bi-directional; subcontracting.	Rationalised producer of one or a few elements in the value chain.	Strong at some points of value chain, weak in others.	Open trade and FDI regimes, at least bilaterally; non-equity arrangements permissible.
Complex integration at the regional or global levels (e.g. networks).	All functions; mostly multi-directional.	Product or process specialist; functional specialisation.	Potentially strong throughout value chain.	Open trade, technology FDI and related regimes; use of advanced information technology; convergence in tastes, heightened competition, low communication and transportation costs.

Source: Adapted from UN 1994a: 137

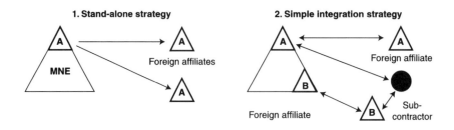

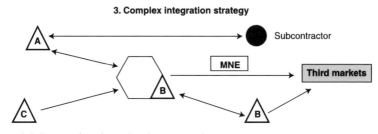

Figure 1.1 International production strategies
Source: UN 1994a: 136. UNCTAD, Division on Transnational Corporations and Investment, *World Investment Report 1994, Transnational Corporations, Employment and the Workplace* (United Nations, Sales No. E. 94. II. A. 14) fig. I.1 and fig. II.2

represent the predominant form of corporate organisation. This is supported by the observation of a few simple facts. One estimate suggests that the top 500 MNEs account for nearly three-quarters of international trade and about half of world output. Around 40 per cent of international trade flows are thought to occur at the intra-firm level, that is trade between the divisions and subsidiaries of the same firm (OECD 1992a). Many multinationals have annual products that are proximate to some of the smaller developed nations.

It should, however, be noted that the global reach of most MNEs remains somewhat limited with most only active in a few countries while the operations of even the largest are still epitomised by their regionalised concentration (see Table 8.2, p. 269). The endurance of such trends undermines the notion of a globalised world economy, although the latter makes for greater interdependence at the regional level. However, an extrapolation of current general trends in international trade and FDI flows (over the last decade or so, FDI has grown four times faster than world output and three times that of international trade) together with the current evolutionary path of how international production is being organised provides, at minimal, the basis for a more complete globalisation of economic activity in the future.

Further support for this view has come from the recent surge of inward FDI flows to developing countries, particularly in the East Asian region, due to the growing locational and strategic attractions of a low cost base and future market prosperity. Foreign investments, together with international subcontracting and other collaborative ventures, have played a crucial part in integrating these countries into the world economic system.

A world economy in which a rising number of developing countries are reaching NIC status and simultaneously becoming more fully participative in moves towards globalisation has posed a series of challenges for the Triad powers. These challenges take different but strongly related forms. As the techno-industrial base of an NIC is upgraded so is its capability to compete more effectively in higher value-added sectors. In order to maintain their competitive position, firms from developed market economies are faced with a number of options.

To compete on the same cost and price terms is the most untenable option owing to the considerable comparative disadvantages now faced, for example on labour and certain other factor input costs. Where possible, a shift to value-added activities within the industry, or those related, which are at least a grade above those being entered by the NICs, would enable the firm to develop new, more unassailable competitive strengths. This would depend on both its technological and managerial capabilities as well as access to a better educated and trained labour force able to handle higher degrees of knowledge-intensive work. The combination of such a strategy with one whereby specific elements of the value-added chain are outsourced to NIC producers constitutes a deeper recognition of global interdependence. This may go deeper still if foreign investment is driven by strategic market motivations in addition to those of cost competitiveness. Intensified competition at home will naturally supply the extra provocation to follow this approach.

As this text will make clear in subsequent chapters, European companies have performed poorly in meeting many of these challenges. They have been relatively slow to take advantage of the investment opportunities that are being presented, especially in the more distant poles of new economic growth. Levels of new investment have even been disappointing with respect to those opportunities that exist closest to home, namely in the 'transitional' economies of Central and Eastern Europe. The response of certain sectors of European business to the threat of the 'new competition' from the NICs has also been criticised by those who highlight the restructuring still required more fully to adapt to global competitive realities. Furthermore, Europe maintains a competitive advantage in comparatively few high-tech, high-growth industries where the industrial battleground between the Triad economies will be the fiercest in decades to come. Thus, there are a number of fronts on which Europe needs to raise its level of endeavour to meet the challenge of global interdependence. We shall soon turn to those strategies that are being formulated with this intention in mind.

The interface between the twin forces

There are strong interconnections between regionalism and globalisation that cover a variety of issues and draw on similar motivational forces. Actions leading to the advancement of both can, at a general level, be interpreted as risk averse, strategic responses to counter apparent extraneous pressures while consolidating a more impregnable defence against them and any other future potential threats. These will include efforts to improve the efficiency, competitiveness and international stature of those parties involved and collaborative enterprises with compatible partners.

Such an approach is further to be expected in a world economy where global and regional interdependence both feed on themselves and each other. A policy of risk aversion pursued through collaboration or diversification is made more critical by the increasing number of permutations arising from greater degrees of interdependency existing between affected parties. This can be shown by the convoluted network of international strategic alliances which has evolved, especially in high-tech industries, and the overlapping regional agreements entered into by countries which can induce similar complex outcomes. The process is self-perpetuating as efforts to collaborate and diversify as part of both defensive and offensive strategies only serve to generate more permutations faced by all parties.

Extra complications are added by the mutually reinforcing effects that regionalism and globalisation can have on one another. In the last twenty-five years, world trade has risen by a factor of twelve, but trade among regional groups increased by a factor of seventeen, largely due to the stimulus given by market integration processes. Hence, internationalised firms will seek more extensive access to these markets through exporting or targeted FDI. The erection of protectionist walls by regional members around their markets will only award more incentive to seek an 'insider' position through inward foreign investments. Motives to develop a position of this kind are heightened by the dynamic efficiencies that are conferred by regional integration. These may be used to the benefit of the company in that regional market or in another if the cost efficiencies acquired can be put to purpose elsewhere. The marked acceleration of Japanese inward FDI to Europe, which coincided with the implementation of the SEM programme, and the huge inflows of US investment that preceded earlier stages of European integration have been strongly associated here. Strong evidence suggests that a positive relationship exists between regional integration and FDI inflows.

An acknowledgement of this has partially motivated countries regionally to integrate. In most circumstances, inward foreign investment is generally accepted to have a significant beneficial effect upon the host economy through accompanying technology transfers, the implementation and diffusion of superior management and production techniques, employment growth and the injection of new capital. Regionalised efforts to attract third country multinationals have also entailed the use of supporting measures and policies, for instance tax allowances and a more simplified regulatory environment for business. However, the foreign operations of MNEs are also frequently subject to various constraints that either aim to check any potential abuse of their market power or extract optimum benefits from their activities (e.g. rules on local content). While these are still mainly administered at a national level, many of the major RIAs have made recent moves towards their regionalised harmonisation. This has largely been accomplished through the establishment of investment codes that themselves may be soon negotiated at a multilateral level.

Given the existence of a more open and interdependent global competitive environment, the view that neighbouring countries need to work together mutually to improve their competitiveness has been increasingly subscribed to. This has supplied a prime economic motivation behind the SEM programme and its core objectives. It may, therefore, seem ironic that such closer regional integration may benefit third country producers either directly if they have acquired 'insider' status through foreign investments, or indirectly through the growth-induced demand for imports. This must be balanced by the improved competitive position of the regional members both in their own collective market and those outside it. Globalisation makes it more and more difficult, though, to disaggregate the economic activities of producers with domestic origins from those that are foreign. Hence, regional integration can only generate potential gains for the combined community of enterprises that functions within its own borders. Attempts may be made in certain strategic sectors to close off the participation of external producers in specific areas, such as the EU's ESPRIT programme on information technologies. Global interdependence has made this approach a more arduous task which, in the case of ESPRIT, was clearly illustrated by the international strategic alliance that Siemens (a key participant in the project) had formed with IBM and Toshiba in the early 1990s.

We have already mentioned that national and harmonised regional policies have been adapted to meet the challenges posed by globalisation. There has also been the need for policy convergence between regional and national powers as economic activities have become more globally dispersed. This has already been well established in the field of trade policy under the auspices of the GATT and now the WTO multilateral framework. Other newer policy areas that have become more relevant include those on competition and foreign investment. As trade barriers have been successively removed and markets more comprehensively integrated so have the remaining domestic level impediments to international competition and cross-border investments been made more transparent. The low import and inward investment penetration made by foreign companies into Japan has been attributed to such impediments that have been termed as 'structural' in nature. Multinationals that have developed a dominant market position straddling more than one regional market present a prima facie case for cooperation on competition policy between the authoritative powers involved. This recently occurred with the respective Trans-Atlantic authorities over the Microsoft case of 1994.

Similarly, MNEs require a degree of commonality to be applied on competition and investment rules for the sake of consistency and predictability. This may also apply to other policy fields, for example on environmental protection and labour standards. A further obligation that rests with governments to converge on policy relates to how companies will seek to exploit certain inconsistencies that advantage them to the detriment of either the host country or those that are indirectly affected. Convergence would to some extent help avoid power-based inter-regional or international relations developing in the future by its provision of a firmer rule-based framework. Parts of this are already in place or soon will be. Since the 1980s, the OECD Secretariat has supplied non-mandatory codes of conduct on competition and foreign investment policy at a plurilateral level. The WTO should serve in a stronger multilateral function for these to be negotiated in forthcoming years. However, a plurilateral approach between the developed countries of the OECD group may prove more appropriate as many developing countries would be unable to bear specific burdens which compliance would incur.

Finally, global networking at an inter-regional as well as a corporate level could well become a main feature of a globally interdependent world economy. This is likely to arise in areas where mutual strategic advantage can be jointly advanced, for example, through scientific and technological cooperation. Motive may also come from the priority to form closer political and cultural ties between the regional groups involved or collaborate on solving commonly held or global problems; for instance, population ageing and environmental degradation.

THE EUROPEAN RESPONSE: IMPROVING COMPETITIVENESS AND PROMOTING COLLABORATION

We have already exposed many of the important challenges for the European economy in the interdependent world economy. Let us now consider the two broad and overlaying categories into which they fall, these being the need to improve European competitiveness and establish firmer collaborative relations with accordant regional and national partners. Frequently, the objective of meeting the challenges bound in one category has been congruent with realising those in the other. This has particularly applied where inter-regional or third country co-operation has both enabled European business to strengthen the competitive position and, together with policy-makers, exert considerable influence over any ensuing rule-based structures designed to govern the new global economy. Thus, European responses to global and regional interdependence have taken on a distinct strategic dimension when meeting both types of challenge.

Improving European competitiveness

Despite the post-war technological and industrial advances that helped reassert the European economy's status in the world, by the 1980s the term 'Eurosclerosis' had come to denote a cumulative inertness displayed in a wide range of its sectors and a general lack of dynamic growth potential. These were symptomatic of flagging European competitiveness and deep structural constraints that would continue to disadvantage European business if they persisted. Changes taking place within the new global competitive environment only served to amplify Europe's problems: the USA extended its dominance across many high-tech industries and international markets; the industrial prowess of Japanese producers continued to be demonstrated in a growing number of activities; in lower technology sectors the NICs were progressively strengthening their competitive advantage.

However, the revitalisation of the common market concept and the resulting SEM programme which embodied it has supplied some antidotal relief to Europe's failing condition. While deeper regional integration still lies at the centre of the EU's struggle to improve its competitiveness, other key initiatives have been required to act in a fortifying and complementary manner. These have mainly arisen in the fields of science and technology, human capital development, various forms of industrial policy and measures aimed at enhancing social as well as economic cohesion across the Union.

The beginnings of a more coherent approach to improving European competitiveness that also made fuller acknowledgement of global and regional interdependence came in the form of a 1990 Commission study document (CEC 1990a). Its main aim was clearly to establish the division of responsibilities between business and public authorities in creating a dynamic environment favourable for industrial development. Furthermore, it called for a marked departure from the defensive, protectionist sectoral approaches that had been previously adhered to. According to the Commission, this made it possible to: accept the realities of global interdependence; highlight the problem of different national approaches to similar problems; devise a more modern approach on industrial policy.

This was followed in June 1993 by the European Council asking the Commission to prepare a broad-ranging policy position culminating in a White Paper that set out a medium-term development strategy for growth, competitiveness and employment. The White Paper was presented a few months later in December (CEC 1993a) and has since provided the main analytical focus on the structural problems confronting the European economy as well as a framework of measures aimed at resolving them. With the

Box 1.1 Gauging an economy's competitiveness

Attempts to measure the competitive position of an economy relative to others is a complex task, made even more so by the processes of globalisation and regionalism. The OECD's (1992d: 242) own definition of national competitiveness describes it as the ability to "meet the test of international markets while simultaneously maintaining and expanding the real incomes of its citizens". Traditionally, competitiveness has been expressed in either microeconomic or macroeconomic terms.

The microeconomic or firm level approach comprises of an examination of product price, quality, design, technological content, after-sales service and the extent to which these aspects are being commercially exploited. Comparative profitability and debt levels, foreign and domestic market shares in internationalised markets and other indicators can be used to gauge competitiveness. An evaluation of more dynamic processes may include the effective exploitation of economies of scale and scope, the installation of new flexible production techniques and the relative product lead times (i.e. the time taken to develop and produce new products). Measuring macroeconomic competitiveness requires a consideration of general price and unit costs levels throughout the economy, its exchange and interest rates and the relative stability of the macroeconomic environment.

The firm's competitive capabilities are partly determined by its own interaction with those capabilities which are predisposed within national or regional systems (Ostry 1990). This not only refers to those shaped by macroeconomic conditions but a miscellaneous range of structural features found within the economy. These in themselves may be quite unique and unable to be replicated elsewhere, or may arise through a combination of factors that are mutually reinforcing (see Porter 1990). Such features can be infrastructural, cultural, economic, institutional or technological in nature. Consequently, efforts to define an economy's 'structural' competitiveness have been more highly prioritised in recent times.

assistance of this document, we shall mainly examine the issue of European competitiveness.

In its opening pages, the Paper insisted that there was no miracle cure nor were reversion to protectionism, a dash for economic liberalisation, drastic cuts in labour costs and social provisions to form any part of strategies to be implemented. This paid respect to the conventional wisdom underpinning the 1990 study document, while alluding that Europe's 'social market' model was not to be ditched in favour of another (e.g. the US's 'free market' counterpart) but rather re-engineered. Growth, competitiveness and employment were perceived as mutually reinforcing economic objectives. The latter of these was given especial relevance by the fact that the White Paper's overarching objective was the creation of fifteen million new European jobs by the end of the decade.

Employment growth was seen as a key component in any future competitiveness strategy while simultaneously ensuring that economic and social progress went hand in hand, in keeping with the social market model. Recent European performance on employment growth had been comparatively poor. By 1994, this was reflected by an EU unemployment rate of 11.2 per cent that was nearly twice that for the USA (6.1 per cent) and around four times greater than Japan's rate of 2.9 per cent (see Figure 1.2). A reversion of these trends was necessary to reduce the considerable drag factor that high rates of unemployment were placing on European competitiveness. Not only did this situation represent a significant loss to current and potential growth but also the incurrence of large public and social costs on the European economy. Moreover, the issue of how Europe manages its human resources lay at the centre of other related challenges. Forthcoming demographic changes, most notably population ageing, add further imperative for more flexible forms of work organisation to be introduced and a re-examination of social policy. Technological change and the rise of the new competition require a European workforce that is adept with more knowledge-intensive forms of industrial activity. This too carries important implications for the way in which education and training systems are resourced and organised. Improving the employability of European labour was thus crucial, particularly in the new growth industries of the next century.

To achieve these ends and generally enhance the EU's competitive position in the world economy, the White Paper drew together a combination of measures, the vast majority of which were to be implemented at member state level. The proposals were largely non-binding, although their main objectives were accepted as strategically critical if not somewhat ambitious in some cases. In broad terms, these measures were covered under the following themes:

- New patterns of practice in labour markets and the management of human resources: the implementation of more flexible work arrangements through the removal or adjustment of regulations causing labour market rigidities, less passive and more active labour market policies (e.g. training) and the promotion of other initiatives conducive to creating employment. The reduction of non-wage labour costs (target amount of 1–2 per cent of GDP equivalent) and greater moderation in wage payments, particularly in labour-intensive industries, to help stimulate employment growth. A stronger emphasis placed on human capital investment and lifelong learning.
- Large scale infrastructure projects: to help to optimise the benefits of regional integration and ensure greater economic and social cohesion in the EU. These were primarily aimed at accelerating the establishment of Trans-European Networks (TENs) in transport, energy and

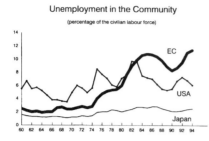

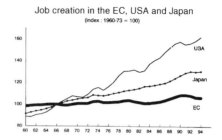

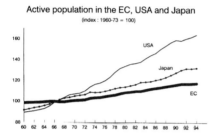

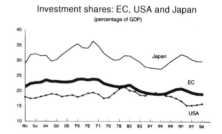

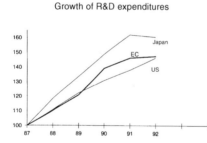

Figure 1.2 Competitiveness indicators: Europe and the Triad
Source: Compilation of evidence from GCE White Paper, CEC 1993a

communications that relied on a mobilisation of funds that nearly amounted to ECU 400bn up to the year 2000. In addition to these were environmental projects valued at a total ECU 174bn over a similar period that were intended as part of a new 'sustainable' development paradigm. Finance for these measures was to be raised mainly at member state level through both private and public capital, with the EU committing structural funds and new 'Union Bonds' (subsequently withdrawn) in support.

- More balanced and co-ordinated macroeconomic policies across the EU: this was essential to restore the confidence and stability in the European economy. Moves towards the convergence criteria of EMU on public finances, exchange rates and interest rates were seen to provide favourable macroeconomic conditions for growth, competitiveness and employment.

Links between what had to be achieved internally to unlock Europe's competitive abilities and their external ramifications were made with an acknowledgement of the further globalisation of markets and economies. Chapter 2A of the White Paper stated that this had made it 'no longer possible to divide industry and geographical areas into clearly identified and relatively independent segments' (71), and hence the solutions proposed to improve European competitiveness had to be adapted to consider this. For example, it suggested a flexible approach to be adopted on international strategic alliances: the creation of welfare reducing oligopolistic situations were to be avoided, whereas a different view was taken if they are able to counterbalance the power of their US and Japanese competitors.

Additional guidelines proposed for a policy of global competitiveness included exploiting the competitive advantages associated with a gradual shift towards a knowledge-based society, promoting a sustainable path of industrial development and reducing time-lags between the pace and change in supply and the corresponding adjustments in demand. The measures suggested within these guidelines served only as a frame of reference from which future business and policy initiatives could take their cue (see Table 1.3). Apart from the gains yet to be had from completing the SEM, the role of TENs and the need to accommodate new technological realities in future economic activity, the designated section on 'competitiveness' within the White Paper also stressed the importance of maintaining an open economy and the EU being perceived as a reliable global partner.

Once past the opening moral rhetoric concerning the need to integrate better the developing countries into the world economy and extend and deepen multilateral processes, more revealing motives are bared. The developing and transitional countries on the EU's southern and eastern peripheral regions are particularly targeted for assistance, with the CEE economies providing a future low cost techno-industrial base to be exploited within Europe. The NICs of East Asia and Latin America are chosen for the new regional market opportunities they present and a means by which European competitiveness can be further sponsored. According to the White Paper, the building of robust multilateral frameworks should be

Table 1.3 Guidelines for a policy of global competitiveness

Objectives	Means
1 Helping European firms to adapt to the new globalised and interdependent competitive situation	● capitalising on the Community's industrial strengths; ● developing an active policy of industrial cooperation; ● establishing a concerted approach to strategic alliances; ● targeting measures to ensure the competitive functioning of markets.
2 Exploiting the competitive advantages associated with the gradual shift to a knowledge-based economy	● reforming tax policies so as not to create employment disincentives and to promote incentives for the efficient use of scarce resources; ● developing a policy to encourage 'non-physical' investment (training, research, technical assistance); ● bolstering policies to streamline and rationalise rules and regulations; ● reviewing the criteria governing the use of public instruments in support of industry so as to enhance their impact on the growth of value-added and employment; ● launching a European policy aimed at quality.
3 Promote a sustainable development of industry	● increase substantially and co-ordinate R&D efforts in the field of clean technology; ● develop economic incentives to support the diffusion of R&D results into products and processes.
4 Reducing the time-lag between the pace of change in supply and the corresponding adjustments in demand	**Demand-side measures**: ● pursuing initiatives aimed at facilitating a concerted revival in consumption at world level; ● promoting the emergence of new markets. **Supply-side measures**: ● encouraging continuing structural adjustment by supporting privatisations; ● underpinning the dynamism of SMEs. **Measures to improve the relationship between supply and demand**: ● facilitating partnerships between large firms and their subcontractors; ● improving the interfaces between producers and users; ● establishing collaboration networks so as to develop clusters of competitive activities.

Source: GCE White Paper, CEC 1993a: 81

accompanied by more harmonious and enforceable rule structures. This suits the EU's strategic interests in that it is well positioned to exert strong influence over these. Moreover, this could potentially lead to the EU pushing for rules that aim to create a more level playing field between itself and its competitors that systematically advantages European business. The possibility of such multilateral rules being implemented in the future may be vindicated on the basis of social or environmental 'righteousness', as recently shown by arrangements within NAFTA and new trade clauses to be introduced into the EU's own Generalised System of Preferences (GSP) scheme by 1998.

However, more overt strategic uses of trade or any other policy have been increasingly seen within the EU as undesirable. Nevertheless, even the most liberal minded member states have defended a coercive approach both to maintain the multilateral rules they have helped to forge and against those third countries found guilty of conducting illicit commercial practices. Put another way, 'fair' competition must prevail, though this relies on an objective interpretation of what exactly is fair and what is not. More importantly, an individual economy's ability to meet the challenges posed by a more globalised world economy is to a large extent dependent on its own relative openness regarding its policy and regulatory frameworks. Without it, the economy may lack the capacity to participate effectively in the integration strategies of multinationals and attain the recipient benefits that are conferred by doing so.

As part of its final analysis on improving competitiveness, the White Paper contended that European policy frameworks needed to converge more where appropriate while also displaying more sensitivity to the imperatives of global and regional interdependence. This was necessary to remove the structural distortions within the European economy that still hinder its progress on several fronts. Although adherence to the plans for EMU in Europe will obviously produce a considerable degree of macroeconomic policy convergence between member states, an asymmetric pattern still typifies many microeconomic policies pursued across the EU. What approach to adopt is dependent on a number of considerations.

Convergence can lead to joint actions which produce synergetic gains, avoid duplication of effort and serve mutually to enhance the competitiveness of active partners. This has been clearly illustrated in science and technology (S&T) collaborations and other forms of industrial co-operation. It can also entail the common compliance to a particular policy that is known to yield an assortment of economic benefits, such as shifting the tax burden from labour and capital on to environmental malpractices. Certain policy fields will, though, require some autonomy in order to retain the flexibility needed to respond to unique localised conditions and structures. Such requirements are supposed to be safeguarded by the subsidiarity principle which, through proper application, can also have a positive impact on European competitiveness. The suitability of deploying convergent policy strategies can thus vary in terms of what convergence entails and its actual relevance to the policy field in question.

Nonetheless, the Commission has generally urged member states to adopt a more common approach on similarly shared problems in subsequent communications that have led from the White Paper on Growth, Competitiveness and Employment (e.g. CEC 1994a, 1995a). This has been supported by mechanisms that have been installed at EU level to facilitate the exchange of information, experience and best practice between relevant agents. At both a member state and EU level, the recasting of policy to befit an increasingly globally and regionally interdependent world economy has

mainly involved recourse to measures conducive towards inward investment and export promotion, the extending of influence over governing
international rules and the building of collaborative links with other
national and regional powers. The last of these aspects has particularly
acquired special significance in recent years owing to their accelerated
proliferation and strategically important nature.

Establishing firmer inter-regional and third country collaborative relations

Since its conception, the external relations of the EU have been mainly
determined or influenced by its external trade policy, or Common Commercial Policy (CCP). This itself has been shaped into a pyramidal structure of preferential trade relations in which countries on the EU's external
periphery are placed at its apex. Triadic trade matters have been largely
resolved through GATT rounds and a series of bilateral negotiations that
have lately become set within more resolute frameworks. Relations with
more distant developing countries are mostly settled through the Lomé
Conventions, for the Africa Caribbean Pacific (ACP) ex-colonial states,
and the GSP scheme.

However, in more recent times, the EU has sought to broaden the scope
of its external relations. This has primarily entailed a widespread introduction of collaborative initiatives on an inter-regional basis or with third
countries usually contained within 'useful bilateral economic packages'
of measures (CEC 1995b). Another related trend has been the greater
emphasis placed on inter-regional trade relations which have often formed
part of the collaborative agreement signed. While this development has
been reactive to global and regional interdependence, the motivation
behind it has not been purely economic.

Closer political ties have been achieved between the EU and other
powers through such arrangements. In some cases, joint actions to overcome specific related problems have been the focus of co-operation, such
as the special 'drugs' provisions in relations with the Andean Pact countries. The rich nations which form the EU are also under a moral obligation
to extend numerous forms of assistance to the poorer developing countries
in particular. Global or regionalised environmental degradation has also
compelled the EU's member states to help co-ordinate international solutions to them.

Economic feedback effects from such collaborations have nevertheless
been positive from the benefits conferred by the further extension of
Europe's geopolitical influence and greater degrees of global and regional
stability that are attained. Networking the EU's inter-regional and third
country collaborative ventures has, though, been driven principally by
strong economic motives that must be understood in the context of global
and regional interdependence. Nearest to home, these have been formalised

through the Europe Agreements that have been signed with six of the CEE states, while the recent inauguration of the Euro-Med Partnership has established a new pattern of co-operation with those nations on the EU's southern periphery. The existence of close cultural and historic ties combined with the considerable economic potential of the CEE states, both as a market and production base, has spurred the EU particularly to prioritise reintegration into the world economy. Up to now, this has been primarily achieved by first integrating back into the core European economy.

Further afield, the EU has taken a strong interest in assisting the regional integration that has been undertaken by non-European countries (CEC 1995c). The reasons for this are numerous. Its encouragement is likely to lead to a growth-induced increase in import demand and enable foreign investors better to rationalise production and distribution networks in the region. These benefits will be additionally forthcoming for European firms by the technical, financial and other forms of assistance being granted by the inter-regional agreement. The links consolidated by these actions could make the partner region more economically dependent on the EU in certain respects, for example, in a technological sense. While this is to be avoided it may not be possible, especially for developing countries. Meanwhile, European producers may find themselves in a position to exploit relatively captured markets as an outcome. Integration at the corporate level could also prove beneficial. From the late 1980s onwards, the European Community Investment Partnership (ECIP) scheme has attempted to provide the advantageous conditions under which these links can prosper.

Inter-regional collaboration may also enable the stronger party to fashion the structure of its partner's trade so as to lead to a consequential improvement in its own balance. Such gains involved may be mutual, although any resultant trade diversion will have a negative impact on third countries and global welfare levels. The EU's collaborations with developing countries, whether they form part of a negotiable regional group or not, have often comprised of measures to promote their compliance to established multilateral rules. Where it has been able to exert significant influence over their formation, the EU has obviously been especially eager to assert.

The EU has signed a growing number of inter-regional agreements in recent years. These include those with Mercosur, the Andean Pact and CARICOM in Latin America, ASEAN in East Asia and the Gulf Co-operation Council (GCC) in the Middle East (see Table 2.4 on page 58). While the relatively limited extent of collaboration within these agreements has admittedly denied them of current global significance, the network links which have been instituted may soon prove their future worth. This will depend on the strategic importance of the EU's partner regions and the degree to which regionalism will shape the contours of global economic relations. In a scenario where RIAs become more the norm, inter-regional agreements can also be expected to flourish. They may be encouraged by the broad opportunities they offer to improve mutual economic security in an ever uncertain and interdependent world economy.

As might be expected, collaborations have tended to be of a higher order between the EU and its Triad rivals. Co-operation in the fields of finance, macroeconomic policy, science and technology, education and a range of others is well developed, especially those of a Trans-Atlantic nature. However, in areas distinguished by their strategic sensitivity, collaboration has been either restrained or not permitted. One frequently cited example of the latter has been the US's Sematech semi-conductor programme. Perhaps the more important issues have centred on how the Triad powers have sought to establish sets of rules to be abided by between themselves and those designed at a plurilateral or multilateral level (Winters 1993).

With the increased globalisation of markets and economies has come the need to implement new rules and converged policies in order to maintain an effective state of governance over cross-border activities. High ratios of Trans-Atlantic FDI and intra-firm trade flows have meant that a considerable degree of interdependence exists between the EU and US economies. The regulatory capabilities of both powers have enabled them to forge a more common approach in areas such as competition policy and rules on foreign investments with the assistance of organisational bodies like the Transatlantic Policy Network. This has led to greater interpenetration whereby each party has affected the laws of the other or displayed extra comity for them (CEC 1995d).

While Trans-Atlantic co-operation over such rule setting has not been without its frictions, the tone of triadic negotiations involving the Japanese has been markedly different. The adoption of a more coercive approach taken in most dialogues with Japan, particularly by the USA, has arisen owing to three main factors. First, Western reactions to the ascendant economic superpower have comprised of measures aimed to contain its direct and indirect impacts upon their own economies. These have mainly been targeted at reducing Japan's huge post-war trade surpluses. Second, the benefits of Japanese economic growth do not appear to have been distributed externally. The country's low import propensity and low ratio of inward FDI flows have been blamed on the existence of varied 'structural impediments', which accordingly have been a prime focus of more recent negotiations. As a consequence of both these factors, the other Triad members have frequently sought to exert considerable *gaiatsu* (foreign pressure) on Japan to make compensatory adjustments (Strange 1995). The inability of Japan to translate its international economic stature into its political equivalent forms a third factor, and has meant that the Japanese have found it difficult either to resist *gaiatsu* from both the EU and the USA or to influence the forming of global rules to the same effective degree; the ability to achieve the latter would assist its cause with the former. The Uruguay Round of GATT clearly demonstrated the capability of the Trans-Atlantic powers more or less to determine both the parameters of multilateral negotiations and the main body of subsequent rules to emerge from them.

Bilateral collaborative agreements with certain distant third countries have proved useful to the EU where it has not been able to extend some form of control or support with respect to their development through multilateral mechanisms. This has especially applied to East Asian nations and, most recently and notably, China (CEC 1995e). The need to claim some form of participatory role in China's future development is crucial, given both the country's enormous economic potential and the range of unpredictable outcomes which depend on how and to what extent this potential is realised. This relates as much to global warming as it does to global trade and investment flows.

Formulating new collaborative relationships with the other dynamic Asian economies will also be necessary due to the growing importance of the Pacific region. The imminent 'graduation' of many of them from the EU's GSP scheme, the recent inauguration of the Commission's 'New Asia Strategy' and the first of many planned Asia–Europe Meetings (ASEM) held in March 1996 have already signalled Europe's intentions to establish a different and more substantial form of partnership. In a recent communication, the Commission admitted that 'reinforcing links with ASEAN . . . or with individual countries of the Asian region would also help to ensure that Asian regional integration occurs in a way compatible to EU interests', and that 'if the countries of East Asia were, as a result of regulatory co-operation within APEC, to align their regulatory systems practices to those of the United States, this would place the EU at a competitive disadvantage, at least to the extent that a large and dynamic part of the world economy developed as result of a system which diverged significantly from that of the Union' (CEC 1995b). Drawing closer ties with Asia could thus prove to be Europe's most critical challenge well into the next century.

CONCLUDING REMARKS

The advance of global and regional interdependence poses some strategically important challenges for Europe at various levels and in many fields of endeavour. The cursory glance we have made at the European economy and the geo-political position it currently occupies suggests that there is much work ahead if it is effectively to rise to meet such challenges. The increased globalisation of economic activity also means that it has sometimes become difficult to identify what actually is a constituent part of that economy, who exactly its agents are and to what purpose they are working. Thus, any study of it and the challenges to be confronted in the next century has to be set within the context outlined in this chapter. This also applies to those that subsequently follow.

2 Regional integration

The next three chapters focus on the theme of European regionalism. This chapter is mainly concerned with the theoretical and historical evolution of regional integration in Europe. First, consideration is given to the concepts of regional integration that been developed (n.b. the term 'regional integration' will be used most frequently to depict the formal or institutionalised regionalism that has emerged as the predominant global form). An examination of custom union theory and other preferential trade agreement concepts which have underpinned the rationale for forming regional trade blocs will then be followed by an overview of the historical context of economic integration in Europe. Other regional integration arrangements (RIAs) will also be analysed, together with the EU's inter-regional links which have been nurtured in recent years. Chapter 3 will continue to focus on the more progressive stages of regionalism, namely the creation of Europe's single or internal market and economic and monetary union (EMU). Chapter 4 will concentrate on the widening of European regional integration within the perspective of recent and future enlargements of the EU.

CONCEPTS OF REGIONAL INTEGRATION

The progressive stages

Before embarking on an in-depth theoretical analysis of free trade areas and customs unions it is first necessary to define key concepts. Let us begin by exploring the conventional framework, introduced by Balassa (1961), within which five main stages of progressive regional integration could be said to exist. We shall start with the simplest form of RIA, the free trade area (FTA).

Free trade area (FTA)

A free trade area is essentially a preferential trade agreement between countries that commits them to remove all tariff and quota restrictions on each other's exports. This entails the creation of a free trade zone or area between them while retaining the ability of each country autonomously to formulate its own external trade policy. One disadvantage of FTAs is that trade deflection is likely to occur, whereby external imports arrive in the lowest tariff country to be re-routed to other member states. Thus, the more protectionist external trade policies of partner FTA members are circumvented.

Let us assume that three countries decide to establish an FTA and each has set its external tariff at a different level: member state A at 5 per cent, member state B at 10 per cent and member state C at 30 per cent. Suppose that member state C wishes to protect its domestic farmers by applying a high tariff wall on the agricultural imports of non-member states. The latter decide to target member state A as their prime export market for agri-products owing to its relatively low external tariff rates. The potential re-export of these goods into member state C could now threaten the protectionist policy it wanted to adopt to safeguard its own farmers' livelihoods. For these reasons, functional FTAs devise 'rules of origin' on all imports transacted between their member states which help determine the nationality of traded products.

Customs union

A customs union arrangement builds on the structure of an FTA with the adoption of a common external tariff (CET). All member states now apply a CET upon every external import entering the union while maintaining an FTA between themselves. In complying to the CET, each member state now forgoes its right to determine its own external trade arrangements. On the positive side, the establishment of a customs union solves the problem of trade deflection as external producers are now prevented from discriminately targeting one specific member state as a port of entry to re-route exports.

Common or internal markets

The next stage of regional integration is a common or internal market. A common market involves the elimination of the remaining barriers that impede trade between its participants. In addition, businesses enjoy the same rights of establishment irrespective of their own national identity or where they wish to conduct business activity. Factors of production enjoy freedom of movement within this integrational arrangement, just as traded products do. Thus, a 'level playing field' is created for goods, services, people and capital by a common market, as aspired to in the EU's Single European Market (SEM) programme.

Economic and monetary union (EMU)

The most important element of economic and monetary union (EMU) is the adoption of a common currency by member states. Monetary union implies that the countries involved must collaborate to a much closer degree on a variety of economic policies. For example, fiscal policy will be significantly affected by this form of integration. Common supra-national institutions, such as a union central bank, will also be necessary to co-ordinate policy and take responsibility on behalf of member states for decisions made. In many ways, EMU is the next logical step for a group of countries which have committed themselves to setting up a common market arrangement. A single market requires a single money if it is to function at an optimal level.

Economic and political union (EPU)

Economic and political union (EPU) is the final stage of regional integration. An EPU amounts to forging an all-embracing federal union between the concurring members. The USA provides a useful historical example of such a union. Under EPU, common political institutions would be formed that further extend the fraternity of supra-national organisations to manage the union's affairs. The national sovereignty of member states is forgone and their peoples would be obliged to adopt union citizenship.

Positive and negative integration

Regional integration can involve a wide range of measures, each designed to achieve their own integrational objectives. Tinbergen (1954) has made the distinction between those measures that aim to eliminate certain obstacles or impediments to integration and others designated to creating the harmonised conditions for improved integrational co-ordination to take place. The former can be categorised as 'negative' integrational measures, while the latter fall into the 'positive' integration category. An example of negative integration would be the deregulation of localised administrative procedures that are deemed to prevent the free movement of products or factors of production. Positive integration tends to entail a greater political commitment as it implies the adoption of common institutions and policies by concerned member states. Hence, examples of positive integration become more frequent as progressive integrational stages are reached.

Natural and strategic integration

Natural and strategic concepts of integration widen our focus to consider the external impact of an RIA. Natural integration involves geographically proximate countries which decide to pursue a relatively open external trade policy towards third countries. Strategic integration represents an alternative situation whereby an RIA adopts protectionist, 'beggar thy neighbour' measures against external imports. There is much debate as to which type of integration should be ascribed to the EU (Jacquemin and Sapir 1991). The 'Fortress Europe' view obviously implies the latter, while the EU's concessionary arrangements with numerous trade partners provide evidence for the former case.

Within the triad scenario of the global economy it is, however, possible that natural integration could very well reinforce strategic integrational tendencies. Each triad bloc may seek to extend their own RIA to neighbouring countries, which simultaneously acts as a defensive, non-cooperative manoeuvre against rival blocs.

Federalists, functionalists and nationalists

The distinction between federalist, functionalist and nationalist approaches to regional integration arises within more of a political than an economic dimension. The federalist approach argues that the creation of a supranational framework of institutions is required for any RIA to prove effective. These institutions would be designed to conduct a common set of policies and would thus possess executive powers that superseded those held by their counterparts at national level. The union central bank would be an example of this type of institution.

The functionalist approach comprises of facilitating a looser set of institutional arrangements than those proposed by federalists. Jointly run institutions would be established between participating member states whose executive decisions could be vetoed at national ministerial level, thus indicating a greater emphasis on inter-governmentalism. Functionalism thus places a stronger emphasis on forging integrational links through extending mutual co-operation at a more gradualised pace than federalism.

As might be expected, the main priority of nationalists in the regional integration process is the maintenance of national sovereignty. Nationalists would thus resist any federalist or functionalist steps taken that undermined it. If they were to support any form of RIA, it would therefore be one that sought less emphasis on positive integration such as the adoption of a single currency within an EMU arrangement. The UK and Denmark's present opt-out of Stage 3 of EMU represents a nationalist position taken on this matter. As will be apparent from further reading, there is much variance within the EU concerning member states' adherence to, and prescription of, the above three concepts.

THE THEORETICAL BASIS OF REGIONAL INTEGRATION: EARLY CONSIDERATIONS

Static customs union theory

Much of the original work developed on customs union theory can be attributed to Viner (1950). He wrote at a time when there was much contemporaneous interest in European integration, but was to demonstrate that RIAs could only aspire to a secure 'second best' position. According to Viner, non-discriminatory trade concessions negotiated at a multilateral level would always provide superior welfare-inducing effects compared to selective preferential trade agreements. This was not the first time that this argument had been postulated. Robson (1987) notes that both Adam Smith and David Ricardo were critical of the counter-free trade 1703 Methuen Treaty signed between Britain and Portugal which enabled British wool and Portuguese wine into each other's respective markets on preferential terms. The basis for Viner's own theory rested on the twin concepts of trade creation and trade diversion.

Trade creation and trade diversion

Trade creation entailed the displacement of one member's domestically produced goods by cheaper imports from more efficient partners. Trade diversion, on the other hand, involved cheaper external imports being replaced by more expensive partner equivalents as a consequence of the CET's imposition on the former. Viner argued that while trade creation may generate higher welfare levels, trade diversion effects diminishes them (see Figure 2.1).

Two countries decide to enter into a preferential trading arrangement. Figure 2.1 illustrates the market situation of the home country. S_h and D_h represent its respective supply and demand schedules for the product in study. S_w is the world's own product supply schedule while S_p denotes the supply schedule from the partner country. Both schedules are assumed to be perfectively price elastic and, in our initial position, face an import tariff (t) that induces the effective supply schedules of S_w' and S_P'.

Price P_w is derived from the more competitive external producers and undercuts below price P_P of the partner country's producers in the home country's market when no tariff is imposed. If we now apply preferential trading terms, external producers will be put at a disadvantage with respect to the partner country. The latter now enjoys tariff-free conditions for its exports of the product in the home country depicted by the reduction in their supply price from P_{P+t} to P_P ($S_P' - S_P$). External producers, on the other hand, are still confronted with price P_{w+t} for their exports.

The application of these preferential trading terms has both trade creating and trade diverting effects. Before their adoption, the home coun-

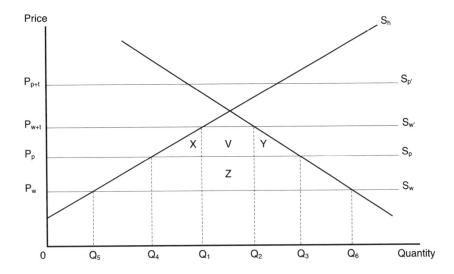

Figure 2.1 Trade creation and trade diversion

try demanded $0Q_1$ supply from its domestic producers and Q_1Q_2 was imported from competitive external producers at price P_{w+t}. Combined area VZ is the tariff revenue acquired by the home country. The removal of tariffs on the partner country's exports lowers the price faced by the home country's consumers to P_P. Consequently, consumption increases from $0Q_2$ to $0Q_3$ as do total imports from Q_1Q_2 to Q_4Q_3, which now all originate from the partner country. It can also be noted that the diversion of trade away from external world producers amounts to Q_1Q_2.

In addition, the partner country is now responsible for the trade creation represented by Q_4Q_1 derived from the partner country supplying the product at more competitive terms than domestic producers. This in turn enables domestic producers to concentrate more on activities where they possess a comparative advantage over their partner country. Area X denotes the gain in consumer surplus from this development (production effect) and, along with area Y (consumption effect), combines to form the welfare improvements associated with trade creation.

Area V is simply the loss of import tariff revenue arising from preferential trading terms, but simultaneously depicts a welfare gain to consumers in the shape of reduced prices. The same case is applicable to area U, though the transfer originates from a producer surplus loss. Meanwhile, area Z accounts for the loss of tariff revenue that is not passed on to consumers, and hence constitutes a trade diversion cost arising from supplanting imports from essentially low-cost producers with those from a higher cost equivalent (i.e. the partner country).

An evaluation of the preferential trading arrangement's net welfare effect rests on the calculation $X+Y-Z$. A positive outcome would obviously indicate that the trade creation gains outweigh the trade diversion costs, while a negative outcome would suggest the opposite. The result would depend on such factors as the size of the initial tariff imposed, the relative efficiency of both home and partner producers to their external rivals and the elasticities of demand and supply for the product.

It would also depend on the degree to which the participating countries shared competitive or complementary industrial profiles. If the countries possessed a similar range of industries (e.g. Germany and the UK), then their competitive nature would propagate greater scope for trade creation. This is due to a wider range of lower cost producers being granted the chance to exploit improved trading opportunities. The scope is narrowed by the more significant degrees of complementarity that exist between countries (e.g. Germany and Portugal) and increases the risk of trade diversion.

Johnson (1965) noted that both trade creation and trade diversion yield gains to RIA members – with trade diversion directly benefiting the members to whom preference is deferred – while disadvantaging its more competitive third party rivals. Moreover, Viner and others have argued that whatever consequences evolved from the agreement, a universal reduction of tariffs produces superior welfare gains as external producers would then be able to expand trade creation to Q_5Q_1 and increased consumption Q_3 to Q_6. Hence, the relevance of the preferential trade arrangement offering only a 'second best' option.

The economics of a free trade area

In addition to those points made in the previous section on FTAs, let us assume that the partner country shown in Figure 2.2 possesses a relatively elastic supply schedule and that T_P and T_h are the respective tariff-induced price levels for the partner country and home country.

Under pre-FTA circumstances, the home country's domestic producers supply 0A to the market with AC derived from the imports of competitive external producers. Again, combined area VZ is the tariff revenue collected by the home country's government. The partner country's tariff ensures that its own domestic producers supply the total market's needs at price T_P and quantity 0B. If an FTA now operates between the two countries the following events unfold.

The FTA's total supply at price T_P would amount to 0A' plus 0B between the two countries. This would lead to unsatisfied demand within the FTA (0A'+0C'). As this shortfall is less than the partner country's capacity to produce at T_P – that being 0B – it would have the incentive to supply the home country's market with A'C' (=A''B), domestically pro-

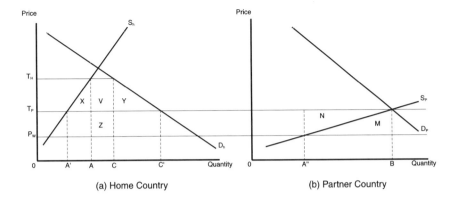

Figure 2.2 The economics of a free trade area

duce 0A″ and import the remainder (A″B) from external producers. Consequently the partner country would acquire the tariff revenue aggregated in area M (Figure 2.2b) and cause an indirect trade deflection effect. Moreover, price T_P effectively becomes the equilibrium price for our product concerned within the FTA. Areas X+Y and Z (Figure 2.2a) again represent the respective trade creation and trade diversion zones. In the example shown, we can also conclude that external producers will enjoy an improved position from the increase in export demand from AC to A″B. The net welfare balance will once more rely on the same determining factors discussed earlier.

The economics of a customs union

In our partial equilibrium analysis below, the same two countries now commit themselves to forging a customs union and their CET is formulated at the arithmetic average of preceding tariff levels.

From Figures 2.3a and 2.3b it can be ascertained that union supply at the CET price level exceeds demand. As a result, the CET will only set the ceiling price within the market. The equilibrium price P_{cu} will arise if it emerges that the excess supply in the partner country's market (GB″) equates with the supply deficiency in the home country's market (JF). Trade creation's production and consumption effects (X+Y) are again evident, but are diminished owing to the higher equilibrium price of P_{cu} over T_P. Trade diversion costs therefore rise accordingly, illustrated by an expanded area Z.

In the progression from an FTA to a customs union it is the partner country in our example, though, which will be most affected. A prevailing union market price of P_{cu} will entail a contraction of demand from B to G

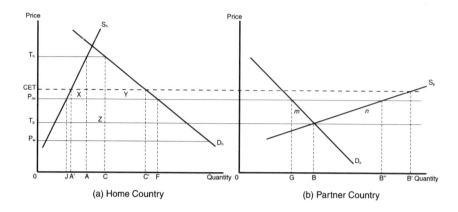

Figure 2.3 The economics of a customs union

and a consumer surplus loss of *m*. A concurrent producer surplus increase is represented by area *n*. The imposition of this relatively high CET denies the access of lower cost external producers to either market, unless they are able in the future to reduce P_w to such an extent that even when inflated by the CET their import price undercuts P_{cu}. Meanwhile, with no imports entering into the union, the partner country is also denied the tariff revenue it once enjoyed under previous arrangements. Thus, only the decision to adopt a CET based on the lowest pre-union tariff of any member would circumvent the adverse welfare effects relative to the FTA of our analysis.

Dynamic customs union theory

Traditional or Vinerian customs union theory (also associated with Meade 1955, Lipsey 1957, and others) concentrates on the detrimental, 'one-off' effects produced by preferential trading arrangements and has therefore been duly labelled as a 'static' form of analysis. Dynamic customs union theory, on the other hand, considers the longer term advantages that evolve, concentrating on how productive capacity is duly affected, as opposed to the allocative efficiency focus of static theory. These advantages are usually borne from the opportunities presented by enlarged markets, a liberalised competitive environment and a widened scope for mutually beneficial collaborations between business and industry. It should be noted that the larger the membership of the customs union the more distinct these opportunities become. Let us now examine the forces at work within this theory.

Economies of scale

As regional integration deepens, the opportunities to exploit economies of scale become more frequent. Corden (1972) has specifically referred to these as 'economies of time'. The conditions for internal specialisation created within a customs union will lead to cost efficiencies that in turn engender welfare gains. Each member will specialise according to their own comparative advantages being able to expand production within a larger and commonly protected market. The larger the customs union, the more likely it is that it will encompass the more competitive producers necessary to secure these gains. One would expect that larger union members would be in the better position to exploit scale economies. However, what is perhaps more relevant is a participating country's industrial structure. An illustration of this is given by Davenport (1982) who claims that many Dutch and Belgian multinational companies have flourished within the integrated European market which has included similarly structured economies.

Increased competition

The effective opening up of the union's market will intensify the competitive pressures exerted on domestic producers from their partner equivalents. These pressures should force firms to reduce prices, invest in new technologies and strive to improve efficiency in order to survive and prosper in the new competitive environment. In theory, monopoly power will either be undermined by increased competition or consolidated by broadened opportunities to exploit scale economies. Third countries can benefit from the structural changes brought about by both economies of scale and intensified competition: efficiency gains will lower the prices of their imports from the RIA, while RIA demand for their exports should rise from the increased growth rates induced from those changes.

Terms of trade effects

The terms of trade refer to the relationship between export and import prices. If a country or RIA experiences an increased price for its exports and a reduced price for its imports, its terms of trade are said to improve. Depending on the size of the customs union, the imposition of its CET could eventually force external producers to lower the price of their own exports in an attempt to circumvent the CET's effects. The larger the customs union, the more success it has in instigating this situation and, in addition, manipulating the welfare gains that are admittedly appropriated at the rest of the world's expense.

Benefits derived from closer collaboration

A variety of advantages are to be had from union members establishing closer collaborative links with each other. The extension of joint ventures and other forms of strategic alliances between businesses should result in a greater transfer of technology and skills across the membership and additional synergetic effects. By acting as one party, union members may also benefit from an improved international bargaining position, enabling particularly smaller member countries to 'punch over their weight' on the world stage.

In conclusion, the accumulation of those dynamic effects discussed will provide the incentive for more progressive forms of regional integration. Moreover, Pryce (1973) and Jansen and DeVree (1985) have contended that FTAs and customs unions ultimately constitute an unsustainable set of arrangements between member countries, and argue that further integrational steps need to be taken to repel the external forces opposed to the RIA's existence.

Europe, trade creation and trade diversion – the evidence

Most studies that have been conducted on the trade effects of European integration use a static theoretical and *ex ante* mode of analysis. Even though static theory would seem to underplay the welfare gains generated by RIAs, most studies indicate that regional integration in Europe has provided trade creation benefits which significantly outweigh the trade diversion costs (see Mayes 1978). This has been particularly revealed as more progressive forms of integration have evolved.

Dynamic and *ex post* studies have been few and far between, mainly due to the difficulties arising from isolating various relevant variables in order to evaluate the longer term effects of integration. Major disturbances such as oil shocks complicate this task to a significant degree. Furthermore, Markheim (1994) has observed that most *ex ante* studies encounter methodological problems arising from a miscalculation of *ex post* adjusted supply elasticities that consequently underestimate new trade volume flows. This has also led to an understatement of the effect of tariff rate changes on valuing the resources that have been subsequently redirected to exporting activity. *Ex post* studies have generally adopted the 'anti-monde' hypothesis which considers what would have occurred to a country's pattern of trade had it not joined an RIA, with trade creation and trade diversion effects then estimated from this position. The central problem of using the anti-monde model is that rather simplistic assumptions have to be built into it for it to be at all manageable.

In a more recent study, Sapir (1992) analysed the consumption patterns of the EC9 from 1980 to 1991 using the 'three-source' method to determine more contemporary trends in European trade creation and trade diversion.

His analysis differentiated consumption for all processed products from that for food, drink and tobacco (FDT). The continued rise in the first of these groups for both intra-EC imports and extra-EC imports implied that a considerable net trade creation effect had emerged as a consequence of EC integration over the period. The same could not be said for the FDT group which experienced a general falling trend in extra-EC imported products. These adverse trade diversion effects have been blamed on the Community's heavily protectionist Common Agricultural Policy and the strategic form of regional integration that it represents.

Regional integration and intra-industry trade

Much of the early theoretical work on regional integration predicted that customs unions would boost trends of inter-industry trade as union members increasingly specialised in accordance with comparative advantage principles. It was not long, though, before studies on regional integration began to build in the increasingly more realistic assumptions pertaining to intra-industry trade patterns (see Verdoorn 1960; Balassa 1966; Grubel 1967). According to Drabek and Greenaway (1984) intra-industry trade (defined as the simultaneous import and export of goods from the same industries) constituted two-thirds of total intra-EC trade by 1977 and had continued to grow faster than inter-industry trade up to the end of the 1970s, albeit at a slower rate than in the previous decade. This trend can be broadly explained by a number of factors:

- a convergence in Community competitive industrial profiles which have encouraged horizontal specialisation aimed at exploiting economies of scale and scope;
- the existence of strong overlapping consumer tastes between EC member states owing to similar per capita income levels and a 'Europeanisation' of consumer culture to some degree;
- the gradual adoption of common industrial standards across the Community which have encouraged common industrial practices.

While it is true that intra-industry links across West Europe were strong even before any post-war RIA was established, the relatively competitive industrial profiles of EU countries have fortified them. The main point here is that the development of intra-industry trade in the Community has widened the scope for trade creation opportunities. If the EU consisted of a more complementary collection of countries, inter-industry trade would be more prevalent, as would the risk of trade diversion.

Returning to Sapir's (1992) work there is more up-to-date evidence to suggest deepening predominance of intra-industry trade in intra-EC trade. Sapir observed that this has been the shared experience of the EEC6 since the EEC itself was conceived in 1958. Between 1970 and 1987, Italy was the only member state to have encountered a falling trend. Furthermore,

Greece, Spain and Portugal – who all joined the Community in the 1980s – appear to have met with larger increases in intra-industry trade than their more developed Community partners over the decade. While the shares of the former still lie at considerably lower levels than those of the latter, we can speculate with some degree of confidence that these levels will converge as the EU integrational process continues. However, the 1980s enlargement that encompassed these poorer nations injected a dose of complementarity into the Community's combined industrial profile. This is reflected by the generally slower pace of intra-industry trade found between member states from 1980 to 1987 (see Robson 1987 and Baldwin 1994 for a more extensive exposition on integration theory).

Box 2.1 The European Free Trade Association (EFTA)

The European Free Trade Association (EFTA) was created at the Stockholm Conference of 1960 with eight original members, namely Austria, Denmark, Norway, Sweden, Switzerland, Liechtenstein, Portugal and the UK. EFTA had, as the term suggests, less ambitious integrational intentions than the EEC. The free trade arrangements covered mainly manufactured goods, with this regime becoming fully realised in 1966. Finland had become an associate member in 1961 and Iceland a member in 1970.

There were a number of factors that differentiated the original EFTA eight from the EEC six. The EFTA nations were less geographically proximate and income levels, industrial profile and resource endowments more dissimilar. EFTA was effectively dominated by one large economy (i.e. the UK), whereas the EEC was composed of a more even balance of members. The EFTA partners favoured a looser integrational agreement to that signed at the Paris and Rome Treaties. Each had their own particular reasons for limiting the scope of the arrangement to this. The Nordic and Alpine countries wished to maintain their traditional neutral independent positions in Europe, while keeping some form of respective association between their immediate neighbours.

The Community and EFTA may have initially been perceived as rival organisations, but the frequent and co-operative dialogue that had always been a feature of their relationship revealed that the two blocs were more comrades than competitors. Both organisations remained each other's largest trading partners for some time, as have a range of co-operative arrangements. In the same year that both the UK and Denmark's application for EC membership had been accepted, along with non-EFTA member Ireland, the Community signed a number of bilateral free trade agreements with the remaining EFTA members in 1972.

By 1977, most of the tariffs on industrial goods had been removed between the members of supra-national organisations, and in 1983 a free trade regime on non-agricultural products was secured. The following year saw the first full ministerial meeting between EFTA and the EC in Luxembourg. A variety of issues was discussed covering the grounds where further co-operative

Box 2.1 *continued*

measures could be formulated. These included co-ordination in many areas of policy, infrastructure projects, joint efforts in research and development and the adoption of similar education and technical standards. In addition, the High-level Contact Group was formed which would meet twice yearly to oversee the progress of these measures and review the scope of extending such activities into other fields.

It was also in Luxembourg that the term 'European economic space' was first introduced by French Foreign Minister, Claude Cheyson, to denote a future framework within which both the EC and EFTA could weave together joint patterns of European integration. The Lugano and Tampere Conventions of 1988 built on the work of the 1984 Luxembourg Declaration. Co-operation on civil and commercial matters was explored resulting in closer collaboration on competition policy, technical standards and the adoption of the Single Administration Document for customs clearance. Towards the end of the 1980s, the momentum of collaboration slowed while the Community became preoccupied with its own internal market agenda. The 1993 European Economic Area (EEA) deal, which came into effect on 1 July, offered EFTA access to many of the benefits of the SEM programme, although both Switzerland and Liechtenstein decided to remain outside the EEA (the latter joined in 1995). While the EEA gave EFTA less to fear regarding a 'Fortress Europe' scenario, some members still aspired to join the Community based on the view that their relative competitiveness would be improved by full accession status.

On 1 January 1995, the EU welcomed Austria, Finland and Sweden as its newest recruits, thus leaving EFTA with a diminished set of small nations: Norway, Iceland, Switzerland and Liechtenstein. There was talk of EFTA folding if Norway's November 1994 referendum had not resulted in a 'no' vote against joining. Nevertheless, the future of EFTA still remains uncertain, given both the haemorrhage of recent participants and the extent to which its economy is integrated into the EU's. These two factors deny EFTA of most of its viable reasons for continuing its existence. A more expansive analysis on EFTA and the EU enlargement issue can be found in Chapter 4.

THE HISTORICAL CONTEXT OF EUROPEAN REGIONAL INTEGRATION

Pre-1945 trends and developments

The French Revolution and the Industrial Revolution did much to remove many of the ancient obstacles which had prevented integration between Europe's markets and factors of production, both on a national and continental scale. Molle (1990) summarised these impediments as:

- feudal structures and transport methods that constrained factor mobility;
- mercantilist trade policies that limited the scope for free trade and promoted autarkic independence;

• miscellaneous factors, such as parochialised customs, standards (e.g. measuring systems) and extensive toll levies.

The French Revolution dismantled numerous institutional barriers which enabled local and regional economies to integrate more effectively into a national economy. Examples of these reforms included the abolition of serfdom, the privileges of the guilds and rules impeding the free traffic of goods and people, the building of new infrastructure and the application of extra-national customs duties. Certain aspects of these policies were emulated by others. Meanwhile, the Industrial Revolution was generating new methods, practices and innovations that gave Britain in particular a leading edge over her European counterparts. Much of the economic success enjoyed by Britain could be attributed to the dynamic integrational effects brought about by the harnessing of new sources of energy, improved infrastructure and increasingly interlinked and sophisticated markets.

Napoleon's Continental System, which was established at the turn of the nineteenth century, whereby the French emperor sought to isolate British trade from his continental empire, forms an early example of an integrational arrangement driven more from political and military motivation rather than economic. The attempt failed largely owing to the strength of counter economic forces at work, namely the logic of the continental European economy having access to British markets and capital. After the Napoleonic wars, many countries adopted more standardised national currencies, partly in an endeavour to fortify a new order of stability in Europe.

The formation of the Zollverein customs union in 1834 brought together 23.5 million people across eighteen different German states into one market for the first time. The consequential integration of both markets and infrastructure – in particular the railway network – invigorated economic activity and mutually shared economic progress, and gave the pretext for eventual political unification in 1870. Among the interesting observations made by Pollard (1974) was that the Zollverein remained intact even when certain participating states were at war with each other. In addition, its CET was lower for imports of European origin than for those from 'colonial' sources.

Perhaps the most significant trading arrangement signed in the mid-nineteenth century was the Cobden–Chevalier Treaty of 1860 which essentially allowed France extended access to superior and less expensive British coal and iron. Towards the end of the century, a heightened tension that had originated from an environment of increasing imperial and industrial competition among the European powers engendered isolationist reasoning and policies that limited the scope for any negotiations towards further economic or regional integrational arrangements being made. However, this period was not devoid of such aspirations, for example:

- Between 1885–6, the Hungarians proposed the creation of a central European union.
- There were unofficial and unsuccessful French efforts to forge a customs union with Germany in 1888.
- From the 1880s to World War I, a proposal for establishing a Central European Economic Association between Germany, Austria–Hungary, Belgium, Holland, Switzerland, Denmark, Italy, Romania and Sweden was raised.

Post-World War I international relations were, in many ways, as badly managed as the war itself. The damaging reparations imposed on Germany, border disputes between old and newly formed nation-states, the collapse of the Gold Standard, destabilising levels of unemployment and protectionist trade policies were all primary contributants to the Great Depression. These factors perpetuated the fragmentary conditions in Europe, with the period being described as one of 'national economic integration and international disintegration' (Myrdal 1956).

The post-war period

After enduring nearly a century of such conditions and the horror and waste of two world wars, the European nations and their associates were ready for change. Initial attempts at constructing a more harmonious world order centred around a clutch of inter-related, Western-led institutions that were established in the mid-1940s. These included the International Monetary Fund (IMF), the General Agreement on Tariffs and Trade (GATT), the International Bank for Reconstruction and Development (IBRD) – commonly known as the World Bank – and the United Nations (UN). This institutional framework provided part of the necessary conditions in which the European nations could seek to work together. The USA also desired this objective for a variety of economic and political reasons. In 1948, the Organisation for European Economic Co-operation (OEEC) – which later evolved into the OECD in 1961 – was formed to help co-ordinate the European Recovery Plan (ERP), or Marshall Plan. Around $20bn was channelled to assist in the reconstruction of Western Europe via the Plan and the OEEC. The OEEC also orchestrated a new system of bilateral currency payments between West European nations which paved the way for liberalised trade relations. The American offer of general aid to the continent was extended to East European nations, but was refused on their behalf by the Soviet Union who had assembled its own package of aid assistance in the form of the Molotov Plan.

By 1948, the Benelux nations (Belgium, Netherlands, Luxembourg) had established a customs union between them. It is worth noting that earlier attempts to achieve a union had failed in 1919 and 1932. France and Italy made plans to follow suit in 1949, but the agreement was not ratified before that of the proposed European Coal and Steel Community (ECSC) was signed at the Treaty of Paris on 18 April 1951.

The ECSC was at the time the most ambitious regional integration agreement to date. Signatories included Germany, France, Italy and the Benelux countries who subsequently had committed themselves to the sectoral integration of their coal and steel industries. The French Foreign Minister, Robert Schuman, and the French Commissaire au Plan, Jean Monnet, were the two main architects of the agreement and shared functionalist views on European integration. The draft plans of the ECSC derived largely from the Schuman Plan of 1950 which comprised France's designs to avoid future military conflict with Germany by coupling their own engines of war – coal and steel – together under a pact of mutual control. The plans also held longer term aims to extend integration into other areas, albeit by adopting an incremental approach. Germany saw ECSC membership as a further step towards her readmittance into the world community. Italy took a similar stance while also expressing the wish to be included in such a strategically important development. The negotiations with France were an additional binding factor. For the Benelux countries the motives to join lay mainly in their relative small size and they had only to gain from an association with countries possessing larger markets. Moreover, there were certain advantages implied from membership that would ensure their national security in the event of future international unrest in Europe.

Britain was also invited to join the ECSC, but declined the offer. It envisaged a 'United States of Europe', as Churchill himself coined the phrase in 1946, but with Britain outside it. British interests were then oriented by its Commonwealth and the relations that lay therein, its eponymous 'special relationship' with the USA and the perception that it still remained a world power in its own right. However, many observers believed British faith in these factors to have been misplaced arguing that the interests of the country would have been better served if it had sought to tie its destiny to Europe when first given the opportunity. Indeed, Jean Monnet prophetically told a British delegation that, 'There is one thing that you British will never understand: an idea; and there is one thing you are supremely good at grasping: a hard fact. We will build Europe without you, but then you will come and join us.'

The ECSC Treaty was ratified on 23 July 1952 and the ECSC commenced operation on 1 January 1953. The Treaty comprised of 100 constitutional articles that involved inaugurating a free trade area over a five-year transitional period in coal and steel products. Under the influence of the French, somewhat interventionist policies were adopted in the venture to modernise coal and steel industries.

Milward (1984) has referred to the ECSC as a 'protoplasmic organisation' in that it retained a malleability which gave the six nations the chance ultimately to fashion it into what they wanted. Indeed, within the

Paris Treaty lay the seeds that eventually germinated into an internal market for all goods. Thus, the ECSC was essentially the precursor of the European Economic Community (EEC). The Council of Ministers, the European Court of Justice and the European Commission (then called the High Authority) all have their roots in the original ECSC institutions. Soon after the ECSC had become operational, Monnet and others had begun to draw up the blueprints for the EEC itself. The ECSC six nations were already experiencing rapid growth and developing stronger intra-bloc trade patterns, and thus observing the mutual gains that sectoral integration on its own had achieved by the time the common market ideal of the EEC was proposed. The EEC Treaty of Rome was signed on 25 March 1957. In contrast with the ECSC Treaty, the tone of the 248 articles of the Treaty of Rome was far more market oriented (see Table 2.1). Article 1 encapsulated the broad objectives of the Treaty with the following statement:

Table 2.1 Contents of the Treaty of Rome

Contents		*Articles*
Preamble		
Part One.	Basic principles	1–8
Part Two.	Foundations of the Community	
Title I.	Free Movement of Goods, including creation of the customs union, elimination of quantitative restrictions	9–37
Title II.	Agriculture	38–47
Title III.	Free Movement of Persons, Services, and Capital	48–73
Title IV.	Transport	74–84
Part Three.	Policy of the Community	
Title I.	Common Rules, including on competition policy, state aids, tax provisions, and the harmonisation of laws	85–102
Title II.	Economic Policy, principally the commercial policy	103–16
Title III.	Social Policy	117–28
Title IV.	The European Investment Bank	129–30
Part Four.	Association of Overseas Countries and Territories	131–36
Part Five.	Institutions of the Community	
Title I.	Provisions Governing the Institutions	137–98
Title II.	Financial Provisions (concerning the EEC budget)	199–209
Part Six.	General and Final Provisions	210–48

Source: Artis and Lee 1994. Reproduced by permission of Oxford University Press.
Note: The details relate to the 1957 EEC Treaty. They do not incorporate changes introduced by subsequent treaty amendments.

The achievement of a harmonious development of the economy within the whole Community, a continuous and balanced economic expansion, increased economic stability, a more rapid improvement in living standards, and closer relations between the member countries.

The EEC's first set of scheduled objectives consisted of the gradual elimination of intra-bloc tariffs and quantitative restrictions and the implementation of a CET by 1970, thus forming a customs union. This was actually achieved eighteen months before the deadline in July 1968. Article 9 of the Treaty of Rome outlines the basis of the EEC's customs union. Articles 12–29 are devoted to tariff reductions and the CET, while Articles 30–37 deal with the removal of quantitative trade restrictions between member states.

Agriculture and transport were seen initially as the two key areas of integration in which the EEC should develop common policies in addition to the installation of the common market and a compatible external trade policy (or Common Commercial Policy). The agricultural sector then employed around 20 per cent of the combined EEC6 workforce and constituted 8 per cent of EEC GNP. The development of a common transport policy was necessary to build the infrastructural links required for the internal market to function effectively. Other policy areas had their roots either in a direct (e.g. competition policy), or indirect (e.g. regional and industrial policy) sense in the Treaty of Rome. The European Atomic Energy Community (EAEC) established in 1958 integrated the activities and policies of the EEC6 in this field, and in turn broadened their interlocking membership over three different Communities – the EEC, ECSC and now the EAEC.

Elsewhere in Europe, other RIAs were being initiated. In 1949, the Council for Mutual Economic Assistance (CMEA) was set up under the co-ordination of the Soviet Union, which together with the satellite communist states in Central and Eastern Europe formed its membership. As a rival RIA to the EEC in Western Europe, the European Free Trade Association (EFTA) was established in 1960 with, as the name implies, a less ambitious integrational agenda (see Box 2.1).

The Dillon and Kennedy Rounds of GATT talks of the 1960s gave the European Commission its first opportunities to present itself on the international stage as the interlocutor for the EEC6. Tsoukalis (1993) comments that it had a profound effect on both the balance of power within the international community and the self-perception of the Community nations. In the negotiations, the Community played an instrumental part in securing a liberalised international trade regime. This was partly reflective of its own generally open trade policy to third countries, especially with respect to industrial and consumer goods, but perhaps more importantly from the substantial liberalisation taking place within the trade bloc. Hufbauer (1990) contends that France, Germany and Italy may not have made the trade concessions they did at multilateral trade talks had it not been for integrational forces of the EEC. In addition, Messerlin (1992) argues that the Community created the macroeconomic conditions that 'allowed the progressive opening' of the French economy.

This being said, the Community's own Common Agricultural Policy (CAP) has on numerous occasions threatened the multilateral trade concessions gained from previous GATT talks, and at one point the very existence of the Community itself. For some, the CAP contradicts the market-orientation accent of the Treaty of Rome. The CAP's expensive, wasteful and heavily protectionist properties are well documented. The CAP dispute of 1965–6 that arose over France's refusal to accept certain changes to the regime nearly brought the Community to the brink of implosion.

The 1967 Merger Treaty of the three Communities was the first constitutional amendment made to the Treaty of Rome and the derivative of the term 'European Community' (EC). After the installation of the full customs union in 1968, the EC sought to study further progressive stages of economic integration. The Werner Plan of 1970 was the EC's first investigation into the possibility of devising an economic and monetary union between member states. Any such attempts at further deepening the integrational process within the EC fell foul of a number of countervailing forces at work during the early 1970s. The eventual collapse of the Bretton Woods exchange rate regime over 1971–2, the 1973–4 oil crisis and the accession of three new member states – the UK, Denmark and Ireland – in 1973 provided the EC with alternative and competing preoccupations.

The general malaise of the European and world economy during much of the 1970s undermined the EC's confidence, ambition and sense of long range vision. The persistence of non-tariff barriers (NTBs) between the now expanded EC9 arose as defensive measures in uncertain times. This was to the obvious detriment to the Community's integrational cause of achieving a common market. The recovery from the deep recession of the early 1980s and a recently expanded EC to ten members – with Greece joining in 1981 – roughly coincided with the appointment of a new President of the European Commission, Jacques Delors, in 1984.

Delors's arrival at the Commission heralded a new era for the EC, revitalising the vision of a European common market as a realisable goal. Delors proved to be the 'new architect of the House of Europe', as Thurow (1992) phrased it, in a similar mould to Schuman and Monnet. As early as 1985, the Single European Act (SEA) had been drafted by the Commission which aimed to inaugurate a single European market by the end of 1992.

THE WIDER GLOBAL CONTEXT OF REGIONAL INTEGRATION

Thus far, we have mainly focused on the European perspective of regional integration. Let us now analyse the European experience in global terms by contrasting it against those of other regions. To do this, we must examine both the extent to which regionalism has emerged outside Europe and how primarily the EU has responded to such development.

The global setting

Regionalism and globalisation have been the principal driving forces that have underpinned the fundamental changes in today's world economy. The main outcome of their exertions has been to increase the level of inter-dependence that exists at both a political–economic and corporate level. Formal and informal regionalism have particularly engendered this between proximate member states through enhancing both intra-regional trade and investment flows and the scope for convergent policy-making. In a recent report, the World Trade Organisation (WTO) stated that the GATT Secretariat had been notified of the establishment of 108 RIAs over the period between 1948 and 1994 (see Figure 2.4), and that 33 of these had occurred in the early 1990s (WTO 1995). These have varied enormously in terms of their degrees of sophistication, with the EU being the most advanced. We have already established that the motives for regional integration lie in an historic mixture of political, economic, cultural and strategic imperatives. Let us summarise what factors are thought to be conducive to an economically successful RIA:

- A large number of participating countries: the larger the membership of the RIA, the more likely it is that low cost producers will be involved, hence increasing the chances of trade creation. Populous RIA membership will also lead to a stronger international negotiating position in world affairs. Other benefits such as reduced distribution costs will be derived from members lying geographically proximate to each other within a compact area.
- Similar or competitive industrial profiles: an RIA that contains countries with competitive industrial profiles can be expected to generate higher degrees of trade creation. Having said this, a broad variety of industrial, commercial and consumer products will be required from producers to provide a multifarious, welfare inducing choice to the RIA's end markets.
- Close pre-RIA trade links: the more established are trade links before an RIA is formed between its members, the greater the probability of trade creation and miscellaneous dynamic gains. A rise in intra-industry trade is a conceivable side effect of integration, especially if the participating countries retain mutual competitive industry characteristics.
- Members that are already major trading powers: the strength of the RIA's international status and global bargaining power will be enhanced by the inclusion of major trading countries which are able to assist the RIA to assert this power on the world stage.

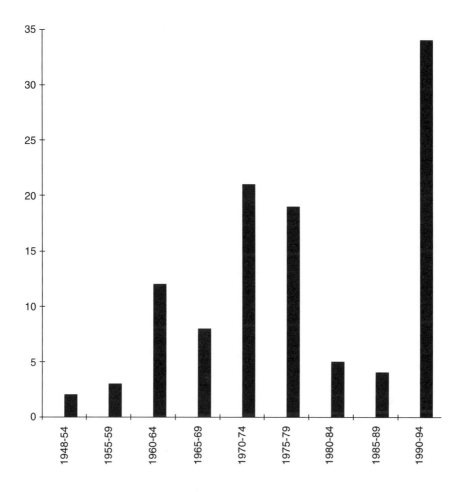

Figure 2.4 Number of RIAs notified to GATT, 1948–94
Source: WTO 1995

The EU scores well when compared against this set of determinants. Its fourth stage of enlargement took place in January 1995, bringing Austria, Finland and Sweden into the fold and extending its membership to fifteen OECD nations within a reasonable degree of propinquity. Though some variance of GDP per capita levels exists, the EU contains essentially parallel economies, some of which have historic integrational links with each other. It is therefore not surprising that Western Europe's intra-regional trade ratio had been the highest among the major global regions for some time (see Figure 2.5).

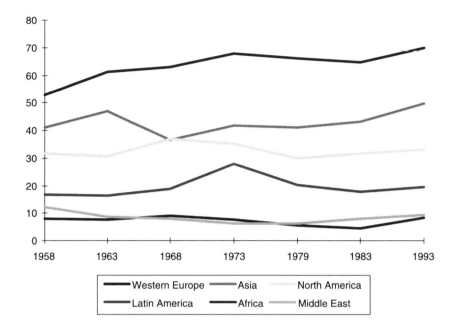

Figure 2.5 Intra-regional trade as a percentage of total trade, 1958–93
Source: WTO 1995

Regional integration in developing countries

Low per capita incomes, underdeveloped commercial sectors and limited trade links with neighbouring developing countries have generally restricted the foundations on which any RIAs between them have been based. Dissimilar levels of development have also worked against aspirations of this kind. Despite these impediments, bold efforts have been made to establish such ties. These spring from the desire to find mutually beneficial paths to improved economic development and ways of projecting national interests onto the larger screen which an RIA confers.

Integrational gains of a more dynamic than static nature require a long-term commitment to pursuing a number of objectives. These will take the form of members being allowed to specialise with respect to their own comparative advantages, the appropriate structuring of industry based on import substitution and export orientation principles and releasing the dynamic of creating regional markets. Many of these objectives will involve short-term sacrifices, the distribution of which is typically asymmetric. Thus, commensurate political and economic interests, as well as political stability, are necessary to exist for a reasonable length of time before any real benefits of the RIA can filter through. Such conditions have been in reality difficult to sustain and cumulative tensions have usually exerted critical pressures on RIAs between developing countries which cause them eventually to collapse. Consequently, the turnover rate of such RIAs is very high, or tends to exist only on paper.

American regional integration

The first North American RIA of any significance was the USA–Canada Auto Pact of 1965 which established sectoral free trade in the automotive industry between the two signatories. In 1988, Canada and the USA embraced a total free trade regional agreement (CUSFTA). At the time, both countries were each other's biggest trading partners and 80 per cent of Canada's trade with the USA already enjoyed duty-free conditions. CUSFTA supplied the framework for the 1993 North American Free Trade Agreement (NAFTA), the continent's most recent development in regional integration, which invited Mexico into the agreement (see Box 5.1 on page 139). Since the early 1990s, Chile has also sought to negotiate for NAFTA membership. The USA's recent interest in building firmer regional alliances corresponds with what Bhagwati (1990) has coined the 'diminished giant syndrome': that is, to some analysts both CUSFTA and NAFTA represent defensive moves made by the USA to counter its reduced world power status, while simultaneously displaying its loss of faith in the multilateral system to assist meeting its wider global objectives.

The experience of regional integration by Latin American countries predates their northern counterparts (see Table 2.2). The first RIA in the region was the ill-fated Latin American Free Trade Association (LAFTA), established by the Montevideo Agreement of February 1960 between Mexico and the Spanish- and Portuguese-speaking nations of South America. The envisaged free trade area never materialised and LAFTA subsequently folded. It was superseded by the less ambitious Latin American Integration Association (LAIA/Aladi) in 1980 that still binds together the ex-LAFTA countries in its membership, but whose organisational apparatus wields limited power among them. The LAIA exists as an umbrella organisation whose main function is to act as a forum for bilateral and sub-regional sectoral negotiations and agreements between members. Despite its modest level of operations, the LAIA has stated its ultimate objective to inaugurate a single common Latin American market. A mechanism for multilateral concessions, the Preferencia Arancelaria Regional, was introduced in 1984 to provide the initial impetus towards this goal.

Latin and North American countries, other than the USA, all share one common denominator, their desire to acquire preferential access to the US market, which for practically all of them represents their largest export market. Moreover, the USA's GNP dwarfs the combined Latin American GNP by a factor of five to one. The fact that relatively small economies tend to seek refuge in the 'safe haven' offered by an RIA with much larger

Table 2.2 Major Latin American RIAs

RIA and date est.	Members	Objectives/history
Andean Pact 1969	Bolivia, Columbia, Ecuador, Peru, Venezuela.	Free internal trade by 1992. Customs union between Columbia, Peru and Venezuela by end of 1993 (others by 1995). Common market by end of 1995.
Association of Caribbean States 1995	CARICOM, Columbia, Cuba, Dominican Republic, Haiti, Mexico, Venezuela and the Central American states.	Aims to reduce trade barriers between members in part preparations for the FTAA.
Caribbean Basin Economic Market Recovery Act (CBERA) 1984	US plus 28 Caribbean and Central American countries.	Duty free entry to USA on selected products.
Caribbean Common Market (CARICOM) 1973	Antigua, Barbados, Belize, Dominica, Grenada, Guyana, Jamaica, Montserrat, St. Kitts-Nevis-Anguilla, St. Lucia, St. Vincent, Trinidad and Tobago.	Caribbean FTA as precursor to CARICOM (1965). CET common external trade policy provisions.
Central American Common Market (CACM) 1960	Guatemala, Honduras, El Salvador, Nicaragua, Costa Rica.	Arrangements broke down in 1970s. Treaty due to expire in 1981, but revived plans for integration made. Liberalised trade on agri-products by 1992. Free trade agreements with Mexico and Venezuela in same year.
LAFTA (1960), LAIA (1980)	Spanish- and Portuguese-speaking countries of South America.	See main text.
Mercosur 1991	Argentina, Brazil, Paraguay, Uruguay.	Southern Cone Common Market by 1995, although more close to a customs union with an 85 per cent complete CET by January that year. Some macro-economic policy co-ordination, removal of selected NTBs and extended regional co-operation initiatives.

Sources: Whalley 1992, CEC 1993b and various journalistic sources 1995

economies is also not lost on Canada. This need is amplified if the multilateral system of trade negotiations appears to be on the brink of collapse.

For its part, the USA has made a number of trade arrangements on a Pan-American scale. The Enterprise for the Americas Initiative announced by

President Bush in 1990 was intended to create more favourable conditions for intra-continental trade, investment and debt management. The trade element included a series of agreements between the USA, the Mercosur group, Chile and Venezuela aimed at establishing areas of mutual interests and grounds for negotiation on trading matters. In 1984, the CBERA had already extended similar trade concessions into the Caribbean and Central America. Closer co-operation is also occurring between the Latin American RIAs. In August 1995, the Association of Caribbean States was inaugurated with the aim of liberalising trade regimes between countries in the central American zone, while the Andean Pact and Mercosur signed an important inter-regional trade agreement in 1996.

At the All-Americas summit of December 1994 in Miami between thirty-four American nations, draft plans were laid out for creating the Free Trade Area of the Americas (FTAA) by 2005. The previous summit of this kind took place in 1967 where preparations were made to establish a Latin American Common Market within fifteen years. This never came to fruition, and a similar fate could well await the FTAA. The push for a date as early as 2005 by certain Latin American countries as a deadline (Argentina wanted it to be even earlier) is five years before the first stage of APEC's free trade schedule. This strategically motivated decision may ultimately prove to be based on over-ambitious intentions. Such a conclusion can be drawn from the USA's insistence that the NAFTA arrangement should set the benchmark for the FTAA. The environmental and social clauses of NAFTA will prove difficult for most South and Central American countries to comply with. The diverse map of Latin American RIAs could also generate incompatibilities with the NAFTA framework.

Asian regional integration

Of all the major continents, Asia has witnessed the least active levels of regional integration. Despite the relative dearth of Asian RIAs, regionalised trade in the continent has grown at a remarkable pace, from 40 per cent in 1979 to 50 per cent by 1993 (see Figure 2.5). This has been particularly pronounced in the East Asian region to which we shall devote most of our analysis. Young (1993) attributes the growth in East Asian intra-regional trade to the following main reasons:

- a rapid increase in East Asia's trade growth in general, on average 16 per cent per annum since 1970;
- the continued attraction of foreign direct investment (FDI) into the region owing to factor and market advantages. Many investments have been cross-networked within the region.
- huge infrastructure investments that have reduced intra-regional trade costs;

- cultural assimilation across East Asia that has to some extent reduced marketing and other related costs.

While East Asia retains a generally diverse complexion, the region is taking on increasingly competitive and complementary characteristics, which have in some way been shaped by the strategic roles played by both Japan and the USA. Both first and second generation East Asian newly industrialised countries (NICs) have pursued successful export-orientation policies that are progressively being tuned to the vibrant rhythms of their own, and not the West's, emerging markets.

The Association of South East Asian Nations (ASEAN), established in 1967 and consisting of Brunei, Indonesia, Malaysia, the Philippines, Singapore, Thailand and Vietnam (its most recent member), forms the most advanced RIA in Asia. Its initial objectives were more political than economic with the primary purpose being to found an anti-communist bulwark in the region with the assistance of the USA. Until recent years, ASEAN only functioned as a forum of debate and co-operation on ad hoc matters. In 1977, a preferential trade agreement was signed covering a limited number of sectoral areas. More ambitious ideas were tabled at its 1992 and 1995 summits, their main outcome comprising of plans to create a free trade area (AFTA) by 2003. Cambodia and Laos are set to become members in 1997 and Myanmar by 1999. The regional integration achieved by ASEAN has been minimal, and the organisation carries at most moderate economic weight in East Asia, although membership could well grow on the ascent to AFTA. Hine (1992) has proposed a series of factors that have constrained the development of East Asian regional integration:

- the legacy of past colonial and other extra-regional ties that still draw interests outside of the region;
- the pace of economic growth that has been achieved independent of any RIA;
- the diversity of political, cultural and other interests in East Asia;
- the lingering memories of Japan's imperial Co-Prosperity Sphere of the 1930s and 1940s.

In the 1990s, the most notable regional arrangements involving Asian countries have been of an inter-regional nature. The Asia–Pacific Economic Co-operation (APEC) forum presently binds together eighteen Pacific Rim nations within a Trans-Pacific alliance with the intention of forming a gradualised free trade area (PAFTA) by 2020, with the more advanced participants scheduled to realise this by 2010. This development is discussed in greater detail in Chapter 5, but the only other forum of debate on regional integration to rival APEC is the East Asian Economic Caucus (EAEC). The EAEC has been keenly promoted by Malaysia's Asia-centric Prime Minister, Mahathir Mohamad, from an inclination to maintain East Asian interests only in any RIA that materialises in the region. In addition, there is the private sector run Pacific Basin Economic Council which provides a framework for regional business co-operation, as well as the Pacific Economic Co-operation Conference consisting of an amalgam of government, business and academic representatives which aims to explore new areas of common interest and collaboration in the region. Finally, the South Asia Association for Regional Co-operation – that has India, Pakistan, Bangladesh, Sri Lanka, Nepal, Bhutan and the Maldives as its members – was established in 1985, based on the prime objectives of accelerating the process of economic and social development and strengthening self-reliance through joint actions.

The future of regionalised trade in East Asia is dependent on a wider set of variables. The region's export-oriented economies are more reliant on an invigorated multilateral trading structure than most (Dent 1995). The substantial array of NTBs placed on East Asian exports by the EU in particular has not assisted their cause. East Asia's economies have thus more to gain from natural integration than from strategic integration. Young (1993) suggests that a formula of further opening up regional markets on a unilateral basis, continued investments in intra-regional infrastructure and occasional co-operation on industrial standards and other similar measures should be followed which 'reduce physical, communicative and cultural gaps'. In essence, this relates more to establishing links based on regional co-operation than regional integration. Given the high degree of economic complementarity that exists both in East Asia and across the Pacific the expected trade diversion of an RIA seems likely, though, to produce a negative global welfare effect in a static analysis. Thus, smaller scale regionalism may prove more universally beneficial, such as the example presented by ASEAN.

African and Middle Eastern regional integration

Efforts to forge alliances with neighbouring countries have been part of a post-colonial strategy in Africa with the aim of establishing a new political and economic order (see Table 2.3). The continent has witnessed numerous attempts at regional integration, but a high proportion have failed or not progressed to the same state of sophistication that many Latin American counterparts have achieved. This has been largely due to the especial applicability of those factors that can impede the formation of an RIA. There have, though, been some recent successes. In 1994, the UEMOA created a monetary union between seven West African francophone states based on the CFA Franc. After the demise of apartheid in South Africa, the country joined the SADC and helped revitalise regional co-operation and integrational ambitions among neighbouring economies. The considerable structural problems still faced by sub-Saharan Africa and its continued marginalisation within

Table 2.3 Major African RIAs

RIA and date est.	Members	Objectives/history
Arab Maghreb Union (AMU) 1989	Algeria, Libya, Mauritania, Morocco, Tunisia.	Immediate goals to remove mutual trade barriers, improve transport links and establish common institutions (investment bank, common airline). Eventual goal to establish a proximate federal union.
Economic and Monetary Union of West Africa (UEMOA) 1994	Benin, Burkina Faso, Ivory Coast, Mali, Niger, Senegal, Togo.	Francophone nations who first sought to re-establish colonial economic links under the CEAO (1973). Reduced tariff and NTBs, measures to enhance labour mobility and specialisation. Monetary union based on the French Treasury backed CFA Franc.
Communauté Economique de Pays des Grands Lac (CEPGL) 1976	Burundi, Rwanda, Zaire.	Mutual liberalisation and co-operation in a limited number of sectors, such as agriculture, energy, geo-technology and finance. More recently preoccupied with border security and refugee problems.
Communauté Economique des Etats de l'Afrique Centrale (CEEAC) 1983	UDEAC and CEPGL plus Chad, Equatorial Guinea and São Tomé et Príncipe.	Similar arrangements to those made in ECOWAS.
East African Community (EAC) 1928	Kenya, Uganda, Tanzania	One time economic and monetary union. Dissolved in 1978. Calls for reinstatement made in 1995.
Economic Community of West African States (ECOWAS) 1975	16 anglophone, francophone and luscophone members.	Plans for trade liberalisation and a CET, but progress has been slow. Links and membership with UEMOA, MRU and UDEAC.
Mano River Union (MRU) 1973	Liberia and Sierra Leone, Guinea (1980).	Customs union and other co-operative arrangements (e.g. 'union' industries).
Preferential Trade Area for Eastern and Southern Africa (PTA) 1981	15 members, some of whom are also participants in CEPGL and SADC.	Sectoral trading arrangements between members. From 1994, attempts to create a common market arrangement (COMESA).

Southern African Customs Union (SACU) 1969	Botswana, Lesotho, South Africa, Swaziland.	
Southern African Development Community (SADC) 1980	Angola, Botswana, Lesotho, Malawi, Mauritius, Mozambique, Namibia, South Africa, Swaziland, Tanzania, Zambia, Zimbabwe.	Origins in a loose set of economic co-operative and development measures aimed at breaking an economic dependence on South Africa under the preceding SADDC framework. Now work together to encourage regional co-operation.
Union Douanière et Economique de l'Afrique Centrale (UDEAC) 1964	Cameroon, Central African Republic, Chad, Congo, Gabon.	Customs union to which Equatorial Guinea is also a member. Shared investment code. Aspirations for future monetary union.

Sources: Robson 1987; Economist Atlas 1989; CEC 1993b; Pomfret 1992; and various journalistic sources 1995.

the world economy remain both as prime incentives regionally to integrate and major obstacles towards it. Weaning off a dependency on hard currency country markets and boosting intra-regional patterns of trade would present a useful first step forward by stimulating greater specialisation between member states.

Most participating members in the agreements shown in Table 2.3 have been sub-Saharan countries. The Arab Maghreb Union (AMU), formed in September 1989, represents the only serious attempt made by a North African group to establish an RIA. Initial declarations of developing somewhat ambitious integrational links based on perceived complementarities in the region have not yet materialised and intra-regional trade patterns remain weak (only 3 per cent by the early 1990s). Pomfret (1992) states the prime reason for this as being their similar range of primary products and labour-intensive manufactured goods which allow only limited internal specialisation to evolve between them. Some North African countries have forged regional alliances with the Arabic countries of the Middle East owing to the close economic and socio-religious links that lie between them. The Arab League and Organisation of Arab Petroleum Exporting Countries (OAPEC, a subset of OPEC) are both examples of inter-regional co-operative organisations whose membership consists of the countries from these two regions.

The leading regional agreement to be signed between Middle Eastern countries has been the Gulf Co-operation Council (GCC) formed as a reaction to the Iran–Iraq war in 1981 between Bahrain, Kuwait, Oman, Qatar, Saudi Arabia and the United Arab Emirates. The GCC has been only marginally more successful than the AUM at deepening integrational trade links with at least some tariff and NTB concessions being achieved. Some progress has also been made in co-ordinating monetary policy and enabling the free movement of people between members.

The EU's global inter-regional links

The emergence of the EU as an international interlocutor has entailed a broad and complex set of inter-regional relations being developed between itself and other groups of countries. As noted in Chapter 1, these relations have become increasing significant in a world of deepening regionalisation and global interdependence. The EU has also taken an active role in assisting regional integration initiatives between third countries through these relations and mechanisms, such as the regional cumulation provisions, that aim to encourage economic co-operation between countries within an RIA (CEC 1995b, c). This has been motivated by the belief that inter-regional negotiations offer a potentially more efficient and effective alternative to conducting international relations than a convoluted series of group-to-country arrangements. Of course, the pooling of national sovereignty required for inter-regional relations to function effectively has been a source of difficulty for the EU and other regional groups. This has limited the scale of relations that the EU has wished to foster on this basis, or led to variant agreements with individual countries in some cases. It should also be noted that some of the EU's inter-regional agreements have contained asymmetric conditions applied to singled out third member countries.

The EU's inter-regional relations have also not been free of global 'power' politics. For instance, certain Latin American countries have been enthusiastic advocates of closer ties with the EU as a means to counterbalance US economic and political influence in the region. This is confirmed by Grabbendorff (1990) who also highlights the differences of opinion within the EU between the Iberian member states, which were keen to develop such links, and the UK which expressed concerns over the apparent meddling in the USA's 'backyard'. When President Reagan called for a trade embargo on Nicaragua in 1985, the Community was split on the issue of whether to comply. Closer relations with the EU were also sought by ASEAN member countries to help check Japan's growing dominance in East Asia. Furthermore, Mols (1990) comments that ASEAN approached the Community to seek its support after the US withdrawal from Indochina in the mid-1970s. For the EU, ASEAN has represented a stepping stone to the Pacific from which it can extend its zonal influence.

The marginal shares of total EU trade taken by the non-European regional groups (with the exception of NAFTA) also led Regelsberger (1990) to suggest that these relations are more politically driven than economic. The pyramidal hierarchy of preferential trade terms granted within the EU's

Common Commercial Policy (CCP) clearly reflects this with ex-colonial countries and those on the EU's external periphery (i.e. EFTA, the CEE and Mediterranean Basin countries) placed at its apex. It is also the case that some of the EU's inter-relations have functioned on a formal political dialogue basis, such as those with the Front Line States.

There are, however, important economic factors that play their part in determining the EU's inter-regional links. First, there is their key role in the EU's development policy, although this is still skewed heavily towards the ACP beneficiaries of the Lomé Conventions. The professed 'economic morality' on which the EU's global trade relations are said to be founded (Brittan 1993) has at least nominally provided the guiding principle on which these politico-economic relations are based. The EU has also stated its similar commitment to 'open regionalism', both regarding its own conduct and that of others. Hence, it has offered assistance to deregulate the cumbersome and protectionist trade regimes of other RIAs when requested. This commitment has become increasingly crucial at a time when the newly inaugurated WTO will more closely monitor the impact of further regionalisation and deepening inter-regional relations which accompany it. Yet arguably the most crucial economic function that the EU's inter-regional links performs is in relation to the strategic dimension in which Europe has been able both to extend and satisfy its global interests (see Chapter 1).

Association agreements and co-operation agreements have traditionally been used as the EU's regional instruments. The former possess a more extensive array of measures and apply to regional neighbours. Articles 113 and 238 have usually served as the legislative basis on which association agreements are founded, while the more limited co-operation agreements draw on Article 113 as well as Article 235 for this purpose. Although the character and text of both kinds of agreement vary, they nevertheless share common features. These include unlimited duty-free access for industrial goods, various tariff concessions on specific agricultural products and financial assistance from the European Investment Bank (EIB) to help facilitate industrial development and diverse co-operative initiatives. Revisionary adjustments have been made to both forms of instrument over the years in order to maintain their relevance to changing global circumstances and develop a greater degree of functional flexibility. Some co-operation agreements may be non-preferential in nature which ensures that they exceed the beneficiary conditions already enjoyed under the EU's GSP scheme. In addition to those signed with some RIAs, the EU has also signed a number of non-preferential co-operation agreements with countries such as India, Pakistan, Sri Lanka, China, North Yemen, Mexico, Chile and South Korea. An overview of the EU's inter-regional relations is given in Table 2.4.

The EU's relations with Latin America from the mid-1980s onwards have largely concentrated on consolidating the process of democratisation

Table 2.4 The EU's main inter-regional relations with non-European countries

Regional group	Relations with the EU
African Caribbean Pacific (ACP) 70 country group	Yaoundé and Lomé Conventions since 1963 (see Chapter 6)
Andean Pact	Co-operation Agreement (1983), implemented 1987 covering economy, trade and development co-operation. Some provisions aimed at tackling drug trafficking. GSP beneficiaries.
Arab League	Memorandum signed in 1975 covering economic, social, and cultural co-operation, investments, trade and technology assistance. GSP beneficiaries.
ASEAN	EC–ASEAN Agreement (1980) covering economy, trade and development co-operation, GSP, investments, joint ventures and broader economic matters. Both parties to study the ways and means of eliminating trade barriers.
Asia–Europe Meetings (ASEM)	First formal inter-regional dialogue established in 1996. Main aims to encourage further trade and investment links and explore the scope for dialogue on political and security issues. Next meetings scheduled: UK (1998), South Korea (2000).
Central American states (Contadora Group and CACM members)	Co-operation Agreement (1985), implemented 1987 covering economy, trade and development co-operation.
GCC	Co-operation Agreement (1990) covering non-energy trade, agriculture, fishery, R&D, technology, environment and investment. Seeking a free trade agreement from the EU on industrial goods by 1995. GSP beneficiaries.
Mediterranean Basin countries	Association and Co-operation Agreements reinforced by Euro-Med Partnership policy framework. Customs union agreement with Turkey. Special trading arrangement with Israel (see Chapter 4).
Mercosur	Co-operation Agreement signed in 1992 covering economy, trade and development co-operation. Future objective of a free trade agreement in 'non-sensitive' trade. GSP beneficiaries.
Rio Group (Contadora Group and its support group: G8)	Consultations began in 1987 between foreign ministers. Rome Declaration signed in 1990.
SADC	Co-operation Agreement signed in 1994 covering economy, trade and development co-operation.

Sources: Regelsberger 1990; Nuttall 1990; the CEC and various journalistic sources.

in the region. This has largely taken the form of special provisions targeted to deal with drug production and trafficking in the region, financial assistance in managing the debt crisis and active promotion of regional integration. The signing of a co-operation agreement with the Andean Pact members in 1983 was the earliest example of institutionalised relations between both parties. A new basis for EU–Latin American relations was established in 1985 by the creation of the so-called 'San José' process involving a co-operation agreement with CACM members plus those of the Contadora Group, namely, Columbia, Mexico, Panama and Venezuela. Two years later, a parallel forum for more informal relations was introduced when the Rio Group brought together foreign ministers from the Contadora Group and its Support Group (Argentina, Brazil, Peru and Uruguay) for semi-annual discussions with the Community.

The basis of the Rio Group meetings was more formalised within the provisions of the Rome Declaration signed in 1990, while the breadth of issues covered has also widened to encompass a range of socio-economic and environmental fields. In 1992, the EU further broadened its inter-regional links with Latin America by signing a Co-operation Agreement with the Mercosur Group. Although the EU would have appeared to have developed an extensive network of relations in the region, Latin American countries have been somewhat disappointed at the level of assistance granted to them with respect to both access to the SEM and investment aid. Some of the poorer states have in particular sought higher priority assistance similar to that enjoyed by the ACP countries under the Lomé Conventions.

The generally underdeveloped level of African RIAs and, more importantly, the supplanting role played by the Lomé Convention explain why the EU's inter-regional links with African countries remain relatively limited. The provisions of Lomé do, however, include measures (e.g. the Cross-Border Initiative) to promote regional integration but little success has been achieved. Collier and Gunning (1995) have recommended that reciprocal free trade access between the EU and African states would establish the credibility in trade reform required in which intra-regional arrangements could be rooted. This would depend on how institutionally and economically burdensome it will prove for the latter to manage such a regime.

Elsewhere, South Africa's dismantlement of apartheid has revived EU interest in developing more meaningful relations with the SADC. In October 1995, the Commission dedicated funds totalling ECU 11.5m towards a new rehabilitation programme for the region. A possible free trade agreement could also soon be signed between the EU and South Africa. Most North African countries, with the exception of Libya, currently join the Mashreq group of Middle Eastern nations, Turkey, Malta, Israel and Cyprus in the Euro-Med Partnership (EMP) with the EU. This was established in 1995 evolving from a well-established inter-regional relationship, although admittedly characterised by a series of bilateral arrangements. The EMP hopes to change this primarily with plans to set up a free trade area between the two regions by 2010. Relations between the EU and other Middle Eastern states have mainly included the GCC. The EU has been generally cautious to extend economic concessions to the GCC members, for example, in industrial trade and technology. Brandenburg (1994) notes that this has principally arisen from a protectionist stance taken with respect to the EU's petrochemical industry. However, this caution may evaporate in a future world economy where the Gulf will become the increasingly dominant supplier of oil by early next century.

In Asia, the EU continues to maintain well-established relations with ASEAN, although more recently these have been somewhat soured by the Commission's decision to graduate many of its members from the EU's Generalised System of Preferences (GSP). Furthermore, the regular imposition of protectionist measures against ASEAN imports have provided additional grievances harboured by their member states against the EU. The monitoring of how the APEC forum evolves over future years is likely to become the top priority for the EU in the region, as will the strengthening of ties through the ASEAN dialogues. This issue will be discussed in some detail in Chapter 5.

CONCLUDING REMARKS

Regionalism and the globalisation of business activity have together been the most significant forces to shape the post-war world economy. Europe has played a crucial instrumental role, providing the model and organisational template on which many RIAs have been built. As Molle (1990) observes, the history of European integration can be seen from one perspective as a by-product of technological progress, and from another as a collective aspiration for political and continental unity, given the capacities of European nations for both military conflict and economic disintegration. Ex-Yugoslavia supplies us with a modern example of the latter. Other global regions have recently endeavoured to initiate or extend existing regional agreements, perhaps most importantly in the Pacific Rim area. Latin American countries are seeking the USA's attention to build a Pan-American RIA that enables them to acquire improved access to US markets. Although many African RIAs have risen and fallen, a sizeable collection of them survive today bearing the common feature of overlapping membership.

We have analysed the different concepts of regional integration and how the economics of free trade areas and customs unions produce trade creation and trade diversion effects which respectively increase and decrease levels of welfare. They also generate dynamic gains that have been used to defend them against critics which accuse preferential trading agreements of undermining the multilateral system of liberalising world trade and thus being a 'second best' route to free trade itself. It can be concluded from the studies that have been commissioned that net welfare gains can be attributed to the EU on this account. According to Lawrence (1991) regional integration in Europe has provided the 'building blocks, not the stumbling blocks' for securing a stable world economy. This being said, trade creation benefits might have been higher had it not been for detrimental NTBs applied within the EU in the 1970s in particular.

3 Single market, single money

At the beginning of the 1990s, the European Union set itself an ambitious agenda for deepening the integrational links between its member states. This was embodied within the terms of the Maastricht Treaty which envisaged some form of economic and monetary union (EMU) by the end of the decade. These aspirations built on the single European market (SEM) programme which by the end of its target date of 1992 had installed most of the components for an internal market within the Community. In addition to political factors, a common belief which united such ambitions was that a more integrated EU would improve its competitive position within the world economy, thus leading Europe onto a higher path of prosperity in the twenty-first century. Both the SEM programme and plans for EMU must therefore be seen at least partly as strategic reactions to external forces being impinged on the Community. In this chapter, we shall examine the composition and intent behind these progressive stages of European economic integration and the potential benefits as well as costs that they bring. In addition, the global dimensions of both the SEM and EMU will also be considered.

A SINGLE MARKET FOR EUROPE

The origins of the SEM programme

As we know from Chapter 2, the single market ideal has roots in the Treaty of Rome. However, it was not until the mid-1980s that a culmination of factors had combined to overcome previous inertia which had hindered any plans for its realisation. We must also evaluate the SEM process in the perspective of global competition and the globalisation of business activity. The Community's position was slipping in an increasing number of high-growth industries due to a combination of successful business strategies conducted by US and Japanese companies and the respective advances made in new product and process technologies. Europe's competitiveness was also being undermined in more mature industries from newly industrialised countries. Thus, European producers were being pincered at both ends of the industrial scale. Given these conditions, it is perhaps easy to see why the formation of the single market can be viewed in defensive or strategic integrational terms.

The Single European Act (SEA) of 1986, drafted by the then newly appointed Commission President, Jacques Delors, outlined the scheduled programme of measures aimed at forming a single European market by the end of 1992. The SEA was not only concerned with the single market, but also widened the constitutional scope of the Rome Treaty, with extra provisions being made on matters such as policy co-ordination, strengthening the institutional powers of the European Parliament, codifying the basis of a joint foreign policy position and other issues. Lord Cockfield's White Paper *Completing the Internal Market* (CEC 1985a) laid out a series of 282 proposals for implementing the single market which provided the schematic guidance for the SEM programme. The White Paper categorised the barriers that hindered the completion of a common market into those of a physical, technical and fiscal nature. By the 1992 deadline 92 per cent of the proposals for removing these barriers had been implemented by the member states.

The European Commission reports on the single market: hurdles and hopes identified

Initial investigations into the SEM's potential benefits and the impediments obstructing them were made by two parallel Commission studies (CEC 1988a; Cecchini 1988) that formed the basis of the 'Costs of a Non-Europe' research project. These examined what remaining obstacles existed to creating a common or internal market in the Community and calculated estimates of both the static and dynamic benefits generated from their removal. Tariff and quantitative restrictions had been mostly eliminated by the late 1980s, but the studies identified a number of major barriers to trade that still persisted within the Community. These were:

- asymmetric technical standards and regulations between member states;
- complex and lengthy administrative procedures on customs transactions on intra-Community trade;
- restrictions on public procurement purchases that limited market scope to national boundaries;
- lack of market integration in certain service industries within the Community that constrained their growth and limited consumer choice.

As Robson (1987) notes, traditional common market theory underplays the role of factor mobility in the integrational process, thus denying it of one of its most critical advantages. The SEM programme aspires to the harmonised integration of both factor and product markets providing allocative and productive efficiency gains. The creation of a functional common market in the Community thus held the aims of presenting both consumer and producer with a more competitive and dynamic market environment, resulting in four principal consequences:

- a reduction in both private and public sector costs from different types of scale economies being exploited;
- improved efficiency through industrial reorganisation and a more competitive environment;
- new patterns of competition emerging in markets and industries;
- increased innovative activity, new business practices and processes.

The measures within the SEM programme were essentially microeconomic in nature, but had obvious macroeconomic implications. Their ability to yield these main benefits rested on producing an effective market integration in which the eponymous 'four freedoms' of capital, labour, goods and services were released. Figure 3.1 illustrates the microeconomic effects that are triggered by the elimination of the remaining non-tariff barriers (NTBs) within a common market area. Let us analyse each of the main forces that are at work.

Economies of scale and cost efficiencies

The single market will help firms to exploit potential economies of scale both from its spur to inter-industry and intra-industry restructuring and the increased production volumes derived from higher levels of expected domestic and foreign demand via improved price competitiveness. These will manifest themselves in a variety of guises. Technical economies will be generated from the opportunity to expand production within a more harmonised and integrated marketplace which has been bound together by common standards. Marketing economies are to be had from the improved distributional efficiencies, while the liberalisation of financial services offers opportunities for financial economies.

Additional economies may be generated from firms seeking to collaborate with new or existing European partners on research and development projects. Continued participation in the SEM would also give rise to economies of experience whereby workers and managers learn cost-reducing methods. Firms will furthermore be impelled to look for ways to reduce X-inefficiencies as a means to cope with the intensified competitive pressures that can be expected under SEM conditions.

Price and profit levels

A combination of price discriminatory practice, asymmetrical technical standards and distributional factors contributes to the uneven price levels that can be found on similar products between countries. The SEM should both harmonise those differences and lower price levels through improved cost efficiency and competitive pressures. Profit levels could initially rise

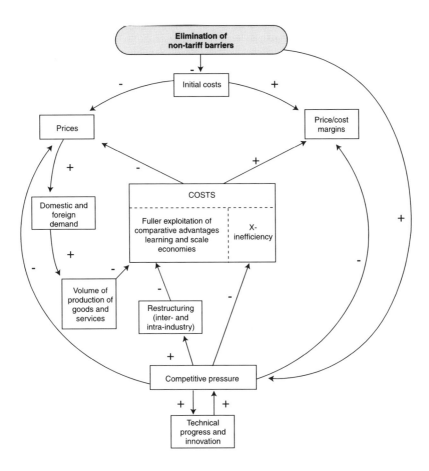

Figure 3.1 Integration and the effects on size of markets: schematic presentation
Notes: The sign + indicates an increase
         The sign − indicates a reduction
Source: CEC 1988a: 125

from new found efficiencies induced by the SEM, but these would be repressed by competitive threats from abroad. Those companies that enjoyed artificially high profit margins which were protected by national market boundaries would be most exposed. The microeconomic effects of the SEM will to an extent highlight inefficient companies that will face the prospect of bankruptcy in the face of unfamiliar competitive realities. To quote Cecchini (1988) the profitable gain from the single market is to be 'earned, not inherited'.

Technical progress and innovation

We have already mentioned that the SEM will motivate firms to seek mutual scale economies through collaborative R&D ventures. The general intensification of innovative activity in the single market environment will be driven by firms' reactions to raised competitive pressures from existing and new rivals in the marketplace. This will be demonstrated by new product and process developments in addition to investments made in new technologies to resist such pressure. In an attempt to galvanise innovative activities and the diffusion of new technologies across Europe, the EU has extended its framework of R&D policy to meet these objectives (see Chapter 9). The fusing together of such activities should enable EU firms to compete more successfully in high-tech industry in particular. The Cecchini Report estimated that in terms of economic welfare the total potential gains of the SEM's microeconomic effects would lie between the equivalent of 4.3 to 6.4 per cent of Community GDP, which if converted into 1988 prices stood at an ECU 216bn average. The full breakdown of those gains is shown in Table 3.1.

Changes brought about by the single market at a microeconomic level will have a series of macroeconomic effects. Consequential improvements to public finances, balances of trade, inflation and unemployment levels would be made by the market integration process of the SEM. Studies of the 'Costs of a Non-Europe' attributed these to four main determining factors which are shown in Figure 3.2.

The elimination of border controls will improve the competitiveness of intra-EU imports not only in relation to domestically produced products but also to extra-EU imports, potentially resulting in trade creation and trade

Table 3.1 The single market's estimated gains in economic welfare from direct microeconomic effects

	ECU bn (1988 prices)	% GDP
The removal of barriers affecting trade	8–9	0.2–0.3
The removal of barriers affecting overall production	57–71	2.0–2.4
The fuller exploitation of economies of scale	61	2.1
Intensified competition reducing business inefficiencies and monopoly profits	46	1.6
Gains from market integration alternative estimate to above two estimates combined	62–107	2.1–3.7
Total (for EC12)	174–258	4.3–6.4
Average	216	5.3

Source: Cecchini 1988

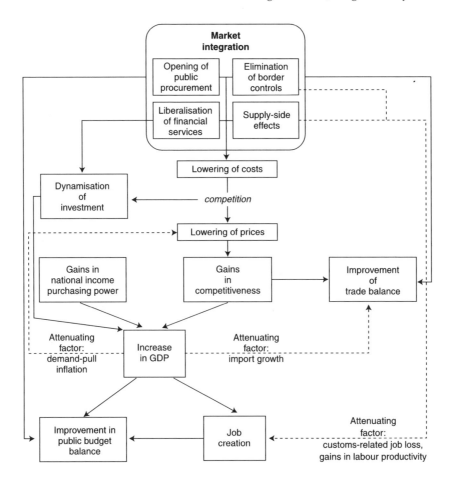

Figure 3.2 Macroeconomic changes associated with the completion of the SEM
Source: CEC 1988a

diversion respectively. There should be an improvement in member states' terms of trade as cheaper imports become more accessible and from a concomitant fall in inflation levels.

The opening of the public procurement markets to enable cross-bidding between producers in different member states for public sector contracts will relieve pressure on both public finances and the taxpayer. Companies that will be mostly affected are those in transport, energy, telecommunications and construction industries.

The liberalisation of financial services is intended to release a dynamism of investment across the SEM. This should arise from a further integration of Europe's financial markets that generates a more efficient allocation of capital flows in an enhanced competitive environment. Further gains may occur from the improved facilitation of pan-European business activity and more favourable conditions for economic and monetary union.

An assortment of supply-side effects that originate from heightened business competition can be expected to be generally positive on the macroeconomic account. Although increased productivity gains are likely in the short run to lead to job losses, longer term gains in employment and output are thought to be substantial. Table 3.2 outlines the macroeconomic benefits that were estimated by the Commission's studies. Their research concluded that if other economic policy measures accompanied these effects then an increase of 7 per cent in Community GDP and 5 million new jobs would be attainable over the medium term.

The Commission's studies of the 'Cost of a Non-Europe' have been criticised by many as being incorrigibly optimistic. This is partly due to the assumption that all SEM legislation would be in place by the 1992 deadline which, as Table 3.3 testifies, will possibly not be the case until 1999 at the earliest. However, most criticism rests on other erroneous assumptions and the methodological approaches employed. For example, the studies made no attempt to estimate the effects of fiscal harmonisation or the differential impacts upon individual member states or regions. Assumptions were also made that labour made redundant from the rationalisation of firms would be re-employed with relative ease and that NTBs were the essential impediment to the four freedoms.

Moreover, the Sutherland Report (CEC 1992a) noted that the SEM's legislative framework suffered from serious procedural flaws and a lack of clarity over issues such as consumer protection rights. Subsequent Commission documents that aimed to reinforce the strategic aspects of the SEM programme also noted the need for a more robust external trade policy (e.g. more recourse to Article 113 of the Common Commercial Policy (CCP);

Table 3.2 Estimated macroeconomic gains from single market integration in the medium term

Total	Customs formalities	Public procurement	Financial services	Supply side	
Relative changes (%)					
GDP	0.4	0.5	1.5	2.1	4.5
Consumer prices	−1.0	−1.4	−1.4	−2.3	−6.1
Absolute changes					
Employment (millions)	200	350	400	850	1800
Budgetary balance (% of GDP)	0.2	0.3	1.1	0.6	2.2
External balance (% of GDP)	0.2	0.1	0.3	0.4	1.0

Source: CEC 1988a

Table 3.3 Outstanding SEM measures to be implemented, 1994–9

Date	Measures
1994	Higher education diplomas recognised across EU.
	Open competition for all public authority contracts, including utilities.
	Insurance companies unrestricted to sell policies throughout the EU.
1996	Stockbrokers to gain open access to operate from anywhere in the EU.
	Banks able to deal on all EU stock exchanges with the exception of Greece, Portugal and Spain.
1997	Application of a single VAT system, if member states agree to a permanent change.
	Airlines able to fly any route EU airspace.
1999	The curtailment of duty-free sales on ferry crossings and flights.
	Free internal market for cars by the end of the year. Trade restraints on Japanese imports must be lifted by all member states.

Source: *Financial Times*, 4 January 1993

see Chapter 6). Consideration needed to be given to the external dimension of EU competition policy if the integrity of the internal market was to remain intact (CEC 1993c). Special measures to assist SMEs through the transitional process and the role played by Trans-European Networks (TENs) were among other initiatives discussed, as well as a commitment to establishing more sustainable patterns of economic development. The Commission furthermore accepted the need to 'ensure conformity and transparency in the transposition of Community directives into national law' and announced that a major study of the economic effects of the SEM programme was to be published in a 1996 report (CEC 1993d).

In a sense, it should come as no surprise that the initial studies sketched an alluring picture of a future single market. Its objectivity must obviously be questioned owing to the composition of its authorship. We can therefore contend that the studies were, at least partially, a marketing exercise to promote the SEM.

Accommodating the single market

Thus far, we have conversed in the somewhat optimistic tone of the Commission's studies. There are also costs associated with implementing the SEM programme in addition to important factors that have undermined the benefits envisaged from reaching their full potential.

The costs of compliance

The SEM programme implies a degree of adjustment to be made by participating private and public sector organisations, the significance of which will vary from industry to industry. Newly harmonised standards and regulations may incur large administrative costs, with the new procedures for VAT across the EU being a prime example. Those industries which were either reliant on state aid or protected domestic markets for public procurement contracts will also find the costs of compliance to the single market's rigours relatively high. In the long run, however, the costs incurred from creating a more level playing field across the EU will progressively diminish while the attributed benefits will become more apparent.

Coping with threats as well as opportunities

The market-oriented principles of the single market imply a wider range of threats for firms from the 'survival of the fittest' ethos that underpins them. We have already discussed how the SEM is intended to expose inefficiencies and inefficient firms. An increased level of bankruptcies bred from the harsher realities created by the SEM could be seen both as unpalatable and potentially more damaging in the long run. A valid case could be made for some firms which momentarily fail the single market's test to be eligible for appropriate support to assist them through the transition period. These could be newly established and inexperienced firms on the verge of developing strategically important products for EU industry. The widening of a future output gap might result from the lack of selected transitional assistance. Such an approach would, however, run the risk of undermining one of the main benefits of the SEM, that of creating a more competitive environment within the EU.

Regional, social and environmental impacts

A similar dilemma arises if we consider the potential regional impact of the SEM. Certain regions in the EU will be more prone to threat than opportunity from the programme's measures. This is particularly relevant if we adhere to the core–periphery view of regional development which dictates that more liberalised market conditions will exacerbate the process of divergence between richer core regions and poorer peripheral ones. The alternative neo-classical view, based on the counter-belief of market forces working towards a convergent equilibrium position, argues that the SEM's effects would be contributive ultimately to greater regional balance. The Commission and most member states have embraced the former view more warmly. The SEA contained proposals to double the EU's Structural Funds as a compensatory measure against the anticipated detrimental impact of the SEM upon peripheral regions.

The single market is the centrepiece of the 'Business Europe' ideal, but the parallel ideal of building a 'Social Europe' can at times oppose the objectives of the former. The SEM's market-orientation may well encourage businesses to conduct themselves in a more competitive manner, but social costs may be generated in the process. Industries in structural decline and having to cope with the pressures imposed by the transition to the single market may seek increased protection from extra-EU importers in the form of weaker social provisions that allow them to be more cost competitive. On a more positive side, EU firms may call for the authorities to fund training and other human resource schemes that better exploit opportunities for workers and companies handling new technologies diffused from the SEM process. Extra Structural Fund provision has been set aside by the EU to help meet these identified needs.

Increased economic activity and growth are prime aims of the single market programme. Concern has therefore been expressed regarding the SEM's adverse environmental consequences. In attempts to remain competitive within the single market, some firms may decide to avoid costly environmental management procedures. However, an alternative thesis asserts that rising prosperity levels can actually help ease ecological pressures by the resources now freed up to install environmental protection measures on a wider scale. The EU has nevertheless increased both the funding and scope of its own environmental policy and has made a systematic attempt to integrate it into other policy fields.

Recasting competition and industrial policies

The competitive environment will experience a climatic shift under single market conditions. The new patterns of competition that are beginning to emerge in Europe as a result have forced the EU to adjust the framework of its competition and industrial policies accordingly. While the SEM should generally raise the pitch of competition between business in the EU, Catinat (1988) notes that the enhanced potential for economies of scale increases the risk of cartelisation. Greater efforts to co-ordinate member states' own competition policies have also been arranged to achieve a more harmonised approach across the single market.

State aid to industry has been argued by many as incompatible with the SEM's free market principles owing to the distortions and asymmetries that it generates in industrial competition. Those member states who pursue relatively interventionist industrial policies at the effective expense of business located elsewhere in the EU can be placed in this context. However, the alternative case for supporting particular firms and industries through the SEM's transitional period has been used to defend the continued use of state aid, for instance that which is still granted to the Airbus consortium.

A case of bad timing?

It was perhaps rather unfortunate that the single market's arrival coincided with the major recession experienced across the EU in the early 1990s. The main concern to our analysis is how these cyclical conditions affected both the SEM's inauguration and subsequent trajectory. A range of responses was made by organisations in the light of both circumstances. On the one hand it caused some firms to seek harder for the market opportunities which the SEM offered, although recessional factors restrained the resources required to adopt more Europe-oriented strategies. For others, the combination of the twin pressures proved burdensome to the point of bankruptcy. While markets had become liberalised under the single market, the recession impeded the consolidation of the reforms made. Public finances, also under cyclical pressure, failed to secure the fiscal gains promised by the Commission's studies. Other estimates made by the Commission's *ex ante* research obviously had to be revised downwards.

It is perhaps too early to judge the extent to which the early 1990s recession affected the positive impact of the SEM. We can state with some certainty that it deflected attention away from the opportunities which were offered to business. However, most of the benefits promised by the single market were of a dynamic, and not static, nature. Business confidence in the SEM programme, albeit initially knocked, should grow with further acquaintance as factors such as economies of experience connected to working within the single market gradually reveal themselves. Thus, the full potential of the SEM will take years to be realised, but will depend upon effectively and sustainably deployed corporate strategies in a stable macroeconomic environment.

Outstanding work to be done

Many of the proposals that had been outlined in the Commission's White Paper (CEC 1985a) had already been installed by member states well before the 31 December 1992 deadline. Thus, the SEM's 'big bang' effect proved to be of limited magnitude. What is more important to recognise is that the complete legislative apparatus of the single market will not technically be in place until around the end of the decade. Table 3.3 shows the outstanding measures that remained unimplemented after 1993. As well as these, extra proposals in support of the SEM programme have been introduced.

There are also many measures subject to derogation agreements which primarily grant delays for specified durations to transpose fully certain aspects of legislation. For example, this has applied to Greece, Portugal and Spain in the case of EU rules governing public procurement. The generally uneven response across the EU in complying to the SEM's Directives (1,308 in total) should also be noted.

Strategies for the single market

Strategies deployed by business in response to the challenge posed by the single market will be largely determined by the structural environment of their own industry. This is because the scope and character of the opportunities presented will be largely fashioned by this environment and the parameters set by it.

Nevertheless, there is a series of considerations that all firms need to make if they are to unlock the latent potential of the SEM. A re-assessment of the forces driving new competitive conditions as well as the firm's own relative strengths and weaknesses would need to be conducted. New patterns of competition bring with them redisguised threats from familiar sources and fresh threats of a previously unknown origin. The recognition of these threats is essential in formulating a company's own tactical, strategic and logistical response. More discerning consumers will arise from the removal of NTBs leading to more sophisticated expectations regarding market products.

The creation of a large internal market carries implications for restructuring, concentration and co-operation for companies and their industries. Restructuring in accordance to the SEM will involve a rationalisation of a firm's organisational structure, major changes made to main product lines and attempts to extend the geographical coverage of operations. An incentive to merge or take over other European companies will arise in an endeavour to generate greater scale economy gains and other competitive advantages.

Increases in industrial concentration have obvious implications for competition policy, with vertical integration activity generally bearing the highest welfare costs. Firms seeking to make co-operative arrangements with like-minded European partners could take many forms. Strategic alliances made over new product developments, R&D efforts, distributional networks and various other aspects of business may prove mutually beneficial. Larger firms may be able to resource their own organic growth within the SEM simply by widening their geographical coverage and adopting appropriate European marketing strategies.

One of the overarching intentions held by the architects of the single market was the transformation of the firm's culture. Promotion of the pan-European focus was essential to the subsequent success of the programme. This specially applied to somewhat introspective firms which had not yet reached their own potential to operate effectively across the European marketplace.

THE SINGLE MARKET: A FIRST GLANCE AT THE EXTERNAL DIMENSION

The purpose of this section will be to examine the external dimension of the SEM. This will largely entail trade and investment issues which, along with other related aspects of this dimension, will be explored in other chapters. Hence, in some cases, the analysis will be introductory in nature.

The trade effects of the single market

The term 'Fortress Europe' has been used by those concerned about the adverse effects which the SEM will have on third countries. To the extreme, these fears relate to the building of vertiginous protectionist walls around the world's largest unified market from the possessive and insular behaviour of its member states. The evidence regarding this issue is still inconclusive. The continued growth of intra-EU trade (see Table 6.2 on page 172) and the extensive range of tariff and NTBs that are still applied on external imports, especially on those from 'sensitive' industries (i.e. those in structural decline owing to lost comparative advantage and other factors) provide vindication for such concerns.

On the other hand, the EU's contribution to the success of the Uruguay Round of the GATT multilateral trade talks could be interpreted as a desire to maintain an open extra-trade policy in keeping with the ethos of liberalisation championed by the SEM. Furthermore, around half of imports coming into the SEM enter under preferential terms. The recipients of EU trade concessions include those on its external periphery and almost all developing countries via the Lomé Convention and the EU's Generalised System of Preferences (GSP) scheme.

Theoretical concerns over the external dimension of the SEM largely focus on the trade diversion effects produced. In brief, this arises from member state producers acquiring preferential treatment in partner markets relative to and at the expense of competitive external producers. With the creation of a common market the regional producer's position is strengthened through the harmonisation of intra-RIA rules of market access encoded between its members. Hence, the scope for trade diversion is widened. Further cause for this may come from the act of certain home producers seeking compensation from the EU's commercial policy-makers in the form of external protectionist measures. These firms will fall into one or both of the following positions: where high adjustment costs have been incurred from compliance to the common market's regime; where greater degrees of threat than opportunity have been experienced in the new competitive environment (see Dornbusch 1990). These pressures are most likely to surface in member states with a high ratio of 'sensitive' industries.

If the authorities are unwilling to provide such compensatory protectionist measures then uncompetitive home producers may propose other alternatives. This could include the dilution of social legislation or state aid to improve their own sectoral competitiveness *vis à vis* foreign producers. An open single market where liberal trade conditions exist for third countries will expose the cost of business regulation within the EU (Wolf 1994). This would further oblige the EU and its member states to scale down social charges and similar regulatory constraints deemed to undermine competitiveness. Breaching the walls of Fortress Europe would also check the monopoly power evolving from SEM-induced industrial concentration. Foreign firms competing from outside the single market with those inside will be better able to exert competitive pressures on them under the governance of freer trade, hence leading to raised welfare levels. As Winters (1992b: 21) states, 'the most important policy conclusion is that competition, and especially external competition, must be preserved'.

While the Commission's 'Costs of a Non-Europe' studies failed fully to consider the external dimension of the SEM programme, they did discuss the static trade diversion effects of removing internal market barriers across the EU upon extra-EU imports. These were categorised into twin Stages: (i) and (ii). Stage (i) concentrated on the direct cost reductions in products traded between EU member states that were generated from the barrier removal process. The direct and indirect production cost effects from the same process on EU-produced goods, whether traded or not, were allocated to Stage (ii).

The combined trade diversion effects from both categories has been calculated at a reduction of over ECU 37bn in extra-EU imports (CEC 1988a). On a sectoral basis these range from a 0.12 per cent fall for agricultural products to 33.33 per cent for beverages. Only coal and coke sectors were expected to experience trade creation effects and five sectors are deemed to encounter neutral balances from Stages (i) and (ii). Milner and Allen (1992) have attributed this to cost savings made by both exporters and importers from the elimination of certain technical barriers once differentiated by the specifications of individual member states. However, the Commission's analysis is bound both by the fact that only the largest seven EU members were included and by its assumption that the market integration process is complete. The impact on third countries will depend on the scale of the trade relationship with the EU in those sectors analysed and any countervailing effects from concessionary trade arrangements that have been established. Studies undertaken by Norman (1989, 1991) and Haaland (1990) seem to suggest that the EFTA countries would be hardest hit, particularly in high-tech industries, thus lending further incentive to acquire access beyond the European Economic Area (see Box 4.1 on page 108).

Third countries will also be affected by the dynamic processes of the single market. Those EU-based firms that have exploited the opportunities it affords to improve corporate competitiveness will be in a stronger position both to defend existing market shares and to challenge more effectively those of external producers elsewhere. On the positive side, the growth and efficiency effects of the SEM programme will both boost EU demand for foreign products and lower import prices for EU products. Davenport and Page (1991) estimated that developing countries could experience a 3 per cent increase in demand for primary products from the first of these effects. Technological and industrial development will also be stimulated if this applies to the production of intermediate or component products, depending on the level of sophistication involved. Cheaper imported EU capital goods will similarly serve this cause.

Foreign investment in a competitive single market

One of the essential purposes of a common market is to improve the competitive position of its members within the world economy. The main competitive advantage will arise from reduced unit costs and a more conducive macroeconomic environment for growth. However, globalisation's blurring of national and indeed regional boundaries requires us also to consider the gains accrued by foreign multinational enterprises (MNEs) residing inside the EU. The SEM offers existing and potential inward investors similar opportunities to those enjoyed by European MNEs. An integrated market of 367 million high-income consumers is just as accessible to insider producers as it is to indigenous ones. Foreign MNEs already well established on EU soil have sought to develop more coherent pan-European strategies in anticipation of the SEM, while newcomers have made endeavours to acquire an initial foothold. The spectre of Fortress Europe has added further imperative to obtaining wider SEM access, enabling companies to circumvent future trade barriers that are allied to such a scenario.

The recognition by American MNEs of the European common market's potential long predates the SEM programme itself. During the original development of the Community, many US companies were actively pursuing inward investment strategies based on the respective defensive and offensive objectives of sidestepping the customs union's CET and securing a bridgehead in the most crucial market in Europe. Yannopoulous (1990) observed that between 1957 and 1964, US inward FDI to the EEC trebled. Current US investment interests still remain strong in the EU, with American firms accounting for 42 per cent of the EU's inward cumulative total in 1993.

Japanese investment activity in the EU accelerated sharply after the advent of the SEA, with inward FDI flows trebling between 1984 and 1988 (see Table 8.4 on page 271). Japanese MNEs have continued to expand their outward FDI interests in the EU during the 1990s. However, this must be tempered by a consideration of other relevant developments. The corporate strategies of Japanese companies have become increasingly globalised, spurred on by the emerging market potential of the East Asia region and the rising yen. During the early 1990s, there were signs that Japanese foreign investment in Europe was flagging, owing to recessional factors and perhaps more importantly the perception held by some that the EU represented a mature market region with relatively limited growth prospects. Nevertheless, the scope for further Japanese investment in Europe remains capacious. Progressive integrational moves towards EMU and the EU expansion into Central and Eastern Europe may reinvigorate Japanese inward investment over forthcoming years. Furthermore, Japanese outward FDI in manufacturing only accounts for 7 per cent of total Japanese manufacturing output compared to 20 per cent for the USA, perhaps suggesting that global aspirations are yet to be fully realised. The decision of Japanese firms to shift more production activity to Europe will obviously have some impact upon the EU–Japanese trade balance which squarely lies in the latter's favour. Not only would it have the effect of reducing export levels from Japan, but in addition Japanese producers in the EU would be in a position to export back to Japan on the EU's behalf. This is dependent, though, on the investment–trade relationship established as it is conceivable that intermediate product imports from Japan will increase from serving their European production requirements.

From the early 1990s, an increasing number of South Korean firms have made direct investments in Europe's single market. Recent evidence suggests that their motives have been driven by the need to counteract both current and future protectionist measures from the EU on their products (Young *et al.* 1991). A similar pattern is likely to emerge from multinationals originating from other newly industrialised countries (NICs) in the East Asia region. This is due to both the high proportion of the EU's NTBs that they attract and the intentions to 'graduate' most of them from the GSP scheme.

The SEM and tensions in an uncommon common commercial policy

We have already explored to some degree the SEM's implications for both intra-EU trade and extra-EU trade issues, both on a separate and mutually related basis. Other tensions, originating from what the EU's authorities preach at home and practise abroad, also require examination. Criticism has been made of the EU's external trade policy – the CCP – based on certain inconsistencies apparent within its framework. The most high profile case in this matter concerns the past imposition of bilateral voluntary export restraints (VERs) on Japanese car imports by France, Italy, Portugal, Spain and the UK. Such barriers belong to a group of 'grey area' protectionist measures that have proved particularly evasive to the GATT's negotiable remit. Moreover, they have fuelled fears of a Fortress Europe scenario and a subsequent lack of faith in the EU as a trustworthy global partner. The EU's position would be exacerbated if it were to adopt extensive trade restraints as common policy. As it is, the bilateral arrangements on Japanese car imports were supplanted by an EU-based VER due to be phased out by 1999.

The French government's use of VERs was partially a reaction against the UK acting in the role of a 'Trojan horse' within Fortress Europe. The favoured location of the UK for inward investment in Europe, especially by Japanese and South Korean companies in recent years, has been attributed notably by the French to a series of 'beggar thy neighbour' national policies pursued at the expense of fellow member states. Examples of these policies have been the relatively low levels of social provision found in the UK and the vigorous attempts made by the Thatcher administration in the 1980s to lure Japanese companies with an array of miscellaneous incentives. However, the Maastricht Treaty's revisions to Article 115 ensure that member states will find it increasingly difficult to take recourse to unilateral or bilateral protectionist measures to resist trade deflected imports.

Further apprehensions contained within the Fortress Europe scenario concern the standards and certification procedures associated with installing the SEM. Compliance to these could potentially involve non-EU firms in complex administrative proceedings with EU authorities. Alternatively, non-EU firms and industries may find that their own products have been-purposely made incompatible with EU standards and certification. Both eventualities could be contrived as part of an active protectionist policy. Organisations outside the EU, especially from the USA, were particularly keen to seek representation on the SEM programme's standards and certification boards. The EU has also made efforts to assist developing country producers to manufacture in accordance with new harmonised European standards (CEC 1995f).

Strict EU rules of origin and local content requirements on foreign producers based in the region have been another area of concern. This policy has been deemed acceptable if member states have expressed anxiety over the production bases of foreign MNEs that are simply 'screwdriver plants', whereby huge volumes of imported component parts from the home country are merely assembled from 'completely knock-down' kit form. Stringent demands placed on these firms to incorporate high levels of an indigenous EU contribution to both product and factor content would make the situation somewhat more palatable to member states. However, they run the risk of being viewed by external producers as protectionist posturing. The EU's future behaviour will be affected by the recently signed trade-related investment measures (TRIMs) agreement from the Uruguay Round of GATT which attempts to bind its signatories to limited use of these measures.

More tension between the EU and its trade and investment partners may be caused by reciprocity provisions built into the framework of the SEM programme. This quid pro quo policy of allocating trade concessions to non-EU countries in return for similar compensation could be seen as playing of the EU's upper hand to full effect. The US finance sector expressed strong concern on this issue over the Second Banking Co-ordination Directive, while similar fears were articulated by US telecommunication companies over access to EU public procurement contracts. In general, agreements of this kind between the EU and third countries have been resolved by mutual consensus. Incidents of reciprocal granting of preferential access to the SEM have anyway been few and far between and usually arise as a low-key retaliatory measure where they do occur.

Product and factor market distortions, as well as welfare losses from overt trade diversion, are prone to occur from a single market apparatus built around strategic integrational principles. We have discussed how some idiosyncratic aspects of the CCP have been at least partially to blame for these distortions while also threatening the integrity of the SEM itself, for instance through bilateral arrangements. Efforts to establish an open and uniform exterior to the single market have been hampered by competing internal interests that seek to maximise the opportunities conferred by the SEM programme. Where the member states and EU institutions have been able to forge a convergence of interest it has resulted in one of two outcomes. The first of these concerns the mutually possessive behaviour that entails the continued maintenance of protectionist barriers around the single market. The second evolves from the realisation that an open SEM is of long-term benefit to all countries for reasons explained above. The EU's engagement in multilateral negotiation processes (especially the GATT/WTO) has obviously helped produce more outcomes of the second type. Thoughts on what pattern of action will emerge in a future world economy where the Pacific Rim hosts its largest unified market still remain largely conjecture, but of increasing significance to European business and policy-makers.

ECONOMIC AND MONETARY UNION IN EUROPE

Economic and monetary union is the next stage of regional integration to follow on from a common market. While the SEM programme essentially consisted of a series of microeconomic measures, the proposals for an EMU are mainly of a macroeconomic nature. Both stages of integration are strongly interdependent with respect to each other. The installation and functioning of a monetary union requires financial markets to be harmonised to enable the free flow of capital across the currency area. Factor mobility inherent to a common market is needed to help absorb the asymmetric shocks and transitional instabilities that monetary integration incurs. The obvious benefit that EMU brings to a single market is the introduction of a single money. The existence of a common medium of exchange for the SEM will help realise the potential of many of its remaining inert aspects.

In this section, we shall look at the plans for the development of EMU as intended by the European Union, concentrating on its internal facets and implications for Europe. The broader global context of EMU is explored in the last section of this chapter.

Towards EMU in Europe

A confusion often arises over the exact definition of EMU as outlined in the Maastricht Treaty. Some use the term to denote European monetary union and not economic and monetary union, which is, strictly speaking, the correct definition since it includes the wider economic policy issues on which the Maastricht Treaty seeks extension of co-operation and co-ordination from member states. It would be helpful at this point to define the various types of monetary union that can be arranged between countries. Vaubel (1988) has outlined four different theoretical models for us to explore:

1 Currency union: a currency union commits member countries to adopting a common single currency. Monetary policy independence ceases to exist along with, of course, the national currency. A union central bank is necessary to operate a common monetary policy in accordance with an agenda set by member country representation. The co-ordination of a series of other economic policies is implied.
2 Exchange rate union: this is simply where member countries agree irrevocably to fix the cross-values of their exchange rates. A central monetary authority will only be required to assist the co-ordination of monetary policy between countries. The credibility of this arrangement will be undermined by the fact that this union is far easier to dismantle than a full currency union.
3 Free intercirculation union: another possible monetary union could involve the free movement of member countries' currencies across the union area. A currency competition may develop whereby those currencies not deemed to hold a sustainable market value are driven out of circulation. Fixed exchange rates may be required to maintain disciplinary conditions.
4 Parallel currency union: a parallel currency union bears some resemblance to the free intercirculation model, but with the addition of a parallel currency circulating between member countries which competes with existing national currencies for market dominance. The ultimate objective is likely to be the eventual establishment of the parallel currency as the common single currency, provided it passes the test of the marketplace.

The ancestral history of European EMU is shown in Table 3.4. Plans to create a full-blown currency union in the Community predate the Maastricht Treaty by over two decades. The Werner Report's ambition to do so

Table 3.4 The EU's progress towards EMU

1970	Werner Report Plans for EMU by 1980 made, but never fully implemented owing to global shocks. Calls for closer economic and monetary co-operation and joint exchange rate management laid down the partial foundations of events that followed in the 1970s.
1972	Basle Agreement: The Snake in the Tunnel The fixing of bilateral exchange rates between the EC6 after the collapse of the Bretton Woods system. EC6 currencies within 2.25 per cent band (the 'Snake'), and in a 4.5 per cent band against the US dollar (the 'Tunnel').
1973–8	European Monetary Co-operation Fund (EMCF) established in 1973 to assist the co-ordination of the Snake and some further discussion on EMU. Italy leaves Snake in 1973. France leaves in 1974, rejoins 1975, leaves again 1976. Germany leads 'mini-Snake' arrangement with Benelux, Denmark, Sweden and Norway until 1978. Numerous realignments made.
1978	European Currency Unit (ECU) ECU concept conceived at December European Council meeting in anticipation of the EMS.
1979	European Monetary System (EMS) Established in March between all EC9. UK opts out of the exchange rate mechanism (ERM), a quasi-fixed exchange rate system and the main element of the EMS. Very Short Term Financing Facility (VSTFF) set up to assist EMCF with EMS management. ECU as basket currency. ERM bands set at 2.25 per cent around a central rate. Italy uses 6 per cent band, but joins narrow band in January 1990.
1983	Germany and the Netherlands form an exchange rate union.
1986	Single European Act (SEA) Economic and social cohesion expressed as one of the main principles of the SEA. Commits signatories to an eventual single currency.
1989	Delors Plan Proposals outlined for EMU to be embodied in the Maastricht Treaty. European Council meetings held in Madrid and Strasbourg to discuss the proposals and others contained in the Maastricht Treaty. Spain joins the ERM in July within the wider 6 per cent band.
1990	UK joins the ERM in October within the 6 per cent band.
1991	Maastricht Treaty on European Union Plans for EMU based on the Delors Plan. Single currency envisaged by as early as 1997 or by 1999 at latest between the majority of EU members. Convergence criteria targets on monetary and fiscal variables. Three-stage schedule set. Other economic policy co-ordination measures included. Both the UK and Denmark opt out of the final (single currency) stage of EMU.

1992　Portugal enters the ERM at wide band rate in April. By the end of September, the UK and Italy forced to drop out of the ERM. Other currencies come under severe pressure in the foreign exchange markets. The peseta and the escudo devalue later on that year.

1993　Devaluation of the punt in February and the peseta and escudo in May.

Recasting of the ERM
ERM implodes owing to renewed market pressure in August. A 15 per cent band set for participating members as a defensive move to salvage the system.

Maastricht Treaty finally ratified in all member states by November.

1994　All remaining members of the ERM manage to stay within the new bands.

1995　On accession, Austria decides to join the ERM but Sweden and Finland do not. Further devaluations of the peseta and the escudo in March.
At the Madrid Summit in December, EU leaders decide upon the name 'euro' for the future single currency.

by 1980 was never realised, but did set the original framework for the development of more robust monetary policy co-ordination within the EU. Despite the tribulations of the 'Snake' and 'Tunnel' exchange rate systems during the turbulent 1970s, member states were not discouraged to embark on the more demanding European Monetary System (EMS). The EMS is thought by many to have played a major positive contribution to the Community economy during the 1980s. Its success in achieving exchange rate stability and macroeconomic convergence towards a low inflation, high growth equilibrium illustrated the benefits of closer economic co-operation in this field.

However, Masera (1994) argues that the 'no realignments' period of the EMS between 1987 and 1992 created the rigidities in the system which produced the eventual fatal faultlines. The lack of exchange rate flexibility at the advent of a world recession and the SEM programme's installation only served to build up the pressurised conditions that led to the effective implosion of the EMS over 1992–3. Other contributive factors to have played their part were as follows:

- The costs of German reunification: a high interest policy was pursued by the Bundesbank to contain the inflationary costs of reconstructing the East German economy. As the anchor currency of the EMS, German monetary policy set the tone for interest rates across Europe. The austere policy stance compounded the effects of the recession in Europe and the manoeuvrability of policy-makers to sustain exchange rate stability.
- The emergent power of the speculative foreign exchange markets: the gradual relinquishment of capital controls by member states over the 1980s had encouraged the growth of the speculative market for foreign

exchange. In London alone, private dealers were trading around £450bn worth of foreign exchange on an average day by the early 1990s (see Minikin 1993).

Thus, the power of speculative capital had by this time dwarfed the resources held by central banks used to stabilise exchange rate values. Recessional factors and the market's lack of faith in the member states' commitment to the EMS and Maastricht's EMU schedule led to the 'bearish' behaviour of the speculative dealers that forced out sterling and the lira from the ERM in September 1992. The later devaluations of the escudo, peseta and punt compounded the pressures on the EMS to recast itself.

- The weakening of the Franco-German alliance: the Franco-German relationship, seen by many as the cornerstone of the EU, came under strain in the early 1990s, mainly from differences expressed over what form EU policy should take towards Central and Eastern Europe. The tension that arose between the Germans – who desired a bolder policy option – and the French was partly transmitted into the foreign exchange markets, proving contributive to the events outlined above.

As Table 3.4 shows, these events caused the EMS to pursue a less robust disciplinary framework by widening the ERM's 'normal' bands from 2.25 per cent to 15 per cent, although Germany and the Netherlands maintain the former arrangement. Around this time the Maastricht Treaty on European Union had been ratified by member states which set out the plans and schedule for EMU by the end of the century. As we shall discuss later, the EMS's 1992–3 experience had a damaging impact on the Maastricht Treaty's EMU proposals and ambitions.

Box 3.1 Optimum currency areas

Many critical observers of the events of 1992–3 have argued that the EU lacks the preconditions to establish an optimum currency area (OCA). The early development of OCA theory is associated with Mundell (1961), McKinnon (1963) and Kenen (1969). Mundell defined an optimum currency area as fundamentally 'a domain in which exchange rates are fixed' and proposed that for countries to forge an OCA near perfect factor mobility was necessary. Making the exchange rate redundant required the use of other adjustment channels if asymmetric shocks were to be managed and structural equilibrium restored. As early as 1957, Meade had argued that the low levels of labour mobility meant that Europe had to maintain flexible exchange rate systems.

However, Mundell's use of a 'one country–one sector' model has been criticised in retrospect for being too simplistic and unrealistic. For example, the role played by expectations is overlooked, while the assumption of comparative advantage as the prevailing determinant of trade patterns lacks

Box 3.1 *continued*

validity in a world dominated by intra-industry patterns of exchange, particularly within the Triad. Mundell's theory also ignores the advantages of improved levels of certainty and the reduced transaction costs and other microeconomic benefits that are attributable to monetary integration.

While labour mobility in Europe remains low (but this is also the case in the USA) other productive factors have become increasingly mobile since the 1960s, especially financial capital, compensating for any potential loss in relative price change mechanisms provided by the exchange rate. Furthermore, the degree of international financial integration radically alters the context within which OCA theory should now be applied, while also introducing an alternative adjustment channel of cross-border financing which has to be considered. Although Mundell's work has become somewhat outdated, it has been revised by some analysts in seeking to explain the adverse distributional effects of monetary union through the loss of the exchange rate as a policy instrument to tackle short-term disequilibria.

The general debate was expanded by McKinnon who explored the relationship between an OCA and the relative openness of economies within it. His main premise was that negative asymmetric demand shocks would cause workers in a country with a large trade sector to push for compensatory measures after witnessing the ensuing fall in their standards of living. This could take the form of a currency devaluation that would simply result in more than proportionate inflationary effects in that country through the transmission of higher priced imports. Thus, an OCA would provide greater disciplinary benefits to more open economies through the removal of the devaluation option. Many European economies are among the most open in the world and high intra-bloc rates of trade have become well established. Extra-EU trade ratios are also higher than those for the USA and Japan, thus proving its eligibility for an OCA once a single currency had been well established.

Kenen's thesis postulated that the more structural diversification that existed across the OCA, the greater the chance that any asymmetric demand shocks would average out within the industrial sectors of those participating, therefore reducing the need to adjust exchange rates and the terms of trade. Most EU economies can be typified by their highly diverse industrial profiles, thus also qualifying them on this account. Indeed, studies conducted by Bini Smaghi and Vori (1993) indicated that a positively applicable case could be made here by the EU than by the USA. Other commentators have also pointed out the need for fiscal harmonisation between members to facilitate transitional and future adjustments, while large OCAs run the risk of denying relatively weaker countries of flexible monetary policy options. Hence, plans for any EMU in Europe must be accompanied by parallel measures that aim to address the above.

The Maastricht Treaty's agenda for EMU

The present commitments made by EU member states to a single currency actually has its roots in the SEA, but the Maastricht Treaty formalised this into a working schedule based on a progressive three-stage approach with concomitant macroeconomic convergence criteria. These guiding principles of Maastricht's EMU agenda have their origins in the Delors Plan of 1989, which was responsible for setting the convergence criteria for EMU participants. These consisted of:

1 Price stability: an average rate of inflation that does not exceed by more than 1.5 per cent that of the three best performing member states.
2 Interest rates: an average nominal long-term interest rate that does not exceed by more than 2 per cent that of the three best performing member states in terms of price stability.
3 Exchange rates: participation in the ERM's normal bands without devaluations from the beginning of EMU's Stage 3 (i.e. at least two years).
4 Budget deficits: a government budget deficit of less than 3 per cent of GDP under sustainable conditions.
5 National debt: a government national debt of less than 60 per cent of GDP.

Although the Delors Plan recommended a three-stage approach to EMU and set the process rolling from July 1990, it was left to the Maastricht Treaty's negotiators to agree on the timetabled schedule. Table 3.5 charts the progress of those three stages to the final adoption of a single currency by at least a small coterie of member states by 1999. A single currency was envisaged as early as 1997 if a majority was able to meet the convergence criteria by then.

There was much debate over the Maastricht Treaty's plans for EMU ranging from the decision of the UK and Denmark to opt out of the critical Stage 3 owing to concerns expressed over the political and economic costs of submitting to a single currency, to the disquiet made known regarding the macroeconomic convergence criteria that had been formulated. Anxieties that arose over the latter issue were founded on the somewhat strict constraints that the convergence criteria targets placed on member state governments attempting to meet wider policy objectives leading up to the Stage 3. Its critics argued that this predicament was exaggerated in times when an economy experienced downward cyclical trends. The EMU's architects, who were largely influenced by central bankers, defended their case by stating that EMU candidates were required to be tested by rigorous macroeconomic discipline if a successful transition was to be secured. However, even core EU member states have appeared to face extreme difficulty in meeting EMU's prerequisitory challenges.

Table 3.5 Maastricht's three progressive stages to EMU

Stage 1 (Single Market)

- Tied into consolidating the SEM. Economic and social cohesion policy co-operation on regional, competition, industrial and other policy areas.
- All member states to join the narrow band of the ERM.
- Financial deregulation leading to the creation of a single financial area. ECU made more accessible for the private sector.
- Enhancing of economic policy co-ordination across the EU.
- To be completed by the end of 1993.

Stage 2 (Transitional)

- To commence from January 1994.
- European Monetary Institute (EMI) established as precursor to European Central Bank (ECB).
- EU currencies to remain in ERM's normal bands without devaluations for at least two years.

Stage 3 (Monetary Union)

- European System of Central Banks (ESCB) established between EU members to co-ordinate central bank policy.
- The majority of EU member states are required to meet the convergence criteria targets for a single currency to be adopted between them.
- If this is not achieved by 1997, then 1999 is set as the next reconvenable date for the EMU but a minority number of member states are allowed to proceed this time.
- ECB to employ monetary policy for participating EMU members.

The benefits and costs of EMU evaluated

The overarching objectives of any economic and monetary union are to enhance both welfare levels and the competitive position of those countries taking part. European EMU should therefore be seen fundamentally as an endeavour to strengthen EU business competitiveness in relation to its global rivals. The advantages that EMU bring are in many ways an extension of those associated with the SEM programme. The benefits of improved factor mobility, wider scope for scale economies and productivity gains, higher levels of intra-regional trade and more efficiency policy co-ordination are common to both. Let us consider, though, the competitive advantages that can be more specifically attributed to EMU itself:

- Lower business costs: the irrevocable fixing of exchange rates under EMU will remove the costs associated with having to monitor and hedge against adverse exchange rate variability. Increased efficiency in corporate planning should arise from the more predictable business environment created by fixed rates. The eradication of exchange rate transaction costs from the EMU process has been estimated at between 0.5 to 2.0 per cent of EU GDP equivalent.

- A more conducive environment for economic growth: the common use of the euro should lead to more efficient price mechanisms and improved capital mobility within the EU. Consequently, one could expect greater price stability to be achieved and an improved exploitation of market opportunities within the SEM. An accumulation of these factors among others will engender a more favourable environment for economic growth in the EU.

- Dynamic gains from further economic integration: EMU establishes a single currency for the single market, thus exploiting the SEM's fuller potential and the more dynamic integrational benefits. Dynamic gains can also be expected from the increase in intra-EU trade and investment under more unified and liberalised market conditions. This will widen the scope for both intra-industry and comparative advantage specialisation, as well as synergetic joint ventures and other forms of strategic alliances between EU firms.

- Lower inflation: the effects of more efficient unit cost management will generally lower EU inflation levels. The European Central Bank's (ECB) prime objectives of price stability and constitutional independence are aligned to those of the Bundesbank model. This is intended to provide the institutional framework on which a credible and non-inflationary EU monetary policy can be formulated in the future.

- Lower interest rates: these could result from a combination of low inflationary expectations (inferred from above), greater exchange rate certainty and more stable patterns of economic growth induced by EMU. An ECB founded on those principles noted earlier will reinforce the possibility of maintaining sustainably low interest rates.

These points are primarily focused on the internalised improvements to EU business competitiveness which EMU is expected by its supporters to produce. An analysis of the impact of a globally circulating euro and the specific benefits which it will bestow is made in the following section. But what of the disadvantages of EMU in Europe? It has often been cited that the political costs involved in surrendering national sovereignty and control over crucial policy instruments to common Community institutions are more relevant than the potential economic costs. For many opponents of EMU, the two types of cost are inextricably linked. This is based on the notion that the dissolution of political self-determination over national economic policy incapacitates a member state to respond to the potentially damaging vicissitudes which affect them more directly than others. For example, it may be appropriate for one country to set its exchange rates and interest rates at levels different to those of partner countries in reaction to an asymmetric demand shock. This may then inflict a proportionately greater inflationary impact for that specific country. However, this argument assumes that countries are able to conduct independent monetary policies in an increasingly interdependent world economy. Key advances made in telecommunication technologies, financial market innovation and deregulation along with the diversification of currency portfolios have all weakened the old grasp of national authorities on domestic monetary control. Indeed, this trend would appear to make a case for a greater degree of international control to be applied.

Another familiar and related cost attributed to EMU is its abdication of the national exchange rate as a policy instrument. The ability of a country to devalue its currency and either improve the competitiveness of its exports or act as a shock absorber to asymmetric shocks, or achieve both simultaneously, is an option no longer available under EMU. A stronger argument can generally be made for using a floating exchange rate as a shock absorber device than for devaluations. The long run effects on competitiveness may prove detrimental by insulating domestic producers from the disciplinary conditions imposed under a fixed system with regard to containing their unit costs. Moreover, within an RIA with highly developed patterns of intra-regional trade, a country's decision to devalue could be easily construed as a 'beggar thy neighbour' policy.

Additional problems with EMU have been highlighted by Minford (1992). In tests within his 'stochastic simulation' model, he subjected a number of EU member state economies to hypothetical global shocks in order to evaluate the welfare costs generated by both floating exchange rate and EMU conditions. Minford found that particular countries, such as the UK, benefited more under a floating exchange rate regime. He went on to express concern over the discrepancy between how foreign exchange markets and policy makers react to global shocks. The former, he argued, are able to anticipate and adjust quickly to new conditions, while the latter respond in a relatively lethargic manner, causing price, wage and interest rate levels to lag behind. According to Minford, this predicament implied that only a floating exchange rate could offer a solution to the nominal rigidities and inflexibilities that could potentially accumulate from managing a fixed rate system. The EMS's 1992–3 experience lends some support to this thesis.

We have already noted that the SEM and EMU share the basis of common advantages. A corollary of this is that they share common disadvantages too. The same regional, social and environmental impacts of the single market analysed earlier in this chapter may under certain circumstances manifest themselves more readily under EMU. Eichengreen (1990) focused on the structural imbalances caused by EMU and the implications carried for regional development. He estimated that only 1 per cent of any regional or national fall in GDP is compensated by EU funds directed for regional policy purposes. While the EU is committed to double this allocation of funds, Eichengreen suggests this still remains vastly inadequate. Other analysts have furthered the argument by drawing on OCA theory and asserting that larger fiscal transfers are necessary to offset the insufficient diversification of the EU economy to absorb those structural imbalances incurred by EMU. However, evidence gathered by Krugman (1991) led him to conclude that the EU's regional variance in its industrial production structure would accommodate asymmetric shocks that arose in the process of establishing EMU and would, additionally, lead to further diversification of this kind.

The outlook for EMU in Europe

We have already hinted that the plans of the Maastricht Treaty for EMU have been shaken by various events and developments of the early 1990s. Despite the difficulties experienced, Thygesen (1993) advocates that to keep any remaining credibility of the EMS intact attempts should be made by member states to return to the narrow bands of the ERM as soon as possible. Masera (1994) also upholds this objective, stating both the SEM's dependency on exchange rate stability and the avoidance of recourse to the devaluation option, but adds that more flexibility needs to be built into Maastricht's EMU framework.

EMU's future still rests on a firm Franco-German alliance – providing the foundation stone even if only a small core of member states are able to meet the convergence criteria targets on time. There are indications that French integrational aspirations lie more in the deepening process as opposed to growing German opinion and intentions to widen EU membership to the east. Such a divergence arising within the alliance could seriously set back EMU's prospects for success. The plans to enlarge the EU further will necessitate a review of its institutional functions that could include the treaties that lie therein.

OECD forecasts made over 1994–5 estimated that only five member states (Denmark, Germany, Ireland, Luxembourg, Netherlands) are likely to meet the budget deficit target by the end of 1996, as against an estimate of nine made in 1991. The forecast is worse for the national debt target in which only four countries (France, Germany, Luxembourg, UK) seem set to achieve success here as opposed to an eight country estimate made previously. Even if the Maastricht Treaty's fiscal preconditions are considerably loosened, certain 'core' countries will still have an arduous task ahead in meeting them. Belgium, for example, was burdened with a national debt in the region of 134.4 per cent of its GDP by 1995 (see Table 3.6). Its finance ministry calculated that even satisfying the Maastricht criteria of 60 per cent by 2009 would require consistent budget surpluses of 6 per cent of GDP on an annual basis up to that date. Some discretion is allowed by the Treaty's provisions, though, on meeting the public debt targets if the ratio is declining substantially and continually, or an excess can be proven as either temporary or has arisen under exceptional circumstances.

There has been much debate over the costs and benefits of creating a 'multi-speed' Europe which entails core member states participating in an

Table 3.6 Maastricht convergence criteria for EMU (1995[1])

	Inflation rate (%)	Long-term interest rate (%)	Budget deficit (% GDP)	Public debt ratio (% GDP)	No. of criteria fulfilled[2]
Austria	2.5	7.4	5.5	68.0	2
Belgium	1.6	7.9	4.5	134.4	2
Denmark	2.1	8.6	2.0	73.6	3
Finland	1.3	9.4	5.4	63.2	2
France	1.7	7.8	5.0	51.5	3
Germany	2.1	7.1	2.9	58.8	4
Greece	9.9	18.8	9.3	114.4	0
Ireland	2.5	8.5	2.7	85.9	3
Italy	4.9	12.3	7.4	124.9	0
Luxembourg	2.1	6.2	+0.4	6.3	4
Netherlands	2.2	7.2	3.1	78.4	2
Portugal	4.2	11.7	5.4	70.5	0
Spain	4.7	11.5	5.9	64.8	0
Sweden	2.8	10.8	7.0	81.4	1
UK	2.7	8.4	5.1	52.5	3

Sources: Reuters; European Monetary Institute
Notes:
1 Twelve-month period ending September 1995 for inflation and long-term interest rate; budget deficit and public debt ratios are Commission estimates for 1995.
2 Does not include exchange rate convergence.

EMU and leaving other members to catch up when they are willing and able to do so. This approach, if pursued, could form either a platform from which eventual EMU between all member states could be engineered, or conversely a lasting wedge between members stuck at a lower level of integration while others have progressed on. Provisions made within the Maastricht Treaty stipulate that the European Council must agree to a two-thirds majority to allow EMU to be initiated between even a minority of member states. A sufficient number of countries who fear being left in a slow-track Europe could thus hold back those destined for the fast track.

Current plans to introduce a European single currency derive from Green Papers submitted by both the Commission and the EMI in 1995. The preferred scenario chosen in these documents was a three-phase transition period starting in 1999 and ending in 2002. Briefly, it was envisaged that a series of gradualised preliminary actions would be required successfully to implement full EMU, ending in the abolition of national currencies and the installation of the euro as legal tender. These actions included: central banks and other financial institutions initially conducting their transactions in a hard euro; building the supportive legal framework; a vast public information campaign; manufacturing the new notes and coins which would take some time to produce.

While the commitment to forge ahead with EMU from 1999 onwards remains more or less strong, increased political manoeuvrings between EU member states can be expected as this date approaches. By late 1995, the German government had, for example, tabled proposals for a 'stability pact' which was designed to enforce budgetary discipline through the imposition of harsh fines on non-compliant countries. It also expressed concern over the accuracy of national data submitted with respect to the convergence criteria targets. These and a variety of other issues, as they become apparent, will keep economists and policy-makers with an interest or stake in EMU very busy until the end of the decade.

THE GLOBAL IMPACT OF EMU

A central economic objective of EMU is to improve the EU's competitive position in the world economy. Monetary integration between even a core of EU member states will cause global repercussions of a significant magnitude and help to fashion a new international monetary regime in the twenty-first century. The effects of EMU on EU competitiveness have already been investigated in an internalised context, but what international role will the euro play in the EMU process? This will serve as the main topic for discussion in this section, which draws largely upon the theoretical work of two Commission studies (1990b, 1992b).

The international position of the euro

The ascendancy of the euro as a tradable currency is obviously tied to the progress and destiny of European EMU. If successful, EMU could propel the euro to challenge the US dollar's current status as the prime global currency. The process would be assisted by the continued relative decline of the US economy, yet the historic experience of sterling provides increasingly valid evidence that the dollar will remain predominant for some time owing to a range of factors. First, the world economy favours a single standard for technical reasons as it may be able to perform the convenient function of providing it with a universally acceptable medium of exchange. Hysteresis effects may supply the distortions and time lags to ensure that despite the over-proportionate role attributed to the fading nation's currency, other countries will desire internationally to trade with it. This can cause a variety of problems for the country itself, as the UK experienced in the inter-war period when sterling became 'bigger' than the UK economy, imposing the overburdening global supply and demand forces that proved contributive to the UK's relative decline.

The euro's global monetary functions

The main advantages bestowed by possessing the global standard currency are the lower transaction costs derived from borrowing and trading in your own currency and the shifting of more exchange rate risk onto other countries. Monetary integration as intended under EMU will bring with it additional savings and gains that can be interpreted in global terms which will be discussed later. The principal disadvantage that accompanies this role is the increased exposure of monetary policy to global shocks. This will also have considerable knock-on effects to other areas of policy. In the Commission's report (1990b), the authors explored the potential international role of the euro (or ECU) across three functions traditionally performed by money, namely those of a means of payment function, a unit of account and finally as a store of value.

The means of payment function

Countries require foreign exchange reserves which have to be accumulated if they are to participate in conventional world trade. They are also needed to manage exchange rate policy conducted by central banks. Krugman (1984) commented that 'probably the most important reason for holding reserves in dollars is that the dollar is an intervention currency'. Although the dollar's role as the international intervention currency has diminished, its predominance remains intact. However, this will be further eroded by EMU as compliant member states will subsequently have no need to utilise dollars for this purpose.

The euro may also be increasingly used as a vehicle currency by the private sector's foreign exchange reserve dealers. A vehicle currency is used to perform the task of being money's own money. Where a double coincidence of wants is difficult to establish for a dealer who, for example, wishes to exchange escudoes for punts, it may prove more convenient and less costly to use the euro as a vehicle currency, whereby the escudoes are first exchanged for it and then into punts. As the European integration process deepens and widens, dealers should encounter a greater incentive effect to use euros as a viable alternative to the dollar as a vehicle currency. The SEM and the ensuing rise in intra-EU trade have already made preparatory contributions to this.

The unit of account function

EU firms invoice their exports primarily in their own national currencies. Most of the world's other regions, especially Latin America, the OPEC countries and most developing nations, invoice exports in dollars. Euro invoicing, drawn out from the EMU process, will generate scale economies released by the merging of European national currencies. These benefits would also be shared by those nations with close regional ties with the EU (i.e. EFTA, Central and Eastern Europe, the Mediterranean Basin) who may also tend to transact exports and imports in euros. However, dollar patterns of trade are likely to remain entrenched by the growing importance of Trans-Pacific trade and investment, as well as the very conceivable persistence of oil trade in dollar terms and an aggregation of other factors raised in this section.

The extent to which other countries will wish to peg their own currency against the euro will depend upon both the relative strength of the dollar and the success of building the reputation of the euro on that of the Bundesbank model. Those countries on the EU's external periphery are the most likely candidates to seek inclusion in any future euro zone which emerges.

The store of value function

The motives for private investors to hold euro assets will be determined by the evolution of a euro zone with respect to the substitute 'safe haven' it offers for storing the value of their funds. The stability of the zone will in turn rely on the institutional fortification and credibility that is associated with the ECB. More progressive financial market integration and liberalisation are also required to persuade further investment in euro denominated assets. However, the extent to which global asset portfolios have become diversified in attempts by fund managers to minimalise exchange rate risk led the Commission to conclude that EMU will only induce a 5 per cent increase in expanded euro asset demand here. This would still represent a substantial rise in demand for euros and the EU would need to respond by raising the level of supply to avoid resultant exchange rate instability.

Despite the relatively small euro holdings on the international bond market, the growth of euro/ECU bonds will continue to outpace most rival currencies and will possess much greater stature when EMU is complete. Nevertheless, continued financial globalisation may prove to consolidate the dollar's role as the global standard store of value. Developments in regional integration on a pan-American and Trans-Pacific scale could have a similar effect.

Global co-operation and co-ordination

Since 1985, the G7 summits held between the world's seven major industrial nations have provided the framework for macroeconomic policy co-ordination between them and associated countries. Four of the G7's members – France, Germany, Italy and the UK – are EU members, and therefore we can expect EMU to have a substantial effect upon the co-ordination and co-operation process at this level. Under EMU, the EU's representation at G7 summits will effectively reduce the number of representatives to four on monetary policy co-ordination. The corollary of this is that all EU members taking part in EMU will now have some voice at negotiations of this kind. The political and economic weight of the EU would rise in accordance with this change, but fiscal policy co-ordination is likely to remain limited to the four largest EU members within the G7 structure. This may develop into a similar G4 arrangement as EMU extends within Europe with consequential effects upon the fiscal management of EU member states, especially if progressive moves are made towards economic and political union (EPU), the ultimate stage of regional integration.

In the meantime, the loss of monetary policy autonomy at national level incurred from EMU implies that fiscal policy measures become more crucial in achieving macroeconomic stability at home. This infers that there will be less room for manoeuvre within international fiscal co-ordination, and in turn increased pressure on global monetary policy co-operation to accomplish its aims successfully. The fiscal convergence criteria laid down in the Delors Plan and the timetable to which convergence is scheduled have made and will also continue to make a considerable impression here. The expanded representation of EU membership will affect the policy stance of other G7 members – USA, Japan and Canada – which would now have to adjust to accommodate the increase of the EU's 'spill-over' effects arising from the policies of a strengthened EU position. The global impact of the common and combined policies of the EU would outweigh that of the individual member states who were also original G7 members. The level of interdependence is thus raised within G7, while the USA, Japan and Canada now have a greater imperative to work together to achieve global macroeconomic stability to avoid the higher negative externalities associated with not doing so.

European EMU is unlikely to make any significant changes to the operation of the IMF. At present, the EU's aggregated quota obligations and allocated voting rights surpass both those of the USA and Japan combined. The EU has well over the 15 per cent necessary to form a blocking veto against initiatives with which it does not agree. The only possible influence EMU may have would originate from a subsequent removing of intra-EU trade as international trade itself. It is highly doubtful whether this development, if it did actually occur, would diminish the EU's allocated voting rights owing to overriding political factors. Hence, the concentration of EU representation at the IMF can only work to its advantage in global affairs.

Potential savings and gains from EMU

EMU should render a number of potential savings and gains made principally by the EU but also by third countries. The adoption of a common euro will make foreign exchange reserves used for intervention purposes redundant. The elimination of the need to hold these funds has been estimated to produce a saving equivalent to 4 per cent of EU GDP. Other attributable gains will come with the increased use of the euro as the intervention currency used by EMU participants in non-EU dealings. An estimate for seniorage revenue gains from foreign euro cash holdings has been put at 0.045 per cent of EU GDP per annum.

The microeconomic gains of the euro acting as EMU's vehicle currency are threefold. The reduction of transaction costs on the foreign exchange market for external trade contracts could produce a saving of up to 0.05 per cent of EU GDP. It has also been calculated by the Commission that the lowering of exchange rate risk from the subsequent development of euro invoicing could lead to a 10 per cent increase of EU trade. In addition, European banks would be presented with expanded opportunities for using the euro in trade invoicing and global currency transactions, as well as be positioned to offer euro-based financial services on a wider global scale.

The alteration of a G7 to a G4 membership should engender an improved global co-ordination process of macroeconomic policy (monetary policy in particular as discussed above) merely by its less fragmented structure. The converted welfare gains derived from this should be distributed on a global scale and offer non-summit countries the public good of greater macro-economic stability in the world economy.

Raising a new standard? The euro as a prime global currency

The ascendancy of the euro via the EMU process poses a new set of challenges for the EU and the world economy. It is doubtful that the euro will replace the dollar as the global standard currency in the foreseeable or even semi-distant future. This is despite the fact that the ability of the latter to play the role has looked less convincing in recent years. The US record on exchange rate stability and fiscal rectitude clearly confirms this, as does the economy's diminished international status.

What is most likely to emerge is a more balanced tripolar structure within the global monetary system based on the roughly proportionate weightings of the Triad powers. There are some, such as Kindleberger (1973), who have expressed concern over such a scenario arising, arguing that the system requires a hegemonic structure for it to function in a sustainable manner. This is largely predicated on the need for the leading currency to act in the capacity of the international 'lender of the last resort'. However, Eichengreen (1990) contends that this is only tenable when that leading currency is supported by symmetrical global market power, which is certainly no longer as applicable with respect to the US economy.

Other commentators have noted that past transitions between the old and new order currencies have led to a destabilised world economy, citing the inter-war period as a prime example. Emerson and Huhne (1991) assert that this was mainly due to the lack of joint responsibility taken by the major industrial nations to co-ordinate and manage the transitional process. The G7 summit and other internationally binding institutions presently exist to provide the context and framework for this to be potentially achievable. The division of the system along tripolar lines has also raised fears that future Triad members' endeavours to deepen regional integrational links may concentrate global power into mutually repelling blocs. This argument, however, subscribes to the view of a prevailing strategic approach to regional integration by each region. Recent evidence generally undermines the validity of this view.

The EU is left with important outstanding objectives to achieve if it wishes to promote the euro as a credible and responsible global currency in the future. First, the relative thinness of Europe's financial markets compared to the USA will impede the development of the euro into such. However, in inaugurated EMU conditions the euro could play a crucial part in this development by its galvanisation of the European market and the subsequent erosion of various asymmetries that hinder its progress in becoming a viable denominational option to private asset holders. The US market currently dominates the world's financial asset markets, but the UK's own innovative and sophisticated financial sector may provide some form of future springboard for the euro. A British 'opt-in' to Stage 3 of EMU would obviously be required for this to be fully realised.

We have discussed earlier the relevance of the Bundesbank model in the EMU process. A Bundesbank style ECB should give the euro the inbuilt reputation needed to secure credibility in the world's financial markets and elsewhere. The endurance of the ECB's reputation will in time, however, increasingly rest on its own actions. To a large extent these will be influenced by a diversity of elements brewing within the EU, for instance its own political accountability and relationship to the Council of Ministers, the new EMU fiscal realities facing individual member states and certain industrial lobby groups pressing for compensatory measures to be taken such as a devaluation of the euro. The ECB's place in the EU institutional apparatus will therefore have to be very carefully considered if the euro is to sustain a credible position as a prime global currency.

CONCLUDING REMARKS

Post-war European integration has been at least partly driven by a series of global economic events and developments. Most recently, the construction of Europe's single market was intended to provide a firmer platform from which European business could build a more competitive position in world markets. It has also given European powers a more valuable bargaining chip in international negotiations, especially where the reciprocity issue has been played to the chagrin of external parties. However, increased globalisation has meant that foreign 'insiders' (i.e. MNEs) have been able to exploit the benefits of the SEM to the sometime disadvantage of European firms. Furthermore, some European firms have shifted production and services facilities to low-cost overseas locations in order to compete in the more intense competitive environment that has been created by the

SEM process. The impact of Europe's internal market can only therefore be fully understood by considering its external dimension.

Plans for European EMU have been broadly impelled by similar motives to those behind the SEM programme. Assessing the full global impact of a single European currency is, though, much harder to predict. On the one hand, the efficiencies associated with adopting a single money for a single market must imply an improved competitive position for Europe. This will, however, be largely dependent on how well both the currency's introduction and subsequent management are conducted. Some unforeseen difficulties could combine or lead to a chain reaction of events that might spell disaster for certain member states. Uncertainty also exists over whether the euro will replace the dollar as the global standard currency, with inevitable ramifications for the world economy. Finally, EMU has also demonstrated that the centripetal forces of economics often come into conflict with the centrifugal pull of maintaining national and political sovereignty in the integrational process. Overcoming political resistance to deeper European integration thus remains EMU's most significant obstacle.

4 EU enlargement

While the European Union has harboured ambitions throughout its history to deepen the integrational links between its member states, similar aspirations have been held to widen its membership. This has manifested itself in the accession of three ex-EFTA countries to EU membership in January 1995 and intended plans to make Central and Eastern European (CEE) countries members by the turn of the century. The magnetic pull of the Community, demonstrated by its expansion from six to fifteen member states over the four decades of its existence, has shaped the geo-political complexion of Europe in its own image. Moreover, its progressive enlargement has carried, and will continue to carry, enormous ramifications for the world economy. The focus of this chapter will be to examine the main bases of these two issues.

We shall first consider some of the key common issues that face both the EU and prospective members. Second, an evaluation of the EFTA countries will be conducted in the context of recent accession to membership granted to Austria, Finland and Sweden. In the third section, we shall make an in-depth analysis of EU plans to prepare the CEE countries for membership and the obstacles to be overcome in doing so. Finally, the potential for a further southward enlargement will be contemplated in addition to the development of a more robust EU Mediterranean policy.

INTRODUCTORY CONSIDERATIONS

In this section, we shall discuss four key common issues at the centre of the enlargement debate, namely the balance between widening EU membership and deepening integration within it, the prerequisites to EU membership, how enlargement is to be accommodated by the EU, and the general global impact of enlargement.

Widening and deepening the EU

With the collapse of the CMEA and the dwindling membership of EFTA, the EU now stands almost totally dominant in the European economy. The evolutionary path of the EU may be explained by the 'multiplier effect'; as the critical mass of regional members grows, so does the lure of joining to those remaining on its periphery (Wijkman 1993; Pedersen 1994). This is particularly the case if intra-regional trade patterns are strong. However, the EU's intentions to widen its integrational links to encompass the CEE countries by the turn of the century represent to many an enlargement too far. This view has been expressed by the French who are worried that such intentions will deflect the EU from its path to integrate deeper, in accordance with the provisions of the Maastricht Treaty. Although such opinions are peppered by other motives (i.e. that a CEE enlargement would place Germany at the geo-political centre of the EU), there are valid grounds for concern regarding the balance between deepening and widening membership. These are largely predicated on the argument that the greater the number of countries involved in membership, the more chance there is that common denominators on which to build deeper integration will not be found. To understand fully the reasons for this we first need to investigate the motives which countries have for wanting to join. These can be summarised as:

- improved access to EU markets;
- the opportunity to influence directly the formation of EU policy and law
  – the *acquis communautaire*;
- membership of the world's largest trading bloc and the benefits which it affords;
- the economic assistance that can be acquired through eligibility for Structural and Cohesion Funds.

While prospective members essentially have to accept the dictates of the *acquis communautaire* on joining, the EU could be caught in a potential 'adverse selection' predicament. The expressed desire of countries seeking membership is likely to be based on the net gains to be afforded on doing so, especially with regard to budgetary transfers. The relationship between the magnitude of these transfers and the structural underdevelopment or imbalances of the national economies concerned can be expected to be positively related. Both aspects would put strain on any plans laid for deeper integration across the membership. Nugent (1992) adds that other pressures complicate the issue. For example, widening membership would broaden the diversity of national interests that could destabilise the policy-making and policy-implementing process. He also notes that as the EU integration deepens so will the expectations of prospective entrants.

At this point, we need to consider the evidence of recent years. Applications from certain Mediterranean Basin countries have either been rejected or indefinitely delayed on the basis of the arguments proposed above. Indeed, even the earlier attempts of some EFTA countries to secure accession to the Community in the late 1980s were stalled owing to the preoccupation of existing member states with the SEM programme. However, both ambitions to widen and deepen the EU in the 1990s have not been deemed irreconcilable. The 1980s southern enlargement, whereby Greece, Portugal and Spain acquired membership, demonstrated the degree to which an interdependent relationship could exist between the two. The accession of these countries pressured the Community's decision-making apparatus to adopt qualified majority voting (QMV) on an increasingly regular basis, thus leading the way for the institutional flexibility required to formulate the Maastricht Treaty on European Union.

Evaluating the compatibility between widening and deepening an RIA will also depend upon key conditions that we have discussed in previous chapters. If prospective members possess similar and competitive industrial profiles to incumbent members, we can expect that opportunities for trade creation will make themselves available. Welfare losses through trade diversion will be minimised if the pre-existing tariff and quantitative barriers between them are negligible. Both these conditions hold true for the three ex-EFTA countries which joined the EU in 1995. The CEE and Mediterranean Basin countries, though, do not measure up so squarely.

Moreover, any dynamic integrational benefits will ultimately depend upon how successfully business integrates within the enlarged market area. Again, evidence suggests that for the moment this is more likely to occur between companies based in EU and EFTA nations which have developed well-established patterns of intra-industry trade and investment. Dynamic integrational outcomes derived from expanding membership will in particular have some influence over the extent to which an RIA can deepen links between member states. If wider microeconomic integration is difficult to establish between businesses and markets in the new area it is likely that macroeconomic integration will be hindered. We shall delay until later the formation of any firm conclusions regarding each region's impact upon the balance of this relationship.

Prerequisites to membership

The notion of building a unified Europe that stretched from the Atlantic to the Urals was proposed by Charles de Gaulle many decades ago. The strength of any union between European states will depend on the level of integration intended as well as the potency of political, cultural and socio-religious bonding agents that bind together common objectives. These are required to set more sustainable conditions under which the future direction of the union can be mutually determined and plotted. Any country aspiring to join the EU must therefore meet particular pre-requisites aimed at maintaining the centripetal forces that keep the union together. At the EU's Lisbon summit in June 1992, the Commission submitted a report which has come closest to outlining the form of those prerequisites; a summary of these is listed below:

- a relatively strong and stable economy;
- firmly installed democratic institutions and a good record on human rights;
- widening must not be at the expense of deepening integration;
- no significant current conflicts with existing member states;
- a geographical and cultural claim to being European.

Most of the above criteria were used by the Community to delay indefinitely the application of Turkey to membership made in 1987. Turkey's current GDP per capita level of $1,815 stands at around an eighth of the EU average and nearly half its workforce is employed in agriculture. Its record on human rights is poor and it is still embroiled in hostilities with Greece over Cyprus and the Aegean Islands which have persisted for a number of decades. The country's cultural and religious heritage is inherently different to that of mainstream Europe, while the fact that only 4 per cent of its land mass is actually inside the continent has not worked in Turkey's favour. Nevertheless, the Community decided not to reject the application outright, as it did with Morocco's in the same year, and agreed to form a customs union with Turkey in 1995. It has also in principle accepted the qualification of Turkish membership when the 'time was right'.

Such concessions granted by the EU raise the question of how the fundamental objective to expand membership can override the prerequisitional terms identified. Austria, Finland and Sweden all had no difficulty in meeting those terms, but the CEE countries would at present fail to do so, especially on the first condition. It may take some time before the economies of these countries are able to be sustained within the framework of the EU, but Germany and member states are keen to set a fast track for them to join. On a general level, this enthusiasm is to be perceived in the context of supporting the CEE countries' own transformation into market democracies and exploiting the gains from the post-Cold War peace dividend. Individual member states may, though, be willing to promote a CEE accession for more idiosyncratic motives. The validity of French apprehensions regarding how Germany could stand to benefit from this enlargement may be very pertinent, while the UK's Conservative government sees the more diluted prerequisitional terms as a vehicle to suppress further ambitions to deepen EU integration. This approach, though, implies a commitment to bear the higher costs involved from both assisting the transitional process to membership and the increased transfer payments incurred once the CEE states have joined.

Accomodating enlargement

By the early twenty-first century, the EU could be comprised of over twenty member states, more than a threefold increase on its original number. The EU's institutions and the *acquis communautaire* were designed in accordance with the EEC6's requirements. It was commonly agreed that an EU15 would place inordinate pressures upon the existing framework which would lead to recasting where appropriate. This does not necessarily infer that radical changes will need to take place. The *acquis communautaire* is not completely immutable. Almost all member states have negotiated customised exemptions from it, especially when entering membership (for further details see Nicolaides and Close 1994). The UK and Denmark's opt-out from Stage 3 of EMU is perhaps the most familiar example of one secured by incumbent members. The three ex-EFTA countries have been granted their own exemptions which mainly cover eligibility to receive regional policy funding for remote areas, although they were also able to negotiate a four-year transitional period in which they could maintain their higher standards on the environment, health and safety matters.

Furthermore, the Maastricht Treaty's Article 0 restatement of the Treaty of Rome's similar proposition (embodied in its own Article 237) that any European country could apply for membership reflects the willingness of existing member states to accommodate additional ones. Nicolaides and Close (1994) comment that the institutional implications for the EU will involve only a greater use of QMV and more pressure to extend the powers of the European Parliament. This could consequently centralise more power in the hands of the EU's institutions, but simultaneously reduce the so-called 'democratic deficit'.

The global impact of enlargement: initial comments

The economies of EFTA and the EU are already well integrated in terms of trade and investment flows, in addition to the provisions made under the European Economic Area (see Box 4.1). The EU is already the world's largest integrated common market, but intentions to make it even larger will have a greater impact on the world economy. A synopsis of these is given below to set the general global context of enlargement. We shall explore most of these issues in greater depth in subsequent sections.

- The EU's share of total world trade from 40 per cent to 45 per cent owing to the 1995 enlargement, improves its negotiating position still further on the international stage.
- A wider geo-political consequence of EU enlargement may entail the establishment of new trading blocs or the reinforcement of existing ones as a counter-balancing reaction. Another reaction may consist of non-EU powers seeking closer integration (e.g. a Trans-Atlantic free trade area).
- EU membership gives the three ex-EFTA countries full access to the SEM, reinforcing intra-industry links and the trade creation and dynamic

integrational gains to be had from wider intra-regional collaborations between business. This should in theory improve EU competitiveness.

- The likely trade diversion costs arising from further EU enlargement are unclear. Although Rollo (1995) suggests these are likely to be low, he notes that the added difficulties to EU decision-making that an expanded number of member states would incur is likely to make it more inward looking.
- Any new member states can expect to attract more foreign investment from being inside the SEM. The transnationalisation of economic activity between EU member states should also increase.
- If European EMU is established an enlarged EU will amplify the impact of a common euro as a global standard currency. As preparation for membership, prospective members may wish to peg their own currency to the euro's exchange rate and join the 'euro' zone.
- The accession of the CEE countries could potentially incur the most significant impact of all. This low-cost production base could provide the EU with considerable trade creation gains and a platform from which to compete against the NICs of East Asia.

THE EU'S ENLARGEMENT AND EFTA

By 5 April 1993, four EFTA countries had entered negotiations with the EU to acquire membership. The 1995 enlargement saw three of those countries – Austria, Finland and Sweden – realise their accession to the EU. Norway, the fourth country, had to decline the offer of membership resulting from a 'no' vote in its national referendum, repeating a similar response given in 1972 when it could have joined the following year with Denmark, Ireland and the UK. Nevertheless, the expansion of membership to an EU15 represented the most significant enlargement since its first in 1973.

EFTA's qualifications for EU membership

The EFTA countries possess characteristics that in many ways make them model EU member states. Their workforces are well educated and skilled, they have developed sophisticated management structures and infrastructural systems that enhance factor mobility, and they are rich – half of the world's top ten richest nations are Nordic or Alpine countries (see Table 4.1). High-tech industry plays a prominent role in the structure of most EFTA economies. The level of environmental, health and safety standards is among the highest in the world and their generous welfare provisions and overseas development aid (ODA) donations epitomise the innate sense of civic responsibility found within their peoples. In addition, the cultural, social and religious ties between EFTA and EU countries run deep.

Table 4.1 The EFTA Seven: general economic indicators (latest figures)

	GNP per capita ($)	Unemployment (%)	Inflation (%)	Trade balance ($bn)
Austria	22,790	4.2	3.8	−8.4
Finland	23,050	20.8	1.6	+3.9
Iceland	22,575	5.0	4.1	+0.2
Liechtenstein	33,000	0.2	5.2	—
Norway	25,810	5.5	1.4	+0.8
Sweden	26,800	14.0	2.9	+8.4
Switzerland	36,280	4.6	3.4	+3.5

Sources: WOI 1995c; *The Economist* 1994

Furthermore, EFTA and EU member states share common bonds that have been forged by a series of institutional arrangements and an ever-developing process of cross-regional integration. Many EFTA nations have pegged their currencies' exchange rate to that of the Deutschmark and the ECU for much longer than a number of existing EU member states (see Table 3.4 on page 81). The European Economic Area (EEA) has given EFTA the opportunity to participate in most aspects of the single market and co-operative involvement in other fields. Most EFTA countries have been more trade dependent on EU markets than on intra-EFTA trade, with between 45.4 per cent and 66.6 per cent of EFTA exports being destined for EU markets in 1993 (see Figure 4.1). In the same year 22.0 per cent of EU's external imports originated from EFTA, maintaining its position as the EU's biggest trade partner, with the US's 17.4 per cent share placing it second. EFTA and EU countries are also closely bound by the integral patterns of intra-industry trade. As Table 4.2 shows, some EFTA countries

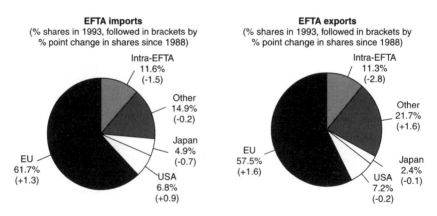

Figure 4.1 EFTA imports and export markets by major partners, 1993
Source: Eurostat

Table 4.2 Percentages of EU12, EFTA and CEE countries' intra-industry trade with the EU, 1988–90

	EU12 members		
France	82	Denmark	63
Netherlands	77	Ireland	59
UK	77	Portugal	42
Belgium–Luxembourg	76	Greece	29
Germany	75		
Spain	73		
Italy	63		
	EFTA6		**CEE**
Switzerland	77	Hungary	50
Sweden	70	Czechoslovakia	46
Austria	68	Poland	42
Finland	39	Bulgaria	41
Norway	36	Romania	34
Iceland	4		

Source: CEPR 1993

have higher intra-industry trade ratios with EU member states than incumbent ones. This improves the opportunity for trade creation to be realised.

This particularly applies to Switzerland, Sweden and Austria, with percentage ratios of 77, 70 and 68 respectively. From a close examination of their economies, this can be explained by their competitive industrial profiles relative to EU economies and a high degree of transnationalised business activity in general. Nestlé, the Swiss multinational, is the world's largest food producer and enjoys a dominant market position across the EU. The Swedish firm Electrolux is Europe's largest manufacturer of household appliances and has production bases in most other EU member states. The somewhat lower percentage ratios for Norway, Finland and Iceland are due to a relatively higher export dependency on their natural resource bases.

The 1995 enlargement: some general considerations

Given EFTA's level of access to the single market via the EEA and their rich, stable economies, the economic rationale for seeking EU membership is, at first hand, hard to establish. The political rationale, however, is more obvious owing to the EFTA countries having to accept and subsequently comply to any further changes made to the EEA agreement under the *acquis communautaire*. The lack of political representation within the EU has thus proved to be the principal motive for seeking accession, removing what Baldwin and Flam (1995) have termed the 'influence deficit' that is inherent in the EEA. The institutional changes incurred will entail an expanded European Parliament to 626 MEPs that includes 22 from Sweden, 21 from Austria and 16 from Finland. Each country has submitted one commissioner taking the total number up to 20, while both Sweden and Austria will wield four votes in the Council of Ministers and Finland three. Whether the loading of these three additional member states onto the EU's institutional apparatus will spotlight any existing or potential faultlines remains to be seen.

The 1995 enlargement also stirs up a number of important economic contemplations. Subsidised agricultural production within EFTA is even more generous than the EU's Common Agricultural Policy (68 per cent of agricultural output value as opposed to the EU's 49 per cent in 1991). Discussions over agricultural, fisheries, forestry and other primary industries proved to be the most protracted of all accession negotiations. As Table 4.3 reveals, the three new EU members all have the least subsidised agricultural policies, and the high level of support given by Norway provides a partial explanation towards why it rejected membership. The embracing of the CAP will render welfare gains with respect to higher consumer surpluses and lower fiscal costs from the softening of government support to farmers (see Table 4.4).

The EFTA countries' support to farmers has been justified on account of the remote geographical conditions in which they work. During the accession negotiations, the EU agreed to create a supplementary regional policy framework, embodied in the new Objective 6 area, that was assigned direct aid to sparsely populated regions with densities of under eight people per sq. km. This was intended as a compensatory measure for subsidy losses borne from engaging with the CAP. The wider global impact of combining the agricultural sectors of the EU with three ex-EFTA members will most notably arise from the newly broadened CAP and its trade diversion effects. A study by the CEPR (1993) estimated that EFTA's participation in CAP could reduce US grain exports to EFTA by up to 75 per cent through trade diversion effects.

In the early 1990s, EFTA countries had an average 40 per cent higher GDP per capita than EU member states. It is expected that Austria and Sweden will make significant net contributions to the EU budget (ECU

Table 4.3 EU12 and EFTA countries' support for agriculture, 1991

		$ per capita			*Producers' subsidy*
	Total ($bn)	*Taxpayers*	*Consumers*	*Total*	*equivalent (%)*
EU12	142.0	168	241	409	49
Austria	4.1	143	381	524	52
Sweden	3.6	100	316	416	59
Finland	5.9	460	677	1,137	71
Norway	4.2	493	494	987	77
Switzerland	6.4	236	689	925	80

Source: CEPR 1993

Table 4.4 The estimated welfare effects from the 1995 EFTA enlargement (% of GDP)

	Austria	*Finland*	*Sweden*
Net transfers to/from the EU	−0.52	−0.30	−0.64
billion ECU	(−0.9)	(−0.2)	(−1.0)
Consumer surplus			
Food demand	0.41	0.81	0.12
Import demand	0.27	0.03	—
Producer surplus	−0.41	—	0.38
Government revenue			
Agriculture	0.23	0.16	0.14
Tariffs	−0.27	−0.03	—
Transactions costs in trade	0.37	0.19	0.22
Net effect	0.08	0.86	0.22

Source: Baldwin and Flam 1995

0.9bn and ECU 1bn respectively estimated for 1995) while Finland will give smaller net transfers (ECU 200m) owing primarily from recast regional policy provisions in post-enlargement conditions. The welfare-minded EFTA nations are likely to lend support to the Social Europe ideal. However, this should be balanced by their free trading convictions as demonstrated by external commercial policies more liberal than the EU's. Having said this, the only acceding nation in the 1995 enlargement to have an average CET on industrial goods lower than the EU's 3.0 per cent on entry was Sweden with 2.9 per cent (Finland 3.6 per cent; Austria 7.3 per cent). In those sectors where the new EU external tariff was higher (e.g. computer components) the USA was particularly keen to acquire due compensation under the WTO's Article XXIV(6) provisions on RIAs. According to one estimate, this amounted to between $150–200m for the USA alone (Agence Europe, 28 December 1994).

There is also evidence to suggest that significant welfare gains from the dynamic integration process could be created for the EU as a whole. Many of these benefits would come from intensifying the pro-competitive forces originating from the EEA agreement upon EFTA's relatively more carte-lised markets. Additional gains would be captured from extending cross-border investment across the widened EU market, thus broadening the opportunities for scale economies – which drives much of existing EFTA–EU trade and investment – to be exploited. Most of this investment should be directed into incoming EFTA countries who *de facto* become full partakers of the SEM programme. Domestic and non-EU foreign investment should also rise as a consequence, thus redressing any imbalanced regional development that may have occurred from not participating in the single market.

The impact of the 1995 enlargement on third countries will be mixed. We have already noted how trade in agricultural products will be diverted in EFTA markets by the effects of a unified CAP. Some agri-products group producers may benefit though from lower CAP tariffs on goods not produced in the EU (e.g. tropical fruits). Developing countries may also profit from both the further growth-induced demand for imports originating from an enlarged SEM in additon to higher levels of EU overseas development aid from the political influence of the new EFTA entrants. The Nordic countries in particular have been strong in their support for good governance and for human rights and democracy issues abroad (Granell 1994: 7). The EFTA3 have, though, expressed their reluctance to promote the EU's Lomé Conventions which allow ex-colonial developing countries (the Africa Caribbean Pacific, or ACP group) preferential market access over other LDCs in the Asian and Latin American regions. Along with Germany, they would like to see a restructured 'global' trade and aid policy towards the developing countries that is less discriminatory. If these wishes are realised this may lead to a collapse of the Lomé Conventions into a wholly new Generalised System of Preferences (GSP) scheme. The developed countries in general will not be too greatly affected by the recent EU enlargement. Intra-regional trade within Europe is already well developed and characterised by intra-industry trade flows, thus diminishing the scope for trade diversion. The most notable difference may come from political–economic ramifications of an EU which now represents well over half of the OECD nations.

Box 4.1 The European Economic Area (EEA)

The creation of the European Economic Area (EEA) on 1 July 1993 represented the culmination of open and natural regionalism that had over years been cultivated between the EU and EFTA. The EEA essentially provides mutual market access for member states in both blocs under proximate SEM conditions. Its origins are rooted in the Luxembourg Declaration of 1984 and its intention to establish a European Economic Space between the two blocs. The agreement in its current form did not take shape until 1989 and was then effectively postponed by the EU until the SEM programme was inaugurated. Switzerland remains outside the EEA owing to a referendum held on the issue, but the EEA nevertheless remains the world's largest marketplace with 381 million consumers and containing 47 per cent of total world trade. The main features of the EEA are:

- The adoption of most of the SEM legislation by the EFTA countries participating allowing the four freedoms of the single market to apply within the EEA. A convergence of technical standards and administrative formalities was seen as the most important barrier to trade removed.
- An EEA competition regime that is based on the EU's competition policy framework.

Box 4.1 *continued*

- Closer co-operation between the two blocs on other policy issues such as research and development, education, the environment and regional development.
- A number of separate EEA organisations will be set up to administer and monitor the progress of the agreement (e.g. The EEA Council and Joint Committee).

Certain trade barriers will nevertheless remain in place and EFTA will not join the EU's Common Commercial Policy (CCP), CAP or Common Fisheries Policy. No fiscal harmonisation will take place between the two blocs and EFTA countries will continue to stay outside the EMS and any future EMU. Gains from full integration into the single market will arise from reduced administration, especially on country of origin declarations, with estimates at 1.4 per cent savings on transaction costs being suggested (Baldwin and Flam 1995). From the EFTA3's move from the EEA to the SEM, the same estimates translated into percentage GDP static savings of 0.37 per cent for Austria, 0.19 per cent for Finland and 0.22 per cent for Sweden (see Table 4.4).

The EU and EFTA are each other's largest trading partners with 67 per cent and 73 per cent of respective imports derived from across the EEA's membership. A free trade arrangement on most EU–EFTA industrial goods had existed since 1977. Low external tariff rates on both groups' manufactures have mitigated any trade diversion welfare losses between the two. Some trade creation gains were expected from the competitive intra-industry profiles that EEA economies shared. Estimates made by Haaland and Norman (1992) seem to point to the EEA agreement increasing EFTA GDP by up to 5 per cent over the medium term. Their studies also suggest that the investment diversion expected from the EEA would bring higher proportionate benefits to EFTA than the EU in terms of real income changes and returns on both capital and labour.

However, Baldwin and Flam (1995) contend that the outlook for the EEA remains bleak, not only in retrospect of the 1995 EFTA enlargement. They state that the competitiveness of EFTA firms will become increasingly compromised as the direction taken by the *acquis communautaire* will gradually come to favour their EU rivals who are in a much stronger position to influence it. It is also noted that with Norway and Iceland as the only remaining non-EU signatories to the agreement the EEA will be prone to institutional top-heaviness.

EMU and the political economy of enlargement

The three new EU member states may experience difficulty in meeting the convergence criteria of EMU, yet their relative position to many other EU countries still remains optimistic. In Chapter 3 it was noted that even the so-called 'core' national economies face serious fiscal impediments in meeting those criteria (see Table 3.6 on page 90). Some ex-EFTA member states (i.e. Denmark and the UK) have presently opted out of EMU's final stage. In addition, Austria, Finland and Sweden have been parallel members of the EMS for longer than many of the EU12 have been full participants, while the inflationary record of the former compares more favourably to that of the latter. The CEPR (1993) also found evidence over the period between 1960 to 1990 to infer a strong correlation between EFTA's cyclical trends with that of the EU economy. Austria, Finland and Sweden all scored highly on this cyclical synchronisation test. From these results, it is therefore conceivable that EFTA countries are well positioned both to achieve closer fiscal harmonisation with the EU while narrowing the asymmetry of any shock adjustment effects from EMU participation.

There are also wider political economy forces that now interplay within an enlarged EU15 membership. The prosperous, generally net budget contributing new members may align with others in similar circumstances to resist any extensive transfer of funds to poorer nations. This will impede the economic and social cohesion process first encoded in the SEA and increase the probability of a multi-speed Europe evolving in the future. Any plans to expand membership eastwards could be similarly hamstrung under this scenario.

One other notable aspect of the EFTA enlargement concerns the future of a possible economic and political union (EPU) in Europe. Denmark's initial rejection of the Maastricht Treaty may have been at least partly based on a small country's lack of enthusiasm for surrendering national sovereignty to the EU. This is because in theory compliance to the Treaty represented a proportionately higher loss of political control over promoting its own national interests than for a larger country, which would be better able to influence the direction of the EU. Thus, by this argument, the UK should seek to play a more active role in the European integration process (CEPR 1993). An inverse case could be made founded on the premise that the gains associated with EU representation in international affairs may outweigh the costs that are attributable to forgone political independence. Economic geography may also determine the cost–benefit balance of EPU for smaller countries. The propinquity of the Benelux countries to France and Germany, for instance, may enable them to gain from spillover effects afforded by being located at the EU's core. In conclusion, however, the long tradition of neutrality that has existed in EFTA countries suggests that any forthcoming plans for European EPU can be expected to prove unpalatable.

EU MEMBERSHIP FOR CENTRAL AND EASTERN EUROPE

Current plans to offer membership to the CEE countries presents the EU with one of its biggest challenges to date. Not only are they comparatively poor (see Table 4.5), but their still incomplete transformation from centrally planned to market economies harbours a number of residual uncertainties. The potential political and economic advantages for Europe of conferring EU membership to CEE countries, though, are too significant to be ignored. This section will examine the relevant issues at stake and will be divided into three parts. The first deals with the transformation process, concentrating on the transitional problems and prospects for the CEE countries. Preparations that both the EU and the CEE countries are making for EU membership will then be investigated, followed by an evaluation of the costs and benefits involved of an eastwards EU enlargement.

The transformation process

Since the collapse of the communist ideological and economic system in Central and Eastern Europe, the countries in the region have embarked on programmes of transforming themselves into fledgling market democracies. This has involved an almost complete reshaping of the political–economic landscape. To engender a deeper understanding of the impediments encountered in the CEE's transformation process, we must first consider the broad microeconomic and macroeconomic problems that had accumulated within the incumbent planned economy system.

Microeconomic dislocation

- The absence of market mechanisms, discipline and information on prices and costs: meeting planned output targets as the primary objective led to little emphasis on quality and the mass stockpiling of labour and capital. Inefficient resource allocation was exacerbated by denying enterprise managers access to market-sensitive data and subsequent over-production of unmarketable products. Low productivity levels and innovation rates were also a feature.
- Sectoral disequilibria: these arose from the overdevelopment of heavy industry, underdeveloped industries for consumer goods and services, acute environmental problems, an incoherently organised agricultural sector and infrastructural and political barriers that hindered factor mobility.
- Institutional, legal and regulatory conditions: the planned system was built on a complex hierarchical apparatus of agencies that co-ordinated economic activity in a somewhat convoluted manner. There was no real basis for a commercial and company legal structure in addition to a rudimentary financial sector and fiscal system.
- Motivational problems: generated from the absence of competitive forces, non-existent property rights and profit incentive, the superiority of political over professional qualifications and the general suppression of an individualist based culture.

Macroeconomic imbalances

- Repressed inflationary pressures: arising from the extensive application of price and wage controls.
- Monetary policy: soft budgetary controls and the reliance on foreign debt in some countries created poor financial disciplinary conditions. Multiple and inconvertible exchange rates led to distorted market prices for both imports and exports and impeded integration into the world economy.
- Inappropriate patterns of investment: from the huge transfer of funds to heavy industry and the military–industrial complex at the expense of consumer-based industries.
- Mass hidden unemployment: resulting from the ideological imperative that unemployment per se should not exist.

The transitional process of converting a centrally planned economy into a market economy involves comprehensive structural and institutional changes which can amplify all these problems. During the early 1990s, when the transition process began in earnest, the CEE6 countries experienced tremendous hardship. Output and investment rates plummeted to Great Depression levels while inflation and unemployment soared in most of the group. Inter-enterprise debts rose as managers conspired to the mutual non-payment of accounts between them. Many enterprises, especially those that were actually adding negative value to the economy, collapsed under the pressures of a market economy environment. Attempts to achieve macroeconomic stability were hindered by the persistent application of soft budgetary controls, or in some cases over-zealously austere monetary policies. While many of the CEE states are still struggling to come to terms with the market reforms required and adverse conditions still persist, recent data suggest that some have perhaps passed through the most difficult stages of transition (see Figure 4.2).

At this point it may be useful to consider what broad elements and objectives are involved in the transitional process. It must be remembered that it entailed not only a transformation of the economy but also the creation of a new society: that is the formation of a market democracy. Rychetnik (1992) makes the distinction between the elements of transition that belong to forming a market economy and those that can be attributed to establishing a market society:

Market economy

- Legal–institutional framework: constitutional and civil laws (private ownership and contracts); commercial and business laws (company formation and bankruptcy); competition policy and taxation system.
- Deregulation: the removal of controls on foreign investment, interna-

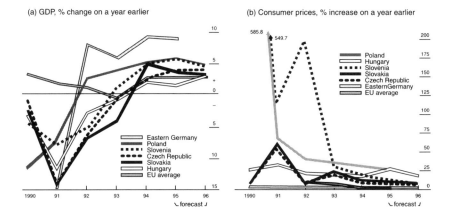

Figure 4.2 Recent trends in CEE inflation and GDP growth rates
Source: EIU, 19 November 1995

tional trade, foreign exchange and other controls that impede the development of a competitive private sector.

- Macroeconomic stabilisation: fiscal rectitude; tightening of monetary policy; appropriate incomes and balance of payments controls during the transitional period.
- Monetarisation: price liberalisation; the unification and convertibility of the exchange rate; a restructuring of the financial and banking sector.
- Institutional and organisational transformation: the dismantling of the state planning agencies; a large-scale privatisation programme, organisational, financial and corporate restructuring; the inauguration of capital market institutions (stock exchange, etc.).

Market society

- Establishing 'social partner' relationships: industrial confederations, chambers of commerce, trade unions.
- Social welfare: welfare safety net provisions, employment and training agencies, public education and health systems.
- Cultural and social transformation: entrepreneurship, individualism, social segmentation and the development of civic society.
- Political economy: political pluralism, the adoption of neo-liberalism or social market ideology and policy.

Paying the costs incurred from establishing a market economy have generally taken priority over the creation of a full market society in CEE countries. Some elements of the latter were already existent before the transition process began – trade unions, public education, health and other institutionalised welfare systems – and these have tended to be financially compromised as a compensatory measure. Balcerowicz (1993) alerts us to other critical conditions under which the CEE countries have transformed. He cites the examples of South Korea and Taiwan whose economic reforms in the early 1960s took place while the political system remained intact. Inversely, the economic systems of mid-1970s Spain and late 1980s South Korea were unaltered during times of comprehensive political changes.

For the CEE countries, however, both political and economic transformation have coincided, creating a historical precedent. As Balcerowicz suggests, the dualistic transitional process may cause tensions generated by the different speeds at which each type of transformation is able to develop. Political change is generally easier and quicker to cement than economic change. Free elections and a multi-party political system can be established in a relatively short period of time. On the other hand, effective economic transformation relies on the creation of deeper institutional relationships and the development of convergent expectations among economic agents regarding the fundamental cultural and psychological adjustment that has taken place within society. This runs counter to the typical experience of capitalist society whereby evolving economic relationships have bred eventual pluralist democratic systems. It is perhaps too early to judge the sustainability of the CEE countries' transformation under these unique conditions, but early evidence suggests that it is likely to succeed. The plans set in motion for their EU membership by the turn of the century will substantially raise the probability of that success.

The approaches taken by CEE countries to transformation have tended to fall into one of two categories: the rapid 'shock therapy' approach and the 'gradualist' approach. The shock therapy method involves a catalytic dash for change and stability based on an astringent series of liberalising reforms. Poland has been perhaps the most successful exponent of this method, which is aimed at jolting economic agents into the realities of a market economy within a very short time scale. External support is required to help alleviate the painful adjustments incurred by this approach in terms of preferential access to OECD markets, technical and financial assistance, the redesigning of the institutional functions and the management of privatisation schemes. The gradualist method to stabilisation will be appropriate to deploy if macroeconomic imbalances are not as pronounced. The process of transformation is longer but intense economic discomfort is supposedly avoided. Hence, it is therefore less likely to produce negative political feedback. Czechoslovakia, before and after its division, has pursued a more gradualist set of economic reforms with some success.

The Visegrad countries include Poland, Hungary, Czech Republic and Slovakia. They met on 15 February 1991 in the Hungarian town of Visegrad to discuss plans to implement a free trade area – CEFTA – between them by 2002. These countries have already entered the final stages of the transformation process. A vibrant and expanding private sector is ingraining the psychology of marketisation within society. The institutions necessary to support the functions of a market economy have more or less been configurated and made operable. Economic, political and civic freedoms have become assimilated into their cultural milieu. Businesses are beginning to enter global markets and to take on foreign competition at home. With regard to the last of these points, some CEE countries have encountered difficulty in reorienting their patterns of trade away from the CMEA structure. The legacy of the CMEA has meant that many CEE industries and enterprises have been exposed to global competition for the first time during the transformation process. Apart from the obvious strategic political reasons, the old planned system would not easily accommodate and internalise the market determined transactions of Western trade. The lack of hard currency reserves also hampered the development of an extra-CMEA trade sector.

Moreover, Lipton and Sachs (1990) note that the chronic levels of excess demand led to major shortages of inputs in the old planned system and, in particular, imported inputs, which encouraged shadow economy pricing and other production and consumption distortions. A consequential rise in the price of importables relative to exportables followed, which in turn led to enterprise managers switching away from the production of goods for export to import substitution. Thus, domestic overconsumption of potential exports and an underconsumption of imports was incurred that further diminished the scope of the external trade sector to flourish. The wider exposure of an external trade sector should assist the removal of any residual consumption and production distortions that have been created by the above process, as well as consolidate transformation by further integration into the world economy. Greater access to EU and other OECD markets will provide the essential incentives for the CEE economies to re-orientate their industries to export-led growth strategies and exploit the trade growth potential that could benefit both sides of Europe.

Preparing for membership

Although trade and other forms of economic partnership have been at the centre of the EU's new Ostpolitik, the ideological transformation of the CEE countries has produced a wider dimension to the normalising of relations between West and East Europeans. The 'new European architecture', as Kramer (1993) terms it, is based on a broad relationship of closer economic, political, cultural and security co-operation. New channels of political dialogue set within a firm institutional framework have helped to forge this relationship, as have new post-Cold War security arrangements based on the foundations of the Western European Union, the North Atlantic Co-operation Council and the Conference on Security and Co-operation in Europe.

Table 4.5 outlines the development of the EU's new Ostpolitik policy since the reform process began in CEE from the late 1980s onwards. This was initially founded on a series of bilateral Trade and Co-operation Agreements that were soon followed by an accession to the EU's GSP scheme once the transformation process had begun. A Most Favoured Nation (MFN) duty was placed on most CEE imports prior to these with some attracting non-tariff barriers (NTBs), such as VERs on steel and iron. Some degree of reciprocity was built into these 'First Generation' agreements with respect to market liberalisation, with the introduction for the first time of the principle of 'political conditionality' into the EU's relations with the CEE countries (Kramer 1993). This meant that the economic concessions granted by the EU could be perceived as a means to lever in political and constitutional changes aimed at founding market democracies in the region.

Before some CEE countries had even signed the First Generation agreements, the two countries at the vanguard of the reforms – Hungary and Poland – had received particular attention in the form of the PHARE programme. This initiative not only involved EU member states but also other participants in the G24 group of OECD nations. The programme contained various measures that aimed both to relieve the pain of transition and to improve the chances of a functional market economy evolving. Other countries soon applied for PHARE assistance as their own reform programmes accelerated. The G24 group subsequently broadened its scope of commitment by extending PHARE membership, adding new measures to the programme, extending the expiry date of the programme from 1992 to 1997 and setting up the European Bank for Reconstruction and Development (EBRD), which was to raise and co-ordinate funding for investment projects not only in CEE but also in Asiatic former Soviet Union republics. Although the EU has shared the responsibility of managing the PHARE programme, it has set its general tone and been at the centre of co-ordinating its activities via the Commission. It has also provided around two-thirds of the programme's total funding (ECU 38.7bn over 1990–94).

Having played the pivotal role in these initiatives, the EU sought to raise the level of partnership with the CEE countries through the vehicle of the Europe Agreements. Signed in 1992 and 1993, these constituted 'Second Generation' agreements between both sides of the continent and contemplated the CEE6's accession to the EU for the first time. Trade liberalisation was the key theme of these arrangements with the goal set of establishing a free trade zone in industrial goods over a ten-year period. The existing framework of co-operation in other economic, political, scientific and cultural fields was also deepened and widened as well as

Table 4.5 The 'new Ostpolitik': the development of EU initiatives towards Central and Eastern Europe

'First generation' bilateral Trade and Co-operation Agreements
EC and the CEE countries arrange a series of bilateral agreements covering trade and co-operative measures starting in the late 1980s as a consequence of Gorbachev's 'Sinatra Doctrine'. Hungary the first to sign (September 1988), then Czechoslovakia (December 1988), Poland (September 1989), the Soviet Union (December 1989), GDR and Bulgaria (both May 1990), Romania (March 1991), Albania, Baltic Republics, Slovenia (1992).

GSP membership
Extended to the Visegrad Four from 1990–92, Bulgaria and Romania from 1990–93, the Baltic states from 1992–4 and the CIS and Georgia from 1993 onwards.

PHARE programme
Established at the June 1989 Group of 24 (G24) meeting as an endeavour to support Poland and Hungary through their early reform process (PHARE stands for the Poland and Hungary Assistance Reconstruction Economic programme). Initial programme measures consisted of finance to help restructure and modernise industry, widened market access to Western markets, the setting up of the EBRD, funds to relieve pressing environmental problems and vocational training for managers, executives and students in key roles.

Other nations applied for PHARE programme assistance in 1990 as the market reforms spread to other parts of the CEE. By mid-1990s, PHARE has become the EU's main instrument for economic and technical assistance under the Europe Agreements and was extended in 1995 to allow more funding for infrastructure on a multiannual financial framework.

Ten countries now benefit from the programme and its allocated funds have tripled. Main aim remains to support economic reform and structural adjustment. Continues to work closely with the EBRD and the European Investment Bank (EIB). ECU 7.072bn has been allocated for expenditure over 1995–9.

European Bank for Reconstruction and Development (EBRD)
Principal role to co-ordinate financial assistance to CEE and former Soviet Union republics for infrastructure projects and technology transfers. Operates as part of the PHARE programme framework. Established in 1990 with a share capital of ECU 10bn (the EU has a share holding of 51 per cent) with 40 country representatives plus the EIB and Commission as members.

Europe Agreements
Ten-year timetable for phasing out trade barriers on industrial goods between the EU and CEE6 countries. EU to phase out its tariffs within the first five years and then the CEE6 to do the same in the second five years. Tariffs and other protectionist measures still applied by EU on a variety of 'sensitive' industrial products (i.e. steel, textiles, chemicals).

Other aspects include technical and financial assistance, a more developed framework for political dialogue, compliance to some aspects of EU law, information exchange and cultural co-operation. Operated since 1992 for Visegrad nations, since 1993 for Bulgaria and Romania and since 1995 for the Baltic states. Russia and Ukraine signed Partnership and Co-operation Agreements with the EU in 1994.

Builds on the 'first generation' agreements made at the advent of the transformation process with the intention of creating a European political area within which CEE countries can be eventually absorbed into EU membership.

The 1995 White Paper
Identified key measures required in each sector to prepare the CEE6 countries for integration into the SEM. Suggested a sequence in which the approximation of legislation should be introduced. To complement this the Paper laid out plans to establish the adequate structures required to facilitate integration and ensure future compliance and enforcement of the *acquis communautaire*. Provisions on social, environmental and other policy fields were also included to lend balance to the Paper's proposals.

setting a multilateral context for future negotiations. The political and economic conditionality of the Europe Agreements require much firmer guarantees made by the CEE6 to implement substantial market democratic reforms. The CEE signatories' obligation to approximate the commercial and civic laws to those of the EU's acts both as an example of that commitment and also part of the essential prerequisites to EU membership. EFTA had made similar trading arrangements to those embodied in the EU's Europe Agreements with the CEE countries in the early 1990s.

More formalised preparations for the accession of CEE states followed from events that unravelled from 1994 onwards. In April of that year, Hungary and Poland formally applied for EU membership. Meanwhile, the Council agreed to speed up the schedule for eradicating EU trade barriers and improve the efficiency of the financial assistance programmes by allowing PHARE to be used in major infrastructure investments. Based upon plans outlined at the previous Corfu Council meeting in June (CEC 1994b), the Essen Council of December 1994 adopted a broad pre-accession strategy for the EU and CEE6 states. At the next Council meeting in June 1995, a White Paper on preparing the associated countries for integration into the SEM was presented (CEC 1995g). The document recognised that a phased adoption of the SEM-related *acquis communautaire* was required of acceding nations and carried a number of provisions with this objective in mind.

The relationship between the EU and Russia has been most recently shaped by a Partnership and Co-operation Agreement signed between the two parties in 1994. Establishing economic and political stability in Russia and the Commonwealth of Independent States (CIS) is a major priority for countries on both sides of Europe. The Agreement's provisions hence contained measures aimed to support purposeful economic restructuring in Russia and its integration into the world economy. This included backing of Russian membership to the WTO, initiatives to stimulate European FDI in the country, the promise of a free trade pact with the EU by 1998 pending sufficient advancement of the reform process and a boost to existing programmes introduced to foster market transition such as TACIS (CEC 1995h).

For the CEE countries, the emerging patterns of closer co-operation with Western Europe in the 1990s represent what Skak (1993) has called the process of 'Europeanisation'. This can be interpreted as an active policy pursued especially by the Visegrad Four that marks a return to the participation in 'West European cultural, political and economic exchange' and an attempt to reintegrate back into the mainstream European economy. Efforts are simultaneously being made by the CEE countries to find their own positions on the wider international stage. The East Asian NICs provide one role model for them based on a formula of pursuing export-led growth strategies. The EU could play a crucial part if this approach was to be adopted. The ensuing expansion of trade between the EU and the CEE countries from the market reform process and the trade concessions granted has provided a pretext for both an EU eastern enlargement and the development of Central and Eastern Europe into an export production platform with formidable potential.

However, trade is not the only precondition for a successful integration between the EU and the CEE6. While free trade may smooth the path to an eastern enlargement, an overwhelming array of centrifugal forces may be released if the transition to EU membership is not carefully engineered. The CEE6 still possess relatively low income levels (in 1992 Greece, the poorest EU member state, had a GNP per capita 2.7 times greater than Hungary, the richest CEE6 state). The prolongation of this disadvantageous position is likely to augment the various asymmetric shocks that can be expected to arise from adherence to the EU's deeper integrational agenda. A premature engagement with the SEM programme may also generate a mass migration from east to west owing to CEE wage rates which will remain a fraction of those in the EU until greater convergence is reached (see Figure 4.4). An early accession would also commit incumbent members to finance substantial transfers to help correct the many structural imbalances that are likely to persist for some time. With EU membership comes a range of responsibilities encoded in the *acquis communautaire*. Compliance to certain aspects, such as its provision on social and environmental protection, may prove too burdensome for some CEE countries, despite the provisions made by the 1995 White Paper.

While these may be valid concerns and worthy of circumspection, the EU must also be careful not to confine its eastern neighbours to a low growth trajectory into the medium term. The preparations made thus far for the CEE6's accession carry sound intentions, but the financial commitment behind them may be judged in retrospect as being deficient. This is likely to become more apparent as the spillover effects increase from the further development of integrational links across the continent.

The costs and benefits of an eastern enlargement further investigated

We have already hinted at what costs and benefits may arise from the plans to integrate the CEE countries into the EU. Let us now consider these in greater detail and pay particular reference to the global dimension of such a development where appropriate.

The EU budget

An eastern enlargement of the EU commits the incumbent member states to offer more systematic financial assistance to the CEE states. This would mainly take the form of CAP and Structural Fund transfers for which the new entrants would be eligible. Estimates that have been made on the costs incurred to the EU budget are shown in Tables 4.6 and 4.7. Anderson and

Table 4.6 Budgetary cost of admitting the Visegrad Group in the year 2000 (ECU bn, 1991 prices)

	CAP cost	Structural Fund cost	Contribution	Net budget cost
Visegrad 4	37.6	26.0	5.5	58.1

Sources: CAP costs from Anderson and Tyres 1993; Structural Fund costs from CEC 1993e

Table 4.7 Annual budget costs at 1991 incomes and agricultural shares

		ECU (per capita)		ECU (billion)
	Gross receipts	Gross contribution	Net contribution	Total budget cost
Czech Rep.	256	60	−196	0.2
Hungary	271	48	−223	2.0
Poland	209	37	−172	6.5
Slovakia	211	31	−180	0.9
Visegrad				9.6
Bulgaria	293	39	−254	2.3
Romania	458	54	−404	9.3
CEE6				21.2

Source: Baldwin 1994

Tyres (1993) have calculated that the combined net annual budgetary cost will sum to ECU 58.1bn alone for the Visegrad group based on a year 2000 entry at 1991 prices. Figures produced by Baldwin (1994), though, suggest that a CEE accession will impose lower scale pressures with the extra cost to the EU's budget being only ECU 21.2bn for the CEE6. However, this still represented 40 per cent of the EU12's 1991 budgetary outlays of ECU 55.6bn but, as Baldwin notes, this is simultaneously a mere fraction of total EU GDP.

It is unclear how these costs will be apportioned between CAP and the Structural Funds and which member states will be most responsible for paying them. Despite the comprehensive restructuring of the agricultural sector that is still necessary, the immense structural imbalances that lie elsewhere in the economy may require greater priority, thus pointing to larger Structural Fund transfers than those through CAP. Poorer incumbent member states and farmers can be expected to be most adversely affected by the need both to deconstruct the CAP framework and raise additional revenues (Baldwin 1994). Richer member states, especially Germany, may only be willing to make significant extra contributions to the EU budget if they are positioned to receive compensatory feedback effects from CEE membership (e.g. stimulated export demand). Others will be reluctant to act in a proportionately generous manner in an enlarged EU with a higher ratio of relatively poorer members.

An east to west migration?

Enduring structural imbalances in agriculture and heavy industry sectors may generate persistently high rates of unemployment which in turn may cause an outward migration to the west under SEM conditions. Certain mitigating factors could, however, reduce the incentive of CEE citizens to migrate. Agricultural workers may wish to savour the new-found freedoms generated by decollectivisation and the counter-incentives offered by land reforms. Inward foreign investment and trade growth will play their parts in converging wage and income differentials over time, although such a convergence could act to repel future inward FDI. This, though, may be largely unrealistic as the market potential of the CEE region and other strategic considerations are likely to pull in considerable levels of foreign investment over the next few decades. This prospect will also ease migrational urges. However, it must also be noted that CEE workers are generally well educated and may be able to offer human capital opportunities to EU-based multinationals, especially those established in poorer member states where educational standards are generally lower.

Competition and intra-industry trade

Widening the SEM to encompass the CEE region will undoubtedly confront certain existing EU producers with competitive threats of some magnitude. How well they cope with the experience will depend on a mixture of circumstance and the perception and response to the challenge posed. However, the EU can anticipate to benefit from sizeable trade creation gains owing not only to the low production cost advantages possessed by the CEE countries, but also the surprisingly high intra-industry trade links with the EU, suggesting the existence of competitive industrial profiles between them. Table 4.2 shows that the Visegrad countries in particular have well-developed ties of this kind that supersede those of Portugal, Finland and Greece, while all CEE6 have higher percentage rates than the latter. Intra-industry trade patterns should deepen as foreign investment in the CEE region expands and sectoral adjustments are made in accordance with the greater imprint imposed by the dynamics of the EU economy. This has been most recently and clearly demonstrated by Hungary whose EU–CEE intra-industry trade ratio had risen to 61 per cent by 1994 from 50 per cent in 1988/90.

Trade: the wider issues at stake

It is now generally accepted that CEE producers are offering a wider selection of globally marketable products and are gradually shifting away from many of the low-tech, labour-intensive industries that have been traditionally associated with them. The CEE region is endowed with the necessary combination of factors required to experience rapid trade growth, yet certain countervailing forces and circumstances may deny this potential being realised. The EU has come under most criticism on this account. The European Agreements, for instance, will maintain protectionist measures on many 'sensitive' industry products from the CEE6 for a prolonged period. These are industries where the CEE6 have competitive advantage and hence the greatest export potential. The EBRD (1995) has shown that 'sensitive' sectors make up between 40 per cent and 70 per cent of CEE exports to the EU. A continued block against the export-oriented development of these industries will no doubt protect the EU's own domestic producers. However, the reversal of this policy could open up benefits that would far outweigh the potential costs involved. Significant trade creation gains would be derived from lower cost production. Trade liberalisation would help to accelerate the transformation of the CEE countries into market economies. The nurturing of their export-oriented industries could provide Europe with the low cost production base required to face global competition in certain key sectors. More generous trade concessions and greater investment interest would also improve the probability of the CEE countries emulating the high growth rates of East Asian NICs and thus present the EU with an emerging market with huge potential on its doorstep.

The EU is by far the largest export market for all the CEE6 countries with at least 60 per cent of total CEE6 exports destined for member states during the early 1990s. Jim Rollo, a trade policy expert at the RIIA, contends that the CEE region could be responsible for around $400bn of annual import demand (at 1990 prices) up to 2010 (*Financial Times*, 7 June 1993). This would depend on more liberal trade concessions made by the EU, which Rollo calculates would receive over half of this demand, equivalent to nearly twice that of the EU's current US export market. In another study, Collins and Rodrik (1991) estimated that the CEE countries could account for about 27 to 28 per cent of future total EU trade, around three times its current proportion.

An early indication of this potential is revealed by Figure 4.3 which shows that after approximately a decade of having a trade deficit with the CEE6, the EU moved into a trade surplus by the early 1990s (ECU 6.4bn in 1994). A rapid increase of trade has concurrently occurred with EU exports to and imports from the region rising by 130 per cent and 82 per cent respectively between 1988 and 1992, and a more marked acceleration of trade flows in 1993 and 1994. While the EU has achieved or maintained a positive balance in certain 'sensitive' sectors (e.g. agriculture/food and chemicals/plastic products), a significant degree of import penetration has been made by CEE producers in textiles, footwear and miscellaneous manufactures (ECU 2.5bn surplus in 1994), timber, stone and base metals (ECU 3.8bn surplus) and mineral products, including oil (ECU 1.5bn surplus). Where penetration has been most pronounced there is likely to

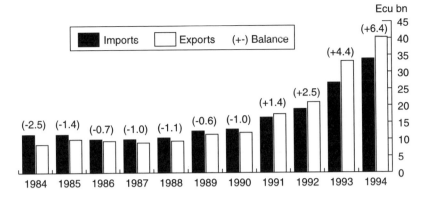

Figure 4.3 EU trade and trade balance with the CEE countries, 1984–94
Source: Financial Times, 7 June 1993

be corresponding pressure from European business leaders to maintain the protectionist provisions of the Europe Agreements.

A somewhat more qualified concern has been expressed by the East Asian NICs which see the Europe Agreements and any subsequent preferential trade arrangements made with the CEE countries as essentially trade diverting with respect to themselves in these 'sensitive' sectors. On a wider scale, the relationship between the two regions could have a number of fascinating aspects. A further development of business integration between West and East Europe of both a natural and strategic nature could improve the competitive position of the European economy *vis-à-vis* the East Asian 'tiger' economies. The CEE states possess many of the competitive advantages with which the East Asians started: a low-cost production base, scope for impressive productivity gains, a mass educated workforce and Western political interest in securing economic success in the region. The ability of the CEE countries to build on those advantages may well rest on the closer collaborative activities with incumbent EU member states that an eastern enlargement would bring. However, the costs of the capital transfers that would have to be diverted to the region may have an adverse effect on European competitiveness if the CEE economy proves to be a 'black hole' for investment funds.

Another side to the relationship between the CEE states and East Asian NICs concerns their mutual interest in forming closer collaborative links. The East Asians have much to teach in the field of export-led growth strategies, consumer product development, global marketing and business management. The CEE countries have the natural resources and certain high-tech industries – such as aviation, optics and electronic beam technologies – which the East Asian countries lack.

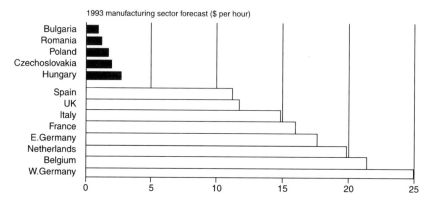

Figure 4.4 Manufacturing labour costs in Europe, 1993
Source: *Financial Times*, 7 June 1993

Global capital flows

Another important global dimension to the CEE transformation process regards its impact on international capital flows. According to a study by Collins and Rodrik (1991) an annual $1.5 trillion would have to be invested in the region for a ten-year period to achieve parity in levels of productivity between CEE and Western workers. Their analysis also evaluated the capital inflows that the CEE states could expect to receive (see Table 4.8). Three scenarios based on different combinations of assumptions were formulated, Scenario (A) being the most pessimistic and Scenario (C) the most optimistic. One of the most striking features of the study is the high proportion of capital flows that Eastern Germany was expected to attract. After the reunification of Germany, the GDR effectively became subsumed into the EU. The huge volume of capital investment and other transfers from West to East Germany is well documented and largely explains the figures. The momentum of capital investment set rolling by Germany in its eastern Länder has had a cumulative causation effect,

Table 4.8 Capital inflows to CEE countries ($bn annually)

| | Scenario | | |
	(A)	*(B)*	*(C)*
Eastern Europe	12	18	24
(CEE6 plus ex-Yugoslavia)			
Former Soviet Union	−4	2	6
Eastern Germany	22	35	60
Total	30	55	90

Source: IIE 1991
Note: Scenario (A) contains the most pessimistic assumptions made by the IIE study, Scenario (C) their most optimistic. Scenario (B) is the study's best estimate.

pulling in foreign investment to exploit the external economies that have been made available.

The increased flow of capital into the CEE region implies either a rerouting of capital away from other developing countries or, *ceteris paribus*, higher global interest rates. Collins and Rodrik estimated that these rates could rise in real terms by between 1 per cent and 3 per cent if capital flows to other developing countries were unchanged. Conversely, these countries could expect to see inward investment fall by between 0.8 per cent and 2.3 per cent of their GDP if global rates of interest remained the same. Some perspective is brought to bear if we consider Blackhurst's (1991) calculation that a 1 per cent rise in the US saving rate could generate Collins and Rodrik's best estimate figure of $55 bn. The issue of foreign investment is discussed in much greater depth in Chapter 8. Suffice to say at this point, though, that their estimates for investment entering into the CEE region are reflective of the somewhat disappointing FDI inflows which have occurred to date.

THE MEDITERRANEAN BASIN AND ENLARGEMENT

Formal links between the Community and the Mediterranean Basin countries long predate those held by the CEE countries, ranging back to the 1960s. Past colonial ties between individual member states date back even further (France with Algeria, Lebanon, Morocco, Syria and Tunisia; Britain with Cyprus, Egypt, Israel and Malta; Italy with Tunisia). As part of the legacy of these ties, the Community initially sought to maintain the socio-political and economic stability of the Mediterranean Basin through a series of separate Co-operation and Association Agreements among other collaborative ventures. The Mediterranean Basin can be broadly divided into the following geo-political groups:

- Northern Mediterranean group: which includes Turkey, Cyprus, Malta. All three countries have applied for EU membership and are the most likely to succeed in doing so.
- The Maghreb group: consisting of Algeria, Libya, Morocco and Tunisia – lying to the west of the Mediterranean Basin.
- The Mashreq group: comprising of Egypt, Jordan, Lebanon and Syria – Middle East nations to the east of the region.
- Miscellaneous non-related grouping: Israel, Albania and certain ex-Yugoslavia republics.

The recent EFTA enlargement and preparations made to envelop the CEE6 into membership has effectively marginalised the prospects of the Mediterranean Basin countries to accession. This has been compounded by a complex mixture of economic, political, cultural and socio-religious factors that have relegated the region to a third division status among the EU's peripheral zones. In this section, we shall consider the development of the

EU's policy towards the Mediterranean Basin, attempts made by countries from this region to secure membership and the emergence of a possible European–Mediterranean Economic Area in the future.

The development of an EU Mediterranean Policy

The historical objective of the EU's Mediterranean Policy has been to create a sphere of influence for itself in its southern peripheral zone. We have already noted the pre-Community interests in the region held by certain member states. However, more contemporary issues and developments of a strategic nature have caused the EU to maintain an active presence in the region. The Mediterranean has been the main route for the Community's OPEC oil supplies and a theatre for recent military conflict (the Arab–Israeli war, the Turkish invasion of Cyprus, the implosion of Yugoslavia). Hence, the focus of this Policy has had a strong orientation towards security-based issues and promoting political stability in the region.

According to Grilli (1993) the first phase of the EU's Mediterranean Policy began in a rather incoherent manner through a series of 'case-by-case', bilaterally negotiated Association and Trade Agreements. Hager (1974: 231) too has commented that 'nowhere on the periphery [of the Community] has the process of establishing a mode of relations with its neighbours been so accidental as it has been towards the South'. The contractual links established in these agreements mainly concerned trade matters (e.g. GSP concessions) but these were to broaden to include economic and financial co-operation initiatives under the Policy's second phase. This new approach was encapsulated in the Community's Global Mediterranean Policy (GMP) which has its origins in the October 1972 Paris Summit. While the term 'global' appears somewhat misplaced, it was supposed to mark a more coherent and rational view to Community–Mediterranean Basin relations.

However, standardising the arrangements within the GMP framework proved a more difficult task than expected. The Mediterranean Basin's diversity meant that the intended principles of commonality and non-discrimination which the GMP was supposed to uphold were compromised. Different political imperatives within international relations and heterogeneous conditions found across agricultural production, industrial structure and patterns of trade all conspired to constrain the adoption of a holistic approach. Grilli (1993) also partly blames the Community for its lack of clarity over plans to treat the region in such a way but adds that fragmentation of the GMP on a sub-group basis was probably sensible given the above.

Subsequently, a Free Trade Agreement on manufactured exports was made only with Israel in 1975 in addition to preferential treatment on agricultural exports and other measures to assist its industrial development. Co-operation Agreements were signed with the Maghreb countries in 1976 (with Libya excepted) and with the Mashreq countries in 1977. Yugoslavia was signatory to a similar agreement in 1980, but this was dissolved after the commencement of civil war from 1991 onwards. The Community and Albania signed a 'First Generation' Trade and Co-operation Agreement in 1992 but as part of the former's new Ostpolitik. Hence, Libya remains the only country in the group not to have been offered any concessions.

Since 1978, the associated countries in the Mediterranean Basin have been covered by five-year financial protocols in which funds have been earmarked from the Community's budget and through EIB loans. Between 1978 and 1991, the Maghreb and Mashreq countries received ECU 1,337m in budget funds and ECU 1,965m in EIB loans. The latter figure includes funds dedicated to Israel which, because it is the most developed country in the region, is only eligible for EIB resources. In the fourth financial protocol (1992–6) ECU 1,075m and ECU 1,300m allocations were made respectively. The Northern Mediterranean group have received ECU 672.5m from the EU budget and EIB loans valued at ECU 262m over the period between 1965 and 1993. In subsequent initiatives that followed the GMP there was both a formulaic adjustment to the allocation of these funds and a significant increase in them.

The arrival of the 1980s saw the GMP come under intensified pressures from various quarters, not least from within the Mediterranean region itself. The accession to the Community of Greece in 1981 and Spain and Portugal in 1986 and their concomitant integration into the CAP improved its self-sufficiency levels in agricultural goods and other products where the Mediterranean Basin countries possessed a comparative advantage. The injurious impact of this enlargement was exacerbated by the disposal of CAP surpluses in international markets which had the effect of depressing world market prices (Pomfret 1992). A further undermining of the GMP came from the agreements made at the Tokyo Round of GATT. Multilateral reductions in tariffs on industrial goods effectively lowered the marginal advantage of preference conferred on the Mediterranean Basin countries through the GMP's trade provisions. Furthermore, both the CAP and numerous NTBs on 'sensitive' sector products (e.g. VERs and the Multi-Fibre Agreement) still erected a substantial protectionist barrier against those industries where a clear comparative advantage existed for Mediterranean producers.

One notable achievement of the GMP, though, was that over the 1980s the relative trade shares of most Mediterranean Basin countries with the Community increased. By the end of the decade, it had become the biggest trade partner for all countries in the region with the exception of Jordan. Those who were most reliant on Community markets were Malta (76 per cent), Tunisia (74 per cent), Morocco (65 per cent), Cyprus (55 per cent) and Turkey (47 per cent). In sub-group terms, Maghreb countries saw their own share of total exports to the EC9 rise from 44.2 per cent in 1977 to 58.0 per cent by 1987. The GMP also had greatest success with this group with regard to stimulating industrial exports, especially in manufactures, fertilisers, clothing, textiles and footwear products.

Initial attempts at accession

While the preferential trade terms conceded by the Community were gratefully received and provided impetus to the region's industrial development, the gains to be had from membership were far greater. Turkey and Morocco were the first to apply for accession in 1987 at the time when the Single European Act had just been ratified. The latter's application was rejected outright on the basis of the criteria discussed in the opening section of this chapter. Turkey's application was neither completely rejected nor accepted. Instead, the Community stated that it would eventually accede Turkey to membership, but alluded to no deadline or detailed criteria as to when and how this would occur. Compensatory measures were set in motion by the Community that essentially enhanced the conditions of Turkey's associate membership. A central feature of this was the establishment of a customs union by the end of 1995. Efforts have also been made by the EU to help Turkey develop a regional leadership role in the Central Asian region.

In 1990, the other countries in the Northern Mediterranean group – Cyprus and Malta – also applied for EU membership. A similar response to that of Turkey was given by the Community to the two countries, albeit for different reasons. Turkey's chances of securing ultimate accession to the EU are impeded by its large and expanding poor population, divergent cultural and religious traditions to those of the European mainstream and weak democratic institutions. Cyprus and Malta, on the other hand, are notably richer (see Table 4.9), much smaller and possess more convergent traditions with mainland Europe.

The size of these island states (Cyprus has a population of around 0.7m and Malta 0.4m) has proved to be both an advantage and a disadvantage to their prospects to accession. While their negative budgetary impact would be minor, concerns have been raised regarding their capacity to cope with the administrative pressures of membership and management of its representation within EU institutions and at inter-governmental meetings. Calculating new QMV formulas would be particularly troublesome. Additional political factors have also generated doubts. The Greek–Turkish territorial division of Cyprus, while it persists, is likely to deter the EU from acceding it to membership. Maltese aspirations to join the EU have been impaired by Labour governments of the 1980s who have expressed not only their hostility to membership, but to the Community itself.

The failure of Morocco to be even remotely considered for EU membership subsequently undermined the confidence of the North African and

Table 4.9 The Mediterranean Basin: general economic indicators (latest figures)

	GNP per capita	GNP real growth (%)	Unemployment (%)	Inflation (%)	Trade ($bn) balance
Northern					
Cyprus	9,820	6.0	2.5	3.5	−2.1
Malta	8,000	6.0	4.5	4.5	+0.7
Turkey	2,125	5.1	12.7	73.6	−14.0
Maghreb					
Algeria	1,830	5.0	—	25.0	+3.5
Libya	6,160	0.0	—	8.0	+1.4
Morocco	1,040	3.0	—	4.1	+3.7
Tunisia	1,700	6.5	14.0	4.0	−0.9
Mashreq					
Egypt	658	4.0	20.0	11.4	−5.5
Jordan	1,150	10.0	15.0	4.5	−1.8
Lebanon	1,075	7.0	—	100.0	+0.2
Syria	1,185	8.0	—	5.7	
Other					
Albania	500	11.0	40.0	23.5	−4.9
Israel	13,762	4.0	—	11.0	−0.9

Sources: WOI 1995a, d; EIU 1995; *The Economist* 1995

Middle Eastern countries to apply for accession. However, the motives for doing so will endure. The entry of Greece, Portugal and Spain to the Community under the 1980s southern enlargement can be interpreted as part of an active policy pursued by these countries to modernise their economy, society and political institutions. Nevertheless, an accession to EU membership will incur calculated risks made on behalf of the new entrant. Although higher levels of foreign investment are likely to be induced by membership (Spain and Portugal both saw rapid increases from the mid-1980s onwards), new member states can expect to see their trade balances tend towards a deficit position. At present, the Mediterranean Basin countries enjoy preferential trade terms with the EU. On accession, these terms will be removed by the reciprocal provisions laid down within a common market arrangement, opening up domestic producers to a tide of unfamiliar competitive pressures originating from incumbent member states.

The experience of other Mediterranean countries – Greece, Portugal and Spain – has provided evidence of this. Tsoukalis (1981) has noted the additional risks that are carried by aspirant member states regarding the pressures placed by membership on institutional structures of countries. If these rest on weak democratic foundations, as the three 1980s entrants did at the time, there exists a distinct possibility that considerable economic and political troubles would ensue. It should also be commented that membership does not yield an automatic path to prosperity for a relatively underdeveloped new entrant. The heavily interventionist domestic policies pursued by Greece in the 1980s deflected much of the foreign investment that would have been directed towards it after accession in 1981. In addition, the Greek government failed fully to exploit the country's eligibility for transferred funds from within the EU budget on a consistent basis (Redmond 1993).

Towards a European–Mediterranean Economic Area (EMEA)

By the end of the 1980s, the Commission came under increasing pressure to review the GMP. This took place in 1989 (CEC 1989a) from which the conception of a new framework for relations with the Southern periphery was established: the New Mediterranean Policy (NMP). The NMP did not constitute a radical departure from its predecessor but rather built on existing structures. An extension of preferential rates of duty for agricultural exports was introduced as well as a sizeable boost to funds channelled in the fourth financial protocol. There were, though, some new features including the MED-INVEST mechanism that was targeted at assisting economic structural reform. This entailed support for the NMP's broader training and rural development programmes. The fourth financial protocol also set aside ECU 230m for regional co-operation measures and an extra ECU 1,800m of EIB loans for these and other measures relating to environmental protection.

However, the NMP was soon to be superseded by more ambitious intentions from within Europe. At the Lisbon Council meeting of 1992 the growing significance of the Mediterranean Basin region was accepted. In addition to the traditionally expressed need to maintain security and political stability the principle of promoting socio-economic development was also formally considered. This centred on the objective of closing the prosperity gap between the Community and its southerly neighbours which was likely to diverge if no counter actions were taken. In October 1994, the Commission called upon EU member states to develop a more ambitious and comprehensive policy towards relations with the Mediterranean countries. It was suggested that the foundations of this policy could be based on the creation of a European–Mediterranean Economic Area (EMEA) that worked on the similar organising principles of the EEA (CEC 1994c). By 1995, proposals for a Euro-Med Partnership (EMP) were published with the idea of the EMEA as its main focal point (CEC 1995i). Financing the Partnership would involve ECU 4.7bn over its first period (1995–9) supplemented by a correspondingly substantial increase in EIB loans guarantees. The principal aspects of the proposed EMEA were:

- A Euro-Med free trade area by 2010: this would be WTO-compatible and apply EU-based rules of origin to trade flows. Existing agreements would be strengthened to enable the arrangement to function effectively (e.g. new assistance on transport networks and customs procedures). The gradual and reciprocal liberalisation of agricultural and other 'sensitive' sectors trade is also implied.

- Measures to promote the private sector in the Mediterranean Basin: these were aimed at encouraging new business formation (especially SMEs), training, industrial restructuring and modernisation, improving legal and regulatory environments, joint ventures and other alliances with EU firms.
- Promotion of European private investment in the region: through MED-INVEST, the EU's Investment Partners scheme and other means to lever in European private capital to the Mediterranean countries.
- Upgrading of the economic and social infrastructure: to reinforce the effectiveness of the above measures.

Overall, the EMP marked a more comprehensive and coherent approach by the EU to the region than any previous policy frameworks. While the new emphasis on achieving a greater socio-economic balance in the region still acknowledged the primacy of security and political stability as the key policy goals, it also recognised that a broader range of objectives was required if more harmonious and prosperous relations were to be achieved. Those measures designed to promote regional integration both within the Mediterranean Basin (i.e. through the adoption of similar rules of origin) and with the EU should improve the chances of future EU accession for countries in the region.

However, the prospects of another southern enlargement and the EU's relations with the Mediterranean Basin countries remain unclear. Existing EU member states with a Mediterranean identity will be more inclined to promote further the EMP if not only to counter-balance the 'eastern' distractions of other members. A full-scale accession of the CEE states by the turn of the next century would significantly alter the EU's centre of gravity to the detriment of the former. Thus, the future of the EMP could be embroiled in this possible power struggle within the EU on this issue. Generally speaking it is more conceivable that any subsequent enlargements of the EU will press on towards the Urals rather than turn further southwards owing, if nothing else, to a more commonly shared cultural and socio-religious heritage between east and west.

CONCLUDING REMARKS

The EU has increasingly come to represent the embodiment of the European economy. Its expansion from six to fifteen countries is also reflective of the benefits to be had from membership. Moreover, as the EU has grown so have the perceived costs of remaining outside. Progressive enlargements have meant that Europe has been able to speak with a louder voice on the international stage. This has related not only to political matters but also to those of an economic nature as Europe's common market has also enlarged. While the endeavour of the SEM programme and subsequent plans for further European integration have been fraught with various difficulties, the economic clout of a deeper and broader integrated Europe is widely recognised both within and outside the EU.

Future enlargement of the EU will carry its biggest challenges yet. Expanding membership into the CEE region entails considerable degrees of risk but also potential opportunities of a similar magnitude. An eastern enlargement could play a key part in strengthening the competitive position of the European economy, providing both its regional low-cost production base and new capacious markets. On the other hand, the initiative could generate burdens on existing member states to the significant detriment of that position. The chances of southern enlargement are less favourable due to the perception that the balance of risk and opportunity is tilted even more to the former. Despite the new tone adopted within the EMP, the EU still appears more interested in political rather than economic gains to be had in the Mediterranean Basin region, with particular respect to security and immigration imperatives. It is likely, though, that EU accession will be granted to 'lower risk' Mediterranean countries sometime next century. Yet ultimately all such decisions must consider their international and global impact as well as the more specific effects within the EU.

5 Europe and the Triad

In George Orwell's *1984*, the ruling world order was dominated by three powers – Oceania, Eurasia and Eastasia. Orwell's vision of the future turned out to be only partially true. Many of the post-war totalitarian states have toppled, but a tripolar division of global economic and political power is certainly apparent. For centuries, Europe has considered itself at the very heart of the global economy. This perception remained intact despite a post-war world which has been largely dominated by an economically dynamic and powerful USA. However, as the post-war years progressed a newly resuscitated Japan emerged as a third rival economic power to challenge the hegemony of the West. The Treaty of Rome's creation of a supra-national entity was intended to compensate for the European nation-state's own relative loss of political and economic weight on the post-imperial world stage.

The US, Japan and European Union thus form a 'Triad' of global economic superpowers, to use Ohmae's (1985a, b) term. We can, though, widen the frame to the North American Free Trade Agreement (NAFTA), East Asia and Europe to represent the extension of regional agreements that have recently taken place. The NAFTA countries – USA, Canada and Mexico – may seek to deepen the links of integration between them using the EU as a prototype model. The gathering momentum of intra-East Asia trade and the progressive discussions made in recent Asia Pacific Economic Co-operation (APEC) fora could well lead to a free trade area being established between both sides of the Pacific Rim by 2020. In 1995, the EU welcomed Austria, Finland and Sweden into membership while preparations for the accession of six Central and Eastern European states by the turn of the century currently preoccupy its policy-makers. The magnetic effect of the world's major economic poles could continue to pull a number of neighbouring, non-aligned countries into future Triad membership.

Explaining the gravitational forces which the Triad exerts on other nations is relatively simple. The extended Triad family of members presides over an approximate 70 per cent of world GDP, international trade (see Table 5.1) and investment flows. They are also in possession of the

Table 5.1 The tripolarisation of world trade

	(% of total world imports)	
	1980	*1993*
Intra-bloc		
Western Europe	28.0	31.0
North America	5.9	7.5
East Asia	6.1	11.2
	40.0	49.7
Inter-bloc		
W. Europe–N. America	7.7	7.2
E. Asia–N. America	7.1	11.1
W. Europe–E. Asia	4.6	7.5
Total	59.4	75.5

Source: IMF

largest and most sophisticated markets and are the primary source of new technological developments and innovations. Where possible, non-aligned countries will thus seek to align or at least associate themselves with a Triad power. Geographical location and the assets which countries have to offer to existing members will primarily determine the level of entry permitted. Triad competition can either take the form of rival protectionist-orientated trade blocs, or each Triad group seeking to compete on more co-operative grounds. The globalisation of business has perhaps shown the advantages of joint ventures, consortium agreements and other forms of strategic alliance collaborations between firms across the Triad spectrum. The Triad's political powers, boosted by the confidence of a successfully negotiated final GATT round, are attempting to strike up similar partnerships realising that it is better to compete from within than from outside.

Nevertheless, the principle of improved competitiveness leading to improved prosperity remains central to the motivation and decision-making processes of business and policy-makers alike. Serious questions are therefore being asked by economists, politicians and others as to which Triad power will acquire the ultimate competitive edge in the twenty-first century and thus seek to claim the period as its own. In this chapter, we shall be investigating the backgrounds of Europe's Triad rivals to engender a firmer understanding of its own global position. We will also focus on the emergence of a possible fourth pole, that of China (see Table 5.2), and its potential ramifications for the world economy. Finally, a discussion on Europe's position within the likely scenario of the next century evolving into the 'Pacific Century' will be held, whereby Europe faces the challenge of a possible Trans-Pacific alliance between its Triad counterparts that could effectively marginalise that position.

Table 5.2 Europe's Triad rivals: general economic indicators

	GDP ($bn 1995)	GDP p/capita ($bn 1995)	Annual ave. growth rate (1985–93)	Annual ave. inflation rate (1989–94)	Investment (% of GDP 1995)
USA	6,388	24,753	2.3	3.8	15.4
Japan	3,927	31,451	3.5	2.1	29.7
China*	2,200	1,950	9.2	11.5	36.0

Sources: The Economist (1996), World Bank (1992)
* Estimates for China's GDP vary greatly. GDP and GDP per capita figures are hence derived from middle order estimates (World Bank 1992).

THE USA: A DIMINISHING GIANT?

A general profile

After World War II, the USA dominated the world economy, accounting for around 35 per cent of total world GDP in the late 1940s. It was by far the most technologically advanced nation at the time, in possession of the world's most dynamic companies and domestic markets, productivity levels that were up to twice the rate of most of its rivals and at the forefront of new product and process innovations. The USA has long held the post of free market capitalism's standard bearer. The pioneering spirit and confidence of its entrepreneurs led the way in the USA's rise to the top of the industrial league of nations. Bountiful natural resources and a seemingly self-sustainable home market provided the necessary conditions required for initial business expansion. American companies took an early lead in mass production industries and technologies that were later to prove their huge growth potential, such as Ford in automobiles and IBM in office equipment and computers. The USA was also the first to develop the concepts of standardised, disposable and convenience goods which were affordable to most households.

The internationalisation of American business accelerated in the early post-war years owing to the need to restore the damaged sinews of the world economy. The USA was the only nation with the industrial capability and capital resources to perform this task. Soon the pace of American foreign investment gathered momentum as the market potential of reconstructed economies expanded. The unregulated nature of the American economy and its low tax structure both exemplify a tradition of minimalist state intervention. Welfare systems in the USA are not as extensive as those found in European countries, especially where they have adhered to the guiding principles of social market ideology. However the US government has taken a dirigiste interest in the defence industry, with a significant part of the federal budget spent on its procurement. The dedication of the Reagan administration in the 1980s to increase the military capability of the USA contributed significantly to the ballooning federal budget deficit, as well as its commitment to reducing personal and corporate taxation.

Although the USA is still the world's largest nation trader of visibles and invisibles, at 13.9 per cent and 13.0 per cent of the world totals respectively, the economy currently stands as the world's sixth least trade dependent with exports and imports at only 8 per cent of GDP. The self-sufficiency of the US economy with its well-endowed resource base and huge domestic market is largely responsible for creating this apparently autarkic situation. The former condition also explains partly why a sizeable proportion of US exports are relatively resource intensive at 24.2 per cent of total national exports. This compares to Germany at 12.4 per cent and Japan at 2.7 per cent. Only Sweden appears to share the USA's ability to combine significant world class positions in both resource-intensive and knowledge-intensive industries.

The rise and stumble of the USA: the Cold War years

By the 1950s and 1960s, US companies had developed a supremacy in a wide spectrum of industries. This was exhibited in many high-tech and high-growth sectors such as civil aviation, office equipment and computers, defence-related products, synthetic materials, telecommunications, power generation and distribution, chemicals and electronics. By 1971, the USA produced over three-quarters of total world aircraft exports. In the field of finance and other commercial services, the USA had similar depth and strength. Abundant capital resources linked to a flexible, accessible capital market and comparatively low real interest rates were key determinants to the US economy's dynamic growth. The domestic market became increasingly affluent, and subsequently during this time its consumers were the most sophisticated in the world. It also became an essential source of economic growth and expansion for other economies, most significantly for Japan and other emerging nations in the Pacific Rim. The well-known phrase regarding the implications of the USA sneezing was telling of the effects of the US business cycle upon the world economy. High levels of productivity, innovative activity and general dynamism were sustained partly by a much envied college education system. The economy's infrastructure was the world's most advanced, with its networks of interstate highways and state-of-the-art telecommunication systems.

Yet as the post-war years wore on, the USA's hegemonic position was exposed to a series of mounting pressures. The involvement in the Vietnam War and subsequent defeat coupled with the shock of the 1973–4 Oil Crisis dealt severe psychological blows to American society. The gradual loss of American dominance in an increasing number of industries and world markets further undermined confidence. Both Japan and Germany had begun seriously to challenge the USA's status as the world's most technologically advanced nation by taking the lead in many process technologies, new material sciences and complex electronic products. Japanese companies were beginning to accumulate an impressive variety of patents in the US market and beating home-produced products on quality, rates of new product development and service. The same could also be applied to certain European firms in a narrower field of industries.

The 1990s: the present picture and outlook

The inevitable questions have been raised as to whether the USA is set for an inexorable decline akin to that which Britain experienced from the late nineteenth century onwards. The USA's share of total world GDP has now fallen to under 25 per cent and the EU is the world's largest unified marketplace. We have already noted how other nations have managed to blunt the USA's competitive edge in a range of industries as the post-war years progressed. However, the very recent performance of the US economy calls us to be somewhat more circumspect. A weak dollar, low wage growth, committed efficiency drives and the willingness to adapt to new realities have all contributed to the USA's recently improved competitiveness. Its ability to breed and nurture small business formation remains a salient feature of its economy. Many of its hard-core industries such as automobiles, machine tools and steel have undergone extensive restructuring in the early 1990s based on a further embracing of total quality management (TQM) and reorganised production along more flexible lines. Many commentators believe that focus on the competitive challenges posed by Japan has spurred US companies recently to undergo this process of transformation (*Financial Times*, 7 February 1994).

In a variety of high-tech industries, the USA has reasserted its superiority. Silicon Valley has not lost its creative flair or its venture capital sponsors and continues to spawn a number of world-beating companies. These continue to hold lead positions in computing, be it software (Microsoft), semiconductors (IBM), personal computers (Compaq, Dell, Apple) or microprocessors (Intel). A similar American presence can also be felt in the telecommunications field, where a more competitive and less regulated domestic market has made firms refocus strategy and new product developments. The USA has made considerably greater progress at linking up information superhighways than any other country. In the new core technology clusters – information technology, biotechnology and new material sciences – and their associated high-tech applications, US companies either lead or share lead at the frontier of their development. It is perhaps not surprising then that the US government negotiated so hard on the intellectual property rights issue in the Uruguay Round of GATT talks. One must note that the strength of the USA also persists in a variety of tradable service sectors from films to finance to fast food chains. On the subject of trade, the USA appears to have rediscovered the advantages of export-led growth. Trade as a percentage of GDP has been gradually rising for some time, with exports growing at an average rate of 8 per cent between 1985 and 1993. This compares to Japan's 2.6 per cent and Germany's 2.3 per cent. The further exploitation of the emerging market potential of the Pacific Rim economies will no doubt enhance both trends.

With regard to productivity levels, the USA again fares well by comparison. Many overlook the huge lead the USA still enjoys over its main rivals in this area. 'All business' productivity rates for 1993 showed that the USA held a 15 per cent lead over both Germany and France and a 27 per cent lead over Britain while Japan lay a somewhat startling 42 per cent behind (*Economist*, 15 January 1994). In manufacturing, the USA possessed a 20 per cent advantage over both Germany and Japan. Suppressed wage growth and a 2.8 per cent productivity rate achieved between 1991 and 1994 that outperformed its other Triad competitors have enabled the USA to contain unit labour costs in manufacturing far more successfully than both Japan and Germany.

However, fundamental problems continue to threaten the longer term health and condition of the US economy. The quality of US primary and secondary education has fallen in relative terms with comparative standards of science and technical education reached at these levels being particularly weak. Consequently, the USA's young do not fare well in international tests of numeracy and literacy. In 1992, the estimated market value for US employers buying remedial reading books for their employees totalled over $500m. While some universities can still be considered of a world class standard, the average higher education institution is below par when compared to its equivalents across the Triad. It is also worth noting that up to 40 per cent of PhDs awarded in the USA are currently collected by non-Americans, most of them being East Asians. Many graduates seek to pursue careers in law, accountancy, finance or those with a more glamorous appeal such as entertainment and marketing. While this trend lends support to the USA's competitive advantage in these areas, the dearth of talented graduates in manufacturing industries, perhaps with the exception of computers, could prove to be a future strategic weakness. Moreover, corporate training programmes in US companies have become relatively mediocre and limited in scope and application. The USA may need to overhaul radically parts of its education system if it is to call on a highly skilled and educated workforce to sustain its lead in knowledge-intensive industries.

Another potential weak spot that has been identified by some analysts concerns the structure of the USA's capital market. This follows the 'Anglo-Saxon' model whereby capital ownership is dominated by large institutional investors. In 1990, these held 60 per cent of total US shares as opposed to 8 per cent in 1950. The primary objectives of these institutions are geared towards extruding short-term gains from stock holdings which are constantly churned over to achieve best possible returns on minimal scales of time. The relatively small shareholdings held across a wide cross-section of companies exacerbates the problem of commitment. This whole process can create an unstable environment for businesses to engage in longer term strategic investments and has been blamed by some for the USA's low investment ratio and low rate of technological upgrading in recent times. This can be partly demonstrated with specific respect to long-term R&D, where US companies compare unfavourably, with only 21 per cent of its total R&D expenditure being dedicated to this end in 1995 – against Japan's 47 per cent and Germany's 61 per cent. A tax system that generally favours consumption has provided a further structural impediment to investment and innovative activities.

Although the Clinton administration has made bold endeavours to reduce the huge fiscal deficit, the associated macroeconomic constraints still remain considerable. Other deep-rooted problems which have been identified include the diverging social equity gap between the USA's rich and poor, in addition to the apparent legislative gridlock on health care reforms. Both of these developments could help swell the country's growing 'underclass' which itself may prove the source of a number of socio-economic impediments to the future progress of the US economy.

Box 5.1 The North American Free Trade Agreement (NAFTA)

In 1993, the USA, Canada and Mexico signed the North American Free Trade Agreement (NAFTA). The objective of NAFTA was to set a series of measures in motion from 1 January 1994 with the aim of establishing a free trade zone between the three countries within fifteen years. A free trade agreement has existed between Canada and the USA since 1989 (CUSFTA). The main impact of NAFTA thus concerns the integration of Mexico into the North American economy and its extended association with a Triad power (see Figure 5.1).

NAFTA has had, and will have, an obvious wider impact. Its profile of a combined GDP of close on $7 trillion and population of 360 million is similar to that of the EU. The evolution of another regional integration agreement at the time of delicate Uruguay Round GATT negotiations could have upset the balance of the multilateral trade system. The USA's East Asian trade and investment partners were also worried about the trade diverting effects of NAFTA and the USA's subsequent use of Mexico as a low-cost production base and emerging market. Other Latin American countries have expressed their desire to join NAFTA (e.g. Chile) in their aspiration to obtain a privileged access to the US economy and its markets.

The global impact of NAFTA remains uncertain. On the one hand it could further consolidate the structure of the world economy into rival power blocs and hence reduce the essence of international trade relations down to power-based rather than rule-based negotiations. Smith (1993a), however, argues

Box 5.1 *continued*

the counter case by stating that the past experience of the EU indicates that
NAFTA will have a generally benign effect on the world's economic order.
Multilateral trade relations have survived since the EU inaugurated their free
trade area in 1968, a date forty years before the NAFTA members plan to do
the same. The USA's primary trading interests still lie in sustaining this
environment within which most of its activity exists. Mexico may actually
prove to be a strategic production base from which East Asian and other
investors could acquire easier access into the US market. Perhaps the most
important global dimension to NAFTA concerns that of a North American
allegiance seeking to achieve common objectives in any Trans-Pacific alliance forged in the future.

JAPAN: THE NEW ECONOMIC SUPERPOWER

A brief economic history

Japan's path to the status of modern industrial nation is not limited to post-
war history. Wide-ranging reforms that were conducted in the mid-
nineteenth century onwards under the Meiji Restoration first marked its
quest to rival the economic hegemony of the Western powers. Part of this
process entailed Japan becoming the first Asiatic country to embrace
modern capitalism. The subsequent economic and industrial progress
which was achieved up to World War II made Japan a formidable force
in the conflict. Considerable financial aid and other assistance administered
under the caretaker leadership of the USA between 1945 and 1953 effectively gave Japan a second chance to realise its century-old ambition.

Inheriting the legacy of a disintegrated industrial base and domestic
market, Japan sought to exploit the only advantages which were available.
The workforce remained well educated and highly skilled. American capital was invested into building the productive capacity purposely geared
towards export-led growth. The lack of natural resources lent more imperative to Japan's efforts to manufacture her way back into the world economy. From an early stage, Japanese businesses possessed global vision.
The accelerated expansion in international trade in the 1950s and 1960s
gave them the initial momentum required to consolidate Japan's reconstruction. However, during this time, Japan's exporters faced an initial
image problem. Many of their products were synonymous in the West
with poor quality. These perceptions soon began to change as their now
familiar focus on product quality and TQM gradually began to provide
Japanese products with a competitive advantage over their rivals. The
contemporary prowess of Japanese business is based on a combination of
product and service quality, responsive technological upgrading and rapid
adaptation to the new needs of consumers.

GENERAL PROVISIONS

- Tariffs reduced over 15 years, depending on sector.
- Investment restrictions lifted in most sectors, with exception of oil in Mexico, culture in Canada, and airline and radio communications in the USA.
- Immigration excluded, except some movement of white-collar workers to be eased.
- Any country can leave the treaty with six months' notice.
- Treaty allows for the inclusion of any additional country.
- Government procurement opened up over 10 years, mainly affecting Mexico, which reserves some contracts for Mexican companies.
- Dispute resolution panels of independent arbitrators to resolve disagreements arising out of treaty.
- Some snap-back tariffs if surge of imports hurts a domestic industry.

INDUSTRIES

- Agriculture: Most tariffs between USA and Mexico removed immediately. Tariffs on 6 per cent of products – corn, sugar, and some fruits and vegetables – fully eliminated only after 15 years. For Canada, existing agreement with the USA applies.
- Cars: Tariffs removed over 10 years; Mexico's quotas on imports lifted over the same period; cars eventually to meet 62.5 per cent local content rule to be free of tariffs.
- Energy: Mexican ban on private sector exploration continues, but procurement by state oil company opened up to USA and Canada.
- Financial services: Mexico gradually opens financial sector to US and Canadian investment, eliminating barriers by 2007.
- Textiles: Treaty eliminates Mexican, US and Canadian tariffs over 10 years. Clothes eligible for tariff breaks to be sewn with fabric woven in North America.
- Trucking: North American trucks could drive anywhere in the three countries by the year 2000.

SIDE AGREEMENTS

- Environment: The three countries liable to fines, and Mexico and US sanctions, if a panel finds repeated pattern of not enforcing environment laws.
- Labour: Countries liable for penalties for non-enforcement of child, minimum wage and health and safety laws.

OTHER DEALS

- The USA and Mexico to set up a North American Development Bank to help finance clean-up of the US border.
- The USA to spend about $90m in the first 18 months retraining workers losing their jobs because of treaty.

Figure 5.1 NAFTA: the details
Source: *Financial Times*, 17 November 1993

This combination of factors, together with others to be examined, enabled the Japanese economy to overhaul all of its Western industrial rivals by the 1970s, apart from the USA. Porter (1990) notes that by the 1980s Japan had come to dominate several key manufacturing industries, being responsible for 82 per cent of total world exports for motorcycles, 80.7 per cent of TV image and sound recorders and 62 per cent of still cameras and flash apparatus by 1985. In 1965, Japan's nominal GDP was 10 per cent of the USA's. By 1991 it had risen to 58.9 per cent due to an average economic growth rate around three times that of the USA.

The Japanese economy: main features identified

There has been much academic study on the development of the modern Japanese economy. Part of the fascination relates to the very different environment *vis-à-vis* its Western industrial counterparts in which this development has evolved. Its distinguishing characteristics have included unique cultural specific and institution specific factors, as well as embodying general economic efficiencies. The most significant of these are highlighted below:

● Producer economics: this term was coined by Thurow (1992) to describe the emphasis placed on achieving predominance in manufacturing and process technologies. Production, as opposed to rent-seeking activities, has long been perceived as the key strategic determinant to national economic success.
● Global corporate vision and global reach: Japan remains committed to extending its interests on a global scale through the export of products, globalisation of business activity and the acquisition of foreign capital. The accumulation of enormous trade surpluses has generated huge foreign exchange reserves. A combination of the above has extended the global reach of Japanese businesses, especially in recent years, through accelerated foreign direct investments (FDI) and portfolio acquisitions. The Japanese economy has provided an important role model for economic development in East Asia and is the central pole of economic activity in the region.
● High saving and investment rates: owing to cultural reasons and postwar policy initiatives, Japan generated high rates of savings that in turn provided the investment funds required for the progressive upgrading of the economy's techno-industrial base.
● Innovative production and management techniques: Japanese companies pioneered many of the production and management methods that have revolutionised the conventional wisdom. Lean production and TQM are perhaps the most familiar examples.
● A highly educated and skilled workforce: Japan's education system is generally perceived as having the world's highest standards of achieve-

ment. This is particularly so in primary and secondary education. Many of the talented graduates from the system enter careers in industry.

- Key structural relationships: these have been the most unique feature of the post-war Japanese economy. The main examples are the special collaborative relationship between government, the *keiretsu* industrial groups, business and employment relations.

In making a closer examination of the key structural relationships that have helped to define the Japanese economy in recent decades, we should first observe that the *keiretsu* (which in Japanese means linkage, lineage or just 'system') evolved out of the handful of large diversified business groups called *zaibatsu* that dominated the economy in the pre-war years. These were family based and normally comprised of a holding company that controlled a number of core operating companies and their subsidiaries. The *zaibatsu* were formally dissolved by the early post-war American administration, but the *keiretsu* emerged in the 1950s in the shape of former *zaibatsu*-affiliated companies with most in association with a group bank (for the six major *keiretsu* these were the Fuji, Dai-ichi Kangyo, Mitsubishi, Mitsui, Sanwa and Sumitomo banks).

Each group also had a general trading company (*sogo shosha*) which developed wide intelligence networks whose main aims were to seek out potential export markets and cheap import sources. Although the links between *keiretsu* members were looser than their *zaibatsu* predecessors, they were connected by both interlocking share ownership and company directorships. This gave each stakeholder a part to play in meeting the group's 'shared destiny' (*unmekyodatai*) corporate objectives. The specific role of the group banks was to provide extended financial capital for the group. It has also meant that Japan's capital markets have developed in a contrasting manner to the 'Anglo-Saxon' model, aligning the interests of finance and industry more closely together and producing a relative absence of take-overs, especially of the hostile kind. A combination of these arrangements has encouraged longer term planning, technological transfer, subcontracting and general synergetic effects across the group. The extent of their influence was revealed in a recent study which reported that the six major *keiretsu* accounted for around a quarter of Japan's post-war GDP while their trading companies currently handle two-thirds of Japanese imports (OTA 1993).

However, not all of Japan's large firms grew in such a way (e.g. Sony and Honda), while the vast majority of Japan's businesses consists of small and medium-sized enterprises (SMEs) which are mostly independent of *keiretsu* groups. There is a generally high level of rivalry between Japanese firms both in domestic and foreign markets. The *keiretsu*, though, have been blamed for cartelisation and other forms of restrictive practices. Such criticism has particularly come from Triad powers which have expressed concern over the so-called 'structural impediments' to foreign competition.

This is illustrated by the discriminatory contracting between *keiretsu* members to the frequent exclusion of foreign counterparts. Efforts to dismantle this structural relationship have been resisted, not least on the grounds of clearly demonstrated past successes.

The formation of the *keiretsu* helped to co-ordinate the policy of partnership that the Japanese government wished to engender with big business. The Ministry of International Trade and Industry (MITI), and the Ministry of Finance have played key roles in developing such a relationship. In collaboration with business they formed the framework of an overall indicative plan which, according to Komine (1993), kept to three basic objectives:

- to forecast the way in which the economy ought to and can develop;
- to indicate the fundamental direction that government medium-term and long-term economic policy should take, as well as identify priority objectives and methods;
- to provide the basic guidelines for both corporate and household decisions.

In addition to the *keiretsu* groups, policy-makers also communicated with several industry associations in whose establishment MITI had been involved. The inauguration of a number of deliberative councils (e.g. the Industrial Rationalisation Council and Industrial Structure Advisory Council), attended by both government officials and business personnel, provided other fora on which Japan's industrial and commercial policy was grounded. The partnership was further reinforced by various informal ties such as *amakudari*, whereby some retiring government officials would take up high executive level positions in business or their representative bodies.

This overarching framework within which these structural relationships were nurtured assisted in creating the favourable conditions for business development. The policy approach followed by MITI has adjusted over time to suit contemporary needs. During the 1950s and 1960s this involved protectionist measures to shield key infant industries from foreign competition and strict controls over foreign exchange and the licensing of imported technology to modulate contact with the vigours of the early post-war world economy. As the economy transformed, the focus of policy soon began to shift away from low-tech, labour-intensive industries and their markets to more high-tech, capital-intensive activities. From 1974 onwards, MITI began to collaborate with industry in fabricating the consensual 'long-term visions' for the development of the economy.

Japanese employment relations form the third special structural relationship in study. These have been founded on strong mutual loyalties between employer and employee. A socio-cultural relationship derived from the old feudal and clan traditions of benevolent lord and obedient peasant is thought to have fermented these relations. The Confucian group ethic also acts as a bonding agent between employer and employee. The four main outcomes of these relations have been summarised by Whitehill (1991) as being: lifetime employment agreements, especially in large companies; consensus decision-making; seniority wage and promotion; enterprise unionism.

Employees are expected to work long hours of unpaid overtime in many companies. According to the OECD (1994a) the average annual hours worked by Japanese employees in 1992 was 1,965. This compares against 1,768 for the USA, 1,618 for Germany, 1,666 for France and 1,485 for Sweden. Annual leave for Japanese workers normally ranges from ten to twenty days depending on seniority level. This compares to an average of twenty-eight days in Germany. However, most employees fail to take their full entitlement of leave in the fear that it may reflect a lack of loyalty to the company. Many Japanese workers will only take three or four days vacation a year. The Ministry of Labour has gone so far as to launch various campaigns to encourage workers to take up their full holiday entitlement.

In return for this devotion to the company, Japanese employers can offer their employees a reward package designed to provide security and inspire further self-sacrifice. Large firms will more than likely agree to a lifetime contract of employment for certain new recruits. Even in times of recession, Japanese firms are reluctant to dispose of excess personnel in the belief that releasing an employee is a lost investment for the future. Within a *keiretsu* group, personnel in overmanned sections in one company are simply redeployed to companies elsewhere within the group which can more easily absorb extra employment. This may involve a temporary move (*shukko*) or a permanent one (*tenseki*).

Japan's domestic market

Japan's present population of 125 million is the seventh largest in the world; it is also one the richest. However, certain aspects of Japan's domestic market have caused it to acquire an external perception of impenetrability from foreign business and policy-makers. This has been the origin of much recent international negotiation with other Triad members. A range of determinants has influenced the features of this market. The Japanese are an ethnically and culturally homogeneous people. They are also among the world's most sophisticated consumers, demanding high standards on product quality, choice and service. Owing to Japan's mountainous topography and seismic activity, the mass of its population is concentrated into huge conurbations, mainly on the southern seaboard of Honshu, the country's largest island. Compact living conditions have required compact goods that are also multifunctional and lightweight. Japan's competitive advantage in electronic consumer durable goods such as the hi-fi stereo and video cassette recorder were partly driven by these conditional necessities.

Status is bestowed upon Japan's conspicuous consumers from obtaining the very latest model or new product on the market. Minimal leisure time and relatively high levels of disposable income have led to such spending behaviour representing a form of personal expression and identity. Conscious of this, Japanese companies have sought to concentrate on sub-segmenting market demand, incremental product innovations and other upgrading activity. The strong desire for product originality has also encouraged the Japanese to consider new production methods aided by microchip technologies which enable them to achieve shorter lead times in product development and 'customise' mass-produced goods.

It has been said that the Japanese display chauvinistic tendencies in their purchasing. Although the more protectionist trade policies pursued in the past may have partially engineered this situation, a more relevant explanation lies in the perceived superior quality and technology vested in Japanese-made products. In 1994, a Bozell–Gallup survey conducted among 20,000 consumers across 20 countries found that Japanese products enjoyed a higher quality perception rating than any rival nations. These findings simply reflect the long held emphasis that Japanese companies have placed on quality in both product and process technologies.

Some weaknesses and fault lines revealed

Although the post-war rise of the Japanese economy has been impressive, we must note a number of weaknesses that have been carried through the period as well as those fault lines which have recently appeared. One of the most important points regards the fact that the breadth of Japan's seemingly invincible industrial strength is somewhat limited in scope. While an undisputed manufacturing prowess has been developed by its companies in the key sectors, such as automotive, electrical/electronic and some high-tech industries, large structural gaps are to be found elsewhere. Japan's aerospace, pharmaceutical and chemical industries lag some way behind both Europe and the USA. In certain service sector industries (e.g. retailing) Japanese firms are also at a competitive disadvantage, although this is not the case in banking and financial services. The predominant position it once had in numerous staple industries has now diminished. Japanese textile, steel, shipbuilding and semiconductor industries have all faced severe competitive pressures from the 'tiger' economies of East Asia. Japan's reliance on imported raw materials still presents a strategic industrial concern. This is particularly the case for oil and other key mineral resources.

The period of rapid export-led growth has come to a halt for Japanese companies. Importing countries have partly contributed through the imposition of formal and informal protectionist measures upon Japanese goods. The continued rising value of the yen has further undermined the relative price competitiveness of Japan's exports, approximately quadrupling in value against the US dollar since the collapse of the Bretton Woods exchange rate system. Japanese companies have reacted by relocating and extending production capabilities offshore.

Although Japan's education system still provides an exemplar to others, many feel that the ethos and structure which underpins it is in need of re-examination. Intuitive and independent thought is not actively encouraged in the schools and universities. The knowledge-intensive growth industries of the twenty-first century will require a blend of technocratically adroit and creatively inventive individuals. Japan may find itself deficient on the second account in forthcoming years if it fails to adapt to these new realities. Another challenge facing the management of Japan's human resources is its ageing population. The country possesses one of the highest dependency ratios in the world, derived from a combination of low birth rates and the highest life expectancy rates of any nation at 75 years for men and 81 for women. By 2025 an estimated 40.3 per cent of Japan's population will be 65 years old and above. This poses an obvious threat to Japan's future wealth generating potential. Furthermore, the intensity of the Japanese work ethic has come under threat from an emerging generation of 'new human beings' who have reacted against the competitive pressures of an achievement-oriented society within both the education system and corporate strata. This has been replaced by a more extensively articulated desire among Japan's young to spend more time dedicated to leisure pursuits.

Pressures have also mounted on the institution of lifetime employment, particularly since the early 1990s recession. An estimate made by Meryll Lynch economists suggested that Japanese firms held up to two million surplus employees in 1993, the equivalent of 3 per cent of the country's total workforce. Companies have sought to retract offers of lifetime employment contracts for new recruits while also cutting back on their intake of graduates. The recession also weakened the bonds of the *keiretsu* enterprise networks as members have sought to improve corporate flexibility by linking up with more competitive outsiders. This has sometimes manifested itself in the form of international strategic alliances that have established with Triad counterparts.

One of the most surprising aspects of the Japanese economy is its relatively underdeveloped infrastructure and housing. The quality of Japan's rail and road networks is comparatively poor. Less than half of Japan's tenements are connected to sewage systems. Living space is a premium commodity and houses and apartments are cramped. The expense of real estate in core urban areas forces many workers to commute vast distances. In the early 1990s, one square metre of real estate in Tokyo's central business district had a market value of $50,000, while the complete real estate value of Tokyo exceeded that of the entire USA. Such conditions will continue to suppress effective Japanese standards of living despite high GDP per capita figures, and persistent infrastructure bottlenecks are likely to hamper a more complete economic development.

The future of the Japanese economy: a brief comment

The ability of Japanese manufacturers to apply new technological developments and compete effectively on product quality has been retained, providing exporters with a significant competitive advantage over their rivals. The compulsion to relocate production and other operations offshore will remain strong, driven by attempts to circumvent the uncompetitive effects of a strong yen and the rationale of globalisation. These future relocations will take the form of an increasing variety of relatively lower-tech industrial activities that can be accommodated by neighbouring East Asian countries whose own economic development has followed in Japan's wake. Domestic production will consequently make a shift towards more high-tech, knowledge-intensive activities.

Despite the attention that has been afforded to Japanese foreign investment, the country's substantial trading surpluses persist in causing the main shockwaves in the international community. In 1993, Japan's total trade surplus reached $141.43bn, with the USA and South East Asia responsible for around a third each of this amount. Such commercial successes have generated political frictions between Japan and the other Triad powers, and have eclipsed most other issues in any negotiations that have occurred. There is considerable debate as to what extent Japan's trade policy can be held to blame over the matter. Japan's average tariffs on industrial goods have been lower than those of the USA and the EU. Non-tariff barriers on Japanese imports have been specifically highlighted by some, but these have generally not been extensive enough to warrant prime concern. This has been directed to the existence of 'structural impediments' which have been described as 'the habits and attitudes bred of Japan's vertically and horizontally integrated industrial, commercial and financial groups' (CEC 1985b). The contracting relationships of the *keiretsu* groups have been a typifying example of this, as have been the relatively underdeveloped retail distribution networks and the low consumption propensity of Japanese consumers. The removal of structural impediments will continue to take priority position in any foreseeable trade negotiations (this debate is further elaborated upon in Chapters 6 and 8).

There has also been much discussion over Japan's international role now that it has acquired the status of a mature and significant industrial country. While it has by no means developed the stature to replace the USA as the world's hegemonic economic power it may be able to play this part on a regional basis. This depends on the reaction of other East Asian nations and the process of regionalisation that emerges between them in the future. Whatever the outcome, we must construct a different set of expectations regarding Japan's future role in the world economy and the developmental path it will take in forthcoming decades.

CHINA: THE BIRTH OF THE QUAD?

China in historical and contemporary perspective

The notion of the world economy taking its orientation around three poles of economic activity is thought by some to be increasingly erroneous. The recent arrival of the Chinese economy into the global community poses all other members of that community a number of critical questions to be answered both now and well into the next century. Such is the potential of China that observers are already referring to it as the new 'quad' economic superpower. For much of recorded history, China has held the position of the most advanced nation on earth. While medieval European kingdoms were continually locked in conflict and combat, China was preoccupied with developing new materials such as gunpowder, inventing new devices such as the compass, attempting to harness steam as an energy source and landing explorers on the east coast of Africa.

Napoleon has been attributed with stating, 'Let China sleep. When China wakes it will shake the world.' China's apparent slumber behind the Great Wall left it in isolation during the European and North American industrial revolutions. Decline followed, as did military defeats against modern nineteenth-century powers who desired to apply their superior technological know-how and industrial muscle to prize open China for the purposes of foreign trade and investment. In many ways, Chinese history seems to be repeating itself with foreign investors making a participatory contribution to China's current economic resurgence. Economic reforms were introduced under the new leadership of Den Xiaoping in 1978. Certain aspects of the economy were radically transformed, leading to what was eventually termed a 'socialist market economy' by the Chinese Communist Party in November 1993. The policy measures marked a clear break with the previous Maoist era, best known for the catastrophic Cultural Revolution and Great Leap Forward. The two main aims of Den Xiaoping's reforms were to integrate China back into the world economy and to reorganise the domestic economy along more capitalist lines. These were to be achieved by pursuing the following objectives:

- introduction of a number of palatable market-based reforms into agriculture and industry;
- decentralisation of political and economic control;
- removal of barriers to foreign trade and creation of incentives to attract foreign investment, or 'Open Door' policy;
- establishment of the basis of a commercial legal system to underpin these aims.

The flagship of the reforms was the creation of four Special Economic Zones (SEZs) in 1979. The SEZs gave tax concessions and other locational incentives to foreign investors. Extensive market-based reforms also assisted new business formation in these areas. It was no accident that three of the SEZs – Shenzhen, Shantou and Zhuhai – were situated in the Guangdong province, directly above Hong Kong. The fourth, Xiamen, lay next door in the Fujian province and hence in close proximity to the other East Asian tiger economy with common ethnic links, namely Taiwan. A fifth SEZ – Hainan, an island near Hong Kong – has been subsequently introduced, as have been the 'opening' of foreign investment to fourteen coastal cities, the creation of new Free Trade Zones and five Open Economic Zones. Consequently, the whole Chinese coast and parts of its hinterland have experienced progressive economic liberalisation, and now produce over a third of the country's GNP with only a sixth of its population.

The economic success of China's recent reforms cannot be easily overestimated. Between 1978 and 1993, economic growth has averaged at an annual rate of 9 per cent, consumption at 7.9 per cent and investment at 10.7 per cent. China's economy has consequently experienced a 260 per cent expansion over this period. The SEZs have occasionally registered annual industrial growth rates of over 30 per cent. Elsewhere, the Chinese have taken the opportunities generated by the reform process. State-owned enterprises (SOEs) have been crowded out of the economy, not by a privatisation programme but from the rapid expansion of the number of new collectively run businesses called township and village enterprises (TVEs).

Estimates vary over the true and potential global stature of China but the World Bank currently places the Chinese economy as the world's third largest. By 2020, it is set to become the largest with a 40 per cent lead over its nearest rival, the USA (see Figure 5.2). However, the world's largest economy is not necessarily the most powerful. China's economic weight lies in her population, still roughly one-fifth of the planet's total. Although appreciable rises in standards of living have occurred, the country remains among the world's poorest. Nevertheless, China may debatably be only a generation or so away from what the more advanced East Asian tiger economies have lately achieved. They have provided the role model for China of how to modernise through such measures as land reform, export-led growth and opening up to foreign investment. China itself is increasingly lending more significant levels of momentum to the economic development of the region, both as a cost base and marketplace.

Such connections are particularly strong with the approximately 40 million overseas Chinese who live in other East Asian countries. The mainland Chinese have developed an extensive network of business contacts (*guanxi*) with Hong Kong and Taiwan in particular, their two most ethnically akin neighbours. The common Confucian traditions of preser-

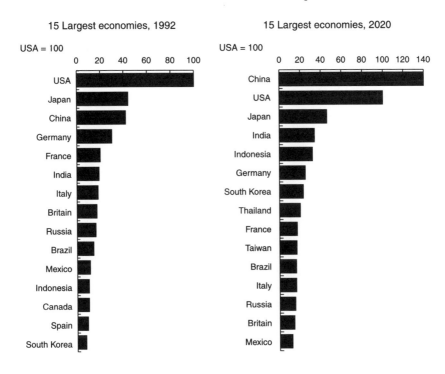

Figure 5.2 The world's fifteen largest economies: 1992, 2020
Source: World Bank; © *The Economist* (October 1994)

ving family structures, close-knit social groups and strong work ethic have sought to underpin the connections between them. Hong Kong is, of course, set to be absorbed back into China in July 1997. There is discussion in certain quarters of some Taiwanese being reconciled to sharing the same destiny within a few decades. The Chinese diaspora also scatters into Singapore, Malaysia, Indonesia, the Philippines, Vietnam and Brunei. Thus, the scope for extending *guanxi*, and ultimately China's political and economic interests is considerable.

The evolving shape of industry

Despite the radical changes that have taken place within the Chinese economy, the agriculture sector remains almost completely non-mechanised and the preponderance of workers stay lodged in SOEs. The service sector only accounts for a mere 20 per cent of GDP. Despite such inertia, the complexion of Chinese industry is altering. The key factors that have been contributive to this are:

- foreign direct investment mainly in terms of 'greenfield' business developments and joint ventures;
- export orientation as a result of liberalised trade regulations and extensive foreign investment;
- the growth of TVEs that have been mainly located in rural areas;
- a deepening competitive environment within industries from both the retreat of the state planning apparatus and rivalry between newly established private and collective businesses.

One of the most startling developments to have been spawned from recent reforms has been the growth of the TVEs. In essence, they are a new form of corporate organisation which does not fully belong either to the state or non-state sector. Instead, they are usually controlled by a mixture of representatives from local government, private companies and foreign investors and are run on a collective basis with managers ultimately answerable to local government. TVEs first emerged from Den Xiaoping's early reform plans that concentrated on rural development with the aim of attempting to introduce free market principles in the countryside. What resulted was the rapid rise of rural-based industries that numbered 1.5m in 1978 and 19m by 1991. The initial intention of the policy was to liberalise family-run farms but the 55 per cent majority of TVEs are now light and heavy industry producers competing directly with SOEs. Their expansion has hence been mainly at the expense of the state sector. They are generally small and have become intensely competitive both in domestic and world markets. The proliferation of TVEs has taken central government by surprise. It is also worth noting that a large number of them have disappeared due to the pressures induced from highly competitive rivalry.

Inward flows of foreign investment are also making an impact upon the shape of China's industry. Currently it receives nearly half of total FDI destined for developing countries and has experienced an accelerated surge in the 1990s. In 1993, $26bn of foreign investment entered the country compared to $11bn in 1992 and around $4bn in 1991. An average of 20,000 joint venture contracts are made each year between foreign and Chinese enterprises. About three-quarters of Chinese inward FDI comes from Hong Kong and Taiwan, where domestic labour costs are currently in the region of ten times those of China.

Not only does China present itself as an inexpensive production base, but also as a marketplace with a potential to rival the EU's own single market. China's population is well over the combined total for the OECD nations. Although the population is poor, companies such as Unilever have long taken an interest in China's market capacity and expect the demand for its products to rise from $200m in 1994 to $1.5bn in 1999 (*Financial Times*, 7 November 1994). Foreign investment has brought with it important benefits to the Chinese economy in the form of much needed technology transfers, the introduction of new production and management methods and in 1993 roughly two-thirds of its exports and 5 per cent of total output. Given a stable political environment and huge market potential there is no reason to doubt that one day China will become the world's primary centre of gravity of inward FDI.

Trade and trade relations

China's trading sector has expanded rapidly since the first of the Open Door policies was implemented in 1978. In 1977, its share of world merchandise trade stood at 0.6 per cent but by 1993 this had risen to 2.5 per cent. There has been a corresponding growth in trade as a proportion of GDP from 5 per cent in 1978 to 20 per cent by 1991. Nominal trade growth has averaged at just over 16 per cent a year. China's trade with the EU over 1979 to 1993 has grown by thirteen times from ECU 2.4bn to ECU 31bn, making it the EU's fifth largest trading partner. An ECU 8.2bn trade surplus was registered in the same year to the former's advantage.

Before the reform process commenced, China's exports reflected its comparative advantage in resource-intensive products with manufactures only making a 50 per cent contribution. By 1994, this contribution had risen to 83 per cent, based on largely low-tech goods such as textiles and clothing, footwear, travel goods, miscellaneous manufactured items and basic chemicals. This structural change in China's trade has partly forced more advanced East Asian economies to move upstream to medium-tech and high-tech industries, while moving their own low-tech, more labour-intensive production to China. Trading activity, once monopolised by a central government agency, now lies in the hands of nearly 4,000 companies. China's currency, the yuan, was unified in early 1994 with plans to make it fully convertible in the near future.

The most pressing objective for China's trade policy-makers has been securing WTO membership. A World Bank estimate suggested that a 50 per cent reduction of the Triad economies' tariffs derived from accession to the WTO could boost China's exports by up to 38 per cent, compared to 15 per cent for an average developing country (*Financial Times*, 7 November 1994). The USA has conducted negotiations on behalf of the WTO fraternity with China over the matter, and even though President Clinton decided in May 1994 to remove the human rights issue from the agenda other hurdles exist. China has frequently been found guilty of breaching the intellectual property rights of foreign companies – one of a new area of negotiated agreements in the Uruguay Round – particularly in audio-visual products and computer software. A wide range of relatively high tariffs are still imposed on China's imports, and these can vary from one coastal province to another. However, given the increasing global significance of the Chinese economy any future multilateral trade negotiations must seek to include China in the process.

An assured future?

While considerable advances have been made there are a number of problem areas that still hamper China's aspirations to modernise. The contradictions of sustaining a 'socialist market economy', as the party line has phrased it, may prove an impossible juggling act to perform. A liberalised economy must give way to political freedom unless palpable rises in living standards can provide an appropriate counter-balance. Uncertainty concerning Den Xiaoping's successor and signs that the pace of reforms is slowing down casts further complications and doubts into the equation.

Since the early 1990s the Chinese central government has attempted to stop the economy from overheating. Inflation stood at 27.4 per cent in September 1994 fuelled by unreined economic growth and uncapped agricultural prices. The policy option of pursuing austere macroeconomic measures may force many of the loss-making SOEs, constituting around 40 per cent of the total by official calculations in 1994, into bankruptcy. This may prove beneficial to the economy in the long run but unofficial estimates of unemployment running as high as 20 per cent in some urban areas would increase the attached socio-political risks. On the other hand, the alternative option of continuing to grant soft loans to SOEs may incubate the chaos that has beset the post-perestroika Russian economy.

China's fiscal system is under immense pressure from both difficulties arising in collecting revenue from SOEs and a faltering tax structure that requires urgent reform and restructuring. A considerable array of bureaucratic controls are still applied to foreign exchange, credit rationing and agri-product price intervention. Heavily subsidised SOEs continue to dominate Chinese industry with around 60 per cent of total fixed investment being sunk into them. The country's inordinate reliance on inward foreign investment to generate exports may prove a strategically dangerous position to maintain in the longer term. Stimulating the further development of the TVEs may provide the most hopeful solution to some of these problems.

Additional difficulties have originated from the relatively slow pace of China's infrastructural development during the reform period which has lagged well behind its economic growth. Consequently, serious bottlenecks have surfaced across most parts of the economy: electricity supplies have been estimated to be between 20 per cent to 30 per cent deficient of demand; the country's rail network is utilised three times more extensively than the USA's; Tokyo possesses more telephones than the whole of China combined; factories being built in the middle of agricultural plots wait for roads to catch them up a few kilometres away.

Severe environmental degradation has also accompanied economic growth in China, and looks likely to continue to do so for some time. The economy's 75 per cent energy dependency on coal, the dirtiest of the carbon fuels, makes China the fourth biggest generator of greenhouse gases. The general ecological implications carried by the rise in its population's purchasing power are enormous. These and other matters of global significance require European policy-makers and business leaders to be prepared for all possible scenarios that could eventuate from China's future path to modernisation and reform.

EAST ASIA'S 'TIGER' ECONOMIES

An introduction

Both Japan and China have been part of a broader economic phenomenon that has taken place in their region. In the most recent decades the dynamism of the East Asian economy has increasingly originated from the so-called 'tiger' economies. These are the region's newly industrialising countries (NICs) which together with Japan and China have produced the fastest economic growth rates ever recorded both individually and by a global region over a sustained period. The economic development of these NICs could be said to have occurred in waves or generations. The first generation has consisted of South Korea, Taiwan, Singapore and Hong Kong; the second generation group is made up of Thailand, Indonesia, Malaysia and the Philippines; the less well-defined third generation comprises countries located in Indochina, such as Vietnam, Cambodia and Laos.

Japan has been the primary role model for this development but it has been mainly the USA that has supplied the most strategically important markets and thus the main impetus for growth and expansion. However, the growing size of the 'tiger' economies' own markets and the level of sophistication found in the techno-industrial base of these countries is beginning to provide its own momentum in the region. This has been demonstrated by the rising trend of both intra-regional trade and investment flows in East Asia. At present, there appear to be no signs of this dynamism waning (see Table 5.3).

Patterns of development

One of the main questions posed by the rise of the 'tiger' economies concerns the pattern of development which they have followed. This has obviously been of most interest to aspiring NICs in other global regions. Attempts to answer this question have generated much academic study which has proved somewhat arduous owing to the different developmental paths taken and methods deployed. The general pattern of development for most NICs has followed an initial period of efforts to improve agricultural productivity that in turn released the workforce from the countryside to join factories engaged in the throes of an import substitution policy. However,

Table 5.3 The East Asian NICs: general economic profile, 1993–4

	Population (millions, 1995)	GDP per capita ($, 1995)	Average annual GDP real growth (%) 1985–93	Average annual Inflation (%) 1989–94
Hong Kong	5.9	17,842	6.8	9.6
Singapore	2.9	19,293	7.8	2.9
South Korea	44.1	7,673	8.9	6.8
Taiwan	20.8	10,404	6.7	4.0
Indonesia	187.2	732	6.4	9.0
Malaysia	19.0	3,156	7.4	3.6
Philippines	65.8	830	3.1	11.7
Thailand	58.8	2,044	9.1	5.0

Source: *The Economist* 1996

most East Asian NICs made a relatively early switch to export orientation policies. This entailed persuading domestic producers to face the challenge of bigger markets and competitive forces further abroad, while simultaneously receiving support in their home markets in the form of protectionist trade measures. Such support was especially granted to infant industries deemed to have potential strategic importance to the economy in the future.

Export-led growth strategies have been a key aspect of the 'tiger' economies' development. In many ways this was a logical choice to make. Their own domestic markets were small while they possessed an initial comparative advantage in well-established, labour-intensive industries in which they could compete against Western rivals with some degree of success. The internationalisation of their economies, as indicated by their increasing openness shown in Table 5.4, produced other general benefits. For instance, economic development was commonly advanced through the acquisition of foreign technology and other forms of strategic capital. This was achieved

Table 5.4 Openness ratios for the East Asian NICs: 1965, 1990 (exports of goods and non-factor services as a per cent of GDP)

	1965	1990
Hong Kong	71	137
Singapore	123	190
South Korea	9	32
Taiwan	21	57
Indonesia	5	26
Malaysia	42	79
Philippines	17	28
Thailand	16	38

Sources: IMF; Grant *et al.* 1993

through arms-length measures, such as licensing arrangements or reverse engineering techniques, or by the selective inward foreign investments which brought with them the means to upgrade the techno-industrial base of the economy.

The game of technological catch-up has been admirably played by the 'tiger' economies. Singapore has become the world's biggest producer of semiconductors. Taiwan has developed an aerospace industry that is collaborating with a number of Western companies (e.g. British Aerospace). Hong Kong possesses an innovative and world class financial centre. By 1988, South Korea's share of the world's total high-tech exports had risen to 2.9 per cent, nearly half of the UK's and France's own share in the same year, and up from 0.1 per cent twenty years earlier.

As Figure 5.2 indicates, current estimates have forecasted that many of the East Asian NICs will be among the world's largest nations by the early stages of the twenty-first century. The ambition to overtake those belonging to the OECD group of rich countries certainly remains strong in East Asia. Many bold development plans have been formulated to help reach this objective. The Taiwanese have embarked on a US$300bn project to establish extensive and upgraded infrastructure networks in their country by the end of the century. Malaysia, with a GDP per capita of only US$3,156 in 1995, has set itself the target of the year 2020 to achieve full industrial modernity. An estimated 7.5 per cent annual growth rate will be required to meet the deadline. All of the first generation 'tiger' economies are preoccupied with gearing to more technology intensive forms of production while increasingly outsourcing low-tech business activity to their younger generation counterparts.

A successful combination

Our analysis so far has only revealed the appearance of East Asian NICs' pattern of development and not the underlying factors that have enabled it. Let us now consider these and the wider context of this development and its global impact. We must first remember that East Asia is one of the most culturally diverse regions in the world. Political and economic conditions and traditions also vary enormously. There has thus been much debate among economists as to establishing any common denominators or model that can explain the foundations of East Asia's modern economic miracle. The most comprehensive study on the issue was made in a World Bank (1993) report which suggested a series of measures and preconditions in supporting its own theories. The dynamics of the model that was constructed by the report are shown in Figure 5.3. A stable macroeconomy, high rates of saving, an openness to foreign technology, selective export promoting devices and substantial investments in education are among those elements cited as having provided the ingredients for East Asia's success.

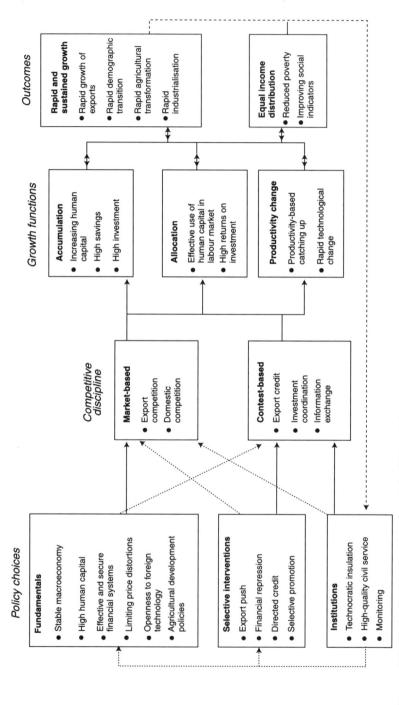

Figure 5.3 World Bank's functional model of East Asian growth
Source: World Bank 1993

The management of human resources has attracted much attention relating not only to how the 'tiger' economies have exploitcd their cheap sources of labour but also the education policies that they have pursued. What has generally set these policies apart from those of other developing nations has been their specific targeting of funds towards educating the mass section of the population as opposed to a university trained elite (see Figure 5.4). This has followed the lead taken by Japan in the early post-war years and has resulted in the formation of a technically adept and highly numerate workforce. The wider benefits of such an approach have been confirmed by studies which show that the social returns of mass education at lower levels are greater than those at a higher level (Psacharopoulos 1993).

Education needs to maintain a priority position for the East Asian NICs owing to new strategic imperatives that have emerged. For example, China's ever-enlarging capability to produce lower-tech goods and attract commensurate foreign investment flows will require them to upgrade their education and training systems to compete in higher value-added fields. The continual move towards both flexible production processes and knowledge-intensive industrial activities will demand a more imaginative and adaptive workforce. This increasingly applies to the 'tiger' economies as they progress to higher technology sectors.

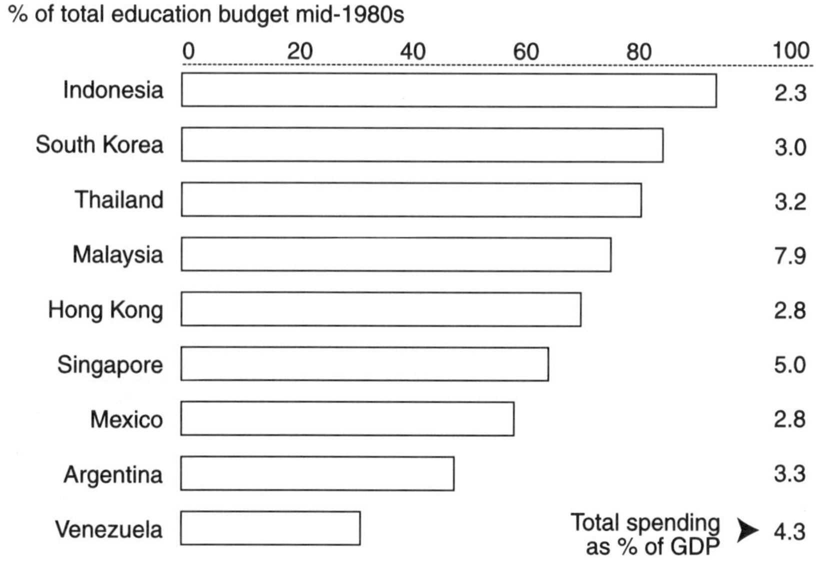

% of total education budget mid-1980s

	0	20	40	60	80	100	
Indonesia							2.3
South Korea							3.0
Thailand							3.2
Malaysia							7.9
Hong Kong							2.8
Singapore							5.0
Mexico							2.8
Argentina							3.3
Venezuela							4.3

Total spending as % of GDP ➤

Figure 5.4 Spending on primary and secondary education, selected NICs
Source: World Bank, UN; © *The Economist* (October 1993)

The use of a singular set of cultural determinants must in most cases be avoided when studying the development of any region. However, strands from the ethical codes of Confucianism, Buddhism and other systems of belief have produced a somewhat distinct 'collectivist' cultural and philosophical tradition which is in contrast to Western 'individualist' axioms. Consequently, many aspects of society reflect a strong 'group ethic' and consensual approach to decision-making at work. More specific elements of this tradition include filial respect and a formal deference to elders; an elevated view of education; meritocratic forms of personal advancement and development; virtue in discipline, harmony, obedience, duty and hard work; the common ownership of intellectual property. In turn, these help to explain why certain economic structures and forms of economic behaviour from producers and workers in East Asian countries have arisen. Some examples of these include:

- the close-knit bonds that lie between the *keiretsu* industrial groups in Japan and their near equivalent *chaebol* groups in South Korea;
- the consensual approach to decision-making and bonds of loyalty which lie between employer and employee;
- the priority given to the mass education programmes;
- the strong work ethic in evidence in most East Asian workforces;
- the absence of guilt over pirating the intellectual property rights of others.

Favourable external conditions have also contributed to East Asia's rapid development. The switch to export-led growth policies coincided with the greatest ever expansion in world trade. As in Japan, certain 'tiger' economies have been recipients of American economic assistance in one form or another. The USA's post-war military activities in the region (e.g. Korea, Vietnam, Cambodia) have required logistical support that many proximate developing nations were happy and able to provide. More direct aid has been granted by the US government with the aim of placing a bulwark against further communist penetration into East Asia. The USA also provided the export markets for the 'tiger' economies dating back to their earliest stages of development.

Japan played a different role and one which has at times been analogously related to the 'flying geese formation'. Geese fly in a 'V' formation with the flock's strongest member in lead position, breaking down the air's resistance and thus allowing those behind to follow in its slipstream. In many ways this position has been Japan's in that it has provided best practice exemplars in production and management methods and the acquisition and application of technological know-how. It is also the largest foreign investor in the region, accounting for around 45 per cent of cumulative inflows between 1970 and 1988, ahead of the USA with 37 per cent and the Community with 14 per cent.

One other pattern of development established by Japan that has been emulated by some its neighbours concerns the evolving government–business relationship and the influence this has had on shaping the structure of their economies. This has been the most contentious of debates between economists who have studied the development of the region. The level of collaboration has varied between those at the minimal end of the scale, such as the *laissez-faire* Hong Kong, to countries like South Korea and Taiwan where the government has worked very closely with industry. Collaboration has been a key operative term to describe the relationship as the primary purpose of government intervention has been to promote the interests of the business sector as a whole. According to the UN (1994c: 50) this has been achieved by the assisting role played by its agencies in 'creating new wealth through capital accumulation and productivity improvement rather than by redistributing a given national income away from workers, farmers and other social classes'. Thus, East Asian governments have not adopted an adversarial, corrective-type approach that has characterised much of Western post-war industrial policy but rather one in keeping with its cultural determinants.

The World Bank's model of East Asian growth illustrated in Figure 5.3 has highlighted the most successful and commonly adhered to government policies, the institutions it created and the competitive discipline it nurtured within the business environment. Interventions could be classed as either 'functional', which were intended to affect the overall framework of structural transformation, or 'selective' whereby specific actions were taken within the context of special exigencies that normally involved key industries and firms. Endeavours to upgrade the techno-industrial base of the economy have avoided the complications entailed of 'picking winners' to lead at frontier technological development. Instead a more simplified game of 'catch-up' has been followed through policies aimed at improving the mastery of well-established and available technologies. Private sector innovation and investment have also been stimulated by the higher rents engineered via government measures, such as repressed interest rates. In many cases this provided the initial level of profit that was able to set a virtuous circle in motion, leading to higher propensities of saving, investment and innovation.

In conclusion, the success of East Asia's 'tiger' economies holds a number of lessons for other countries and important geo-political implications for the rest of the world. European business and policy-makers who up to now have remained relatively distant from these events cannot afford to ignore their impact. In a world economy that seems destined to be increasingly preoccupied with the activities of the Pacific Rim powers, Europe needs to take appropriate actions to strengthen the weak link in the Triad set of relationships if it is to claim a stake in East Asia's future. It is this issue that we shall now discuss in some depth.

LOOKING FORWARD TO THE PACIFIC CENTURY?

Back to the future

Future historians may well conclude that during the 1990s the EU's pre-occupations could be categorised into two distinct periods. In the first years of the decade, it followed an introspective agenda of consolidating the SEM and the Maastricht Treaty's provisions, counteracting against the internal squabbles that arose from them. The mid-1990s onwards were spent preparing for the single currency and new entrant candidates from Central and Eastern Europe, attempting to reduce politically dangerous levels of unemployment and establishing a credible and robust common foreign and security policy (CFSP). What, though, will be their judgement on Europe's efforts to adjust to the global realities of the time: a time when the global shift of political and economic interests gravitated away from the old Trans-Atlantic poles to its Trans-Pacific equivalents? The early signals were there; from 1983 trade flows across the latter overtook the former, while by 1992 EU trade with East Asia became larger in volume and value than its trade with North America. In forthcoming years, a similar pattern could be observed with investment flows.

Hence, Europe must come to terms with the fact that the early twenty-first century at least is most likely to belong to the Pacific powers. East Asia's economic growth potential has not yet been fully realised. China and the younger generations of 'tiger' economies still possess the low cost advantages and spare market capacity to accommodate further spectacular growth rates. Their more advanced neighbours, Japan and the first genera-tion 'tigers', will provide the region with its own capital and techno-industrial base to underpin East Asia's ability to raise its levels of prosper-ity and global influence. Moreover, the stated intentions of the USA to play a more active role in the Pacific economy underscore its future global significance.

The Trans-Pacific alliance

The USA and its other NAFTA partners recognised long before the EU the significance and magnitude of East Asia's post-war economic miracle. A wider array of historical and geo-political imperatives have forced them to do so. The USA has been the largest market for most of East Asia's exports for decades, while the machinations of its foreign policy have determined the shape ultimately taken by major political events and developments in the region.

The recently invigorated APEC forum provides North America with the institutionalised framework in which to exploit trade and investment opportunities in East Asia, as well as forge closer political ties across the Pacific. APEC's eighteen members include Japan, China, the more developed 'tiger' economies, Australasia, NAFTA and Chile (see Table 1.1, on page 6). Established in 1989, it took until the 1993 summit meeting in Seattle to make any serious progress towards forming a consensus over reciprocated trade concessions of any note. The 1994 summit held in Bogor, Indonesia, had a more ambitious agenda, with the proposal of creating a free trade area between APEC members by 2020. A gradualised and sequential removal of trade barriers would be set in motion under the scheme. North America, Australasia and Japan would be the first to yield their borders by 2010, followed by the advanced tiger economies, with the less advanced finally capitulating and thus completing the last stage of this integration.

At the 1995 Osaka summit, APEC's Eminent Persons Group submitted a report recommending that it should implement the Uruguay Round's liberalisation measures within half the period set (APEC 1995). This would commit the developed countries to a quicker phasing out of the Multi-Fibre Agreement and other protectionist frameworks. Meanwhile, APEC's developing countries would have to adjust more hastily to the new multilateral rules on property rights, export subsidies and trade-related investment measures.

However, proposals for establishing a Pacific Free Trade Area (PAFTA) are felt by some to be unrealistic. Trade regimes across East Asia vary enormously from the liberal and open trade policies pursued by Singapore, Malaysia and Thailand to protectionist Indonesia, where import tariffs average out at 20 per cent. Malaysia's Asiacentric leader, Dr Mahathir, is also sceptical of developing APEC to any level of formal integration involving Western countries, preferring instead to promote the East Asian Economic Caucus (EAEC) as an alternative forum. Differences in culture and political tradition that exist between East Asian members, let alone those that lie on all sides of the Pacific, may also hinder progress. Furthermore, while most Western members favour a formal structure with more steadfast rules, many Asian countries prefer to maintain a looser institutional relationship. The progress of PAFTA may also be impeded by strong US sectoral lobby groups representing industries in structural decline.

Nevertheless APEC's members would still have much to gain from closer co-operation and integration. The development of APEC trade flows gives a reasonable pretext for this. APEC's share of total world trade in 1993 was 46 per cent, placing it higher than the EU's at just under 40 per cent. The intra-APEC trade ratio of 70 per cent in the same year has likewise risen above that of the EU's at 63 per cent, although this belies a somewhat unbalanced pattern of trade integration across APEC. A more telling picture is given by observing intra-APEC trade between East Asian members which has risen from 32 per cent in 1983 to 43 per cent in 1993. The proportion of East Asian exports to the USA and other APEC members has actually declined over the past decade or so. There are opportunities to be explored by members of this Trans-Pacific alliance by further mutual exploitation of each other's markets and converting the significance of these statistics into global political capital.

The ability of APEC's members to achieve this is largely dependent on the particular interests of the group's big three, namely the USA, Japan and China. Aware of its widening trade deficit with East Asia, the USA's prime objective in the alliance is to open markets for American exports. Oddly enough, US exports to the west Pacific Rim are more resource intensive than average, while its imports from the region mainly consist of manufactured goods. The USA is aiming to redress the imbalance, although American high-tech products continue to sell well. For its part, Japan will be concerned with similar trade and investment objectives. In 1994 it traded a third more with East Asia than with the USA – roles that were reversed ten years earlier. East Asian imports into Japan totalled $60bn in 1993, compared with $50bn from the USA and only $24bn EU imports. More importantly, Japan will be looking for the lead position of any East Asian bloc that emerges in the next century. China has used APEC membership as a vehicle to negotiate entry to the GATT–WTO community. There is no doubt that its ambitions at any future negotiating table within the APEC forum, and anywhere else for that matter, will be raised to much higher levels. The weight of the big three will be such that the remaining APEC members may have to play them off against each other at times to achieve any specific and collectively shared objectives of their own.

The new Trans-Atlanticism: providing a counterbalance?

Thus far, we have not commented on the oldest of the Triad relationships, that between Europe and the USA. Trans-Atlantic ties have generally come under increasing pressure from the attention diverting dynamism of the Pacific economy and the perception that Europe offers only mature markets with marginal potential for exports. Nevertheless, there is reason to believe that Euro-American bonds will remain formidable for a long time. Both Triad members possess the same cultural and liberal democratic traditions which have engendered a reasonably similar *Weltanschauung* on what shape the new world order should take. Moreover, the EU and the USA still remain principally responsible for overseeing the world's international economic, financial and monetary systems and have sought, to varying degrees, to help integrate the developing and 'transition' economies. It must also be remembered that the economic links between the two powers are considerable: North American and Europe are each other's largest single trading partner; the respective stocks of Trans-Atlantic FDI in each other's territory are nearly half the global totals for both; in the mid-1990s, an EU growth rate of 3 per cent still translated into a one year market size increase ($210bn) equivalent to that for the entire Taiwanese market.

However, geo-political change provided the catalyst for a new phase in Europe–US relations. The thawing of the Cold War had effectively loosened the underpinnings of a security relationship which had held the two powers together for over forty years. Calls for a 'New Trans-Atlanticism' thus sought to modify the basis of the partnership to one driven more by common economic objectives. Consequently, the EU and USA signed the Trans-Atlantic Declaration (TAD) in November 1990 which confirmed the intentions of both parties to work towards these ends. For the USA, this was also used as a vehicle to articulate support for further intended European integration and simultaneously to extend its influence within the EU and over its future role in international affairs. In addition, the TAD led to an easing of the frictions that had been generated by American fears concerning a 'Fortress Europe' being built by the SEM programme (Smith and Woolcock 1993).

The recasting of the old alliance gave both sides the assurance that some degree of geo-political balance would be maintained. In light of the Pacific century scenario, this has been particularly imperative for Europe, although also implying that a much firmer relationship needed to be established with Asia. According to Peterson (1993), foreign policy in general has increasingly had to incorporate trade, FDI and environmental protection issues into core areas of negotiation. New sources of conflict and constraint within EU–US relations could surface as these move more to the centre ground, thus heightening the importance of embracing these issues in future diplomatic agreements.

By the mid-1990s, the EU and USA had been key signatories to GATT's successful Uruguay Round and continued to build on the reconstructed partnership with the introduction of the New Trans-Atlantic Agenda (NTA), produced from the EU–US summit of December 1995. The overarching framework of the NTA provided clearer guidance for a range of bilateral activities and arrangements. Germany and the UK had been among those that favoured the idea of a Trans-Atlantic free trade area (TAFTA) to be included as part of the agreement, but this was shelved for further progressive and reciprocal liberalisation of trade.

Under the NTA, the scope for co-operation in various fields was broadened (e.g. in science and technology, education and environmental protection) and efforts to complete outstanding bilateral agreements, such as on government procurement and telecommunications, were prioritised. Preparatory developments leading up to the signing of the NTA involved inauguration of the Trans-Atlantic Business Dialogue, whose main objective was to legitimise a business influence over events shaping any Trans-Atlantic economic space to emerge from political negotiations (see CEC 1995d). Its representatives, consisting of a mixture of EU and US corporate executives, were especially eager to press for a Mutual Recognition agreement by 1 January 1997, covering product standards, certification and testing procedures. In acknowledgement of the deep level of EU–US interdependence and interpenetration – for example, through close policy co-operation and comity for each other's laws – the NTA also comprised appointed measures to install or extend mutually compatible regulatory frameworks.

Although the NTA did not signify a commitment from the USA to engage in a free trade agreement that paralleled its APEC obligations, the Trans-Atlantic relationship draws global significance from its considerable breadth. The ability of the EU and USA to be able to find so much common ground on which to collaborate is a sign of the relationship's undisputed strength. Closeness, though, does not necessarily imply harmony. The surfacing of new conflicts and constraints, together with the global shift of politico-economic power to the Pacific, could still work to decouple the hinges of the New Trans-Atlanticism. However, for the foreseeable future, based on what we have considered, such an outcome is likely to persist only temporarily.

The Triad's weak link

The sinews that bind the European and East Asian economies together have traditionally been the weakest within the Triad. This is beginning to change in line with the new patterns of trade. In acknowledgement of the opportunities presented by the dynamic Asian economy and the possible looming of the Pacific century, the Commission introduced its New Asia Strategy in 1994 (CEC 1994d). The broad aim of the initiative was to adopt a more proactive and coherent approach towards the region. Such attempts to construct strategies in response to the Pacific global shift have been few and far between at this level. Part of the problem has also been a strong East Asian perception of the EU as a trade bloc rather than a trading partner. This was due not only to the SEM programme but also the defensive, protectionist stance that had very often characterised the EU position.

Before publication of its New Asia Strategy, the EU's existing links with the region consisted of a disparate set of bilateral arrangements. To be fair, this represented the diverse selection of countries to be found on the continent, even between contiguous states. In 1991, the EU–Japanese Declaration was signed, which was modelled on the TAD and aimed to establish closer ties between the two powers and also counterbalance the stronger US–Japanese ties that had developed. Trade and Co-operation Agreements have been made with South Korea, some Indian sub-continent states and China. With respect to the latter, the EU has sought to help integrate China into the international community through promoting its membership for the WTO and other multilateral fora, offered assistance where appropriate to the continuing reform process and most importantly extended trade and investment interests in the country as part of a longer term policy (CEC 1995e). Since 1980, the EU has had a regional framework agreement with the Association of South-East Asian Nations (ASEAN) and most countries in the region are beneficiaries of the EU's

Generalised System of Preferences (GSP) scheme of trade concessions, although the many 'tiger' economies will soon 'graduate' from this by the end of the decade.

The intentions of the EU's new Asia policy are not to dismantle these existing links but rather to make them part of a more rational strategy. This would also include plans for business and government agencies to work separately or in unison towards raising the EU's profile and interests in Asia. Furthermore, the Commission saw a supportive role for the EU in redressing regional imbalances and advocating sustainable development processes. The progress that Europe can expect to make towards more significant inroads into the region is still unclear. The EU is lobbying for observer status in APEC but has received a less than enthusiastic response. Some form of participation will be essential to ensure that Europe has some connections with any APEC specific regulatory environments that emerge. This reaction to the assertion of European interests may alter as certain Pacific–Asian members may wish to involve Europe in order to counteract the US influence. A role for Europe could be facilitated through the newly established, biannual Asian–Europe Meetings (ASEM), the first of which took place at Bangkok in March 1996 between the EU and ASEAN, China, Japan and South Korea. The set agenda follows a similar theme of partnership for greater mutual growth as outlined in the New Asia Strategy. This may at least constitute the beginning of a closer and more comprehensive relationship between the two regions in the future.

CONCLUDING REMARKS

What then is the way forward for Europe as it faces the prospect of a world economy most likely to be oriented between the poles of a Trans-Pacific alliance? On a political level, it makes sense for the EU to be represented by one voice in inter-regional negotiations, as has been recently proved at the Uruguay Round. The development of a coherent and well-focused new Asia policy will bolster this process in the future, providing the EU with a firmer platform on which future trade, investment and regulatory issues can be more effectively brokered with APEC.

There is still much debate over what strategies Europe should adopt given the Pacific century scenario. Should it proceed as a federalised EU economy, or as a 'Europe by menu' approach with European economies selecting aspects of integration and collaboration from agricultural policy to sharing a common currency? European business must lead with a more proactive approach by extending and creating network links in Asia through FDI, strategic alliance-making or other means. Whatever proves the more effective, Europe must revitalise and restore its competitive advantages and position in a fast changing world economy: a world economy that is working to the principles of new realities that are, in many ways, unfamiliar to Europe.

6 EU external trade and trade relations

In this chapter we shall be investigating recent trends in EU trade and trade relations with its global partners. A structural overview of this position will first take account of geographical and sectoral patterns of EU external trade. An examination of the EU's Common Commercial Policy (CCP) and the GATT/WTO multilateral framework for international trade will then follow. We will also evaluate how the EU's trade relations with developing nations have emerged through the Lomé Conventions and Generalised System of Preferences (GSP). Finally, the EU's trade relations with its Triad rivals will form the basis of discussion for the last sections of the chapter.

A STRUCTURAL OVERVIEW OF RECENT TRADE PATTERNS

A global analysis

The growth of world trade has consistently outstripped rates of world output in post-war years, a trend that has continued to play a key role in the internationalisation of economic activity and to deepen global inter-dependence of regions and nations. In 1994 world trade was valued at $5.14 trillion, an increase of 9 per cent on the previous year, and consisted of $4.06 trillion merchandise trade (manufactures and materials) while service trade amounted to $1.08 trillion.

As Table 6.1 indicates, the EU is the world's largest international trader, having consistently taken around 40 per cent of the world's per annum total during the 1990s. With progressive achievements made in European integration in recent years it perhaps comes as no surprise that intra-EU trade has flourished, rising from an 18.1 per cent share of total world trade in 1982 to a 24.7 per cent share by 1994. Even with this aspect of European trade removed, the EU remains the world's largest external trading entity. However, between 1987 and 1993 the EU has experienced a worsening of its trade balance equivalent to 0.7 per cent of its GDP owing to a 10.6 per

Table 6.1 Patterns of world trade, 1960–94

	1960	*1970*	*1980*	*1990*	*1994*
World exports (% of total)					
Intra-EU[1]	13.8	19.7	19.3	24.4	24.7
Extra-EU	19.9	17.3	15.1	15.6	15.1
USA	15.8	13.7	11.1	11.5	11.9
Japan	3.2	6.2	6.5	8.4	9.2
Canada	4.3	4.0	3.6	3.7	3.8
Australasia	1.9	1.8	1.4	1.4	1.4
EFTA[2]	5.6	6.4	6.1	6.6	5.5
DEVELOPED COUNTRIES	64.5	69.1	63.1	71.6	71.6
China	2.0	n/a	0.1	1.8	2.8
Asian NICs[3]	1.8	1.7	3.0	7.8	10.2
Latin America	8.8	4.4	5.6	3.7[+]	3.7[+]
Africa	4.9	4.1	6.2	2.5	2.2*
Rest of world	18.0	20.7	22.2	12.6	9.5
World imports (% of total)					
Intra-EU	13.1	19.9	18.6	23.7	24.5
Extra-EU	21.5	18.8	19.1	16.5	14.4
USA	10.8	12.2	11.7	15.1	16.3
Japan	3.7	5.7	6.9	6.9	6.5
Canada	4.2	4.0	2.9	3.6	3.7
Australasia	2.0	1.7	1.3	1.5	1.5
EFTA	7.6	7.1	7.3	6.7	5.3
DEVELOPED COUNTRIES	62.9	69.4	67.8	74.0	72.2
China	1.8	n/a	0.1	1.5	2.7
Asian NICs	2.5	2.8	3.6	7.8	10.7
Latin America	8.6	4.4	4.5	3.3[+]	4.7[+]
Africa	5.9	3.4	4.6	2.2	1.9
Rest of world	18.3	20.0	19.2	11.2	7.8

Sources: Eurostat, IMF
Notes:
[+] Figures include Caribbean countries.
* 1993 figure.
[1] Intra-EU refers to EC12 for total period.
[2] EFTA 7: Austria, Finland, Iceland, Liechtenstein, Norway, Sweden, Switzerland for total period.
[3] Hong Kong, Singapore, South Korea, Taiwan.

cent deterioration in its cost performance but despite a 6.4 per cent effective depreciation in EU currencies over the period (CEC 1994e).

The East Asian region, led by Japan, has made the most noticeable advances in its share of world trade. In 1960, Japan, China and the

Asian NICs accounted for 7.0 per cent of total world exports and imports. By 1994, this share had risen to 22.2 per cent for exports and 19.9 per cent for imports. Meanwhile, the USA has seen its traditional trade surpluses converted into considerable deficits, with a simultaneous downward trend in its share of world exports (15.8 per cent to 11.9 per cent) and upward trend in its share of world imports (10.3 per cent to 16.3 per cent).

The proportion of world trade taken by other developed countries (i.e. Canada, Australasia and the EFTA group) has remained more or less stable over the period. However, there has been a general upward trend in the combined share of world trade of the developed countries that has been led by Japan and the EU. The growing marginalisation of the developing countries is indicated by the falling shares for both Latin America and Africa. The almost consistent decline in these shares was broken in the mid-to-late 1970s and early 1980s by the effect of inflated oil prices on export and import values. For example, in 1980 Africa's three main oil producers, Algeria, Libya and Nigeria, were responsible for around 40 per cent of total exports. The burden of debt constrained growth in both regions during the 1980s, although Latin American countries have shown signs of recovery partly illustrated by the stabilisation of world trade shares in the 1990s. Deeper rooted economic problems still beset the African countries (particularly in the sub-Saharan region) whose trade share has continued to slide during this decade.

EU trade with the world

The developed countries

The USA has remained the EU's single most important trade partner, maintaining an average share for both exports and imports of just under 20 per cent. However, EFTA, as a regional trade partner, has played an even more significant role up to 1994, taking a 22.2 per cent share of total extra-EU exports and 22.9 per cent of imports in that year compared to a respective 17.6 per cent and 17.3 per cent shares for the USA. From the EU's major trade partners in 1994, five EFTA countries were placed in the top ten imports table and four in the top ten exports table. Switzerland was the third largest importer into the EU with 7.6 per cent of the total in 1994 (more than the CEE countries combined) while also being the EU's second largest export market at 8.1 per cent (more than Latin America and China combined). In 1993, both Austria (6.0 per cent of extra-EU exports) and Sweden (4.9 per cent) were then larger individual export markets than Japan (4.7 per cent). The 1995 EFTA enlargement of the EU has thus raised the intra-EU trade ratio and effectively relegated EFTA as an EU regional trade partner.

The EU's diminished trade position with both Canada and Australasia, as shown in Table 6.2, has been affected by two main factors. The first has arisen from the UK's accession to the Community in 1973, resulting in considerable trade diversion which affected the British Commonwealth countries. This entailed a subsequent denial of preferential treatment from the UK's own trade regimes and the imposition of an EU common external tariff (CET) on their exports after a transitional period had passed. New Zealand was particularly affected, with up to a third of its total exports destined for the UK market at the time. Although by the 1970s Japan had already become the biggest market for Australian exports, the UK still represented its most significant source of imported goods. Both countries have been prominent members of the Cairns Group of agricultural producers who proved to be instrumental in pressuring the EU into reforming the Common Agricultural Policy (CAP) in compliance with the Uruguay Round negotiations. Lodge (1992) suggests that the concentration of their efforts within the Cairns Group has probably been the most logical strategy to pursue in trade relations with the EU, given their small trader status. For its part, Canada was less affected by the UK's accession on account of its exceptionally close trade relationship with the USA where around three-quarters of its trade is linked.

However, the second and most important factor to affect EU trade relations with Canada, Australia and New Zealand has been greater alignment of trade relations on a more regional basis. The recent dynamic growth of the Pacific economy has played a key role in nurturing these relations. Canada can expect to deepen its already extensive trade links with fellow NAFTA members in the future. Australia is currently contemplating severing some of the cultural and institutional ties with Europe by seeking to establish itself as a republic in its search for a more distinct Pacific-oriented identity. All three countries are members of the APEC forum, and thus could be fellow participants in a Pacific free trade agreement by the early twenty-first century.

Japan's share of EU trade has consistently grown decade on decade in post-war years. The same could also be said of its considerable trade surpluses with the EU which have dominated the agenda of most trade discussions between both parties. As we shall discuss later, certain initiatives have been undertaken by Japan in attempts to redress the imbalance in the relationship.

The CEE countries

It is generally accepted that the growth of trade between the EU and the CEE since the market transformation process began has been somewhat disappointing. The region's share of total EU imports rose from 6.3 per cent in 1990 to 7 per cent in 1994. Meanwhile, the CEE's share of total EU exports has risen from 5.6 per cent to 7.7 per cent. Moreover, Table 6.2

Table 6.2 Geographical breakdown of the structure of EU external trade (all products), 1970–94

	1970	1982	1990	1994
Exports (% of total)				
USA	18.0	15.7	18.4	17.6
Japan	2.6	2.3	5.5	4.9
Canada	2.8	1.8*	2.2	1.8
EFTA	25.1	22.1	26.8	22.2
Australasia	3.4	1.9*	2.0	1.7
CEE[1]	7.3	6.3	5.6	7.7
Mediterranean Basin[2]	10.3	12.9	11.0	10.2
OPEC[3]	7.5	20.7	8.5	6.9
Latin America[4]	6.7	5.2	3.8	5.3
ACP[5]	7.6	7.2	4.0	2.8
Asian NICs[6]	2.1	3.0	5.6	7.6
ASEAN[7]	2.3	3.1*	3.9	5.2
China	0.1	0.1*	1.3	2.3
Imports (% of total)				
USA	21.7	17.7	18.5	17.3
Japan	3.4	5.7	10.0	9.0
Canada	4.9	2.0*	2.0	1.7
EFTA	17.4	17.2	23.5	22.9
Australasia	3.1	1.3*	1.4	1.1
CEE[1]	6.4	8.2	6.3	7.0
Mediterranean Basin[2]	9.4	10.0	9.2	7.9
OPEC[3]	16.3	24.6	9.8	7.5
Latin America[4]	7.9	6.5	5.5	5.0
ACP[5]	8.9	6.0	4.4	3.4
Asian NICs[6]	1.5	3.2	5.7	6.2
ASEAN[7]	2.0	2.4*	3.6	5.5
China	0.1	0.1*	2.3	4.5

Source: Eurostat

Notes: The country groupings are not mutually exclusive, thereby giving rise to some double counting. Figures refer to EC12 external trade.

* denote 1983 figures.

[1] Former USSR, GDR, Albania, Bulgaria, Czech Republic, Hungary, Poland, Romania and Slovakia (1970, 1982); omit GDR for 1990 and 1994.

[2] Ceuta and Melilla, Gibraltar, Malta, Cyprus, Turkey, Maghreb and Mashreq countries, Israel, Albania, ex-Yugoslavia. Ceuta and Melilla omitted for 1990 and 1994.

[3] Algeria, Ecuador, Gabon, Indonesia, Iran, Iraq, Kuwait, Libya, Nigeria, Qatar, Saudi Arabia, UAE, Venezuela.

[4] Argentina, Bolivia, Brazil, Chile, Columbia, Costa Rica, Cuba, Dominican Republic, Ecuador, El Salvador, Guatamala, Haiti, Honduras, Mexico, Nicaragua, Panama, Paraguay, Peru, Uruguay, Venezuela.

[5] The African, Caribbean and Pacific signatories of the Lomé Convention. Membership has expanded over the period.

[6] Hong Kong, Singapore, South Korea, Taiwan.

[7] Brunei, Indonesia, Malaysia, Philippines, Singapore, Thailand.

reveals that on a longer term trend the EU appears to have strengthened its position, with the CEE's share of EU exports rising between 1982 and 1994, while the region's share of EU imports over the period fell from 8.2 per cent to 7.0 per cent. Throughout the 1980s, the CMEA members maintained a consistent surplus with the EU. This was buoyed up by inflated oil prices in the early years of the decade and limited access for EU consumer goods. Conditions created by the market reforms have reversed the balance in favour of the EU. Throughout the early 1990s, the CEE countries' trade surpluses with the EU were being gradually eroded. The first deficit with the EU for many years was recorded in 1991 at ECU 2bn (see also Figure 4.3, p. 123). For the CEE6, which on a collective basis had been in deficit since 1991, the figure was ECU 4.7bn. Future trade relations will be shaped by plans to establish free trade arrangements in industrial products under the Europe Agreements.

The Mediterranean Basin countries

The volume of EU trade with the Mediterranean Basin countries has remained relatively stable over the past two decades. However, in recent years a decline in EU imports from the region has become increasingly apparent. In 1990, the region's share of EU imports stood at 9.2 per cent but by 1994 it had fallen to 7.9 per cent, leaving the Mediterranean Basin countries with an ECU 12.3bn deficit with the EU that year. The CEE countries may have been responsible for creating some trade diversion that caused this situation to arise, but the trend may well be reversed pending future success of the European–Mediterranean Economic Area and its intentions to establish a free trade area by 2010 (see Chapter 4). The EU is likely to continue to deepen trade relations with countries on its external periphery through such frameworks as part of preparatory measures for accession.

EU–OPEC trade

The OPEC countries have experienced the sharpest decline in trade with the EU in the past decade or so. At its peak in 1975, OPEC accounted for 27.9 per cent of EU imports and until the early 1980s was one of the EU's most important trading partners. By 1994, OPEC's share of total EU imports had shrunk to 7.5 per cent while the total share of EU exports destined to the group had fallen to 6.9 per cent from 20.7 per cent in 1982. This pronounced oscillation in trade patterns between the EU and OPEC can be almost completely explained by an examination of events and developments within the oil industry. First, the Oil Crises of 1973–4 and 1979–80, instigated by conflictual events in the Middle East, considerably inflated the price of oil. Around this time, OPEC controlled between 70 per cent and 80 per cent of total world oil production, thus further enhancing the inelasticity of the price of oil and inflated value in trade. Processed oil products such as petrochemicals, which the EU exported back to the OPEC group, were also cost inflated. By the mid-1980s, the glut of oil on world markets led to a drastic price fall. The exploitation of North Sea oil and gas fields, in addition to the decline in OPEC market power, led to further weakening of EU–OPEC trade links.

Latin America and the ACP

A particularly noticeable trend in extra-EU trade in recent years has been the decline of trade with the less developed countries (LDCs). This is clearly illustrated by an examination of extra-EU trade flows with Latin America and the seventy-country African Caribbean Pacific (ACP) group. Between 1970 and 1994 the ACP countries have experienced a persistent decline in their share of EU imports, falling from 8.9 per cent to a mere 3.4 per cent in the period. The relative proportion of EU exports finding their way to ACP markets has also dipped sharply from 7.6 per cent to 2.8 per cent. These trends are despite concerted efforts by the EU through the Lomé Conventions to achieve the opposite effect.

A very similar story applies for the Latin American countries which have also witnessed a dwindling share of their exports in EU markets over the period in study. In 1970, imports from Latin American countries constituted 7.9 per cent of the EU total, but by 1994 this had receded to 5 per cent. The long-term trend for the flow of EU exports to the region has also been one of decline, falling from 6.7 per cent of the total in 1970 to 3.8 per cent in 1990. However, this share has recently increased to 5.3 per cent in 1994 giving the EU a trade surplus of ECU 1.2bn. Although the Latin American countries receive less favourable trade terms than the ACP countries under the EU's CCP, we have already made note in Chapter 2 of the trade stimulating provisions within the EU's recently developed inter-regional arrangements with these countries. However, many of these provisions, such as the proposed free trade agreement between the EU and Mercosur, may take some time to make an impact in reversing these trends.

EU–East Asia trade

The East Asian 'tiger' economies and China represent the EU's most dynamic trading partners. We have already examined the foundations on which the recent East Asian 'miracle' of economic development has been based and the role that export-oriented strategies have played. The extent to which EU industry, particularly in 'sensitive' sectors, has come under intense pressure from East Asian producers is well documented. China and the ASEAN countries continue to attain expanding trade surpluses with the EU. However, in 1993 the EU achieved a trade surplus of ECU

2.8bn with the four Asian NICs, for the first time since 1980. While EU exports to the Asian NICs, China and ASEAN have expanded quite rapidly, they still amounted to only 13.4 per cent of total exports compared to 16.8 per cent for the USA and 36.1 per cent for Japan in 1994, thus indicating that EU companies compare poorly against their Triad counterparts in terms of taking advantage of today's most dynamic markets.

A sectoral analysis

In general terms, the sectoral trade relationship between the EU and other developed countries is characterised by intra-industry patterns of trade. This is also increasingly the case for the NICs and the more advanced developing countries. Patterns of trade with the developing countries, on the other hand, are still largely determined by inter-industry trade and thus the dictates of comparative advantage.

The most significant structural change to EU imports in sectoral terms has been the shift away from primary products to manufactures. In 1980, 60 per cent of EU imports comprised of the former but by 1993 this figure had fallen to 29 per cent. The marked decline in fuel imports largely explains this shift for reasons outlined in the analysis of EU–OPEC trade above. The proportions of EU machinery and transport equipment imports have roughly doubled over the period. The share of chemical, textile and clothing imports have also shown growth, but to a lesser degree, while other manufactured products have increased their share of EU imports by just over two-thirds.

The Triad context

In comparing the current structure of EU imports with that of its main trade rivals, the USA and Japan, some notable contrasts arise. Japan still maintains a considerable resource dependency on other nations, with primary products taking 52 per cent of imports in 1993. The resource abundant USA maintains the lowest dependency rate on foreign primary products, with primary sector imports amounting to only 19.5 per cent of its total. All Triad members have similar import ratios for chemicals, textiles and clothing. The USA, however, has an import ratio on transport equipment almost twice that of the EU's and over three times that of Japan's, resonate of the market penetration made by Japanese automobile producers in recent years. Figure 6.1 also indicates how European and American manufacturers have found it difficult to establish a presence in Japan's own market, with manufactures as a whole making up only 48 per cent of total Japanese merchandise imports in 1993, compared to 68 per cent for the EU and 77 per cent for the USA (for further analysis see Figures 6.2 and 6.3).

At first glance, there appears to have been relatively little change to the sectoral structure of EU exports between 1980 and 1993. Total primary

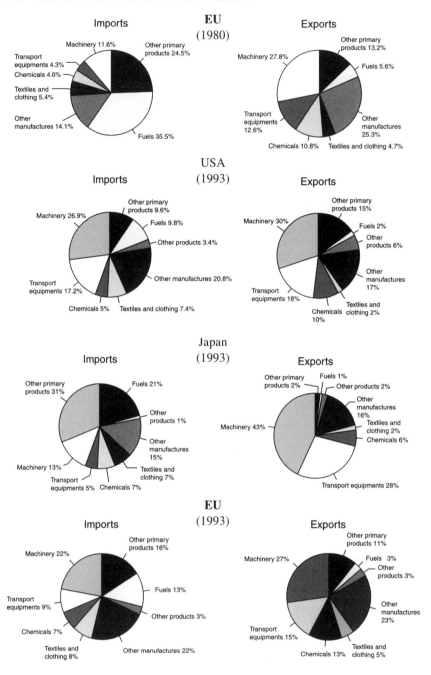

Figure 6.1 Product breakdown of merchandise trade of the USA, EU and Japan
Source: CEC 1993b: 23

product exports have decreased slightly from 18.8 per cent to 14 per cent, and most manufactures have remained at very similar shares with chemicals and transport equipment achieving the most significant improvements. Figure 6.1 illustrates that the US economy possesses a reasonably proximate sectoral export structure to that of the EU, but an inspection of Japan's exports reveals a stark contrast. In 1993, 95.9 per cent of Japan's exports were in manufactured goods, compared to 83 per cent for the EU and 77 per cent for the USA. Japan has maintained such a structural orientation of its exports for some time built on a manufacturing prowess developed in key sectors. A closer examination of the EU sectoral trade structure is required to consider how it has been affected by recent competitive threats from its traditional Triad rivals and the emerging 'new competition' of the NICs.

Trade and competitiveness: recent findings

Competitiveness can be defined as the ability of a country or region to reconcile growth with external equilibrium (CEC 1994e). Price and cost factors have been the traditional focus of analysis, but trade performance also necessitates a consideration of structural factors such as productivity levels and investment in physical and human capital (see Box 1.1, p. 15). An examination of recent trends indicates that the EU's competitiveness *vis-à-vis* its main and newly emerging trade rivals has been eroded. A variety of factors can be held attributable, but in particular the EU's failure in strong demand, technology intensive world markets.

Table 6.3 reveals the EU's comparative weakness within the Triad in strong demand sectors, with only 23.4 per cent of its exports falling into this category, whereas the USA has 29 per cent and Japan 33.6 per cent. In moderate demand sectors the EU also lags behind, with a 46.6 per cent share compared to 52.8 per cent for the USA and 52.2 per cent for Japan. A relatively large proportion of EU exports (30.1 per cent) are located in weak demand sectors. Further evidence put forward by the Commission suggested that EU levels of investment in the more dynamic growth sectors are comparatively inferior, thus undermining the EU's ability to meet both internal and external demand for products in these sectors (CEC 1994e).

In an earlier analysis, the Commission found that between 1982 and 1990 EU high technology imports rose by an annual 11.4 per cent, but high-tech exports by only 6 per cent, thus converting an ECU 5bn surplus on high technology trade in 1982 into a ECU 23bn deficit by the end of the decade (CEC 1993b). This being said, more recent evidence which is analysed in Chapter 9 suggests that the combined West European high technology trade balance has stabilised (see Figure 9.4, p. 321).

In conclusion, the recent poor performance of the EU economy is clearly unveiled by a closer examination of sectoral trade developments. Its comparative failure to restructure from weak demand, low-tech industrial

Table 6.3 Sectoral distribution of manufacturing exports in the EU, USA, Japan and the Triad, 1992

	Strong demand sectors				Moderate demand sectors				Weak demand sectors			
	EU	USA	Japan	Triad	EU	USA	Japan	Triad	EU	USA	Japan	Triad
					Market share (%)							
World	23.4	29.0	33.6	26.1	46.6	52.8	52.2	48.7	30.1	18.3	14.2	25.2
EC	21.2	32.1	39.0	23.4	46.4	54.8	53.1	47.6	32.4	13.1	8.0	29.0
EFTA	23.4	32.2	27.8	24.2	42.3	57.5	62.6	44.4	34.3	10.3	9.6	31.5
USA and Canada	26.3	23.7	31.6	27.5	52.2	55.1	59.7	55.8	21.5	21.3	8.7	16.7
Japan	31.7	30.4	–	30.9	42.2	46.4	–	44.8	26.0	23.2	–	24.3
NICs	30.5	36.8	42.9	38.4	43.6	46.0	35.9	40.5	25.9	17.3	21.3	21.2
China	23.4	20.0	28.9	25.1	62.0	61.4	39.3	51.6	14.6	18.6	31.8	23.3
Latin America	30.2	29.3	24.7	28.9	52.1	46.8	67.5	50.9	17.8	23.9	7.9	20.2
ACP	22.1	20.5	7.4	19.5	53.7	45.6	82.1	56.3	24.2	33.9	10.5	24.2
Rest of the world	28.1	25.8	26.6	27.4	46.5	62.2	53.2	50.3	25.5	12.0	20.2	22.2

Source: CEC 1995j: 126

Notes:

Strong demand sectors: chemicals, pharmaceuticals, office and data processing products, precision and optical instruments and electrical goods. Based on 3.5 per cent plus average annual growth rate of gross value added between 1980–91 at 1985 prices.

Moderate demand sectors: machinery, transport equipment, food, beverages and tobacco, paper and printing products and rubber and plastic products. Criteria as above: 1–3.5 per cent.

Weak demand sectors: ferrous and non-ferrous metals, non-metallic minerals, metal products, textiles, clothing, leather and footwear and other manufactured products. Criteria as above: less than 1 per cent.

activity to strong demand, technology intensive sectors is indicative of a broader industrial malaise which the SEM programme, EMU and other integrative policy initiatives have been charged with rectifying.

THE COMMON COMMERCIAL POLICY

An introduction to the CCP

The EU's external trade relations are primarily determined by a complex array of bilateral and multilateral arrangements that are managed via its Common Commercial Policy (CCP). Along with agriculture and transport, the CCP was one of the three 'common' policies first envisaged in the Treaty of Rome where exclusive competence was given to the Commission to act on behalf of the member states in an executive role. Naturally, this has entailed a loss of national sovereignty in what most member states would consider to be in a key strategic area of policy. This must, though, be balanced with the advantages attributed to operating an integrated common trade policy as confirmed by a Commission report (CEC 1977). The most significant of these include:

- The enhanced international bargaining power of the Community which has enabled it both to protect and assert wider European interests on the world stage. This had been demonstrated since the Dillon Round (1961–2) of GATT when the Community's stature as an international inter-locutor was first recognised.
- The reduction of spillover effects mainly arising from unilateral actions undertaken by member states (e.g. generous export subsidies) that affect the competitive position of others in third country markets.
- The integrity of the internal market being maintained by the managing of a technically uniform external trade policy aimed at improving the functional efficiency of the Community as a trade bloc.

Most areas of external trade are covered directly by the CCP, but in some sectors only indirect influence has been granted owing to its competence lying in the EEC pillar of the Maastricht Treaty. Thus, the CAP still wields direct governance over the EU's agricultural trade while trade in coal and steel products is covered by the terms and procedures of the ECSC. Nevertheless, the CCP still manages over 16,000 joint tariff headings under the Combined Nomenclature system and represents one of the most integrated EU policies.

Coping with external and internal pressures

It was not until 1968, when the community's common external tariff (CET) established a full customs union between the EEC6, that the CCP was officially inaugurated. However, this was a relatively simple accomplishment in comparison with handling the internal and external pressures imposed on the CCP in subsequent years. The inability of European industry to undertake the necessary restructuring from the stagflation period onwards subsequently led to more vocal pleas from industry lobby groups for a more pliable and protectionist CCP regime. Rising unemployment and accompanying social costs gave additional vindication for such positions of policy, as did new competitive threats emerging from the NICs, especially in 'sensitive' industrial sectors. The 1970s macroeconomic 'shocks' – the collapse of the Bretton Woods exchange rate system and two oil crises – brought their own demands upon the CCP to perform a compensatory role. A more stable and neo-liberal global economic environment in the 1980s brought new challenges to the CCP, as did the most ambitious agenda ever set for a GATT Round in 1986 at Punta del Este, Uruguay.

Other pressures have been of the Community's making. First, the enlargement of the EEC6 to the EU15 has brought considerable complexity to formulating trade policy. The inclusion of new member states has increased the probability of compromise decisions being made in internal negotiations, although the recent introduction of qualified majority voting (QMV) has partly solved this. While new member states have brought with them valuable trade relationships with third countries based on past colonial or other ties, the CCP's architecture has become further complicated by extending similar preferential terms to these countries where the EU has obliged. The UK and the British Commonwealth countries and the Iberian countries and Latin America present cases in point here.

The same effect can be observed with respect to the dispensing of preferential treatments to peripheral regions of the EU. For example, the accession of the Iberian countries in 1986 shifted the political balance within the Community's membership towards the Mediterranean Basin countries, while German reunification in 1990 has had some influence over the orientation of EU trade policy towards central and eastern Europe. Another pressure from within has been the expansive development of preferential trading arrangements granted by the EU, which in 1993 covered around two-thirds of all external trade. Some difficulties have originated from sustaining a trade regime of this nature alongside the EU's stated commitment to supporting the multilateral 'free trade' structure of GATT and the WTO.

Furthermore, some member states have bilaterally negotiated or imposed their own NTBs with third countries. The most common of these have been voluntary export restraints (VERs) which are a type of quota that is negotiated between the parties in the importing and exporting countries. They have become one of the most common forms of NTBs to be deployed in recent years playing a central role in the 'new protectionism'. VERs may be contracted between national governments or on an industry-to-industry basis such as the arrangement made in 1975 between UK and Japanese car producers to limit Japanese car imports to 11 per cent of the UK market. A VER agreement is usually established as an alternative to retaliatory measures that could potentially occur. Variations on VERs are the orderly marketing arrangements (OMAs) which are multilateral voluntary restraints on exports. However, all bilateral VERs and most other bilateral trade arrangements have either been replaced with EU-level equivalents or are intended to be phased out altogether.

While these pressures have no doubt been significant, Woolcock (1995) has criticised the CCP as being 'excessively reactive', which has led to an undermining of its ability to fulfil the EU's responsibilities to the GATT/ WTO system and uphold unified European interests abroad. Moreover, Winters (1994) believes that the technocratic management structure of the CCP has produced complexities which have induced a more protectionist approach being adopted.

The CCP's principles and basis

The Treaty of Rome's provisions for the operation of a full customs union between member states are outlined in Article 3 and Articles 9 to 37. The establishment of a CET remains contained within Articles 18 to 29, but the more specific basis for the CCP was detailed in Articles 110 to 116. The Maastricht Treaty made three of these, Articles 111 and 114 (transitional period) and Article 116 (common action in economic organisations) redundant, with only minor revisions made to the remainder which presently embody the guiding principles of the CCP.

Article 110 (Purposes)

This sets out the broad aims of the CCP. The tone of the text is characterised by its support of a liberal world trading order, stating that:

> By establishing a customs union between themselves Member States aim to contribute, in the common interest, to the harmonious development of world trade, the progressive abolition of restrictions on international trade and the lowering of customs barriers. The CCP shall take into account the favourable effect which the abolition of customs duties between Member States may have on the increase in the competitive strength of undertakings in those States.

Article 112 (Aid for exports)

This outlines the need for EU member states to 'progressively harmonise the systems whereby they grant aid for exports to third countries'. Most promotional efforts for EU exports take place at national level. Article 112 therefore provides for at least a convergence and co-ordination between member states in this area to avoid any possible distortions to competitive opportunities that exist for EU exports. In addition to Article 112, the EU is also a signatory to the 1978 OECD 'consensus' on rules and codes for export credits.

Article 113 (Uniformity principle, implementation and decision-making)

Section 1 of this Article states that a principle of uniformity on tariff rates, trade agreements, trade liberalisation, export policy and anti-dumping measures must be complied to by member states. Section 2 grants the Commission its exclusive competence over handling the CCP itself. The implementation of and decision-making process of the CCP is contained within Sections 3 and 4.

Article 115 (Trade deflection)

Rules concerning trade deflection are detailed in Article 115. This legislation has traditionally allowed member states to maintain certain bilateral trade barriers against third country imports, both direct from that country or those that have been indirectly routed through other member states. However, this is only permitted if the Commission can be convinced that significant material injury to domestic producers was being caused. An amendment in the Maastricht Treaty strengthened the Commission's hand by denying member states to take unilateral decisions whereby trade deflection would ensue.

   These new provisions to this Article state that the deployment of protectionist measures by individual member states should 'cause the least disturbance to the functioning of the common market'. Article 115 also notes that member states affected by such cases should first endeavour to resolve the dispute between themselves. Owing to Commission efforts to remove any potential impediments to completing the single market, references to the provisions of Article 115 are now rare. For instance, in 1994 no measures based on Article 115 were adopted.

Articles 228 and 238

In addition to those above, Articles 228 and 238 outline the framework for EU relations with international organisations and special arrangements with third party countries and regional groupings. This legislative base forms the foundation of the numerous Association and Co-operation Agreements which the EU has established with some of its trading partners. The EU's external trade relations may also be determined by Articles 130u–y which encompass development co-operation policy.

The EU's external trade policy instruments

The Common External Tariff (CET)

On joining the EU, new member states have to adopt its CET on all third country imports over a negotiated transitional period. Most of the EU tariff rates are *ad valorem* in character. Under the GATT Rounds these have been lowered to levels where the EU's average rate on industrial products now lies at around 3 per cent. This compares to a CET of 5.7 per cent on the eve of the Uruguay Round. The concessions granted by the EU at GATT talks on mainstream tariff rates have been roughly similar to those conceded by its main trading partners, and there is currently very little variance between these rates. Agricultural and other 'sensitive' industry products have attracted much higher tariffs as part of a systematic protectionist position that has been adopted.

The formula for CET rates are provided in Article 19, although variations to the uniform CET regime apply in a number of circumstances. If the domestic price of the imported product is found to be higher than its actual import price then the CET valuation is set to the former. In situations of strategic emergency tariffs may be suspended, for example on food and high-tech products. Intermediate products of EU firms engaged in out-sourced production in low factor cost locations may re-enter the EU for further processing at zero or reduced tariff rates. Similar provisions exist for inward processing for re-export from the EU.

Tariff quotas allow certain countries to export up to threshold, or 'ceiling' levels before tariffs are imposed, but tariff impositions are not usually automatic. Such devices have been deployed within the EU's preferential trade arrangements. Finally, imports from non-GATT countries attract 'conventional' duties that are normally higher than GATT member imports. Where these are lower, GATT members must also benefit from them.

Safeguard measures

Article XIX of the GATT serves its members with a 'safeguard clause' whereby protectionist measures may be applied in cases where a sudden surge of imports is found to have caused material injury to domestic producers and other adversely affected groups. Under such circumstances, the EU has normally employed quantitative restrictions (QRs) to diminish these injurious effects from competitive external producers. These have sometimes taken the form of 'grey area' measures such as VERs and OMAs, so called because their informal character has made encompassing them within the competence of trade policy somewhat difficult.

Products from 'sensitive' industries tend to attract the vast majority of QRs which have also been the most popular type of NTB used by the EU in recent decades. The employment of surveillance measures, such as import licence requirements, may be the initial step taken by those gathering evidence which the Commission requires before any action on safeguard measures can be qualified. The GATT's Article XIX states that all contracting parties affected by the safeguard measure must be consulted and compensation granted to exporting countries in other product areas. Retaliation is permitted if this procedure is not followed.

Throughout the 1960s, all EEC6 member states had a series of bilateral

QRs on Japanese textile and clothing products. In 1969, the first collectively negotiated VER on cotton textiles was achieved, replacing the equivalent bilateral arrangement. By 1994, the Commission had abolished all member state QRs as part of removing distortions which bilateral agreements can cause to a fully functional single market. EU-level QRs were introduced to replace these, establishing the administrative procedure as well as a uniform import licence valid throughout the EU. The Commission also intends to eliminate all VERs and OMAs as soon as possible.

Anti-Dumping Duties (ADDs) and Countervailing Duties (CVDs)

The use of these measures is normally defended on the grounds that 'fair trade' is of tantamount importance to free trade. Dumping occurs when the price of incoming imports is deliberately set at very low levels in an attempt by the exporting producer to knock other producers out of the market and hence establish a dominant market position. Anti-dumping duties (ADDs) are employed to counter such tactics and their application must comply to international obligations laid down in Article VI of the GATT and the 1979 Anti-Dumping Code. These state that the ADD imposed is to be no greater than the difference between the lower export market price and the average price found in the exporter's domestic market. Under CCP regulations, a full factual investigation is required by the Commission before ADDs can be applied.

Similar codes of conduct apply to countervailing duties (CVDs) which impose punitive tariff rates on those imports found to have gained an 'unfair' competitive advantage through subsidies granted by the government of the exporting country concerned. Thus, CVDs must be no higher than the incidence of the subsidy enjoyed by the exporting producer.

The introduction of the EU's regulations for ADDs coincided with the timing of the CET's introduction in July 1968, but it was not until 1976 that ADDs were actually utilised, the first case being on Taiwanese bicycle chains. By 1994, the EU had 150 ADD and CVD measures in force, with 58 of these imposed against state trading countries. China had the most with 23; other prominent countries included Turkey and Japan with 18 each and South Korea with 12 (CEC 1995k). However, the general trend for resorting to ADD and CVD measures is downwards and covers a mere fraction of EU external trade. In 1987, only 0.9 per cent of EU imports were affected by ADDs and CVDs, but even this had fallen to 0.6 per cent by 1994. There are, though, signs that the Commission plans to deploy CVDs on a more regular basis in the future. This comes from taking a looser definition of third country subsidies to producers along the lines of a US-style interpretation of them (*Financial Times*, 27 October 1994).

Products from the EU's main trading partners which currently attract these duties are characterised by their high-tech content (e.g. Japanese television cameras and US ethanolamines), thus their imposition is motivated by strategic reasoning. This is in contrast to products originating from low factor cost countries (e.g. Chinese bicycles and photo albums, Polish seamless steel) which mainly affect the EU's 'sensitive' sectors. Pressures have come from EU industrial lobby groups for the compensatory effects that ADDs and CVDs are able to generate. However, policy-makers have been reluctant completely to insulate business from these pressures, knowing that restructuring these industries is essential.

Rules of origin

The main functions performed by rules of origin are to establish an import's identity and thus avoid trade deflection from occurring. This is determined from the EU's customs nomenclature which abides by either the process or value-added rule. The process rule is concerned with where the product was processed and substantial transformation took place. The basis of the value-added rule is founded on the proportion of the import's ex-factory price represented by value-added criteria. Rules of origin are obviously required to determine which aspect of the CCP should apply to any EU import.

They are also used to manage disputes in trade-related investment issues owing to disagreements arising over the local content of EU-based foreign production plants targeting EU markets. Under the EU's 1988 'screwdriver plant' legislation (Regulation 2423/88), ADDs were imposed on foreign multinationals deemed guilty of circumventing these duties by establishing low local content production and service facilities within the EU. However, in 1990 a GATT panel upheld a formal complaint by Japan against this legislation on account of its market distorting effects.

The New Commercial Policy Instrument

Becoming operational in 1985, the New Commercial Policy Instrument (NCPI) was modelled on the USA's Section 301 provisions on unfair trade. The main aim of the NCPI was to streamline procedures which improved the EU's ability to exercise its international rights against third country illicit commercial practices. It can also be applied where export interests are threatened by like actions. A range of retaliatory measures may be applied under the NCPI's provisions including suspension or withdrawal of trade concessions and increased tariff rates. These were revised as part of implementing the outcomes of the Uruguay Round. However, the NCPI has rarely been invoked and lacks the same degree of potency possessed by its US equivalent. In compliance to the WTO's rules and codes, the EU may take cases of illicit commercial practice through its dispute settlement procedures.

Sectoral aspects

In an attempt to protect producers in certain sectors of EU industry, the CCP has developed a series of NTB measures alongside its CET system.

Most of the measures outlined in the section above have been introduced to perform this purpose, while in some cases the CCP complies with wider international agreements such as the Multi-Fibre Agreement (MFA). We have already noted that the CCP is not directly responsible for all aspects of EU trade policy. Therefore, in accordance with its permitted competence, it has played only an indirect role in shaping some areas of the external trade policy regime.

Textiles and clothing

The EU has remained in the MFA since it replaced the Long Term Arrangement on Cotton Textile Trade (LTA) in 1974. Although the MFA extended QRs to other textile and clothing products, its ultimate objective was to allow time for producers in developed countries to rationalise and restructure production towards more high value-added activities while simultaneously phasing in a progressively liberal system of bilateral trade arrangements. At the Uruguay Round, the EU and other participating members agreed totally to phase out the MFA by 2005 with QRs being replaced by tariff rates ('tariffication') as a parallel part of the process. EU member states had maintained restrictions on 77 per cent of the MFA's textile and clothing categories against external producers under the last MFA(IV) agreement, many of whom have been from CEE and Mediterranean Basin countries. From 1993, the EU's internal market for textiles was completely administered by a system of centralised quotas complying to both the requirements of the SEM programme and the Uruguay Round agreement on textiles.

Steel

Competitive Japanese steel producers attracted the EU's first VER within this sector in 1972. In 1977, the Davignon Plan provided internal guidelines for import delivery schedules and prices in support of the CCP's own provisions. Since then, tensions over the EU's steel trade have arisen not only with East Asian and CEE producers, but also with the USA. From the early 1980s, both sides have imposed ADDs and CVDs on each other's exports which is clearly indicative of both offensive and defensive endeavours to protect ailing domestic industries. A similar struggle could be observed between EU and EFTA producers. In 1991, three of the EU's ten restraint agreements on steel were on EFTA products (see Hayes 1993). The failure of the Uruguay Round talks to establish a multilateral steel arrangement suggests that these tensions will continue to simmer, although the EU and other affected parties expressed their commitment to pursue negotiations until such a settlement is completed.

Automobiles

The application of QRs by EU member states on automobiles has been one of the highest profile trade issues. Most of these have taken the form of bilateral VERs on Japanese cars. Italy's VER with Japanese producers actually predated the EEC being negotiated in 1955, and up to 1970 did not permit any Japanese car imports. France and the UK agreed their own VERs with Japanese producers in the mid-1970s, limiting them to 3 per cent and 11 per cent of their domestic markets respectively. Spain and Portugal had also imposed VER conditions upon Japanese car exporters. From the beginning of 1993, the Commission replaced the bilateral VERs with an EU-level equivalent arrangement that is due to be phased out in 1999. This represents an attempt partially to reconcile the CCP with the overriding objectives of the SEM programme by removing the market distortions inflicted in such circumstances.

Agriculture

This has been the EU's most comprehensively protected sector, although owing to the EU's preferential trading arrangements about 55 per cent of agri-imports entered the EU market CET-free in 1993. Nevertheless, almost 34 per cent are subject to customs duties or a combination of duties, levies and CVDs, with a remaining 11 per cent attracting a levy (CEC 1993b). Peterson (1993) also notes that more than 80 per cent of US legal actions against the EU within GATT derived from agricultural or fishery disputes.

Consumer electronics

Japan has again been the traditional target for QRs on consumer electronic goods with the earliest example dating back to France's 1962 ban on all Japanese products in this sector. From as early as the 1970s, East Asian producers from other countries such as Taiwan and South Korea had joined Japan in attracting an imposition of QRs, ADDs and CVDs on their products. The relatively technology intensive and strong growth character of these products has resulted in rather extreme defensive measures being adopted by certain member states in the past.

Sectoral interests within the EU wield considerable influence over the CCP. Policy-makers are usually caught in the dilemma of balancing two key objectives with respect to 'sensitive' industries. On the one hand is the desire to minimise the social costs associated with restructuring in the face of global competitive realities, while on the other is the need to rationalise domestic industry to meet future challenges that lie ahead. The adjustment process within which this balance of objectives exists must be carefully managed and involve the appropriate scheduling of phased-in changes.

In the late 1970s, the OECD emphasised the need for 'positive adjustment policies' based on market forces, factor mobility and capital development. In addition, 'sensitive' industry producers needed to find new competitive advantages in higher value-added activities. EU producers in relatively technology intensive sectors have enjoyed promotional support in the form of export subsidies in a bid to develop strategic advantage in these key markets. Nevertheless, some NICs have managed to compete effectively even in these sectors, thus attracting defensive as well as offensive measures under the CCP.

Member state and international influences

Over time the CCP has altered its complexion in accordance with the influence of a variety of internal and external factors. In the first instance, the traditional views held by member states on trade policy have had considerable sway over the direction which the CCP has taken. These range from mercantilist views that have usually predominated in France and Italy which are partly derived from the conventions of *dirigiste* policy frameworks. In the past, member states which have prescribed to these views have pressed for most of the derogations from the CCP to pursue their own unilateral or bilateral actions. However, in recent years moves towards a more 'Euro-protectionist' stance have been supported, illustrated by the development of such CCP instruments as the NCPI (Pearce *et al.* 1985).

These views are in contrast to those upheld by liberal traders like Germany and the Netherlands with their belief that only free trade and an open trade policy can secure longer term benefits to the economy through exposing industry to the rigours of foreign competition. A more pragmatic line has been taken by countries such as the UK which may be keen to stress their free trade credentials, but in practice adjust their stance on CCP matters according to the circumstances that are presented. The view adopted towards the role of the CCP will depend to some degree on a member state's openness to trade. For example, we could expect the Benelux countries, with their very high trade ratios, to place great importance on attempting to influence the direction of the CCP. Relatively closed economies would not be expected to make equivalent efforts.

We have already noted the obligations which the CCP must meet with regard to those trade rules and codes set by the GATT/WTO and other relevant international organisations. Indeed, to some degree it should be expected that the EU would more readily comply to these obligations as a consequence of the European integration process. This is due to EU member states progressively having to accept more rule-based or adjudicative methods of resolving disputes through the ECJ. It is proposed by Woolcock (1993) that this has made it harder for the EU to argue against the GATT's dispute settlement procedures. Further commonality and influence can be observed from the similar approaches adopted to both European liberalisation (i.e. the SEM programme) and multilateral liberalisation under the Uruguay Round over a parallel time period.

As a result, an interdependent development process has evolved that at times has manifested itself in a joint search to establish common rules on technical barriers to trade and other related issues. This has been demonstrated in negotiations on the MFA. Moreover, the EU has wished to confirm the compatibility between the SEM programme and the GATT outcomes to third countries by stressing the commitment to maintaining an 'open Europe' and 'partner Europe' position with regards to external trade relations.

GATT, WTO AND INTERNATIONAL TRADE ORDER

General Agreement on Tariffs and Trade (GATT): an introduction

The General Agreement on Tariffs and Trade (GATT) was established in 1947 as an attempt to avoid the 'zero-sum game' protectionism that had characterised inter-war international trade relations. Many commentators have blamed this protectionist environment for aggravating the political tensions that ultimately led to World War II, while there was little doubt over its adverse contribution to the Great Depression. Emerging as part of the Bretton Woods community of post-war international organisations (i.e. the IMF, World Bank), GATT was charged with the prime objective of building a stable multilateral framework for international trade. This was to be achieved by establishing common rules and codes on which international trade was to be conducted by GATT members and a series of 'Rounds' in which negotiated reductions in tariff rates and other impediments to free trade were to be eradicated. This system was actually a substitute for the original plans for a permanent International Trade Organisation (ITO) to govern such matters which the US Congress rejected on the grounds that it would impair the sovereignty of American trade policy.

At the first GATT Round held at Geneva in 1947 there were only 23 members – or 'contracting parties' (CPs) – present with the volume of trade under negotiation then valued at $10bn. By the time of the eighth and last GATT Round (Uruguay Round), 117 CPs were participating in talks concerning trade volumes estimated in excess of $1 trillion. One of the main roles played by the pre-Kennedy Rounds was to enable the USA to grant tariff concessions to Western Europe to assist the post-war recovery process (Greenaway 1991). This policy altered once the European producers had developed their competitive advantage in a substantial number of sectors.

The Kennedy and Toyko Rounds began to extend the scope of GATT beyond tariffs into areas such as dumping, technical standards, import licences and customs regulations. Regarding the issue of tariffs the 'product by product' approach, based on negotiations between their principal suppliers which were then extended to all other CPs, was ditched in favour of the 'linear' approach. Hine (1985) notes that the former method of negotiation was found to be too prone to protectionist lobby group pressures and free riding by small countries which enjoyed the benefit of tariff cuts under the MFN rule without having to grant their own concessions. The linear method avoided these problems by setting a target rate of tariff cuts to be negotiated between all CPs which would then have the opportunity to propose exceptions to form the basis of further discussions.

The progression of the GATT Rounds, as shown in Table 6.4, gives some indication of its main achievements. First, it has gradually managed to encompass the vast majority of the world's nations into a multilateral forum for trade negotiations. The volume and value of trade negotiated has increased largely in proportion to this expansion of members, but also from an enlarging of the GATT agenda. This has no doubt been contributive to securing the relatively stable post-war economic and political international relations that have existed. The other main area of success is on the unprecedented reductions in tariff rates between nations which in turn have played their part in stimulating the most rapid international trade growth rates ever recorded. Over the eight Rounds of GATT talks the average tariff rate for industrial goods had fallen from 40 per cent in 1947 to just 4 per cent in 1993. In the same period, the volume of trade had increased sixteen-fold.

These accomplishments must also be judged with respect to recent developments in trade policy. Michalski (1991) has conveniently provided an analytical framework – the 'two-track' approach – in which these can be understood. The first track has consisted of measures with a reliance on selective contingency protection such as ADDs and CVDs, 'grey area' measures (e.g. VERs) and other NTBs. These are 'defensive' in character and have formed the basis of the 'new protectionism' that has entailed the expansive use of bilateral measures, in particular quantitative restrictions which are accompanied by the threat of unilateral action, such as VERs. In contrast, second track 'offensive' measures have been based on reciprocity measures primarily aimed at surplus countries. This has involved pressure being applied on these countries to revalue their currency, widen domestic

Table 6.4 The eight GATT rounds, 1947–93

Round	Dates	No. of CPs	Value of trade
Geneva	1947	23	$10.0bn
Annecy	1949	33	n/a
Torquay	1950	34	n/a
Geneva	1956	22	$2.5bn
Dillon	1961–2	45	$4.9bn
Kennedy	1962–7	48	$40.0bn
Tokyo	1973–9	99	$155.0bn
Uruguay	1986–93	117	$1000.0bn+

Source: Greenaway 1991

market access to imports and graduation to full GATT (MFN) status. Non-compliance with such requests normally leads to denied or limited access to the deficit country's home market. The USA in particular has taken frequent recourse to such actions on a unilateral basis. This is owing both to its continued slide from being a major trade surplus to a trade deficit country and its ability effectively to assert its interests due to the size and stature of the economy.

Despite the tactical and strategic orientation of trade policy that has persisted throughout the post-war era, the GATT framework has remained intact and more importantly managed consecutively weightier agendas. In the view of those who prescribe to the 'bicycle theory' of GATT, by which the bicycle falls over if it loses forward momentum (Nguyen *et al.* 1993), this has been a crucial achievement. One corollary of this view is that the failed completion of GATT Rounds would lead to its own demise and be followed by a new era of protectionism.

GATT/WTO's main principles

GATT and its successor, the World Trade Organisation (WTO), have been guided by a number of principles that are embodied in 38 Articles. These main principles of the GATT/WTO framework are outlined below.

Non-discriminatory trade

This is often referred to as the cornerstone principle of the GATT/WTO framework and is encoded in two key provisions: the 'Most-Favoured-Nation' (MFN) clause and the 'national treatment' clause. The MFN clause is based on a reciprocity rule which implies that tariff concessions granted by one CP to another must be returned in kind. Furthermore, Article I of GATT states that any advantage, favour, privilege or immunity affecting tariffs or other trade regulation instruments, which are granted to one of the GATT members, must immediately be granted to all other members as well. The principle of 'national treatment' involves upholding a parity between domestic and foreign producers in respect to all laws, regulations and other administrative purposes that affect internal sales.

Multilateral negotiation and free trade

The ultimate objective of GATT/WTO is to establish free trade between all participating CPs. This can only be achieved through the multilateral negotiation of tariff reductions, trading disputes and other trade-related issues between members. Thus, in principle, GATT/WTO attempts to deter settlement by unilateral, bilateral or plurilateral means but in reality derogations of this nature have been conceded as part of a compromise solution. The most significant achievements of GATT Rounds have been in the multilateral reductions of tariff rates and more recently the inclusion of an expanding number of trade-related issues concerning impediments to free trade.

The prohibition of quantitative restrictions

Article XI of GATT/WTO details provisions that seek to eliminate the use of QRs by contracting parties. The relatively less transparent nature of QRs with respect to tariffs has made them both a prime target of more recent GATT Rounds while also more intractable to negotiate. In the Tokyo and Uruguay Rounds, endeavours were thus made at the 'tariffication' of QRs and other NTBs entailing the conversion where possible of these trade barriers into tariff equivalents.

However, a number of exceptions to Article XI were written into GATT's constitution. These have included, until recently, QRs being permitted on agricultural imports, those countries experiencing serious balance of payments difficulties (Article XII) and developing countries wishing to protect infant industries (Article XVIII). Article XIX contains a safeguard clause that allows a CP to deploy quantitative restrictions on a sudden surge of imports that can be proved to cause material injury to domestic producers. If this procedure is followed by a CP it must do so on a non-discriminatory basis and the use of QRs must be accompanied by compensatory measures in other product areas. Yet as Trebilcock and Howse (1995) note, compliance to these GATT/WTO counter-actions has fuelled the incentive for CPs to turn to 'grey area' measures such as VERs and OMAs whose informal contractual character has eluded the reach of GATT/WTO. This has compounded the difficulties experienced by GATT/WTO in effectively prohibiting quantitative restrictions in general.

Article XXIV: An exception to the 'MFN' rule for RIAs

Article XXIV allows CPs to enter into RIAs owing to the 'second best' notion of trade liberalisation that they present. The GATT/WTO rules stress trade creation as the overarching objective of these arrangements and also lay down operations guidelines. These are:

- that the RIA be established within a 'reasonable length of time';
- a universal coverage of trade between members;
- a uniform application of CET rates;
- an intention progressively to reduce CET rates.

Under the provisions of Article XXIV(6), if a new member has to raise tariffs to comply to the CET regulations then all GATT contracting parties are eligible for compensation. This applied to the EU's 1995 EFTA enlargement. In general, third country CPs have been more or less willing to accept the formation of RIAs provided that these guidelines and compensatory regulations have been complied with. It is conceivable that they may even favour the initiative if they can derive any benefits from the dynamic integrational processes that take place, such as those offered by the SEM programme. The growing number of countries participating in RIAs has diminished the scope for disputes to be raised on this issue. Nevertheless, Stevens and Andrieu (1991) state that any multilateral system for trade negotiations must be founded on a rule-based system and warn that the proliferation of RIAs could lead to a deterioration of that system by being progressively dependent on a power-based structure.

Box 6.1 The Uruguay Round

The Uruguay Round was launched at Punta del Este in September 1986 with the most ambitious and complex agenda of any GATT talks. At the end of the talks in December 1993, 15 different negotiating groups had involved up to 117 CPs. Hoekman (1993) comments that the expansion of issues tackled within the Uruguay Round reflected its intention to confront the recent transformations to the world economy brought about by the continued globalisation of economic activity. These involved the impact that foreign investment flows, global structural changes, new flexible manufacturing techniques, growth of tradable services and cross-border transfers of technology had imposed on patterns and relations of international trade.

This was also the first Round since the original to discuss major changes to GATT systems and procedures, culminating in the establishment of the WTO in January 1995. New fields of competence were extended to the GATT that some CPs believed were beyond its constitutional remit. For example, international compliance to patents, copyrights and trademarks has been overseen by the World Intellectual Property Organisation for some time, although membership was by no means universal. Many CPs also made known their views that trade-related investment measures (TRIMs) were a matter of national policy only. The main items on the Uruguay Round agenda can be summarised as:

● The reduction of tariffs in those sectors with particularly high rates.
● General agreement on the trade in services (GATS) now that services account for around 20 per cent of world trade.
● Trade-related intellectual property rights (TRIPs) owing to the recent proliferation of breaches made on patents, copyrights and other forms of intellectual property rights.
● Trade-related investment measures (TRIMs) from both the impact of a significant growth of foreign investment flows on international trade and the actions taken at national and sub-national level to regulate it.
● Removing protectionist measures on agriculture (e.g. the EU's CAP system).
● Allowing developing countries more access to OECD markets (e.g. textiles, steel and agriculture).

Box 6.1 *continued*

- Reforming GATT's procedures which also involved strengthening the facilities to monitor and manage international trade agreements. The WTO was established for this purpose. Streamlining the dispute settlement procedure was another priority.

The Uruguay Round has undoubtedly been the most difficult and protracted of all. The course of the negotiations was consistently hampered by a variety of disputes arising between CPs on an individual and collective basis. One consequence of this was that the Round ran way over its intended 1986 to 1990 schedule. Some disputes that surfaced between the major trading powers at times threatened to jeopardise the whole Round of talks. A summary of the main difficulties is given below:

- The proliferation of 'grey area' measures such as VERs that have been able to circumvent the GATT rules and codes of conduct.
- Agricultural subsidies, especially those employed by the EU and USA.
- EU steel tariffs and state aid to domestic producers in addition to EU state aid to its aerospace industry (e.g. the Airbus consortium).
- Japanese and other East Asian protectionism of domestic markets and dumping of exports on world markets.
- The Multi-Fibre Agreement (MFA) affecting textile imports from non-OECD nations.
- US insistence on maintaining a series of unilateral agreements and policy instruments.

At the successful completion of the Uruguay Round by the end of 1993, its Final Act document, containing 23 international agreements, was formally signed at a ministerial conference in April 1994 at Marrakesh (CEC 1994g). The main outcomes of the Round were:

- Industrial tariffs cut by developed countries by over a third. Over 40 per cent of imports to enter tariff free.
- On agriculture, trade distorting subsidies and import barriers to be cut up to the end of 2000. Domestic farm supports reduced by 20 per cent, the value of subsidised exports by 36 per cent and by 21 per cent in volume. The tariffication of import barriers and these tariff rates to be cut to 36 per cent. Tropical product tariffs cut by over 40 per cent.
- GATS rules and codes established. A framework set for further talks on provisions for financial services and telecommunications.
- The dismantling of the MFA over a ten-year period with developing countries also reducing some trade barriers on textile and clothing imports.
- An agreement on TRIPs and TRIMs signed. International standards of protection on intellectual property rights and means for their effective enforcement to be managed by the WTO. Local sourcing and minimum export requirements imposed by host authorities on foreign investors are now prohibited.

Box 6.1 *continued*

- Revision and clarification to rules and codes on the use of ADDs and CVDs established resulting in a more difficult use of ADDs and tighter regulations on subsidised exports.
- Strengthening of the safeguard regime by introducing firmer time limits on safeguard measures (four years) which must be progressively liberalised over that period. Multilateral notification and surveillance procedures improved and 'grey area' measures to comply to new regime or be terminated.
- The expansion and revision of the Government Procurement Code that encompasses additional areas such as procurement by sub-national governments and public utilities.
- The establishment of the WTO provides a permanent world trade body to continue the work of the Uruguay Round and beyond.
- Other issues included the improvement of provisions on dispute settlement mechanisms, technical trade barriers and miscellaneous GATT regulations such as import licensing and rules of origin.

Estimates have been made regarding the expected welfare gains generated by the trade liberalising effects of the Round (see Table 6.5). The initial estimate made by OECD/GATT in 1993 was valued at $235bn per annum for a subsequent ten-year period. This soon had to be revised as broader and wider dynamic effects had not been considered. A year later, the new GATT/ WTO Secretariat estimate recalculated on these criteria was almost twice the original at $510bn. A geographical breakdown of the gains revealed that the EU would become the main beneficiary of the Uruguay Round largely through reforms made on trade in agriculture and textiles and improved competitive effects upon EU industry from a more open global competitive environment. The USA was also found to be a major beneficiary for similar reasons. Developing countries would primarily benefit from improved market access to OECD markets and subsequent developmental effects this generates.

Table 6.5 Estimated future welfare gains from the Uruguay Round ($bn per annum, 1995–2004)

USA	122.4
EU	163.5
Japan	26.7
Canada	12.4
EFTA (7)	33.5
Australasia	5.8
China	18.7
Taiwan	10.2
Rest of world	116.8
TOTAL	510.0

Source: Reuters, 10 November 1994

WTO and the future of the international trade order

The WTO was established on 1 January 1995 to act as the successor to GATT but exists as a permanent negotiating forum. Its main aim is to provide a stronger and more coherent framework for accelerating the trade liberalisation process. This will still entail an adherence to GATT's underlying precepts. Although the WTO enjoys the use of enhanced international trade rules (e.g. WTO rulings can be rejected only by a unanimous vote) and a more effective advocacy of a liberalised world trade system, its powers of enforcement, like those of its predecessor, are almost non-existent. Most decisions taken by the WTO are dependent on the consensus of its members. With no other resources to draw on except its operational budget (an initial £57m per annum) the effectiveness of WTO will ultimately rest on its credibility. The reputation of GATT, built on those achievements highlighted earlier, should serve it well. However, there are a number of new challenges inherited from the Uruguay Round that will soon put the WTO to the test. These include:

- The administration not only of international trade in goods but also trade in services under the GATS agreement and trade in products covered by intellectual property rights. The opening up of banking and insurance markets in East Asia and Latin America has become a significant issue for both the EU and the USA.
- Additional new trade-related areas to be managed consist of environmental protection, TRIMs, trade and development, government procurement and others.
- Overseeing the dismantling of trade barriers in agriculture and textile sectors and the possible negotiation for a multilateral steel arrangement.
- The greater transparency that is supposed to be applied to WTO procedures and actions will make it vulnerable to pressures emanating from a wider range of interest groups (e.g. NGOs and environmentalists).
- Assisting in the co-ordination of global economic policy making through close collaboration with the IMF, World Bank and other relevant bodies.

As well as those tasks, the WTO has a number of important general duties to manage and expectations to meet. These will also have to be successfully handled if its credibility is to remain intact. The most critical of these include:

- Convincing the USA of the adequacy of its mechanisms in redressing the illicit commercial practices of certain countries and thus reducing its incentive to resort to compensatory unilateral actions. However, US Congress may wish to install its own 'safeguards' against WTO rulings.
- Integrating the developing countries into the global economy to ensure that they are not marginalised in the globalisation process.
- The continued proliferation of RIAs pose a potential threat to the multilateral trade order. In April 1995, a WTO report stated that 33 regional

arrangements had been made over the 1990–94 period, nearly a third of all arrangements since 1948. The possibility of a Trans-Atlantic free trade area has caused particular consternation.

- The possible inclusion of an increasing number of trade-related issues on the WTO's agenda, such as multilateral rules on competition policy and foreign direct investment, international trade and company law, labour standards and immigration.

Overall then, it can be seen that the breadth of the WTO remit is considerably greater than that of GATT. This is further demonstrated by its thirty councils and standing committees on trade-related issues – twice the number administered by its preceding framework. Furthermore, by April 1995 there were twenty-five countries waiting to become WTO members, many from the former Soviet Union. The obligations laid out in the WTO's Agreements require of those seeking accession to make a more significant commitment to free trade than under GATT's arrangements. As a UN report commented, 'This will substantially reduce the flexibility which developing countries have enjoyed under the multilateral trading system with respect to trade policies in certain areas previously considered to fall within the domestic policy sphere' (UN 1994b: 125). However, it conceded that they would still benefit from favourable treatment from developed countries, for example under GSP regimes. Developing countries should also gain from the WTO's new rules which aim to provide better protection against the 'grey area' measures.

The accession of China presents a particular challenge to the WTO in this field, given both its future prospects and the impediments to membership that still persist. A recent attempt to make China an original WTO member failed owing to the protracted nature of negotiations over issues such as market access, intellectual property rights, state trading measures and various others. The gravitational pull of China's economy will make any major multilateral trade negotiations that do not include the Chinese increasingly meaningless based on the persistence of current trends.

The expansion of WTO membership is likely to present less difficulty to the organisation compared to the widening range of trade-related issues which it anticipates managing in the future. Both the EU and USA have expressed their desire to have social and environmental clauses written into WTO agreements and have already used them in certain trading arrangements. However, extending WTO interests into these new areas will only make some countries more aware of the asymmetric conditions and trade advantages enjoyed. Attempting to establish a 'level playing field' will prove extremely arduous and thus some WTO members may feel vindicated in adopting counteractive protectionist measures.

A final key issue concerns one that has been identified by the WTO's head, Renato Ruggiero, who contended that the logical conclusion of globalisation implied that replacement of trade policy by competition policy will be required as the main method of keeping these markets open (*Financial Times*, 1 May 1995). While this remains a very distant prospect, the setting of plurilateral rules on restrictive practices and other forms of anti-competitive behaviour have been informally discussed between the EU and USA. As traditional national demarcations are broken down by the globalisation process, the interface between trade and competition policies can be expected to become more manifest. Hence, tackling certain new trade-related areas may be unavoidable for the WTO.

LOMÉ AND THE ACP COUNTRIES

The background to the Lomé Conventions

As part of the EU's hierarchy of preferential trade arrangements, the Lomé Conventions have granted trade concessions to countries belonging to the Africa Caribbean and Pacific (ACP) group since 1975. These preferential terms have been buttressed by an integrated development co-operation and aid policy aimed at assisting the economic development of ACP members through structural adjustments and trade promotion. The precursors to Lomé were the two Yaoundé Conventions, the first of which was established in 1963 and the second in 1969 involving eighteen countries with which Community member states had strong ex-colonial ties.

A number of factors led to the introduction of the Lomé Conventions and their gradual expansion over the years. First, by the early 1970s there were increasing calls from certain Community members – especially those with strong ex-colonial links such as France and Belgium – for a more comprehensive trade and aid policy towards the ACP group. This coincided with the UN's own proposals for a 'New International Economic Order' which aspired to recast international economic and political relations more in favour of developing countries. Consequently, the Lomé Conventions replaced the provisions of its Yaoundé predecessor in 1973 with a much broader range of functions and revised principles, becoming operational from 1975 onwards.

Lomé was a departure from Yaoundé in the sense that its principles were founded more on 'partnership and mutual respect' and interdependence than on lingering traces of imperial deference and dependence. In terms of its functions, Lomé took a more directly active role in development of the ACP in addition to extending the scope of the preferential trade regime. The reciprocal preferential treatment the Community expected under the Yaoundé Conventions in some cases with respect to other developed country imports was also retracted. The accession of new EU member states brought their own ex-colonial trade relations such as the UK and its Commonwealth Preference system. These relations have been subsumed into Lomé where the countries concerned are eligible to join the ACP group. Developing countries that fall outside the group are considered for the EU's GSP scheme. These and other developments have thus expanded the number of current Lomé signatories to seventy ACP countries.

The first three Lomé Conventions covered five-year financial protocol periods. However, the current Lomé IV Convention was set to last for ten years between 1990 and 2000, with a mid-term review undertaken in 1995 for the second protocol period. In the Uruguay Round, a dispensation was given to Lomé IV to continue its preferential trade regime among ACP states for this period. This was of some concern to other developing nations who receive less favourable trade terms under the EU's own GSP scheme.

As Table 6.6 indicates, the financial resources devoted by the EU to the Lomé Conventions have progressively increased in real terms. Lomé IV was the first, though, to give a real increase on a per capita basis to ACP states amounting to 3 per cent on the previous Convention. In the second financial protocol of Lomé IV, the budget was increased to ECU 14,625m with an additional ECU 1.6bn allocated for specific aid resources from the EU budget. These funds provide the group with its main source of aid and other forms of economic assistance. Yet in an empirical analysis conducted by Davenport (1992) on Lomé's particular impact on sub-Saharan

Table 6.6 The Lomé Conventions

Convention	Period	Members	Financial resources ECUm (current prices)	Real change	Real p/cap change
Lomé I	1975–80	46	3,450		
Lomé II	1980–85	57	5,700	+5.0%	−7.0%
Lomé III	1985–90	65	8,500	+15.7%	−5.0%
Lomé IV(1)	1990–95	70	12,000	+14.8%	+3.0%

Lomé IV(2) Breakdown of financial resources for 1995–2000

8th EDF	12,967
of which:	
Investment aid	9,592
which includes:	
Structural adjustment	1,400
Long-term development aid	260
STABEX	1,800
SYSMIN	575
Venture capital	1,000
EIB own resources	1 658
Total	14,625

Source: CEC 1995m; Agence Europe, 9 November 1995

Africa countries it was concluded that the elimination of the Convention's privileges would have long-term beneficial effects. These would occur from relieving their customary dependency on traditional EU markets and forcing them to search, develop and diversify into new, more dynamic ones. On a similar theme of dependency, Schmuck (1990) considers the potential for ACP countries to develop closer economic integrational ties, but concludes that their collective lack of propinquity and the fact that most are members of localised RIAs would make this essentially unworkable.

Lomé's main provisions

The provisions of the Lomé Conventions include a range of functions to assist the economic development process in the ACP countries. These have broadly consisted of preferential trade terms within the CCP, CAP concessions on variable import levies, the STABEX and SYSMIN funds and facilities and EDF investment aid.

Preferential trade terms

These are aimed at enabling trade to play a developmental role in the ACP economies. The EU is the largest market for ACP exports taking around 40 per cent of total ACP export earnings. In effect the ACP states receive free and non-reciprocal access to the EU market for almost all their exports. Lomé also offers derogations from CCP regulations on rules of origin, with ACP exports allowed up to 45 per cent of their content to be derived from EU or other ACP sources, whereas normally a 10 per cent foreign content ceiling applies. Although CAP products still attract import levies, ACP producers receive special treatment not reserved for those in other developing nations. Separate protocols on aspects of commodity trade, such as sugar, bananas, rum, beef and veal, involve quota arrangements that are complemented by financial advantages conferred from the EU agreeing to purchase minimum volume levels at a guaranteed price. Lomé IV banana protocol provisions have been the cause of dispute between the EU and Latin American banana producers who have argued that the regime unfairly discriminates against them in favour of less efficient Caribbean producers. The USA has supported the case of the Latin American countries, accusing the EU's banana policy of trade diversion.

Under the Lomé Conventions, the EU has bestowed increasing generous preferential trade terms to the ACP countries. This must be partly understood as an attempt to reverse the trend of a steadily decreasing relative share of ACP trade in EU total trade. A number of factors have undermined the endeavours of Lomé's preferential trade regime in achieving this:

- The vast bulk of ACP exports – typically tropical foodstuffs and raw materials enter the EU at zero CET rates largely owing to similar terms granted to GSP beneficiaries. Thus, the potential for trade creation and trade diversion gains for ACP countries on this account is removed.
- GATT Rounds have successively marginalised the ACP's preferential advantage where tariffs have been applied on their exports.
- The complementary industrial profiles of the EU and ACP countries have reduced the scope for trade creation between the two regional groups. QRs have been imposed on ACP exports in many sectors where a competitive overlap exists (e.g. textiles and the MFA).
- There has been limited potential from trade diversion benefiting the ACP countries in their manufacturing exports (Hine 1985). Under the EU's GSP and other global arrangements many foreign manufactures enter the EU market CET-free. ACP states could have taken advantage of the fixed and flexible QRs that were imposed on GSP imports before 1995, but their ability to do so has been hampered by their low levels of industrialisation.

This would seem to suggest that the EU needs to concentrate its efforts to help restructure, diversify and upgrade the industrial base of ACP economies while also awarding greater access to ACP manufacturing exports. The Uruguay Round outcomes have already forced the EU to act on the latter, for example reforms to the CAP and the phasing out of the MFA. There still remains much to achieve as the profile of ACP exports to Europe illustrated in Table 6.7 shows, with agricultural and mineral products constituting 62.8 per cent of the total in 1994.

STABEX

Owing to the dependency of many ACP countries on just a few commodities for their export earnings (e.g. Uganda and coffee: 95 per cent; Ghana

Table 6.7 ACP exports to the EU, by sector, 1994

Sector	MECU	% total
Agricultural products	6,297	34.0
Mineral products	5,345	28.8
Metals, pearls	2,618	14.1
Raw hides, textiles, footwear	1,260	6.8
Wood, cork, paper	1,251	6.7
Machinery, transport equipment	898	4.8
Chemicals	625	3.8
Other	195	1.0
Total	18,489	100.0

Source: Eurostat

and cocoa: 59 per cent), Lomé I introduced the STABEX scheme in an effort to stabilise export prices for non-mineral commodities. The scheme operates funds and facilities whereby cash transfers are bestowed on ACP countries to counteract the adverse effects that fluctuations in commodity market prices have on export earnings. The financial resources that have been devoted to STABEX in Lomé IV(2) amount to ECU 1.8bn. To be eligible for STABEX assistance certain criteria must be met, the main one being that the product in question must be of significant importance to the country's balance of payments. STABEX funds are released once a product or product group has reached a trigger threshold of at least a 5 per cent contribution to export earnings and where the product's earnings have fallen by at least 4.5 per cent.

There must also be verification that the product originated from that country and that the decline in export earnings has not been artificially induced by deliberate trade policy actions. If these criteria are met the transfer of STABEX funds usually takes the form of grant payments made to ACP governments which are then obliged to dispense financial assistance to affected sector producers. For some more developed ACP states these transfers have been based on interest free loan payments repayable over a formulated period.

The ACP states have generally viewed STABEX as a crucial instrument in achieving Lomé's intended objectives. However, there have been many criticisms of the STABEX scheme. These have included the cumbersome bureaucratic mechanisms of both systems and the paucity of financial resources dedicated to it. The erratic fluctuations in commodity prices (exacerbated by the typical demand and supply inelasticities of commodities) and the general downward or static trend observed in many of their market prices have highlighted the deficiencies of the latter in particular. The EU has also been reproached for not extending the scope of such a scheme to the ACP's industrial exports. The arbitrarily determined trigger thresholds have been criticised for not taking account of the country's overall export earnings by the adoption of the product-by-product approach. This approach has also meant that STABEX fails to consider the allocation of financial support proportionate to GDP per capita levels found among ACP countries.

Furthermore, concern has been expressed over the dispensement mechanisms of STABEX funds that have queried not only the time lag in payments made but also how ACP governments have been allowed to use the funds as general tax revenue. Lomé IV has included provisions for ACP governments to undertake a 'substantial analysis' on how they intend to allocate STABEX funds. Additional allowances have also been made for financial resources under the scheme to help promote greater product diversification and capital formation in agriculture.

SYSMIN

In Lomé II, the SYSMIN scheme was introduced to provide similar assistance to that provided by STABEX but for mineral producers in the ACP group. Many ACP members faced the same dilemma of dependency on mineral products to generate export earnings (e.g. Zambia and copper: 98 per cent; Niger and uranium: 85 per cent), but the main objective of SYSMIN has been to ensure that the productive mining capacity of ACP producers has been sustained when income has fallen. No formulaic trigger thresholds for releasing SYSMIN funds are used but instead it is left to the Commission's discretion to decide when intervention is necessary, although Marin (1994) notes that in practice this tended to be around a 10 per cent fall in capacity and a 15 per cent fall in export earnings (10 per cent for the poorest ACP).

As with the STABEX scheme, SYSMIN has been prone to some misappropriation of funds. Nevertheless, Lomé III sought to broaden the scope of SYSMIN fund allocation by allowing it to be channelled to other development projects in the mining industry provided they did not impair its productive capacity. Lomé IV also introduced improved monitoring facilities of how these funds were deployed. While SYSMIN has performed a valuable function for ACP producers, the main criticism that has been made of the scheme is that it is limited only to a few mineral products, these being aluminium, bauxite, copper, iron, manganese, phosphate, tin and uranium.

EDF investment aid

The ACP countries are the main recipients of EU official development assistance (ODA). Most of this is channelled through the European Development Fund (EDF) which has made up an increasing majority of Lomé's financial resource allocation. The EDF actually dates back to 1958 since when it has been a flexible financial instrument which has grown in size with each successive appropriation. The main objective of the EDF investment aid grants, which totalled ECU 9,592m for Lomé IV(2), is to assist the developmental process within the ACP countries by providing aid for investment projects aimed at broadening their industrial base and improving infrastructure, and technical assistance on related matters. Thus, the EDF acts in a parallel role to other Lomé provisions by attempting to create favourable conditions for improving ACP trade prospects.

Criticisms have also been levelled at EDF funding in general. These have included charges that the principle of additionality has been contravened by associated reductions in bilateral aid given to EU member states. Concern has also been expressed over the predominant 'tied' nature of this aid with respect to EU firms securing important contracts out of EDF fund flows at the occasional direct expense of ACP firms. Fierce debate surrounded the budgetary allocation for the 8th EDF and Lomé IV(2) in which France, pushing for a substantial increase to the fund, was left virtually isolated against fellow member states. Counter-arguments for such an increase were put forward by Germany, which has long supported a more global approach to EU development aid policy and has become more absorbed with the CEE countries, and the UK which has pressed for more autonomy for members' state bilateral programmes. The new EFTA members, who are already among the most generous donors of ODA, also expressed their reluctance to fund what they perceived as an anachronistic post-colonial policy. As it transpires, the EDF received a considerable boost in resources but tensions aroused in the debate are likely to surface again in future attempts to rationalise the EU's trade policy towards developing countries.

THE EU'S GENERALISED SYSTEM OF PREFERENCES (GSP)

The background to the GSP

The EU's Generalised System of Preferences (GSP) and the Lomé Conventions have largely determined its trade and wider economic relations with developing countries. While the Lomé Conventions extend selected preferential trade and aid terms to the ACP countries, the GSP offers mainly Latin American and Asian countries a series of concessions in its trade relations with the EU. Other beneficiaries of the scheme have included the Mediterranean Basin and CEE countries in attempts to foster economic development on the EU's external periphery.

The notion of the developed countries adhering to a GSP scheme within which developing economies would benefit from treatment was first proposed at the 1964 UNCTAD Conference at Geneva, in particular the removal of tariffs on industrial products aimed at assisting the development process. This was formally accepted by the UN at a following UNCTAD Conference at New Delhi in 1968 where the principles of GSP were first established. These principles of non-reciprocal concessions and internal non-discrimination ran counter to GATT's own MFN principle. Consequently, an 'enabling clause' was authorised by GATT on 25 June 1971 that allowed GSP schemes to be adopted, with the EU first to do so on 1 July 1971. The EU has reviewed its GSP in 1981, 1986, 1990 and 1995, and a detailed account of the major revisions made in the most recent of these is discussed below.

The GSP operates as an autonomous instrument of the CCP with its main objective being to provide the means to facilitate industrial development in developing countries through tariff reductions on industrial goods. Before 1995, most of these products from GSP beneficiaries entered the EU market tariff free but under fixed and flexible quantitative restrictions. Textile products were only granted limited access through the separate arrangements of the MFA. The ECSC legislative framework has offered GSP concessions on iron and steel products to a small number of beneficiaries as it excludes Albania, South Africa and the ex-Soviet republics, while being only partially applicable to China. The constraints of the CAP, as well as the GSP's objective of industrial development, have meant that agricultural products from temperate zones are excluded from the scheme. However, a limited range of products has been eligible for tariff concessions (e.g. tropical products).

At negotiations held in 1977 at the Tokyo Round of GATT talks, the EU established the basis for special preferential treatment to be awarded to the least developed countries (LLDCs). Most nations in this category were already Lomé beneficiaries, but a significant catchment were not, namely Afghanistan, Bangladesh, Bhutan, Cambodia, Laos, the Maldives, Myanmar, Nepal and Yemen. Under the EU's GSP, the LLDCs receive CET exemptions on all industrial products and admission on a wider range of agricultural products at zero-CET rates. Nevertheless, safeguard measures which may still be applied to LLDC imports were judged appropriate.

While the usual strict conditions apply to EU imports regarding their rules of origin under the GSP scheme, certain derogations have been made aimed at encouraging successive processing between regional groups of beneficiaries. These 'regional cumulation' provisions are currently applied to ASEAN and Andean Pact countries with plans to extend the conditions to the CACM, the CIS and the Baltic States in the near future. Beneficiaries of the GSP can also expect to receive technical assistance from the EU aimed mainly at exploiting the opportunities afforded to them through the scheme.

The review and revisions

The 1995 review of the GSP introduced a set of radical changes and new provisions that was intended to underlie the EU's Uruguay Round commitments more fully to integrate the developing countries into the international trade system (CEC 1994h). There was also a shift away from the traditional annual system to a multi-annual system of making adjustments to the scheme. Certain adaptations to the GSP heralded by the 1995 review, for example the graduation scheme, were scheduled to be implemented over a subsequent three-year period. The review as a whole, though, inaugurated revisions to the old system that were to remain valid up to 2004. A summary of these revisions is given below:

Tariff modulation

The old fixed and flexible QRs on industrial products were replaced by preferential CET duty concessions granted according to their 'sensitivity' classification. Unlimited market access was also offered to GSP imports, although safeguard measures were still applicable under certain circumstances. These revisions meant that GSP imports were no longer eligible for automatic zero-CET rates, but attracted a modulated preferential duty (MPD) commensurate with the degree of sectoral sensitivity associated with the products in question. Four types of classification exist:

1 Very sensitive: an MPD equivalent to 85 per cent of the CET. Examples mainly include textiles and ferro-alloys.
2 Sensitive: a 70 per cent MPD rate. A wide range of products is covered, including chemicals, electronics, cars and footwear.
3 Semi-sensitive: a 35 per cent MPD rate. A similarly diverse range of products in less sensitive sectors than the above (e.g. jewellery, calculators, watches).
4 Non-sensitive: a zero MPD rate applied to products deemed not to possess any degree of sectoral sensitivity.

This sectoral approach to granting preferential trade terms under the GSP scheme represented a deviation from that which preceded whereby allowances were made according to the beneficiary's general level of competitiveness (see 'accentuated differentiation' below) or that found in some specific product groups. The 1995 review provisions thus apply the same tariff conditions to all GSP members without distinction, although the LLDCs and countries benefiting from special 'drugs' arrangements still receive exemptions.

The GSP's restructured tariff regime may appear to have penalised its beneficiaries by the imposition of MPDs on some goods that entered CET-free under the previous system. The use of 'sensitivity' classifications could also be perceived as counter-productive, given that those products attracting higher MPDs originate from industries that are spearheading the industrial development of the scheme's members. However, successive GATT rounds have negotiated down the tariff rates on industrial products to minimal levels, and thus the removal of quantitative restrictions on GSP imports into the EU has been more effective. Many GSP imports in 'sensitive' industry sectors have attracted separate tariff arrangements (e.g. textiles and the MFA) or other protectionist measures in the past, such as VERs on cars and electronics. Hence, the new regime is not so much a departure from the practices of the previous system, but rather a rationalisation of it.

Graduation from the GSP

Over the years, a number of GSP beneficiaries have acquired NIC status. The competitive advantages afforded to these countries through the GSP has caused some of the EU's domestic producers to argue for their removal from the scheme. The EU was also concerned with the competitive advantages held by the NICs over other GSP members in the EU and other key world markets. It was also found that the bulk of GSP imports were originating from a handful of highly competitive countries. The 'accentuated differentiation' provisions were thus introduced to the GSP under its 1986 review as a response to redress these perceived imbalances within the system. Consequently, the preferential terms afforded to the NICs were either withdrawn or reduced with the benefits redistributed to less competitive members.

We have already noted above that the new tariff modulation provisions appeared to have partly eradicated this internal discrimination between GSP members. However, in keeping to the accentuated differentiation's objectives, the 1995 review introduced a 'graduation' mechanism involving an evaluation of the industrial capacity on a sectoral basis to determine which beneficiary required GSP assistance to sustain satisfactory export levels. Where this was no longer deemed necessary, such assistance is to be withdrawn in accordance to specialisation and development indices criteria. Graduation from the GSP scheme on this sectoral basis follows two phases, with Phase 1 consisting of the preferential margin between the CET and MPD being halved and Phase 2 seeing this margin being eliminated altogether. The phased timing of GSP graduation corresponds to the GNP per capita levels of those beneficiaries that qualify. Those with a level above US$6,000 in 1991 were to enter Phase 1 in April 1995 and Phase 2 in January 1996, while those with a level under this amount were to enter the phases in January 1997 and January 1998 respectively. There are three broad exceptions to the new graduation mechanism:

- The eventual exclusion of the most advanced countries altogether by January 1998, thus taking GSP graduation beyond its basic 'sectoral' mechanism. These will include many of the East Asian NICs.
- The 'lion's share' clause in which the graduation mechanism will apply to those countries' exports which exceed 25 per cent of eligible products in their sector, despite the fact that the basic mechanism's criteria may not be met.
- The 'minimal share' clause grants exemption from the graduation mechanism to countries whose share of graduation sector exports does not exceed 2 per cent.

The overlapping between the conditions created by the old accentuated differentiation provisions and new graduation mechanism gave rise to potential anomalies within the GSP. The tariff modulation terms offered the more advanced beneficiaries a relatively favourable GSP regime, albeit for a short period during the graduation mechanism's transitional phase. To overcome this problem, products already excluded from the GSP under the dictates of accentuated differentiation remained so. The Commission also stated that safeguard measures would be deployed if necessary during the transitional period.

Special incentive arrangements

Perhaps the most radical new provisions introduced by the 1995 review to the GSP were the special incentive arrangements which built environmental and social dimensions into the scheme. This initiative was partly a response to recent International Labour Organisation (ILO) and International Tropical Timber Organisation (ITTO) conventions that called for the compliance of international trading activity to higher social and environmental standards and practices. The arrangements thus offered GSP members wider preferential tariff margins, up to an additional 25 per cent, if evidence of their adherence to these conventions could be shown and were due to commence from January 1998. The social incentive clause focuses on the GSP member's record on trade union freedom, collective bargaining rights and child labour, while the environmental incentive clause deals with sustainable tropical forest management issues.

These new provisions have been interpreted as either a cloaked form of protectionism or a genuine attempt to encourage more environmentally and socially acceptable trade-related practices on a global scale. The similar social clause built into the NAFTA agreement demonstrates that such arrangements should not be seen as an isolated trend. To many developing countries these measures represented a means in which further conditions could be levered into the GSP scheme in the future. Some GSP beneficiaries, such as Malaysia, have accused the incentive arrangements of improving the EU's competitive position at the ultimate expense of the growth and development of the scheme's members. However, the new provisions are of a 'positive reinforcement' nature, offering additional concessions to those already conferred, although a case could be argued that these have been introduced when the whole scheme has undergone a comprehensive overhaul and are thus disguised to this extent.

Additional outcomes of the review

Under the 1995 review, ECSC products were to be included in the GSP's industrial scheme for the first time, but those originally excluded from receiving previous concessions will continue to be so. The Latin American countries have received extra preferential treatment under the GSP to help facilitate the combating of drug trafficking. These conditions were extended for a further four years for industrial products and one year for agricultural products from 1995 onwards. Part of these provisions have involved efforts to diversify the export base of these countries away from drug crops, in particular coca. In addition to the GSP's regional cumulation rules of origin, the review introduced provisions on donor country content which allow intermediate products from EU producers to be considered as originating from the GSP beneficiary. This parallels similar provisions granted under Lomé IV for ACP countries and is aimed at fostering joint ventures and other forms of industrial co-operation between GSP beneficiaries and EU suppliers.

The EU's trade with developing countries: a general note

The management of the EU's hierarchy of preferential trade terms offered to developing nations through the Lomé Conventions and GSP scheme has been fraught with difficulties. We have already noted the assertions made by some member states for a more global approach to the EU's trade and development policy and criticism of the apparent incompatibilities between the two regimes that lie therein. Future political manoeuvrings inside the EU over this issue will determine whether or not Lomé-type conditions will be extended to GSP beneficiaries, with particular respect to EDF assistance.

Furthermore, maintaining internal non-discrimination within both regimes has been made laborious owing not only to the vicissitudes of international political relations but also the imbalances caused within the regimes' membership by the ascendancy of NICs. The latter is demonstrated by the fact that both the Lomé and GSP regimes are dominated by a handful of producers: in 1994 just ten of the seventy ACP states accounted for two-thirds of Lomé exports to the EU, while those countries that constitute the Chinese diaspora (China, Taiwan, Hong Kong and Singapore) made up over 50 per cent of the EU's imports from Asia (CEC 1995f). Meanwhile attempts made to meet other objectives, such as the encouragement of integration through the regional cumulation rules of origin, have been an additional source of the regimes' discrimination between participating developing nations. The overlapping of initiatives such as the Euro-Mediterranean Agreements, the EU's 'New Asia Strategy' and its regional agreements with Latin American countries and groupings (e.g. Mercosur) obviously add their own complications to this issue.

The operation of complex preferential trade arrangements has also been at odds with the multilateral apparatus of the GATT/WTO. Although the 1971 'enabling clause' and Articles XXXVI and XXXVII provide the means to bestow such terms on developing countries, some have argued that this two-tier system should be rationalised or removed altogether. These arguments are partly based on the notion that developing nations are in a more favourable position to contribute to the GATT/WTO's reciprocity process. An OECD study (OECD 1992b) suggested that only those developing countries that have emerged as successful exporters have benefited from preferential trade terms. The study further comments that a fuller participation of developing countries in the GATT/WTO framework and a rationalisation and liberalisation of their import regimes would create the conducive environment for their growth and development. While there is perhaps some validity in this first assertion, the second is certainly more open to dispute, although the present and future obligations of WTO membership may induce such a response.

Certainly, the EU's parallel support of developing nation exports in the form of investment aid, STABEX and other provisions found within the Lomé Conventions provides a model on which all trade relations with developing countries could be based. The funding and management of such an approach on a global scale would, though, prove a burden which the EU is not likely to want to bear unless shared by other Triad members.

EU–US TRADE RELATIONS

Introductory comments on the relationship

The Uruguay Round of GATT talks clearly revealed that the EU–US trade relationship has maintained its global strategic importance. The bipolar axis formed between the USA and Western Europe in post-war years has forged the underlying character of this trade relationship. This was initially founded on US attempts to assist the post-war European recovery and a progressive mutual 'interpenetration' of shared social, political and economic denominators (Smith 1993b). Similar cultural and political traditions, as well as the scale of Trans-Atlantic trade flows, have ensured that dialogue within the relationship has been both comprehensible and continuous. The 1990 Trans-Atlantic Declaration was an important step in formalising the channels for this dialogue by six-monthly ministerial consultations between the EU and USA. However, a prime reason for this initiative was an attempt to deal with the growing discord within the relationship that had arisen over issues such as the protection of 'sensitive' industries, market access, agricultural trade, public procurement and more strategic trade-related issues.

Both sides have shared similar global challenges. This was illustrated by the proximity of issues that the EU and USA pressed to be placed on the Uruguay Round agenda, such as tradable services, TRIPs and TRIMs. The Trans-Atlantic powers have also had to confront the new competitive threats posed by Japanese and NIC producers while seeking to acquire market access to their emerging markets. At the same time, EU–US trade relations have become increasingly strained owing to challenges that each pose to the other. For the USA, this has mainly involved market access and reciprocity problems related to the formation of the SEM. The EU, on the other hand, has been particularly concerned over the USA's drift towards unilateralism in the past decade or so. Smith and Woolcock (1993) comment that these and other domestic structural and political preoccupations had undermined their commitment to the multilateral process leading up to and during the Uruguay Round. Despite the regular threats that Trans-Atlantic trade frictions directed towards the whole GATT/WTO system at this time, both parties nevertheless succeeded in overcoming their differences and thus helped to secure the Round's completion. More recent EU–US talks may produce a broader framework in which trade relations will flourish in a more harmonious political environment, as we shall discuss later.

Sectoral issues

While sectoral flows of trade across the Atlantic have remained broadly symmetrical (Figure 6.2), disputes over sectoral issues have at times dominated Trans-Atlantic trade relations. These cover three main areas. The first concerns the shared predicament of how to manage the restructuring of similar industries in structural decline having lost their comparative advantage, particularly to the more advanced developing countries. Deployment of both offensive and defensive trade policy measures in attempts to protect or reinvigorate these industrial sectors have embroiled both powers in bitter exchanges. The respective importance of each other's market has meant that significant volumes of subsidised 'sensitive' industry exports have been targeted there. The adoption of strategies of this kind has been further vindicated by lost market share at home and abroad to NIC producers. This has been accompanied by the mutual application of countervailing tariff rates on similar subsidised export product groups.

The EU's 'social market' traditions as opposed to the USA's more 'free market' equivalent at least partly explain why the former has more frequently resorted to the subsidy option. Trade disputes over agricultural trade and policies have been especially protracted. Peterson (1993) has estimated that EU spending on agricultural subsidies has been around ten times greater than that directed to more competitive US farmers. The conflicts at the Uruguay Round over agriculture between the EU and USA nearly derailed the talks on this single issue. The Cairns Group, consisting of Australasia, Canada and other major agricultural producers, joined the USA in an attempt to isolate the EU into reforming the CAP. Subsequent negotiations between these parties resulted in the Blair House accord whereby the EU agreed to undertake certain reforms, thus sustaining the momentum of the Round. However, this and other sectoral based issues denied the Bush administration's 'fast track formula' initiative aimed at completing the Uruguay Round by March 1991.

The second area of dispute centres on more technology intensive sectors. The future strategic importance and high growth potential of these industries have motivated both the EU and USA to use trade and industry policy instruments as a means to develop competitive advantages against each other. This has been demonstrated over the EU's Airbus project where three-quarters of the development costs have been publicly funded. The US government and producers, such as Boeing and McDonnell Douglas, complained to the Commission over the unfair advantage granted to the Airbus consortium through this policy of subsidisation. The dispute was settled in

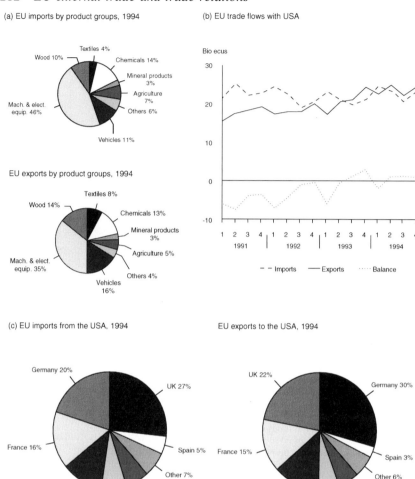

Figure 6.2 Trans-Atlantic patterns of trade
Source: Eurostat

1992 but Airbus continues to challenge Boeing's from its long held position as the world's largest civil aviation producer.

Third, Trans-Atlantic sectoral trade disputes have also focused on issues
of market access. The debate over market access and structural impediments is discussed in a fuller sense below. More specific sectoral matters
have involved respective access to service industry markets and public
procurement contracts. The forces of globalisation have stimulated the
growth of tradable services but the regulatory environment of each market
remains   bound   by   a   diverse   array   of   domestically   determined

arrangements. By design or fault, some of these arrangements award bias towards home firms. The SEM programme has sought to harmonise this regulatory environment between EU member states. Yet the USA and others have argued that this has been at the expense of third countries as the bias still lingers, with financial services held up as a prime example of where this is manifest. However, the EU has made similar accusations at the way in which US markets are structured at a national, regional as well as sub-regional level. Almost identical charges have been made on each other regarding limited market access to public procurement contracts. One of the most important successes achieved by the Uruguay Round was the Government Procurement Agreement with its stated objective of the joint opening up of public sector markets. This has been estimated to be worth around $103bn each to the EU and USA in reduced public procurement costs. Talks on similar arrangements on telecommunications, financial services and other sectors continue between both sides.

US unilateralism

One of the EU's main aims at the Uruguay Round was to neutralise the unilateralism that had recently come to characterise US trade policy. This had its roots in the gradual erosion of the USA's post-war trade surpluses from the 1970s onwards (see Table 6.1) and simultaneous disenchantment with the multilateral system of world trade. The penetration made by Japanese exporters into the US market seemed to expose particularly the weaknesses and diminishing comparative advantages of US industry in the face of foreign competition. Within influential political circles in the USA the mounting trade deficits with Japan, and others who had begun to make significant inroads into US markets, were perceived to be the result of unfair trade practices. A growing consensus on such views culminated in the 1974 Trade Act which included the Section 301 provisions for discretionary unilateral action to be taken by the executive arm of the US government against illicit commercial practices undertaken by US trade partners. Owing to continued congressional and industrial lobby pressures during the 1980s for a more results-based 'fair' trade policy, the 1988 Omnibus Trade and Competitiveness Act marked an even deeper relapse into an aggressive unilateralist policy position. Industrial policy measures also formed a constituent part of the Act to reinforce this position. The centrepiece of the 1988 Act was the introduction of the Super 301 policy instrument as part of Section 301's provisions, giving these provisions powers of specific reciprocity to be applied against offending countries. The failure of the offending country to retract its illicit commercial practices would entail measures aimed at denying access to US markets. The Super 301 provisions were targeted primarily at Japan and the East Asian 'tiger' economies, although EU oil seeds and telecommunications were also considered.

Peterson (1993) has suggested that this shift in US trade policy had entailed a move away from 'generalised' reciprocity, as embodied in GATT's multilateral rules and processes, to 'specific' reciprocity owing to circumstances which had caused a loss of faith in the former. In addition, the principles of 'fair' trade rather than those of free trade have provided the USA with the vindication and *modus operandi* on which these unilateral provisions are based. What constitutes unfair trade and what does not is, of course, highly subjective and ideally requires a multilateral forum to determine such cases. Furthermore, Sandholtz and Zysman (1989) have criticised the USA's notion of fair trade for being founded on balanced outcomes with regard to their own position rather than a balanced process of policy. However, the withdrawal of the Super 301 instrument in 1990 and the USA's role in the completion of the Uruguay Round did perhaps hint at a recovered faith in multilateralism. This being said, the reintroduction of Super 301 in 1994 by President Clinton, ironically in the same year in which the Uruguay Round was ratified, indicates that US trade policy continues to be at least partly based on the unilateralist option.

Market access and structural impediments

The unified nature and free market principles of the US economy have presented exporters with few structural impediments in acquiring market access. A structural impediment can be defined as a barrier to market access when there exists an absence of effective competition or transparency in that market. The SEM programme was principally designed to remove many structural impediments between EU member states, but also for third countries seeking an interest in a more unified European marketplace. While the introduction of some new statutory measures may have had an impeding effect, the GATT/WTO's multilateral rules and processes have had considerably more success in eradicating these measures. This partly explains why the USA has taken recourse to unilateralism in recent years. Most barriers to the US market were statutory regulations whose transparency has been easier to negotiate away within the GATT process compared to those of a more structural nature. The failure of multilateral negotiations to deliver parallel benefits for US exporters thus gave rise to results based unilateral actions and the preoccupation of the US Trade Representative Office (USTR) with market access issues (Woolcock 1991).

With respect to the EU, this has largely comprised of US fears of an introspective Fortress Europe being built by the SEM programme. The extension of the EU's regulatory sphere of influence, as illustrated by the EEA agreement and the CEE countries' adoption of some aspects of the *acquis communautaire*, has also roused interest among the US business community and policy-makers. While private sector links between both sides of the Atlantic are strong, the corporate response of US firms to the SEM has been dependent on sectoral background and more importantly whether a firm possesses an 'insider' or 'outsider' status regarding the European market. Those that could be categorised as 'insiders' were typically large firms which had adapted to the diverse conditions of the European market through well-established trade or investment activities. 'Outsiders' could be classified as usually small or medium-sized firms with no current direct interests in the EU market, but who sought to exploit the opportunities and minimise any potential threats engendered by the SEM.

Speeches given in 1988 by the then EU External Affairs Commissioner, Willy de Clerq, on EU expectations of reciprocity from third countries owing to the benefits European liberalisation would confer on them and a subsequent Commission document (CEC 1988b) were of particular concern to outsider firms. The reciprocity terms encoded within the SEM programme's Second Banking Co-ordination Directive (SBCD) that was introduced in December 1989 came to exemplify this apparent position then taken by the EU. The political impact of the SEM programme had not been fully considered by the Community at the time. At an address given at Boston University in May earlier that year, President Bush commented: 'We must work hard to ensure that the Europe of 1992 will adopt the lower barriers of the modern economy, not the high walls and the moats of medieval commerce.'

Endeavours were subsequently made to erase the Fortress Europe image conjured up by such statements. Smith (1993b) notes that over 20 US federal agencies were engaged in their own strategic analyses in response to the emergence of the potential Fortress Europe scenario, ranging from the State Department to the CIA. The results of the economic studies indicated, however, that further European integration would be generally beneficial for both insider and outsider US producers. This was mainly due to the removal of structural impediments to both trade and investment.

Leading up to 1992, there was a marked upsurge in the number of strategic alliances being formed between EU and US firms as 'outsiders' sought to acquire an 'insider' status. The USA also pressed for representation on the SEM programme's standards and certification discussions and on rules pertaining to public procurement contracts. Partial success in this area has consequently led to greater convergence in trading procedures and practices, but on wider issues such as developing the standard for High Definition Television (HDTV) the EU and USA remain as rivals.

The new Trans-Atlanticism and trade

As the 1990s have progressed, EU–US trade relations appear to have been increasingly shaped by wider geopolitical and global events. The thawing of the Cold War has meant that the economic dimension of the Trans-

Atlantic relationship has acquired new meaning and a relatively higher priority. Completion of the Uruguay Round and the subsequent establishment of the WTO have also had a significant influence on the emerging new framework within which these relations must now evolve. Although the New Trans-Atlantic Agenda (NTA) failed to include plans for a future free trade area (TAFTA), trade relations between the two powers will retain their global significance for some considerable time. Moreover, the NTA contained numerous provisions that aimed to reinforce existing EU–US commercial links and to seek a common understanding on meeting similar global economic challenges, in particular to ensure the future integrity of the WTO.

Whether the NTA heralds the start of a more benign era for Trans-Atlantic trade relations remains to be seen. Major difficulties still persist in a variety of 'sensitive' sectors, and these will ultimately defer the creation of TAFTA for as long as they do so. The USA's complete support for the WTO is likely to be conditional on its demonstrated ability to tackle market access and structural impediment issues. Pressures from similar sources within the USA to adopt a more circumspect view towards the EU, especially from Congress, could eventually prevail, and hence cause a relapse into the adversarial posturing that has characterised recent past relations. Thus, while the new Trans-Atlanticism has sought to provide the pretext for more harmonious trade relations between the EU and USA, many threats still lurk in familiar corners.

EU–JAPANESE TRADE RELATIONS

Evolving post-war trade relations

Trade issues have tended to dominate most aspects of the EU–Japan relationship. For both the EU and USA, coming to terms with this emergent economic superpower has primarily entailed a policy of reactionary measures to the intense competitive pressures exerted by Japanese producers on their domestic counterparts. Different cultural and social traditions have made it difficult for the formation of a broader relationship between the EU and Japan, and have meanwhile only served to create or pronounce the mutual misunderstandings over trade disputes.

In the early post-war years, European nations were wary of re-establishing trade links with Japan, not only on account of it being a former Axis power but also because of enduring memories of aggressive pre-war trade practices. These had taken the form of dumping textile products in European markets, regular breaches of intellectual property rights and a highly protected domestic market. The US reconstruction programme between 1945 and 1953 had given Japan the opportunity to re-enter the international community and its companies a base on which successful export-led growth strategies were pursued. The competitive threat emanating from

Japanese producers in key industrial sectors was recognised from a relatively early stage. In 1955, Japan secured GATT membership, but some European countries – the UK, France and Belgium – refused to grant it MFN status using Article 35 in exoneration.

The dynamic economic forces working within the Japanese economy continued to produce spectacular results as the 1950s and 1960s progressed. In 1958, Japan's commercial vehicle production stood at 138,000 units compared to the Community's 384,000 units. By 1968, Japanese producers were turning out an annual two million vehicles, over three times the Community's 634,000 figure. However, the rapid growth of the Japanese economy was not accompanied by an expanding market for foreign imports. In the same year the volume of Community exports to Spain was larger than those going to Japan, representing only 2.1 per cent of their total. By the early 1970s, the trade deficit with Japan began to gather momentum, almost tripling between 1969 and 1972. A noticeable aspect of these deficits was reflected in what Ishikawa (1990) refers to as the 'concentrated penetration' made by Japanese producers in certain industrial sectors, such as consumer electronics, cars, motorcycles, ships and steel. The imbalance within the trade relationship was acknowledged by both sides. As early as 1971, the Japanese Federation of Economic Organisations (the *Keidanren*) met with European business leaders to discuss the application of VERs and OMAs to Japanese imports. These measures were palatable to both sides as they gave Japanese business some voice and representation on European protectionist decisions and actions taken. By shortening their supply to European markets, the Japanese were also able to exact higher economic rents from European consumers. A year later, the first VER on Japanese consumer electronics imports was negotiated between some European countries and Japan.

Formalised trade agreement negotiations between the Commission and the Japanese government began in 1970. In the talks, the Commission resisted Japanese pressure to resolve the growing number of trade disputes that had arisen between them through GATT's mechanisms and procedures. Instead, it pressed for assurances from Japan that certain administrative NTBs and other structural impediments be removed. However, negotiations throughout the 1970s did very little to diffuse the tensions building up within trade relations. The Community's deficit with Japan continued to accelerate at a time when its trade balance with the rest of the world was mostly in surplus. European industry faced intensified competition from Japanese firms which led to a flourishing number of bilateral industry-to-industry restraint arrangements between them. By the end of the decade, the Japanese trade surplus with the Community had become a serious political issue. Mounting tension between them culminated in the infamous 1979 Commission working paper which talked of Japan as 'only recently emerging from a feudal past' and as 'a country of workaholics who lived in what Westerners would regard as little better than rabbit hutches'.

Over a decade earlier, President de Gaulle had dismissed Japan's prime minister as being a 'travelling transistor salesman'. Such comments were obviously of great detriment to the relationship.

Desperate talk was matched by desperate actions in some European countries. A high profile example of the latter concerned the French government's decision to route all imported video cassette recorders through a tiny customs office at Poitiers staffed by only eight people. Consequently, a mere 8,000 imports were processed per month instead of the projected 75,000 to 100,000 as estimated by importers, most of which were Japanese. While criticism from both inside and outside the Community forced France to withdraw this system after a few months, the incident demonstrated the willingness of some European authorities to resort to extreme and unorthodox protectionist measures against Japanese imports. This development more than any other had the additional effects of highlighting the uncommon nature of the CCP and the dissonance between the opinions of Community member states over trade policy in general.

From the mid-1980s onwards a number of factors led to more cordial trade relations between the EC and Japan. The end of the world recession of the early 1980s generally helped ease international relations between the developed nations. A further framework for dialogue and policy co-ordination was established within the Plaza Accord agreement signed at the historic G7 meeting in 1985, where Japan agreed to revalue the yen in an attempt to depress trade surpluses held against both its Triad partners. A third factor comprised of more convincing efforts made by Japan to open up its own markets to imports. In 1985, an Action Programme was launched with this specific objective, one of the measures being the introduction of more competitive tendering for public procurement contracts which sought to engage foreign firms. The UK firm Cable and Wireless was successful in securing an important contract to upgrade Japan's international telecommunications network partly as a result of the initiative.

As a further indication of more harmonious Community–Japanese trade relations, the number of nationally imposed quantitative restrictions on Japanese imports had fallen from 466 in 1962 to 131 in 1988. A further forty-two were removed a year later in negotiations by the Commission as a response to engender a more open trade environment between them. Around this time, the Community's trade deficit with Japan began to stabilise and in 1988 exports to Japan actually increased almost 50 per cent faster than Japanese exports to Community markets. In preparations made for the SEM programme, the Commission announced its intentions to substitute national level QRs with Community-based measures but that 'these measures would not result in a higher level of protection than exists at present' (CEC 1988c). A similar arrangement was made for VERs on Japanese car imports whereby bilateral measures that had been separately applied by five member states were replaced with a Community-level equivalent. In the agreement, these imports were limited to 11 per cent of the EC market in 1993 with annual negotiations on further volumes set to take place up to 1999 when all restrictions on them will be removed. These decisions were a signal to Japan that while a more rationalised CCP would result from the SEM programme the same problems that had dominated trade disputes between them would be met by already established actions.

One reason why Japanese export growth to the Community appeared to slow down was due to the rapid acceleration of Japanese FDI into Europe. This acted to displace certain export activities from the home country. However, the arrival of Japanese multinationals on Community soil gave rise to various concerns. Some saw the strategy as a means to circumvent protectionist measures imposed upon them by installing low value-added 'screwdriver' assembly plants within the European market. The first 'screwdriver' regulations were introduced by the Commission in 1987 which enabled ADDs to be deployed on foreign imports now produced in the Community that once attracted ADDs previously. Related and associated products could also be targeted for similar treatment in accordance with stated criteria. Local content rules applied the same measures against lower value-added foreign assembly plants. Under the general rules of this regulation, foreign assembly plants were obliged to acquire at least 40 per cent of their materials and components from domestic European sources. Previous investigations had revealed that the effective local content found in some Japanese assembly plants varied from 4 per cent to 25 per cent, and in one case the only local material used was the packaging for electronic typewriters (Kaikati 1990).

The regulations were first invoked in July 1987 against Japanese ball-bearing producers. The Commission had even imposed a 20 per cent ADD on Ricoh photocopiers assembled in the USA on account of their low local content which thus categorised them as Japanese products. When a string of other cases followed, Japan made a formal complaint to GATT on account that they contravened the 'national treatment' principle of Article III. Furthermore, the Commission had failed to follow the Anti-Dumping Code procedures as laid out in Article VI. Additional arguments put forward regarding the difficulties Japanese producers had faced in acquiring intermediate products locally and of a suitable quality were proposed by both the Japanese government and the *Keidanren*. In March 1990, a GATT panel upheld Japan's complaint and the Commission had to adjust its policies accordingly.

Japanese firms have shared similar concerns to their US counterparts over market access issues and the SEM programme whose associated directives in banking (e.g. the SBCD), capital movements and public procurement were accused of seeking reciprocity in third markets. At the European Council meeting at Rhodes in 1988 this reciprocity was defined as one being based on a 'balance of mutual advantages'. Put alternatively, guarantees of similar or at least non-discriminatory opportunities for firms from the Community to operate in those markets on the same basis as local firms would be sought. Thus, the Commission was in a sense appealing to GATT's 'national treatment' principle in playing the SEM card.

For both the Community and Japan, the tradable services had become an increasingly important issue. Japan's financial sector firms had spearheaded the surge in Japanese FDI flows into Europe during the 1980s, representing around 80 per cent of the total. The Commission thus sought to argue the reciprocity case for Community firms in return for the advantages that a harmonised European marketplace offered these Japanese firms. Motives for seeking such access lay largely in the perception of Japan's own market as being highly insulated from foreign competition.

Although the CCP still wields a variety of protectionist measures against Japanese imports, the EU has generally accepted that in order to compete against Japan it must do so more on its terms. This has involved the adoption of Japanese production and management methods as well as competitive strategies more in tune with global realities. The focus of current EU–Japanese trade relations has shifted more towards removing structural impediments to mutual trade. The persistent trade surpluses still maintained by Japan against the EU have meant that this has been concentrated primarily on Japanese markets. We shall now examine this issue and how a firmer trade relationship has developed in more recent years.

Towards a firmer relationship?

The EC–Japan Declaration signed in July 1991 marked an important step forward in fostering closer bilateral relations and understanding between the two world powers, not only in economic matters but also political and cultural ones. In wider global terms it was also seen as a means to redress the skewed imbalance within the Triad frame of relationships. However, trade issues dominated both the tone of the agreement and its outcomes. The Community was keen to emphasise the 'equitable access' aspect of the Declaration with its objective of seeking to eradicate any structural impediments to trade. While the Community disapproved of the USA's Structural Impediments Initiative (SII) of 1989–90 which had compelled Japan into prising open some of its more closed markets, it nevertheless agreed with its broad aims. However, the Community did not have the equivalent commercial policy instruments or the political leverage to achieve the same (Bridges 1992). Thus, the Declaration provided some foundation on which at least the latter could be exploited by the EU in the future.

The structural impediments issue had first been raised by the Community as far back as 1969, when it then chose to refer to the problem as Japan's 'low import propensity'. By the 1980s the predicament was described as one arising from 'the protracted and unpredictable technical certification and registration procedures and above all the habits and attitudes bred of Japan's vertically and horizontally integrated industrial, commercial and financial groups' (CEC 1985b). When Japan entered the Uruguay Round its tariffs on industrial goods were among the lowest of any country. Yet, its trading partners stated that specific structural features of the Japanese economy provided more effective barriers to trade. These have included:

- the *keiretsu* business groups whose interlocking corporate relationships have had the supposed effect of excluding foreign competition;
- the lack of independent dealership networks and an underdeveloped retail sector;
- a particularly idiosyncratic trade financing system and business associations which have influential government involvement;
- a convoluted system of multiple layers of wholesalers which have advantaged domestic producers at the expense of foreign rivals.

In its defence, Japan has stressed that structural impediments to its imported trade are only part of the problem and that equal blame should be attached to the deficient entrepreneurism of European firms. A supporting argument was developed by El-Agraa (1992) who inculpated European business and bureaucrats of holding superannuated notions about the Japanese economy and society as a whole. Moreover, Saxonhouse (1983) goes so far as to say that these features simply represent Japan's distinctive trading structure in comparison with those found in Europe and the USA and that abnormalities in Japanese trade and industrial practices do not exist.

Recourse to more positive actions taken by some member states has entailed export promotion schemes, such as the UK's 'Priority Japan' and France's 'Le Japon: C'est Possible' campaigns in the early 1990s. The EU's own 'Gateway to Japan' export promotion campaign was launched in 1994. However, while Japanese demand for luxury imports from the EU remains strong, Japan has criticised its producers for their lack of endeavour to diversify into other markets. In their defence, the Commission has stated that the lack of consumption led growth in Japan in the past has been a further source of frustration for EU exporters. Since the Declaration, Japan has commenced certain initiatives aimed at removing identifiable structural impediments to improve market access to EU imports.

- A government action plan and administration procedure laws were introduced in 1993 to add transparency and rationalise the regulatory environment encountered by EU firms in Japan.
- The profile of the Fair Trade Commission, Japan's main competition policy agency, has been enhanced by boosted resources and a remit to take a more strict interpretation of the Anti-Monopoly Act.
- Japan's financial services sector has been deregulated and reformed. Procedural improvements have been made, especially to the insurance sector, to allow foreign firms to compete more effectively.
- Larger scale retail stores laws have given greater operational flexibility for larger retail outlets. This has been of particular benefit to the more

sophisticated Western retailers who require large store space (e.g. super-markets).

Although these reforms to remove Japan's structural impediments have been welcomed by the EU and USA, their scope and the lack of speed with which they have been embraced have been criticised. However, Ishikawa (1990) argues that considerable efforts are required to deconstruct the social and economic infrastructure and networks. Moreover, the Japanese tradition for consensus decision-making and the number of affected groups involved in these processes helps to explain the apparent procrastination here.

Future EU–Japanese trade relations

Trade relations between the EU and Japan are likely to be determined by a similar set of issues that have shaped them in the past, namely the impact of European integration, structural impediments in the Japanese economy and relative positions of competitiveness. Woolcock and Yamane (1993) have contended that the discord found within EU–Japanese trade relations mainly originates from different perceptions over the fundamental 'rules of the game'. They state that the EU's perception continues to be based on equivalent competitive opportunities for both European and Japanese firms whereby bilateral protectionist measures are applied in those sectors possessing an imbalance against them. As Figure 6.3 illustratively confirms, this has most frequently arisen in machinery and electrical products as well as transport equipment imports from Japan.

Owing to key competitive advantages recently developed by Japan, its perceptions are founded on the appropriate use of the GATT/WTO mechanisms in solving trade disputes. It has also stressed that more effective corporate strategies must be developed by European companies if they are to compete in Japanese markets. However, inconsistencies with respect to the Japanese position are apparent in sectors such as chemicals and plastics where European firms hold the competitive advantage. Thus, Woolcock and Yamane conclude that competitiveness, rather than structural impediments still represents the main contributant to present and future EU–Japanese trade tensions.

Whatever view one adheres to, the EU can still be expected to regard trade relations with Japan as a top policy priority in its international economic affairs. The emergence of a more formalised Pacific economic community in the twenty-first century will reinforce this, largely due to the pivotal role played by Japan in the region. An equal-treatment agreement signed in 1994, which aims to ensure national treatment for EU goods in Japan, has been particularly crucial considering the advantages that have been gained by US firms through a series of similar bilateral arrangements. Up to now, these have been at the expense of their European rivals, as

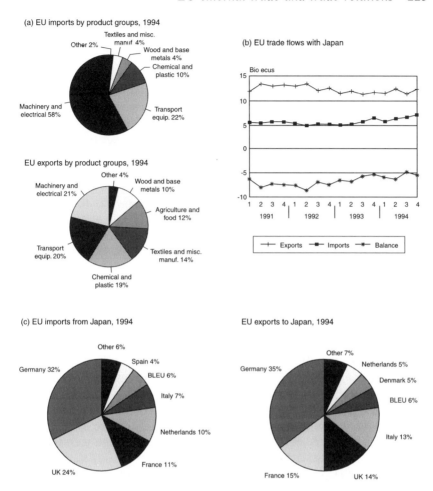

Figure 6.3 EU–Japanese patterns of trade
Source: Eurostat

demonstrated by Europe's falling market share in the Japanese auto components sector from 40 per cent to 22 per cent, as opposed to an increase in the USA's share from 25 per cent to 40 per cent (*Financial Times*, 9 September 1995). The announcement by the Japanese government in March 1995 that it was to introduce plans for a wide-ranging five-year deregulation programme was also warmly welcomed by the EU. With such concessions made by Japan, the initiative lies more firmly on European business to exploit the new opportunities that are, albeit slowly, presented to them.

CONCLUDING REMARKS

The post-war growth of international trade has led to the EU's trade relations playing an increasingly major role in determining Europe's position in the world economy. We have seen in this chapter how the CCP – which primarily orientates these relations – has had to adapt to various internal and external pressures over that time. Considerable tensions have surfaced in trade with its Triad rivals, some of which have been depressurised while others still persist. Another notable aspect of Triadic trade relations has been the necessity to establish clearer trade rules, and hence help to set the parameters for the competition environment in which they all must play. For both the EU and USA, this has also entailed attempts to negotiate for removal of the structural impediments that hinder 'fairer' trade in Japan's domestic market, for right or for wrong motives.

The main pressure on the EU with respect to the developing and 'transition' countries has naturally been to widen their access to the single market. Many have acquired such concessionary terms, especially those states that are signatories to EU Association and Co-operation Agreements or the Lomé Convention. However, there have been calls from both within and outside the EU to rationalise the CCP by delayering the pyramidal structure of preferential treatments so as to present a more global trade policy towards the developing economies. This will prove difficult as many EU member states still retain strong bilateral links with ex-colonial countries in particular. Having said this, the Lomé Convention could be terminated when Lomé IV expires in the year 2000.

Our analysis in this chapter also revealed that Europe must concentrate its efforts in those industrial sectors and markets where future growth potential is most apparent. This principally refers to high-tech industries and the dynamic East Asian economy. Chapter 5 has already stated the case for the latter. In Chapter 9, we shall examine Europe's position with respect to technology, innovation and trade in further detail.

7 Internationalisation and globalisation

Mr Jensen: You get up on your little 21-inch screen and howl about America and democracy. There is no America. There is no democracy. There is only IBM, ITT, AT&T, Dupont, Dow, Union Carbide and Exxon. Those are the nations of the world today. . . . The world is a college of corporations, inexorably determined by the inimitable bylaws of business. The world is a business, Mr Beale . . . and our children will live to see that perfect world in which there is no war or famine or brutality, one vast and ecumenical holding company for who all men will work to serve a common profit, in which all men will hold a share of stock, all necessities provided, all anxieties tranquillised, all boredom amused. And I have chosen you, Mr Beale, to preach this evangel.
Mr Beale: Why me?
Mr Jensen: Because you are on television, dummy!

(From the film *Network* 1976)

The scenario framed by this quotation reveals a world economy dominated by debatably benign multinational enterprises (MNEs) that operate in accordance with their own divisional demarcations while transcending the seemingly redundant frontiers drawn up by nation-states. The logical conclusion that is inferred above is just one of many interpretations of what is meant by 'globalisation'. Notions surrounding this term are still rather subjective, ill-defined or somewhat vague. This is not surprising as it encompasses a complex array of dynamic, interacting forces whose own parameters are not easy to establish.

For the sake of clarity, though, let us begin with definitions that have been put forward by Dicken (1992: 1) who describes 'internationalisation' as 'the increasing geographical dispersion of economic activities across national borders' and 'globalisation' as 'a more advanced form of internationalisation which implies a degree of functional integration between internationally dispersed economic activities'. According to Grant (1992: 1) economic globalisation can be referred to as 'a process in which transactions across the borders of nation-states increase in importance relative to those within nation-states; and whereby national boundaries cease to be a significant impediment to the movement of goods or services'. Thus, globalisation extends well beyond the act of exporting products – the oldest form of internationalisation – and marks the advent of a new phase of business activity that has the following characteristics:

- The accelerated growth of foreign direct investment (FDI) in post-war years, but most notably in very recent years.
- The role played by MNEs in world trade and the corresponding rise in intra-firm trade. This has involved the growing use of international 'sourcing' of intermediate inputs produced in one location which are then exported for final production elsewhere.
- Highly concentrated international supply structures which have emerged as a resultant mix of global restructuring, cross-border mergers and acquisitions and the formation of international strategic alliances.

The deepening of internationalisation and globalisation activities make a contextualised 'European' study of these processes rather arduous as continental borders have arguably become just as dissolvable as national ones. Moreover, by its very nature globalisation means that it is some-times difficult to distinguish the corporate identity of firms and their business practices. The European economy has spawned indigenous com-panies that conduct most of their operations in other global regions. It has also nurtured a vast array of foreign subsidiary companies, with some having been active in Europe for at least a century. Thus, the aim of this chapter is to introduce an historical and theoretical context to both internationalisation and globalisation – adding a European perspective where possible and appropriate – and hence providing useful points of reference for themes covered in other chapters. Chapter 8 will, however, be devoted to examining how both inward and outward flows of FDI – the most dynamic aspect of globalisation – have affected the European economy.

In this chapter, we shall first investigate the historical background to internationalisation and globalisation by analysing the evolution of inter-national competition. An overview of the theories on international produc-tion and global competition will be made followed by a discussion on the future prospects for globalisation. In conclusion, the role of the nation-state will be examined in closer detail with respect to a globalised world economy.

THE EVOLUTION OF INTERNATIONAL COMPETITION

The first preconditions

International trading activity has ancient historical roots. However, the rise of the European maritime nations from the late fifteenth century onwards – England, Spain, Holland, Portugal, France – spurred a great expansion of trading activity on a substantially wider world scale. Mercantilist trading companies, such as the East India Company and the Hudson Bay Company, gradually opened up a growing network of overseas markets. The advent of European imperialism was partially determined by the development of commercial interests overseas. The new technological possibilities attributable to industrialisation and its appetite for natural resources further extended and deepened patterns of international trade and competition, accelerating the pace of market expansion that had already begun in the late eighteenth century.

The introduction of new production techniques, mass production machinery, the harnessing of new sources of energy and the development of key technologies in communications (e.g. the telegraph) enabled the first multinational companies strategically to position themselves across national borders by the end of the nineteenth century. As Chandler (1986: 405–6) states, 'changing technologies and expanded markets enhanced the advantages of managerial co-ordination and at the same time intensified competition between such managerial enterprises. As the technologies of production and distribution and the markets for products became more homogeneous, such competition forced multinationals to acquire a broader, more global perspective.' This helped to produce the self-contained, multi-unit, multifunctional companies that were bound together by multi-level hierarchical structures around the time of the 1850s and 1860s.

By the 1880s and 1890s, many of these firms had become vertically integrated – mainly in a forward sense to meet immediate marketing and distribution objectives – and were primarily concentrated in high volume production industries. Foreign direct investment (FDI), which may be defined as the transfer of a firm's resources into a foreign business venture with the objective of acquiring control of the venture (Meyer 1994), at first evolved within this category of industries. Empire provided the market framework for many of these firms up to the mid-twentieth century, both as supply sources and end destinations for processed goods. Imperialism was also initially responsible for the internationalisation of capital as empire builders sought to protect and support their colonial markets, infrastructure projects and trade servicing facilities being principal examples.

This development in many ways prefigured the rise of FDI itself, serving the conditions in which companies could confidently expand their own interests into other nations. Foreign portfolio investment (FPI) – which can be differentiated from FDI on account of originating agents not seeking to acquire control but simply some degree of ownership (the OECD use a 10 per cent equity stake benchmark for this) – has its origins in this export of capital, and was up to the early post-war years the most prevalent form of foreign investment.

The early twentieth century

By 1914, European and particularly British companies were at the forefront of establishing production and service facilities overseas. Table 7.1 shows that the UK could claim 45.5 per cent of total world cumulative FDI outflows just before World War I, and a combined Europe 77.1 per cent. The UK's preponderance reflected the extent of her empire and the reach of both the City of London's financial institutions and emerging multinationalised companies. The majority of European outflows were supporting resource-intensive industrial activities based in colonial countries. The mono-structure of the countries' economies, which still persists today, is a direct legacy of this imperial division of labour and specialisation. For example, Zambia's exports of copper currently make up 98 per cent of its total exports and for Uganda coffee exports make up 95 per cent of its total (Oxfam 1993).

Before 1914 most US outward investment lay in Canada, but a number of American manufacturing companies had begun to venture across the Atlantic at the turn of the century. The UK was the primary Trans-Atlantic location sought by US firms who established a notable presence in agricultural machinery, sewing machines and armaments. Pre-war, intra-European FDI was similarly technology intensive.

The inter-war years

The general collapse of confidence in the world economy during the interwar period did not hamper the continued growth of MNEs, and indeed provided some of the conditions which gave provocation for their activities. This stimulus took the form of a more urgent need to protect existing

Table 7.1 Percentage shares of total world cumulative FDI outflows, 1914–71

	1914	*1938*	*1960*	*1971*
UK	45.5	39.8	16.2	13.8
Germany	10.5	1.3	1.2	4.2
France	12.2	9.5	6.1	4.2
Belgium			1.9	1.4
Italy			1.6	1.7
Netherlands	8.9[a]	13.3[a]	10.5	8.0
Sweden			0.6	1.4
Switzerland			3.0	5.5
Australasia/South Africa	1.3	1.1	2.2	1.4
Japan	0.1	2.8	0.7	4.4
USA	18.5	27.7	49.2	48.1
Other	3.0	4.5	6.8	5.9

Sources: Dunning 1983; OECD 1989a
[a] Combined figure for Belgium, Italy, Netherlands, Sweden and Switzerland

overseas markets and penetrate new ones. The hiking up of tariff rates gave further motive for FDI intended to circumvent protectionist measures. As Porter (1986a) noted, MNEs evolved more into a 'federation of autonomous subsidiaries' as a consequence of the inter-war business environment.

The period is also marked by the advance of US firms into world markets which was to some extent made possible by the contraction of multinational activity by many European firms. This can be clearly observed in Table 7.1 where the USA's share of cumulative FDI rose from 18.5 per cent in 1914 to 27.7 per cent by 1938, whereas the European nations' share had fallen to 63.9 per cent. During this period, the competitive edge enjoyed by many American companies over their European rivals was becoming increasingly apparent across an ever broader range of industries. This was largely owing to superior development and application of new technologies, management and production methods. The size of the home market and rising prosperity levels also enabled American firms to exploit scale economies to greater effect while serving as a test-bed for new product developments. An anti-trust policy geared towards penalising monopoly, but not oligopoly, gave US multinationals additional advantages over European counterparts who were constrained by extensive cartelisation and the subsequent loss of competitive dynamism that this implied. Chandler (1986: 433) comments that for European firms, 'market power was achieved and maintained in the domestic market far more by contractual co-operation than through functional and strategic efficiencies'. However, contractual co-operation proved difficult to sustain, especially as international competition became increasingly characterised by the American oligopoly model rather than the European pattern of collusive monopoly.

The dominance of US multinationals particularly lay in the production and distribution of consumer goods and light industrial machinery. British MNEs retained world leadership in a variety of consumer branded goods, while German multinational strength was to be found in technologically advanced chemicals and machinery. Table 7.1 indicates the minor but growing role played by Japanese MNEs at this time, accounting for only 0.1 per cent of cumulative FDI in 1914 but 2.8 per cent by 1938.

International competition in the inter-war period can also be understood in terms of how well firms adapted to cost advantages of scale and the pace of technological change. Scale economies encouraged the centralisation of some industries and decentralisation in others, the latter being compounded by the rising tide of protectionism that sought to fragment MNEs' organisational structure and narrow the scope for rationalisation gains. Europe's fall in its share of cumulative FDI was partly due to this relative loss of competitiveness, but perhaps more importantly to fragile intra-European relations and idiosyncratic political developments in certain countries in the 1920s and 1930s. As part of its war reparations, German MNEs had many of their overseas manufacturing and servicing facilities and other international capital confiscated. This and the subsequent discouragement of German foreign investment is illustrated by the slump of its cumulative FDI share from 10.5 per cent to 1.3 per cent over the period, accounting for nearly three-quarters of the decline in Europe's share.

The post-war period

Unprecedented trade and investment growth ensued out of the post-war reconstruction process driven largely by the ideals of a *Pax Americana* and by a group of international consensus building institutions that had their origins in the 1944 Bretton Woods agreement, namely the IMF, IBRD and GATT. The improved state of equilibrium reversed some of the trends of the inter-war period, such as the need to operate a series of country centred strategies owing to the highly charged environment of protectionism.

However, other trends persisted. The dominance of USA firms in international competition grew into the vacuum that a devastated European economy in particular had left behind. American MNEs were given a principal role in the reconstruction process. By 1960, the US had come to account for 49.2 per cent of total world FDI outflows, over three times greater than the UK, the next largest country investor at 16.2 per cent. Between 1950 and 1967 the number of foreign manufacturing subsidiaries under US control more than trebled from 988 to 3,646. Foreign investment from US multinationals almost trebled from $29.7bn in 1959 to $110.2bn in 1974.

The large encampment of US firms in Europe, and to a lesser extent in Japan, partly led to an increased diffusion of American technology to the other Triad regions. Consequently, the USA's lead in industries where it had been dominant for so long – automobiles, light industrial machinery, domestic appliances – gradually eroded. The rise of newly emergent Japanese multinationals was to some extent built on their ability to absorb and exploit commercially these technologies to greater effect, simultaneously deepening their home market as a platform for this development. A diffusion of American corporate administrative and financial control systems, which were generally considered superior to others at the time, also occurred for similar reasons. The subsequent weakening of US export performance led to a weakened US dollar that was not allowed to depreciate due to commitments to the Bretton Woods exchange rate system. This further stimulated outward FDI from US firms who were offered relatively cheap dollar purchases of foreign – especially European – assets and in some cases a more cost effective export production base.

The new technological developments of the post-war period had a greater impact on international competition than those preceding it. Advances in communication and transport technologies made vital contributions by extending the range of international business operations. By

1965 the first commercial satellite was placed in orbit. The rise of accumulative civil aviation passenger miles from 26 million in 1960 to 152 billion by 1974 gives some indication of how 'space shrinking' technologies were being exploited. While these improvements enabled firms to benefit by shifting production from relatively high-cost to low-cost production locations, they would only embark on such a strategy if the geographical distances involved did not impose higher net costs and effective organisational co-ordination could still be maintained.

The micro-chip revolution, that had its origins in the first commercial application of the computer in the late 1950s, provided the basis for a new 'Kondratiev wave' of technologies from which emerged a vast array of industries. The application of micro-chip technologies to almost all other existing industries allowed more flexible and efficient production and service techniques to be developed. For example, Porter (1986b) observed that the minimum efficiency scale levels in auto assembly plants roughly tripled between 1960 and 1975. Moreover, firms could now produce multi-models for a single country instead of or as well as single models for multi-country markets (Doz 1980).

The period has also been characterised by a series of inter-related trends that has emerged in international trade, production and investment. First, export growth rates have consistently outpaced output growth, but foreign investment flows have accelerated fastest of all. The rise of the East Asian economy to establish a firmer tripolar core structure within the world economy and the significant shift of manufacturing activity to the region largely based on export-orientated production has already been documented in Chapter 5. Intra-firm trade has risen sharply as a general consequence of increasing multinational activity and has helped to found a firmer basis for the relationship between trade and investment. The scope of this relationship has also been broadened by the use of FDI as a means of advancing the paramount objectives of exporting strategies and has particularly applied to initial phases of Japanese FDI outflows to the West. The expansion of tradable services is another notable development that has been facilitated primarily by the further expansion of internationalised capital, considerable improvements in communicative technologies and a variety of deregulatory factors recently undertaken by national governments.

During the 1980s and early 1990s, FPI has made a marked comeback within international transactions flows rising above FDI's comparable 2 per cent of the world total in 1980 to a 6 per cent share by 1992, equivalent to twice that of FDI in the same year (see Figure 7.1). In absolute terms, FPI flows experienced an over elevenfold increase between 1980 and 1992, from $30bn to $340bn, placing the total stock of world FPI at $1,700bn at the end of the period, thus overtaking total FDI which had accumulated at $1,650bn. This development, tied to the expansion of FDI, generated higher international flows of investment income, enlarging its own share

(a)   OECD total: International transactions, growth trends, 1980-92*

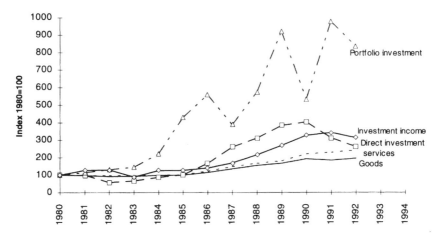

* Annual averages for exports and imports, not excluding intra-OECD flows

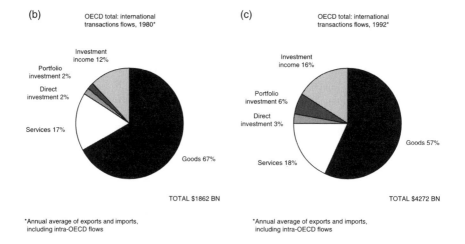

Figure 7.1 OECD international transactions, growth trends and flows, 1980–92
Source: CEC 1994i

from 12 per cent to 16 per cent of the total over the period. The rising FPI trend indicates how firms have sought to pursue defensive and offensive competitive strategies through internationalised equity holdings that offer the opportunity for diversified sources of profit, a wider spread of risk and the forming of cross-border collaborative ventures.

Foreign investment had become increasingly concentrated in developed market economies up to the 1980s, although developing countries have increasingly played host to inward FDI at the expense of OECD countries (see Figures 8.2, 8.3, 8.4 on pages 266–8). Nevertheless, the vast majority of outward FDI is still accounted for by the latter. A concomitant shift towards more technology intensive FDI activity has occurred, driven by rising convergent incomes in Western countries and the mass-produced consumer goods industries that have thrived as a consequence. A related outcome of this has been the growth of global standard products targeted at reaching the identifiable market segments that have emerged in recent years. But Caves (1971) has also observed that more sophisticated forms of market strategies based on product differentiation have driven both intra-industry trade and FDI from the need more accurately to discern nuances in consumer tastes in localised market segments. Industrial restructuring has also been increasingly achieved through FDI in response to the rapidly changing conditions of global competition.

Another important trend concerns how firms have sought to engage in creative exchanges with others in response to global competitive forces. These international strategic alliances have been founded on the perception that synergetically generated and mutually shared benefits of improved market penetration, higher volume production and technological advantages are more attainable by joint actions of this kind (see Box 7.2). Such collaborations may or may not involve cross-equity holding arrangements lasting for a specified time period and have become especially prevalent in high-tech industries where the characteristics of heavy entry and product development costs, scale economies, rapid technological change and high associated risks make collaboration an attractive option.

International subcontracting has also emerged as another network relationship to have gained more prominence in recent years owing to similar competitive pressures and the enabling role played by technology. Dynamic networks, or flexible integrated organisational forms, have evolved as a hybrid of both international strategic alliances and international subcontracting. These are based on a company acting as a broker between a series of co-ordinated producers, designers, distributors, suppliers and other agents in the business value chain. The company may employ only a small core workforce whose prime task is to orchestrate the network of corporate relationships. While FDI has made it more difficult to determine the extent and boundaries of competition between nations, the proliferation of these different forms of inter-firm co-operative arrangements further complicate the issue by obscuring the exact borders between competing firms.

Box 7.1 The multinational enterprise (MNE)

A multinational enterprise (MNE) can be defined as one which owns and controls production or service facilities in two or more countries. Its operations are usually vertically integrated to some degree with intra-firm exchanges of intermediate products taking place on a regular and extensive cross-border basis. According to a United Nations report (UN 1993), they have surpassed international trade flows as the most important single source of international economic exchange on account of the FDI and intra-firm trade they generate. The term 'transnational' is preferred by some as 'multinational' infers that the organisation's presence is spread over many countries. The debate is further perplexed by those who hold that a true transnational corporation is defined by its faded home nation identity and the implications this carries for its conduct. Most of the world's current 37,000 MNEs are relatively small. In 1988, the United Nation Centre on Transnational Corporations (UNCTC) calculated that the largest 74 MNEs accounted for around half the sales of the top 600. For the majority of MNEs their home nation identity holds a large degree of significance with top executive posts and core activities (e.g. R&D, marketing) originating there (see Figure 7.2). With these points considered, the term 'multinational' will be adopted for our analysis except where a transnational distinction is necessary.

The opening quotation to this chapter hints at the status that MNEs have acquired in contemporary times. The notion of MNEs usurping the nation-state as the prime economic unit for studying the world economy is a potent one, carrying with it issues regarding the distribution and control of economic power, how the world economy is structured and organised and the political dimension to these changes.

Multinationals are the main source of new technological developments and other innovative activities and are thus key engines of economic growth for the world economy. Of the world's largest 100 economic entities, half are MNEs and half are countries. It has been estimated that the top 500 MNEs are responsible for around 50 per cent of world GNP and about 70 per cent of world trade and investment. In addition, intra-firm trade between the world's largest 350 MNEs is thought to constitute at least 40 per cent of total world trade (OECD 1992c). The top fifty MNEs are listed in Table 7.2.

The conflicts of interest that have arisen between MNEs and countries are well documented. During the 1960s and 1970s, the debate over the rise of multinational power intensified as some nation-states began to recognise the threat posed to their national autonomy. The dislocation of economic policy, adverse cultural effects, industrial dominance and technological dependence were the main concerns expressed regarding the negative impact of multinational activity.

However, in the neo-liberal political climate of the 1980s, an increasing number of governments adopted a different policy stance towards MNEs and FDI as the perceived effects of playing host to foreign investors became more favourable. These included new capital formation, technology and skills transfer, regional and sectoral development and improved internal

Box 7.1 *continued*

competition, entrepreneurship, export potential and employment creation. A 1994 OECD report concluded that FDI has a significant net benefit effect on employment, productivity, research, technological transfer and trade in the host country (OECD 1994b). Foreign MNEs generally paid higher wages compared to their indigenous rivals, but R&D activity was more likely to occur back home. They were also noted for introducing best practices into the host country in terms of management, skills and technological considerations.

While MNEs originating from Europe, North America and Japan still provide the norm, a growing number are emanating from the NICs. For example, the multi-industrial *chaebol* firms of South Korea have already begun to make significant foreign investments both in Europe and the USA. By the late 1990s, Europe is expected to play host to five South Korean automobile manufacturers. Taiwanese producers of electronic goods and chemicals have also established a presence in key Triad locations.

Table 7.2 The world's 50 largest MNEs, 1993

Rank	Name	Country	Turnover (million ECU)	Profit (million ECU)	Net worth (million ECU)	Employees	Return on assets (%)	Major sector of activity
1	General Motors	USA	114,145	2,106	5,166	711,000	1.5	Motor vehicles and parts
2	Ford Motor	USA	92,703	2,160	14,549	322,213	1.3	Motor vehicles and parts
3	Exxon	USA	83,566	4,510	29,721	91,000	6.3	Petroleum refining
4	Royal Dutch Shell	UK/NL	81,290	7,426	44,731	117,000	8.6	Petroleum refining
5	Toyota Motor	JPN	67,498	1,167	30,980	73,046	1.9	Motor vehicles and parts
6	Hitachi	JPN	59,447	548	23,772	330,637	0.8	Electrical engineering
7	IBM	USA	53,575	−6,823	16,861	256,207	−9.8	Computers and office equip.
8	Matsushita Electric	JPN	53,209	197	26,421	254,059	0.3	Electrical engineering
9	General Electric	USA	51,107	3,779	22,060	222,000	1.8	Electrical engineering
10	Daimler-Benz	D	50,535	311	9,092	366,736	0.6	Motor vehicles and parts
11	Mobil	USA	48,330	1,780	14,725	61,900	5.1	Petroleum refining
12	Nissan Motor	JPN	46,585	−698	10,136	143,310	−1.2	Motor vehicles and parts
13	Samsung	KOR	45,811	464	6,489	191,303	1.1	Electrical engineering
14	IRI	I	45,080	−5,556	N/A	366,471	N/A	Conglomerate
15	British Petroleum	UK	44,847	789	12,509	84,500	2.0	Petroleum refining
16	Philip Morris	USA	43,243	3,048	9,932	173,000	7.0	Food, drink and tobacco
17	Siemens	D	41,992	927	9,810	391,000	1.9	Electrical engineering

18	Volkswagen	D	39,599	−1,054	5,821	251,643	−2.6	Motor vehicles and parts
19	Chrysler	USA	37,245	2,063	5,840	128,000	5.8	Motor vehicles and parts
20	Toshiba	JPN	37,201	98	8,979	175,000	0.2	Computers and office equip.
21	Unilever	UK/NL	35,734	1,663	6,216	302,000	7.5	Food, drink and tobacco
22	Nestlé	CH	33,238	1,669	9,055	209,755	6.5	Food, drink and tobacco
23	Veba	D	31,692	427	7,801	128,348	1.5	Conglomerate
24	Elf Aquitaine	F	31,669	111	12,700	94,300	0.3	Petroleum refining
25	Honda Motor	JPN	31,030	190	7,771	91,300	0.8	Motor vehicles and parts
26	Sony	JPN	29,994	123	10,681	130,000	0.4	Electrical engineering
27	ENI	I	29,711	228	8,073	106,391	0.5	Petroleum refining
28	FIAT	I	29,651	−969	9,472	261,500	−2.1	Motor vehicles and parts
29	Nec	JPN	28,757	66	6,282	147,910	0.2	Computers and office equip.
30	Texaco	USA	28,399	912	8,781	32,514	4.0	Petroleum refining
31	EI Du Pont De Nemours	USA	27,862	474	9,592	114,000	1.5	Chemicals
32	Chevron	USA	27,441	1,081	11,957	47,576	3.6	Petroleum refining
33	Philips Electronics	NL	27,080	394	5,270	238,469	1.8	Electrical engineering
34	Daewoo	KOR	26,382	412	6,292	76,986	1.1	Electrical engineering
35	Renault	F	25,644	162	5,117	139,733	0.5	Motor vehicles and parts
36	Fujitsu	JPN	25,219	−303	8,498	54,091	−1.0	Computers and office equip.
37	Mitsubishi Electric	JPN	24,947	209	6,506	49,842	0.8	Electrical engineering
38	ABB Asea Brown Boveri	CH/S	24,180	58	3,013	206,490	0.3	Electrical engineering
39	Procter & Gamble	USA	24,120	213	5,897	104,941	1.1	Chemicals
40	Hoechst	D	23,809	295	5,773	170,161	1.4	Chemicals
41	Mitsubishi Motors	JPN	23,688	45	3,119	26,654	0.2	Motor vehicles and parts
42	Alcatel Alsthom	F	23,612	1,055	8,743	196,500	2.7	Electrical engineering
43	RWE	D	22,895	447	3,903	105,572	1.4	Conglomerate
44	Pemex	MEX	22,692	829	29,642	106,951	2.0	Petroleum refining
45	Mitsubishi Heavy	JPN	22,368	642	8,990	44,077	2.0	Mechanical engineering
46	Nippon Steel	JPN	22,087	−435	7,799	34,619	−1.2	Metallurgy
47	Peugeot	F	21,965	−213	7,633	143,900	−1.2	Motor vehicles and parts
48	Boeing	USA	21,730	1,063	7,823	125,500	6.1	Aerospace
49	Amoco	USA	21,643	1,555	11,673	46,317	6.4	Petroleum refining
50	Pepsico	USA	21,374	1,356	5,415	423,000	6.7	Food, drink and tobacco

Source: CEC 1994j: 83

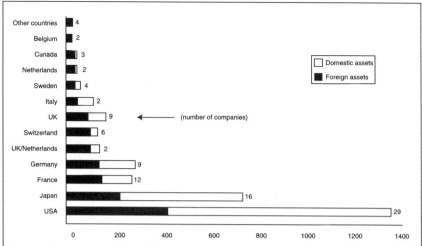

Figure 7.2 The top 100 MNEs: number of companies and assets by home country, 1992 (number of companies and billions of dollars)
Source: UN 1994a. UNCTAD, Division on Transnational Corporations and Investment, *World Investment Report 1994, Transnational Corporations, Employment and the Workplace* (United Nations, Sales No. E. 94. II. A. 14) fig. I.1 and fig. II.2

THEORIES OF INTERNATIONAL PRODUCTION

As the internationalisation of capital and MNE activity have become more ingrained within the world economy, so have theories that seek to explain the processes involved. International production theories primarily originate from the debate on why firms pursue internationalisation strategies beyond those based primarily on exporting. The development of these theories has drawn on six different branches of economics: international capital movements, trade, location, industrial organisation, innovation and firm theory (Cantwell *et al.* 1986). They also have involved analysis at the microeconomic, mesoeconomic (interactions between firms at the industrial level) and macroeconomic levels. Each theory under scrutiny adopts its own distinctive approach to its respective study of internationalisation and globalisation, although theory building has been partially evolutionary with some protagonists drawing upon the founding work of others.

Weber's location theory

In 1909, Alfred Weber published his work *Theory of the Location of Industries*, which is generally considered to be the first complete study on why firms had sought to extend production facilities overseas. Weber's theory rested on the idea that certain 'location-specific' factors provided the incentive for multinational firms to expand. The most important or 'primary' locational factors consisted of lower attainable transport and labour costs. Weber recognised that transport costs could be minimised by locating production nearer to the destination market and that the employment and relatively cheap labour could also prove to be a valuable route to improving a company's profitability.

'Secondary' locational factors were related to the external economies of scale that were afforded to companies deciding to locate in a particular region. Weber proposed that a regional concentration of industrial activity may generate these benefits, especially if the companies located there are functionally connected to each other in some manner. In many ways, Weber's theory was founded on the axioms of classical trade theory with the comparative advantage of countries determining the modes of production and exchange.

The Heckscher–Ohlin 'factor endowment' model

The Heckscher–Ohlin (H–O) model was initially constructed as an attempt to explain a country's international trade patterns by analysing its relative factor endowments. It also has been used to help examine broader patterns of internationalisation. The fundamental premise of the H–O model with respect to internationalised production is that FDI flows should be greatest between countries whose proportional factor endowments have the most pronounced contrast.

The initial rapid export-led growth of the NICs, for example, can be to some extent explained by the labour-intensive industries that were effectively geared to achieving this success. The decision to locate a high-technology production plant overseas may be determined by the capital intensity of a country and its capacity to generate high value-added activity. However, like Weber's theory, the fundamental premises of the 'classical' theory on which the H–O model is based lack the sophistication required to explain the complexities of today's global economy, although certain elements do retain some degree of relevance.

Hymer's 'market power' theory

In Hymer's doctoral treatise on multinationals (1976), he articulated what he believed to be the deficiencies of traditional international production theory and proposed an alternative. This in turn became what is generally accepted as the first pioneering academic study on modern multinational enterprise. Traditional theory held that flows of international trade and capital would occur between two countries with dissimilar production factor profiles. This was based on the assumption that capital would be exported to less developed countries where potential returns were higher owing to relative capital scarcity. Hymer criticised this approach on account of its failure to explain the nature of post-war FDI flows which were mainly channelled between the developed market economies. Instead, he contended that the motives which lay behind a firm's decision to locate production and service facilities abroad were part of its wider corporate objectives to improve and exploit its own market position within the industry.

According to Hymer, this process is essentially rooted in the oligopolistic market conditions within which most MNEs operate. In conducting global competitive strategies, multinationals attempt to utilise their idiosyncratic 'ownership-specific' advantages (e.g. a patented technology) against other MNEs on a cross-border basis and the 'location-specific' advantages enjoyed by domestic producers in the host country. In exploring this particular dimension to international competition, Hymer was the first to consider the relevance and application of this advantage type that enabled the firm to sustain a significant market position and impelled it to adopt an FDI strategy. He also suggested that one consequence of a multinational's oligopolistic behaviour may lead it to form a strategic alliance or a merger as a defensive or offensive competitive manoeuvre against others in the industry.

Such potential outcomes and the capacity of MNEs to exert and exploit a dominant market position within a host country led Hymer to conclude that multinational activity could be closely monitored and counter-checked where appropriate.

In Kindleberger's (1969) adaptation of Hymer's theory greater stress was placed on the monopolistic competition model where production differentiation holds more relevance than oligopolistic interdependence. This issue also interested Caves (1971) who explored and related the role played by an MNE's ownership advantages. In a much later work, Cowling and Sugden (1987) analysed the capacity of multinational market power to generate higher labour surplus induced profit levels. This was achieved in two ways: first, by MNE's engagement of 'divide and rule' tactics when negotiating wage and work conditions across national borders; second, the fragmentation of production processes by use of local and international subcontracting among the firm's network of dependent agents, leading to a weakening trade union position. Market power theorists have emphasised different aspects of structural market failure associated with monopolistic–oligopolistic competition and share some similarities with NIDL theorists noted below.

The product life cycle theory of internationalisation

This theory was first developed by Vernon (1966) and applies the principles of the product life cycle to understanding the sequential development of the internationalisation process while adding a locational dimension to the theory. One of Vernon's prime assumptions was that the US economy was the main source of new product developments. In the initial stage of the cycle, where new products are introduced to the market, production remains in the USA and firms export to foreign markets. Here the products are first tested or demonstrated. Vernon surmised that as demand for the product increased so would be the incentive to commence production in Western Europe. This argument rested on two further assumptions. First, at the time this theory was introduced only Western European nations possessed the technological capacity to manage production at this developmental stage (see Table 7.3). Second, the need to closer proximate the product specifications to suit localised preferences will strengthen the imperative to locate nearer to destination markets, especially where demand is high owing to similar income levels to those in the USA.

The location of a US firm's production in Western Europe will incur a displacement effect on US exports of the same product, diverting them to markets in other less developed economies. Vernon notes that this Trans-Atlantic pattern of FDI was particularly noticeable in domestic appliance goods such as washing machines and vacuum cleaners. As demand in the major markets falls in the third and fourth phases, US subsidiaries in Western Europe begin to export, first to less developed countries whose demand for the product rises from relative price and income changes, and second to the USA owing to the cost advantages enjoyed by the newer production plant conditions of those subsidiaries. Market extension strategies may be adopted to boost flagging sales through cheaper prices, product differentiation or improved product quality. In the last phase, as greater product standardisation occurs, offshore production will shift to NICs which then export the product back into the developed market economies. A gradual convergence of the NICs' techno-industrial capability and income levels with those of the USA and Western Europe will provide the incentive to relocate progressively higher forms of value-added activities in the former.

Table 7.3 The product life cycle and its suggested locational effects

	Production	*Exports*	*US net trade position*
Phase 1	All production located in the USA	US exports to many countries	Exporter
Phase 2	Production commences in Europe	US exports mostly to LDCs	Exporter
Phase 3	Europe exports to LDCs	US exports to LDCs displaced	Exporter/importer
Phase 4	Europe exports to USA		Importer
Phase 5	LDCs export to USA		Importer

Source: Adapted from Wells 1972

The relative decline of the USA's hegemony in new product developments required Vernon's theory to be refocused, especially regarding Japan's contribution to global innovatory activity. Many European economies and even some NICs have been the source of an increasing number of patented products in recent decades. In recognition of this, Vernon (1971, 1974) attempted to build in features of oligopolistic competition into his 'mark II' model. This proposed that after an initial innovative phase, established firms would seek a cost advantage position through scale economies rather than maintain technological superiority in a mature product market. Other competitive international industry approaches have considered the importance of technological competition between multinationals and ways in which they accumulate technology and the knowledge that underpinned it. Some connection also exists between the PLC model and the macroeconomic development model of international production which has attempted to analyse the effects of national economic development upon internationalised economic activity.

Internalisation and transaction cost theory

The extent to which an MNE's success is attributable to the 'internalisation' of its international operations and our understanding of how a multinational functions according to this principle lay at the centre of Buckley and Casson's (1976) thesis. This work was the first systematically to formalise a modern analysis on internalisation, although Coase (1937) had conducted some of the theoretical grounding by discussing internalised efficiencies arising from transactions between units of productive activity. Buckley and Casson first suggested that location-specific advantages will depend on those proposed by both Weber and Hymer. In addition, the related factors arising from host government policies and the need for production to be accompanied by other corporate activities, such as marketing and R&D, were also of importance. The authors went on to state that 'location decisions will be influenced by the ownership effect or the extent to which the internalisation of markets in the firm modify the above considerations'. Thus, the basis on which a company made locational decisions was more complex than traditional theory, with its ideal assumptions of competitive conditions, would have predicted.

A main tenet of the theory was that the internalisation of ownership-specific advantages enables an MNE both to protect against and exploit market failure. Time lags between external market transactions and production planning decisions, unstable bargaining positions and buyer uncertainty from the existence of asymmetric information are citable examples. The cross-border, intra-firm movement of various inputs between different corporate divisions or subsidiaries is priced according to internalised formulae known as transfer pricing. A multinational's transfer pricing in these exchanges can be designed to minimise tax and tariff payments or assist the rerouting of profits to a low tax country. The incentive for MNEs to internalise markets in this way is largely derived from market imperfections which make external market transactions costly in comparison or those that compel the firm to look for ways to circumvent them. Further incentive lies in the multinational's actual ability to exploit its particular ownership-specific advantages to these ends. Access to internal and external market information together with the ownership-specific advantages at the command of the MNE strengthen the position of the subsidiary relative to domestically bound producers in host countries. This will be more pronounced by the existence of market imperfections.

However, there are costs involved in maintaining internalised markets, such as the organisation and monitoring of market mechanisms required for intra-firm exchange, rectification of any distortions that arise and so on. Buckley and Casson (1976) proposed that the ability of an MNE to service its final markets will depend on its own blend of ownership-specific advantages working within an internal market structure. Moreover, the internalised dispersion of its international operations over and between national markets will depend upon the interaction between the following:

- industry-specific factors: for example, product nature, existing market structure, the scope for scale economies;
- regional-specific factors: for example, factor costs, access to material and inputs, geographical and social distances between regions;
- national-specific factors: for example, fiscal structures, political environment, infrastructure and other supportive networks;
- firm-specific factors: the MNE's organisational competency to co-ordinate corporate activities and internal market frameworks.

The different branches of internalisation and transaction cost analysis now more or less dominate the theory of international production. The Hymerian emphasis on structural market failure (e.g. oligopoly–monopoly power) has tended to be rejected, in favour of the theory that firms internalise in response to 'natural' market failures. In other words, it was not the structure of the end product market that ultimately determines profitability, but the efficient inter-divisional exchange of intermediate products.

The new international division of labour (NIDL)

Frobel *et al.* (1980) explored further some of the themes that Hymer had identified in his market power approach. They sought to explain MNE activity within the context of its own human capital and how it was organised and controlled on an international basis. For NIDL theorists, three key factors have enabled MNEs to drive down their labour costs to minimal levels: advances made in transport and communications technology which help create the network links of international production; advances made in production process technologies which have fragmented and standardised specific tasks that can now be contracted out to inexpensive unskilled labour; the growth of a worldwide reservoir of potential labour power. It is suggested that the existence of these factors, tied with the oligopolistic nature and conduct of MNE competitive practices in pursuit of global profit, essentially explains why there has been export of manufacturing jobs from developed industrial economies to less developed ones.

Criticisms made of NIDL theory centre on its somewhat reductionist approach that either denies or underplays key determinants which add greater complexity to the issue of why firms internationalise. For example, the role played by state policies to MNEs and the wider considerations that form part of corporate strategic decision-making are not discussed to any level of significance. Marginson and Sisson (1994) also point out its failure to account for the fact that most FDI is a two-way exchange between developed countries. However, developing countries are increasingly playing host to foreign capital especially in low-technology, labour-intensive industries that have fallen into structural decline in developed market economies on the basis of lost comparative advantage. It is within this context that NIDL theory tends to have most validity.

The eclectic 'OLI' paradigm

In our analysis so far, we have seen the central role played by ownership-specific, location-specific and internalisation advantages in formulating our understanding of how and why firms are able to attain and sustain internationalised and increasingly globalised business activity. In an endeavour to fuse these three determinants into an holistic framework of analysis, Dunning (1983, 1988) produced the 'Ownership–Locational–Internalisation' (OLI) paradigm within which this analysis could function. We should already be familiar with the nature of the OLI constituents, but let us consider some examples of them below as proposed by Dunning:

- Ownership-specific advantages: product innovations, management skills, organisational and marketing systems, non-codifiable knowledge, favoured market access, product diversity, economies of scale, scope and experience, operational flexibility.
- Location-specific variables: factor endowments, transport and communications infrastructure, market size and composition, the existence of market imperfections, government policies, political stability, cross-country linguistic, ideological and cultural differences.
- Internalisation incentive advantages: the avoidance of search and negotiating costs, the need of seller to protect quality of both intermediate and final products, to avoid or exploit government market intervention (e.g. tariffs, price controls, quotas), control of market outlets.

Dunning noted that MNEs are able to deploy ownership-specific advantages, which are internal to the firm, to compete effectively against the host country's indigenous firms. Location-specific variables, which are external to the firm and can take on public good characteristics, attract appropriate forms of foreign investment but may serve the interests of both the domestic and foreign producer. However, for reasons discussed earlier in Buckley and Casson's (1976) study, the MNE may possess a superior ability to exploit these. Internalisation incentive advantages give a firm cause to integrate production and service facilities on a cross-border basis.

The purpose behind Dunning's integration of these various strands of theory was to postulate that FDI could not take place unless it was based on a considered interaction of all three factors. Let us take the car industry as an example. International production of this kind is based on a rationalised specialisation of the product and its components. Ownership-specific advantages in the form of technology, capital, management and organisational skills would not be able to function without the opportunity to exploit the location-specific advantages of economies of product specialisation and concentration, or without taking advantage of the gains borne from internalisation, such as the transfer priced exchange between vertically integrated stages of production and the economies that lie therein. In conclusion, while Dunning's model for analysing MNE behaviour has been criticised for simply offering a series of inter-related factors that identify that behaviour rather than providing a deeper explanation for it, the eclectic character of the OLI paradigm does supply us with a theoretical synthesis in which the complexities of international production can be more commonly understood.

Box 7.2 International strategic alliances

The intensification of global competition and the pace of technological change mean that not even the most powerful MNEs can afford to act independently. As both a defensive and offensive reaction to the global economic environment, inter-firm co-operation has developed on a variety of levels. The need to share the costs and reduce the risks associated with internationalisation provides the essential basis for these international strategic alliances between enterprises to be formed. It has become increasingly the case for a firm to enter into a network of alliances and not just maintain a single, monogamous relationship. Combined with the fact that most collaborations are made between competitors, what has frequently arisen is an overlapping of alliances within many industries which has shrouded the frontiers of participating firms. Strategic alliances may be formal or informal, with joint equity holdings tending to formalise them. Their time span will vary according to the nature of the objectives pursued. Examples of the different types of strategic alliances are explored below.

Box 7.2 *continued*

Informal co-operations

No binding agreement exists between partners in this arrangement. Examples of co-operative activities include a two-way exchange of information about new products, processes and technologies and personnel. Partners are not usually direct competitors to each other and are comparatively sized. The bond of the relationship may be based on friendships, family ties or other forms of common association. Informal corporations may well be an initial step towards a more developed form of strategic alliance.

Contractual agreements

Like informal co-operations, contractual agreements are non-equity based arrangements but require a greater degree of commitment between participating partners. Enterprises may wish to enter into joint projects with others to share the costs of R&D, marketing and distribution activities. These are very common in high-tech industries where R&D costs are particularly high. For example, Renault and Volvo have developed new engines and new auto technologies together for a number of years.

Joint ventures

These involve two or more enterprises with a shared new equity base. The participating partners may be wholly private sector enterprises or include private sector and public sector enterprises. Examples of the latter are commonly found in China where multinational firms have established jointly run production and service facilities in partnership with government agencies. Joint ventures usually entail a long-term relationship and may be the only way for some firms to enter a specific market. The benefits arising from the pooled resources, more effective market access, the scope for specialisation and greater flexibility make joint ventures attractive.

Consortia

Consortia consist of a number of enterprises that may or may not be bound by joint equity holdings. The high costs and risks involved in research and technology-intensive production projects normally provide the pretext for the formation of consortia. Governments may play the key role in putting together a consortium of firms such as Sematech in the USA (semi conductors) and Airbus in the EU (civil aviation). The potential improvements made to national strategic advantage explain the main reason for state support. The EU's own R&D Framework Programmes are designed to galvanise the efforts of European consortia in high-tech fields of industrial activity (e.g. ESPRIT in information technology).

Box 7.2 *continued*

Relationship enterprises

These are one of the newest forms of strategic alliance to have emerged in recent years. Relationship enterprises are inherently different from other forms of inter-firm co-operations in that they involve partners from different industries. Participants are usually large firms whose established common objective is based on a project of significant proportions. For example, Boeing (aircraft manufacturer), British Airways (airline), Siemens (electronics), TNT (distribution), and SNECMA (aircraft engine manufacturer) submitted a proposal to build new airports in China in the early 1990s. Mutual benefits would arise from British Airways and TNT receiving preferential routes and landing slots, new aircraft contracts being secured by Boeing and the demand for air traffic control systems to be installed by SNECMA and Siemens.

The evolution of global business networks owes much to the proliferation of international strategic alliances. At certain levels, this has provided the greater opportunities for smaller firms to internationalise their corporate objectives and activities. Such alliances have also given firms more flexible options in terms of market expansion, cost reductions and creative product and process developments. However, such collaborations may have adverse effects. Jacquemin (1986) has found that most international strategic alliances have been horizontally driven by an oligopolistic desire to reduce levels of combative competition and refashion the structure of the market at the expense of consumers. Furthermore, Porter (1990) believes that these 'coalitions', as he terms them, are often costly both in strategic and organisational terms which usually lends to an instability that triggers their demise. He concludes that the most successful alliances are those which are highly specific in nature and are orientated to obtaining access to a certain market or the acquisition of new technology.

Cross-border strategic alliance relationships look likely to continue as a significant global trend. Although measuring the extent and impact of inter-firm co-operation is notoriously complex, it is conceivable that international strategic alliances will become a key route to internationalisation for an increasing number of firms in the twenty-first century.

GLOBAL COMPETITION THEORIES

Theories of international production are now complemented by recent analytical work that focuses on the current nature of global competition and the prevailing trends of globalisation. We shall concentrate on four influential ideas which have been developed by contemporary analysts in this field.

Triad powers within a borderless world

Against the backdrop of a tripolarised world economy, Ohmae's (1985a, b) 'Triad Power' thesis concentrated on three fundamental forces of change that had shaped the essential nature of international production and competition. These were:

● the growth of capital-intensive manufacturing;
● the accelerated pace of technological development;
● concentrated patterns of consumption across the Triad.

Ohmae contended that the first of these forces had made labour costs less relevant to production considerations. This relevance was further diminished by more competitive firms who tend to possess higher levels of capital intensity. While this may be more applicable to some industries than others, it was proposed that the main corollary of this is that the location of production facilities in low labour cost countries has lost some of its strategic importance.

The rapid pace of technological change has required firms to devote more time and resources to innovative activities in order to retain and sustain a competitive advantage over rivals. Rising R&D costs have compelled some rival firms to collaborate on joint projects. Companies will also need to proximate their operations where positive technological spillover effects are likely to occur. These are most likely to arise within the Triad, where the world's most sophisticated techno-industrial activities are located. Ohmae's third force of change concerns the concentrated patterns of consumption which have emerged for both capital and consumer goods across the Triad. These have arisen from convergent levels of income found in Triad countries and the global homogenisation of certain products, such as electronic consumer goods, sportswear and other branded items that are able to project a global image.

For firms to become global competitors, Ohmae stresses the imperative to acquire an 'insider' presence within each Triad region owing to the fundamental forces of change that have occurred. New process technologies, such as automation, may only be able to function successfully in capital-intensive economies. The pace of technological change requires that firms either establish their own operations in each of the Triad regions in order to capture the diffusion of new strategically relevant technologies, or form strategic alliances with Triad Power partners. An insider position will also enable firms more effectively to familiarise themselves with the localised demand conditions that exist in the world's most important markets and customise products to suit idiosyncratic tastes. Ohmae notes that a closer examination of Triad rivals in their own domestic context will assist firms in formulating more successful competitive strategies in their own home and other Triad markets. Neo-protectionism adds further incentives for globally competitive firms to establish separate Triad locations.

The organisational structure of a Triad Power should ideally have a decentralised corporate centre with a strong insider position in other Triad regions. These positions should be characterised by:

- well-established management systems in each part of the Triad;
- a full set of organisational functions that are fully responsive to local and regional conditions;
- continuity of management, mostly with home grown and overseas trained personnel;
- swift, autonomous decision-making, fully synchronised with the rest of the corporation;
- strong 'staying power' in key markets and the capacity to respond creatively to new market challenges;
- constantly active communications within the corporation;
- intolerance of the customary 'it is out of my control' excuses for shortcomings and mistakes;
- significant presence and weight in the communities where operations are located;
- a corporate headquarters that functions simultaneously in three roles: as resource mobiliser, as interface lubricator and as strategic sensitiser.

While Ohmae is a general advocate of strategic alliance building, he advises similar caution to that expressed by his contemporaries (see Box 7.2), mainly emphasising that potential Triad Power partners should base such collaboration on existing similarities. In conclusion, Ohmae states that true Triad Powers will be distinguished by a global corporate infrastructure that possesses the flexibility to adapt quickly to new competitive challenges and where 'domestic operations can be only a part of the global whole'.

In a further development of his ideas, Ohmae (1990) introduced the concept of the increasingly 'nationality-less' multinational company. This 'Borderless World' thesis is essentially concerned with the transformation of MNEs into transnational organisations where the usual geopolitical frontiers hold less relevance to how they conduct and organise their worldwide operations. Ohmae proposes his set of 'five C's' as an alternative framework in which global competition and production can be understood: customers, competitors, company, country and currency.

The company must find ways to relate to the interdependent significance of each of these elements to the other. The competitive environment has been radically altered by an expanding web of strategic alliances that interlink firms across the world. This has produced, to varying degrees, a growing number of shared destiny relationships. It has also been affected by the rapid dispersion of new technologies across borders and the expanding number of global products and market segments. The volatility of currency movements and the subsequent disruptions they impose on corporate transactions will give incentive for the multinational to adopt a 'currency neutral' position. Essentially, this constitutes an exercise in risk aversion that can be achieved by further internationalisation of the MNE's activities.

Ohmae extends his analysis of 'insiderisation' when he considers the need for multinationals to pursue a 'global localisation' strategy within host countries. The co-ordination of production and servicing is still orchestrated on a globally integrative scale but sensitive to national level conditions. This requires a deeper understanding of customer needs, their segmentation and potential market opportunities. Prevailing political risks in the country or region concerned must also be closely examined. The role of national governments in this Borderless World scenario of global competition primarily lies in adapting to the increasingly pluralist strands that interconnect today's world economy. Setting domestic policy within an international context provides a means to achieve this.

The EPRG strategic predispositions

Heenan and Perlmutter (1979) and Chakravarthy and Perlmutter (1985) devised an analytical framework in which an MNE's strategic management and competitive strategies could be studied. Chakravarthy and Perlmutter (1985) recognised that a globally focused firm calls on its worldwide system of operations and resources to compete in a string of national markets. In order to maintain a globally competitive position these need to be closely integrated and co-ordinated across the different aspects of the business value chain. This can be defined as the firm's 'economic imperative'. The increasing pressure placed on multinationals to comply to the wishes of its stakeholders was also identified. Moreover, governments were noted as the most acute source of this pressure in their attempts to determine the legitimacy of MNE activities and the commensurability of their objectives with those of host countries' own interests. Compliance to different elements of the host government's policy framework forms the firm's 'political imperative'.

Thus, the challenge to MNEs lay in balancing the two, as efforts to satisfy both could pull the firm in opposite directions. For example, the metering out of subsidiary autonomy to pursue a more nationally responsive corporate strategy with respect to the host country's policy agenda may be at odds with the need to comply to the overarching strategic objectives held commonly between all subsidiaries. With this tension considered, the firm had to come to terms with a different dimensional challenge of which strategic predisposition to assume. Four modes of strategic predisposition were suggested:

- Ethnocentrism: strategic decisions are derived from the parent company's own value system and interests. Legitimacy in the home country normally only considered.

- Polycentrism: some elements of strategy responsive to subsidiaries' own immediate environment, but a centralised organisational structure is still retained.
- Regiocentrism: the compounding of parent and subsidiary interests to some degree, at least at a regional level.
- Geocentrism: the adoption of a global systems approach to decision-making that reflects a more decentralised, globally flexible corporate culture and organisation. This will manifest itself in closer collaborative links with stakeholders and competitor firms.

Firms will not be camped in one mode or another but possess overlapping elements of at least two predispositions. Most current MNEs, though, hold strong ethnocentric characteristics focusing on bottom line profits and perceiving all political imperatives as 'unnecessary constraints'. However, Jacoby (1984) predicts that multinationals will eventually tend towards other modes of strategic predispositions. Chakravarthy and Perlmutter (1985) seem to support this view by forecasting that firms seeking to conspire with competitors and key stakeholders to 'proactively simplify' the competitive environment will become the future norm. Put alternatively, to meet the challenge of functioning both in a globally integrative and nationally responsive manner, MNEs will have to become more regiocentric and geocentric to survive. They conclude by stating that appropriate human resource management policies are the most effective way of re-orienting the strategic predisposition of the multinational, principally through developing a truly multinational citizenship within the upper strata of the firm's hierarchy.

Competitive advantage within multidomestic and global industries

Porter's (1980, 1985) work on conceptualising how firms develop a 'competitive advantage' over rivals has been much adapted to suit the needs of other theoretical frameworks. Porter partly applies the principles of competitive advantage to provide a basis for his analysis of global scale competition (Porter 1986a, b). A firm's competitive advantage consists of a series of assets and attributes that give one firm a competitive edge over another. He proposed that a firm's competitive advantage could be developed from cost advantages and differentiated products which led to their eventual adoption of three 'generic' competitive strategies:

- Cost leadership: the ability to produce at lower unit cost levels through the use of scale economies, superior technology and organisation, etc.
- Differentiation: the ability to meet the needs of consumers through segmentation, product innovations and upgrading.
- 'Focus': a blend of the above two whereby firms find particular market niches to cater for specialised product demand.

The conditions of international competition make the formulation of an appropriate competitive strategy more complex. In order to explore the implications that international competition carried for strategic decision-making, Porter made the distinction between two types of international industries that could exist:

- Multidomestic industries: whereby competition in each country (or small group of countries) is essentially independent of competition in other countries. Firms adapt strategies to localised conditions and thus the international complexion of the industry is marked by a series of domestic industries (e.g. Porter cites the variance found in commercial banking across Sri Lanka, France and the USA).
- Global industries: where a firm's competitive position in one country is significantly affected by its position in others. Thus, the industry is globally interlinked across national and regional borders with rival firms competing worldwide (e.g. civil aviation and semiconductors).

Firms in multidomestic industries should manage their international activities as a portfolio with subsidiaries given the autonomy to pursue country-centred strategies. Under these competitive conditions, any international strategy that exists concertinas into a series of domestic strategies. In global industries, firms need to integrate their activities to capture the linkages that exist between countries. A global overview must drive the firm's core strategy, but there still exists a requirement to maintain some country-centred perspective. It is apparent that Porter's analysis shares much in common with Heenan and Perlmutter (1979) and Chakravarthy and Perlmutter (1985). These similarities continue as Porter moves on to consider the strategic implications of the multidomestic–global industry distinction for developing the firm's competitive advantages and the configuration and co-ordination of different elements of the existing value chain.

The international configuration and co-ordination of value chain activities determines how firms compete in world markets. Configuration considerations involve locational decisions that dictate where the value chain activities are performed. Co-ordination considerations deal with how these activities are conducted between each other. In his analysis on the future of international competition, Porter predicts a shift from multidomestic to global industrial competition. The more extensive use of flexible manufacturing techniques would, for example, improve a firm's responsiveness to country-centred demand patterns while retaining a globally integrative strategy. A broader, more general role played by technology is also intimated in its enhancement of both the configuration and co-ordination of value chain activities across a wider geographical dispersion.

Porter also comments on the future prospects of Triad MNEs. For Japanese firms a major challenge will lie in their ability to develop a more definitive global vision. This approach had provided the basis of a successful strategy used against foreign rivals but mainly concerned exporting activity. Compared to other parts of the Triad, Japan retains a high proportion of domestically located industry. Hence, another important challenge that was noted consisted of learning how to exploit fully their competitive advantages in overseas based operations. For US and European multinationals, difficulties may arise in endeavours to co-ordinate and rationalise a relatively wider geographical dispersion of more autonomous subsidiaries. Porter suggests that the country-centred tradition is more a legacy of European MNEs, but strengths lie in their experience of operating in local market conditions and working alongside host governments.

Global shift theory

In his seminal work, *Global Shift*, Dicken (1992: xiii) describes the globalisation process as essentially 'the outcome of the complex interaction between transnational corporations and nation-states set within the context of a volatile technological environment'. While he accepted that MNEs were the primary agents of globalisation, he also recognised that an interdependent relationship existed with national governments that bound them together inextricably within the process. Both pursue their own set of specific objectives: multinationals seek to acquire global profits through extending their operational presence across national borders while national governments generally attempt to improve the welfare and wealth of their citizens. These objectives may overlap, especially if formed by consensus between both parties. For example, governments may agree to adapt their fiscal systems or upgrade infrastructures to suit the needs of MNE operations and in doing so empower them to improve efficiency levels within the economy. According to this theory, globalisation will also be shaped by government trade and investment policies and the regulatory framework within which multinationals have to operate. These may be geared either to encourage or inhibit MNE activity, and hence the tone of the interdependent relationship will modulate.

Rapid advances in technological development have served to overcome geographical distances that had hampered the ability of MNEs to function in a globally integrative way. Dicken also notes that new technologies have standardised and fragmented production processes, thus allowing them to extract the benefits of specialisation aligned to an international division of labour. One major consequence of the interplay between globalisation's three strands discussed by Dicken is the perforation of national economies as the singular containers of production. Some industries can only be understood within a globally integrative context as a 'kaleidoscopic complexity' of production and service networks are organised across national boundaries. The notion that products possess a national identity – a British car, a German camera – is being eroded by globalisation. Products become 'global', and hence competition between affected rival firms also takes on a global dimension. However, Dicken observed that the disparate strands of globalisation have evolved in a very uneven manner across and between countries, regions and industries. Indeed, the inevitability of globalisation is by no means secured, and this will form the theme of the following debate.

GLOBALISATION: IS IT INEVITABLE?

From our analysis so far, we have examined the historical and theoretical foundation of globalisation while certain impediments which potentially hinder its realisation have also been noted. Some, however, have expressed the belief that these will prove ephemeral and that the onset of globalisation cannot be resisted due to the conducive technological, economic and political forces which are at work. Others have disputed such claims, emphasising the counteracting factors which will obstruct progress towards a completely globalised world economy, either indefinitely or for some considerable time to come.

The viability of global products

For some, a key aspect of globalisation implies that globally standardised products become the predominant form of goods and services sold in the marketplace. Levitt (1983) argues that it is very likely as such products enjoy a superior competitive position over customised products. The cost efficiencies associated with the mass production of global products would make them not only cheaper but also more advanced and reliable than their customised counterparts. Levitt's argument further stated that consumers were willing to sacrifice product differentiation for higher quality, lower priced goods and that firms should concentrate on 'what everybody wants, not about the details of what everyone *thinks* they might like'. The increasing homogeneity of consumer needs and interests was also noted as a key determinant. While it was recognised that MNEs do endeavour to acclimatise and adjust to variances in market conditions, they do so not without attempts to influence these conditions to suit their own objectives. Moreover, product standardisation improved the aptitude of firms to harness the 'two vectors of technology and globalisation' to achieve wider corporate objectives.

This 'Model T' approach to global products and production was criticised by Douglas and Wind (1987). They contended that Levitt's ideas were based on a product-oriented marketing strategy, which represented one of numerous strategies that could be followed. Circumstances may deem it more appropriate to pursue a market-oriented strategy, while specific barriers to adopting a global product approach may exist. Porter (1980, 1985) offers examples of what form these barriers could take, namely protectionism, preferential treatment given to domestic firms, pronounced differences in country-centred consumer demand patterns and the existence of various institutional constraints. The tension between balancing the 'economic imperatives' and 'political imperatives' that we discussed in the analysis of EPRG strategic predispositions may require the firm to comply in a nationally responsive manner while rationalising operations across national borders.

Huszagh *et al.* (1985) contend that global product standardisation may be suitable in some industries but not in others. Consumers of industrial goods, for example, will be most interested in the functional aspects of the product and not any aesthetic differentiation that exists between them. Purchasing firms will be guided by similar procurement criteria that have been determined by the competitive dictates of their sector. The extent to which these products can be sold in a standardised format will partly depend on whether multidomestic or global competition is faced. Luxury products such as cameras, watches and perfumes are able to convey an association of 'status', and will therefore be able to sell on this basis. This is less applicable to more essential products. Nestlé, for example, adopts different marketing strategies for its Findus product lines across Europe: fish fingers and fish cakes in the UK, beef bourguignon and coq au vin in France, vitello con funghi and braviola in Italy.

While Douglas and Wind accept that global market segments may emerge as trans-border tastes, preferences and other socio-cultural factors converge – hence providing a wider apex for global standard products – they recognised that certain countervailing forces are acting to diminish their prospects. Micro-chip technologies have spawned flexible production techniques that are able to 'mass customise' products by cost efficient methods. External and internal operational constraints will reduce the scope for global standardisation. We have already noted examples of the former given by Porter above. An additional external constraint could lie in the nature of resource markets and their relative cost implications. This largely explains why plastic packaging is used more in Europe than in the USA where paper packaging is more predominant. The variance found in existing internationalised organisational structures and subsidiary management cultures can be the cause of internal constraints to global standardisation.

The political–economy dimension

The process of establishing a globalised world economy is in many ways as much political as it is economic. One of the main reasons why politicians have a vested interest in determining its associated outcomes is that serious changes to the world's political structures are implicated in this process. However, multinationals must work in the environment created by these structures, the composition of which may impose its own constraints upon globalisation. For this and other reasons, the political dimension of globalisation will always remain relevant. In framing his political–economy analysis of globalisation, Hirst (1993) outlines four key fcatures that lead to a situation where:

- a globalised world economy is determined by international processes, not national economic performances. Domestic policy objectives become subsumed into those dictated by the interests of international business. Governments effectively become local service providers.
- TNCs and not MNEs become the norm. The importance of home origin for a globalised firm fades. Core activities are more geographically dispersed.
- the political influence of organised labour diminishes. Labour forces, which by their very nature are localised, compete with each other with the aid of government to attract internationalised capital.
- globalisation undermines the political role of the state from being subjected to the overriding economic rationale and power of international business. Industrial sanctions that can be applied by MNEs on certain countries become more effective than military sanctions imposed by stronger national powers.

Hirst acknowledges that these essential features of globalisation have increasingly come to characterise the nature of today's world economy. However, he casts doubt on the ability of the forces that underpin these features to secure globalisation's inevitability. The growing importance of regional integration agreements (RIAs) has served to denude the impact and fluidity of international processes through fragmentation of the world economy into distinct trading blocs. Supranational decision-making can also have a similar effect. The 'level playing field' on social policy conditions that the Social Chapter has attempted to create across the EU has provided certain benefits for multinationals that outweigh those which could be derived from playing off one workforce against another.

MNEs are likely to hold out as the conventional mode of internationalised firm. Most of the world's largest companies are strongly ethnocentric and have made relatively limited progress towards joining the small group of true TNCs which actually exist. This runs counter to Reich's (1991) belief that TNCs, through their expanding globally integrative networks, will become the dominant model of corporate organisation in the twenty-first century. Hirst concludes by stating his belief in a 'loosely structured' internationalised economy which will persist into the foreseeable future and that RIAs, countries and regions make imperfect institutions for economic governance but still politicise it enough to resist the power of international business.

The debate concerning the inevitability of a globalised world economy is likely to continue for some time. The complexities involved in the process also serve to provide a range of interrelated imponderables that make forecasting outcomes particularly difficult. Further complications are added by the discrepancy that exists between analysts over exactly what is meant by the term. What is clear from our discussion thus far is that some industries will encounter less resistance to become more globally integrated than others.

THE POSITION OF THE NATION-STATE: A CLOSER EXAMINATION

The evolving relationship between nation-state and MNE

At several points in this chapter we have debated the position of the nation-state in a globalised world economy. It has been noted that this position has had to adjust to the new realities imposed by the conditions of globalisation. The nation-state is an invention of relatively modern historical times dating back to the seventeenth century from where it emerged as the dominant economic unit of study, administering international economic relations and acting as a prime source of technocratic influence over international economic activity. This role has, of course, been challenged by the MNE.

Nevertheless, all firms have to participate in a political dimension whose tone is still set by governments. Yet it has become more common for firms successfully to exert influence on the political environment in which they operate. Governments have recognised that MNEs can generate crucial improvements to society's welfare. This has often led to both nation-states and multinationals working in concert with each towards common objectives. The nature of such collusion will be influenced by the political ideology of the government, the relative size and prosperity of the national economy and its position in the world economy, the nation-state's resource endowment (Dicken 1992).

Policy-makers will obviously attempt to deploy measures designed to extract as many benefits from multinational activity as possible. However, attempts to elicit welfare benefits from multinational activity will backfire if such policies appear relatively burdensome. The 1973 Community Action Programme on MNEs, for example, was criticised by business as being too adversarial. As a more amenable view was taken towards multinationals, European governments saw the need to adopt more relaxed policies, if only to assist the restructuring of European industry to compete globally against US and Japanese firms. Foreign firms, in attempting to reduce political risk, may follow a defensive strategy aimed at increasing the cost of government intervention. This may be based on high exporting ratios, technological development and other high value-added activities in the host country. These are likely to meet the objectives held by governments for inward FDI, or provide further grounds on which negotiations between governments and MNEs can reach common objectives (Poynter 1986).

The concern of the nation-state with respect to outward FDI lies mainly in the loss of both actual and future potential value-added activity. The issue was high on the US political agenda in the 1960s and in the UK and Sweden in more recent times, with huge investment outflows (e.g. around a quarter of GNP equivalent for the UK) being made by its home-based companies. Its impact, though, need not necessarily be negative. Allowing home nation MNEs to seek optimal locations for their operations should yield higher levels of repatriated profits which can then be redistributed throughout the economy via improved domestic investments, tax revenues and other conduits. If the firm's core activities and key suppliers are based at home, a positive stimulus to the domestic economy can be expected, for example, by an increase in intra-firm exports. Government policy towards outward FDI will depend on a mixture of both its own ideological stance and more pragmatic conditional responses. Exchange control and compliance to formal government approval have been the most frequently used means to regulate the outward investment of home MNEs.

Triangular diplomacy

The way in which nation-states relate to international business and changes to the global competitive environment of the 1990s was explored by Stopford *et al.* (1991). They noted that governments were seeking to establish an ever broader basis of negotiation with MNEs, which at times may include international and supranational institutions. This is mainly based on the contention that the pace at which global structural changes occur has meant that governments need to co-operate with multinationals on a wider range of issues which relate not only to foreign investment. Other areas have included the key financial and technological innovations that have been made by MNEs which carry particularly significant economic, social and political implications. To support their thesis, Stopford *et al.* made six general propositions:

1 Nation-states are now competing more to create wealth within their own territory than to maintain and extend power over more territory. Wealth is used more as a means for power than *vice versa*.
2 Product quality, not just product costs, has become more critical in global competition. Responses made by governments to attract new investment include improvements made to infrastructure, education and training.
3 Small, poor countries face increased barriers to entry into industries where global competition is the most intense.
4 The above changes have meant that states must negotiate with MNEs as well as other states within a 'triangular diplomacy' relationship on issues relating to globalised economic activity.
5 The implications of this emergent relationship are that policy option

permutations have increased with the number of potential outcomes from negotiations between participating agents. This in turn complicates the balancing of multiple economic and political agendas.

6 All of these shifts have increased the volatility of change and the divergence of outcomes.

In looking ahead to the future role of the nation-state, Stopford *et al.* argue that governments must acknowledge the extent to which independence has been lost in the globalisation process and that the game theory of bargaining within the triangular diplomacy relationship must be learnt. However, the adoption of more outward looking policies may be constrained by counteractive endogenous forces. Powerful lobby groups founded on purely national interests and similarly oriented and influential agents may undermine the consensus required to push forward with this policy approach. Germany and Japan have been cited as exemplary examples of countries that have followed a successful path of subordinating national policy to the overriding objective of strengthening their position in the globalised world economy (Drucker 1986). Moreover, some nation-states have achieved similar results by actively competing against others to attract inward FDI.

The competitive advantage of nations

In his seminal work, *The Competitive Advantage of Nations*, Porter (1990) was concerned with how nation-states were able to achieve international success in certain industries. He proposed that four generic determinants shaped the environment in which firms compete which either promoted or hindered a nation's competitive advantage in that industry or industries.

1 Factor conditions: the factors of production found in a country, such as skilled labour or infrastructure, which enabled it to compete in a given industry.
2 Demand conditions: the nature of home demand for the industry's product and service.
3 Related and supporting industries: the presence or absence in the nation of supplier industries and related industries that are internationally competitive.
4 Firm strategy, structure and rivalry: the conditions in the nation governing how companies are created, organised and managed, and the nature of domestic rivalry.

These four factors were bound into a mutually reinforcing 'diamond' system whereby cross-contingent relationships existed between them. For example, intense rivalry between firms would broaden home demand and breed more discerning consumers. More sophisticated expectations from domestic consumers would exert competitive pressures on firms to upgrade their product range. A well-trained, skilled and educated workforce would bring benefits to all other determinants in the 'diamond'. Porter noted that a national economy did not necessarily require a balance of advantages in all four factors to succeed internationally. Smaller countries, such as Belgium and Denmark, lacking the same scale of domestic rivalry enjoyed by larger countries, can compensate by adopting an open position to foreign competition. Competitive advantages are sustained by nation-states through perpetual efforts to broaden and upgrade their sources via investment and innovation.

From his research, Porter found that there was a tendency for rival firms and their related and supporting industries to form a cluster within a geographical location of the nation-state. In Italy, the vast majority of its woollen textile producers are located in just two towns. Basel is the home base for Switzerland's three largest pharmaceutical companies. This has served to intensify domestic rivalry, but has also provided more conducive conditions for a flow of ideas and new technologies to take place where collaborative ventures exist. The close proximity of related and supported industries allow them more effectively to participate up and down the value-added chain of activities. This may take the role of supplier, source of transferable factor creation or a new entrant to the industry. Family or quasi-family ties between firms, common ownership and interlocking directorships within a cluster may lead to a congruence of corporate objectives.

While industry clusters will form on a localised or regionalised basis, national level considerations remain vital. The policy framework established by governments, capital market conditions and the social, cultural and political values of the nation will all exert influence on the competitive advantage of its industries. Certain implications are therefore carried by the European integration process which could aggregate such factors across and between member states. However, many country-specific differentials relevant to Porter's model will endure, even within a federalised Europe.

The transplanting of a country's 'diamond' elements will be of particular relevance and importance to home firms wishing to internationalise, but this feat may prove difficult owing to a number of considerations. First, some elements will be non-exportable, such as the sophistication of home consumers, although the firm may find that consumers in the host market are just as able to perform the same function. Second, we may wish to use the analogous notion that other elements 'may not travel well'. This could apply to smaller Japanese supplier firms within pyramidal subcontracting relationships that have followed major assemblers into Europe. Third, the diamond system will have developed through an evolutionary process within a country-specific environment. This implies that some kind of alchemy is required for the system to be emulated outside that environment. Thus, both multinationals and host governments are likely to fail in their attempts to re-engineer industry clusters and the cross-contingent links between the 'diamond' determinants in the host country. As Porter himself states:

> Competitive advantage is created and sustained through a highly loca-lised process. Differences in national economic structures, values, cul-tures, institutions and histories contribute profoundly to competitive success. . . . With fewer impediments to trade to shelter uncompetitive domestic firms and industries, the home nation takes on growing sig-nificance because it is the source of the skills and technology that underpin competitive advantage.
>
> (Porter 1990: 19)

It can be inferred from this that countries and global regions such as Europe are limited to the extent to which 'best practice' aspects of the value-added chain can be imported or copied. Similarly, the nation-state's own compe-titive advantage is to some degree protected from piracy by the 'highly localised process' which broadly underpins it. Thus, understanding the composite nature of the competitive advantages of European nation-states is required more fully to recognise Europe's position within the world economy and the process of globalisation.

CONCLUDING REMARKS

We have explored the historical and theoretical foundations of interna-tionalisation and globalisation while paying reference to the European economy where possible and appropriate. It is clear that the issues which relate to these global processes are increasingly complex and interdepen-dent. We must also acknowledge that much debate exists over the extent to which these processes are recasting and reconfiguring the relationships and activities that drive the world economy. In Chapter 8 we shall examine these matters in closer detail by investigating global flows of FDI and Europe's association with them. The application of concepts and theories discussed in this chapter will enable us to frame a clearer and more detailed picture of globalisation.

8 Foreign direct investment

The previous chapter discussed the historical and theoretical context in which internationalisation and globalisation could be understood. In this chapter, we shall make a closer examination of the European economy's position in these global processes by analysing foreign direct investment (FDI) trends, relationships and related issues. The subject of FDI has been chosen because it has endured as the most dynamic element of globalisation since the mid-1980s. As the host and source of some of the world's largest flows of FDI in recent years, Europe has been a prime focus for global investors and policy-makers alike. The themes of this chapter shall cover recent trends in FDI on a global, European, extra-regional and intra-regional basis; the connections between European integration and foreign investment; Europe's Trans-Atlantic FDI relationship; Japanese FDI flows; FDI and central and eastern Europe.

RECENT TRENDS IN FDI

General global trends

1967 to 1990

All OECD countries experienced a rising trend for FDI inflows and out-flows over the period between 1967 and 1990. Between 1983 and 1990, FDI grew at an annual rate of 29 per cent for the developed market economies, compared to their output growth of 7.8 per cent per annum and trade growth of 9.4 per cent per annum. Europe was both host to and source of the world's largest flows of FDI, with the EC and EFTA countries combined taking around two-thirds of total OECD flows. Table 8.1b shows that Western Europe's share of total world inward FDI rose from 29.8 per cent in 1967 to 44.3 per cent by 1990. As we shall discuss in some depth, the European market integration process has been contributory to this by exerting its own gravitational pull on overseas investment funds. The USA experienced an even sharper increase in its share from 9.3 per cent to 24.2

per cent, which was most pronounced over the latter end of the period, partly owing to the Reagan administration's expansionary fiscal policies during the 1980s. However, Japan's 0.6 per cent share of the total in 1990 was identical to its percentage share in 1967, a further indication for some of the Japanese economy's 'closed system' character.

The fall in percentage share of the Latin American and Caribbean countries, from 17.5 per cent to 7.3 per cent can be partly explained by a resistance to foreign investment of many countries in the region during the 1960s and 1970s. The debt crisis in the late 1970s and early 1980s and accompanying recessionary factors had their own adverse effects on FDI inflows. The introduction of debt–equity conversion schemes and the softening of regulations on FDI (e.g. the Andean Pact's Decision 220) towards the end of the period did manage to halt this trend in some countries, most notably Mexico, Argentina and Colombia. The USA remained the largest investor in the region with extensive interests in the primary sector. This contrasts with European firms whose most significant investment activities have rested in manufacturing sectors: automobiles and chemicals from Germany; food from the UK; tyres, automobiles and office machines from Italy (Pio and Vannini 1992: 104–5).

Africa's share of total world FDI fell from a relatively smaller base figure than that of Latin America of 5.3 per cent to 2.1 per cent, a reflection of the persistent fundamental problems that have hindered the continent's development for some time. The debt crisis also exacerbated the already deep-seated structural difficulties that had beset the region. Moreover, the primary product and import substituting character of FDI in Africa meant that both the volume and value of exports generated were insufficient to service the cost of investments. In addition, an import dependency on component parts made the region particularly exposed to foreign exchange shortages as export commodity prices fell and oil prices rose (Pio and Vannini 1992: 108–9). Due to geographical proximity and past colonial links, Europe has traditionally been the largest source of inward FDI, being accountable for around 60 per cent of cumulative flows over the period, which compares to roughly 30 per cent for the USA and 10 per cent for Japan.

Unlike the other developing regions, Asia managed to secure an increase in its regional share of world FDI, rising from 7.8 per cent to 9.4 per cent by 1990. The attraction of FDI flows has been instrumental to the development process of most East Asian NICs, particularly later generation 'tiger' economies as a strategy to catch up with more advanced neighbours. Foreign investments have usually been characterised by their export-orientated nature, but as regional levels of prosperity have risen so has FDI geared towards production that meets the domestic market demands of these countries. Japan has been the most prominent investor in the region with nearly 45 per cent of FDI inflows between 1970 and 1988, followed by the USA with 37 per cent and the Community with 14 per cent.

Table 8.1(a) reveals that while the USA remained the dominant (single country) source of FDI outflows, its total world share had almost halved from 50.4 per cent in 1967 to 25.6 per cent in 1990. On a regional basis, Europe overtook North America as the world's largest FDI source in the mid-1980s with 49.2 per cent of the total in 1986 as compared to a

Table 8.1(a) Stocks of outward FDI flows, 1967–90 (US$ bn)

Countries/regions	1967 % of total	1973 % of total	1980 % of total	1990 % of total
Developed market economies	97.3	97.1	97.2	95.7
USA	50.4	48.0	40.0	25.6
UK	14.1	13.0	14.8	14.7
Japan	1.3	4.9	6.6	12.1
Germany (FDR)	2.7	5.6	7.8	9.3
Switzerland	2.2	3.4	7.0	3.9
Netherlands	9.8	7.5	7.6	5.9
Canada	3.3	3.7	3.9	4.5
France	5.3	4.2	3.8	6.9
Italy	1.9	1.5	1.3	3.6
Sweden	1.5	1.4	1.3	3.0
Other*	4.8	9.5	3.2	4.8
Developing countries	2.7	2.9	2.8	3.1
Total	100.0	100.0	100.0	100.0

Source: Dunning, J.H. (1993) *The Globalisation of Business*, 288, 290
* Australia, Austria, Belgium, Denmark, Finland, Greece, Ireland, New Zealand, Norway, Portugal, South Africa, Spain.

Table 8.1(b) Stocks of inward FDI flows, 1967–90 (US$ bn)

Countries/regions	1967 % of total	1973 % of total	1980 % of total	1990 % of total
Developed market economies	69.4	74.0	78.0	81.2
Western Europe	29.8	38.4	42.0	44.3
UK	7.5	11.6	12.5	12.5
Germany	3.4	6.3	9.5	8.1
Switzerland	2.0	2.1	2.8	2.6
USA	9.3	9.9	16.4	24.2
Other*	30.2	25.6	19.7	12.6
Japan	0.6	0.8	0.7	0.6
Developing countries	30.6	26.1	22.0	18.9
Africa	5.3	4.9	2.6	2.1
Asia	7.8	7.4	7.1	9.4
Latin America and the Caribbean	17.5	13.9	12.3	7.3
Total	100.0	100.0	100.0	100.0

Source: Dunning, J.H. (1993) *The Globalisation of Business*, 288, 290
* Other developed – Australia, Canada, Japan, New Zealand, South Africa, sub-Saharan Africa, Algeria, Egypt, Tunisia, Morocco.

combined US and Canadian share of 39.0 per cent. By 1990, European FDI outflows had reached 51.9 per cent of the world total, twice the share taken by the USA. It perhaps comes as no surprise to observe that Germany (FDR) and in particular Japan have been responsible for progressively increasing percentage shares, rising from 2.7 to 9.3 per cent and 1.3 to 12.1 per cent respectively over the period.

Worthy of similar note is the fact that despite the general post-war malaise of the UK economy, its companies had retained and even slightly increased the UK's share of total world outflows of FDI from 14.1 per cent to 14.7 per cent, thus maintaining the country's position as the world's second largest, and Europe's largest outward investor. The Netherlands, a country with a similar multinational profile to the UK, was the only European country separately listed that experienced a fall in share, with France ousted from its slot as Europe's third most important outward investor by 1990. In terms of Triad FDI balances, Figure 8.1 shows that:

- Europe kept a more or less stable net outflow position (Figure 8.1a);
- the gap between US inflows and outflows almost completely converged over the period, thus eradicating a huge net outflow balance (Figure 8.1b);
- Japan also saw a dramatic change in its own balance but concerning one of growing divergence in favour of net outflows (Figure 8.1c).

The early 1990s

While most relative positions of the major regions and countries remained unaltered during the early 1990s, there were some important changes to global trends. Total world FDI inflows actually peaked at the very beginning of the decade at $160bn with outflows falling from their 1989 $180bn peak in consecutive years between 1990 and 1992 (Figure 8.2). This would appear to confirm Julius and Thomsen's (1988) proposition of a strong correlation existing between FDI and business cycle. Outward investment from Japanese and EU companies fell most significantly during this time, primarily affecting US inward flows. Recovery from the recession in 1993 led to an increase in outflows from around $100bn in 1992 to $118bn in 1993.

Although the OECD countries still dominate outward FDI flows with 95 per cent of the 1991–3 world total, the most startling trend that emerged in the early 1990s was the decline in their share of world inflows which dropped from around 80 per cent in the late 1980s to 42 per cent by 1993 (excluding intra-EU flows). This has been due to the expansion of investment flows towards the developing countries, which in 1993 had attracted 55 per cent of total inward FDI with the remainder going to the central and eastern Europe (CEE) countries (see Figure 8.3). During the 1980s, the annual average of the developing countries was only 21 per cent.

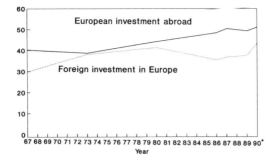

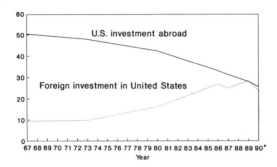

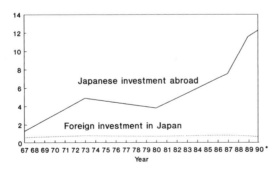

Figure 8.1 Triad FDI balances
Source: Wallace and Kline (1992) *EC 1992 and Changing Global Investment Patterns*, 10–13. Reproduced by permission of the Center for Strategic and International Studies
8.1(a) Europe as host and home to FDI, 1967–90
8.1(b) USA as host and home to FDI, 1967–90
8.1(c) Japan as host and home to FDI, 1967–90

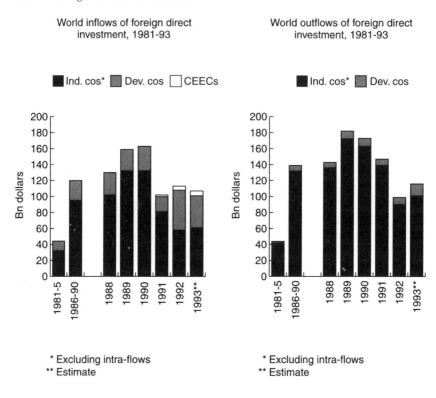

Figure 8.2 World inflows and outflows of FDI, 1981–93
Source: CEC 1994i: 5

Private FDI entering into developing countries has also overtaken overseas development aid (ODA) as their main net resource flows at 55 per cent of the total in 1994.

Over two-thirds of this new investment has been mostly concentrated in the East Asian NICs and China. Latin American NICs were also notable recipients of these inflows. The more positive policy stance taken by countries in the region towards inward FDI and the further deepening of regional integration agreements (RIAs) between them, such as the formation of Mercosur's Southern Cone Common Market in 1995, served to reverse the trend of the middle post-war years. The continued marginalisation of the sub-Saharan economy in the world context would appear to offer limited scope for inward flows of FDI, although, of course, it would prove part of the elixir required to boost its general prospects. Again, regional integration may provide the conditions conducive for FDI interest to be nurtured, while South Africa should attract considerable investment inflows from Western market democracies as the 1990s progress.

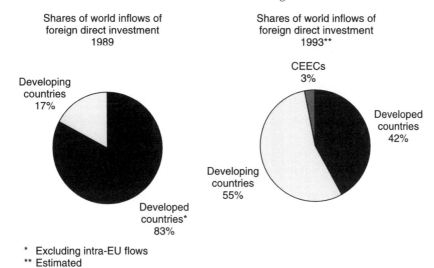

Shares of world inflows of
foreign direct investment
1989

Shares of world inflows of
foreign direct investment
1993**

Developing
countries
17%

Developed
countries*
83%

CEECs
3%

Developed
countries
42%

Developing
countries
55%

* Excluding intra-EU flows
** Estimated

Figure 8.3 Shares of world inflows of FDI: 1989, 1993
Source: CEC 1994i: 6

In order to promote FDI in developing countries the Community established the Investment Partners (ECIP) scheme in 1988 which acts as a
financial instrument within the EU's development policy. Its main aims are
to encourage joint ventures of mutual interest between EU and developing
country producers, with small and medium-sized enterprises (SMEs) particularly targeted. This is achieved through decentralised and flexible management structures that network together financial institutions and
investment promotion agencies. The framework of the scheme is based
around four financial facilities:

- project identification;
- feasibility study and pilot projects;
- capital financing;
- management assistance and human capital development.

Hence, the ECIP is not a substitute for private FDI but rather performs the
function of creating stimulatory conditions within developing countries.
Between 1988 and 1994, 909 projects were sponsored by the scheme.

Figure 8.4 indicates that the developing countries kept pace with the
USA as hosts to inward FDI flows between 1980 and 1992, and that the EU
retained its position as the world's most important host to inward investment. Mergers and acquisitions have remained the most predominant form
of FDI, being responsible for almost three-quarters of outward investment
in recent years. In 1970, service sector FDI represented around a quarter of
total inward stocks but by 1993 this proportion had risen to almost 50 per

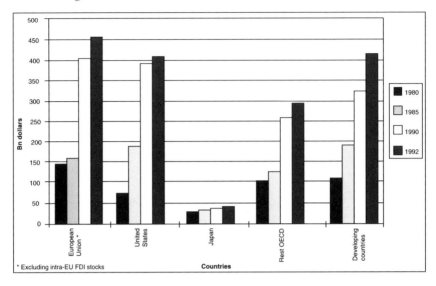

Figure 8.4 Stock of inward FDI by host region and economy, 1980–92
Source: CEC 1994i

cent. Around two-thirds of service sector FDI is concentrated in finance and trade-related activities in the OECD countries. Primary sector and manufacturing industries have traditionally predominated inward FDI flows in developing countries, but here too they are losing ground to services which now constitute approximately one-third of the total FDI stock accumulated there. A Commission study on trade and investment (CEC 1994i) links this trend to the development and growth of internationally tradable services that have been reinforced by widespread privatisation and deregulation programmes. The necessity of the service provider in most cases to establish an end market presence in the form of a service outlet furnishes the connection between FDI and trade in services, often referred to as 'establishment trade'.

Finally, it should be noted that FDI flows are still characterised by strong patterns of regional concentration. This can be explained by a range of political and cultural factors in addition to those of a more economic nature. Table 8.2 reveals that these patterns have formed along the lines of geographical proximity and where historical ties have been closest. These trends have persisted owing to the continued existence of local and regional economies of agglomeration. Regional integration has impelled home multinationals from participating countries to maintain cross-border investments within the bloc, while attracting third country firms where dynamic efficiency gains and improved market opportunities are made accessible. Where these are substantial, regionalism has helped to break down the home region bias of FDI flows and create stronger inter-

Table 8.2 The intensity of FDI, by host region, 1990[a]

Region	North America	Latin America	Europe	Africa	Middle East	South Asia	East Asia
North America	1.97	1.12	0.84	0.49	0.85	0.32	0.8
Europe	0.98	0.53	1.32	1.16	0.79	1.77	0.56
East Asia	1.28	1.09	0.5	1.10	1.12	0.28	1.94

Source: Adapted from UN 1994a: 147
[a] The intensity ratio: share of host region in outward investment stock of a given country, divided by share of host region in worldwide FDI stock.

regional and global patterns. This has been recently demonstrated by the surge of Japanese foreign investment into Europe's single market.

European FDI in a closer global focus

An examination of Table 8.3 that details global patterns of European investment exposes a number of key features regarding both inward and outward European FDI flows. The stock of intra-European FDI inflows by 1991 were twice that of combined US and Japanese foreign investments in Europe. The former clearly predominate over extra-regional inflows in all countries with the exception of the UK and Ireland, both of whom have received significant US investments for some time. British companies were responsible for 41 per cent of all European investment in the US and 17 per cent in Japan, thus confirming the UK as the Europe's largest investor overseas. It is also the most important recipient of inward FDI, accounting for 40 per cent of all inward EU FDI during the 1980s (more than Germany, France, Italy and Spain put together), although recent evidence suggests that the UK's dominance is slipping in a growing number of sectors.

While much attention has been conferred on the recent acceleration of Japanese investments in Europe, both Tables 8.3 and 8.4 demonstrate that Japanese firms have yet to challenge seriously the position of their US counterparts. With respect to European investment outflows, European firms seem to have established only a limited direct presence in Japan. However, any evaluation must be tempered by the minimal penetration made by inward FDI in the country generally, a subject for debate later in the chapter (pp. 291–2). Most recent US direct investment in Europe has consisted of mergers and acquisitions, with 85 per cent of its total value taking this form between 1985 and 1992. Japanese firms, on the other hand, have tended to engage in more greenfield FDI ventures.

The notable growth of both inward and outward flows of European FDI from the mid-1980s has occurred during the time when deregulation, privatisation and other market liberalising policies – converging at the gradual installation of the SEM – were being pursued by most European countries. This helped to create the favourable environment in which

Table 8.3 Global patterns of European FDI (percentage of stock in or from each region, cumulative to 1991)

Inflows	From			
	USA	Japan	Europe	Total stock* (ECU bn)
To				
Belgium–Luxembourg	14	6	71	28.0
France	12	6	75	48.4
Germany	30	7	56	68.0
Ireland	50	3	41	na
Italy	14	2	80	44.8
Netherlands	27	4	66	53.0
Portugal	8	2	80	6.3
Spain	8	3	81	67.8
Sweden	10	na	87	8.9
UK	41	5	39	153.3
Europe	27	5	60	478.4

Outflows	To			
	USA	Japan	Europe	Total stock* (ECU bn)
From				
Denmark	14	1	72	7.8
France	25	0	62	63.0
Germany	23	2	55	112.9
Italy	9	1	68	47.1
Netherlands	31	1	66	78.7
Sweden	14	na	74	3.3
Switzerland	23	na	53	47.7
UK	39	1	28	163.0
Europe	27	1	53	549.7

Source: Reproduced from Thomsen and Woolcock (1993) *Direct Investment and European Integration*, by permission of Pinter Publishers in association with The Royal Institute of International Affairs, London, England
* Some countries do not record stock figures. In these cases, cumulative flows were used.

international competition between firms could flourish. The intensification of competition within the SEM has placed a greater emphasis on acquiring closer market proximity for both EU and non-EU firms alike, which has been mirrored by the increase in strategic alliances and FDI strategies being networked. Furthermore, outsider firms have also been drawn by the efficiency gains to be had from an insider SEM position.

For the majority of European and non-European firms, merger and acquisition (M&A) FDI has presented an easy option quickly to secure the economies of scale attributable to the SEM and the reduction of the accompanying competitive threats. Much of inward European FDI has been

Table 8.4 Geographical breakdown of extra-EU FDI flows, 1984–92 (million ECUs)

	1984	1985	1986	1987	1988	1989	1990	1991	1992
					Outward				
USA	11,537	10,061	17,772	23,885	22,120	24,053	7,155	9,232	5,682
Japan	294	34	104	12	247	682	911	341	412
EFTA	952	722	163	1,789	2,593	1,992	3,226	2,471	2,609
OPEC	153	104	565	56	343	1,801	74	1,502	580
ACP	19	120	66	155	269	322	211	650	731
EX-COMECON	1	6	12	9	74	113	244	1,304	NA
Extra-EU	17,407	15,105	21,932	30,670	31,680	33,282	20,527	26,732	15,487
					Inward				
USA	2,951	1,788	2,660	2,337	2,551	9,846	9,178	5,411	11,142
Japan	390	719	465	1,572	2,584	4,354	5,406	1,682	1,686
EFTA	1,663	1,838	3,258	3,833	8,509	8,351	11,284	6,883	3,533
OPEC	149	421	−543	−119	912	110	306	453	494
ACP	155	61	40	104	15	52	−14	164	136
EX-COMECON	75	18	15	16	18	83	274	201	NA
Extra-EU	**6,152**	**5,711**	**7,119**	**12,991**	**18,141**	**27,943**	**32,753**	**20,933**	**21,129**

Source: Eurostat
Notes: Excludes reinvested profits. 'Other class 1' includes other OECD FDI and excludes intra-EU FDI.

market based, resulting from firms requiring more immediate contact with the highly fragmented, multi-domestic competitive conditions that can exist in the region. A distinctive regional division of labour has also occurred within Europe, based on MNEs exploiting and reacting to differentials in culture, language, unit labour costs, skills and a variety of techno-industrial environmental factors.

According to Rugman and Verbeke (1991) both positive and negative integrational aspects of the SEM should decrease the need for firms to be nationally responsive, but increase the need for global restructuring. This view is based on the expected convergence of market conditions across the EU brought about by the single market's harmonising effects and the organisational implications carried by systematic removal of cross-border impediments. Moreover, the strength of insider firms will rest on their existing or extended distribution and sales networks that will permit them to adapt market strategies more easily than outsiders. The latter may have to pursue more nationally responsive strategies as the corporate integration option is not so open to them. This may manifest itself in a variety of ways, namely a concentration on niche markets, a more amenable access sought via the formation of a strategic alliance with insider firms or through M&A activity.

These modes of entry to the European market will differ according to the nature of the competitive advantages possessed by companies and the structural dimensions of their industries. Outsider firms that have traditionally exported into Europe from a low-wage production base would also have to consider the cost implications involved in securing a high-cost production location within SEM that would be offset by lower transport costs. In addition, a move to a European FDI strategy may run the risk of dissolving concentration advantages in manufacturing, marketing and R&D currently enjoyed from their global export platform and other globally oriented strategies. This may result from potential distractions caused by adopting 'Euro-strategies' at the expense of globalisation, but would ultimately depend on the existing corporate structure and culture of the firm and issues pertaining to matters such as local content and technical standard regulations imposed by the EU (Young *et al.* 1991).

Intra-European FDI flows

European nations are among the world's largest outward investors and most important hosts to FDI. Consequently, intra-regional investment flows in Europe by far outweigh extra-regional FDI. The European integration process has added its own impetus. However, in their analysis of intra-European FDI, Molle and Morsink (1993) proposed that while it has been stimulated by certain push and pull factors, cultural differences and physical distances have been the dominant factors of resistance. The SEM programme, though, served as a considerable spur to intra-EU FDI which has primarily taken the form of M&A. This carried forward the momentum of significant M&A activity that had already commenced in the 1970s from the efforts made by European firms to attain similar size and structure to US rivals. Horizontal M&As have been the norm, thus leading to increased levels of industrial concentration. Furthermore, intra-EC M&As between 1984 and 1991 were especially common in chemicals, food, construction, metals and paper, electronics, banking, insurance and distribution.

Germany is the largest intra-European investor, with 21.3 per cent of total outward FDI stock across the region by 1991, ahead of the UK share of 15.7 per cent and France of 13.4 per cent. Revealing patterns of intra-regional investment emerge from a closer examination of the figures. Thomsen and Woolcock (1993) found that between 29 per cent and 45 per cent of intra-EU FDI by German, French, Dutch and British firms is concentrated in only two countries. For example, UK FDI in the Netherlands represented 37 per cent of the UK's total intra-European total and France 18 per cent up to 1990. In addition to market size, geographical proximity appeared to be a key determinant of how this concentration of FDI was clustered: Germany was seventeen times more likely to invest in Belgium than Greece; Spanish firms have preferred to invest in Portugal and France; strong cross-investments have been made between the Nordic countries. Support to these findings is given by Kay (1990) who contended that a merger between European firms is more likely to cross just one border than two or more. Cultural similarities between adjacent countries may to some extent explain this trend in intra-European FDI as well as more practical considerations such as transport and other distributional costs. However, the clustered formation of foreign investment interests provides an anomaly within the context of the cost-based and market-based opportunities presented by the SEM programme.

Intra-European FDI has a number of other defining characteristics. Many intra-European investment flows are of an intra-industry nature, for example Unilever has invested in Switzerland to levels similar to those of Nestlé in the UK. To some extent, this typifies both the oligopolistic character of multinational competition and the growing concentration of markets and industries across Europe. The strength of investment flows between EU and EFTA countries has tended to be overlooked by some commentators. Between 1984 and 1991, foreign investment by EFTA firms in the EU amounted to ECU 45.1bn, around a quarter more than investment from US firms and three times that of Japanese FDI into the EU. Relative market sizes largely explain why FDI flows from EU firms into EFTA countries only represented 32 per cent of the inward EFTA FDI flows noted above (see Table 8.4). These and other relevant trends and developments will be examined in a more detailed discussion on European integration and FDI flows.

EUROPEAN INTEGRATION AND FDI

Initial considerations

The relationship between regional and corporate integration is key to our understanding of past, present and future patterns of FDI flows in and out of Europe. Both forms of integration share similar motives. Dunning and Robson comment:

> In both cases, an essential prerequisite for integration is a failure of markets to allocate economic activities efficiently among units being integrated – affiliates or associated companies in the case of MNEs, and countries in the case of regional groupings – because of the market imperfections involved which it is envisaged that the integrated governance of the units will reduce.
>
> (Dunning and Robson 1988: 2)

Multinationals try to avoid these market imperfections through internalisation and transfer pricing, though the process is more complex for RIAs. Member states have to consider both the benefits arising from attempts to minimalise market distortions from government intervention and optimising the co-ordination and harmonisation of policies where structural economic conditions allow.

Traditional theory on regional integration did not consider the MNE's ability to bypass the market through internalisation, and thus was fatally flawed. However, an early attempt was made by Kindleberger (1956) to introduce theories on investment creation and diversion. Surprisingly, only limited analytical work has been subsequently developed in this field with even the Cecchini Report (1988) failing properly to address the multinational's role and impact in the SEM.

Multinationals have generally taken a favourable view of regional integration owing to the benefits derived from dynamic efficiency gains, though apprehension may also be expressed in reaction to the heightened competitive threats it can pose. Studies have shown that past RIA activity is more often than not accompanied by higher inflows of US foreign investment, and to a lesser extent increases in intra-regional FDI (Dunning 1972 and Balassa 1977 for the Community; Behrman 1972 for LAFTA; Mytelka 1979 for the Andean Pact). With respect to the relationship between intra-European FDI and the European integration process, a study conducted by Molle and Morsink (1993) drew two main conclusions:

1 The relation between trade and FDI appeared to be non-linear. For FDI to occur trade relations need to reach a minimum level. Beyond that level more trade integration in the EU does not seem to give rise to larger intra-European FDI flows.
2 The exchange rate risk appears to discourage FDI. Monetary integration, by stabilising exchange rates, is likely to stimulate FDI from richer countries to poorer countries in the EU, hence contributing to its cohesion.

This would seem to suggest that the creation of a single money for the single market would induce further intra-European FDI and the associated benefits it would generate.

The impact of European integration on European corporate integration

For intra-EU FDI, the dynamic efficiency gains of the SEM and beyond will reduce the cost of exporting, thus providing some incentive to relocate production back in the home country. This will be tempered by reduced transfer costs across the EU that enable firms better to co-ordinate their cross-border activities. Thus, the option to produce in the lowest cost locations and export from there to the rest of the single market may prove more advantageous. However, the highly idiosyncratic nature of Europe's segmented national markets, due to localised tastes, linguistic and other cultural barriers, requires MNEs to maintain a pan-European presence to some degree. Thomsen and Woolcock's (1993) study of the clustered concentration of intra-European FDI flows between countries would appear to deny the relevance of both the above. In theory, though, vertical integration activity should increase from the scope for rationalised specialisation of a firm's own value chain of operations.

Inward extra-EU investors will be motivated by fears of a trade bloc, protectionism and the opportunities presented by a more integrated market. This can involve a considered trade-off between the costs of producing in lower cost countries but with the EU's CET to pay against the alternative of a higher cost but non-internal tariff EU location able to harvest dynamic efficiency gains over time. An outsider's decision to locate production within the single market will also entail an analysis of whether marginal costs will fall sufficiently from market completion to offset the tariff barriers found in third country export markets. Insider and outsider MNEs may decide to establish plants inside the SEM as a pre-emptive manoeuvre against the emerging domestic producers who flourish under the single market's conditions. Protectionism may deter FDI where imports of intermediate products are highly complementary to FDI, although strict local content regulations may compel the foreign investor to find alternative indigenous suppliers. Import competing sectors that are heavily protected will suck in resources from others, reducing the profitability levels of the latter, which could consequently lead to a decline of foreign investment levels in these sectors (Sodersten and Reed 1994).

The cumulative causation model is deployed by Cantwell (1987) to analyse the response of MNEs to progressive regional integration. According to the assumptions made by the model, MNEs would play a significant contribution to the virtuous and vicious circle effects which affect core and periphery regions respectively as market integration deepens. The compulsion for MNEs to concentrate innovatory and high value-added activity in core areas of the RIA would be strong, as would the incentive to locate low value-added activity in peripheral regions which lack an advanced techno-industrial base to attract R&D and other high value-added activities. Thus, peripheral regions are destined for assembly modes of production and the importation of knowledge-intensive products under the theoretical constructs of this model. Its applicability to the EU's plans for an eastern enlargement and EMU remain to be seen.

The contribution of corporate integration to the objectives of European integration

Two immediate considerations arise on this issue. First, intra-firm transactions, further induced by regional integration, will tend to incur lower costs than those from using external market mechanisms, thus providing a positive contribution to the objectives of European integration. However, the SEM may well enable MNEs to accumulate greater concentrations of oligopolistic–monopolistic market power and bear the accompanying adverse distributional effects. In addition, any remaining barriers to the completion of a fuller functioning single market that owe their origin to MNE cross-border activity (e.g. discriminatory national dealership networks) may be the most difficult to eradicate. Moreover, multinationals already attempt to reduce inefficiencies caused by government intervention by arbitraging national differences in tax rates, interest rates, tariffs and exchange controls (Robson and Wooton 1993). Aliber (1985) has implied that the potential gains from completing the single market will be reduced if MNEs already dominate in the RIA and pursue these practices effectively, although this will depend on the efficiency of existing transfer price systems.

Other considerations for non-EU multinationals concern how the integration of their European activities affects the balance of the global strategies they wish to pursue and what difference any redress of this balance could make to Europe's competitive position. Decisions made by the firm regarding how the benefits originating from European integration are distributed between EU and non-EU stakeholders will also be of relevance. The EU's institutions and its member state governments are able to implement a range of policy initiatives aimed at helping EU firms compete more effectively against non-EU rivals, for example the Trans-European Networks, joint R&D programmes (e.g. ESPIRIT), consortia projects (e.g. Airbus). However, the ultimate success of these initiatives depends on the ability of EU firms to exploit the opportunities presented by the SEM to overcome structural market distortions and transactional market failures. As we shall note later, US multinationals were arguably better able to rationalise in accordance with these principles in the early stages of European integration than were their European rivals.

One of the key economic objectives of European integration is to improve the competitive position of EU firms at home and abroad. The European response to the challenge from the USA has taken different forms, each yielding varied degrees of success. Some larger EU firms, such as Philips, Hoechst and ICI, have tackled US rivals head on. Cross-border mergers, joint ventures and consortia have been formed between other European firms which have granted them the scale and concentration to compete more effectively against their generally larger American counterparts. Certain domestic merger activity was engineered by similar motives. For example, in 1968 the UK's Industrial Reorganisation Commission fused together Leyland Motors and BMC in an attempt to compete against Ford and General Motors.

European integration and state policy towards FDI

In 1962, the implementation of two directives confirmed the Treaty of Rome's commitment to the principles of free capital movements across the Community but left member states free to set their own terms and conditions on FDI flows to and from third countries. Although this situation currently remains the case, the process of European integration has subsequently forged together some implicit aspects of member state policies towards FDI. This has worked through the common adoption of legislation and regulations in industrial, regional, competition, social and other policy areas, and also from preparations for the SEM and EMU. Member states wishing to retain a more resolutely autonomous FDI policy in the face of progressive European integration may encounter difficulties. For example, a more rigorous compliance to the SEM may well be an active method to attract inward FDI. Furthermore, the deepening of regional integration between member states may deny individual states their traditional differentiation against others, although asymmetric economic development may yet uphold this. Additional potential conflicts of interest may arise on other fronts as European integration continues. More liberal policies have tended to be adopted in small industrialised or internationalised countries (e.g. Benelux and the UK) whereas they have been less liberal in more interventionist economies (e.g. France and Italy). Thus, endeavours to formulate a future EU common policy towards FDI may be impeded by this conflict of traditions.

The need to co-ordinate FDI policies across the EU to avoid competition between member states and preserve the integrity of the single market presents another key issue. Problems arising over the fragmentary European approach to policy were illustrated by the 1992 Hoover case when the US multinational announced its intention to shift production from Dijon in France to Glasgow in Scotland owing to the UK's lower social charges. The UK's 'opt out' of the Social Chapter of the Maastricht Treaty was also thought to be instrumental to the decision. Another notable case concerned the Japanese car manufacturer, Nissan. The company established a greenfield foreign investment in Sunderland, UK, in 1986. Although Nissan began its operations based on 'completely knocked down' (CKD) kit production with only a 20 per cent local content ratio, by 1988 it had risen to 60 per cent and was due to rise to 80 per cent by 1991 under its original contract with the UK government. However, these arrangements did not satisfy the French and Italian governments which were imposing voluntary export restraints (VERs) on Japanese car exports to protect production and employment at home. Initially, both countries refused to acknowledge the UK produced Nissan Bluebirds as European, causing the European Commission to intervene in April 1989 – when local content of the cars had reached a 65 per cent ratio – to announce the cars in question as formally European produced.

Endeavours to harmonise policies towards FDI across the EU are further complicated by two other issues. The first concerns the growth of regional governments and sub-regional agents that have developed their own external profiles in response to globalisation. National governments are thus not the only players in transnational relations as district authorities also attempt to attract inward investment to their own localities (Campanella 1995). Second, around 600 bilateral investment treaties have been signed worldwide, many of which involve EU member states and third countries. This has obviously injected a significant degree of complexity into rules governing FDI, although the OECD has a reasonably well-established voluntary investment code for host country treatment of inward investment. Furthermore, the TRIMs agreement of the Uruguay Round incorporated a specific investment discipline in multilateral fora for the first time, albeit that its remit is limited to redressing trade distorting activities.

In 1995, discussions began to establish a firmer base on which FDI rules and codes could be multilateralised. The Commission published its own recommendations based on a three-pronged strategy of providing freer access, upholding the principle of national treatment and introducing an array of accompanying measures to help create a level playing field for foreign investment (CEC 1995n). The WTO is perhaps the most appropriate organisation to take on this responsibility given the substantial links between trade and investment and the principles and institutional mechanisms on which its operative capacity is based. Some countries, most notably the USA, have favoured a more pragmatic agreement between OECD signatories first to substantiate such rules for developed countries to which developing countries can later join. The reasoning behind this proposal is that many developing countries would not be able to sustain the liberal FDI regimes that are pursued by most of the OECD group. However, given the increasing stock of foreign investment being accumulated in non-OECD locations, it would appear sensible to involve them as closely as possible in any future multilateral negotiations on the issue.

The growing significance of SMEs in foreign investments also highlights the need for multilateral governance to guide and protect their investment interests. The alignment of national policies to formulate international regulations on FDI will particularly affect competition policy. The absence of trade-related barriers to investments makes those of any other kind which impede foreign competition more critical to identify. Deliberate discrimination against foreign investors may prove notoriously difficult to establish. This is largely because they may originate from immutable cultural and structural differences that are inherent in all countries. As we shall discuss later, this has become the prime focus of triadic negotiations to open up Japan to more inward investment.

TRANS-ATLANTIC FDI

Foreign investment flows between the USA and Europe still retain their long-standing global significance, accounting for over half the world's cumulative total. Both regions had been export markets for each other's industries, serving to reduce the informational costs borne from Trans-Atlantic FDI activity. By 1993, the EU accounted for 53 per cent of total FDI in the USA, while US foreign investments made up 42 per cent of those made in the EU. Current estimates suggest that about 10 per cent of US manufacturing output is derived from EU firms located there, while US firms based in the EU account for between 15 per cent and 20 per cent of total EU manufacturing output.

The 1950s to the 1980s

The post-war reconstruction of Europe was partially achieved by the involvement of American MNEs working in orchestration with the US government, bringing with them the capital, technology and know-how of the most sophisticated and 'intact' industrial power of the time. Working largely in unison with the Marshall Plan, they provided an essential foundation on which this reconstruction was based. Another notable feature of the involvement of US firms in Europe during the early post-war years was their positive response to the formation of the EEC. Between 1960 and 1985, the share of total US outward FDI taken by the Community nearly doubled from 18.3 per cent to 36.4 per cent. Foreign investments have been particularly active in those industries best positioned to acquire the dynamic efficiencies of vertical integration (e.g. chemicals, pharmaceuticals) where economies of specialisation and common governance are most attainable. This became increasingly apparent as the common market began to unify and after the Community's CET was installed. In his seminal work, *The American Challenge*, Servan-Schreiber (1968) stated that, 'Fifteen years from now it is quite possible that the world's third largest industrial power, just after the US and Russia, will not be Europe, but American industry in Europe. Already, in its ninth year of the Common Market, this European market is basically American in organisation.'

From an early stage, the internalised benefits rendered from the intrafirm trade of Community-based US multinationals combined with fervent rationalisation drives enabled them to develop successful competitive advantages against domestic European producers. The relative imbalance in US–EC investment flows (see Tables 8.5 and 8.6) for most of the period in question was a further source of tension. Certain European nations, in particular France, expressed their concern over the threat posed by American multinational activity not just to their national economic integrity but also over its adverse social and cultural impact.

Table 8.5 US FDI in the EC, 1960–93

	1960	*1970*	*1980*	*1985*	*1990*	*1993*
All EC12 industries ($bn)	6.0	20.9	79.9	84.0	172.9	224.6
Total US outward FDI ($bn)	32.7	78.1	213.4	229.7	421.5	448.3
EC12 share of total US outward FDI (per cent)	18.3	26.7	37.4	36.4	41.2	50.1

Sources: Wallace and Kline 1992, US Treasury 1995, Reinicke 1996

Table 8.6 EC FDI in the USA, 1965–93

	1965	*1975*	*1980*	*1985*	*1990*	*1993*
All industries ($bn)	4.9	15.6	40.0	107.1	229.9	238.0
Total US inward FDI ($bn)	8.8	27.7	68.4	184.6	403.7	449.1
EC12 share of total US inward FDI (per cent)	55.6	56.3	58.5	58.0	56.9	53.0

Sources: Wallace and Kline 1992, US Treasury 1995, Reinicke 1996

Such sentiments had largely subsided by the late 1970s, especially as US companies were not able to resist the diffusion of their advanced technologies and management systems which European firms were able to capture and eventually convert into relative competitive gains on their Trans-Atlantic rivals. This development led partly to the changing circumstances which were to follow. For much of the post-war years, the impact of European FDI in the USA caused comparatively minimal stir in the host nation. By the mid-1980s, as Tables 8.5 and 8.6 reveal, the balance of the Trans-Atlantic investment relationship began to alter with the Community's outward FDI to the USA overhauling US foreign investment in the Community. The gap continued on a divergent path until the end of the decade, as Table 8.4 also testifies. This adjustment in Trans-Atlantic investment flows infers the following:

- improved competitive and ownership advantages of EU firms along with the competitive advantages of the US economy in exploiting these advantages;
- insider Triad power motives have been at work based on the acquisition of new technology and key strategic knowledge (both of US firms and Japanese firms in the USA) as have the opportunities presented by scale and scope economies.

In relation to these points, Dunning (1993: 182) comments, 'In the late 1980s, EC investment in the US was partly a reflection of the economic vitality of the investing countries, and partly a deliberate strategy by European multinational firms to protect or advance their global competitive positions.' It may have appeared strange that huge outflows of European investment coincided with preparations being made by European companies for the SEM. However, we must understand such a strategy in the context of globalisation, and thus as an effort to strengthen their competitive advantages both inside and outside Europe.

Anxieties were soon raised in the USA over the invasion made by European companies in the form of their capital investments. This was compounded by a similar penetration made by Japanese MNEs during the decade. Merger and acquisition FDI was the most prominent feature of European Trans-Atlantic investment in the 1980s, more than doubling between 1984 and 1988. This should also be seen as part of a wider trend of frenzied M&A activity during the decade. Furthermore, the closing of the gap between respective Trans-Atlantic investment flows in the 1980s must be set against the gradual convergence of US inward and outward FDI over the decade, as noted earlier (see Figure 8.1). Up to 1980, the ratio between US FDI inflows to outflows had remained at approximately one-third. By the end of the decade a parity relationship had almost emerged, although in the early 1990s outflows were beginning to pull away from inflows again with an increasing proportion being directed towards the East Asian region.

On a more specific locational basis, the UK has traditionally been the host of US investment in Europe due to a variety of economic factors and cultural similarities. In 1957, when the Treaty of Rome was signed, the UK economy received 54 per cent of all US FDI entering Europe. This pre-dominant position was gradually undermined as the potential of European integration began to be more widely acknowledged by US multinationals. Sales of American manufacturing affiliates in the UK accounted for 3.2 per cent of its GNP in the same year, as opposed to the EEC's 1.8 per cent. By the time the UK joined the Community in 1973, the gap had closed to 6.1 per cent and 5.8 per cent respectively. However, once the UK had more purposely engaged in the European integration process, US outward FDI to the UK actually rose faster than it did for the rest of the Community, increasing from 35.7 per cent to 40.7 per cent of the Community total over 1972 to 1985. It should, though, be noted that US manufacturing invest-ment fell in the UK from 29.4 per cent to 13.1 per cent of the Community total over the same period. European outward FDI flows across the Atlantic have also been dominated by UK multinationals which consistently took a higher share of the direct investment stake in the USA up to the year it acceded Community membership (33.5 per cent in 1972, the EC 27.1 per cent). The UK continued to make sizeable investments in the USA, taking 26.8 per cent of total inflows into the country in 1990, representing 47.1 per cent of the value of all Community investments made there.

The impact of the single market and beyond

It has already been established that US firms had seen Europe as one market long before the launch of the SEM programme. The Single European Act (SEA) of 1986 and its integrational agenda thus served to reinforce this perception. A new wave of US investment followed resulting in a 56.2 per cent increase in sales for Community-based American subsidiaries between 1985 and 1988. The strongest trends lay in those sectors most expected to gain from the SEM's provisions (pharmaceuticals 81.0 per cent; motor vehicles 130.5 per cent; finance, except banking, 176.2 per cent; business services 141.5 per cent). A high propensity of M&A activity and strategic alliance formation were also to be found in these areas. In addition, there was a general shift of US investment interests more towards peripheral member states (especially Spain, Ireland and Germany) that has been largely at the expense of the UK. Other relevant trends emerged:

- US intra-firm trade in Europe also increased tempo as the single market began to take shape, while the growth of US manufacturing output in Europe rose faster than US exports (both intra-EC and Trans-Atlantic) to Europe.
- US firms now currently sell around five times more from production and service facilities inside Europe to European markets than from outside it.
- US manufacturing subsidiaries sell 60 per cent of their output to the market in which they are located. This location specific strategy is particularly pursued in larger market countries.

Apart from the reinvigorated competitive environment that should be created by the SEM programme, a number of other important challenges face Trans-Atlantic investors in the 1990s. These include assisting the economic recovery in central and eastern Europe and safeguarding access in other Triad markets. NAFTA will present an increasingly attractive location as the dynamic benefits of integration appear, while the benefits of penetrating the Japanese market are also considerable. The latter objective may prove more attainable after the signing of two agreements in 1991: the Structural Impediments Initiative between the USA and Japan and the EC–Japanese Co-operation Declaration. Both contained miscellaneous bilateral arrangements aimed at removing barriers that had hindered foreign competition in Japan. Wallace and Kline (1992) propose other key aspects of the US–European investment relationship:

- Changing patterns of corporate investment: in endeavours to minimise liabilities and costs, elaborate Trans-Atlantic strategic alliances have been formed whereby the value-added chain of activities is reconfigurated between involved parties, blurring the focus of their corporate nationality. This had made it difficult for governments to apply national level FDI policy instruments and for MNEs to gain access and eligibility for government programmes aimed to assist them. For example, European incorporated US firms have been allowed only partial admission to the Joint European Submicron Silicon Initiative (JESSI) scheme while US-based EU firms are denied involvement in any government projects with US Defense Department funding such as Sematech, the US equivalent to JESSI.
- US federalism versus EU centralism: a very decentralised FDI policy exists in the USA owing to the autonomous governance given to individual states. These states have established their own offices across Europe and elsewhere to promote inward FDI. The US federal government does have some role to play in setting a national agenda on FDI

policy, largely through common measures on taxation, competition policy, product liability, company disclosure of information, education and technology. The EU, on the other hand, has pursued increasingly centralised policies on industrial organisation and regulation policies originating from the convergence associated with the SEM, the merger regulation and other investment-related policy areas. US firms thus benefit from having to deal more and more with centralised single authorities in the EU, whereas in the USA, EU firms still encounter an assortment of different state laws and practices.

- The US–EU investment relationship and its effects on other players: the sheer magnitude of the Trans-Atlantic FDI and the political and economic interests that are carried by it are a cause for concern for third parties. This has been particularly expressed by Japanese companies which fear the corporate pressures exerted in a 'two-versus-one' scenario involving themselves and Trans-Atlantic alliances. The market and low cost base production potential of the CEE countries could also divert US investment away from other regions.

Towards the end of the 1980s, foreign investors in the USA found that the traditionally very liberal policy stance adopted to FDI inflows had changed. The US Congress became concerned over adverse implications for national security carried by huge inward investments to which the USA had played host during the 1980s. A series of legislative measures was passed which aimed to enhance government control and competence in this field. The Exon-Florio provision of the 1988 Omnibus Trade Act was the first of these measures, strengthening the powers of investigation over foreign takeovers of US firms. Fujitsu's bid for Silicon Valley's Fairchild semiconductor operation was one casualty of the provision, as was the bid made by James Goldsmith, the famous Anglo-French corporate raider, for Goodyear, a major supplier to the US Army. Other legislation has followed in a similar vein into the 1990s.

Many observers believe that the legislation was more a reaction to the strategically sensitive investments made by Japanese firms in addition to their large-scale purchases of US real estate. In Chapter 6, we saw how low value-added investments being made by Japanese firms led to calls within the EU for more effective controls over inward investments. These typically entailed compliance with stricter rules on local content quotants and value-added activities. However, such protectionist posturing is likely to be tempered both by the outcome of negotiations commenced in 1995 on the establishment of multilateral rules on FDI and the inauguration of the New Trans-Atlantic Agenda in the same year.

EU–JAPANESE FDI

Emerging patterns of Japanese FDI

Owing to a number of government restrictions imposed on FDI, it was not until the late 1960s that Japanese firms began to invest overseas to any level of significance. Once such constraints were released, these investments could be said to reflect the various interactive developments working within the Japanese economy at the time. In broad terms, these could be identified as:

- the consequences of industrial restructuring;
- the systematic upgrading and improving of ownership specific advantages;
- the maintaining and advancing of export markets in developed countries;
- the shifting of uncompetitive activities to developing countries.

Particularly in its earlier stages, Japanese foreign investment in Western countries had also been used as a conduit for acquiring new technological knowledge. This has been channelled back to the parent company and converted into successful exporting strategies based on improved product modifications made to the original against which it eventually competes.

Indeed, many analysts have maintained that most of outward Japanese FDI up to the early 1980s was subordinated to the primary corporate and national objective of improving trade performance. Up to 1985, Japanese exports exceeded the value of Japanese overseas subsidiary production in Europe and the USA by ten times. FDI strategies geared towards achieving this objective were based on two types of investment:

- defensive market-seeking investments aimed at protecting export market shares, many taking the form of 'screwdriver' plants modelled on those that operated at home;
- offensive, supply-orientated investments characterised by activities that were engineered to upgrade and rationalise domestic operations with the overarching aims of prising open export markets and widening export distribution networks.

As Figure 8.5 shows, the USA has been seen as the favoured location of Japanese companies, accumulating 42 per cent of their overseas investments between 1951 and 1990. In contrast, Europe failed to match even half of this figure with 19.1 per cent of the total, further highlighting the general imbalance within the Triad relationship. One major consequence of this has been that export performance oriented Japanese FDI has lingered longer in Europe than in the USA which was increasingly playing host to Japanese MNEs with more substantial global objectives. The comparatively stronger magnetic pull of the US economy can be attributed to a variety of factors:

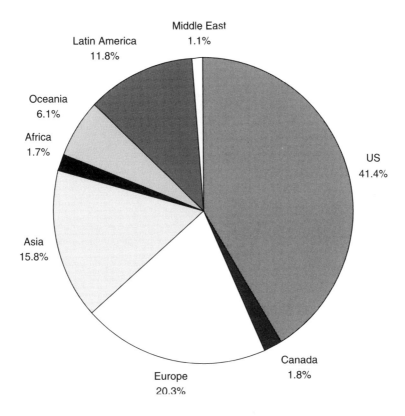

Figure 8.5 Accumulated share of Japanese overseas FDI, 1951–94
Source: Japanese Ministry of Finance

- the nature of the USA–Japan political ties that were nurtured in post-war years and the economic relationship which emerged;
- the opportunities afforded by superior sources of new technology located in the USA;
- the formation of a large, prosperous and well-integrated market in the USA provided Japanese MNEs with more scope for internalising markets and acquiring dynamic efficiency gains;
- the US policy framework for inward FDI has traditionally been more liberal than those found in EU member states.

Although the foreign investments of Japanese manufacturers have perhaps attracted most attention, Japanese FDI in the European and American economies is predominated by services, taking just over two-thirds of total FDI in both. Finance and banking (most of the world's top ten banks are Japanese), insurance, real estate, trading services, hotels and catering are the most important sectors in which the Japanese have established a presence in Europe. Reasonably similar investment patterns are found in the USA with greater sectoral emphasis on wholesale trade and real estate. Japanese service sector MNEs generally arrived well before manufacturers in both Europe and the USA to facilitate home-based exporting activity, largely assisted through the intermediation of balance of payments surpluses (Balasubramanyam and Greenaway 1992). The persistence of surpluses also explains why levels of inward Japanese FPI into Europe are still greater than correspondent FDI inflows. A further wave of service sector FDI followed in support of Japanese manufacturers which arrived *en masse* only from the early 1980s onwards. In manufacturing, Japanese firms have invested most heavily in machinery, transport equipment and electric/electronic goods sectors within the EU, with manufacturing as a whole representing 27.9 per cent of Japanese FDI in 1991.

While there was a marked increase in overseas investments made by Japanese firms in the 1970s after the relinquishment of many government controls, only by the mid-1980s was there a real acceleration of Japanese outward FDI activity. The underlying reasons for this lay mainly in the government's reversal of policy towards one of positive encouragement, the rising value of the yen, the relative shortage and high cost of domestic labour and the emergence of neighbouring NICs as alternative production locations. The shift to more knowledge-intensive industrial activities and the need for a rationalised global strategy were additional key determinants that can be understood in the context of Ohmae's (1985a, b) view of acquiring an insider status within the Triad. This implied a move away from the export performance oriented strategies, on which foreign investments were partly based for so long, to FDI driven by the need to integrate globally corporate activities. This extension of the global reach of Japanese companies first began, as we have noted earlier, in the USA.

The single market in context

The signing of the SEA in 1986, within which lay the blueprint for the single market, acted as an important catalyst for inward Japanese investment. Table 8.4 clearly shows the rapid increases of Japanese FDI that were seemingly triggered in preparation for 1992, a resonant echo of the increased influx of American FDI after the Treaty of Rome was signed decades earlier. In both 1989 and 1990, annual levels of inward Japanese investment had reached well over ECU 4bn, as opposed to the average mid-1980s levels of around ECU 500m, although a significant dip was recorded between 1991 and 1992 owing to recessional factors.

There has nevertheless been much debate over the influence of the SEM programme on the accelerated pace of Japanese FDI in the EU. From their empirical studies, Heitger and Stehn (1990) contended that the increase was a reaction to fears of a future 'Fortress Europe' position being adopted by the EU. This implied a belief in the use of protectionist measures to help insulate the single market from foreign competition while ensuring its benefits could be more fully enjoyed by EU-based firms. European industrial lobbyists, representing those industries that were most adversely affected by the competitive rigours of the single market, were at the forefront of those calling for compensatory external trade protection. Thus, Japanese firms have sought to acquire an 'insider' status within the SEM in order to circumvent any high tariff regime that may afflict their exports. However, Nicolaides and Thomsen (1991) argue that while EU integration does partly explain the raised interest of Japanese MNEs in establishing European locations, other factors demand consideration. The most important of these concerns the growing use of ownership specific advantages by Japanese firms during the mid-1980s onwards on a global strategic scale. In other words, a significant spurt of Japanese investment in Europe may have occurred anyway, regardless of the SEM programme as part of this wider development. Nicolaides and Thomsen also question why certain European industrial lobbies would seek to induce foreign rivals to locate within the protectionist wall and thus have to compete against them on a more direct basis.

While Japanese firms have not yet established themselves on the same scale as American firms, their ownership specific advantages should enable them to capture the microeconomic efficiency gains generated by the SEM to a considerable degree. This will partly depend on their ability to internalise these advantages and transplant particular production and service structures that are distinctly Japanese, which we shall discuss later. Dunning (1993) comments that because Japanese firms have 'less cross-EC institutional impediments to relinquish' compared to European firms, they will not be able to exploit organisational and technical capacities as much as their indigenous rivals. Furthermore, certain parallel measures undertaken with respect to the SEM that have been specifically aimed at supporting European firms (e.g. R&D programmes and competition policy measures) should reinforce their competitive position relative to foreign firms. Many European firms have also learnt from closer observation of Japanese production and management methods. This may potentially result in a similar loss of competitive advantage once held by US firms over European rivals before they encamped themselves in close proximity. The UK, which is consistently attracting between 30 per cent to 40 per cent of all inward Japanese FDI into the EU, is more favourably placed to seize such benefits. The advantages acquired by Rover in its collaborations with Honda from the late 1970s onwards also demonstrated the potential benefits derived from strategic alliances formed with Japanese firms.

Japanese FDI and industrial restructuring: Ozawa's thesis

We have recognised some validity in the argument that up to the early 1980s much of Japanese outward FDI was based on export performance oriented strategies. Ozawa's (1991) contention that patterns of Japanese outward FDI must be understood as an integral part of the restructuring of Japanese industry is also worthy of attention, and owes its theoretical origins to macroeconomic development and product life cycle models of international production. In this thesis, Japanese post-war industrial restructuring was broken down into four distinct but overlapping phases:

- Phase 1: expansion of labour-intensive manufacturing in textiles, sundries and other low-wage goods (1950s to mid-1960s).
- Phase 2: scale-based modernisation of heavy and chemical industries such as steel, aluminium, ship-building, petrochemicals and synthetic fibres (late 1950s to early 1970s).
- Phase 3: assembly-based, subcontracting dependent, mass production of consumer durable products (late 1960s to present day).
- Phase 4: flexible manufacturing of highly differentiated goods utilising CAD/CAM and other micro-chip technologies (early 1980s to present day).

Alongside these four phases of domestic industrial restructuring lay three phases of FDI, namely the 'elementary' stage of offshore production, the 'Ricardo–Hicksian trap' stage of transnationalism and the 'export-substituting-cum-surplus-recycling' stage of multinationalism. The 'elementary' stage of FDI for Japanese firms evolved from the locational advantages of basing labour-intensive production offshore in neighbouring East Asian countries owing to their more competitively waged but relatively well-skilled workforces. In the second FDI phase, Ozawa asserts that the Japanese economy fell into what she terms a 'Ricardo–Hicksian trap' whereby its shift to heavy industry production induced an unsustainable resource dependent position. At the centre of the predicament lay the country's own lack of natural resource endowments. The trap essentially consisted of the constraints placed by an 'irremovable scarcity' of resources upon the economy's ability to generate substantial levels of reinvestable profits. Moreover, acute environmental problems arose from this industrial structuring and were further compounded by the tight demographic clustering of the population around compact industrialised areas. Foreign investment provided a way out of the trap by Japanese companies securing stable supplies of industrial raw materials, the transfer of some resource intensive industrial activity overseas and policy guided moves to restructure Japanese industry towards less resource consuming and more knowledge-intensive industries. Neighbouring Asian countries were the prime target of this phase of FDI where mining in particular has subsequently become the predominant sector to have attracted Japanese foreign investment.

The third stage of restructuring, that of assembly-based mass production of consumer durable goods, developed from this shift in industrial activity. Japan's phenomenal export success of these industries was quickly established and it was not long before protectionist measures were defensively imposed upon them in both Europe and the USA. The accumulation of financial capital from substantial trade surpluses and high rates of domestic saving were recycled to fund and resource what amounted to a series of export substitution exercises conducted by a growing number of Japanese MNEs overseas, with many making their first forage on to European and American territory by the mid-1970s. The more extensive application of protectionist measures gave greater spur to the internationalisation of Japanese firms. This heralded the start of the third and final stage of Japanese outward FDI, according to Ozawa's model.

The introduction of flexible manufacturing techniques relatively early in the fourth stage of industrial restructuring enabled Japanese firms to compete successfully in Europe and to make some adjustments to the multi-domestic competitive conditions that were concentrated across a fairly small geographical expanse. The need to observe more clearly the nuances of Western consumer cultures so as to exploit these new industrial capabilities gave further impetus to raise levels of FDI in both Europe and the USA. It comes as no surprise that automobiles, electric/electronic goods and other high value-added products that form the core of Japanese assembly-based industries have spearheaded most of Japan's foreign manufacturing investment in Europe and the USA. To Ozawa, the five major sources of competitive advantages which have been developed in these sectors have been:

1 Effective use of a multi-layered system of subcontracting.
2 Widespread practice of a 'just-in-time' (JIT) inventory system, combined with 'total quality control'.
3 Successful commercial exploitation of R&D and other innovative activities and the formation of 'new composite technologies'.
4 Ever-sophisticated consumer demand from rising incomes and expectations.
5 Intense rivalry between domestic firms.

The interaction between the above factors has nurtured higher levels of dynamic efficiency in these Japanese industries relative to their Triad counterparts. Yet, somewhat obvious problems arise for internationalising Japanese firms in transplanting these competitive advantages abroad. Factors (1) and (2) present Japanese MNEs with the greatest challenge here. The operation of a JIT system and thus the lean production method itself can only effectively function if a multi-layered pyramid of subcontractors has been established. In the Japanese automobile industry, this pyramid consists of three stages of productive activity below the major assemblers (see Figure 8.6). Static efficiency gains are generated from this intricate

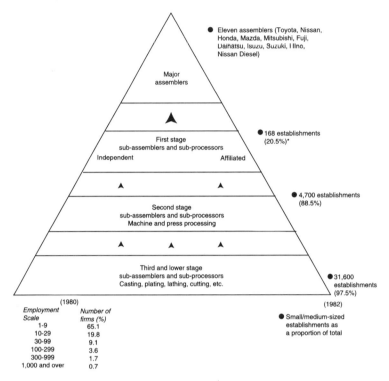

Figure 8.6 Japan's pyramidal system of production: the automobile industry
Source: Ozawa, T. (1991) *Multinationals and Europe 1992*, 148

vertical division of labour based on the orchestrated inter-firm flow of intermediate products. Dynamic gains are also derived from the constant bilateral exchange of information that enables improved strategic decision-making. The major assemblers benefit from the dedication of their sub-contractors' R&D activity to their own cause. Subcontractors benefit from the technical, financial and other forms of assistance granted them by the major assemblers. This reflects the 'shared destiny' relationship that binds all members of the pyramid together, creating the conditions for synergetic collaborations to flourish.

Western production has traditionally been organised on a mono-layered subcontracting principle. However, Ozawa comments that the EU has presented Japanese assembly-based firms with a more favourable environment to anchor a multi-layered system of subcontracting. The regional diversity found in labour market conditions and the high density of SMEs have proved conducive. Peripheral member states, such as Portugal and Spain, have been targeted by the Japanese as locations for more labour-intensive upstream production. The enthusiastic embracing of Japanese-style production and management methods by some European countries, in particular the UK, has also helped support the system. Some of the major assemblers' usual subcontractors have followed them overseas. For example, NSK Bearings, TI-Nihon, SP Tyres, Nissan Yamato and Ikeda-Hoover were among the first of such firms to have clustered around Nissan's car plant in Sunderland. In the process it has been common for many Japanese auto component suppliers to have made joint venture arrangements with indigenous counterparts in both the USA and Europe. This trend, though, is more developed in the USA where it is estimated that between one-quarter to one-half of Japanese suppliers have entered into joint ventures of this kind.

Inward flows of FDI to Japan

As we mentioned earlier in the chapter, there exists a considerable imbalance between Japan's inward and outward foreign investment flows with a heavy skewing towards the latter. Over the period between 1984 and 1991 annual levels of inward FDI to Japan from EU firms ranged from only 3.6 per cent to 10.4 per cent of those outward Japanese FDI flows received by Europe. Government restrictions (particularly on foreign M&A activity), the failure to harmonise with international standards and testing procedures, convoluted distribution networks, the impenetrable nature of the domestic market and *keiretsu* business structures have been cited as key impediments to European companies establishing a presence in this Triad core. While some genuine concern can be construed from these points, at least equal blame must be placed on EU firms which have not familiarised themselves adequately with Japanese business culture, distribution practices and the government regulatory framework. The comparatively small number of strategic alliances to have been formed between European and Japanese firms within the triadic structure is similarly accusatory.

As part of a wider framework to strengthen the weakest link in the Triad, recent efforts have been made to redress the imbalance in the EU–Japanese investment relationship. In March 1995, the Japanese government announced plans for a five-year deregulation programme that would comprise of measures to stimulate inward foreign investment. The success of the programme will, though, ultimately depend on the breadth and depth of response it has been devised to elicit from economic agents and organisations within Japan's domestic economy. Many of those impediments mentioned above possess defining characteristics that are essentially structural or cultural in nature. Hence, efforts to remove them completely may take a very long time to accomplish or, in some cases, may be impossible. This will be reinforced by actions of resistance to *gaiatsu* (foreign pressure) from the perception that Japan's economic as well as societal identity is being threatened. Consequently, the imbalance seems set to remain unless European multinationals are able to construct more innovative investment strategies in Japan or work in closer collaboration with Japanese firms through different forms of strategic alliance. The increasing significance of the East Asian region as an investment centre will undoubtedly create some of the impetus required, with Japan providing the location and resources for higher value-added activities of European investors.

The future of Japanese firms in Europe

Unlike their US counterparts which had already established a bridgehead in Europe decades before, Japanese firms to some degree have had to start from scratch, and consequently paid the higher transaction costs incurred from doing so. The relative lack of socio-cultural similarities also served to raise the potential outlays involved. However, Japanese firms have demonstrated their adroitness in adapting to changing OLI conditions of operation in Europe and the USA which has mainly entailed a shift from an essentially defensive export protection strategy to one based on more offensive global positioning. The success of recent Japanese FDI has been based on ownership specific advantages consisting of advanced managerial and technological capacities, the improved locational advantages of Europe and the USA relative to a home and home region base and the perception of Japanese firms that they possess the organisational capacity to add greater value by internalising productive and service activity. Moreover, Young *et al.* (1991) maintain that the very fact that Japanese firms are relative newcomers to Europe compared to their more entrenched US peers may advantage them in rationalising their operations in a manner sensitive to evolving conditions created by the SEM programme.

It is perhaps too premature still to make any evaluation on how successful has been the transferral and internalisation of Japanese MNEs' ownership specific advantages within their European branch operations. The same could be said of how European firms will react to more direct Japanese competition within the SEM. Although the articulation of partisan attitudes is still expressed in some quarters of the EU predicated on the assumption that Japanese firms remain 'marginal providers' in terms of core R&D and other value-added activities, there is evidence that indicates that European based Japanese firms have improved the competitive advantages of the host economy (Thomsen and Nicolaides 1991). In the opinion of Morris (1991), Japanese manufacturing MNEs in Europe began to move away from their position of being low value-added assembly producers around the start of the 1990s. Young and Hood (1992) support this view, contending that Japanese firms are progressively improving their value-added contributions to the European economy. In the twenty-first century, Japanese firms in Europe could prove just as important a source of competitive advantage to the European economy as American multinationals have been in post-war years.

FDI AND CENTRAL AND EASTERN EUROPE

Earliest beginnings

Despite the ideological frictions that were supposed to arise from most forms of economic contact with the West, the authorities in central and eastern Europe gradually began to develop a more open environment to FDI from as early as the late 1960s onwards. This primarily arose from the recognition that the isolated stance taken by the region in the post-war world economy might soon evolve into one of marginalisation, particularly with respect to technological development. The Yugoslavian government was the first to pass legislation permitting FDI activity in 1967. This was followed by Romania and Hungary in 1972, Poland in 1976, Bulgaria in 1980, Czechoslovakia in 1986, the Soviet Union in 1987 and Albania the last to adopt such legislation in 1990. In attempts to reduce the ideological risks and maximise the capital benefits, a strict regulatory regime was imposed upon inward foreign investments by the CEE communist countries. This was typified by two general limitations. First, foreign capital participation was allowed only in partnership with a host country enterprise with inward investors limited to a minority share (i.e. 49 per cent maximum). Second, the involvement of foreign capital was restricted to certain industries specified by the host country. For example, during the 1970s Hungary banned inward FDI in material production and consumer services (UN 1992a). As a means to protect the interests of their own firms, Western countries have pressed for and secured a number of bilateral investment treaties with the CEE states since the 1970s. Joint ventures or 'international inter-enterprise co-operative agreements' were the more ideologically palatable terms in which CEE governments chose to describe any FDI links that had been forged in the process. Indeed, collaborative ventures between Western and CEE enterprises existed before rules on more formalised FDI were adopted. These had occurred especially in the automobile industry where Fiat, Ford, Citroen, Renault, Volkswagen, General Motors and others had established a series of licensing, co-production and subcontracting agreements with CEE governments dating back to the 1950s.

The restrictive conditions placed on foreign capital had made the CEE region the exception to the rule in that most middle-income countries had generally followed the pattern of receiving inward investments before becoming the source of significant outward investments (Artisien and McMillan 1993). Many CEE enterprises were actively involved in pursuing the strategic objectives of appropriating new forms of Western technology and the need to increase exports to the West to procure much required hard currency from an early stage. State trading companies had also established links with Western sources of supply based on the acquisition of strategically important imports. In addition, some attempts were made to re-establish the trade links that existed in pre-communist times, for example between Hungary and Austria. Most outward FDI flows from the CEE countries have been directed to Western Europe which has been the host to over half the outward investments made.

The transformation process in perspective

The current transformation process in Central and Eastern Europe has radically altered the environment for FDI, presenting both potentially high costs and benefits for the foreign investor. The microeconomic dislocation and macroeconomic imbalances that still persist to varying degrees across the region present a significant scale of risk. On the other hand, considerable opportunities lie in the huge potential market size and the competitively priced and abundant resource base – both natural and human – which the CEE countries possess.

For Western governments eager to assist the transformation process, FDI represents both a means to transplant the sinews of capitalism within the region and to restructure industries in closer accordance with global economic patterns. Multinationals represent the embodiment of the most advanced form of capitalist organisation and corporate activity. Their ownership specific advantages therefore have an important role to play in helping coagulate the formation of the market economy. The EU's attempts to fund investments through the European Bank for Reconstruction and Development (EBRD) and PHARE programme (see Table 4.6, p. 120) have made some contribution to improve the general investment climate for business mainly through its infrastructure, technology transfer and minor industrial restructuring projects. The extent to which FDI has been levered in by these endeavours to ameliorate the location specific advantages of the CEE countries is unclear. The generally recognised paucity of the funds that have been allocated so far would imply that their impact has been insignificant. For those countries that are preparing for EU accession by the early twenty-first century (i.e. the CEE6: Hungary, Poland, the Czech Republic, Slovakia, Bulgaria, Romania) can expect to receive more inflows of FDI leading up to the event. Nevertheless, it is in the interests of the EU to commit itself further to promote FDI inflows to complement or substitute the transfer payments for which these states will be eligible from the EU's Structural, Cohesion and other relevant funds.

The transformation process has also meant that the old state sector MNEs, now newly privatised, have encountered substantial difficulties, particularly in aspects of finance and restructuring. The imperative to extend trade links and to internationalise on a more ambitious scale remains strong. The existing network of foreign affiliates will no doubt be retained as a central part of this strategy. Furthermore, the gradual reintegration of the CEE region with Western Europe and the world economy in general should further assist the process. On a domestic scale, the infusion of new competition from inward foreign investments will assist the restructuring process by helping break down sectoral concentrations. These originated from the predominance of state monopolies in most key sectors. Donges and Wieners (1994) contend that this approach has been more effective in introducing competition to the market than simply breaking up existing incumbent monopolies into competing units. Moreover, it has provided a yardstick for evaluating the performance of domestic producers.

The relationship between FDI and the broader, longer term economic development in the CEE region deserves some special consideration. This is explored in three alternative models as proposed by Dunning (1993). The 'developing country' model proposes that FDI is attracted by the high rates of economic growth, as has been the case for the East Asian NICs. Some doubt has been cast on the applicability of this scenario for the CEE countries whose capacity to attract large influxes of FDI may be compromised by a comparatively weak industrial performance over recent years, a dilapidated infrastructure and the burgeoning interventionist policies still pursued by some central governments. Albania, Bulgaria and Romania are suggested as the most likely CEE countries to follow this model, though it may be some time before any emerging and appropriate patterns of economic development make themselves apparent.

The 'reconstruction' model draws on the early post-war experience of Germany and Japan whose growth path was initially determined by transfers of funds from outside sources and strategies configurated on the basis that neither country was particularly resource rich. German reunification provides the most obvious example of where an ex-Soviet bloc country (i.e. the GDR) has undergone a transfer dependent reconstruction, while Dunning suggests that countries such as Hungary and the Czech Republic are 'two or three steps behind' from attempting to reconstruct through the help of indigenous and foreign investments. Those CEE countries which are abundant in natural resources must particularly not to be distracted from attempting to emulate the strategies of Germany and Japan in developing the key technological, organisational and managerial capabilities required for industrial success. This model, though, does not consider the wider political, social and cultural changes that are also required for effective reconstruction to take place.

The 'systemic' model draws on elements of the previous two models while additionally taking account of micro- and macro-organisational and attitudinal changes necessary for economic development. The parameters of this model are described by Dunning (1993: 230): 'the willingness and ability of foreign (and domestic for that matter) investors rests mainly on the speed and extent to which East European economies can organise both their economic and legal systems, and the ethos of their people towards entrepreneurship and wealth creating activities'. The broader considerations that foreign investors have to make in this model of development may entail a slow initial entry rate of foreign firms. This should quicken as the jigsaw pieces of a fuller transition to a market economy fall into place and the associated costs of establishment subsequently diminish (i.e. through agglomeration effects). As we shall see later, this has particularly worked to the advantage of Hungary and to a lesser extent the Czech Republic in their ability to attract inward FDI flows.

Observations on recent FDI trends and developments

A more outright policy of encouragement has been adopted by all CEE governments towards FDI under the conditions created by the transformation process. This has entailed a general broadening of objectives to include the procuring of transfers of management, financial and marketing skills to assist the transition to market economy status. More original objectives – technology transfer, export market promotion and boosting hard currency reserves – have remained just as critical. Yet in an analysis on FDI trends in the region, Radice (1995: 1) states that, 'East European governments have taken a rather piecemeal and pragmatic approach towards foreign capital, and have given little thought to co-ordinating the wide range of policies that affect both the decisions of foreign capital and the eventual impact of those decisions'. It is further argued that where this is manifest, inward FDI has been used as a 'quick fix' to more immediate problems, such as the acquisition of hard currency through sizeable privatisation share sales to foreign investors which could have possible longer term detrimental effects on the economy.

The conflict that arose between Volkswagen (VW) and the Czech government over the management of Skoda – the once state-owned automobile manufacturer and centrepiece of the Czech privatisation programme – presents an illustrative case study of the tensions that have originated between some foreign investors and CEE governments. In 1991, VW outlined its plans to invest DM9.5bn in Skoda over a ten-year period when it succeeded in its bid to acquire the enterprise with an initial 31 per cent stake rising to 70 per cent by 1996. The German firm established a joint venture plant at Mlada Boleslav with an annual planned production of over 200,000 cars in the first phase and an eventual planned expansion to 450,000 per annum.

Relations were to deteriorate when in September 1993 the company announced that it intended to raise the price of Skoda models by an 8 per cent average on the premise of higher costs incurred from upgrading, marketing and distributing the cars through new networks. It also emerged that Skoda was to consider switching from some original Czech suppliers to German and British producers because of rising cost levels in the host country and other strategic reasons. Such moves would have amounted to Volkswagen reneging on its stated commitment to using indigenous suppliers. In further developments later on that year, VW decided to pull out of a DM1.4bn project partly facilitated by the EBRD and the International

Finance Corporation to assist Skoda's development. New management changes at the top executive level of VW had ushered in scaled down expectations regarding all branches of the company's operations, as a consequence of poor market performance and over-optimistic investments made in the early 1990s. The Czech government, concerned about the combined effects which these decisions would have on domestic inflation and employment, adopted a retaliatory posture by threatening to reduce tariff rates on imported cars. Volkswagen had made raised import tariffs a condition of its investment in 1991, with the Czech government agreeing to terms which would maintain such a regime for at least four years.

By 1994, however, both parties had resolved most of their differences. In a revised deal, Skoda's capital investment over the decade was reduced to DM3.7bn. Plans to develop a new car engine plant were dropped and Skoda's target annual capacity was to fall back to less than 350,000. On the positive side, a second model range was launched in 1996 and Skoda was to be drawn into the parent company's programme to adopt advanced production techniques and methods. VW reconfirmed its commitment to local Czech and Slovak suppliers with around 80 per cent of Skoda's components being sourced from them. However, falling sales in most markets during 1994 led to a decision by VW to cut Skoda's workforce of just over 1,000 employees, although the company expected sales to increase towards the middle end of the decade based on hopes of the 1996 new model range and further productivity gains.

The case demonstrates the nature of some government–MNE relationships that have emerged under the conditions of the CEE's transformation process. Two main points are at issue. First to consider is the extent to which some CEE governments are willing to make major policy concessions to attract larger scale investments from foreign MNEs. This could involve the sacrifice of other policy objectives such as the adoption of a more protectionist trade policy. Second, frictions have surfaced between foreign corporate interests and domestic policy interests in CEE countries. These may arise from one party attempting to exert a position of power over the other or from genuine reactions to economic and political vicissitudes. VW have injected into the Czech economy strategically important transfers of technology and advanced management and production methods, but these have to be weighed against other factors. The scaling down of the initial investment commitment represented a significant potential loss that might not have been incurred if an alternative bid, such as Renault's, had been accepted instead. The reductions made to Skoda's workforce may prove only temporary but nevertheless represent a situation where core socio-economic objectives once held by the government have been at least partly subordinated to the logic of corporate decision-making.

Let us now consider the general trends in inward FDI flows that have been recently attracted into the CEE region. The largest foreign investments have generally been in resource intensive industries (e.g. oil and other mineral investments in Russia and Central Asia) but manufacturing projects seem to be the most popular with 61 per cent of total investment. This has particularly been the case in electricals/electronics, computers and telecommunications, food and beverage production, agri-business and transport equipment. Most of the FDI projects in the CEE region have been on a relatively small scale. For instance, in 1992 the CEE countries accounted for only 1.3 per cent of registered German capital abroad, but for 3.4 per cent of the number of German foreign investments made (Meyer 1994). Yet there still exists a concentration of FDI towards large investments. Hungary presents a good illustration where the top 5 per cent of projects amounted to 85 per cent of all project capital up to 1992 (Lane 1994). It is also worth noting that joint ventures continue to be the most common form of investment, with the wholly owned subsidiary option only rarely been chosen. West European firms have spearheaded the majority of foreign investments into the CEE region. However, American MNEs have been responsible for some of the largest and highly profiled ventures, with petroleum, automobiles, foods and consumer goods being the most notable. Japanese firms, on the other hand, have yet to establish a significant presence.

In the period leading up to German reunification, the Eastern Länder received the largest influx of FDI. Hungary has remained the favourite location for foreign investors if the Eastern Länder are not in the equation, with a cumulative $5,441m taken over 1990–93, representing 44 per cent of the CEE total (see Table 8.7). On an FDI per capita basis, Hungary's figure of $528 is over three times that of a combined Czech and Slovak Republics figure of $167 which between them attracted an estimated $2.6bn of foreign investment in the 1990 to 1993 period, equivalent to 21 per cent of the total for the region. Together with Estonia and Slovenia they accounted for shares of inflows into the region out of proportion to their size. Russia and Poland only managed to acquire 16 per cent and 7 per cent shares respectively. The data thus unveil the somewhat uneven pattern of FDI across the region countries: 81 per cent of the total in the period being concentrated in just four countries while 91 per cent of the CEE population received only 32 per cent of the cumulative inflows. Some correlation between low levels of FDI and relative economic underdevelopment is also apparent (Albania, Bulgaria and Romania), except in countries with huge resource bases (Russia and Kazakhstan). Overall, annual measured FDI inflows into the CEE region rose tenfold during the period, but nevertheless represented only 10 per cent of total inward FDI to developing countries in 1993.

Most foreign investments in the CEE countries have been calculated on market-based and cost-based strategic objectives. Radice (1995) has noted that branded consumer non-durable goods such as cigarettes, detergents, food and toiletries have provided favourable returns on medium-term investments. With investments in consumer durable sectors (see Table

Table 8.7 FDI in Central and Eastern Europe and the former Soviet Union,[1] 1990–93

	FDI (millions of US dollars)				Cumul. 1990–93	% of total	FDI per capita 1990–93	1993	% of PPP $-GNP[3]	% of current $-GDP[4]
	1990	1991	1992	1993[2]						
Albania	—	—	19	20	39	0	13	6	—	—
Bulgaria	4	56	42	62	164	1	19	7	0.18	0.49
Croatia	—	—	16	30	46	0	10	6	—	0.25
Former CFSR	188	592	1,054	—	2,600	21	167	—	—	—
Czech Republic	—	—	983	606	—	—	—	59	0.82	1.92
Slovak Republic	—	—	71	160	—	—	—	30	0.56	1.46
Estonia	—	—	58	122	180	1	113	76	1.31	7.05
Hungary	311	1,459	1,471	2,200	5,441	44	528	214	3.81	6.03
Kazakhstan	—	—	100	300	400	3	24	18	0.42	1.40
Latvia	—	—	43	60	103	0	38	22	0.54	—
Lithuania	—	—	5	40	45	0	12	11	0.34	—
Poland	88	117	284	350	839	7	22	9	0.18	0.41
Romania	−18	37	73	48	140	1	6	2	0.08	0.19
Russia	—	100	800	1,100	2,000	16	13	7	0.14	0.63
Slovenia	−2	41	113	123	275	2	138	62	—	1.03
Uzbekistan	—	—	100	45	145	1	7	2	0.08	0.18
Totals/Averages	571	2,402	4,178	5,266	12,417	100	41	18	0.37	1.17
Central Europe	585	2,209	2,938	3,469	9,201	74	129	49	1.38	2.38
The Baltics	—	—	106	222	326	3	40	27	0.69	—
Southern Europe	−14	93	134	130	343	3	10	4	0.12	0.35
Central Asia	—	—	200	345	545	4	14	9	0.27	0.75

Source: EBRD 1995. Dunning, J.H. (1993) *The Globalisation of Business*
Notes:
[1] FDI values from national balance of payments statistics.
[2] Results for 1993 are preliminary.
[3] 1993 FDI divided by 1993 GNP at purchasing power parity.
[4] 1993 FDI divided by 1993 current dollar GNP.

8.8) a longer term commitment is required as ownership levels are high in some products and income levels are still insufficient for regular patterns of replacement purchases to emerge. In other product areas, the income thresholds needed to trigger significant market demand have not yet been reached. Business, financial and personal services have flourished in the environment created by the transformation process where indigenous firms have not independently been able to form a critical mass of effective competitors in these sectors. A much needed infusion of more advanced managerial and technological capacities has also led to a similar situation arising in relatively backward industrial and infrastructure sectors.

Low-cost production has provided a significant location specific advantage for firms investing in CEE countries which wish to supply world markets from there. While differentials in wages rates are particularly pronounced between Western and CEE producers, the latter also enjoy a cost advantage over many East Asian and Latin American NIC rivals. By 1993, the average labour costs in the manufacturing sectors of Taiwan, Singapore, Hong Kong, South Korea, Mexico and Brazil were all higher than that of Hungary's which held the region's best paid workers. However, Radice (1995: 10) has observed that in some labour intensive sectors

Table 8.8 FDI by sector in Central and Eastern Europe and the former Soviet Union

Sector	Number of projects	Per cent of the total number of projects
Electricals, electronics, computers, telecommunications	472	11.4
Food and beverage production, agri-business	426	10.3
Oil and gas, mining and metals	389	9.4
Automotive, aircraft, railway manufacture, shipbuilding	373	9.0
Financial services	340	8.2
Chemicals, plastics, glass	188	4.5
Engineering, heavy machinery	180	4.4
Building materials, construction	165	4.0
Textiles, fashion, footwear	157	3.8
Miscellaneous services	901	21.8
Miscellaneous manufacturing	544	13.2
Total	4,135	100.0

Source: EBRD 1995

looser contractual arrangements have been adopted instead of FDI strategies, and suggests that 'this is typical of the global sourcing in this sector, and arises because the Western partner's firm-specific advantage lies in market access, rather than in proprietary technology or production management'. Nevertheless, decisions made by MNEs to switch production from original West European locations to lower cost CEE alternatives have particularly affected workers in 'sensitive' labour intensive industries. Consequently, it has been the EU's poorer member states, whose industrial structures carry a preponderance of these industries, which have repeatedly highlighted both the current and future potential damage caused by rediverted investments to the CEE countries while simultaneously pressing for compensatory actions to be made.

In its analysis of recent corporate and academic surveys, the EBRD (1995) noted that market based motivations currently provided the strongest observable pattern for foreign investment in CEE. Low factor costs were not found to be as critical, largely owing to the belief that rising levels of income through prosperity effects would soon eradicate the labour cost advantage of the region. Those investments made based on low labour costs were of the import substituting variety with relatively little manufacturing activity founded on export orientation. To some extent, this represents a lost opportunity to the European economy as a major competitive advantage of the CEE countries appears not to have been exploited. The reasons for this lie in the expressed intentions of many investors to acquire a 'foothold' stake in CEE markets. This in turn has been founded on circumspection regarding the future investment climate of the region. Political risk, legislative uncertainty, macroeconomic instability and miscellaneous regulatory obstacles still appear to be significant impediments to inward flows of FDI to some CEE countries.

The somewhat disappointing levels of FDI across the region in general as well as the noticeable concentration of foreign investment in relatively small, well-democratised and higher income countries (i.e. Hungary, the Czech Republic, Slovakia and Slovenia) can largely be explained by these factors. While many foreign investors in CEE have taken a long-term view, the need to find a politically stable environment becomes even more imperative. Furthermore, the EBRD proposed additional factors that have contributed towards the concentrated pattern of FDI found in the CEE region:

- The geographical and cultural proximity to countries that are the source of FDI. The Czech Republic, Hungary and Slovakia share borders with countries where most of their inward FDI originates, namely Germany, Italy and Austria.
- Those CEE countries who have promoted foreign participation in their privatisation schemes have generally attracted higher levels of FDI.
- Oligopolistic competitive forces have worked to accumulate FDI in clustered locations on the basis of defensive 'follow the leader' strategies being deployed by firms in the same sector.
- Agglomeration effects have influenced inward FDI flows from the critical mass of common supporting services, suppliers, infrastructure and other elements that have grown up around existing projects to reduce the entry costs for new investors.

These factors have complemented the previously mentioned core conditions required for long-term investments to flourish. In addition, they further explain why foreign firms have reacted in an 'elastic' fashion to strategic FDI decision-making. By this reasoning, once CEE countries are able to secure relative macroeconomic and political stability a self-reinforcing effect should lead to a gathering momentum of inward FDI flows. Such findings therefore carry important implications for policy-makers in the region and for other interested parties able to assist them.

CONCLUDING REMARKS

This chapter has analysed Europe's connections with the most dynamic force of globalisation – namely FDI. At present, there appears to be no reason to suggest that the pace of FDI's growth will slow down. This not only applies to the developed industrial countries – the traditional sources and hosts of investment – but increasingly to the developing countries where foreign investment is playing a crucial role in integrating them more into the world economic system. Nonetheless, as we have noted, the new distribution of FDI among them has been concentrated in a few core regions, in particular China and the East Asian NICs. A strong regionalised pattern of investment is also still apparent, in Europe and other parts of the Triad.

Our discussion on European integration and FDI showed that regionalism and globalisation can have mutually compatible objectives. The advantages presented by a common market in Europe were not only recognised from an early stage by European MNEs but also by their US counterparts. Hence, the Trans-Atlantic FDI relationship is both well established and extensive. The advent of the SEM programme in combination with a number of other factors acted as a catalyst for an acceleration of Japanese FDI into the world's largest unified market from the mid-1980s. Other East Asian companies, especially from South Korea, are currently following in the wake. As the CEE economy becomes more closely integrated with that of the EU, it can expect to attract higher FDI inflows from other global regions. For the time being though, the CEE economies must primarily rely on those from Western neighbours. While the somewhat disappointing FDI commitment to the region reflects the considerable perceived risks which are associated, the investment opportunities that are offered could play a key part in the global strategic plans of many European firms.

9 Technology and innovation

Technology and innovation lie at the heart of a number of important challenges facing Europe. This is particularly the case in various high technology industries that are generally accepted to hold the key to future growth and prosperity. Another critical challenge concerns managing the impacts of technological development in a socially and environmentally responsible manner. Hence, the aim of this chapter will be to examine the strategic, developmental and global dimensions to technology and innovation, as well as Europe's own recent technological performance and co-operative efforts in this field, both at a regional and international level.

STRATEGIC, DEVELOPMENTAL AND GLOBAL DIMENSIONS

In this section, we will introduce the key issues that underpin the main discussions of this chapter. These draw on the strategic, developmental and global dimensions to technology and innovation and will consist of the following themes:

- convergence and divergence in (global) technological development;
- new technological paradigms and technology clusters;
- the internationalisation of research and development (R&D) activity;
- strategic technological partnering;
- the state, national systems of innovation and technology.

Throughout this chapter the term 'science and technology' (S&T) will refer to a broader range of activities than that implied by R&D, including large commercial projects (e.g. Concorde) and peripheral actions (e.g. scientific and technical education) that serve the interests of corporate or government R&D.

Convergence and divergence in (global) technological development

Economists have long been interested in the role played by technology and innovation in economic development. Schumpeter (1942) has attributed this role as being the prime motor and driving force behind capitalism and stated that, 'Innovation is the outstanding fact in the economic history of capitalist society. . . . What dominates the picture of capitalist life is innovation, the intrusion into the system of new production functions.' As was the case with Britain in the nineteenth century, the prominence of the US economy in the twentieth century has been founded on a technological superiority that has been nurtured across a wide range of industrial sectors. With the increasing internationalisation of post-war economic activity it was believed that advanced US technologies would be diffused through MNE subsidiaries and other conduits. This would eventuate in a broader geographical dispersal of centres for new technological development. However, while the USA's general technological lead against its main industrial rivals has undoubtedly been undermined, it has nevertheless managed to sustain a more specific lead in an impressive number of high technology sectors.

Furthermore, those rivals that have surpassed the USA in other sectors have been limited to Japan and a handful of European countries, in particular Germany. Thus, a prime characteristic of post-war technological development has been its increasing tripolar concentration that has led to widening technological gaps between the developed and developing countries. Clear evidence for this convergence and divergence is shown by comparative international statistics in R&D activity, patent figures, strategic technological partnerships and other relevant indicators that are presented throughout this chapter.

In attempting to explain this trend, economists have established the concept of 'technological accumulation' whereby the technological advantage of countries, regions and firms is maintained by a so-called 'snowball' effect. An initial critical mass in the form of technological capability is required to provide the basis of this advantage. In metaphoric terms, the extent and position of more 'snow' – the technological environment in which the growth of knowledge depends – will determine future technological development and its trajectory, while the more 'mass' that is absorbed gives rise to yet further momentum. In support of this thesis lies the assumption that technology acquisition and transfer are costly, as demonstrated by rising R&D costs, thus stimulating further divergence by making the game of technological catch-up more arduous for late starters.

Moreover, Patel and Pavitt (1995) assert that technology acquisition is by nature principally dependent on learning processes and these have tended more and more to involve tacit (institution or person embodied) rather than codified (easily transmitted) knowledge. Dosi has suggested that:

Tacitness refers to those elements of knowledge . . . that individuals have which are ill-defined, uncodified and unpublished, which they themselves cannot fully express and which differ from person to person, but which may to some significant degree be shared by collaborators and colleagues who have a common experience.

(Dosi 1988: 1126)

This tacitness is invariably industry specific or firm specific and must also be distinguished from 'blueprint' information that is far more transferable. If Patel and Pavitt are correct, then this further localises the cumulative character of technological development while also providing inertia to technology transfer.

While the East Asian 'tiger' economies represent those developing countries that appeared to have broken into the virtuous circle of technological accumulation, via the successful installation of imported technology, techno-industrial upgrading and human capital strategies, most others remain marginalised. The general trend of post-war FDI flows, as we observed in Chapter 8, has contributed to the marginalisation of many developing regions by denying them the technology transfer potential afforded to them by inward FDI from Triad multinationals. It has also been argued by Lanvin (1990) that 'because globalisation is technology-driven and technology-focused it tends quasi-naturally to perpetuate and reinforce the phenomena of integration and exclusion of most previous technology-based changes in the world economy'. Thus, the ability of localities and regions to attract inward FDI flows is highly dependent on their techno-scientific capabilities in the first place. However, Archibugi and Pianta (1993) note that in addition to a more efficient husbanding of a country's technological resources convergence may be attainable through the wide array of internationalised channels now available, such as patent cross-licensing, trans-border co-operative research projects and other specific forms of technology transfer.

It should also be noted that technological accumulation can also evolve down paths of innovatory diversification from a core R&D base through tangential innovations and the existing potential for economies of scope. Patel and Pavitt (1995: 163) comment that, 'At higher levels of technological accumulation in today's developed countries the central inducement mechanism has often become the cumulative mastery and exploitation on world markets of core technologies with multiple potential applications.' Thus, Switzerland's competitive advantage in maritime diesel engines developed not from any natural resource-related determinants but from the engineering expertise that initially originated from its textile industry.

New technological paradigms and technology clusters

The technological capability of firms, countries and regions is determined by their ability to generate, absorb and adapt to new technologies and innovatory processes. The Schumpeterian notion of 'creative destruction', whereby existing technologies and the economic activities linked to them are displaced or made obsolescent by newer ones, is no more pronounced than when this change entails the introduction of a new technological paradigm. By way of contextualising this statement, let us consider the four categories of technological and innovatory change that Freeman (1987a) has identified:

- Incremental innovations: small, progressive modifications of products and processes.
- Radical innovations: catalytic changes to the nature of existing products and processes through R&D activities. A single innovation of this kind will have limited economic impact unless linked to a series of other related radical innovations.
- Changes of technology system: the emergence of whole new industries associated with such changes (e.g. biotechnology).
- Changes in the techno-economic paradigm: revolutionary economic and social change caused by the development, application and absorption of new core technologies.

Porter (1990: 46) states that 'industries are born when technological change makes a new product feasible' and uses the illustration of the discovery of X-rays in Germany which gave the country the initial lead in medical imaging products. However, technological leadership can be challenged by the introduction of radical innovations originating from elsewhere, for example, new electronics based technologies for X-rays in some applications. Firms that are most reliant on older technologies and their associated products and processes are less likely to perceive emerging alternatives. This can occur even when they have been partly responsible for the founding concepts of the latter, such as IBM and the personal computer.

Early theoretical work on changes in techno-economic paradigms was conducted by the Russian economist, N. D. Kondratiev, who first discussed the idea of long waves in economic activity in the 1920s. According to Kondratiev, economies not only experienced conventional business cycles that lasted every decade or so, but in addition economic cycles of a more fundamental nature that endured for fifty to sixty years. Subsequent theorising suggested that each wave evolved through the convergence of economic, social, demographic, industrial and financial conditions that forces firms to seek new innovations and technologies. This pressure largely derives from the market saturation of products based on old or existing technologies.

Today's current long wave is likely to rest on the core industries around which new 'technology clusters' have been created and on which new technological paradigms could be based in the future. It is generally accepted that three such clusters currently exist:

1 Information Technology (IT): combining computer and communications technologies.

2 Biotechnology: containing elements from pharmaceuticals, chemicals, environmental related, agricultural and medical industries.
3 New material sciences: encompassing the development and application of advanced man-made substances such as polymers, ceramics, new metal alloys and composites that are currently substituting more traditional materials in an increasing range of products.

These technology clusters are underpinned by the 'generic' nature of the core technologies that link them, and have thus served to modify, blur and in some cases break down well-established boundaries between firms and between industries. This has been largely due to the broad common knowledge base upon which firms and industries draw in making technological advances. Furthermore, there has been greater pressure on firms within these clusters to co-operate with oligopolistic rivals based on 'knowledge-based' rather than 'product-based' collaborations (Mytelka 1984).

The development of a strong technological capability in the core industries of these clusters is essential for firms, countries and regions in order to establish a position to create future prosperity and wealth into the next century. They must also consider the stress that contemporary innovation theory places on the importance of 'appropriability regimes', that is the degree to which a firm's core technological competencies can be protected. Under conditions of rapid paradigmatic change only the most innovative firms are best able to sustain strong regimes. In addition, the economic and social impact of new process technologies and innovations upon both work practices and organisation structures must be carefully and judiciously managed. Japan's post-war pattern of economic growth owes much to the capabilities developed by its firms in this area, such as Toyota which pioneered lean production and just-in-time techniques back in the early 1950s.

The internationalisation of R&D activity

The location and organisation of R&D activity will be determined within certain basic parameters such as the evolutionary structure of the firm and its R&D function, particular locational rigidities and the type of R&D activities being considered (Howells and Wood 1994). However, for MNEs the wider arguments for and against the internationalisation of a firm's R&D activities revolve around the internal benefits derived from research concentration (i.e. at the MNE's home base) and those advantages offered by decentralisation and external networking which research dispersal (i.e. internationalisation) presents. The latter is sometimes referred to as 'global switching'. Howells and Wood (1994) and Freeman and Hagedoorn (1995) have proposed the following set of benefits arising from each approach:

Research concentration

- Economies of scale and scope from larger R&D operations;
- minimum efficiency size associated with indivisibilities of certain scientific instruments, facilities or specialist staff;
- the maintenance of good internal communication links within the R&D function;
- research that is able to concentrate on producing original ideas and not be involved in short-term operational problems;
- the ability to capitalise on the accumulated experience in the home base and the technology networks with main suppliers;
- improved security and reduced risk of emulation by rivals or 'leapfrogging' in key research and innovation fields;
- the creation of a well-established dense local innovation network with other research agencies (e.g. universities, research institutes, etc.);
- the need for tighter strategic control over technological development.

Research dispersal

- More effective and applicable R&D efforts focused on the needs of the business and operational units;
- improved communication or 'coupling' between R&D and other key corporate functions, particularly production, sales and marketing (e.g. the need to transfer knowledge to manufacturing facilities);
- the ability to tap pools of scarce research personnel talent;
- monitoring of, and interaction with, localities that possess a technological lead in their field;
- access to key lead suppliers or customers in certain technologies or products;
- customisation, responsiveness and adaptation to local or 'multi-domestic' market conditions and needs;
- rewards offered through government incentive schemes to locate R&D activities in selected areas.

Trans-frontier R&D can be categorised into three forms or methods, namely inter-company technological co-operation agreements, co-operation between universities and companies and the redeployment of in-house R&D (Warrant 1994). None of these emerged to any real degree until the inter-war period, and consisted mainly of a few subsidiary research laboratories. Although the rapid acceleration of post-war FDI has heightened the internationalisation of R&D, Patel and Pavitt (1991) have noted that it is still minimal compared to other aspects of the corporate value chain. Empirical evidence would seem to support this view. A study undertaken by Pearce and Singh (1992) involving 163 parent companies and 60 others indicated a strong tendency for MNEs to retain R&D activity within their home base. Estimates made regarding the internationalisation of R&D

employment by multinational ownership ranged from 2 per cent for Japanese companies to 40 per cent for Swiss MNEs, with 6 per cent for the USA, 7 per cent for Germany and 15 per cent and 18 per cent for France and the UK respectively. The low figure for Japanese MNEs partly reflects the lag in outward manufacturing FDI in comparison to US and European companies. Switzerland's relatively high percentage is largely due to its large companies and small market base.

The findings of a 1992 FAST Report (see Miege 1995) found that European MNEs had established 41 per cent of their R&D laboratories overseas compared to 33 per cent for North American firms and 20 per cent for Japan. A Commission report (1994e) provides further evidence that seems to confirm this with its findings that 99 per cent of the US patenting activity of Japanese firms originates from home-based R&D centres against 92 per cent and 83 per cent rates for US and European companies respectively. In addition, European firms were found to have located 50 per cent of their laboratories outside Europe, with 96 per cent of these being established in the USA. These studies and others have clearly indicated that European multinationals have been more prone to internationalise their R&D activities than other Triad members. The failure both to retain such activities and to attract proportionately more from other Triad-based members would seem to point to certain inadequacies within Europe's techno-scientific base.

Strategic technology partnering

Inter-company technology agreements have existed for some time. Extensive cross-licensing between large firms has been made within the chemicals industry since the 1920s and remains a basic form of collaboration in many sectors today (OECD 1992a). Hagedoorn and Schakenraad (1993: 60) define a strategic technology partnership or alliance as 'those inter-firm agreements aimed at the long-term perspective of the product-market position of at least one partner through a joint effort of which common innovative activities are at least part of the agreement'. They usually possess the following distinctive features:

- Participating firms are usually of equal size and stature and hold complementary assets in relation to each other.
- They are normally involved in different market segments but draw on common generic technologies and scientific knowledge base.
- Prime objectives include the protection or extension of their core technological capabilities and assets and access to global markets.
- Resources are pooled to reduce competitive risks and erect oligopolistic technological entry barriers to others.

Rising R&D costs and shorter product life cycles in high technology sectors are among the main pressures on firms to seek strategic technological partners. The tensions generated by the innovatory commitment and resources required to survive in these sectors can be demonstrated by using the semiconductor industry as an illustration. Rapid technological advances in semiconductors in recent years have meant that each generation lasts for approximately four years. However, an R&D programme leading to commercialisation may take up to five years. There is also a need for the development of new capital equipment and materials associated with each generation to be co-ordinated in the process. Thus, as in the semiconductor and other high technology industries it has become increasingly the case that no one firm is able to command all the resources and knowledge necessary for effective independent R&D, or resist the mutual advantages offered by collaborations with others.

In a comprehensive study, Hagedoorn and Schakenraad (1992) found that around a third of international strategic technology partnerships were based on the prime objective of access to new markets or as a reaction to changes in market structure. However, the prime objective of over 60 per cent of cases was founded on shared R&D costs and the acquisition of new technological know-how. Further evidence has been provided by Hagedoorn (1993) to suggest that research-oriented alliances were more likely to be formed between partners from the same region owing to benefits offered by economic and geographic proximity and shared cultural values towards S&T activities in general.

Market-oriented alliances, though, were more globally focused, being driven by the imperatives to acquire wider market access and critical technology transfers. This has been confirmed by Wegberg and Witteloostuijn (1995) in their analysis of multi-market contact and collusion between firms. Hence, strategic technology alliances are just as much driven by complex S&T determinants as by the compelling forces of globalisation. Table 9.1 also indicates the extent to which strategic technological partnering is dominated by the Triad MNEs. Furthermore, a positive correlation exists between this position of triadic predominance and higher degrees of technology-intensivity.

Another analysis by Hagedoorn and Schakenraad (1993) showed that during the 1980s nearly three-quarters of all strategic technology alliances were made in the new 'technology cluster' industries, with IT constituting 41.2 per cent of the total (see Figure 9.1). It was also noted that in the biotechnology industry, particularly towards the end of the decade, agreements between large MNEs and relatively small R&D intensive firms had become common. Small firms have rarely become involved in international strategic partnering of any kind, but where specialised scientific knowledge has been developed they have sometimes been courted by larger firms with the intention of jointly converting this knowledge into a more fully realised competitive advantage for all partners.

Table 9.1 Distribution of strategic technology alliances by sector, 1980–89

Field of technology	No. of alliances	% for developed economies	% for Triad	% for Triad NICs	% for Triad LDCs	Other
Biotechnology	846	99.1	94.1	0.4	0.1	0.5
New materials	430	96.5	93.5	2.3	1.2	—
Computer	199	98.0	96.0	1.5	0.5	—
Industrial automation	281	96.1	95.0	2.1	1.8	—
Microelectronics	387	95.9	95.1	3.6	—	0.5
Software	346	99.1	96.2	0.6	0.3	—
Telecommunications	368	97.5	92.1	1.6	0.3	0.5
Misc. IT	148	93.3	92.6	5.4	0.7	0.7
Automotive	205	84.9	82.9	9.8	5.4	—
Aviation	228	96.9	94.3	0.9	1.3	0.9
Chemicals	410	87.6	80.0	3.9	7.1	1.5
Food and beverages	42	90.5	76.2	9.5	—	—
Heavy electronics	141	96.5	92.2	1.4	2.1	—
MT/Instr.	95	100.0	100.0	—	—	—
Others	66	90.9	77.3	1.5	4.5	3.0
Total	4192	95.7	91.9	2.3	1.5	0.5

Source: Freeman and Hagedoorn 1995, after MERIT-CATI

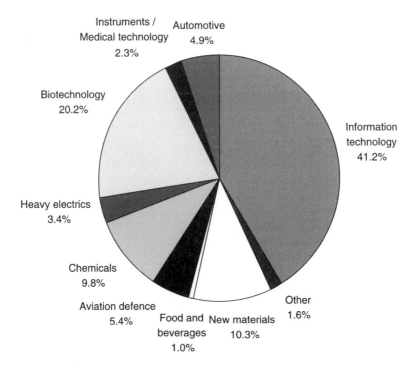

Figure 9.1 Distribution of strategic technology alliances by sector, 1980–89
Source: Hagedoorn and Schakenraad 1993: 66

The state, national systems of innovation and technology

Traditional linear theories on the relationship between technology and economic development were founded on the belief that increasing R&D and other innovatory activities were required to stimulate economic growth. This view is no longer widely subscribed to due to the recognition that various persistent barriers to innovation can stunt this development, such as capital immobility and inadequate human resources (Malecki 1991). Consequently, R&D is seen as integrated into a broader system of innovation at a national or other level. A national system of innovation has been defined as 'the network of institutions in the public and private sectors whose activities and interactions initiate, import, modify and diffuse new technologies' (Freeman 1987b). In recent times, the state's role within this system and its subsequent influence over the technological development of the economy has changed, as Table 9.2 indicates. Some of the original premises on which this role has been justified have been:

- the necessity to fund important basic or 'precompetitive' research that possesses public good characteristics and therefore may not have been undertaken by the private sector;
- some R&D projects require long-term commitment which firms may not be able to meet owing to reasons of market failure;

Table 9.2 Recent trends and changes in S&T policies

	Traditional approach	*Modern approach*
Object	Material aspects (material technology).	In addition, organisational, institutional and cultural aspects (technological practices).
Objective	Economic growth.	In addition, social and ecological compatibility.
Stage of technological innovation process	Stages of little bearing on the market (primarily fundamental research).	Also stages closer to the market (technology transfer).
Policy integration	Part of economic policy (largely implicit R&T policy).	Independent policy field closely interlinked with other policy areas (increasingly implicit technology policy).
Role of the state	Central actor of technological innovation process.	Facilitator and co-ordinator of the self-regulation of the innovation process.
Instrument	Support, regulation.	Provision of infrastructure.
Policy type	Direct control.	Context control.

Source: Schienstock 1994. Reproduced by permission of Walter de Gruyter & Co.

- to tackle the problems of indivisible end market uses (e.g. public health), uncertainty and inappropriability associated with some technological developments;
- the state's 'responsibility' to match the support given by other governments to their domestic industries, especially if viewed as strategically important (e.g. micro-electronics).

The spate of high technology programmes that began in the early 1980s typified the above justifications for state support for R&D. In 1982, Japan's launching of the Fifth Generation Computer Programme prompted similar initiatives a year later from the USA with its DAPRA Strategic Computing Programme, as well as from the EC in the form of ESPRIT (see Box 9.1). The announcement of the US's Strategic Defence Initiative (SDI) in 1984 was soon followed by the pan-European EUREKA project and Japan's Human Frontier Science Programme in 1985. Such programmes have been given huge budgets and the prime objective of developing a key strategic position in the emerging new technology clusters.

However, the general tone and practice of S&T policy within the Triad has adjusted to one where the state plays a more facilitating and less direct role in the economy's technological development. For example, in some countries the state has encouraged cross-institutional research between higher education institutions (HEIs), public research establishments (PREs) and industry (see Malerba *et al.* 1994). The UK has been at the forefront of providing Europe with models of HEI–PRE–industry collaborations which have enabled mutually beneficial technology transfers to pass between involved parties (Charles and Howells 1992). On a more international dimension, inter-state science and technology collaboration has increased as a response to raised awareness and responsibility on common global issues, in particular the environment and health.

State S&T policies have to consider the nature of the national innovation system within which they operate and identify its strengths and weaknesses. This may involve establishing where patterns of revealed technological advantage exist in certain sectors and where they do not. Policymakers are also seeking to understand the existing and potential network relationships between the system's different components as well as the integrative functioning of the system as a whole, for example, human resource considerations and overcoming technological gaps that persist between regions.

Many analysts also believe that the nature of national innovation systems helps to explain much of the inertia to internationalised R&D activity by arguing that a considerable degree of innovatory endeavour is embedded within national or regional level science and technology infrastructures (Freeman 1987b; Nelson 1987; Lundvall 1989; Porter 1990; OECD 1991a). Technological accumulation effects, complex producer–user relationships based on economic and geographic proximity and various cultural and social determinants are thought to contribute to this.

EUROPE'S RECENT TECHNOLOGICAL PERFORMANCE EXAMINED

Many observers have drawn strong correlations between Europe's recent low levels of economic growth and its technological performance compared to its rivals. In this section, we shall examine the evidence that has been presented in order to evaluate Europe's performance across a variety of scientific and technological indicators. These indicators will consist of the extent and nature of R&D activities, scientific and technological outputs and a sectoral analysis on technology intensive industries.

R&D activity

On a global scale research and development activity remains largely concentrated in the leading fifty technological nations which are responsible for 98 per cent of total world R&D expenditure and 94 per cent of R&D employment (CEC 1994k). Figure 9.2 shows the trends in R&D intensity by region over the period between 1981 and 1992. The main identifiable trends are as follows:

- All core Triad regions intensified their R&D activities during the 1980s, although Japan, NAFTA and the EU experienced a decline between 1990 and 1992.

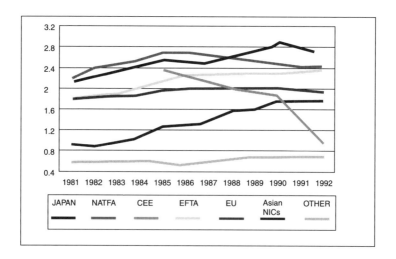

Figure 9.2 Trends in R&D intensity (R&D as percentage of GDP)
Source: CEC 1994k: 16

- Owing to a 6 per cent per annum growth rate, Japan's R&D as a percentage of GDP rose from 2.1 per cent to 2.8 per cent, thus giving it the highest intensity rating by the end of the period.
- Both the EU and NAFTA rates rose only slightly from 1.8 per cent to 2.0 per cent and 2.3 per cent to 2.4 per cent respectively. The EU's annual growth rate was 4 per cent per annum over the period. NAFTA's rate was negative between 1986 and 1991.
- In other European regions, EFTA's R&D intensity rate increased from 1.8 per cent to 2.4 per cent while due to 'transitional factors', such as the collapse of old institutional science and technology structures, the CEE countries have experienced a rapid decline from a 1985 rate of 2.4 per cent to 0.9 per cent by 1992.
- By contrast, the Asian NICs have seen their R&D intensity rate double over the period from 0.9 per cent to 1.8 per cent.

Table 9.3 and Figure 9.3 examine the extent to which R&D activity is military oriented and business funded respectively across a range of countries and regions. The USA, UK, France and Sweden remain the largest spenders on military R&D while Germany, Italy and Japan have devoted only minimal resources to these ends. There is much debate over the commercial potential of military R&D. Many believe that its scope for generating marketable spin-offs is somewhat limited. In 1989, the UK government's former Advisory Council on Science and Technology (ACOST) estimated that only 20 per cent of the military R&D budget could have civil applications. Indeed, the military share of total government R&D expenditure has fallen for most countries since the thawing of the Cold War. Many governments have sought to re-orientate their military R&D programmes to more civil end uses. Nowhere else is this deemed more important than in the CEE countries and the former Soviet Union in particular (Dent 1994).

As regards business-funded R&D, the EU's rate is 52 per cent and EFTA's 61 per cent, compared against NAFTA's 50 per cent (pulled

Table 9.3 Government expenditure on military R&D as a percentage of total government R&D outlays

	1963	*1985*	*1992*
USA	50.3	69.4	58.6
UK	43.1	49.2	45.2
France	52.9	32.7	34.6
Sweden	34.0	26.0	24.5
Germany[1]	36.7	12.1	10.5
Italy	51.7	8.5	7.1
Japan	19.1	n/a	5.9

Sources: OECD 1989b; CEC 1994k
[1] West Germany for 1963 and 1985.

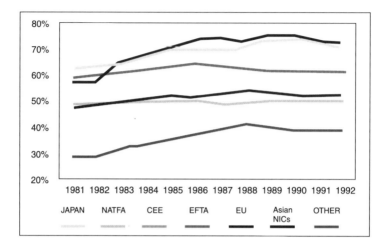

Figure 9.3 Percentage of R&D expenditure financed by business, 1981–92
Source: CEC 1994k: 20

down by the US government's military R&D effect) in 1992, while rates for the Asian NICs and Japan are now firmly placed in the 70 per cent plus range. Higher degrees of private sector R&D are generally considered more conducive to economic growth. This is due to the fact that more R&D is occurring at a 'near market' level. Meanwhile, the lack of interventionist actions from government are likely to be based on the perception that minimal market failures are arising in the economy's technological development. While it appears that Europe scores reasonably well on this account other indicators suggest otherwise. By 1992, the USA had 950,000 research scientists and engineers (RSEs) compared to Europe's 580,000 RSEs. Japan's figure of 520,000 gave it a clear per capita advantage over Europe and the USA.

Additional concern has been expressed over the comparatively low levels of 'near market' research that is conducted by Europe's public and private sector research agencies. Some believe that the emphasis on pre-competitive research reflects the European perception of science as a culture and not a means to generate commercial advantages. This attitude is perhaps changing with many European state science and technology policies adapting a more 'near market' approach (see Table 9.2).

Scientific and technological output indicators

Scientific and technological output indicators provide a useful basis on which technological performance of countries and regions can be contrasted. They can range from fields as diverse as Nobel prize winners to the percentage of total exports taken by high technology products.

Scientific 'output'

Europe's comparative performance on scientific activity and its 'output' is mixed. Its contribution to total world scientific publications remains significant. Over the period between 1981 and 1993, the EU's share rose from 28 per cent to 33 per cent while publications from the EFTA countries maintained a stable 4 per cent share of the total. However, the CEE's decline in output from 10 per cent to 4 per cent pulled down the European average to give a combined share of 41 per cent in 1993, more or less matching the USA's 42 per cent, but by far and above Japan's small but rising 6 per cent. However, Europe's record on producing leading world scientists has been relatively less impressive. Between 1940 and 1990, 143 Nobel prizes in medicine, physics and chemistry have been awarded to US scientists compared to 86 for Europe and only 5 to Japan (*Economist*, 9 January 1993).

On balance, the relatively strong profile that Europe has developed on scientific 'outputs' supports contrasting notions regarding the region's S&T endeavours. The first relates to the view that the higher cultural status afforded to purer scientific activity in Europe, as shown by these indicators, still hampers its ability to produce a sharper commercial focus to these endeavours. Conversely, the concentration on a broader scientific knowledge base is thought by other analysts to provide more effective foundations on which to develop and sustain capabilities in generic technologies. According to the latter notion, the scientific 'bias' to Europe's S&T activities may yet prove advantageous to those firms making efforts to create a deeper impression at the core of the new technological clusters.

Technological output

Patenting activity

The method of examining patenting activity to determine the technological dynamism of firms, countries and regions has been commended and developed by numerous academics, most notably Schmookler (1966) and Griliches (1984). Patents have the advantages of both covering a broad spectrum of innovatory endeavour while giving a precise classification of the new technologies and innovations that are associated with them. For these reasons some believe that they are a more useful indicator than R&D intensity owing to their focus of end products outcomes. However, not all innovations of importance are registered through patenting and there may be some which lack significant economic value.

As Kogut *et al.* (1995: 60) put it, the US economy is still 'the world's seeding ground for technology', and due to this patenting activity in the USA has formed the basis of most comparative analyses in this field. Table 9.4 clearly shows that Europe's performance here gives some cause for

Table 9.4 Shares in US patents granted in all industries

	1981	1987	1993
European Union	23.1	22.4	16.7
of which:			
Germany	11.2	10.8	7.6
France	3.9	3.9	3.2
UK	4.4	3.8	2.6
Italy	1.6	1.6	1.4
EFTA	4.5	4.2	2.8
of which:			
Switzerland	2.2	1.9	1.3
Sweden	1.4	1.3	0.7
CEE countries	1.0	0.5	0.2
TOTAL EUROPE	28.6	27.1	19.7
NAFTA	54.9	48.2	52.4
of which:			
USA	52.8	46.0	50.1
Canada	2.0	2.2	2.2
Japan	14.9	22.7	24.2
Asian NICs	0.2	0.7	2.4
China	0.0	0.0	0.1
Australasia	0.7	0.6	0.4
Israel	0.2	0.5	0.4
South Africa	0.2	0.2	0.1

Source: CEC 1994k

concern with the EU, EFTA and CEE country groups, and its most prominent patenting countries, all experiencing progressive declines in their shares between 1981 and 1993. An analysis of individual sectors reveals that only the EU's aerospace industry was able to record a slight increase of 0.54 per cent during the period while strong representation is still made in pharmaceuticals, chemicals, non-electrical machinery and motor vehicles. Other important trends identified by the data include:

- NAFTA's majority share of US patenting activity has been regained;
- Japan's share has increased by around 62 per cent over the period and is now responsible for more US patents than the whole of Europe combined;
- Asian NICs have increased their share by a factor of 12, rising from 0.2 per cent in 1981 to 2.4 per cent by 1993.

A similar scenario arises when considering Europe's performance in patenting activity within its own backyard. Table 9.5 records consistently declining shares again for all European regions and prominent countries with the exception of Italy. The EU and Europe combined lost the majority

Table 9.5 Shares in European patents granted in all industries

	1981	*1987*	*1993*
European Union	52.8	46.5	42.6
of which:			
Germany	26.0	21.8	19.8
France	10.8	8.8	8.3
UK	8.6	7.7	5.8
Italy	2.3	3.4	3.9
EFTA	8.7	7.4	6.5
of which:			
Switzerland	4.6	3.3	2.9
Sweden	2.3	2.1	1.5
CEE countries	0.3	0.5	0.3
TOTAL EUROPE	61.8	54.4	49.4
NAFTA	27.3	28.1	29.4
of which:			
USA	26.5	27.1	28.4
Canada	0.8	1.0	0.9
Japan	9.4	15.4	19.1
Asian NICs	0.1	0.2	0.6
China	0.0	0.0	0.1
Australasia	0.8	1.2	0.6
Israel	0.1	0.3	0.4
South Africa	0.2	0.2	0.1

Source: CEC 1994k

share of European patenting over the period while both Triad rivals increased theirs, most notably Japan. Additional trends and points worthy of comment include:

- All European regions have faced falling patent shares across almost all industrial sectors with the exception of transport equipment for the EU, aerospace for EFTA and pharmaceuticals and chemicals for the CEE countries.
- European industries are still well protected by patents, but these are located mainly in traditional technologies with stagnated markets.
- Japan's patent share actually declined between 1991 and 1993, peaking in 1991 at 21.9 per cent.
- The Asian NICs have failed to make a similar impact on European patenting with respect to their US patenting score, but have nevertheless recorded the fastest growth rate.

Europe's technological performance on this account is put into even starker contrast by the fact that European firms submitted only 245 patent applications for every million inhabitants to the European Patent Office

(EPO) in 1992 compared to 388 per million for US firms and a remarkable 2,665 figure for Japanese companies (CEC 1995p). This poor record is partly due to the relatively low levels of inventions from European companies that are actually patented in comparison to their other Triad counterparts. For instance, only 25 per cent of those European companies surveyed by the Commission patent close to all their inventions against 42 per cent and 44 per cent of US and Japanese companies respectively. At the other end of the scale, 19 per cent of European companies patent under 10 per cent of their inventions as opposed to 4 per cent for Japan and a mere 2 per cent for the USA (CEC 1995p).

Although this highlights one of the disadvantages of using patenting activity as a technological output indicator and underscores Europe's performance on this account, it nevertheless represents a situation where European companies are not fully exploiting the commercial potential of their innovative efforts. Furthermore, the Commission's survey also found that European firms lagged behind their US and Japanese rivals in orienting their patent activity towards strategic objectives.

High technology exports

An evaluation of our second technological output indicator – high technology exports – reveals somewhat surprising results given what has preceded and conclusions that were drawn in the opening section of Chapter 6. Figure 9.4(a) shows that the combined West European share of high technology exports as a percentage of 40 leading countries has remained relatively stable in recent years falling only fractionally from 51.2 per cent in 1986 to 50.9 per cent by 1992. Moreover, as Table 9.6 illustrates, Europe's top high-tech trading nations compare quite favourably against other leading countries in terms of high-tech trade balances with performances by Germany and Switzerland standing out in particular. This has been supported by reasonable export growth figures for these European countries over the period in question, especially in comparison to their main Triad rivals. With a combined West European share for high-tech imports of 48.2 per cent in 1992 (see Figure 9.4(b)) the region thus achieved a 2.7 per cent surplus on this account. Furthermore, the region also compares well in an analysis of high-tech trade specialisation with seven out of the top twelve countries in this field.

Like Europe, NAFTA's share of high-tech trade has remained relatively stable, although each member country recorded deficits in high-tech trade in 1992. However, it is also worth noting that the USA has a higher share of its high-tech trade in total trade than any European country. Japan's relatively low high-tech export growth between 1986 and 1992 explains its dwindled share of high-tech trade, but as Table 9.6 suggests its high technology credentials remain formidable. Both its specialisation in high-tech trade and its trade balance in these sectors are clearly unparalleled.

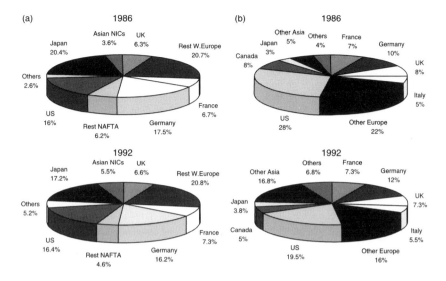

Figure 9.4 Market shares in high-tech exports and imports: 1986, 1992
· *Source*: CEC 1994k: 51, 53
9.4(a) Market shares in high-tech exports (percentage of 40 leading countries), 1986, 1992
9.4(b) Major importers of high-tech (percentage of 40 main countries), 1986, 1992

The technological strengths of Europe's main rivals revealed through high technology trade activity thus still present certain challenges. Other points to consider from data presented are:

• Between 1986 and 1992, the value of high technology exports of the main trading nations increased by 46 per cent, compared to 38 per cent for all other exports. This is to be expected as the rate of trade growth in 'newer' technology products tends to be higher than that of mature products.

• The most rapid increases in high technology exports were registered by the more dynamic Asian economies. However, these have been matched by even more significant propensities to import such products, thus giving them comparatively large high-tech trade deficits, with the exceptions of Singapore and South Korea.

• By contrast, the Latin American NICs – Argentina, Brazil and Mexico – have experienced less pronounced high-tech export growth, but possessed a similar profile of considerable trade deficits in these sectors.

• Some Asian countries have developed high-tech trade specialisations that are increasingly comparable to those of the main industrialised countries. Mexico represents the only Latin American country to approach such a level.

Table 9.6 High technology trade: specialisation and export growth performance
(selected countries from 40 leading country survey)

	Specialisation in high-tech trade (% of high-tech in total trade, 1992)	Growth of high-tech exports, 1982–92 (% increase in value, ECU)	High-tech trade balance as a % of total trade (1992)
Germany	51.0	35.6	+9
France	42.4	60.1	+1
UK	46.0	53.2	−1
Italy	34.1	42.6	−2
Sweden	43.5	18.8	+4
Switzerland	50.4	32.0	+6
Spain	41.1	138.9	−9
Austria	38.5	71.8	−5
Netherlands	30.0	39.6	−2
Japan	69.2	23.2	+31
USA	52.0	50.2	−3
Canada	39.7	7.0	−4
Australia	7.6	124.8	−19
New Zealand	4.9	59.7	−20
South Korea	36.7	114.2	−1
Singapore	52.9	206.2	0
Hong Kong	36.0	36.3	−20
Thailand	23.1	457.4	−13
Malaysia	38.5	216.9	−7
Indonesia	3.7	392.3	−17
China	20.8	1,748.2	−12
India	10.7	92.8	−8
Argentina	8.4	74.2	−13
Brazil	19.8	42.5	−3
Mexico	31.6	27.9	−15
40 leading countries average	42.4	46.2	+1

Source: CEC 1994k

A sectoral analysis

Table 9.7 presents an overview of the EU's 'leading' technology intensive
sectors that details the EU's international position, recent trade performance and other relevant economic indicators across the industries in these
sectors. Using these criteria it can be discerned that European producers
have maintained their traditional dominant position in some sectors but
have yielded important ground in other faster growing sectors.

Europe's apparent strength in scientific output appears also to be
reflected in those technology intensive sectors that have a more pure
scientific base such as pharmaceuticals and chemicals. However, weaknesses lie in a wide range of engineering sub-disciplines as demonstrated

Table 9.7 An overview of the EU's leading technology intensive sectors

	International position and structure	Employment and trade
Aerospace	1993 production level of 42 bn ECU was half the US level but five times that of Japan's. Less concentration than in USA, but high R&D costs led to the formation of the Airbus consortium which has managed to undermine the market share of US rivals Boeing and MDD.	Relatively constant at around 400,000 for the last decade. Rising trend towards intra-sector international trade at around 40 per cent by 1993. Trade deficit with USA, but balanced by exports to other markets.
Pharmaceuticals	The world's largest producer with a 64 bn ECU production level in 1993 that was a third larger than the USA and twice that of Japan. Relative size of top companies are heavily dependent on the relative success of new products. Four of the world's top ten firms are EU-based (one Anglo-US). Global concentration not so pronounced with top ten accounting for only 22 per cent of world output. Similar degree of concentration exists across the Triad.	Core employment in 1993 at 413,000 and rising slowly. EU significant net exporter and around 15 per cent of production is exported. Intra-EU trade tripled over 1985–94. A recent deterioration of the trade balance has occurred owing to increasing US and EFTA imports.
Chemicals	USA overtaken by the EU in the 1980s as the world's largest chemicals producer with a 150 bn ECU production level in 1993. Japan remains well behind Triad rivals, but has experienced rapid growth in this sector. Large number of firms, but top six account for 40 per cent of output. This is similar for other Triad members. Six of the top ten chemicals firms are EU-based.	Still a major employer with a 1.25 million workforce in 1993, but large scale job losses as a result of falling profits have hit the industry. The world's largest exporter but recent trade balance deterioration owing to weak US dollar and stronger petrochemical export performance from the Gulf.
Electrical equipment	Electrical machinery (46 bn ECU) and electrical domestic appliances (24 bn ECU) constituted around 80 per cent of the total EU output of 86 bn ECU in 1993. The EU is home to some of the world's largest companies such as Siemens, Philips, ABB, Electrolux and AEG. The sector covers a heterogeneous set of industries most of which Japanese firms have come to dominate.	1.1 million employees in 1992, and many of these are found in foreign MNEs based in the EU. High degree of internationalisation makes any conclusions hard to draw on EU trade performance here, statistics suggest that imports make up a smaller share of consumption.
Electronics	The EU trails well behind Japan and the USA to a lesser extent in electronic components and consumer electronics subsectors. Strong domestic positions are maintained by EU producers in telecommunications and hold reasonably competitive international positions. Structures vary across the three subsectors with a higher degree of concentration in the EU than in the USA or Japan for the sector as a whole.	Modest decline in employment due to the early 1990s recession but growth in the 1980s. 1993 figure of about 1.2 million. EU trade surplus on telecommunications, but 40 per cent propensity to import consumer electronics which compares to a 25 per cent production for export rate. Significant trade deficit in electronic components as well.

Motor vehicles	With 12 million units and output valued at 250 bn ECU in 1993, the EU industry is the world's largest compared to Japan's 9 million and the USA's 6 million. A strong internal market and variety and strength of producers have enabled Europe to sustain international competitiveness, although Japanese firms have the lead in both product and process-related technologies. EU industry less concentrated than US and Japan.	A 1993 figure of 1.7 million was down on those for the late 1980s owing to recession. Role of exports in decline though intra-European trade has experienced rapid growth. Japanese import penetration rates in the region of 30 per cent in most countries that have not imposed restrictions (Germany around 15 per cent).
Scientific instruments	A relatively small but high growth sector with EU output valued at 24 bn ECU in 1993. The USA is the international leader but both European and Japanese producers (evenly matched themselves) are catching up. A diverse range of subsectors exists within the industry with low concentration in all Triad locations.	Low concentration levels make this sector labour-intensive relative to levels of output. 323,000 employed in the EU in 1992. European producers established themselves in world markets, but trade balance in deterioration since the mid-1980s owing to Japan's growing strength in the optical and photographic subsectors, and also the USA in medical instruments.
Data processing/office equipment	The EU has improved its relative position to the USA with an increased level of production to 44 bn ECU in 1993, though Japan has overtaken both (60 bn ECU in the same year). The USA has maintained strength in computers while Japanese firms such as Canon and Ricoh have developed a dominant position in paper copiers and other office equipment. Europe has only one firm – Olivetti – in the top ten. However, greater concentration exists in Europe than elsewhere owing to the relationship between large firms and public procurements. This has caused problems in an industry where the role of SMEs has increased.	250,000 employed in 1993 with many other sectors dependent for employment on it, such as software production and maintenance organisations. Trade balance deterioration has significantly worsened since late 1980s despite export growth. The deficit accounts for around one third of production.

Source: CEC 1994k

by its deteriorating position in electrical equipment, electronics and data processing and office equipment sectors.

Further European weakness in technology intensive sectors is exposed when patenting activity is examined. Table 9.8 seems to confirm the findings of a 1988 Commission report (CEC 1988d) which stated that of the thirty-seven technology intensive sectors identified as key to future economic prosperity for industrial nations in the twenty-first century, the USA held or shared a technological lead in thirty-one of these, Japan nine and Europe two. The relatively poor scores achieved in patenting activity in the USA across these sectors would seem to suggest a lack of innovative dynamism among European firms and support some of the conclusions drawn earlier. Perhaps more important is the fact that European firms have

Table 9.8 Nationality of the top twenty firms in US patenting, 1986–90

Industry	Japan	USA	Western Europe
Defence-related technologies	0	15	5
Raw materials based technologies	1	16	5
Fine chemicals	1	12	7
Industrial chemicals	1	11	8
Materials	6	11	3
Telecommunications[1]	6	9	4
Electrical machinery	7	10	3
Electrical capital goods	7	10	3
Non-electrical machinery	9	8	3
Motor vehicles and parts	11	4	5
Electronic consumer goods	14	4	2

Source: Patel and Pavitt 1995
[1] The Canadian firm Northern Telecom was the twentieth contributant in this sector.

failed to establish a significant competitive presence at the core of the new technology clusters in which US and Japanese companies have come dominate.

Towards a conclusion

The above largely descriptive analysis has sought to highlight the main strengths and weaknesses and subsequently some causes for concern in Europe's recent technological performance. Attempting to untangle the complexities that have ultimately determined this performance has been an arduous task for European policy-makers and business strategists. However, the Commission's 1988 report on European R&D activity (CEC 1988e) identified research duplication, a strong emphasis on basic research, thin distribution of funds, an underdeveloped venture capital market, lack of the SEM, an unfocused organisation of innovative activity and poor marketing at the main roots of Europe's poor performance. The next section discusses how scientific and technology policy and collaboration have sought to provide some of the solutions to these problems.

SCIENCE AND TECHNOLOGY POLICY AND CO-OPERATION IN EUROPE

Raising the standards of Europe's technological performance will partly rely on improving the patterns of S&T co-operation across the region. This section investigates some aspects of Europe's national innovation systems, the EU's own framework programmes for R&D activities, the extent to which pan-European collaborations have been established and the relevance of European integration to technological processes.

European national innovation systems and S&T policies

The vast majority of Europe's research resources remains funded by individual countries and their firms with the EU's own research programmes amounting to only 3 per cent of total EU expenditure. National European S&T policies initially evolved from a minimalist position based on addressing essential market failures to a more maximalist approach that entailed the promotion of broad scale domestic technological change to counter competitive threats posed by foreign technological capabilities (Sharp and Pavitt 1993). The pursuit of this objective had involved huge S&T projects with bold commercial goals. Many of these ended up as failures on this account (e.g. Concorde and the Fast Breeder Reactor) but some achieved varying degrees of commercial success (e.g. the TGV, Airbus and Ariane). In an overall evaluation of these projects and other forms of more direct intervention, Stevens (1991) comments that they represented 'at best a mediocre record of achievement'.

By the late 1970s, two trends were identifiable in European S&T policy-making. First, there was a shift of support from sunset to sunrise industries. This came from the realisation that insulating the former by shoring up their defences against foreign competition was only forestalling the inevitable. Simultaneously, a sharper focus was required on those industries that embodied the new technological future. The second trend involved the switch to a more generic and less sectoral approach which was a response to the new technological realities that were emerging at the time.

In more recent years, national S&T policies in Europe have increasingly followed the patterns of those trends identified in Table 9.2, becoming more integrated with other related policy areas with the gradual transformation of the state's role into one of a facilitator rather than a direct generator of techno-innovation. This has recently involved the initiation by government agencies of major public debates between different members of the S&T community on the future of national level research and innovation. Examples have included the UK's 'Realising Our Potential – A Strategy for Science, Engineering and Technology' in 1993, France's 'Large-scale National Consultation' in the same year and the establishment in Germany of the 'Council for Research, Technology and Innovation' as a permanent forum for such debate in 1994. At EU level, the recent inauguration of European Science and Technology Assembly aimed to provide a similar set of links between policy-makers and the S&T community. These actions have also broadened the S&T agenda by encompassing a wider range of economic, social and environmental issues. The social impact of technology has become the focus for increasingly common and institutionalised 'technological assessments', while the relationship between technology and the environment has brought a global context and hence more collaborative efforts on an international scale.

Additional policy convergence at national level in Europe has arisen through schemes aimed at identifying future S&T priorities. These have mainly concerned 'foresight' programmes that take consideration of the country's S&T infrastructure, resources and logistics and the current and potential problems faced by society in order to evaluate emerging technologies and their potential applications. The Netherlands was the first European country to undertake such a programme in 1992, followed by the UK and Germany in 1993 and France in 1994. The EU's own R&D policy has been instrumental in developing a congruence between policies at a member state level. This itself has led to a reduction in zero-sum game outcomes arising from what Ostry (1991) has termed 'system frictions' between competing national policy objectives.

Despite the growing convergence in the objectives and implementation procedures of European national level S&T policies, there remain qualitative differences between the national innovation systems across the region. Patel and Pavitt (1991) present two types of system within which such distinctions can be made. In 'myopic' systems, technological activities are treated in the same way as conventional investments and thus must be essentially market driven and accountable to similar rates of discount and risk evaluation criteria. In contrast, 'dynamic' systems do not limit the perceived value of technological and innovative activity simply to tangible outcomes, but in addition the 'intangible by-products in the form of cumulative and irreversible processes of technological, organisational and market learning that enable them to undertake subsequent investments' (ibid.: 55) are also considered. The UK is cited as a prime example of the former and Germany as possessing the latter. The existence of these two different types of system are thought to evolve through both independent and interplaying institutional forces:

- Financial institutions: the short-termist 'Anglo-Saxon' model of financial institutional arrangements is not conducive to supporting new technological development and innovation. The German and Japanese models, whereby financial and industrial powers are aligned with each other through interlocking share ownership and directorateship, are more likely to provide this support.
- Methods of management: innovation and new technology formation will flourish in a management culture where technocrats hold more status than finance directors from the orientation of business strategies that consequently follow.
- Education and training: strong and well-established technical and vocational education programmes supported by effective training schemes are also required for an effective dynamic system to function.

The persistence of such institutional impediments would suggest that technological activity will be inclined to develop unevenly across Europe, notwithstanding patterns of congruence between national S&T policies and the collaborative ventures promoted by the EU's own programmes.

The EU's Research and Development policy

An evolutionary overview

The evolution of the EU's R&D policy formally dates back to the Euratom Treaty of 1957 from which originated the strong emphasis on nuclear research which dominated policy up to the 1970s. Later that decade it became increasingly clear that more stress was required on industrial research as Europe's industries continued to struggle against foreign competition on a wider number of fronts. By the early 1980s, the EU's R&D policy was recast with the introduction of a new range of programmes focused on improving its competitive position in the emerging technology intensive sectors. These included ESPRIT (IT), RACE (communications technologies) and BRITE/EURAM (new industrial materials and manufacturing processes) and a variety of others targeted at particular technological fields (see Table 9.9). The policy's structure and organisation was also rationalised into overlapping multi-annual framework programmes (FPs), the first of which commenced in 1984 (see Table 9.10). As these evolved a generic technology emphasis has progressively come to characterise the schemes within the FPs in response to new technological realities. The main principles on which these FPs were based have been:

- the nurturing of home-grown expertise in new critical technologies, particularly generic technologies that are multi-applicable;
- to enable European companies to acquire scale economies in R&D to place them a similar 'playing field' to US and Japanese rivals;
- the promotion of pan-European collaboration at both a corporate and national policy level to consolidate the ideals and principles of the SEM. This has also been extended to non-EU member states in Europe through support for initiatives such as EUREKA.
- to close technological gaps across the EU's regions by assisting the technological activities of member states with relatively low levels of R&D;
- that research conducted should lead to the development of common European standards and codes of practice.

However, it was not until 1986 that the SEA provided the legal basis for the EU's advanced technology policies for the first time, while also defining its objectives and implementation procedures. A newly revised Article 130f hence stated the overarching objective of the EU's R&D policy as being 'strengthening the scientific and technological bases of Community industry and encouraging it to become more competitive at international level'. The Maastricht Treaty confirmed the role of the Commission in co-

Table 9.9 The EU's main R&D programmes

Programme	Period	Budget (MECU)	Prime objectives
BIOTECH	1992–6	164	Builds on work conducted by precursor programmes, i.e. BAP (1985–9) and BRIDGE (1990–3) to enhance European biotechnology capabilities. More basic research than BRIDGE and includes safety.
BRITE/EURAM: Basic Research in Industrial Materials/ Advanced Materials for Europe	BRITE I: 1985–8 EURAM I: 1986–8 BRITE/EURAM II: 1989–92 BRITE/EURAM III: 1992–6	100 450 663	Support for industrial R&D which upgrades Europe's technological/ materials base of production.
COMMETT: Community Action Programme for Education and Training for Technology	Phase I: 1987–9 Phase II: 1990–94	30 200	University and industry collaborative training programmes through: (a) enterprise partnership schemes and (b) transnational staff exchanges.
ECLAIR: European Linkage of Agriculture and Industry through Research	1989–94	80	Application of advanced collaborative biotechnology to the agro-industrial sector.
Environment R&D Programme	1991–4 1994–8	414 532	Focused on four 'Areas'. 1 Participation in Global Change 2 Technological and Engineering for the Environment 3 Economic and Social Aspects 4 Technological and Natural Risks
ESPRIT: European Strategic Programme for R&D in IT	ESPRIT I: 1984–8 ESPRIT II: 1988–92 ESPRIT III: 1992–4 ESPRIT IV: 1994–8	750 1,600 1,350 1,911	Promotion of EU capabilities and competitiveness in IT with especial focus on microelectronic systems.
MONITOR	1989–93	22	Identification of new directions and priorities for EU R&D programmes.
RACE: R&D in Advanced Communications Technologies in Europe	Definition 1985–7 RACE I: 1990–94 RACE II: 1992–4	21 460 489	Promotion of EU competence in broadband communications equipment, standards and technology necessary for an integrated (IBC) system.
SPRINT: Strategic Programme for Innovation and Technology Transfer	SPRINT I: experimental SPRINT II: 1986–9 SPRINT III: 1989–94	9 90	Promotion of innovation and technology transfer, particularly for SMEs.
TELEMATICS	1990–94 1994–8	380 843	Development of telematic systems. 'Areas' include public administration, transport, health, flexible/distance learning, libraries, linguistic research and engineering, rural areas.
VALUE: Valorisation and Utilisation for Europe	1992–4	66	Dissemination mechanism for assisting the exploitation of programme research findings.

Source: DTI 1991; CEC 1994m

Table 9.10 The EU's R&D framework programmes, 1984–94

Framework Programme	Budget (MECU)	Main objectives
First (1984–7)	3,750	Funds devoted to energy took nearly half the budget at 1,770 MECU. Secondary priorities in order of funds granted included industrial competitiveness (1,060 MECU), improving living and working conditions (385 MECU), development aid (150 MECU), agricultural competitiveness (130 MECU) and management of raw materials (80 MECU).
Second (1987–91)	5,396	Programme reorganised around eight principle areas, including IT and communications which displaced energy (1,173 MECU) as prime objective with around 42 per cent of its funds (2,275 MECU). Other main areas consisted of modernising industrial sectors (845 MECU), 'Quality of Life' (375 MECU), S&T co-operation (288 MECU) and biological resources (280 MECU).
Third (1990–94)	6,660	This overlapped with the previous FP to allow for more complete preparations for the SEM. Further recasting of areas over three broad themes. 1 Enabling technologies: (3,488 MECU) comprising of IT and communications and industrial and materials technologies. 2 Management of natural resources (2,465 MECU) covering environment, life sciences and technologies and energy. 3 Management of intellectual resources (581 MECU) dealing with human capital and mobility.

ordinating national level policies and the EU's own programmes. Important activities that were previously outside the scope of the framework programmes, such as SPRINT, were subsequently integrated into it. This scope was also extended into a broader consideration of how they related and could support other EU policy areas, for instance the environment and transport. The EU's R&D policy is currently implemented through three types of action. These are:

• Shared cost contractual research: this constitutes the main form of intervention through bringing together consortia of companies, research centres and universities across Europe to participate on EU programmes.
• Concerted actions: these involve attempts to co-ordinate research initiatives promoted at national level, but no funds are provided for the research activity itself.

● EU 'own research': this is based on the Joint Research Centre's (JRC) activities which have shifted away from preoccupation with nuclear research to concentrate on new fields such as the environment, materials, remote sensing and assessment of manufacturing risks.

The Fourth Framework Programme

With a budget almost twice that of its predecessor, the Fourth Framework Programme heralded a further consolidation and extension of the EU's R&D policy by building on the structure of the Third FP but also adding new areas of focus and additional innovative measures (see Table 9.11). These can be summarised as follows:

Table 9.11 The Fourth Framework Programme

	Funding	
Activities/areas	*MECU*	*In %*
Activity 1: RTD and Demonstration Programmes	10686	86.9
Information and communication technologies	3405	27.7
Telematics	843	
Communication technologies	630	
Information technologies	1932	
Industrial technologies	1995	16.2
Industrial and materials technologies	1707	
Standardisation, measurements and testing	288	
Environment	1080	8.8
Environment and climate	852	
Marine sciences and technologies	228	
Life sciences and technologies	1572	12.8
Biotechnology	552	
Biomedicine and health	336	
Agriculture and fisheries (including agro-industry, food technologies, forestry, aquaculture and rural development)	684	
Energy	2256	18.3
Non-nuclear energy	1002	
Nuclear fission safety	414	
Controlled thermonuclear fusion	840	
Transport	240	2.0
Transport	240	
Targeted socio-economic research	138	1.1
Targeted socio-economic research	138	
Activity 2: Co-operation with third countries and international organisations	540	4.4
Activity 3: Dissemination and exploitation of results	330	2.7
Activity 4: Stimulation of the training and mobility of researchers	744	6.0
Total	12300	100.0

Source: CEC 1994k: 216

- As already mentioned, the Maastricht Treaty's provisions integrated all EU R&D policies into the FP scheme.
- The introduction of new specific programmes for transport and targeted socio-economic research. The Transport programme will concentrate on strategic research for a Trans-European multi-modal network and network optimisation. Socio-economic research will centre on technological assessments, education and training and social integration and exclusion in Europe.
- International co-operation with a wide range of third countries and international organisations forms a substantive new activity. Of its 540 MECU budget 43 per cent will be directed to co-operation with the CEE and former Soviet Union states. Another 43 per cent is devoted to co-operation with developing countries, 8.5 per cent to co-operation with other S&T fora within Europe and 5.5 per cent towards co-operation with non-European industrialised countries.
- A more comprehensive approach has been adopted to stimulate research by SMEs that draws on the CRAFT facility within the BRITE/EURAM programme.

The Fourth FP has attempted to respond to many of the past criticisms made of previous framework programmes. Perhaps the most notable of these has been the traditional bias of EU-sponsored R&D towards pre-competitive research. A more defined 'near market' focus has thus been introduced to the 4th FP's projects with the aim of converting more R&D activity outcomes into direct commercial gains. The introduction of the new Activity 2 (see Table 9.11) covering international co-operation reflects a recognised need by the EU for its R&D policy to be both more receptive to outside influences and more participative in the S&T activities of other global regions. Assessment of the social and environmental impacts of technological change has also been incorporated into the FP's structure, as has a more integrative approach taken to other policy fields such as the EU's regional and transport policies. Furthermore, the promotion of the EU's human capital base (this has been partly achieved through schemes such as ERASMUS and COMMETT) has acquired greater significance as its inadequacies in education and training have become increasingly apparent and the knowledge intensity of new core technologies more widely recognised. Future FPs and other technology related areas of policy will have to take greater consideration of forthcoming demographic changes, for example, the prospect of an ageing population, and the implications for assimilating and generating new technologies. Figure 9.5 shows the progression of funding priorities and hence emphasis given to different technological fields over all four FPs.

While some of the more traditional areas, like energy and IT, have experienced a decline in funding, their support still remains substantial. Together with industrial and materials technologies, their combined 62.2

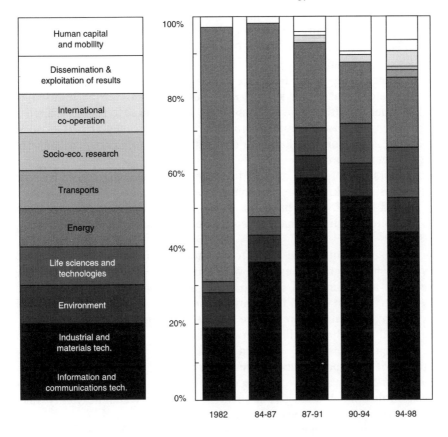

Figure 9.5 Changes in R&D priorities between the framework programmes
Source: CEC 1994k: 219

per cent share of the Fourth FP's budget is illustrative of the strong emphasis which persists on promoting industrial competitiveness. Part of the reason for their decline has been the opening up of the framework programmes to new fields of research and greater priority conferred upon biotechnology – a technology cluster core where Europe has yet to make a sizeable impression.

The impact of the framework programmes on EU industry

The sectoral impact of the EU's R&D policies has obviously varied. Moreover, a Commission study (CEC 1994n) found that the relationship between technology and the business strategies of firms largely determined the effects of the FPs' activities on them. The study identified three types of firm for the purpose of analysing these effects:

- Traditional firms: these operate in mature markets, produce standardised products and usually lack the incentive or capacity to install significant technological change. R&D activities tend to be aimed at cost cutting process innovations.
- New technology based firms: technology and innovation lie at the centre of strategy-making in such firms. 'Soft' products are customised in accordance with contacts established within close customer–supplier relationships. R&D projects are seen as a more integral part of their business environment having a direct impact upon a complete range of management procedures.
- Corporate laboratories of large firms: in recent years these have become increasingly akin to internal contract organisations whose work is contracted by individual business divisions in this manner. Hence, their portfolio of activities has moved further downstream.

In the cases examined the FPs offered traditional firms the opportunity to evaluate new technologies that were orientated towards meeting their needs. It also stimulated them to adopt a more committed approach to R&D activity, but overall their participation in the FPs could be classified as passive. A more comprehensive impact has been made on new technology based firms through their inter-active approach towards the FPs, which in consequence has widely affected the business environment in which they function. For corporate laboratories of large firms, the FPs have sought to match funds dedicated to strategic research where internal funding has not been forthcoming, thus giving them more options and flexibility than would have otherwise been the case.

In attempting to make similar evaluations, Kastrinos (1994) draws the distinction between firms deemed to be either 'technology users' or 'technology producers'. For the former, EU standardisation arising from FP activities may help bring stability to these firms which lack the capability to cope with the pace of technological change and the uncertain environment it generates. The FPs can also assist them in perceiving new technological capabilities and strategies that are within their grasp. In the case of the latter, the FPs have helped focus the extensive technological orientation of their business strategies and have stimulated competition regarding new technology formation. This has produced potential benefits for all European industry, as has the FPs' networking infrastructure which has been able to link firms in co-operative ventures through its shared cost contracted research and concerted actions. The gains derived from collaboration have involved learning benefits from mutual access to complementary skills and knowledge and also shared strategic motivations regarding the development of a European based capacity to compete against US and Japanese rivals. Sustained benefits have additionally been generated from initial collaborations leading to the exploitation of other synergetic opportunities.

In a survey conducted by the Commission (1994e), firms and states felt that it was too early to estimate the impact which FPs have had upon European competitiveness in terms of market share and balance of trade. However, there was broad agreement that they had made important positive contributions to structural competitiveness through improvements to the S&T knowledge base and research skills, and hence the innovative capabilities of European firms.

Pan-European S&T collaborations

There is a range of S&T collaborations working outside the EU's own R&D programmes which seeks to promote pan-European research and innovative activities. We shall consider three main aspects, namely the EUREKA programme, COST and EU–CEE co-operation initiatives. Additional activities such as research undertaken by the European Space Agency, the European Science Foundation and others also exist to promote a pan-European approach.

EUREKA

In November 1985, the EUREKA programme was established as an inter-governmental arrangement between a number of European states with the objective of promoting pan-European research in advanced technologies. In contrast to the EU's R&D programmes, there is no centralised executive control and no central funding. Potential participants propose initiatives which are then interfaced within the programme through a series of national networks of co-ordinators and each proposal is assessed at ministerial conferences. There are currently twenty-two member nations in EUREKA (Hungary, Russia, Slovenia and Turkey are the only non-EU/EFTA countries), while the Commission plays a supportive role.

EUREKA's four main technology areas consist of the environment (22.2 per cent of the ECU 12,463m funding in 1994), biotechnology (18.8 per cent), robotics (18.8 per cent), and IT (14.4 per cent). Its projects are consortia-based and range from 'standard' projects, which normally involve a few partners, to large 'strategic' projects. The Joint European Sub-micron Silicon Initiative (JESSI), which commenced in 1989, has been the most important of these with its main remit to establish a competitive European capability in microelectronics. The High Definition Television (HDTV) project has been another notable example, representing Europe's attempt to establish a global standard for the product ahead of the rival efforts by the USA and Japan. In certain areas 'umbrella' projects have networked together a series of related initiatives, for example the EURO-ENVIRON projects.

Both types of EUREKA projects have a stronger 'near market' approach than EU R&D equivalents. EUREKA collaborations are generally based on pre-existing groupings that are founded on vertical market relationships. A supplier–user relationship typically forms the basis of links between small and large firms with the latter providing the test bed for new product and process applications.

Although the EUREKA programme has produced some commercially and socially useful results it has not been without its problems. For example, the decision of Philips to pull out of the static random-access memory chip project in 1990 nearly caused the collapse of JESSI. Its fundamental objectives were again tested when Siemens agreed to develop new chip technologies with both IBM and Toshiba. There has also been some criticism over the qualification of foreign companies to participate within JESSI (which IBM now does), a situation that does not apply to the USA's counterpart Sematech programme. In contrast, it may be a fallacy to think that pure European research is the most effective route to take in improving European competitiveness given the forces of globalisation at play. Moreover, Flamm (1993) has proposed that inter-regional reciprocity arrangements in R&D programmes may provide the further impetus towards multilateral negotiations on certain global technology issues and the benefits that these bring.

COST

COST is the longest running S&T co-operation programme in Europe, being established at a 1971 European Ministerial Conference. It provides a mechanism for pan-European S&T co-operation and its current membership comprises of the EU and EFTA member states (plus the Commission), Turkey and the Visegrad countries minus Slovakia. COST operates through networked co-operative projects involving a variable number of participants who are committed to undertaking research in common areas of interest. Organisations from non-members are able to join COST projects if approval is granted at appropriate committee levels.

EU co-operation programmes with CEE countries

An important aspect of the communist legacy in the CEE countries was the vast array of research institutes that were produced. However, their activities were determined by strict state economic and military goals which were both highly segregated and secretive. Their recent fate has been closely tied to the political structure that supported them. Halting the 'brain drain' of RSE personnel from CEE countries has been a major priority of their S&T policy. Another has been the conversion of military sector R&D to the civil sector, although a number of factors have made this difficult. The political influence of the military–industrial complex remains strong in some countries. In addition, much military R&D has been concentrated in 'closed cities'. These present certain locational rigidities, especially where they have been established in remote areas.

Some CEE countries have begun to develop an S&T infrastructure that is rooted in their emerging private sectors. This has also involved an integration into the international S&T community. For example, in Poland the number of domestic patents registered had risen from 2,854 in 1989 to 3,443 by 1992. In addition, there has been a promotion of S&T activity in key industrial sectors oriented to new priorities in social and economic development. These have typically covered environment, health care, nuclear safety, the general transformation of industrial processes and a greater priority afforded to developing product technologies.

Against this background, the EU has formulated collaborative programmes to assist in this aspect of the transformation process and establish closer links between EU and CEE S&T communities. Some EU member states had already made pre-reform contacts with CEE countries. However, since the transition period began co-operation at an EU level has been based on four key initiatives:

- The PHARE Programme: contains the TEMPUS (student exchange) and ACE (economists in wider international co-operation) sub-initiatives. These were first commenced in 1990 and 1991 respectively. ACE is an annual programme and TEMPUS began its second four-year phase in 1994.
- Technical Assistance for the CIS (TACIS): has provided special measures aimed at supporting social, economic and political reform in the CIS states since it began in 1991.
- PECO/COPERNICUS: aims to promote S&T co-operation between EU member states and PHARE countries. It was launched in 1992 with five 'action' areas, namely mobility initiatives, networks and conferences, joint research projects, support for participation in the EU's framework programmes and COST.
- INTAS: or the International Association for the Promotion of Co-operation with Scientists in the Newly Independent States of the Former Soviet Union. This is an independent initiative, partly funded by the Commission, with the aim of creating a framework for international S&T co-operation with former Soviet Union countries in non-military research fields.

The former Soviet Union has particularly been targeted by the EU for assistance in S&T fields, although like PHARE, TACIS concentrates primarily on economic development. INTAS was introduced to compensate for this, even though strictly it operates independently of the Commission, but nevertheless receives substantial financial support. Further collaborative efforts through COST, which welcomed three Visegrad countries into membership in 1991, and the EUREKA programme have reinforced the EU's policy of S&T co-operation with the CEE states. Future S&T

co-operation between both regions will be mainly determined through Activity 2 of the Fourth Framework Programme (see Table 9.11). The immediate and longer term aim of the EU will be to act as guardian to the S&T potential of the CEE countries, this being in its economic, political, social and environmental interests (CEC 1995q).

Box 9.1 ESPRIT: A strategic technology response to international competition

The introduction of the ESPRIT programme – the flagship of the EU's new R&D projects launched in the early 1980s – was perceived by many as a direct response by the EC to Japan's Fifth Generation Computer Programme (FGCP) of 1982. To understand its wider background we need to consider previous events and developments. Through military 'demand–pull' effects and the technological superiority of its firms, the USA had established a dominant position in microelectronics since its conception in the 1950s. This position was reinforced by the new entrepreneurial 'merchant chip producers' which have subsequently emerged in the USA.

In recognition of the strategic importance of R&D activity to the country's economic development, Japan's MITI and NTT began to invest considerable resources in this sector from the 1960s. By the end of the next decade, the innovative endeavours of Japan's large computer companies had placed them at the technological frontier of semiconductor production and other micro-electronics sub-sectors. This position was augmented by the FGCP in the early 1980s by which time trade frictions had arisen from Japanese import penetration in both US and European markets.

Additional motives for establishing the ESPRIT programme had been fuelled by the heightened competition originating from Japanese microchip producers, whose operations were becoming vertically integrated by the end of the 1970s. This was of significant concern to European IT systems companies which had previously benefited from lower chip prices brought on by intensifying competition between Japanese firms, which had not yet developed a strong systems capability, and traditional US suppliers (Flamm 1993).

On the one hand, ESPRIT marked a departure from previous European attempts to sponsor 'national champions' by the engineering of pan-European horizontal and vertical collaborations within which each network player was supposed to specialise in their respective technological strengths. On the other, the programme's commercial success was hampered by its designing principles which drew heavily on macroeconomic linear growth models and thus a concentration on broad 'pre-competitive' research. The lack of market focus consequently led to a neglect of the subsequent innovation processes and wider incentive systems that were required to sustain its momentum (Mytelka 1993). It has also been suggested that the initial impetus of ESPRIT 1 was stalled by its concentration on relatively old technologies (e.g. bipolar integrated circuits and silicon substrates), whereas

Box 9.1 *continued*

little was placed on microprocessors and new RISC technologies which came to shape the IT market in the 1990s. Furthermore, within the 'big 12' group of European IT firms, brought together by EC Industry Commissioner Davignon to form the corporate bedrock of the programme, there were considerable differences of opinion or ambivalence over the vision and position of Europe's microelectronics industry.

ESPRIT's early predicaments were further aggravated by developments elsewhere in the Triad. From the mid-1980s, market conditions had become increasingly hard for European IT firms. Scale economies were difficult to come by after the 1985–6 crash of the semiconductor market. The fall of computer sales in the USA and Japanese overcapacity meant a more competitive and contracted marketplace. In addition, the 1987 Semiconductor Trade Agreement (STA) signed between the USA and Japan, which applied minimum floor prices to Japanese semiconductor imports, enabled Japan's producers to attain high rent-seeking profits that were ploughed back into R&D activities. A second STA followed in 1991 after the USA went into deficit on its semiconductor trade balance for the first time. Ernst and O'Connor (1992) note that these developments had led to an 'unstable global oligopoly' existing in the industry between Japanese and US firms which dominated product design and whose technological and organisational capabilities reinforced their control of the main global markets and distribution networks.

Despite the fact that ESPRIT 2 had made some key adjustments to the programme's orientation – for example, it integrated project clusters in which only 37 per cent of its projects were classified as 'pre-competitive' and 49 per cent as those with immediate market application, as opposed to 63 per cent and 23 per cent rates for ESPRIT 1 respectively – the wider global picture made for a poor recipe on which a European catch-up could be based. Circumstances were made worse by the targeting of the European market by Japanese and US firms suffering from excess capacity. Consequently, ESPRIT's participants were forced to adopt a more defensive posture which obviously deflected them from pursuing more focused global strategies.

Mytelka (1993, 1995) has argued that ESPRIT's essential failure in producing a 'tight knot oligopoly' between European IT firms has led ultimately to its unfulfilled potential. Influential members of the 'big 12', such as Philips, have gradually pulled away from the programme, while others were either taken over by non-European firms (e.g. ICL by Fujitsu) or drawn into the orbit of the USA–Japan global oligopoly players (e.g. the Siemens–IBM–Toshiba alliance formed in the early 1990s). The need for greater corporate integration between ESPRIT's participants has been made even more crucial owing to the progressively burdensome sunk development costs that are attributable to each generation of semiconductors. Furthermore, scale economies have not been the only entry barrier which they have encountered. These have now broadened to include newer intangible investments in R&D, management and marketing, while learning economies have become more

Box 9.1 *continued*

complex and firm specific. Other impediments have been caused by the persistence of ESPRIT to concentrate on niche areas with limited commercial spillover effects. The convergence of its projects on mainly upstream activities has also meant that ESPRIT's effect on improving the structural competitiveness of the European IT industry has been underplayed.

THE EU AS A WORLD PARTNER

With the industrialised countries

Strategic technology alliances

At a corporate level, European collaboration with other industrialised countries has occurred most frequently and extensively through strategic technology alliances. The fact that over 90 per cent of all technological agreements and partnerships are between Triad members reflects how the industrialised countries have come to dominate global technology-based networking. The majority of non-Triad alliances has been formed between firms originating from the East Asian NICs. Recent trends in triadic strategic technology alliances are displayed in Figure 9.6.

Before we embark on an analysis of the trends shown it must be noted that the data represented show absolute numbers of strategic alliances made in core technology industries, thus giving no account of their scale or scope. In addition, the work of public sector co-ordination schemes such as the EU's R&D framework programmes has not been included; hence the EU is somewhat under-represented. Nevertheless, certain key trends are clearly identifiable:

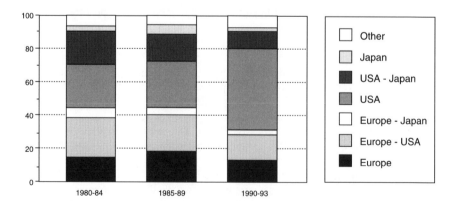

Figure 9.6 Distribution of strategic technology alliances, total core industries
Source: CEC 1994k: 297

- There has been a large increase in intra-US alliances. This is in contrast to the recent experience of the two other Triad members.
- The number of European–Japanese alliances has actually fallen in all core areas since the 1980s.
- Alliances between US and Japanese firms have also fallen over the long term, although the increase of IT alliances formed in the early 1990s has helped to reverse this trend.
- US–European alliances as a proportion of total Triad alliances have fallen slightly but still remain larger in number than US–Japanese equivalents. In the separate core technology industries this lead is most marginal in IT.
- There is a reasonably close correlation between the trends found in all core technology industries: IT, biotechnology and new material sciences.

The developments behind these trends have been analysed by Hagedoorn and Schakenraad (1993, 1994) who conclude that there has been an increasing penchant for regional strategic partnering. Over half the companies investigated followed this pattern, while only 6 per cent had adopted a true global strategy with respect to technology partnering. This is confirmed by the data above whereby US firms in particular appear to be turning towards each other for mutual technological support. This either reflects a dearth of appropriate partners in other Triad regions or a change in the strategic motivations that underpin their alliance-making, or a combination of the two. If the latter of these effects holds most validity, then this would prove commensurate with the findings proposed by Hagedoorn and Schakenraad (1992), Hagedoorn (1993) and Wegberg and Witteloostuijn (1995): intra-US strategic technology alliances have been founded increasingly on research-driven as opposed to market-driven objectives.

The data shown would lead us to assume that European firms have faced a different set of imperatives, given the comprehensive decline in intra-bloc alliances since the mid-1980s. However, any conclusions that can be determined from this must be placed in the context of Europe's falling number of total alliances over the same period. Hence, it is a question of apparent relative decline and, in addition, we have mentioned earlier that FP registered European alliances have not been recorded. Nevertheless, Europe's generally poor technological performance would seem to suggest the need to tap into the S&T activities of other regions at the cutting edge of new technology formation in order to improve its own technological capabilities. Strategic technological partnering offers some of the prime routes by which this can be achieved. The growing search for inter-regional partners may have been further induced by the lack of suitable fellow European counterparts. Further evidence is required to determine the exact influence that the EU's R&D framework programmes have had on countering such developments by their promotion of pan-European research.

Scientific collaboration

The continuous rise of scientific specialisation in research has been partly driven by the pressure to identify fields in which to concentrate their efforts and excel at an international level. Impinging globalisation factors and the benefits offered by sharing the cost of maintaining S&T infrastructures have generated additional centripetal forces for international scientific collaborations.

In a study by Luukkonen *et al.* (1992) it was suggested that the degree to which a country's or region's scientists participate in international collaborations is inversely related to the size of its scientific community. For example, around one-tenth of US scientific papers are co-authored with foreign counterparts, whereas for the UK, France and Germany the proportion is closer to one-fifth. Scientific collaborations between the industrialised countries have also formed into clusters that have been most notably defined by their cultural–linguistic features (CEC 1993a). Five main clusters have emerged in Western countries, based on Germanic, Latin, Nordic and Slavonic groups, involving respective West and East European countries, and an Anglo-Saxon group incorporating the UK, English-speaking North America and Australasia.

The participation of Japanese scientists, while generally limited, has helped to create a Trans-Pacific cluster with the USA. On an inter-regional basis, EU–NAFTA scientific co-publications have been the most frequent, with 46.2 per cent of total EU co-publications. For EFTA countries this figure is 13.9 per cent, with 4.4 per cent for Australasia and only 3.9 per cent for EU–Japanese co-publications. The underdevelopment of this form of scientific collaboration between the EU and Japan has prompted a number of initiatives to promote the international mobility of Japanese scientists. This has been welcomed by Japan as it has become increasingly acknowledged that its general introspection as a nation has impeded the scientific creativity that is required to generate its future prosperity.

Another key dimension to scientific collaborations has been the numerous inter-governmental bilateral scientific agreements signed between the industrialised countries. These have provided the framework for facilitating exchanges and co-operative projects between signatories. By the mid-1990s, most West European states have signed such agreements with the USA and Canada, and a few have general agreements with Japan and Australia. By 1994, the Commission had also been a signatory to agreements with the USA, Canada, Korea and Australia. Trans-Atlantic agreements are the most well established with the first Community–USA agreement being signed in 1958. Since this date around 36 per cent of activities within these agreements have focused on nuclear research, but this misrepresents the significance of new priority areas to have emerged, namely transport, environment and biomedical fields. European countries have also been participants in multilateral scientific agreements that have covered S&T fields with global scope such as the environment and health. In addition, they have sometimes enabled participants to share scientific instruments and facilities on a mutual benefit basis.

With the developing countries

At the beginning of the chapter, we noted how convergent and divergent trends in technological development have tended to marginalise the developing countries. A poor scientific and technological infrastructure, the lack of RSE personnel, unfavourable financial conditions, inadequate communications and transport networks and high levels of political risk have proved far from conducive to supporting new technology formation and innovatory activity. Not only have more technologically advanced nations felt a moral obligation to provide some of the fundamental conditions in which these impediments can be overcome, but they have also increasingly recognised the wide range of damaging spillover effects if they do not. This particularly relates to the environmental, social and health negative externalities that have been generated on a global scale.

Much of the assistance given to developing countries to promote technological development and innovation by the EU takes place at member state level. The pattern of the assistance granted has been largely determined by historical and cultural ties between participating nations. Education and training programmes have formed an important function here providing key investments in human capital for the beneficiary country.

Technical assistance has been conferred to the ACP countries through the Lomé Conventions (see Chapter 6), as well as through the EU's own Association and Co-operation Agreements. The Commission has a number of specific initiatives aimed at providing support for the technological development of LDCs at an EU level, namely the International Scientific Co-operation (ISC) scheme, the Science and Technology for Development (STD) programmes and the AVICENNE initiative.

International Scientific Co-operation (ISC) scheme

The main aim of the ISC scheme is to strengthen the links between the scientific communities of the EU and those in Latin American, Asian and Mediterranean Basin countries. The scheme can be seen as complementary to the general preferential trade terms granted under the EU's GSP to which most of these countries belong. While the extent of assistance provided does not match that given to the ACP countries via the Lomé Conventions, the ISC constitutes a parallel set of measures that aims to support the GSP's objectives of promoting industrial development in recipient states.

The three main elements to the ISC consist of joint research projects (which take 78 per cent of ISC funds), 'Marie Curie' fellowships for LDC scientists and workshops which bring together small groups of EU and third country scientists to discuss particular scientific issues. By 1993 around thirty five developing countries had co-operated in 650 joint research projects. The more advanced of these have been the most active participants in the sub-scheme so far, namely Israel, Mexico, Brazil and Argentina. This characterises the dilemma faced by such programmes in that those countries most in need of them often lack the capacity to exploit the technical assistance on offer. However, this predicament has not arisen so much in the ISC fellowship sub-scheme where countries with relatively low per capita incomes such as China and India have been among the main participants.

Science and Technology for Development (STD) programmes

Unlike the ISC and AVICENNE, the STD programme is open to all developing countries. It was established in 1982 as a response to the Second UN Conference on Science and Technology for Development (UNCSTD) with a focus on agriculture and medicine. The main objective of STD1 (1982–7) was to improve Europe's tropical research potential with contributions made by scientists from developing countries. The STD2 (1987–91) programme extended its scope by actively promoting R&D capabilities. On a regional basis, sub-Saharan African countries were the most active in the STD2 programme, taking part in 46 per cent of its projects, with those from Latin America having a 26 per cent share, Asia 16 per cent and the Mediterranean Basin 12 per cent. The most recently completed programme, STD3 (1991–4), sought to place a stronger emphasis on development. Funding for the STD programmes is generated through the EU's R&D framework programmes and has successively increased its share of budget from 1.06 per cent for STD1 to 1.94 per cent for STD3.

AVICENNE

The objective of the AVICENNE initiative has been the promotion of scientific and technological co-operation between the EU and Mediterranean Basin countries. Within AVICENNE, the EU has sought to enhance the R&D capability of the region in waste water treatment, primary health care and renewable energies. Israel, Algeria and Tunisia have had the highest number of institutions involved in the initiative while environmental projects have more than twice outnumbered those in health and biomedicine.

The EU and global collaboration programmes

As we have seen, there is some debate over whether foreign firms should be allowed to participate in national or regional level R&D programmes. The Sematech project has illustrated the USA's aversion to such participation, while the JESSI scheme showed a tendency for EU and European countries to lay down strict criteria for third country membership. In contrast, Japan's Agency of Industrial Science and Technology (AIST) has positively encouraged foreign firms to join its own funded or sponsored initiatives. These have typically involved high technology industries where Japan has yet to develop a competitive advantage, for example, civil aviation and more basic research-based industries.

Partly in an effort to demonstrate its contribution to the world's research output, Japan has also pioneered initiatives whose main purpose has been to promote global collaboration in S&T activities. These have included the Human Frontier Science Programme (HFSP) that was launched in 1987 with the aim of facilitating basic research on biological functions. In 1989, the Intelligent Manufacturing Systems (IMS) project was initiated by Japan in an attempt to involve other industrialised countries in promoting standardisation, R&D in manufacturing technology and the systemisation of the existing S&T knowledge base in the related sectors.

The higher cost commitments involved in new technology formation across an increasingly broad range of sectors and the forces of globalisation would suggest that inter-regional and global collaboration in S&T activities will become more frequent in the future. Triadic patterns of concentration not only in this form of partnership but also in strategic technology alliances present some cause for concern over the position of developing countries, given additional relevance by the current lack of a multilateral regulatory framework.

CONCLUDING REMARKS

Technological and innovatory considerations are pivotal to all strategies that aim to improve corporate or economic performance. In this chapter, we have discussed how the development of a technological advantage over rival firms or countries remains important, but there have been several notable changes concerning the areas of activity and the accepted means of achievement. It has been stressed that Europe's top priorities are to acquire a much stronger position in the core technology industries and to adapt more comprehensively to the new technological paradigms emerging in production and elsewhere.

Most European governments have already acknowledged that the supportive role played in this process has implied a recasting of traditional S&T policies. This has also entailed taking account of how technology and technological endeavours have become increasingly globalised. Foreign investments have brought with them valuable technology transfers for developed and developing countries alike, while cross-border strategic technology alliances have helped further to diffuse new product and process innovations. European firms have been at the centre of these developments. However, at an industrial level, Europe still lags behind its Triad rivals with respect to the new growth sectors of the next century. If one defining characteristic can be attributed to these it is their high degree of knowledge intensivity. This issue will form a central theme of Chapter 10.

10 The human dimension

The European economy's ability to meet its current and future global challenges is largely dependent on how it manages its human resources. In this chapter, we shall consider four key aspects of its 'human dimension' and analyse how they are specifically related to these challenges. First, the advent of significant demographic changes, particularly population ageing, can be expected to generate a complex range of economic impacts. While both the number and scale of these may be difficult to predict, an attempt will be made to study the main pressures that have to date been most anticipated. Second, we shall discuss why employment growth has become a top economic and political priority within Europe and initiatives that have been set in motion to improve the EU's relatively poor performance on this account. Third, the key issues and challenges surrounding education and training will be examined in closer detail and the emerging role that both have played in developing Europe's human capital. Social policy forms the last section of this chapter in which we shall investigate how it has had to adapt to new priorities recently set within Europe, and to what extent it has become an integral part of strategies aimed at enhancing European competitiveness.

THE IMPACT OF DEMOGRAPHIC CHANGE

The projected growth in world population

Concern over the economic and environmental impact of projected rises in the world's population have existed for some time. It was Thomas Malthus who, in the nineteenth century, first fully articulated the demographic predicaments caused by population growth, stating that 'the natural power of mankind to increase' at a geometric rate was unsustainable given 'the diminishing and limited power of increasing the produce of the soil' (Malthus 1830: 225) which tended to yield only arithmetic increases in food supplies. In more recent years, environmentalists have adopted the basic premises of Malthusian theory to highlight the tensions between an expanding population and environmental resources. Evidence presented by the UN and others suggests that at current estimates the world's population is set nearly to double by the middle of the next century (see Table 10.1). This increase in demographic pressure upon the world's eco-systems must also be considered alongside rising standards of living and the potential for environmental mismanagement of significant magnitude in forthcoming years.

An alternative, more optimistic scenario rests on the ability of new technologies and innovations to provide the means to alleviate future environmental and demographic pressures. For instance, the development of renewable energy sources and biodegradable chemicals that enhance crop yields are among solutions which could lead to a more sustainable path of global economic growth. Furthermore, Table 10.1 reveals that, at least in relative terms, the developed countries' share of world population is falling while those regions set to increase their share up to 2025 – India and in particular Africa and – are among the poorest. However, this argument tends to simplify the issue over the proportionate impact of future per capita consumption rates as it is not only the amount of resources that are consumed that matters, but rather how they are consumed. The post-war energy and industrial practices of the CEE countries clearly illustrate this point. Moreover, there is evidence to suggest that rising levels of prosperity in a country actually help facilitate and improve its environmental protection systems. This forms part of a much wider debate that will be discussed in more detail in Chapter 11.

Table 10.1 Shares in world population: 1955, 1990, 2025 (millions and percentage)

	1955	*1990*	*2025*
World (millions)	2752	5295	8472
World	100.0	100.0	100.0
Developed countries	32.3	22.9	16.6
Developing countries	67.7	77.1	83.4
Europe	15.1	9.6	6.4
North America	6.6	5.2	4.3
Asia	55.0	58.9	57.8
China	22.1	21.8	18.2
India	14.4	16.0	16.5
Africa	9.0	12.1	18.7
Latin America	6.9	8.3	8.3
Oceania	0.5	0.5	0.5
Former USSR*	6.9	5.3	4.1

Source: UN 1992b
* Excluding the Baltic States which are included in Europe.

Ageing populations

Attempting to forecast the future population growth is notoriously difficult and caution must be exercised when dealing with estimated figures as errors in exogenous parameters tend to cumulate over long periods. Nevertheless, we can state with a significant degree of certainty that the populations of particular countries and regions will show more notable signs of ageing by the early twenty-first century. Ageing occurs from the increase in a population's longevity rates and decrease in its fertility rates, thus raising the overall average age. The economic and social implications of ageing largely centre on the increase of the population's dependency ratio (i.e. the number of 'dependent' citizens divided by wealth-generating citizens, normally the working population), its effect upon supply and demand conditions in product and capital markets and potential for affecting the general behaviour of economic agents.

As Table 10.2 indicates, all three Triad regions face future ageing of their own populations, in particular Japan whose 65+ group is estimated to constitute over 40 per cent of its total population by 2025. For Europe and the USA, this share will only reach around 30 per cent. Combined with its low fertility rate, Japan's population will 'dejuvenate', as Cliquet (1993) terms it, and hence experience a gradually declining total population after 2010 according to the OECD's 1995 estimates. Yet, as Table 10.3 shows, Japan's ageing population will be counterbalanced by the support received by a high labour force participation rate in both the 65+ and working age groups.

Other regions will also encounter an ageing of their populations, most notably Asia and Latin America. Raised living standards and the eroded

Table 10.2 Global dependency ratios (percentages): 1990, 2025

	1990			2025		
	Total	*Under 15*	*Over 65*	*Total*	*Under 15*	*Over 65*
World total	62.6	52.6	10.1	53.0	38.1	14.9
Europe	49.7	29.6	20.1	57.2	26.6	30.6
North America	51.4	32.5	18.9	57.1	28.0	29.1
Japan	43.2	26.4	16.8	65.2	25.0	40.3
Asia[1]	61.0	52.9	8.0	48.5	34.3	14.3
Africa	92.5	86.7	7.4	67.4	60.7	6.7
Latin America	68.0	59.9	8.1	49.3	35.6	13.8
Oceania	55.1	40.9	14.2	54.4	33.8	20.5
Former USSR*	54.0	39.7	14.2	56.0	34.0	22.0

Source: UN 1992b
Notes: Total indicates Under 15 plus Over 65, divided by 15–65 population;
Under 15 = U15/15–65; Over 65 = 65+/15–65.
[1] Includes Japan.
* Excluding the Baltic States which are included in Europe.

Table 10.3 Labour force participation: 1990, 2025 (year group, percentages)

| | 1990 | | | | 2025 | | | |
	10–14	15–19	20–24	45–59	10–14	15–19	20–24	45–59
Europe	0.2	40.5	75.5	68.0	0.0	40.4	83.5	67.1
North America	0.0	45.2	78.8	72.0	0.0	50.7	90.6	70.5
Japan	0.0	18.3	73.2	77.0	0.0	20.1	82.0	77.0
Asia[1]	14.5	52.0	74.6	67.8	2.3	34.6	63.0	65.5
Africa	22.9	50.9	66.5	69.4	5.8	43.0	68.4	65.0
Latin America	4.7	36.9	61.7	56.1	0.5	32.2	70.4	57.2
Australasia	0.0	52.7	80.3	68.4	0.0	51.4	84.9	66.4
Former USSR	0.0	34.0	81.1	77.2	0.0	33.8	87.5	76.5

Source: UN 1994c, after ILO statistical database
Note: [1] Includes Japan.

perception of children as family-based economic assets, in both their formative and later years, has increased the average age in many of the regions' NICs in particular (e.g. Singapore and Taiwan). The latter determining trend can be observed in the expected labour force participation of the 10–14 years group in Table 10.3 for both developing regions. Despite the fact that relatively high fertility rates here buoy up their total dependency ratios, they still fall well short of those carried by the developed regions.

Moreover, a total dependency ratio inflated by young dependants, as is the case with Africa, is arguably less burdensome than one expanded by elderly dependants. This can be illustrated in terms of the fiscal pressures caused by rising dependency ratios. Population 'greying' carries with it a need to devote more economic resources to pension incomes as an increasing number of people enter the pensionable age bracket. For example, it has been recently estimated that social security taxes in Germany would have to rise to 30 per cent of wages to maintain pensions at current levels (UN 1994c). The cost of health care provision will also mount as older people tend to be ill more frequently, take longer to recover and contract more serious ailments. Consequently, per capita public health spending on the 65+ group is over quadruple that for those under 65 years (*Financial Times*, 8 March 1994). Where the under 15 group makes up a considerable section of the population (e.g. Kenya at 49.9 per cent in 1992) the country is provided with a large number of potential future wealth generators and hence a broader tax base from which revenue can be sustainably withdrawn.

The same does not apply with an 'aged' population unless they are able to make similar productive contributions. However, the economic development of countries with very high fertility rates may be impeded by difficulties in raising their education spending per pupil levels and also by meeting the needs of resourcing necessary child care facilities. In base economic terms, diverting public or indeed private funds towards education would, though, be perceived as a 'productive' investment as opposed to those devoted to the 'unproductive' ends of financing pensions and elderly health care.

Pensions

The funding of future pension systems is one of the most important challenges that faces Europe. How this task is managed could significantly affect its fiscal structures, levels of saving, investment and employment and ulitmately its industrial competitiveness. Pension expenditure varies quite markedly between the G7 nations owing both to the level of generosity found in each national welfare system and the elderly dependency ratio. In the USA, Canada and the UK pension expenditure represents between 5 per cent to 8 per cent of GDP, whereas rates that range between 15 per cent to 20 per cent are found in France, Germany, Italy and Japan (OECD 1995a). Managing and adjusting pension systems and the resources attributed to them will become increasingly critical to the Triad regions as the burden of population ageing becomes more ponderous.

Of the policy options available to governments concerning adjustments to present pension systems, the OECD Secretariat has favoured raising the retirement age over both the alternatives of lowering pension payments or raising contribution rates. Extending the accepted range of the working population has the dual advantage of both prolonging the contribution made by older workers to the national economic effort and releasing funds earmarked for pensioner incomes. This solution would also arguably carry less political risk, but only if the sacrifice of future leisure time forgone was seen as suitable trade-off for avoiding adverse pecuniary circumstances in the meantime. Means testing methods of assessing eligibility for state pensions, as have been recently introduced to New Zealand, may offer another alternative option, although this may lead to distorted incentive structures for those near the means test thresholds. Such reforms would need to be announced well in advance so as to enable people to adjust their behaviour accordingly prior to implementation, and more often than not involve a phasing in of intended reforms.

The majority of state pension systems are based on a 'pay-as-you-go' (PAYG) principle whereby current contributions to the fund made by the working population are passed on to the current recipients. Hence, under such a system inter-generational imbalances arise as the population progressively ages in favour of earlier generations who carried a proportionately lower burden when making their contributions. The 'fully funded' or capitalisation principle on which private sector pension schemes are devised offers another solution, whereby invested funds are locked into the value of the accumulated capital initially acquired with them (i.e. shares and other securities). The USA has had a well-developed system along these lines for some time. Since 1988, UK citizens have been able to opt out of the supplementary state system, while 5.5 million people have also chosen to accept tax rebates to set up private pension plans.

The main advantage of the fully funded system is that, in theory, it should avoid the considerable social expenditures that are presently associated with state PAYG schemes. A greater role played by private schemes with a maximum freedom to invest should also increase saving rates and capital availability, improve the efficiency of capital markets in Europe and thus help stimulate the capital formation required during the establishment phase of the system (Taverne 1995). However, it is conceivable that market forces would dictate a progressive real depreciation in the invested capital assets owing to diminished demand from a shrinking younger population, thus possibly denying the ability of the whole system to store up purchasing power over time. However, with continued financial globalisation it is increasingly feasible for the value of invested European pension funds to be sustained by new poles of economic growth. This in turn relies on the magnitude of the wealth-generating power of regions such as East Asia to protect the real value of these investments. Ownership and foreign exchange risks will also come attached to pursuing this policy in addition to a number of other foreseen and unforeseen complexities.

Although some degree of inter-generational equity comes with implementing the fully funded system, a major drawback lies in the disproportionate benefits that it confers on those current contributors best able to invest larger capital sums over time. In addition, under any transition period the present generation would have to fund both those already retired as well as its own retirement. Furthermore, the concentration of capital required to make the system widely operable would be enormous (estimated at several times GDP). This raises questions as to the effect on asset price movements and who should own and control such stocks of wealth. Given the above considerations it would seem probable that a dual system will emerge based on a balance between the two approaches.

Saving ratios

Future saving ratios may be under threat from the dissaving tendencies that have been associated with ageing populations (see Modigliani's 1986 'life-cycle hypothesis'). The main reasons for this lie in the normally lower income levels and lack of saving 'objectives' held by elderly, and especially retired people. However, this can only be assumed if a liquidity constraint does actually exist or, if there is no such constraint, the wish to run down assets to facilitate consumption of their current incomes. The latter would, though, be tempered to a considerable degree by the general uncertainty of their life expectancy and reluctance to convert many key assets into an income flow, such as their homes. Evidence from Europe shows that since 1961 Community household savings have been compensated by corporate savings (CEC 1994e), from ageing or any other determining factors, while research for the USA shows that the elderly generally still save, albeit at a lower level (UN 1994). The life cycle hypothesis also predicts that as average family sizes decrease a greater share of parents' income will be saved rather than dedicated to children-related expenditure. Moreover, as individuals witness longevity rate increases they will desire to save more during their working lives.

Supply and demand

An ageing population will create new patterns of demand in product markets and new conventions to marketing wisdom. The demand for health care and elderly related welfare services will rise. Those sectors producing recreational products, such as the music industry and sports manufacturers, will have to consider the changing cultural tastes of society brought about by ageing. Many other firms have already begun to respond to these demographic imperatives by targeting older age groups as the most promising market segments.

Behavioural changes

There are, though, a number of concerns over the behavioural changes related to ageing and their effect on economic performance. Older people are thought to be more risk averse than their younger counterparts. This holds implications for levels of investment – which may themselves be under simultaneous pressure from lower saving ratios as a consequence of ageing – in particular those key strategic investments upon which the optimisation of future economic growth is dependent. On the other hand, the wisdom and circumspection imbied in older management strata may improve economic efficiency. Further advances made in the systems of financial intermediation should also counteract any fall in investment funds through more efficient rerouting and allocation.

Lower levels of motivation may be found among older workers due to the perception of diminished opportunities for career advancement and the acquisition of adequate responsibilities that befit their seniority. Furthermore, lower job mobility rates that are usually attributed to older workers would lead to lower levels of productivity. The effect on unit labour costs would be exacerbated by the adoption of higher, seniority determined wage compensation. Employers can play a pivotal role here by redesigning job specifications and career trajectories while also placing more emphasis on lifelong education and training programmes. The shortage of younger workers will pressure firms into pursuing such policies aimed at improving the productive capacity of their existing human capital.

A further increase in female participation rates may be sought to compensate for falling recruitment rates due to ageing, but this may induce a detrimental effect on the fertility rates required to reverse the trend of population dejuvenation. One solution would be for organisations to improve maternity leave entitlements and crèche facilities in order to support both. It may also be in the wider interest to allow those people who have to combine their commitments to work with care of the elderly enough flexibility to manage them where possible.

Following a more open immigration policy may be perceived as another viable option to widen access to the domestic labour market, but there may be practical limits as to how far this could be taken in terms of accomodating large numbers. The economic and social interaction of immigrants may also cause unpredictable effects, although these may prove to be advantageous. It is improbable, though, that EU member states will conform to such a policy with many having to resist strong migratory pressures from North Africa and from the CEE countries.

The labour shortages associated with population ageing present a special opportunity for resolving high rates of unemployment. Increased employment levels would additionally help meet the political imperative of having to redistribute income from the active to the dependent population. This is because employment growth and the accompanying incomes would compensate for the more extensive transfer payments which are involved with ageing (i.e. increased pensions and health care costs). However, there is also a chance that technological advances may counteract the absorption of the unemployed into the workforce through productivity enhancing innovations. Moreover, higher labour activity rates and full employment can only achieve a one-off countervailing effect on the ageing process. A more durable solution would be to increase the fertility rate, but this may be loaded with significant global environmental implications if applied to the developed countries.

Economic behaviour will also be affected by the extent to which intergenerational solidarity remains intact under circumstances where political and economic power will be, *ceteris paribus*, increasingly vested in the elderly in an ageing population. The desire to protect their incomes and entitlements may well be at the expense of the younger generation if this power can be effectively wielded. However, it is unlikely that investments made in the education and training of young people will be compromised owing to the positive externalities enjoyed by all society which this produces. Nevertheless, where such broad societal advantages are not generated, the young may find their economic interests consequentially marginalised.

Concluding remarks

It has not been the aim of this section specifically to evaluate how Europe will fare against the backdrop of demographic change, but rather to examine the possible contours of that change and discuss its main ramifications for the future. The issues concerned are broad based and different European countries face idiosyncratic circumstances that are being confronted in a similar manner. Moreover, addressing impending demographic change, whatever the outcomes, and assessing Europe's future likely position *vis-à-vis* that change still largely remains a crystal ball gazing exercise.

UNEMPLOYMENT AND EMPLOYMENT

An introduction

Employment growth has acquired new political significance in the 1990s with rising levels of unemployment becoming 'increasingly recognised as a major problem with global dimensions and consequences' (UN 1994c: 157). In March 1994, the G7 summit meeting hosted by President Clinton at Detroit dedicated unemployment as its central theme. It noted that a combination of extended trade with developing countries and the impact of technological change had permanently reduced the demand for low-skill labour in the developed countries. Employment growth strategies were announced as the corollary to this predicament based on the development of more highly skilled, educated and trained workforces.

This then marked a similar challenge for all Triad powers but particularly for the core European economy where unemployment has remained comparatively high and its performance on employment growth poor. The annual economic cost alone to the EU was calculated in 1993 at around ECU 210bn. However, this has not implied the subordination of low inflation as a macroeconomic policy objective to endeavours at lowering unemployment at its expense – as some would typify by the Phillips curve trade off which is usually associated with the pre-stagflation, post-war era – but rather the search for new employment growth strategies which are compatible with achieving both objectives simultaneously.

Recent patterns of employment and unemployment

The European economy has fared particularly unfavourably in its ability to create new jobs and suppress high rates of unemployment when compared to its Triad rivals. Figures 10.1 and 10.2 clearly indicate the extent of that failure over the past two decades. Only the EC12's employment rate trend has fallen both in the short term and long term, and moreover stood at 58 per cent of the total working population at the end of the period compared to rates for the USA and Japan which are well above the 70 per cent mark. While EFTA's rate was just below this its short-term trend like the EC12's is also downward. Actual employment growth figures (see Table 10.4) reveal the EU's inferiority in creating new jobs, and most recently failing even to achieve any growth at all in the early 1990s.

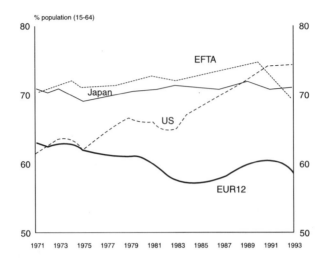

Figure 10.1 Employment rates in the Community and elsewhere, 1971–93
Source: CEC 1994p: 27

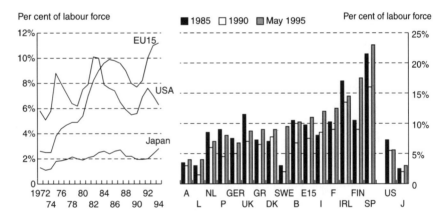

Figure 10.2 Unemployment in the Triad, 1972–94
Source: CEC 1995r

Another determining factor accounting for the variance found between the Triad regions' employment rates lies in the different activity rates of their working populations (i.e. those deemed eligible to be considered part of the working population and their actual participation in the labour market). On average, Community workers retire earlier than their Triad counterparts and are more reluctant to work beyond the pensionable age threshold. In 1992, only 6 per cent of EC males aged over 65 years were still employed in work compared to 15 per cent for US males and 40 per cent for Japanese males. Although the increased participation rate of

Table 10.4 Triad employment patterns

	EU	USA	Japan
Employment growth			
1961–73	0.3	2.0	1.3
1974–90	0.5	1.9	1.0
1991–3	−1.1	0.3	1.3
Labour market participation – females[+]			
1973	44.7	51.1	54.0
1983	49.8	61.8	57.2
1993	53.3[1]	69.1	61.7
Labour market participation – males[+]			
1973	88.7	86.2	90.1
1983	82.3	84.6	89.1
1993	75.1[1]	84.5	90.1
Unit labour costs (nominal, PPS weighted, 1980=100)			
1975	60.6	67.6	80.5
1985	142.5	127.2	104.6
1990	173.4	153.5	109.9
1995	198.3	176.5	114.0
Real compensation per employee (PPS weighted, annual per cent change)			
1971–80	2.9	0.6	5.0
1981–90	0.9	0.7	2.2
1991–5	1.2	1.2	0.1

Sources: Eurostat; OECD 1993, 1994a; CEC 1995j; UN 1994c
[+] OECD Europe for EU
[1] 1992 figure

Community females aged over 55 years has offset the decline for 55+ males, the rates for US and Japanese females are higher here too. The European pattern has provided some degree of improved access to the labour market for younger workers, though it undoubtedly presents some cause for concern to European policy-makers over managing future human resources among an ageing population.

In terms of unemployment, the EC12's rate overtook that of the USA in the early 1980s and has remained considerably higher since, reaching 11.2 per cent by 1994, nearly twice that of the US rate and nearly four times that of Japan (see Table 10.5). EFTA's performance over the period has been marred recently by the impact of the early 1990s recession with its average rate jumping from under 3 per cent in 1990 to almost 8 per cent by 1993. The EU's high unemployment rate cannot be blamed on the labour-displacing effects of relative productivity gains made over Triad rivals in recent

Table 10.5 Thematic patterns of unemployment in the Triad (per cent total)

	EU	USA	Japan
Total workforce			
1961–70	2.1	5.6	1.1
1971–80	4.6	6.5	1.6
1981–90	8.0	6.4	2.1
1991	8.3	6.7	2.1
1994	11.2	6.1	2.9
Long-term (12 months)			
1991	46.0	6.3	17.9
1993	41.2	11.7	17.2
Youth (under 25 years)			
1991	16.5	13.4	4.4
1994	22.3	12.5	5.5
Female			
1991	10.4	6.3	2.2
1994	13.1	6.0	3.0
Male			
1991	7.0	7.0	2.0
1994	10.1	6.2	2.8

Sources: Eurostat; OECD 1993, 1994a; UN 1994c

years. Its labour productivity growth record between 1980 and 1993 compares poorly at a 45 per cent increase against figures for the USA at 64 per cent and Japan at 52 per cent. This performance can be related to the EU's generally inferior levels of investment, which in turn have produced a slow growth rate in manufacturing value-added during the same period at only 14 per cent, in contrast to 45 per cent for the USA and 78 per cent for Japan (CEC 1994e). Japan was able to support comparatively generous rates of employee compensation over a similar period as a result without inflating its unit labour costs, as Table 10.4 indicates. Poor productivity growth coupled with less than abstemious worker compensation have left the EU with the highest level increase of unit labour costs in the Triad between 1980 and 1995, thus providing a further indictment on its employment growth performance.

An analysis of sectoral contributions to employment growth since the 1970s exposes Europe's reliance on the service sector for job creation. The relatively severe deindustrialisation experienced by European countries has meant that its manufacturing and other industrial activities have been unable to generate any positive contribution, unlike the USA and Japan. The more pronounced the deindustrialisation, the more deep seated the structural changes that it inflicts, thus exacerbating the labour market problems such as worker immobilities and skills mismatch which give rise to structural unemployment. It is also generally accepted that the higher value-added by manufacturing activities gives it an advantage over the service sector in terms of employment growth. This largely explains why the USA's record on aggregate factor productivity over the last two decades has actually slowed relative to Europe owing to the disproportionate rise of lower productivity service sector jobs.

The EU's relatively high rates of long-term and youth unemployment have been particularly contributive to the persistence of the high general rate. On female participation rates, the EU again lags behind its main rivals with only a 53.3 per cent rate, in comparison to 69.1 per cent and 61.7 per cent for the USA and Japan respectively in 1993. These rates vary greatly across the EU from around 40 per cent in Spain to 90 per cent in Denmark. The more active role played by women in the labour force, the more scope exists to alleviate demographic pressures while also, of course, contributing to the productive capacity of the economy. Although some anxiety has been expressed over the displacement effect incurred on male workers from increased female participation, it has largely flourished of its own accord amid recent structural and organisational changes. The ascendancy of the service sector and the growth of more flexible norms of work patterns – most notably part-time contracting – has improved employment opportunities and prospects for women in unison with broader societal forces.

However, the confinement of female workers to specific niches – in sectoral, professional and hierarchical terms – found prevalent in all Triad economies ultimately places a constraint on potential output. Owing to the tendency of female workers to be located in more precarious conditions of employment, a high female unemployment rate often accompanies a high participation rate. Table 10.5 shows that only the US appears to have an unemployment rate higher for males than females during the early 1990s. Patterns of part-time working across Europe vary considerably with the European average comparable to the USA for female part-time work (but below Japan) and with all OECD Europe below both Triad rivals on account of male part-time work (Denmark and the Netherlands excepted). This carries implications for the introduction of and adaptation to new flexible work organisation, as we shall examine later.

Evidence and theories of European unemployment

Many academics have offered a series of theories on the causes of high levels of European unemployment. The most prominent work in this field is summarised in Table 10.6. We can observe that there is a general lack of consensus between theorists over the issue with certain determining factors prioritised over, or contradicting those emphasised by others. However, some common ground is discernible. From the mid-1980s, some theorists sought to explain the persistent high rates of unemployment with the aid of the hysteresis concept. Hysteresis occurs when an economy's long-run equilibrium depends on the path which it has followed in the short run

Table 10.6 Views on the causes of European unemployment

Bruno and Sachs (1985)	Pervasive real wage rigidities in Europe's labour markets.
Budd *et al.* (1986)	Long-term unemployed hysteresis effects caused by their atrophication of skills, stigmatisation in the eyes of employers and other adverse effects.
Bean *et al.* (1986); Jackman *et al.* (1990)	Greater flexibility for real wage adjustments exists in corporatist countries (e.g. Germany, Netherlands) than non-corporatist (e.g. UK, Spain) owing to more effective communication and participation in industrial relations.
Blanchard and Summers (1986); Lindbeck and Snower (1988, 1991); Flanagan (1987)	The persistence of insider–outsider hysteresis effects. Insider workers able to maintain disproportionate competitive advantage over outsiders, hence causing labour market distortions.
Burtless (1987)	Aspects of unemployment compensation including eligibility conditions, replacement ratios, duration of benefits and efforts to prevent job avoidance.
Alogoskoufis and Manning (1988)	Europe's comparatively high worker compensation rates.
Blanchard (1990)	Investments made in labour-saving methods have continued even when the general level of investment in Europe has fallen.
Dreze and Bean (1990)	Similar argument to above. Productivity gains have been transferred into real wage increases. This has in turn induced greater incentives for capital intensivity and hence substitution of capital for labour.
Layard and Nickell (1991); Layard *et al.* (1991)	Over-long duration of unemployment benefits and high replacement ratios. May lead to upward pressure on wage rates at lower end of the market and thus make entry into it more difficult. Theories on discouraged worker hysteresis effects also associated with Layard.
Padoa-Schioppa (1991)	Labour immobility more detrimental to labour market flexibility than employment mismatch.
Dreze and Malinvaud (1994)	High social charges and burdensome and inflexible welfare state structures.

Sources: Adapted from CEC 1994e; Symes 1995

(Begg *et al.* 1994). Thus, a short-run fall in aggregate demand can lead to a permanently higher level of unemployment due to a series of hysteresis effects that have occurred within the labour market in the meanwhile. Franz (1995: 66) refers to this situation as one where 'unemployment breeds unemployment'.

Budd *et al.* (1986) express a useful view on hysteresis caused by long-term unemployment. The longer a worker is unemployed, the greater the erosion of skills and the adverse psychological effects associated with being in this state. This affects the ability of the labour market to clear given the existence of an excess supply of labour from the long-term unemployeds' failure to exert enough downward pressure on going wage rates to price themselves back into work. The EU's inordinately high long-term unemployed rate makes this of particular relevance.

Similar hysteresis effects arise in the insider–outsider scenario, first developed by Blanchard and Summers (1986). This can be applied to the case of long-term and youth unemployment, whereby market distortions can ensue when job security becomes a primary objective for insiders (actual employees) at the expense of their own remuneration and to outsiders (potential employees). Furthermore, the insiders' positions are continually strengthened against the outsiders as they accumulate firm-specific skills which make them increasingly indispensable to their employers, and insider knowledge of the firm and the advantages extruded from it. Some labour economists also believe that reforms aimed at introducing more flexibility into labour market conditions only intensify competition between outsiders, hence aggravating existing insider–outsider divisions (Grahl and Teague 1995).

There are both supply-side and demand-side policy implications carried by hysteresis. More active labour market policies are required to improve the human capital potential of outsiders, especially those who are long-term unemployed, in order to address the market failures responsible for shifting the labour market equilibrium to higher natural rates of unemployment. These may also constitute policy measures that are in some way responsive to structural changes, for example, initiatives to improve skills matching. While expansionary demand management policies are almost universally accepted as providing limited assistance to labour market hysteresis, a stabilisation of aggregate demand levels will be required to counteract its further progress.

There also appears to be agreement between many of the scholars listed in Table 10.6 over the contribution that high payroll taxes and generous European worker compensation and social security systems have made in stimulating unemployment. Any attempt to scale down unemployment benefits with the aim of inducing higher employment search and incentives must be accompanied by simultaneous parallel measures, in particular the acute and seemingly intractable high rates of unemployment in Europe's inner city and urban areas. This aspect of European unemployment is of great concern to Symes (1995) who comments that: 'It has become evident that at a local level a more co-ordinated policy concerned with both economic and social policy is needed to combat the longer-term hysteresis effects of generations of unemployed being created and locked into social exclusion.' She advises the promotion of 'social renewal' programmes similar to those recently pioneered in Rotterdam as a means to give virtuous circles of socio-economic rejuvenation their initial momentum. These would help tackle the occupational and geographical immobilities of labour that lie at the root cause of the inner city unemployment and the growth of Europe's underclass.

The technological and international dimension

Technological forces have served to both create and destroy jobs. The introduction of labour displacing, process technologies will obviously have a negative effect, although this depends on: the elasticity of substitution between factors; whether any ensuing unit cost reductions translate into a lower demand for labour; the market conditions confronted by the firm and other considerations. Firms installing these technologies as part of adopting a highly competitive and expansionary corporate strategy are more likely to create growth-induced employment. The application of new process and product innovations that lie at the technological frontier of their industry can be expected to divert demand away from foreign rivals and produce higher value-added gains for the economy as a whole. This positive impact will be further supported by accompanying physical and intangible investments and the gradual diffusion of new technologies to other firms and related sectors.

The conversion of these gains into actual employment will rely on the existence of conducive macroeconomic conditions and institutional factors. It has also become increasingly apparent that a new approach to education and training is required if an economy is to adapt to current patterns of technological change. This entails not only a fuller recognition of the higher priority they deserve but also the heightening strategic importance of both knowledge and lifelong learning. The latter has become more apparent as the demand for skills are continuously changing; technological competition obligates firms to maintain a brisk pace of innovation and hence invest in the necessary human capital in order to facilitate this. Shifts to more knowledge intensive forms of industrial activity amplify the need for business and policy-makers to take education and training more seriously.

This particularly applies in more internationalised sectors. Technological upgrading has become imperative for the 'sensitive' industries (e.g. textiles, steel) of developed countries where the NICs have acquired a competitive advantage. A lower potential level of sectoral employment will arise where smaller market segments exist for higher value-added activities. The highest rates of unemployment have followed among those sectors which have not adapted to new global realities, or where efforts to restructure in light of them have been taken to extremes. Moreover, wages may fall behind productivity increases owing to at least some pressure to compete on lower unit costs. Price and income elasticities of demand for internationally traded products will also bring an influence to bear on what response a firm adopts and its subsequent outcomes. As was discussed at length in Chapter 9, the most important challenge for Europe is to improve its performance in high-tech industries relative to its Triad rivals. This is because their future potential for economic and employment growth is substantial and more assured when compared to those characterised by more traditional technologies. Hence, seeking a stronger position in these industries must be considered an integral part of any employment policy to emerge in Europe.

Employment growth: a new priority?

Since the late 1980s, unemployment has become an increasingly prioritised item on the European political agenda. Recent Commission documents have identified it as the main economic problem facing the EU leading up to the twenty-first century (CEC 1993a, 1994p). The Community's comparatively poor performance on employment growth has been perceived as both a failure of the wider European economy's performance in recent years and a serious impediment to future growth prospects.

The relative inflexibility of the EU's labour markets has been noted as lying at the core of its unemployment problem (CEC 1994e). Consequently, this has yielded slow responses to shocks and policy changes which in turn have undermined the EU's capacity for employment growth and adaptability to technological innovation and increased international competition. In response, the Commission has assembled a number of employment growth strategies that form the basis of a more systematic and coherent EU employment policy. This has its foundation in the EU's White Paper on *Growth, Competitiveness and Employment* (CEC 1993a) that constituted a medium-term development strategy within which it was intended that member states and Community institutions could focus and co-ordinate their efforts in stimulating employment growth.

Reaction to the White Paper in the member states was mixed. Neo-liberal economists and politicians viewed it with some degree of scepticism, fearing the initiative as an excuse for large scale Euro-interventionism. Others were not totally convinced over the value of its objectives. For example, only the year before the UK Chancellor Norman Lamont had stated that 'unemployment was still a price well worth paying' if it led to lower levels of inflation. However, the general consensus across the EU acknowledges that persistent high rates of unemployment undermine any future sustainable growth patterns which the European economy can hope to follow. The White Paper presented a mix of new ideas and established conventional wisdom on which a strategy could be formulated to create new jobs.

As a result, it has been generally accepted as a tenable basis on which such a strategy can be pursued. The European Council initiated a process for implementing its employment action plan by urging member states to transpose elements into a multi-annual programme. This, though, was to be conducted in a manner sensitive to the national characteristics of the employment system and socio-economic conditions. For their part, the EU's institutions were to perform the function of making ongoing comparative analyses of member states' labour markets, disseminate information (e.g. regarding best practices across the EU) and organise joint research and co-operation in the field of employment.

Measures consisted of labour market deregulation and 're-regulation' initiatives, infrastructure projects and macroeconomic policy prescriptions with the main aim of reducing EU unemployment to 5 per cent by creating 15 million new jobs by the end of the century. This implies an annual 2 per cent employment growth rate between 1995 and 2000, which given recent EU performance in this area (see Table 10.5) seems rather ambitious. The White Paper contends that the success of achieving such targets relies on five factors:

1 Balanced and co-ordinated macroeconomic policies management between the EU member states is required to restore the confidence and stability in the wider EU economy, as incarnated in EMU's convergence criteria on public finances, exchange rates, etc.
2 Maintaining an open economy, in particular to the EU's southern and eastern peripheral regions, that enables external competitive pressures to generate a stronger competitive environment. Recourse to protectionism not a viable option.
3 Greater decentralisation through new information-sharing and communication systems. Information superhighways are advocated to help perform this function.
4 Further consolidation of the single market and enhancement of its integrative dynamics are key in determining the extent to which more efficient microeconomic decision-making and flexible market relationships can be established.
5 A series of 'flanking actions' aimed at embracing the Single European Act's (SEA) principles of economic and social cohesion. This included new forms of work organisation, the wider enfranchisement of 'outsiders' in the labour market process and more active policy initiatives.

Any notions of the White Paper representing an expansionary demand–management solution to unemployment were tempered by its key targeting on infrastructure, human capital and R&D investments; these are associated more with employment creation than most public expenditures. Hence, improving competitiveness and tackling unemployment are presented as mutually reinforcing objectives – an attempt to appease policy-makers from all political persuasions. The required funding from both the public and private sectors for the proposed infrastructure projects totalled at just under ECU 400bn over the set period of 1994 to 1999. This would help construct the transport and energy networks, environmental projects and communication systems that would provide greater employment opportunities in the short and longer term.

The option of competing with the NICs on unit labour costs is not seen as viable. Hence, improvements made to European productivity and increased investment in the new technology clusters, with particular support directed to SMEs in these sectors, are promoted in the White Paper as alternatives. In terms of macroeconomic policy, lower interest rates are prescribed both to improve competitiveness and restore confidence. Lower budget deficits and a shift of the tax burden from firms on to environmentally hazardous activities are suggested to achieve this.

The tone adopted by the White Paper can in some ways be interpreted as a departure from the 1989 Social Action Programme which had spawned the Social Chapter. Some of the measures suggested, such as more flexibility of minimum wages for the young, reduction of non-wage labour costs and removal of restrictions on hiring and firing of workers are evidence of this. Conversely, the White Paper and other policy documents that followed have still maintained their commitment to Europe's 'social market' ideals and safeguarding 'fundamental workers' rights'. The regulatory structures of many EU member states are, though, being more closely examined and 'weeding' processes being set in motion to eradicate outmoded and overcomplicated measures.

To flesh out some of the ideas first aired in the 1993 White Paper, the Commission published a follow-up report on *Flexibility and Work Organisation* (CEC 1995a). Flexibility is defined in the report as 'the ability of systems, organisations and individuals to adapt successfully to changed conditions by adopting new structures or patterns of behaviour' (ibid.: 2). In broad terms, it recognised the need to develop a two-pronged approach: a 'defensive flexibility' based on reactive adjustments to new labour market conditions and 'proactive strategies', such as new product developments and technological foresight programmes, that aimed to achieve employment induced economic growth. Making reference to the work of Sengenberger (1994) and Bosch (1994), the report subscribed to the view that 'labour market regulations are responses to massive and pervasive social damage from market failure or uncontrolled economic behaviour'. Sengenberger (1994) noted the three functions of labour market regulation as:

- Participation: the involvement of appropriate social actors in the social dialogue process.
- Protection: of workers from abuses associated with labour market risks (e.g. redundancy, work-related accidents).
- Promotion: of labour productivity, workforce flexibility, etc.

In order to move towards creating more flexible forms of work organisation and employment growth the report submitted that future policy-making in Europe should place more emphasis on the promotion and participation functions relative to that of protection. This echoed calls from other quarters, such as recent reports from the OECD (1993, 1994c), for states to adopt more 'active' (e.g. training) than 'passive' (e.g. unemployment benefits) labour market policies. In addition, more decentralised decision-making that accounted for varying conditions across firms and regions was also prescribed, as well as experimentation with new forms of work hours. The virtues of part-time work were particularly extolled based on the recognised advantages of higher rates of productivity from lower absenteeism and greater work intensity, greater flexibility in coping with demand fluctuations and lower wage and non-wage costs. However, certain disadvantages were also acknowledged, these being higher organisation costs and lower organisational control, poor communications and high rates of employee turnover, while the employee may suffer from worse terms of work, limited career opportunities and higher potential for marginalisation both in the labour market and social security systems. The recommendations made by the report attempted to minimise such risks and emphasised the benefits carried by promoting these new forms of work organisation in Europe which are summarised below:

- Flexible firms: introducing more organisational innovation within firms (e.g. flatter, more responsive organisational structures, cross-divisional teamworking, neural networks). The transfer and diffusion of best practice knowledge where appropriate, the promotion of co-operation between national activities and strengthening European organisational R&D.
- New wage systems: the dissemination of best practice to the appropriate level of firm in accordance with the nature of production and size. Broader job descriptions, fewer pay grades, incentives to acquire higher qualification levels, higher valuation of new job requirements, result rewarded pay.
- Telework: similar to above. A major study to be undertaken and the establishment of codes of practice.
- Working time: time off in lieu as a reward for extra time worked instead of remuneration. Overtime options maintained to help flexibility. Maintenance of the most favourable aspects of the European model on working time.
- Part-time work: identified as a valuable form of flexible work organisation, but part-time workers must be given equal treatment to full-time counterparts. Incentives to the unemployed to accept part-time work reinforced by state-backed training schemes and allowances. Improvements to child care leave and facilities as well as other measures to support part-time work.
- Retraining, short-time and redundancy: During periods of cyclical downturns training programmes should be organised to make up short-time hours worked. Remunerations payable to redundant workers should

partly finance retraining schemes aimed at rehabilitating them back into the labour market. The promotion of transferable skills and 'multi-skilling' to enhance occupational mobility.

In a comparative work organisation analysis, the report also discusses the notion of a European working-time model. The emerging basis for the model rests on the increasing decouplement of working time and operating hours. The more common use of three shift crews in Europe instead of two plus extensive overtime, as more prevalently found in the USA and Japan, has the advantage of generating more employment but the disadvantage of creating higher levels of redundancy in cyclical downturns. To compensate for the latter the report proposes that European companies need mechanisms for reducing capacity in line with these downturns to maintain employment relationships while simultaneously lowering unit costs. These could take the form of state allowances that enable firms to retain their workers at lower levels of operating hours. This has already been practised in Germany where in 1993 up to 700,000 workers drew on short-term state benefits estimated to have avoided 200,000 redundancies. Another proposed option consisted of that experimented by Volkswagen in the same year when in negotiation with the unions working hours were cut to 28 per week for assembly plant workers as an alternative to 30,000 redundancies (estimated to have cost DM741m per annum in unemployment benefits). The VW work-sharing agreement has been a template used by a number of other European companies and agencies since. For example, the Dutch government has introduced a similar contract for certain public sector workers based on a 32-hour week while in Belgium some employees aged 55+ can opt into a half-time work scheme, receiving a mix of pay and pensions.

Nonetheless, alterations to working-time practices carry a number of potential difficulties. There may be pressure in the wage bargaining process to raise real wage levels well above productivity rates to maintain standards of living. If this does occur, the scope for employment growth will be significantly diminished. Shorter working weeks not compensated by productivity gains may increase unit labour costs. Moreover, employment growth will only be sustained in the longer term if utilisation rates of given capacity are not adversely affected, including that capacity hitherto unused by the once unemployed. Rising capital costs and a subsequential depression in investment demand are likely if this is not achieved.

The Commission has repeatedly stressed the importance of avoiding the excesses that are evident in the US labour market model (CEC 1994e, 1995d) despite the superior record of the US economy on employment growth in recent years. This is largely owing to the growing divergence in income inequality that has accompanied US achievements in reducing unemployment; a consequence of a more pronounced *laissez-faire* policy stance. Between 1969 and 1989 the real earnings of US males in the lowest income quintile fell by 37 per cent while those for the upper quintile rose by 11 per cent. An excess supply of unskilled and low-skilled workers in the USA has been the cause of depressed wage levels, but excess demand for highly skilled workers has produced an opposite effect in top income groups. In 1993, 18 per cent of US full-time employees earned less than the official poverty line compared to only 12 per cent in 1979 (*Financial Times*, 14 March 1994).

Although the US model has produced somewhat unpalatable side effects, there has been mounting pressure within Europe to emulate certain of its elements. The relatively less generous benefit system has produced a considerably lower long-term unemployment rate. This is also supported by wage and employment flexibility found in the US labour market that enable both the relative and real wage levels of the less skilled to adjust downwards when required, thus better avoiding hysteresis effects. This has been fortified by a real decline in the minimum wage, low unionisation rates and the large inward migration of less qualified labour.

The apparent differences between European and American policy approach towards labour markets are primarily anchored in their respective 'social market' and 'free market' traditions (see Box 10.1). The complete transposition of the US model, with its more sparsely reticulated safety net of welfare protection, would be culturally and politically unacceptable, even in the most admiring of EU member states such as the UK. Nevertheless, it is likely that future efforts to proximate more closely European labour market and social legislation to the US model will occur *en route* to securing greater flexibility. To both counterbalance and embrace such a direction of policy, more concerted efforts will be required to enhance active labour market policies. The current position of the OECD countries with regard to their resources devoted to active and passive policies is shown in Figure 10.3 and indicates that for most it is the latter rather than the former that enjoys the majority allocated, although the general trend is shifting. European countries clearly devote larger resources to labour market policies than both the USA and Japan, a manifestation of their different policy traditions.

Box 10.1 Key institutions shaping labour market outcomes in the Triad economies

EUROPEAN UNION

1 A relatively generous benefit system in which unemployment benefit is paid at the equivalent to 60–70 per cent of average wages for the low skilled. The duration of benefits varies between twelve and thirty months and extensive income support is granted unrelated to income.

Box 10.1 *continued*

2 Minimum wage levels either set by the state (as in France and Spain) or within industry (as in Germany and Italy) that typically are set between 50–70 per cent of average male median earnings.
3 Declining, but relatively strong union density with some countries close to early 1970s levels (as in Belgium, Denmark, Germany and Italy).
4 Comparatively extensive labour market regulations covering equal opportunities, recruitment and dismissal, redundancy and working hours. Relatively high social charge levels also persist in the EU.
5 Higher education levels that are low in comparison to the USA and Japan, but in some countries the proportion of the workforce with intermediate qualifications (especially Germany) is very high.

USA

1 A relatively severe benefit system with the shortest period of unemployment insurance at twenty-six weeks. This is coupled with limitations on unemployment assistance granted to families.
2 Federal level minimum wage, although higher state specific rates may apply, which is low relative to European standards and affects mainly young workers.
3 Low union density at around 16 per cent and minimal collective bargaining.
4 A highly unregulated labour market which confines regulation primarily to equal opportunity issues. This has given the USA the lowest median tenure rate in the OECD at three years and hence the highest labour turnover rate in the Triad.
5 A higher education system which is largely self-financed. Although the education level of new entrants is high, the rate of increase of degree holding has slowed since the mid-1970s at around 25 per cent for the 25–54 years group.
6 A relatively large influx of immigrant workers from Central America (mainly less qualified) and Asia (mainly qualified).

JAPAN

1 A culture of lifetime employment among Japan's largest firms in particular, although this is being undermined by growing pressures for greater labour market flexibility.
2 Redeployment within *keiretsu* company groupings which may involve a temporary move (*shukko*) or a permanent one (*tenseki*).
3 Enterprise unionism and a highly co-ordinated pay setting system which both engender a more harmonious environment for industrial relations.
4 A very limited duration of unemployment benefit entitlement (at thirty weeks) and no national unemployment assistance system in support.

Box 10.1 *continued*

5 The grading of manufacturing employees according to the level of skill acquired rather than job specifications giving greater flexibility among blue-collar workers by breaking down job demarcations.

6 A notable bonus payment element to wages which consequently leads to less cyclical unemployment, but more impoverished workers during recessions.

7 A highly educated and trained workforce. Japan has been particularly successful in raising the levels of educational attainment of its lower quartile.

Sources: UN 1994c and other miscellaneous

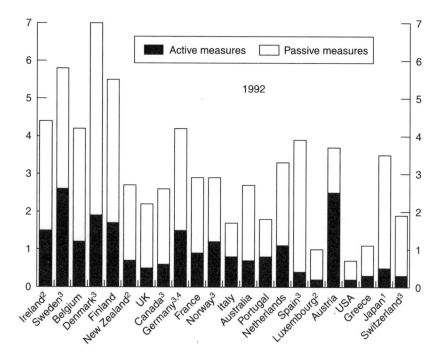

Figure 10.3 Expenditure on labour market measures, OECD countries (percentage of GDP, 1992)
Notes:
Countries are ranked in descending order of their 1985 expenditure on active measures.
Figures in brackets on top of each bar refer to the standardised unemployment rate (national definitions for Austria, Denmark, Greece, Luxembourg and Switzerland).
1 1990
2 1991
3 1993
4 Data for the whole of Germany. Secretariat estimate for the standardised unemployment rate.
Source: OECD Jobs Study 1994

While lessons already drawn from the Japanese labour market model have been salient, adopting certain elements would prove an arduous and complex task due mainly to their entrenchment in socio-cultural and structural relationships particular to Japan. The redeployment of workers within *keiretsu* company groupings is a good example of this. However, European firms have been able to learn from the pioneering efforts of their Japanese counterparts made in innovative forms of work and management organisation in post-war years, such as lean production/Toyotaism techniques, teamworking, total quality management (TQM), enterprise unionism and quality circles. Lam (1994) believes that this has led to a hybrid form of Japanese-style management emerging in Europe which has been forged by adaptation to local conditions. Depending on the evolutionary path of networking between firms through strategic alliances and other means may enable European firms to experiment with *keiretsu*-style redeployment. It remains to be seen, though, how far Europeans would be willing to accept the subordination of private life to corporate goals that is closely associated with the 'Japanisation' of employment practice.

What is clear is the need for more flexible labour markets to be incorporated within the European economy that entails an improvement in both the employee's and employer's ability to participate in the job creation process. A greater emphasis placed on education and training and lifelong learning would make a key contribution to this by providing a more employable workforce which is simultaneously capable of adjusting to the shift to more knowledge intensive economic activities. We shall now turn to this facet of Europe's human dimension.

EDUCATION AND TRAINING: PRACTICE AND POLICY

The key issues and challenges

In recent years, various countries across the world have introduced a series of far-reaching reforms to their education and training (E&T) systems. The prime motivation has been the belief that the development of an economy's human capital is one of the most, if not the most, effective routes to improve national economic performance. As Reich (1991: 301) has commented, 'it is not what we own that counts: it is what we do'. In addition, rapid technological advance and the emergence of the information society have instigated a number of fundamental changes to how work is organised. According to Toffler (1990), the role of knowledge has increasingly moved towards the social centre of gravity, while the strategic importance of 'knowledge workers' who are able to absorb and apply information in response to heterogeneous demands in society will become progressively more critical. Hence, a workforce that is able to handle more 'knowledge-intensive' forms of economic activity is required to enhance future competitiveness. It must also be remembered that education and training have an important role to play in the process of socialisation, integration and reintegration in a society that is becoming increasingly information technology driven.

The forces of globalisation and global competition further amplify the imperative to upgrade a country's E&T systems. An economy's ability to attract higher value-added foreign investment, or indeed retain domestic investment, will to a large extent depend on the quality and skills of its workforce. The advent of wage levels being increasingly set by global market rates implies that richer countries require more productive and adroit workers in order for them to remain competitive in existing markets and from which to enter and sustain positions in high value-added sectors. Implications for any new paradigms of European E&T practice and policy are also carried by the pressures of population ageing and the priority of employment growth.

Evidence provided by Thomas (1995) suggests that recent employment growth has been greatest among those occupational groups which are more E&T intensive. Today's dynamic industry sectors are typified by their knowledge intensive character, and thus call for higher quotients of human capital investment to maintain momentum. Moreover, with the half life of the 'frontier' knowledge that drives these industries diminishing at an ever faster rate, workers need to be integrated into multiple and continuous learning processes that empower them to respond effectively to consequential technological and economic changes. Establishment of these processes has often been reliant on the forming of partnerships involving higher education institutions (HEIs), industry, government agencies, trade unions and relevant parties due to the breadth and complexity of the task encountered. Thus, greater participation, control and responsibility have been conferred upon non-governmental agencies.

Attempts to install more flexible systems of education and training have also created disparate ranges of modular pathways in which different levels of educational and skill attainment can be accredited. Combined with the increasingly important role played by non-government agencies, this has generated problems regarding the mutual recognition and transferability of E&T certification. Hence, governments have aimed to preserve coherent and unified E&T systems while simultaneously aspiring to build in greater flexibility and openness. Policy-makers and business must also take account of the continued blurring of demarcations between the technical disciplines that necessitate workers to acquire more broad generic techno-industrial skills and less career specific programmes of learning. This will particularly apply to professional workers of the future who will need to become adept in three or four of these disciplines, while programmes for continuous training structure will give specialisation when required (CEC 1994q).

Conducting a comparative analysis on the E&T systems of different countries is notoriously difficult. Figures on participation rates, dedicated expenditures and those derived from other indicators can belie a system's effectiveness at producing citizens who are well equipped at meeting current and foreseeable economic and social challenges. This is because the wider determinants that are bound within a country's educational structures, organisations and cultures are of great significance. Hence, a higher per capita proportion of GDP spent on education does not imply an automatic advantage gained over competitor countries. What perhaps is more critical is investigating precisely how and where such expenditures are made.

However, statistical analyses can provide at least some insight into comparative conclusions to be drawn between different countries. The highly idiosyncratic features of Europe's national education systems are partly revealed in our data presented. European countries are among the highest spenders at all levels of education. This is particularly pronounced at the nursery and tertiary level (see Figures 10.4 and 10.5). A strong tradition for vocational education exists in the Germanic countries but until recently has remained a low priority in countries such as the UK.

Many European countries have recently made efforts to boost participation rates at the tertiary level. The rationale behind this policy rests on the notion that the economy's capability to handle more knowledge intensive forms of activity generally requires a larger proportion of the workforce which is university or college trained. For some time now, both the USA and Japan have maintained an impressive record on this account, and past and current economic successes have been at least partially attributed to it. Although investments made at the tertiary level will remain critical, studies have shown that the highest private and social returns are found at the

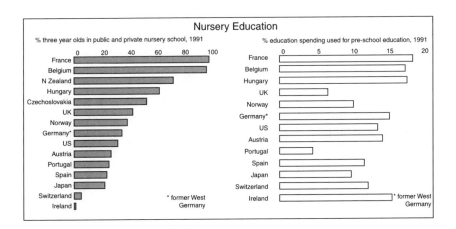

Figure 10.4 Nursery education, 1991
Source: The Independent, 9 December 1993

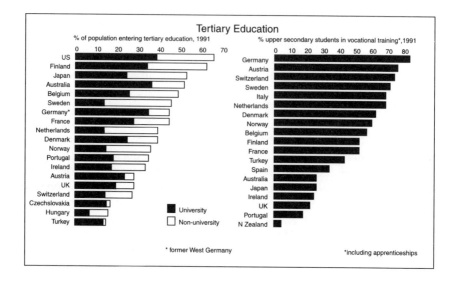

Figure 10.5 Tertiary education, 1991
Source: The Independent, 9 December 1993

primary level (Psacharopoulos 1993). Consequently, nursery education has also received especial attention by policy-makers in many parts of the world. This has been realised in many East Asian countries in particular, such as South Korea which during the 1980s devoted around eightfold more funds to education at basic level relative to that at higher level (World Bank 1993).

The development of the EU's education and training policies

The origins of the Community's E&T policy are rooted in three Treaty articles: Article 118 (co-operation between member states in matters of vocational training); the Maastricht introduced Article 126 (development of quality education by co-operative and supplementary actions); a Maastricht revised Article 127 (implementing the Community's vocational training policy).

However, it was not until the adoption of a Commission decision in 1963 that the operating principles of a common policy were established and appropriate committees formed. These principles remained until 1990 when they were revised by the Social Charter. An EC ministerial meeting on education and training met for the first time in 1971 and four years later the Centre for the Development of Vocational Training (CEDEFOP) was inaugurated. In 1976 came the initiation of the first action programme which aimed to establish closer relations between ministries, compile E&T data across the Community (conducted by EURYDICE), encourage greater HEI co-operation, promote a European dimension to education – initially through language teaching – and more comprehensive equal opportunity measures.

By the 1980s, Europe's education and training systems were brought into sharper focus by moves to continue European integration. The SEM programme's investigative surveys had identified various skills shortages in a number of key areas. A range of new policy initiatives was launched, including EUROTECNET (vocational training in new technologies) in 1983, ERASMUS (promoting student mobility), COMETT (university and industry collaborative training programmes) and PETRA (youth training) in 1987, IRIS (training for women) in 1988, LINGUA (foreign languages) in 1989 and FORCE (access to training programmes for all Community workers) in 1990. Furthermore, in 1988 competence for the Community's E&T policy was removed from DG5, the Commission Directorate for employment and social affairs, and granted independence under a new Task Force for Human Relations, Education, Training and Youth.

Additional change was brought about by a 1989 Commission study on EC labour markets (CEC 1989b) and a meeting of the Education Council in October of the same year which broadened the dimensions of the Community's E&T policy into five main areas. These were intended both to be commensurate with preparations for the SEM programme and to promote a 'social Europe':

1 A Multicultural Europe: the celebration and exploitation of Europe's unique cultural diversity. Both strengths and weaknesses are recognised. Strengths are drawn from the potential sources of creativity and wide global appeal this diversity offers. Weaknesses arise from managing and accommodating a heterogeneous range of cultures and their values.

2 A Mobile Europe: E&T must play its part in promoting 'economic and social cohesion' required for the SEM to function effectively. Linguistic barriers to labour mobility are particularly significant and thus targeted, especially among more peripheral, non-internationalised member states. The need for mutual recognition of qualifications and a common curriculum for professional workers. (A target is set of at least 10 per cent of Community students to study in a foreign EC member state.)

3 A Europe of Training for All: open access for all Community workers to training through COMETT, ERASMUS, IRIS, and HORIZON (disabled people) programmes, European Social Fund (ESF) resources and other more minor initiatives.

4 A Europe of Skills: improved HEI–industry and school–industry links, promotion of retraining opportunities, development of new types of qualifications as the traditional boundaries between jobs become

increasingly blurred and encouraging more open learning systems (the DELTA open and distance learning programme was established for this purpose).

5 A Europe Open to the World: exchanges organised with non-European countries, especially North American and ex-colonial states.

Despite the significant adjustments made to the Community's E&T policy its main objectives had not wavered. These were to encourage co-operation and compatibility rather than the harmonisation of member states' E&T systems, but nevertheless encased within a strong European dimension. However, Beukel (1993) comments that the increased institutionalisation of European level education that these changes embodied may in the future stimulate a bottom-up demand for supra-national level organised education services. However, it is suggested that this will complement and not replace institutionalisation at national level which will no doubt continue to predominate. Beukel goes on to suggest that the 'Europeification', as he terms it, of education policy from the mid-1980s onwards must be understood in the context of endeavours to reinvigorate Europe in response to intensified international competition and the continued ascendancy of the knowledge-based society. The increase of globalisation implies that national education systems must be more open to transnational forces. The growth of the information society and the technology that drives it straddle national borders while some foreign investing firms bring traits of their own national cultures into the workplace. This has been most notably observed by the recent impact which Japanese multinationals in Europe have had upon systems of training.

Rainbird (1993) notes that many of the Community's E&T programmes initiated in the 1980s came under mounting criticism for being too elitist owing to their bias towards higher education. The mutual recognition of qualifications between member states which should assist the operation of labour mobility within the SEM has also progressed slowly. The same applied to occupation classifications, although by 1991 CEDEFOP had attempted to rectify this by collecting information on skilled occupations and constructing comparative tables to establish common reference points across the Community. The European Credit and Transfer System was also launched by the Commission which aimed to provide the basis for easier credit transfers between educational establishments in different member states. More recently, the Commission has taken extended action on improving mutual academic and occupational recognition across the EU largely based on creating networks between academic institutions and occupation-related organisations and establishing systems of quality assessment.

After a far-reaching review that was completed in 1995, the EU's education and training programmes were further rationalised. Two new Community action programmes, SOCRATES and LEONARDO, were introduced to place current programmes into a more coherent and simplified framework. The main aim of SOCRATES is to 'encourage innovation and improve the quality of education through strengthening co-operation between the various educational institutions' (CEC 1994r: 232). SOCRATES has been given a budget of ECU 850m over the period from 1995 to 1999, 50 per cent higher than the previous 1990 to 1994 combined budget dedicated to the programmes which it replaced. It is envisaged that SOCRATES will operate at three levels:

- universities, where student mobility and the acquisition of wider European experience will be promoted;
- schools, where the COMENIUS programme seeks to establish multilateral joint initiatives on language learning, student, teacher and teaching material exchanges, the promotion of IT and facilitating the updating of teachers' knowledge base;
- horizontal measures, such as open and distance learning.

SOCRATES is also supported by the Youth for Europe III(3) programme with a 1995–9 budget of ECU 126m to resource youth exchanges and mobility, activities for youth leaders and educators, youth exchanges with third countries and other similar initiatives.

While SOCRATES encompasses the EU's education and academic exchange initiatives, the main aim of the LEONARDO action programme, with a minimum ECU 620m budget over the 1995–9 period, is to 'ensure the implementation of a vocational training policy which will support and supplement the action of the Member States as a means towards realising an open European area for vocational training and qualifications' (CEC 1994r: 232). The concept of lifelong training also receives significant attention within the action programme; indeed 1996 was ascribed the EU's Year of Lifelong Learning. The rationalisation of training programmes that LEONARDO embodies was partly a response to the 1993 White Paper, although initial developments had already begun in early 1992 under Commissioner Ruberti.

Three types of measures are provided by LEONARDO: design, development and testing of transnational pilot projects; placement and exchange programmes; the accumulation of knowledge on vocational training. All actions within the programme have a European dimension that can be characterised by their:

- transnational nature, involving participants from at least three member states and in some cases four;
- partnership based functions, with a range of actors engaged including businesses, public authorities, training organisations and social partners (i.e. employers organisations and trade unions);
- transversal nature, attempting to concentrate on transferable competencies and innovations across similar generic fields;

- experimentation with new training innovations and subsequent broad dissemination;
- provision of opportunities for cross-border co-operation on training.

In addition, the ADAPT and Employment programmes were introduced to help expand the scope for trans-European co-operation.

Extra flanking actions have been provided by the human capital and mobility (HCM) programme. The HCM forms part of the EU's research and development policy and was first introduced in the Third Framework Programme but evolving out of precursor programmes (e.g. SCIENCE) in the Second Framework Programme. Its activities are divided into providing training fellowships, science and technology co-operation networks, large scale scientific and technical facilities, Euro-conferences and other accompanying measures.

Another notable initiative concerns the establishment of a high-level reflection group on education and training that was first announced in June 1995 by Commissioner Edith Cresson, who at the same time acknowledged that, 'The development of the new technologies and the globalisation of the economy are imposing a model of society in which knowledge is becoming the most precious human resource. The work of this group will be particularly important in promoting within the EU this "intangible" investment – i.e. education and training – on the same level as research and innovation'(*Rapid*, 23 June 1995).

SOCIAL POLICY

Developments in European social policy

The EU's social policy remains one of its most prominent yet controversial fields. Its conduct has had considerable ramifications for European labour markets and the management of Europe's human resources. These have become increasingly significant as the Commission's competence and policy harmonisation between member states have been gradually extended. Since the mid-1980s, EU social policy has been focused by the SEA's overarching aim of distilling 'economic and social cohesion' within the Community. This was perceived as a further commitment to building a 'Social Europe' to counterbalance the 'Business Europe' actions that have accompanied the SEM programme and plans for EMU.

The 'Social Europe' ideal, though, has been in currency for some time via policy initiatives funded through the European Social Fund (ESF), the European Regional Development Fund (ERDF) and others. Articles 117 to 128 in the Treaty of Rome were devoted to social policy issues which stated an expressed need for close co-operation between all member states over such matters as employment, labour legislation, social security, training and health and safety. More recently, social policy measures have been moderated to serve more effectively the interests of improving EU competitiveness. Thus, a reinforcing rather than a countering role has been assigned to it.

Teague (1989) made the distinction between two types of position that have traditionally been taken on social policy. The 'maximalists' – usually championed by DG5 and France – have attempted to push through EU-wide legislation in the belief that the common market requires a social dimension in order to function in both an effective and equitable manner. The 'minimalists' – which have typically been led by employers organisations (e.g. UNICE) and the UK – have emphasised the cost–push factors and inflexibilities that social legislation places on business. According to Teague (1989: 108), the Commission had, after thirty years of European integration, taken the view that 'to compromise too much with a minimalist point of view weakens integrative dynamics'. However, the process that had spawned the 1994 White Paper on EU social policy and its eventual outcomes displayed that the Commission had drawn on both positions, and had, to some extent, endeavoured to reconcile them. This was also in keeping with the position outlined in the *Growth, Competitiveness and Employment* White Paper the year earlier.

Much debate over social policy has focused on the Social Charter – the centrepiece of the 1989 Social Action Programme (SAP). This has represented one of the most important, and certainly the most polemical, EU policy initiatives devised to safeguard the social dimension of the SEM programme and beyond. Its full attributable name was the EC Charter of the Fundamental Social Rights of Workers and formally consisted of twelve of these rights that were systematically applicable to all workers and social groups where identified (CEC 1989b):

1 Right of freedom of movement.
2 Employment and remuneration.
3 Improvement of living and working conditions.
4 Right to social protection.
5 Right to freedom of association and collective bargaining.
6 Right to vocational training.
7 Right of men and women to equal treatment.
8 Right to information, consultation and participation of workers.
9 Right to health protection and safety at the workplace.
10 Protection of children and adolescents.
11 Rights for the elderly.
12 Rights for the disabled.

The forty-seven proposals of the 1989 SAP were intended to implement the principles and practice of the Social Charter, which Gold (1993) categorises into four different types:

- updating existing measures (e.g. the 1975 redundancy directive);
- incorporating those already in progress;
- recasting 'deadlocked' measures (e.g. the European Work Councils, EWCs);
- creating new measures in new areas (e.g. posted workers, maternity leave, etc.).

The Social Charter was incorporated into the legislature of the Maastricht Treaty under its revised title of the 'Social Chapter'. This was done only on a 'protocol' basis after the UK government negotiated an opt out from its proposals.

The controversy that the Social Chapter has attracted revolves largely around its perceived impact on European competitiveness. Addison and Siebert (1993: 23) have referred to it as 'a Canute-type attempt to take the labour market out of competition' and an 'ambitious and continuing exercise in social engineering' (ibid.: 13). Conversely, its supporters state that the fundamental rights it upholds merely reflect best practice among the most forward thinking firms on human resource management.

With regards to other issues, Adnett (1993) argues that Community-wide shocks induced by progressive stages of economic integration will not produce the desired common intra-EU adjustments if member state labour markets have idiosyncratic adjustment processes. We have already discussed certain aspects of this argument in Chapter 3 on optimum currency areas. Thus, the adoption of a common European social policy is a crucial part of the process of creating a single labour market characterised by common wage adjustment and regulatory procedures. Moreover, the intensification of competition between member states within an emergent single market will bring greater incentives for them to manipulate their own social and labour policies to acquire a 'beggar thy neighbour' competitive advantage over each other. In light of this, Van Rompuy *et al.* (1991) assert that EU-level regulations are preferable on 'second best' grounds to prevent such behaviour and any labour market distortions they may generate within the SEM. However, it is also argued that social policy harmonisation undermines the ability of poorer member states to adjust to country-specific shocks, and that progressive European integration only serves to exaggerate the risks involved. It is for this reason that the EU's structural and cohesion funds have been significantly boosted as a means to counterbalance any adverse effects potentially borne from this.

Further concern is articulated by Addison and Siebert (1993: 22), who state that 'since mandated benefits work at the level of the firm, rather than at the level of the tax-transfer system, firms will tend to make countervailing moves which frustrate the re-distributive aims of the policy'. One outcome of this could be that unskilled workers will find themselves unemployed when mandated benefits increase since the accepted wage level cannot adjust downwards to accommodate the rise in social charges.

Thus, the inequality of employment opportunities is substituted for inequalities of wage levels and conditions.

Opponents of the Social Chapter have frequently cited the comparatively high social charges or indirect costs that are imposed on European business and their detrimental impact upon competitiveness. These can comprise of payroll taxes, maternity and paternity pay, training levies and other miscellaneous outlays. Figure 10.6 indicates that such costs are generally higher in Europe than in other developed countries. It should come as no surprise that an even greater variance exists when the newly industrialising countries are considered. Nevertheless, a number of points must be noted. Germany's high labour costs are supported by high productivity rates that enable it to produce at relatively competitive unit cost levels. This is applicable for many other European countries which lie at the top of the labour cost table. Much of the Social Chapter's legislation has not been

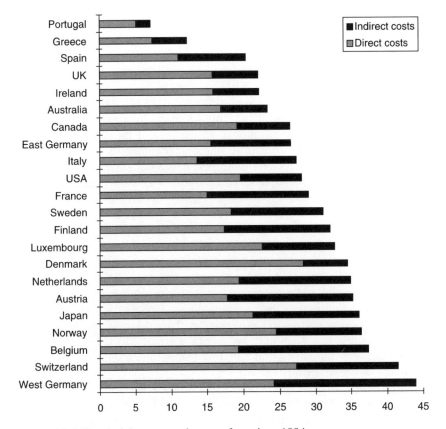

Figure 10.6 Hourly labour costs in manufacturing, 1994
Source: Reproduced with permission from European Industrial Relations Review, August 1995, p. 13, published by IRS/Eclipse Group Ltd, 18–20 Highbury Place, London N5 1QP. Tel: 0171 354 5858

perceived as cost inducing, at least not in the longer term, and has been duly embraced by business. It is interesting to note that a growing number of UK firms (e.g. Coats Viyella, ICI, United Biscuits, Marks and Spencer) have opted into the EWC scheme, and that of the Social Chapter's thirty-seven directives that had been passed by January 1994, the UK was the only member state to have incorporated every one of them.

A change in direction?

In July 1994 the Commission published its plans for EU social policy over the 1995–9 period in a White Paper subtitled *The Way Forward for the Union* (CEC 1994s) and after an 'unprecedently wide-ranging consultative process'. Three main factors provide the background context for the introduction of the document (EIRR, September 1994). First, the 1989 SAP had by now been largely exhausted with almost all of its measures either in place or near completion, hence a fresh sense of direction and retrospective evaluation was required. Second, the Maastricht Treaty had meanwhile significantly altered the legal and institutional framework in which social policy functioned, for instance, by extending qualified majority voting into new fields. Third, unemployment's move towards the top of the political agenda had instigated calls for a revised balance between EU competitiveness and social solidarity that were first voiced in the 1993 White Paper, but not at the expense of social integration or re-integration. Thus, this represented a further attempt to reconcile the European 'social model' in the face of the challenges posed by globalisation and new forms of technological competition.

The White Paper is a longer, more discursive document than the 1989 SAP, consisting of ten chapters which outline its eighty-three different measures. For some this represented a clear departure from the more 'aggressive' elements of 1989 SAP (*Financial Times*, 2 November 1994) and the direction forged ahead by the Social Charter. The four principal objectives of the White Paper for future EU social policy were:

1 Employment as key to social and economic integration: the wealth-creating potential and employment growth were recognised in addition to its ability to preserve the socio-economic fabric of society.
2 Competitiveness and social progress are two sides of the same coin: social progress and economic prosperity are mutually dependable. Key investments in human capital and new technologies seen as a means to support this relationship.
3 Convergence which respects diversity: complete harmonisation of social policies across Europe is not a goal, but meeting common and mutually beneficial objectives will entail some degree of 'progress in harmony towards the fundamental objectives of the Union'.
4 A level playing field of common minimum standards: a stated aim not to overburden the poorer member states with rigorous legislation but also

not to discourage richer member states from implementing higher standards. The avoidance of unfair competitive advantages sought through social policy at the expense of fellow member states (i.e. social dumping).

In the document, the Commission stated that a substantial foundation of social legislation had already been laid down by the Social Chapter and that the need did not exist for a similar approach over the forthcoming period. The measures proposed therefore were intended to consolidate recently implemented legislation while also placing greater emphasis on subsidiarity.

The notably more cautious approach to EU-wide social legislation is also partly a reflection of the changes that have been made within DG5 which have arisen from its new adopted role as a job creation think tank. It was also recognised that social exclusion has become even more pronounced. Rapid and far-reaching social and economic change has marginalised an increasing number of EU citizens so that 52 million of them were living below its poverty line by 1995.

Leading on from its 1994 White Paper, the Commission introduced a medium-term SAP for EU social policy covering the period 1995–7, superseding the previous 1989 SAP. The programme was organised around five key themes: employment; the consolidation and development of legislation; equal opportunities; an active society for all; and a medium-term retrospective analysis on recently implemented policy. The impact of globalisation upon European society and social policy was acknowledged at the outset of the SAP's policy document while also contextualising its general background, particularly with reference to competitiveness and employment growth. In echoing the second stated principal objective of the White Paper it was noted that:

Economic and social dimensions are in fact interdependent and must, therefore, advance hand in hand. There cannot be social progress without competitiveness and economic growth. Conversely, it is not possible to ensure sustainable economic growth without taking the social dimension into account. Social progress and social solidarity must form an integral part of the European approach to competitiveness.

(CEC 1995s: 9)

The SAP's comments on education and training are largely confined to the new LEONARDO and SOCRATES programmes. On 'Building a European Labour Market', the SAP planned to encourage labour mobility by attempting to remove impediments arising from pensions, taxation and social security, rights of residence and in other areas, though no intentions were stated regarding moves towards complete harmonisation of such systems. Providing the function of networking information across the EU on employment opportunities was to be performed by the newly established European Employment Service (EURES), while the Transnational Telematics System (TESS) was given the objective of modernising the exchange mechanisms of information between national social security institutions. This was commensurate with the Commission's own self-appointed role of disseminating useful information across the member states to assist the workings of Europe's labour markets and generally promote employment. At an international and inter-regional level, new frameworks of communication aimed at improving co-operative procedures with the EU's global partners. Five main areas of focus are detailed:

- CEE countries: measures to support PHARE, the Europe Agreements, TEMPUS and the aspects of the SEM programme.
- Third countries and territories of the Mediterranean Basin: linked to the new European–Mediterranean partnership.
- Social issues related to world trade: the social clauses of the EU's GSP scheme, links with the WTO and ILO.
- Bilateral co-operation: co-operation programmes with the USA and Japan on higher education, vocational training and a range of social and employment topics.
- Multilateral co-operation: the Commission to publish a bi-annual report on multilateral co-operation on transnationalised social, employment and industrial relations issues.

It obviously remains to be seen just how determined and effective the change in European social policy will prove to be. Important adjustments have already been made to the social and welfare policies at member state level in light of the pressures identified in this chapter. However, the essential integrity of Europe's 'social market' model can be expected to remain intact. Notwithstanding the undoubted recent success of the American 'free market' model at employment creation, its excesses have generated a variety of social costs that most European governments would view as politically and economically unacceptable. However, seeking a new balance between economic and social objectives that were once held as irreconcilable is likely to lead to a major redefining of 'social market' model and ultimately European social policy.

CONCLUDING REMARKS

This chapter has shown that the effective management of Europe's human resources is central to meeting the anticipated challenges of the twenty-first century. We have seen how mounting demographic pressures, particularly population ageing, will make it increasingly necessary for key decision-makers to affect important structural changes within the economy and establish new conventional forms of economic behaviour. The advocacy of employment growth as a top economic priority within Europe happens to coincide with these objectives. This is because the ability to respond to these pressures will largely depend on the optimum utilisation of its human capital, whether this is already actively engaged or lies dormant. A firm commitment both to improving education and training systems and a recasting of social policy frameworks also has an obvious role to play here. With the heightened globalisation of markets and technology, and the growing knowledge intensivity to be found in the workplace, unlocking the potential of an economy's human resources will thus prove crucial to assuring its future prosperity.

11 The environment

This chapter considers Europe's position with regard to the environment. The main themes of relevance we shall discuss include: its global responsibilities and participation in international co-operative efforts with respect to environmental protection; the EU's environmental policy and the new economic instruments that have been developed to assist it; the relationships between the environment and industry, international trade and foreign investment.

GLOBAL RESPONSIBILITIES AND INTERNATIONAL CO-OPERATION

An introduction

The ecological interlinkings of global interdependence affect the greatest number of people most deeply. Securing more sustainable patterns of economic development is a challenge that faces developed and developing countries alike, both at an autonomous and a collective level. The transborder and global character of many environmental dilemmas implies that a Machiavellian approach of pursuing only national or even regional self-interests is exposed as fatally flawed and ultimately self-defeating (Brenton 1994). By the mid-1980s, the four main global environmental problems that had been recognised were adverse climate change, the depletion of the ozone layer, biodiversity loss and deforestation.

Climate change

It is generally accepted by the scientific community that the increased concentration of so-called 'greenhouse gases' has significantly altered atmospheric conditions. As a consequence, a process of global warming has resulted in which many environmental risks are implicated (e.g. rising sea levels, desertification). Estimates made by the UN's Inter-governmental Panel on Climate Change in 1988 suggest that global warming of 0.3°C and a rise in sea levels by 0.6cm on a per decade basis should be expected extrapolating current trends of practice.

The depletion of the ozone layer

The Earth's layer of ozone lies in its stratospheric reaches, performing the function of protecting the surface from ultraviolet radiation. A range of manmade chemicals – in particular CFCs – are known to be responsible for its depletion that has led to ozone 'holes' at the polar extremes.

Biodiversity loss

Human activities that lead to the destruction of natural habitats and disturbances to eco-systems have been blamed for the loss of around one hundred species per day (CEC 1992e). In addition to the 'psychological spillover' effects from biodiversity loss, the economic well-being of indigenous peoples may be put at risk by eco-system damage as well as the potential to develop new products, especially food and pharmaceuticals, which are dependent on animal and plant species.

Deforestation

The destruction of the planet's rain forests has exacerbated the problems of biodiversity loss and climate change. Most of the world's catalogued and uncatalogued species are located in these regions. The forests also act as 'carbon sinks' by absorbing CO_2 and then converting this into oxygen. The ecological balance is further worsened if the timber is combusted, releasing CO_2 into the atmosphere. It has been estimated that deforestation currently contributes towards between 10 per cent and 30 per cent of all manmade CO_2 emissions (Deutscher Bundstag 1990).

Significant tasks lie ahead of Europe in addressing both global and localised environmental issues. The wider environmental impacts educed from decades of industrialised production and consumption have been considerable. The global level negative externalities generated by the nature and form of such activity have made Europe and the other Triad powers, both on cumulative and current practice terms, the major environmental offenders of the age. Thus, there exists at least a moral obligation on Europe to lead and resource co-operative efforts to help rectify the environmental damage which is attributable to those activities in question. However, ascertaining the environmental viability of nations and organisations can be a highly complex task, as can formulating and maintaining multilateral environmental agreements (MEAs) which attempt to provide a framework for international co-operation.

The burden of Europe's environmental responsibilities is also very regionalised, being home to some of the worst polluted countries in the world. This particularly applies to many CEE countries which, through neglecting numerous technological and market failures, have had to cope with severe environmental damage in certain areas. Substantial socio-economic costs have accompanied poor ecological management in the region. These are now being partially borne by West European nations as part of the measures aimed at assisting the East's reintegration into Europe's market economy.

The structure of the EU's external relations has also obliged it to grant assistance to a wide range of developing countries, in particular those within the ACP and Mediterranean Basin group. Environmental protection and sustainable development have become increasingly key themes to the EU's ODA and external trade policies. In 1992, 47 per cent of Community ODA was dedicated to environmental improvement programmes, while the Lomé IV Convention stated a commitment to screen all aid-funded projects with an environmental impact assessment (EIA). Of the technical and financial assistance granted to the Asian and Latin American countries (ECU 2.75bn over 1991–5) at least 10 per cent must be allocated to environmental projects. We have already noted in Chapter 6 that the EU has recently introduced an environmental clause to its GSP scheme. However, the most important aspects of international co-operation have concerned Europe's role played in MEAs.

Multilateral environmental agreements (MEAs)

As many environmental problems have trans-boundary or global characteristics, international co-operative efforts to overcome them have been essential. Such actions have normally revolved around multilateral environmental agreements (MEAs). The EU has played an important role in establishing MEAs and has been a contracting party to all the major agreements that have emerged since the 1950s. Subsequent to the Stockholm Conference of 1972, MEAs have taken on new significance in terms of the breadth of membership and, more importantly, the magnitude of the environmental issues at stake (see Table 11.1).

There are a number of inherent difficulties involved in designing an MEA that is able to function effectively. These are mainly associated with the divergent levels of economic development between participating countries. Poorer nations are not normally expected to respond as positively as rich nations to environmental challenges but it will become increasingly crucial for them to be accommodated within MEA arrangements. Recalcitrant nations pose another problem. While MEAs are usually accompanied by their own institutionalised mechanisms which are devised to monitor compliance and enforce retributory measures where deemed necessary, these may not be vigorous enough to deliver, by forceful means or otherwise, a set of desirable outcomes. Attempts by contracting parties to work outside the framework of the MEA by deploying more coercive

Table 11.1 From Stockholm to Rio: the major MEAs since the 1970s

Stockholm (1972) UN Conference on the Human Environment
The first MEA to encompass a broad range of global environmental and developmental issues. The main outcomes included the establishment of the UN Environmental Programme (UNEP) and the Action Plan for the Human Environment, which consisted of 109 policy recommendations to be enacted by signatories (but were poorly adhered to). The developing nations stated that their primary aim was economic growth even if this incurred compromises to the environment. The communist bloc countries did not attend.

Convention on International Trade in Endangered Species (CITIES) (1975)
Evolved out of negotiations held at the Stockholm Conference. The most successful of all international treaties to conserve wildlife. By 1994, over 100 ratifications had been secured. CITIES aims to uphold a trade ban on over 600 species and the imposition of controls on 26,000 others.

Vienna Convention (1985) and Montreal Protocol (1987)
The first international agreements on action to address the ozone layer problem. However, there were only 20 signatories to the Vienna Convention and virtually all were developed countries (with the notable exception of Japan). The Montreal Protocol obliged its contracting parties to further cuts in CFC production and consumption. In the London Amendments that followed in 1990 it was agreed to phase out CFC production completely by the year 2000. The EU set itself a target of 1996 (except for essential uses), but accomplished by 1995. By 1994, 74 nations had become signatories.

Basel Convention on Trans-boundary Movements of Hazardous Waste (1989)
Developed from UNEP negotiations between developed and developing countries over the import and export of hazardous waste materials. Mainly expressed developing countries' concern over pressures exerted by developed countries to deposit such materials in the former's proximity. More rigorous supervision and control on shipments agreed upon. Ratified by the EU in 1994 (except Germany and Greece). An EU Regulation (259/93/EEC) bans the export of hazardous wastes to developing countries while allowing exports for recycling only to Convention signatories and/or those with a bilateral agreement with the EU (CEC 1994t).

Rio de Janiero (1992) UN Conference on the Environment and Development
Attended by 117 heads of state and government and by far the most important MEA to date. Sustainable development made the central theme to the summit. The signing of pre-prepared UN framework conventions on Biodiversity and Climate Change (both ratified by the EU in December 1993), and the establishment of Forest Principles principally based on the sustainable management of the rain forests. Two other important outcomes were: (a) Agenda 21 which covered 115 programme areas on environment and development with sections on technology transfer, financial assistance and future institutions; (b) the Rio Declaration (Earth Charter) which outlayed the general principles for sustainable development across a broad multidisciplinary range of issues. The EU's own 5th Environmental Action Programme (EAP) is oriented by the underlying principles of Agenda 21 and the Declaration.

means of persuasion on reneging partners (e.g. trade sanctions) may run the risk of being the target of counteracting measures.

Another impediment involves the potentially heavy initial costs incurred in complying to the MEA's obligations, especially if this burden is carried by just a few participants. This can lead to MEA inertia if more countries are not enticed to join and a critical mass of contracting parties is achieved. The character of the externalities generated by the environmental problem concerned will also have some bearing on the success of an MEA. These can fall into two categories:

- Reciprocal externalities: these arise when every country contributes directly to the problem (e.g. ozone layer depletion).
- Unidirectional externalities: whereby all countries are affected by the problem but may not be the direct cause of it (e.g. deforestation).

With problems possessing reciprocal externality qualities, all MEA signatories benefit from positive action taken to tackle them. Thus, there is an incentive to 'free ride' on the actions undertaken by others. The same disincentives apply to the perpetrators of unidirectional externalities but, unlike the reciprocal externalities position, other contracting parties are not able to punish the offender by environmental reciprocity. Other forms of retaliation are, of course, available if the level of the game is raised say to include trade and ODA (OECD 1991b). This, though, constitutes an undesirable framework for an MEA to operate within unless these peripheral actions were inverted to take the form of positive reinforcement measures.

Coaseian bargains are representative of such measures and work on the 'victim pays' principle. They are based on a socially optimum compromise being achieved through resource transfers made by the victim to the offender which are dedicated to abatement processes. Well-known examples include the assistance granted by Sweden to Poland to reduce acid rain sources. The Montreal Protocol carried provisions to pay China, India and other developing countries not to use CFCs but more expensive alternatives to help protect the ozone layer. These arrangements may at times also reflect a reinterpretation of the basis on which ecological relationships exist between global regions. For example, an alternative to imposing punitive measures on Brazil for the destruction of the Amazonian rain forests may be compensatory payments made for the free 'carbon absorption services' that the country provides to the international community.

Encompassing the developing nations into global MEAs is likely to offer wider scope for finding low-cost solutions to environmental problems, since the marginal diminishing returns on implementing environmental protection systems are considerably higher in the early stages of sophistication. This can be illustrated by recent studies on reforestation programmes in tropical countries where the cost per tonne of carbon stored was estimated to lie between ECU 5–40 (Shunker *et al.* 1992), while the cost of modestly reducing energy-related CO_2 emissions in the EU was thought to be around ECU 50–150 per tonne abated (Coherence 1991).

The growing impact which developing countries are having on environmental problems at a global level also makes their participation in MEAs more imperative. Studies that have sought to establish projected patterns of those factors affecting future climate change present a clear case of this. The baseline scenario of the OECD Secretariat's 'Green' statistical model (OECD 1992d) predicts that coal's contribution to CO_2 emissions from combined fossil fuel sources will rise from 42 per cent in 1985 to 53 per cent by 2020. A main determinant of this trend is the forecasted rise in economic growth for China and India. Both countries are heavily reliant on coal (the 'dirtiest' fossil fuel), highly populous and with huge indigenous reserves. The data shown below help to translate the implications with respect to future climate change. Here, while the annual average growth rate of CO_2 emissions for the OECD group is anticipated at 0.9 per cent between 1990 and 2050, China and India have been attributed rates of 3.7 per cent and 3.9 per cent respectively. The trends shown in Figures 11.1, 11.2 and 11.3 are perhaps more revealing, indicating a regional shift to the developing countries regarding global shares of CO_2, with China's own cumulative share rising from 6 per cent to 20 per cent, the highest of any one single country between 1990 and 2050.

Developing countries may be willing to implement so-called 'no regrets' policy measures – those where economic benefits are attainable even when abstracted from the environmental benefits – as the returns on investments such as input saving capital may prove not only economically favourable, but are also distributed internally. However, the investment return ratio

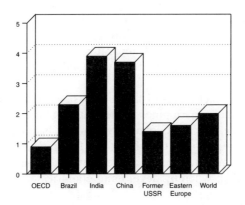

Figure 11.1 Future CO_2 emissions: annual average growth rates
Source: OECD 1992d: 151. © OECD, 1992, *The Costs of Reducing CO_2 Emissions: Evidence from Green*

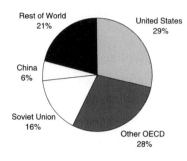

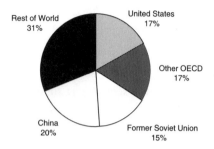

Figure 11.2 Cumulative CO$_2$ emissions: shares by world regions, 1950–90
Source: Burniaux *et al.* 1992

Figure 11.3 Cumulative CO$_2$ emissions: shares by world regions, 1990–2050
Source: Burniaux *et al.* 1992

deteriorates when measures to improve the state of environmental public goods (i.e. environmental media of air, water, waste) are considered due to the attenuated scope for the captured benefits involved (CEC 1992d). Thus, additional economic incentives are required for many developing countries to extend beyond the use of 'no regrets' policies. The Coaseian bargain principle, coupled with the morally defensible and practical view which suggests that the developed countries must currently bear most of the cost of redressing global environmental problems, provides the main basis for facilitating and resourcing the incentive structures required. All MEAs are accompanied by such measures to varying degrees. Examples of these include:

- Technical assistance provisions: these may take the form of technology transfers, mutual co-operation and support in research, environmental monitoring and exchange of key information.
- Helping install an institutional apparatus: necessary for environmental policy measures to function effectively and the MEA feasibly to be complied with.
- Trust funds and other forms of financial assistance: required to resource the transfers and programmes aimed at encouraging lower income country participation. The Global Environment Facility (GEF) trust fund is financed through the World Bank for this purpose to aid countries' efforts towards meeting the objectives outlined at the Rio Conference.
- Double standards: whereby developing countries are offered less stringent terms of compliance. This was applied to the agreement at the Toronto Conference on climate change in 1988.

There are a number of political and economic advantages in deploying incentive structures within MEA arrangements instead of punitive measures. Perhaps the most important advantage is how signatories are bound within a more co-operative framework rather than a potentially adversarial one if the MEA breaks down. The future market potential offered by technology transfers provides the developed countries with some compensation regarding incentive structure costs (Grubb 1989). There is also minimum interference on trade flows and trade policy from these measures, and the self-determination of sovereign states remains unthreatened.

However, as Kummer (1994) notes, difficulties may arise in their successful implementation and maintenance. This mainly concerns their dependency on the willingness of richer countries to resource the incentive provisions and any transfers that have been incorporated. Their role as donors is likely to depend on how they are affected by the nature of the externalities. At a global level, rich countries should be just as inclined to negotiate over reducing those of a reciprocal kind as they are for unidirectional externalities, although the cost benefit ratio of a Coaseian bargain arrangement on the latter may prove relatively more burdensome. However, for more localised externalities with marginal global impact (e.g. desertification) it is conceivable that the developed countries would be less generous. This, though, may be mitigated by the extent to which they were responsible for the environmental problem in the first place (e.g. trade in hazardous waste).

Despite the constraints imposed by the comparative brevity of electoral cycles, political leaders and policy-makers in developed countries may raise their level of donorship if convinced of its transitional nature in the longer run. This may occur for two reasons. First, the transfer of technology and financial resources to the developing countries will equip them to practice more environmentally benign economic activities. In addition, demonstrating the benefits of installing 'no regrets' measures may prove conducive to a more comprehensive programme of environmental protection evolving in the future. There is also evidence to suggest that increased levels of prosperity may assist these processes (see Box 11.1). Second, the moral obligation to address environmental problems that affect the 'global commons' is likely to fall more on the current developing countries as their cumulative contribution grows.

The gradual convergence of adopted roles can, however, only be assumed if the developing countries are willing to subordinate economic objectives to their environmental equivalents, a switch not many have shown signs of contemplating, even when significant localised externalities have had to be tackled. For some developing countries it may be that only when they have progressed beyond the 'catch-up' mentality will their global environmental conscience be fully activated.

The costs and benefits of leadership for Europe

The EU has often been the main protagonist of MEAs and other initiatives on environmental issues at a global level, but what are the costs and benefits of taking the lead role? This was discussed in a Commission report on climate change (CEC 1992d). The 'first mover' advantages that were proposed included the stronger position of European business to compete in tomorrow's markets through technology transfers and structural adjustments made with respect to sustainable development principles. In addition, leadership avoids the risk of strategic behaviour undermining the MEA in the longer run and, depending on the influence of the leader, may be able to exert moral persuasion on other parties to concur. Such attempts may be reinforced by demonstration effects, and by practising what is preached there will be considerable environmental benefits to reap at home. These may be much lower, though, where the investment returns ratio for abatement technology has become increasingly marginal.

The costs of leadership are largely dependent on whether a 'go it alone' or a 'front runner' position is adopted. The application of strict environmental standards on domestic business will to some extent impede its ability to compete in world markets, especially if the main rivals are non-participants to the MEA. However, if the EU was a front runner the adverse effects would be diminished and eventually may work to its advantage. This is because relative price differentials would eventually turn in favour of the front runner, but as a consequence negative income effects would reduce world demand, thus making the net welfare effect uncertain.

There could be wider cost and benefit implications from European leadership, as illustrated by the example of climate change. Efforts to reduce CO_2 emissions would lead to a shift in carbon intensive production to lower cost locations. These would benefit in terms of output and employment, but would have to bear the costs of localised pollution that resulted. Further costs would be borne from fossil fuel exporters to Europe as its demand for imports would simultaneously fall.

THE EU'S ENVIRONMENTAL POLICY

The evolution of EU Environmental Policy

The Treaty of Rome afforded no legal basis for a common environmental policy to be adopted between Community member states. Consequently, the EU's Environmental Policy was a relative 'late developer', not coagulating in any shape or form until the early 1970s. In more recent years, however, its profile has acquired increasing political significance and been reflective of the emerging global ecological concerns. Current EU policy takes its bearings from the principles of sustainable development as outlined at the Rio UNCED of 1992. It has also attempted to pursue a more integral approach both with regard to other policy fields and the mix of instruments deployed.

The conception of the EU's Environmental Policy is generally accepted as occurring at the Paris Summit of October 1972 where member states formally acknowledged the need for a Community-wide policy framework in this field. At the Bonn Conference of Ministers responsible for environmental issues later that month the initial objectives were established to form the policy's guiding principles. These were to be embodied in the first of many Environmental Action Programmes (EAPs) that have provided the main thrust of EU Environmental Policy. The first four EAPs are detailed in Table 11.2.

However, no formal competencies were granted to the Community for actions on environmental matters until the Single European Act (SEA) of

Table 11.2 The first four of the EU's EAPs, 1973–92

First EAP (1973–7)
Concentrated mainly with remedial actions addressing both cumulative and immediate problems facing the Community. Directives on the regulation and elimination of toxic waste discharges. The introduction of water pollution control measures were given particular priority. The *polluter pays* principle established underpinning all policy measures.

Second EAP (1977–82)
A greater emphasis on *preventive action* helped give new orientation to policy to some degree. However, most measures that accompanied this EAP were essentially revisions of those of its predecessor, thus constituting no significant departure from it. It is worth noting that many of the early policy directives in the first two EAPs contained socio-economic derogations that effectively placed their environmental objectives into a subordinate position. For instance, French and Italian tourist industries were in the past allowed to adopt lower compliance levels on beach pollution regulations in order to avoid redundancies in that sector.

Third EAP (1982–7)
The marked ascendancy of environmental issues on the political agenda led to a much higher profile and priority granted to the Third EAP. Its comparatively broader framework relative to previous EAPs encompassed many new areas in addition to the traditional pollution control themes. These included stimulating the development of 'greener' industries, eco-technologies and efforts to promote the recycling, re-use and recovery of environmental resources. The 1985 Directive on Environmental Impact Assessments (EIAs) was introduced, whereby permission for large industrial or infrastructural projects to proceed were made conditional to a prior study of their environmental side-effects.

Fourth EAP (1987–92)
Environmental protection stated as an essential element of all economic and social policies, thus extending the integrational imperatives set within the SEA. Urgent action on the application of agrochemicals, waste management, biodiversity and compliance to the SEM was highlighted. There was also criticism made of member states' past record in complying with EU environmental policy directives.

1987. Article 100a(3) of the SEA stated that environmental protection be promoted within the SEM programme, while Articles 130r and 130s were the first to outline the objective and functional parameters of the EU's Environmental Policy. This included the acceptance that any new environmental legislation should be applied according to the principles of preventive and precautionary action, rectifying environmental damage at source, and that the polluter should pay. Furthermore, the need for greater standardisation over environmental legislation and controls across member states was alerted.

The political priority afforded to environmental issues was further raised by the attention conferred to them by the Maastricht Treaty, in which Article 2 stated a commitment to achieving 'sustainable and non-inflationary growth respecting the environment' and Article 3(k) confirmed the need for 'a policy in the sphere of the environment'. The revisions made by the Treaty to existing Articles enabled the EU's Environmental Policy to be interpreted in a more rigorous manner by an amplification of its essential objectives (Article 130r) and the procedures to which actions are to be taken and measures adopted (Article 130s). This involved the requirement for these to be integrated into other policy fields (Article 130r(2)), thus broadening the scope of environmental objectives within the EU. It was also recognised that member states should be able to implement measures more stringent than those set at an EU-level (Article 130t).

Responsibility for environmental policy currently lies in the hands of DG11 (Environment, Consumer Protection and Nuclear Safety) which is divided into two sub-sections: Directorate A (waste management, prevention and control of pollution, nuclear safety) and Directorate B (protection of water and air, resource conservation). Strubel (1994) has noted that DG11's relative political weakness has led to difficulties over the integration of environmental objectives into other policy fields and the overriding of DG11 proposals in certain fora. An example of the latter was when Community President, Jacques Delors, circumvented the line of mediation adopted by the then Environmental Commissioner, Ripa de Meana, at the Rio UNCED. However, as part of the new integral approach of the Fifth EAP, the Commission decided to appoint a senior high level official at each Directorate General to monitor compliance to the principles of sustainable development.

Other developments have also helped to safeguard environmental concerns within the EU institutions. Collins (1995) has commented that the enhanced post-Maastricht powers bestowed upon the environmentally minded European Parliament – whereby it is now involved in co-decision procedures in certain legislative areas, including proposals based on Articles 100a and 130s – have helped close the democratic deficit in this policy field where public participation is especially vital. Qualified majority voting (QMV) has also been extended into environmental policy matters, thus denying the ability of member states intent on continuing certain environmental malpractices to veto the proposals aimed at curtailing them.

The Fifth EAP: a more coherent approach?

The EU's Fifth EAP (1992–2000) is notably more comprehensive in scale and ambitious in its objectives than any of its predecessors. One of its distinguishing features was the attempt to adopt a 'bottom-up' approach as opposed to one that was more 'top-down' and typified by a prescriptive, legislatively heavy emphasis. Hence, the importance of developing a consultative framework with business and the wider application of the subsidiarity principle were stressed in the Commission document outlining the EAP (CEC 1992c). However, its most important feature lay in the EAP's central theme of sustainable development, thus establishing a commensurability with the Rio UNCED and other recent related MEAs.

Some of the established conventions of previous EAPs were nevertheless retained with the Fifth EAP mainly consisting of principles and objectives that were devised to undergird future environmental policy rather than present a body of legislation to be implemented. There were, though, a number of important new initiatives such as the Environmental Management and Audit Scheme (EMAS), the eco-labelling scheme and further impetus given to establishing the European Environmental Agency. These are discussed in some detail later on. One other new initiative worthy of note was the LIFE financial instrument. This was introduced on the eve of the Fifth EAP with an initial budget of ECU 400m over the period 1992–5 which was set to double over the following four years. Its main purpose has been to help fund demonstration projects, technology transfers, the dissemination of best practice and provisions for third (especially developing) countries.

The Fifth EAP was also designated a sectoral dimension with a special focus on industry, energy, transport, agriculture and tourism. This entailed an examination of their resource implications, environmental impacts and the potential outcomes of actions taken in response to them. The numerous environmental issues identified as requiring particular attention were climate change, acidification and air quality, protection of nature and biodiversity, management of water resources, the urban environment, coastal zones and waste management. The familiarity of many of these issues with respect to preceding EAPs added some sense of continuity. A section on the management of environmental risks and accidents included those that were industry related, nuclear safety and radiation protection, matters of civil protection and environmental emergencies. Another was devoted to broadening the range of instruments, comprising improvements to the gathering and dissemination of environmental data and environmentally related R&D activities, the spatial dimensions to environmental protection and, perhaps most importantly, the adoption of a more economic approach to policy, which included the application of economic instruments (see Box 11.2).

With regard to the Community's wider international role, the importance of continued positive action on the four main global environmental problems – climate change, depletion of the ozone layer, biodiversity loss and deforestation – was stressed. The Fifth EAP subscribes to a more integral approach to environmental policy which applies on various levels:

- The interface with other policy fields: for example, the environmental dimension of the Trans-European Networks (TENs), recent and impending reforms to the Common Agriculture Policy, the 'greening' of the EU's external trade relations, the development of eco-technologies sponsored by the Fourth R&D Framework Programme.
- The defining characteristics of measures being deployed: the 1993 Integrated Pollution Prevention and Control (IPPC) Directive provides a good illustration of this principle. Under the Directive, all three environmental media are systematically embraced under a unified regulatory mechanism. In addition, the IPPC's integral approach includes incentive provisions to encourage a more efficient use of materials, while criteria also exist to help determine if the best available technologies can be employed by firms.
- The configured policy mix used to solve environmental problems: one of the highest priorities given within the Fifth EAP was the more extensive use of economic instruments (e.g. eco-taxes and tradable permits) to reinforce the existing policy framework which is still dominated by the more established 'command and control' regulations.

The Maastricht Treaty helped to facilitate this new course of policy by enhancing both its influence in other spheres and the depth and breadth of the formal competencies from which it draws its *raison d'être*. Moreover, as Murphy and Gouldson comment

> The adoption of this principle of integration began to move the EU past the point where it saw environmental protection as a necessary supplement to economic growth and towards a situation where effective environmental protection was recognised as an integral facet of (if not a prerequisite for) economic development.
>
> (Murphy and Gouldson 1995: 21)

Thus, the integrational issues that concern EU environmental policy are closely related to broader issues of sustainable development.

Accommodating environmental objectives into other EU policy fields is essential if the 'new development model', as conceived in the GCE White Paper (see Box 11.1), is to be realised. The wider application of economic instruments should support this as they are generally accepted to induce a more pro-active response from business to improve their environmental conduct. Their 'market-based' nature also gives them the ability to transcend different aspects of policy, thus providing a multidisciplinary focus from which certain synergetic advantages may be achievable. For example, the introduction of carbon tax will involve policy-makers from various different departments (e.g. transport, energy, consumer affairs, competition, regional development) to consider its impact. Actualising sustainable development should also be assisted by legislation such as the IPPC Directive that aims rationally to combine pre-existing environmental rules so that business is confronted with a more coherent and simplified regulatory framework.

One potential impediment to securing a more integral approach within EU Environmental Policy lies in the subsidiarity principle – whereby Article 3b of the Maastricht Treaty states that relevant EU institutions should not be allowed unlimited interference at member state level. While it is undoubtedly essential for member states to be able to determine their own environmental policy, the fact that many environmental spillovers (most notably pollution) do not respect national or regional borders also requires some form of supra-national co-ordination of policy. As Barnes (1994a) has argued, more extreme applications of subsidiarity may work to undermine both industrial competitiveness and sustainable development owing to the fragmentary influence upon the business environment and subsequent uncertainty effects.

By the end of 1994, the Commission had published its interim review of the Fifth EAP (CEC 1994t). The review recognised that EU environmental policy had reached a critical turning point with many of the EAP's initiatives having struggled to gather momentum. In all, six aspects of policy were considered with their conclusions summarised as follows:

1 Integration: slow progress had been made in making environmental objectives a more integral part of other policy fields, although some important gains had been made in relation to the EU's Structural Funds, state aids, agriculture and the Fourth R&D Framework Programme.
2 Broadening the range of policy instruments: again, slow progress was experienced here over attempts both to implement a carbon tax and new statistical methods and sustainable development indicators aimed at helping internalise environmental costs. However, more streamlined legislative processes had been successfully introduced.
3 Establishing firmer partnerships and shared responsibilities: only seven member states were found to have prepared sustainable development strategies in accordance with Agenda 21 of the Rio UNCED and the Fifth EAP, although some consultative fora had been created at a national level in addition to the EU's own on environmental matters.
4 Changing attitudes and patterns of consumption and production: not much was found to have surfaced on this issue. Fiscal restructuring aimed at switching the tax burden from productive factors to environmental malpractice had been further extolled by the GCE White Paper

(CEC 1993a), while EMAS and the eco-labelling scheme were still evolving.

5 The application of legislation and enforcement: some advances had been made but it was accepted that greater legislative clarification and simplification was still required.

6 The international dimension of the Fifth EAP: the review commented that the momentum of the Rio UNCED's proposals must be maintained.

Some major new elements to EU Environmental Policy

The Environmental Management and Audit Scheme (EMAS)

The EMAS initiative was formally conceived by a Directive released in July 1993. It represents an attempt by the EU to encourage firms to aspire to 'a standard which states that effective systems of managing the environment are in place' (*OJ*, L168, 10 July 1993: 1). Similar environmental management and audit schemes had already been developed at member state level (most notably the UK's BS7750 standard) and some multinationals have conducted eco-audit exercises since the 1970s. The main aspects of the EU's EMAS include:

1 The development of an environmental strategy: which involves the setting of performance criteria by firms regarding the environmental management systems, and establishing patterns of eco-auditing which include methods to generate useful and reliable data to be employed by these systems and the public. A commitment to external validation assessment exercises must also be shown.

2 EMAS is site specific, not company specific: thus, EMAS awards may be dispensed on a locational rather than a corporate basis.

3 EMAS is a voluntary action: firms are free to opt into the scheme. The provisions made for EMAS apply across the EU, therefore no firm can be denied access.

In the short term, the compliance costs will be high, but the cost advantages derived from adhering to EMAS will manifest themselves in the longer run, for example from lower levels of waste and material intensity, reduced insurance premiums from diminished environmental risks and less fine payments from improved compliance to environmental regulations. Further advantages may be had from an enhanced reputation among consumers.

The EMAS is compatible with the more market-based orientation of EU Environmental Policy. The competitive conditions in which a firm finds itself will have to be carefully considered before any decision to embark on the scheme is made, while consumers can exert their own pressures through the acquisition of the environmental information made available to them. However, problems exist over SMEs which face proportionately higher compliance costs relative to larger firms and the site specific awarding of standards which may deter those companies wishing to improve the environmental credentials of the entire corporation in one bold stroke. Furthermore, upstream suppliers may show minimal interest owing to their limited direct contact with end-product users, although downstream purchaser firms may use EMAS membership as selection criteria themselves for the former (Barnes 1994b).

In a survey undertaken by Kok and Saint Bris (1994) across the UK, France, Germany and the Netherlands 'national regulatory constraints' (i.e. environmental legislation) was found to be the main determining factor behind EMAS membership. Pressures from public opinion and marketing considerations also ranked higher, but competitive pressures registered a much lower response.

Eco-labelling

An eco-labelling scheme attempts to promote the production and consumption of environmentally friendly products through the bestowing of an award on products that meet the scheme's criteria for eligibility. The main incentives for firms lie in both the increased demand for eco-labelled products that can be expected from environmentally discerning consumers and the assistance provided towards constructing an environmental management strategy. The first known scheme dates back to 1978 when Germany introduced its 'Blue Angel' eco-label, predating other national schemes by at least ten years. By the early 1990s, though, most developed nations had installed their own schemes.

As part of complying to both the principles of the Fifth EAP and the SEM programme, the EU established its own eco-labelling scheme with subsequent actions following a Regulation introduced in 1992. Like most other schemes, the EU's eco-label will be awarded on a 'cradle to grave' basis, entailing consideration of the entire life cycle of the product from pre-production to disposal. This implies that making cosmetic changes to existing products is insufficient for eligibility as the whole value-added chain of activities will be implicated (Welford 1992). A candidate product will also be assessed on its potential impact across a range of environmental fields, such as environmental media, energy intensivity and material input requirements. The EU's scheme still applies to only a few select product groups, although there are plans progressively to expand the number to be encompassed. In each product group chosen national eco-labels have to make way for the EU equivalent, hence a phasing-in approach from a low base has been adopted to smooth the transitionary process.

Many of the initial product groups involved consumer goods that were either resource intensive in terms of production and consumption (e.g. dishwashers) or chemical based and where their environmental impact was well recognised (e.g. laundry detergents). As the EU scheme's range of product groups broadens the so-called 'fourth hurdle' may be encountered. This refers to questioning the necessity of candidate products with respect to their general contribution towards a more sustainable future (e.g. hair laquer). Ascertaining the 'green' credentials of products in relation to their purpose has been a big grey area for any scheme. Fleming (1992) observes that certain 'displacement activities' could arise over such concerns from the concentration on minor problems while more critical environmental impacts of products are not effectively redressed. This view has been subscribed to by environmentalists who see a contradiction in the term 'green consumerism' and who themselves would suggest the promotion of abstemious behaviour rather than an eco-labelling mandate to consume. In addition, it is argued that environmental risks would be raised from eco-labelling criteria that are easily diluted or abused by the authorities responsible for co-ordinating the scheme (Salzman 1991).

The progress made by the EU's eco-labelling scheme has been somewhat disappointing. Unresolved disagreements between environmentalists and industry over evaluation criteria issues have obstructed many of the implementation processes. There has also been resistance from organisations at national level over how the scheme has been managed and reluctance to substitute the EU eco-label for their own in those product groups selected. Other difficulties have arisen over the exclusivity issue, whereby the EU intends to allow only around 10 per cent of candidate products to be accepted onto the scheme. While this is designed to encourage high standards and competition between firms, criticism has been made of the scheme's high failure rate and the disincentive effect this is likely to have on applications.

The European Environmental Agency

In many countries the day-to-day operation and management of environmental policy is assisted by an environmental agency. Perhaps the most well known of these is the US Environmental Protection Agency which, as well as playing a monitoring role, has been endowed with considerable powers of enforcement. The EU's own agency was first envisaged in a 1990 Regulation, but did not become operational until 1994 from its headquarters in Copenhagen.

The role of the European Environmental Agency is 'to provide the Community and member states with objective, reliable and comparable information at European level, enabling them to take requisite measures to protect the environment, assess the results of such measures and to ensure that the public is properly informed about the state of the environment' (CEC 1990c). In order to provide the apparatus for this role to be achieved, the Agency's primary task has been to establish the Environment Information and Observation Network across the EU. From this, it can be seen that the informative and disseminative functions performed by the Agency have been constructed to help realise some of the specific objectives of the Fifth EAP.

However, reproach has been expressed in some member states (particularly the UK) over the limited scope given to the Agency within the framework of EU Environmental Policy, with critics arguing for a more proximate modelling on the US EPA. The subsidiarity principle makes the likelihood of any inspectorate role being given to the Agency increasingly distant as it implies that this is the task of member states. Changes to the Agency's role in response to such opinions will be made subject to its first review due in 1996.

Box 11.1 Sustainable development

The notion of sustainable development attempts to bring together environment and development into the same conceptual framework from which mutually beneficial objectives may be achieved. Much of the initial work towards constructing this framework can be attributed to the World Commission on Environment and Development and its subsequent report, *Our Common Future*, or Brundtland Report. From this Report we have the commonly quoted definition for sustainable development, that is: 'development which meets the needs of the present without compromising the ability of future generations to meet their own needs' (WCED 1987: 43).

The traditional conflict between environment and development has centred on the adverse ecological consequences that originate from expansions of industrial activity. From a growth-oriented view, environmental protection measures are perceived as constraints to economic development. However, in the longer run the economic potential of future production factors will increasingly depend on the state of environmental conditions. This can be clearly depicted by effects that accumulated pollution levels are known to have on human health and land productivity.

Certain 'evolutionary' trends have, though, provided hope of their own in reducing the marginal environmental impacts of development. Recent innovations in eco-technologies present the basis for a new economic paradigm to be established. Furthermore, the underlying structural changes that have heralded the emergence of a post-industrial society, at least in developed countries, imply the dissolution of many material intensive industries and a simultaneous shift from volume to value production (Janicke *et al.* 1989). Meanwhile, in order for the secondary sector to negate any of its harmful environmental impacts it must, broadly speaking, experience decreasing rates of material intensity at a faster rate than those for industrial expansion, while also seeking to utilise appropriate material contents to the same effect.

The ideas and theories that underpin the principles of sustainable development have been examined and discussed by a number of important Commission policy documents (CEC 1992c, 1992e, 1993a, 1993d, 1994u). Sustainable development was made the centrepiece of the EU's Fifth Environmental Action Programme in alignment with the commitments made at the

Box 11.1 *continued*

1992 UNCED at Rio. In the last chapter of the GCE White Paper (CEC 1993a) the basis for a new development model was explored which focused on the objectives of sustainability. Its opening premise contended that an unsatisfactory situation prevailed in Europe in which labour was under-utilised and environmental resources over-utilised. In order to rectify this fundamental predicament, a number of proposals were made:

- The construction of new infrastructures including extended public transport networks and upgraded water and waste management systems.
- The growth potential of eco-industries and the advantageous technological impacts they confer should be fully acknowledged.
- Longer product life cycles should be encouraged not only on environmental grounds but because they have the added bonus of generating comparatively labour intensive employment (i.e. repair and maintenance activities).
- The introduction of lean technologies to manufacturing processes that enhance product quality and resource efficiencies and provide employment growth through the competitive advantages which they bestow on firms that have adopted them.
- Restructured fiscal systems that shift the burden away from labour to environmental malpractice achieve the proverbial 'killing of two birds with one stone'.

Integrating environmental policy into other policy fields is essential if sustainable development is to succeed. In recognition of the more holistic approach that this intimates, Article 130r of the Maastricht Treaty states the need for all areas of EU policy to make environmental objectives an integral part of any future strategies. In further discussions on this topic, the Commission also suggested that this integration should involve the use of market-based instruments where possible (CEC 1994u).

A case frequently argued is that environmental protection is actually easier to achieve with economic growth than without it. In support of this, a World Bank (1992) report on development and the environment commented that the experience of rich countries showed that growth and pollution can be 'delinked'. It pointed to the fact that since 1970 OECD Europe's growth rate had risen by 80 per cent yet lead emissions had fallen by 50 per cent. In addition, improvements to air quality had been achieved with only a fraction of GDP devoted to abatement measures. Rising levels of prosperity also tend to breed more public desire for an amelioration of environmental media. This may be related to the income thresholds at which more immediate material needs have been perceived to be met. Consequently, government policy-makers may feel predisposed to release resources and funds at their command to these ends once the growth enhanced tax base permits it.

However, such assumptions remain largely theoretical and it may take some time for developing countries to allow more social and environmental objectives to exist on equal terms with their industrial economic counter-

Box 11.1 *continued*

parts. More importantly, Fleming (1994) articulates an opinion still commonly held to in that sustainable development is achievable only by pursuing low output, or even negative growth. Any evaluation of the ecological compatibility of growth will also require the 'greening' of national income accounts to reflect which of its aspects can be interpreted in this way. This will rely on accurate valuations of environmental goods and bads in the marketplace and any negative distributional effects that are relevant.

Impediments to attaining sustainable patterns of development may arise from the dilemma of safeguarding intergenerational equity. Because it is not unusual for decision-making processes and their outcomes to be designed to favour the generation responsible for them, future generations are hence disadvantaged. For this scenario to be inverted implies, in extreme circumstances, that sacrifices should be made now. This would often prove to be politically unpalatable in developed and developing countries alike. Additional problems are created by the length of time taken by many environmental investments to yield results (e.g. reforestation programmes). These mainly concern what discount rates to adopt on these investments. The higher the discount rate, the higher the returns must be to compensate. However, the adoption of lower discount rates may produce environmental projects over and above the social optimum level, or investments of the wrong kind, such as the mass conifer planting schemes in the UK during the 1980s. The challenge posed in securing the right balance of intergenerational equity is one of the keys to unlock the combination of sustainable development.

INDUSTRY AND ENVIRONMENT

Establishing an appropriate relationship between industry and the environment is essential as it is almost entirely the manifestation of industrial activity, at various levels, that is the main cause of environmental degradation and ecological collapse. The discussion below investigates two key aspects of that relationship: industrial competitiveness and environmental protection, and the potential of eco-industries.

Industrial competitiveness and environmental protection

Whether the underlying principles of sustainable development are adopted by business to a significant extent will be determined by the scope for reconciling the objectives of both industrial competitiveness and environmental protection. The view taken by many analysts is that this task is a highly arduous one, particularly for some northern European countries which possess some of the world's most stringent regulatory structures on environmental protection. The EU's own environment policy has produced nearly 300 directives since its formal inception in 1972, with the annual number passed increasing progressively from 1985 to 1994. The main argument against imposing such a regime on business is that there is a strong correlation between the level of rigorousness and the compliance costs it incurs on affected firms. In 1993, for example, CONCAWE, the oil industry's European environmental lobby, claimed that adjustments made to meet the EU's sulphur emission limits on fuel oils would cost the industry $3.3bn in the short term and more than $5bn in the long term (*Financial Times*, 3 March 1994).

Moreover, in many European industries the already infused environmental technologies are at a state of sophistication where diminishing marginal returns on additional investments are now modest. Put illustratively, the cost of 90 per cent abatement may be ECU10m for an enterprise, but the cost involved in reducing emissions by the next 5 per cent could also commit it to a similar expenditure. While environmental policy has a critical role to play in correcting market failures, its measures must be devised in such a way as to exact the most amenable response possible from industry. As Barnes (1994c: 1) has commented, 'It would be unrealistic to expect society in general to accept a significantly lower living standard in order to improve the environment. It is therefore improbable that a business will be willing to reduce its competitiveness for the sake of similar goals.'

In acknowledgement of the cost and constraint implications carried by a robust environmental protection policy for European competitiveness, the Commission explored the areas of compatibility between the two objectives in a document published on the eve of the Fifth EAP (CEC 1992e). The stated aims of the document were based on an examination of two fundamental questions. First, how can industry fulfil its responsibilities towards environmental protection? Second, what was the potential of environmental policy to stimulate industrial competitiveness? In seeking to establish the grounds for a mutually positive relationship the Commission commented:

> In total, the exploitation of positive synergies between industrial competitiveness and protection of the environment is increasingly seen to lie in the introduction of environmentally-sound industrial processes and products rather than through remedying unwanted side-effects of existing patterns of activity. They also respond much better to the requirements of industrial competitiveness by providing a permanent boost to fundamental factors of competitiveness instead of temporary advantage.
>
> (CEC 1992e: 3)

In other words, the ad hoc removal of negative externalities from deleterious environmental practices (e.g. waste abatement) provides only a series of one-off static advantages, as opposed to the dynamic advantages offered by introducing new eco-technologies to product and process design. The latter may take the form of 'pioneer profits' derived from the creation and successful exploitation of new market opportunities and also the general development and diffusion of new clean (less emissions) and lean (less required inputs) technologies across a wide sectoral range. The introduction of such industrial practices is closely aligned to the precepts of the 'new manufacturing paradigm'. These involve lean production techniques entailing less material intensive and more knowledge intensive production, quality maintenance systems that may seek to avoid environmental faults as part of the process and other similar innovations that coincide with a more environmentally benevolent approach. Within this development various eco-technologies have played an integral role in many advanced manufacturing systems.

Additional advantages may originate from a more positive purchasing attitude from environmentally conscious consumers. The market for 'green' products is potentially enormous and presents its own competitive challenge to firms in all industries to varying degrees. For this potential to be realised, though, consumers must embrace more vigorous and sophisticated forms of demand for such products, but will simultaneously need to be suitably informed (e.g. through eco-labelling) and offered appropriate incentives to alter their expenditure patterns accordingly. Nevertheless, some products – and the technology responsible for them – still remain comparatively expensive, while the purchasing capacity of low income consumers is particularly susceptible to cyclical constraints.

Although one evaluation of the SEM's environmental impact has centred on its adverse resource and waste product effects from the stimulation given to growth, there are a number of positive outcomes that should in theory arise. The competitive pressures generated and other microeconomic efficiencies will improve performance on capital and resource utilisation, while investment rates in eco-industries can be expected to rise. The SEM could also play an important role in diffusing new environmental technologies across the EU, assisted by the environmental R&D programme in the Fourth FP. Article 100a of the Maastricht Treaty expresses the need for coherence between environmental policy and the programme. Furthermore, the Commission has accepted both the need to maintain 'the integrity of the Internal Market whilst promoting the protection of the environment at a high level' (CEC 1992e: 11). While excessive environmental legislation can place constraints upon the SEM's potential, the harmonisation of environmental standards and certification systems across Europe has been beneficial.

However, the Commission and others have expressed concern over how smaller firms have risen to these challenges. As Barnes (1994c) has noted, SMEs experience disproportionately high implementation costs when installing many forms of environmental best practice. For example, monitoring equipment incurs the same cost if ten or one million units are produced. Smaller firms also sometimes lack the human and managerial resources to keep abreast of legislation and market opportunities that are available through policy incentive structures. In their role as subcontractors and suppliers to other businesses, pressures may originate from the demands for high environmental standards, especially if the larger firms have adopted eco-audit schemes. The Commission has noted that the SMEs found in eco-industries need to be particularly encouraged given the acknowledged critical innovative role they play. This and the generally more flexible responsiveness of SMEs to consumer demand lends further necessity to their support.

Trying to induce a more pro-active approach by industry on environmental protection rather than a reactive one to legislative pressures is generally more desirable. This will partly rely on there existing a framework for constructive dialogue between industry and policy-makers supported by mechanisms to disseminate environmentally relevant information to business where appropriate, for instance, through voluntary agreements. Barnes (1993) has criticised the Commission for past deficiencies shown here where a prescriptive approach has led to undermined business confidence, discouraged investment and occasional capital flight to non-EU locations. In part response to criticism of this kind, the Commission outlined four organising principles on which those future environment protection policy initiatives affecting business should be based:

1 Predictability: to enable business to make anticipatory actions and hence plan with certainty, thus engendering a long-term approach.
2 Flexibility: to enable business to implement the policy's requirements in an efficient manner.
3 Integration: an effective policy mix may involve a combination of policy instruments or an interface with other policy fields to achieve the best possible outcomes on a particular issue.
4 Cost-effectiveness: optimal least cost solutions should always be pursued so long as environmental integrity is not compromised.

In conclusion, while the extent to which the reconciliation of industrial competitiveness and environmental protection is achievable may still be unclear, the adversarial relationship in which they have been implicated in the past is now less accurate. For its part, the Commission appears to be turning to its policy-makers to provide a regulatory framework and the incentive structures that are more conducive to market development and less encouraging to market distortion, for example, the use of environment protection measures in a protectionist role against imports. These will increasingly include an array of economic instruments to complement and in certain circumstances supplant more traditional regulatory mechanisms.

The potential of eco-industries

Eco-industries can be described as those 'including firms producing goods and services capable of measuring, preventing, limiting or correcting environmental damage such as the pollution of water, air, soil as well as waste and noise-related problems' (CEC 1994j: 53). These are not then to be confused with any definitions involving industries that claim to produce eco-labelled or 'green' products or introduce more environmentally benign production processes.

The potential of eco-industries has been widely recognised both inside and outside Europe. In the 1993 GCE White Paper (CEC 1993a), eco-industries were regarded as key sources of present and future competitive advantage, while large environmental projects – cumulatively valued at ECU 174bn up to the year 2000 – were envisaged that would stimulate the development of European based eco-industries. A report published by the research consultants ECOTEC (1995) forecast a 266,000 increase in eco-industry employment from 1992 to the end of the decade. This is particularly relevant considering the employment growth orientation that has been given to many EU policy fields over the medium term at least.

The OECD Secretariat has formulated its own estimates on eco-industries which suggest that by 1990 their global market had reached a magnitude of $200bn (comparable to that of the aerospace industry), of which the Community market constituted nearly a quarter of this total at $46.9bn, while the US market at $78bn represented a much larger share. A relatively impressive growth rate is also predicted by the OECD at an annual average of 5.5 per cent up to the year 2000 (see Table 11.3), thus increasing the global market for eco-industries to $300bn, although the US EPA forecasts suggest an even higher figure of $600bn (*Financial Times*, 3 March 1994). According to OECD estimates, the US is set to stay ahead of the EU with

Table 11.3 Forecasts of market trends for eco-industries by country

(billion ECU)	1990	2000	Estimated annual growth (%)
Germany	17.0	23.0	4.0
France	10.0	15.0	5.5
UK	7.0	11.0	6.3
Italy	5.0	7.7	6.0
Netherlands	2.7	3.7	4.1
Spain	1.8	3.0	7.4
Belgium	1.4	2.3	6.4
Denmark	1.0	1.2	2.2
Portugal	0.4	0.7	8.3
Ireland	0.3	0.5	6.5
Greece	0.3	0.5	7.4
Total EC	46.9	68.6	4.9
USA	78.0	113.0	5.0
Total world	200.0	300.0	5.5

Source: CEC 1994j: 60

an annual market growth rate that is marginally superior over the period. This predicted continued dominance can be explained by the fact that, with some exceptions, European firms have lagged behind their US counterparts in both the development and assimilation of new eco-technologies.

In terms of OECD trade in eco-industry products, though, Table 11.4 indicates that Europe leads the way with its share of production exported and trade surplus being twice that of the USA and around three times that of Japan in 1990. Germany is Europe's largest eco-industry exporter with about 40 per cent of the total and, with respect to product categories, European exports in water treatment and air pollution abatement technologies are the most important at 40 per cent and 35 per cent of the total respectively. However, import penetration remains less than 5 per cent within the OECD group, partly due to the fact that technology licensing has become an increasingly significant component of international exchanges relative to trade in environmental equipment (CEC 1994j). Europe is expected to remain the Triad's prime exporter in at least the medium term, but along with Japan will lag behind the USA as the world's largest eco-industry producer (see Figure 11.4). Meanwhile, Figure 11.5 and Table 11.5 show that the relative positions of eco-industry's market segments are forecasted to remain similar, while a broadly comparative level of market development across the Triad is also apparent.

The development of eco-industries strongly correlates to the importance afforded to environmental concerns in that country, the prime determinant from this being the regulatory framework for environmental protection. The imposition of environmental regulations confronts many firms with cost and operational encumbrances which they would wish to avoid but simultaneously offers those in eco-industries with corresponding market opportunities. Other lesser influences include the patterns of consumer demand for environmentally benign products and the growing need to integrate environmental risk into decision-making. However, technological considerations are increasingly becoming a key market driver in the formation of eco-industries. For instance, there are eco-technology aspects to all the emerging core generic technologies (i.e. IT, new material sciences and

Table 11.4 OECD trade in eco-industry products, 1990

	Export share (% of production exported)	Trade balance (MECU)
USA	10	3,120
Europe	20	6,240
Germany	40	7,800
UK	17	390
France	14	390
Japan	6	2,340

Source: CEC 1994j

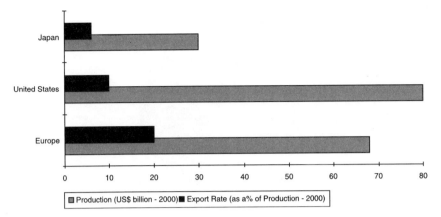

Figure 11.4 Eco-industries production and export, Triad to 2000
Source: CEC 1994a

biotechnology). The R&D content of eco-industrial activity is also high at around 8 per cent to 10 per cent of turnover equivalent for multinationals operating in this field. This is partly attributable to the favourable growth potential which they possess.

Examples of frontier technologies being developed across the different market segments include: for water/effluent treatment, aerobic methods, ion exchange and membrane technologies; for waste, physio-chemical treatments of chemicals, including neutralisation, detoxification and eva-poration; for air, biological scrubbers and filters to treat flue gases, acti-vated charcoal and catalysts to reduce organic emissions and combined particulate and acid gas control through electro-static methods. There have also been endeavours to nurture a more anticipatory 'along pipe' approach to clean technologies, as opposed to the dominant and relatively less desirable 'end of pipe' equivalents which currently hold around 80 per cent of market demand in the industry.

As eco-industries have relatively high technology credentials, the need for a more dynamic and committed long-term managerial approach has been stressed by Murphy and Gouldson (1995). The emphasis on the long-term view happens to coincide with the principles that underpin the general notions of sustainable development. Any interface likely to exist between the two axioms will be contained at the core management culture values of the eco-industry firms, but it is unclear what synergies will be generated as a consequence. However, one may evolve from a deeper appreciation of the 'stakeholder' concept, in which the business accepts a broader responsi-bility for its own actions. This may be especially relevant to firms in eco-industries as they need to place a higher corporate value on investments *per se*, and in addition the social and environmental dimensions of the returns that are accruable on them.

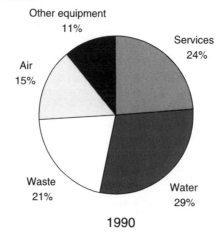

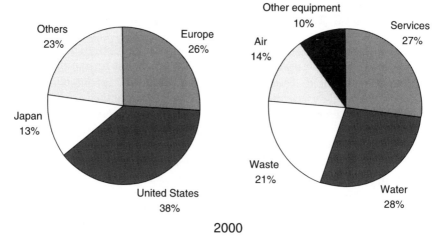

Figure 11.5 Main components of eco-industries, regions and markets, 1990 and 2000 forecasts
Source: CEC 1994j: 55

Table 11.5 Main components of the eco-industries, 1990

(%)	North America	Europe	Japan	Total OECD
Equipment/related services	74	76	79	76
Water and effluents treatment	24	34	22	29
Waste management	25	15	22	21
Air quality control	12	17	25	15
Other (land remediation, noise)	13	10	10	11
General services	26	24	21	24
Total	100	100	100	100

By way of conclusion, it should also be noted that increased rates of market concentration have emerged both in Europe and the USA. This is largely owing to strategic reactions against the high risks associated with the substantial R&D content and the marked degree of market specialisation and fragmentation that both characterise eco-industries. Studies in the USA that have revealed considerably higher returns on investments made by large firms compared to small firms in all sub-sectors would seem to confirm the advantages of concentration. The implications for the competitive dynamics and ultimate growth potential of the eco-industries are as yet unknown since it will depend on whether the gains afforded by scale economies can offset the welfare losses normally attributed to increased monopoly power.

Box 11.2 Economic instruments in environmental policy

Economic instruments have become an increasingly important part of any policy mix charged with helping protect the environment, and there are plans to make them an integral part of the EU's Fifth EAP. In the context of environmental policy, economic instruments have been defined as 'instruments that affect costs and benefits of alternative actions open to economic agents, with the effect of influencing behaviour in a way that is favourable to the environment' (OECD 1989c). They are sometimes referred to as 'market-based' instruments on account that 'the basic objective of economic instruments is to ensure an appropriate pricing of environmental resources' (OECD 1991b). Hence, their main aim consists of attempting to correct the market failures generated by environmental externalities. The most prevalent forms of economic instruments are eco-taxes and charges, tradable permits and deposit refund systems. A brief description of these is given below:

- Eco-taxes and charges: are levied on environmental bad practices, which most commonly involve pollutive activities. They may also be imposed on products to adjust the relative price positions engineered to produce incentive and disincentive effects. Eco-taxes and charges can be specific, *ad valorem*, or differentiated in nature (e.g. those on lead-free petrol).
- Tradable permits: normally take the form of pollution quotas, permits and ceilings, although they have also been used to serve other environmental objectives (e.g. New Zealand's tradable fishing quota permits). These are bought and sold between interested parties within the regulatory parameters set by the authorities.
- Deposit refund systems: have a relatively long history being used in the beverage container industry for a considerable time. Users pay a deposit on the packaging or container concerned and are recompensed when this is returned to be re-used, recycled or disposed of. These systems are now being applied to bulky items such as car hulks.

Box 11.2 *continued*

The Scandinavian countries and the USA have been key pioneers in this field. Estimates suggest that between 1987 and 1993 the number of economic instruments introduced into OECD environmental policies rose by between 25 per cent and 50 per cent, with most of this increase composed of new eco-taxes. The USA currently has the most sophisticated range of tradable permit systems, especially with regard to air pollution where the 1990 Clean Air Act extended their use.

Up to now, environmental policy has been dominated by 'command and control' regulations whereby legislation and the rules that accompany it have acted as a 'stick' to encourage good environmental behaviour. The most common examples of these include total pollution bans, maximum discharge limits, the required implementation of certain eco-technologies or bans on particular production processes or materials (e.g. CFCs). Economic instruments, on the other hand, attempt to work with the grain of the market by aiming positively to reinforce such behaviour through the incentive structures (the 'carrot' approach) that they embody. However, any marked departure from more traditional and well-established policy approaches requires circumspection, and the more widespread application of economic instruments in environmental policy is no exception. Potential difficulties may arise if they are applied in isolation of the legislative framework, while the financial purpose of the instruments must be clearly defined (Barde and Opschoor 1994). The introduction of a carbon tax, for example, may have wide-ranging implications for a country's fiscal structures and systems, or produce unpredictable outcomes which are contrary to wider environmental objectives such as its invigorating effects on the development of the nuclear power industry. Nevertheless, the generally expressed desire by both governments and business to give a higher profile to economic instruments is due to the recognised advantages they possess over 'command and control' regulations:

- Significant administrative cost savings: derived from avoiding the need to monitor compliance and enforce punitive measures on regulatory offenders.
- More flexibility is granted to business: implementation of environmental protection measures as firms are allowed to choose how and where to make reductions in pollution. This is beneficial because producers are likely to know the most appropriate and cost effective methods to achieve the environmental objectives which have been set.
- The provision of continuous incentives to develop less environmentally hazardous products and methods of production: unlike regulations which merely encourage a minimum compliance to standards and quotients set.
- More effective resource conservation and transmission to future generations: promoted by harnessing the market mechanism but this will depend on an appropriate market valuation being placed on environmental goods and bads (see Box 11.1).

Box 11.2 *continued*

● A new source of finance to governments: provided by economic instruments that may enable them to make favourable readjustments to their fiscal policy.

There are, of course, a number of disadvantages associated with economic instruments, and these will be discussed later on in this section when eco-taxes and tradable permits are examined in closer detail. Briefly, these include the adverse distributional effects that may be attributable to eco-taxes and their negative impact on industrial competitiveness. The transitional and longer term impacts of installing economic instruments also have the capacity to generate uncertain sectoral shifts and significant changes to capital market structures which may prove costly in the future (Harrison 1993).

The design of economic instruments should also incorporate inbuilt sensitivities to the ecological dynamics which they encounter. For instance, the marginal impact of the same magnitude of pollution is different in low polluted areas compared to those that are highly polluted. Delbeke (1991) comments that another potential problem lies in whether the economic instruments are applied to mobile sources of environmental damage (e.g. products, some kinds of pollution) or stationary sources (e.g. limited dispersal emissions). This has obvious implications for the level at which economic instruments should be managed (i.e. national, international, global).

THE ENVIRONMENT, INTERNATIONAL TRADE AND FOREIGN INVESTMENT

In this section, we shall examine the environmental dimension of the foreign exchange of products and capital. This will entail a discussion on the 'green' dimensions of international trade and what positions have been adopted by the GATT/WTO framework with respect to trade and the environment. In addition, we shall briefly consider some of the key issues surrounding the relationship between multinationals and the environment.

Green trade?

There has been much debate over the environmental impacts of international trade, which has largely centred on two traditionally opposing views. That which has been usually championed by environmentalists has concentrated on the detrimental growth inducing effects generated by free trade and trade liberalisation measures that encourage it. The other view draws upon two main theoretical arguments. First, that greater resource efficiencies are engendered by a more open, multilateral free trade system. Second, the rise in a country's affluence from intensified trading activity could assist the implementation or improvement of its environmental protection schemes.

Contention also exists over the issue of the positive and negative effects of trade-related environmental measures (TREMs). A number of problem areas have been noted, principally over environmental NTBs, eco-subsidies to firms (e.g. on pollution abatement), environmental clauses in preferential trade regimes and eco-labelling schemes. Antagonism over TREMs may arise at multilateral or bilateral level, or both. For instance, calls for higher international environmental standards in either products or processes by those already proximate to them are likely to be repelled by those on whom disproportionate costs are imposed.

Another area of discussion has centred on trade, the environment and related welfare effects. For instance, it will be more advantageous for countries to import goods that are pollution intensive in production. The reverse position applies to exportable products that are pollution intensive, although some products inherently will be both. Automobiles present a good case, where the production processes involved for most models are thought to incur just as much, if not more, environmental damage in comparison to their fuel combustion effects once in active service.

Returning to the debate on the environmental effects of trade, Stevens (1994) has categorised these into four types: scale, trade in products, structural effects and regulatory effects. Let us now consider these, relating where appropriate to the other points of controversy we have raised above.

1 Scale: trade-driven growth may lead to a range of adverse environmental outcomes, but accompanying higher levels of prosperity may resource and facilitate a wider application of environmental protection measures (as discussed in Box 11.1). However, those enjoying material and financial gains from freer trade must actually want to implement these measures, and thus will be dependent on the opportunity costs perceived at the time. For example, many East Asian 'tiger' economies have devoted export earnings to fund new road-building programmes in response to infrastructural bottlenecks caused by recent high-growth performances.

2 Trade in products: the intensified transportation of general merchandise and the export of ecologically hazardous materials such as oil and toxic wastes carry higher environmental risks. It has been estimated that international trade flows are responsible for around 12 per cent of total world oil consumption (Madeley 1992), but this must be offset against energy efficiencies generated by the dictates of comparative advantage – the more competitive producer may be so due to lower energy inputs required in the production process. In addition, freer trade will help diffuse eco-technologies and eco-industrial products to a greater number of global locations.

3 Structural effects: enabling countries to specialise according to their comparative advantages allows them to exploit resource and capital

efficiencies, thus yielding greater opportunities for less material intensive production and distribution. This, though, assumes that comparative
advantage is the main organising principle underpinning international
trade relations. Further problems may be caused by the absence of
accurately valued environmental assets such as tropical timber. Those
countries that are resource rich are likely to specialise in pollution
intensive production (e.g. the CEE countries), thus aggravating the level
of global environmental damage.

4 Regulatory effects: some NTBs have been vindicated on the basis of
performing a quasi-environmental protection role. Other TREMs have
sought to encourage positive environmental practices from others by
granting preferential trade terms in response to evidence displayed of
this (e.g. the EU's environmental clauses to its GSP). The latter are more
easily legitimised than the former in a multilateral free trade regime,
though pressure to remove the NTBs will limit national governments'
competence in environmental matters. The closer harmonisation of
environmental policies between countries, as found in more advanced
forms of RIAs, will have indirect trade effects from their influence on
product standards, fiscal measures and subsidy structures.

The position of the developing countries in the green trade debate has also
been a focus of concern for some analysts. For instance, Selincourt and
Thussu (1994) have asserted that trade liberalisation enables the more
powerful to exploit the market opportunities and other benefits generated,
thus ultimately compromising the position of poorer countries not able to
respond so favourably to the competitive challenges posed. This may
manifest itself in environmental 'short-cuts' to counteract the ensuing
welfare losses. Furthermore, the recent introduction of environmental
clauses into preferential trade terms for developing countries has been
viewed with suspicion. This is owing to the potential for selective application by the developed countries who wish to chastise out of favour LDCs.
Moreover, Snape (1992) notes that environmental trade clauses may lead to
losses in global welfare levels from any adverse terms of trade and distributional effects that arise.

The GATT/WTO framework and environmental issues

The rules of GATT had contained guiding principles on dealing with
environmental matters for some time, stating quite clearly that environmental policy cannot be used in a protectionist role. However, the Agreement on Technical Barriers to Trade (TBT) acknowledges measures aimed
at environmental protection as the sovereign right of countries. Such
measures are not deemed barriers to trade if they are applied in a non-
discriminatory manner, or if in the course of meeting the scientific objectives set by environmental policy trade is not restricted unnecessarily. This

suggests that the 'first-best' option consists of pursuing environmental protection of the global commons through domestic policy initiatives as opposed to more coercive means available such as trade sanctions. Yet Ekins (1994) has argued that selective trade policy instruments may provide a 'second-best' option where the 'first-best' solutions are not viable, although the incentive structures and transfer schemes of MEAs may provide the external assistance to domestic policy initiatives.

The GATT/WTO rules also state that contracting parties may not deploy unilateral trade policy measures to protect the environment of other members. This not only contravenes the sovereign rights of countries, but also the general ethos of multilateralism embodied in the GATT/WTO framework. Perhaps the most familiar case of this kind was the US ban on Mexican yellow-fin tuna exports in 1993, where a GATT ruling upheld Mexico's complaint that the USA was not acting with proper recourse to GATT's codes. Nevertheless, the GATT panel did not deny the right of the USA and European countries to introduce 'dolphin friendly' labelling of tuna products on account that environmentally discerning consumers would appreciate an awareness of this.

In Europe, similar pressures to adopt TREMs against environmental offenders have arisen, such as the occasion when the European Parliament – currently the most pro-environment EU institution – called upon the Commission to use them against Sarawak's exports of tropical timber in 1990. This was resisted, though, with the Commission expressing a reluctance to operate outside the framework of GATT and the International Tropical Timber Agreement of 1983. Yet, the post-Maastricht competence granted to the European Parliament on EU environmental policy may imply more effective pressure for TREMs to be qualified under Article 130s rather than Article 113, thus leading to a potential reduction of the EU's external coherence on its Common Commercial Policy.

Despite the guidance offered by GATT's Articles on trade and environment issues, there was a slow response in taking a more pro-active stance with respect to them. Although its Group on Environmental Measures in International Trade (GEMIT) was formed in 1971, it was to lie effectively dormant for twenty years until it was convened two decades later when it then proposed its working agenda for the early 1990s. This was divided into three main areas of investigation which, combined, aimed to revise and update GATT's approach on the environment:

1 Trade provisions in MEAs: in a report submitted in October 1993, 19 of the 170 MEAs then in existence were identified as having trade provisions. Among the key issues were the unilateral measures to protect the global commons (e.g. within the Montreal Protocol) and those deployed against third party country exports (e.g. the US ban on Mexican tuna). Article XX allowed exemptions from the MFN principle under special circumstances that could be demonstrated by the protagonist as long as

these were not interpreted as disguised trade restrictions, and no alternative measures with similar effects were achievable.

2 The transparency of TREMs: in its March 1994 meeting, GEMIT stated the need for those countries contemplating the use of TREMs to take appropriate actions that allow affected parties to make the anticipatory and preparatory adjustments necessary. These may include eco-labelling on exported products.

3 Possible trade effects of packaging and labelling requirements: the main concern expressed by GEMIT on this issue regarded the constrictions that national requirements for the re-use, recycling and recovery of product packaging could place on foreign suppliers and hence trade. North American and Brazilian paper and pulp producers have accused the EU's eco-labelling scheme of being trade restrictive, stating that although it is a voluntary scheme, foreign suppliers which are not able to acquire label status due to logistical or other reasons may be discriminated against. This, though, will depend to some degree on the relative balance between consumers who are more price sensitive and those who are more environmentally sensitive. Moreover, such schemes are unlikely to cause significant problems within GATT/WTO if 'national treatment' is extended on equal terms to foreign enterprises competing in the same marketplace.

In additional revisory efforts a special GATT report on trade and the environment (GATT 1992) reiterated its position on trade-related environmental measures and highlighted certain practices of members for criticism. Among those TREMs particularly targeted were agricultural and energy subsidies that both impeded the opportunity for free trade and encouraged resource intensivity. The EU's Common Agricultural Policy was especially singled out on the grounds of being not only highly protectionist but also a prime cause of serious environmental degradation in Europe. In support of this allegation, the report found evidence to suggest that European farmers were using over ten times more fertiliser per hectare than their counterparts in Australia, Argentina and Thailand.

The same report further asserted that trade barriers that frustrate the wealth-creating abilities of countries will also frustrate similar abilities to aspire to higher environmental standards, thus upholding the argument – as one would expect – that freer trade led to a more environmentally advantageous route to development. In addition, some anxiety was expressed over the influence exerted by certain producer groups which, with the sometime partnering of environmentalists, had manipulated trade policy-makers into adopting a protectionist posture based on environmental vindications to their arguments. Theoretically, the success of such partnerships between industrial and environmental lobbyists is dependent on whether production or consumption externalities are implicated and if the environmental group's interests lie at a national or international level. If both former cases apply, the group is likely to favour free trading arrangements (Hillman and Ursprung 1992).

Meanwhile, during the Uruguay Round, a Decision on Trade and the Environment was adopted by contracting parties in December 1993 which focused on two areas:

- the need for international trade to play a prominent role in sustainable development;
- the possible modifications necessary to multilateral trade rules to enhance the interaction of trade and environmental measures with special reference to effects on developing countries, the avoidance of protectionist outcomes and the surveillance of TREMs.

Later at the GATT meeting at Marrakesh in March 1994, a clause on the protection of the environment was written into the WTO's preamble and the Committee on Trade and Environment (CTE) was established. The CTE was given the remit to pursue a similar line of investigation and evaluation taken by GEMIT before it, while also encompassing new relevant and emerging issues. These included the impact of eco-taxes on international trade, a re-examination of the relationship between the disputes mechanism and MEAs, environmental measures and market access – especially with regard to developing countries and the exports of domestically prohibited goods. Perhaps the most difficult issue for the WTO to manage concerns the future exploitation of the environmental clause with means to advantage the developed over the developing countries. The USA has particularly expressed an interest in the WTO, making recourse to environmental provisions a priority – a view also shared in some European quarters.

Multinationals and foreign investment

For many, initial reactive thoughts on the relationship between multinationals and the environment still conjure up images of a state of perpetual antagonism existing between the two. To some extent there is validity in such sentiments, if only for the fact that the world economy is increasingly dominated by MNE activity, which has become representative of ecological pressures attributable to human actions. The ability of MNEs to exploit positions of market power over lesser rivals and poorer countries has undoubtedly led to a number of environmental compromises being made *en route*. This may proceed from MNE trade and investment practices that have had adverse effects on fragile eco-systems. Certain US fast food firms and their notorious burger ranches in Latin America were a high profile example of this during the 1980s. Runnalls and Cosbey (1992) state that MNEs have been prone frequently to adopting a 'regulatory chill' position against those countries attempting to maintain high environmental standards on account of the threat posed to competitiveness. In their defence, multinationals have also been responsible for developing some of the most advanced eco-technologies and environmentally benign process systems yet to be introduced. Furthermore, globalisation has enabled them to diffuse and disperse these across a wider breadth of locations.

Whatever view is prescribed to, globalisation implies that future international actions on managing global environmental problems must increasingly involve MNEs. The need to establish firmer MNE accountability on environmental issues has also been raised by those concerned over deficiencies in the institutional apparatus and jurisdictional mechanisms capable of confronting them at an international level, although the UNCED at Rio did go some way to address this (UN 1994d).

The future proliferation of MEAs should further diminish to some extent the ability of multinationals to exploit the diverse regulatory conditions between countries, but certain advantages may be drawn from the approach that this engenders. Where it is feasible, the adherence to a set of core environmental standards across the MNE should yield the efficiencies afforded by global consistency. This could also work to improve the corporate image by being seen not to adopt double standards on environmental protection. There may, though, be impediments to adopting a consistent approach. By way of an illustration, variances existing between national legal systems imply that different liabilities arise over the ownership of pollution from contrary interpretations of each country's laws on property rights.

A multidisciplinary approach may also be required to meet the company's environmental objectives towards risk assessment and liability prevention. This is because the traditional demarcations between environmental, health and safety regulatory fields are becoming increasingly blurred (Whitehead 1993). Corporate environmental programmes are increasingly concerned with packaging, labelling, product recovery and recycling, the employee's vulnerability when handling potentially hazardous products and processes in addition to the more well-established issues regarding emissions into environmental media. This has created the need for a broader combination of personnel within the company to manage these programmes.

CONCLUDING REMARKS

Protecting the environment and establishing sustainable patterns of economic development are the ultimate global challenges. Europe can and must play a vital part in these processes. This chapter has outlined the nature and extent of Europe's global responsibilities concerning the environment and some of the means by which it is able to work with other countries and regions on such issues. Its eco-industries have the potential to generate many of the solutions to the environmental problems which face humankind. They are also a growth industry, yielding new sources of wealth and employment for Europe. We have discussed at length the debate over industrial competitiveness and environmental protection. While current conventional wisdom is shifting more towards the view that economic growth and expansion of international trade and investment flows can be commensurate with maintenance of the ecological balance, the resource intensive patterns of development presently being adopted by most of the world's dynamic developing economies should be of significant concern to all nations. Dealing with the legacy of wide-scale ecological neglect in the CEE states presents Europe with its own specific regional problem that is, however, likely to preoccupy it at the expense of those elsewhere.

The EU and its member states, through their bilateral and multilateral links, nevertheless remain able to assist less developed countries in the installation of more environmentally friendly practices. Part of this assistance may take the form of new innovative policy measures that are being gradually introduced into the EU's own policy framework. As we have seen, though, the integration of a disparate range of countries into international agreements and common policy structures is an arduous task. A central dilemma entails persuading developing countries to desist from subordinating environmental objectives too far down the government's policy agenda. The *realpolitik* of averting further environmental degradation on a global scale necessitates that the developed countries must still make considerable sacrifices, at least in the medium term, in order to facilitate more sustainable patterns of development not just at home but also overseas. Therefore, key decision-makers in Europe have some very critical judgements to make with respect to the future of our planet.

References

Addison, J.T. and Siebert, W.S. (1993) 'The EC Social Charter: The Nature of the Beast', *National Westminster Bank Quarterly Review*, February, pp. 13–28.

Adnett, N. (1993) 'The Social Charter: Unnecessary Regulation or Pre-requisite for Convergence?', *British Review of Economic Issues*, vol. 15, pp. 63–79.

Aliber, R.S. (1970) 'A Theory of Direct Foreign Investment', in C. Kindleberger (ed.) *The International Corporation: A Symposium*, MIT Press, Cambridge, Massachusetts.

Aliber, R.S. (1985) 'Transfer Pricing: A Taxonomy of Impacts on Economic Welfare', in A. Rugman and L. Eden (eds) *Multinationals and Transfer Pricing*, Croom Helm, London.

Alogoskoufis, G. and Manning, A. (1988) 'On the Persistence of Unemployment', *Economic Policy*, vol. 3, pp. 427–469.

Anderson, K. (1991) 'Europe 1992 and the Western Pacific Economies', *Economic Journal*, vol. 101, pp. 1538–1552.

Anderson, K. and Blackhurst, R. (eds) (1992) *The Greening of World Trade Issues*, Harvester Wheatsheaf, Hemel Hempstead.

—— (1993) *Regional Integration and the Global Trading System*, Harvester Wheatsheaf, Hemel Hempstead.

Anderson, K. and Norheim, H. (1993) 'History, Geography and Regional Economic Integration', in K. Anderson and R. Blackhurst (eds) *Regional Integration and the Global Trading System*, Harvester Wheatsheaf, Hemel Hempstead.

Anderson, K. and Tyres, R. (1993) *Implications of EC Expansion for European Agricultural Policies, Trade and Welfare*, CEPR, London.

APEC (1995) *Implementing the APEC Vision*, Third Report of the Eminent Persons Group, August, Singapore.

Archibugi, D. and Pianta, M. (1993) 'Patterns of Technological Specialisation and Growth of Innovative Activities in Advanced Countries', in K. Hughes (ed.) *European Competitiveness*, Cambridge University Press, Cambridge.

Artis, M.J. and Lee, N. (eds) (1994) *The Economics of the European Union*, Oxford University Press, Oxford.

Artisien, P. and McMillan, C.H. (1993) 'Some Contextual and Thematic Aspects of East–West Industrial Cooperation, with Special Reference to Yugoslav Multinationals', in P. Artisien, M. Rojec and M. Svetlicic (eds) *Foreign Investment in Central and Eastern Europe*, Macmillan, London.

Balassa, B. (1961) *The Theory of Economic Integration*, Irwin, Boston.

—— (1966) 'Trade Reductions and Trade in Manufactures Among Industrialised Countries', *Manchester School of Economic and Social Studies*, vol. 33, pp. 99–123.

—— (1967) 'Trade Creation and Trade Diversion in the European Common Market', *Economic Journal*, vol. 77, pp. 1–21.

—— (1974) 'Trade Creation and Trade Diversion in the European Common Market: An Appraisal of the Evidence', *Manchester School of Economic and Social Studies*, vol. 42, pp. 99–135.

—— (ed.) (1975) *European Economic Integration*, North-Holland/Elsevier, Amsterdam.

—— (1977) 'Effects of Commercial Policy on International Trade, the Location of Production and Factor Movements', in B. Ohlin *et al.* (eds) *The International Allocation of Economic Activity*, Macmillan, London.

Balasubramanyam, V.N. and Greenaway, D. (1992) 'Economic Integration and Foreign Direct Investment: Japanese Investment in the EC', *Journal of Common Market Studies*, vol. 30, pp. 175–193.

Balcerowicz, L. (1993) 'Transition to a Market Economy: Central and East European Countries in Comparative Perspective', *British Review of Economic Studies*, vol. 15, pp. 33–41.

Baldwin, R.E. (1994) *Towards an Integrated Europe*, CEPR, London.

Baldwin, R.E. and Flam, H. (1995) *Enlargement of the European Union: The Economic Consequences for the Scandinavian Countries*, CEPR, London.

Bangemann, M. (1992) *Meeting the Global Challenge: Establishing a Successful European Industrial Policy*, Kogan Page, London.

Barde, J-P. and Opschoor, J.B. (1994) 'From Stick to Carrot in the Environment', *OECD Observer*, No.186, pp. 23–27.

Barnes, P. (1993) 'Industrial Competitiveness and the Environment: The Need for EU Policy Integration', *European Environment*, vol. 3, pp. 11–15.

—— (1994a) *Subsidiarity: A Green Light to Distort Industrial Competitiveness?*, paper given at the 2nd ECSA World Conference, Brussels, 5–6 May

—— (1994b) 'The Environmental Audit Scheme', *EIU European Trends*, third quarter, pp. 80–86.

—— (1994c) *Integrating Industrial and Environmental Policy Objectives to Policy*, paper given at Kings College, London, 25 March.

Beamish, P. (1991) 'The Internationalisation Process', in P. Beamish *et al.* (eds) *International Management: Text and Cases*, Irwin, Boston.

Bean, C.R., Layard, R. and Nickell, S. (1986) 'The Rise In Unemployment: A Multi-Country Study', *Economica*, vol. 35, No. 210.

Begg, D., Fischer, S. and Dornbusch, R. (1994) *Economics*, McGraw Hill, London.

Behrman, J.N. (1972) *The Role of International Companies in Latin American Integration*, Lexington Books, Lexington, Massachusetts.

Beukel, E. (1993) 'Education', in S. Anderson and K. Eliassen (eds) *Making Policy in Europe: The Europeification of National Policy-making*, Sage, London.

Bhagwati, J. (1990) *Multilateralism at Risk*, The Harry Johnson Memorial Lecture, London, July.

—— (1992) *Regionalism and Multilateralism: An Overview*, Columbia University, Discussion Paper Series No. 603, April.

Bini Smaghi, L. and Vori, S. (1993) 'Rating the EU as an Optimal Currency Area', *Banca d'Italia Temi di Discussione*, No. 187, January.

Blackhurst, R. (1991) *Implications of the Changes in Eastern Europe for the World Economy*, Kiel Institute of World Economics, Kiel.

Blackwell, B. and Eilon, S. (1991) *The Global Challenge of Innovation*, Butterworth Heinemann, Oxford.

Blanchard, O.J. (1990) 'Unemployment: Getting the Questions Right – and Some of the Answers', in J. Dreze and C. Bean (eds) *Europe's Unemployment Problem*, MIT Press, Massachusetts.

Blanchard, O.J. and Summers, L.H. (1986) 'Hysteresis and the European Unemployment Problem', *NBER Macroeconomic Annual*, MIT Press, Massachusetts.

Bochniarz, Z. and Jermakowisz, W. (1993) 'Foreign Direct Investment in Poland: 1986–1990', in P. Artisien, M. Rojec and M. Svetlicic (eds) *Foreign Investment in Central and Eastern Europe*, Macmillan, London.

Bofinger, P. (1994) 'Is Europe an Optimum Currency Area?', in A. Steinherr (ed.) *Thirty Years of European Monetary Integration*, Longman, London.

Bollard, A. and Mayes, D. (1992) 'Regionalism in the Pacific Rim', *Journal of Common Market Studies*, vol. 30, pp. 195–209.

Brandenburg, U. (1994) 'The European Community and the Gulf Co-operation Council: Co-operation or Conflict', *European Access*, No. 2, pp. 10–12.

Brenton, T. (1994) *The Greening of Machiavelli: The Evolution of International Environmental Politics*, Earthscan, London.

Bridges, B. (1992) *EC–Japanese Relations: In Search of a Partnership*, Royal Institute for International Affairs, London.

Brittan, L. (1993) 'Shaping a Framework for Global Trade: The Challenge for the European Community', *European Access*, No. 3, pp. 8–13.

Brock, C. and Tulasiewicz, W. (eds) (1994) *Education in a Single Europe*, Routledge, London.

Bruno, M. and Sachs, J. (1985) *The Economics of Worldwide Stagflation*, Harvard University Press, Massachusetts.

Buckley, P.J. and Artisien, P. (1988) 'Policy Issues of Intra-EC Direct Investment: British, French and German Multinationals in Greece, Portugal and Spain with Special Reference to Employment Effects', in J.H. Dunning and P. Robson (eds) *Multinationals and the European Community*, Blackwell, Oxford.

Buckley, P.J. and Casson, M. (1976) *The Future of the Multinational Enterprise*, Macmillan, London.

Budd, A., Levine, P. and Smith, P. (1986) 'The Problem of Long-term Unemployment', *Economic Outlook 1985–89*, vol. 10, London Business School Centre for Economic Forecasting, London.

Burniaux, J.M., Martin, J.P., Nicoletti, G. and Martins, J. (1992) 'The Cost of International Agreements to Reduce CO_2 Emissions', *European Economy*, special edition No. 1, Office for Official Publications for the EC, Luxembourg.

Burtless, G. (1987) 'Jobless Pay and High European Unemployment', in R.Z. Lawrence and C.L. Schultz (eds) *Barriers to European Growth: A Trans-Atlantic View*, Brookings Institution, Washington DC.

Campanella, M. (1995) 'The Effects of Globalisation and the Turbulence on Policy-Making Processes', in J. Drew (ed.) *Readings in the International Enterprise*, Routledge, London.

Cantwell, J.A. (1987) 'The Reorganisation of European Industries After Integration: Selected Evidence on the Role of Mulitnational Enterprise Activities', *Journal of Common Market Studies*, vol. 26, pp. 127–151.

—— (1991) 'A Survey of Theories of International Production', in C.N. Pitelis and R. Sugden (eds) *The Nature of the Transnational Firm*, Routledge, London.

Cantwell, J.A., Corley, T.A.B. and Dunning, J.H. (1986) 'An Exploration of Some Historical Antecedents to the Modern Theory of International Production', in G. Jones and P. Hertner (eds) *Multinationals: Theory and History*, Gower, Farnborough.

Catinat, M. (1988) 'The Large Internal Market under the Microscope: Problems and Challenges', in A. Jacquemin and and D. Wright (eds) *The European Challenges: Shaping Factors, Shaping Actors*, Edward Elgar, Aldershot.

Caves, R. (1971) 'Industrial Corporations: The Industrial Economics of Foreign Investment', *Economica*, vol. 38, pp. 1–27.

—— (1982) *The Multinational Enterprise and Economic Growth*, Cambridge University Press, Cambridge.

Cecchini, P. (1988) *The European Challenge: 1992 The Benefits of a Single Market*, Wildwood House, Aldershot.

Centre for Economic Policy Research (1993) *Is Bigger Better?: The Economics of EC Enlargement*, CEPR, London.

Chakravarthy, B.S. and Perlmutter, H. (1985) 'Strategic Planning for a Global Business', *Columbia Journal of World Business*, summer, pp. 3–10.

Chandler, A.D. (1986) 'The Evolution of Modern Global Competition', in M. Porter (ed.) *Competition in Global Industries*, Harvard Business School Press, Boston.

Charles, D. and Howells, J. (1992) *Technology Transfer in Europe: Public and Private Networks*, Belhaven, London.

Church, C.H. and Phinnemore, D. (1994) *European Union and European Community: A Handbook and Commentary on the Post-Maastricht Treaties*, Harvester Wheatsheaf, Hemel Hempstead.

Cliquet, R. (ed.) (1993) *The Future of Europe's Population*, Council of Europe, Strasbourg.

Coase, R.H. (1937) 'The Nature of the Firm', *Economica*, vol. 4, pp. 386–405.

Coherence (1991) *Cost-effectiveness Analysis of CO_2 Reduction Options*, Report for the Commission of the European Communities, DG XII, May.

Collier, P. and Gunning, J.W. (1995) 'Trade Policy and Regional Integration: Implications for Relations Between Europe and Africa', *World Economy*, vol. 18, pp. 387–410.

Collins, K. (1995) 'Plans and Prospects for the European Parliament in Shaping Future Environmental Policy', *European Environmental Law Review*, March, pp. 74–77.

Collins, S. and Rodrik, D. (1991) *Eastern Europe and the Soviet Union in the World Economy*, Institute for International Economics, Washington DC.

Commission of the European Communities (1977) *Report of the [MacDougall] Study Group on the Role of Public Finance in European Integration*, Collection Studies Economic and Financial Series, vol. 2, No. B13, Brussels.

—— (1979) *Japan: Consultations in Train and Envisaged*, Brussels.

—— (1985a) *Completing the Internal Market*, White Paper, Brussels.

—— (1985b) *Analysis of the Relations Between the Community and Japan*, Brussels.

—— (1988a) 'The Economics of 1992: An Assessment of the Potential Economic Effects of Completing the Internal Market of the European Community', *European Economy*, No. 35, Office for Official Publications for the EC, Luxembourg.

—— (1988b) *European Economy: Creation of a European Financial Area*, Office for Official Publications for the EC, Luxembourg.

—— (1988c) *Europe 1992: Europe World Partner*, Brussels.

—— (1988d) *Research and Technological Development Policy*, Office for Official Publications for the EC, Luxembourg.

—— (1988e) *Telecommunications: The New Highways for the Single European Market*, Office for Official Publications for the EC, Luxembourg.

—— (1989a) *Redirecting the Community's Mediterranean Policy*, SEC(89) 1961 final, Brussels.

—— (1989b) *Communication from the Commission Concerning its Action Programme Relating to Implementation of the Community Charter for Basic Social Rights for Workers*, COM(89) 568 final, Brussels.

—— (1990a) *Industrial Policy in an Open and Competitive Environment*, COM(90) 556, Brussels.

—— (1990b) 'One Market, One Money', *European Economy*, No. 44, Office for Official Publications for the EC, Luxembourg.

—— (1990c) *On the Establishment of the European Environmental Agency and the European Environment Information and Observation Network*, Council Regulation No.1210/90, Brussels.

—— (1992a) *The Internal Market After 1992 – Meeting the Challenge*, Office for Official Publications for the EC, Luxembourg.

—— (1992b) 'The Economics of EMU', *European Economy*, special edition No. 1, No. 44, Office for Official Publications for the EC, Luxembourg.

—— (1992c) *A Community Programme of Policy and Action in Relation to the Environment and Sustainable Development (the Fifth Action Programme)*, COM(92) 23 final, Brussels.

—— (1992d) 'The Climate Challenge: Economic Aspects of the Community's Strategy for Limiting CO_2 Emissions', *European Economy*, No. 51, Office for Official Publications for the EC, Luxembourg.

—— (1992e) *Industrial Competitiveness and Protection of the Environment*, SEC(92) 1986 final, Brussels.

—— (1992f) 'The Economics of Limiting CO_2 Emissions', *European Economy*, special edition No. 1, Office for Official Publications for the EC, Luxembourg.

—— (1993a) *Growth, Competitiveness and Employment: The Challenges and Ways Forward into the 21st Century*, White Paper, Office for Official Publications for the EC, Luxembourg.

—— (1993b) 'The European Community as a World Trade Partner', *European Economy*, No. 52, Office for Official Publications for the EC, Luxembourg.

—— (1993c) *Towards a Strategic Programme for the Internal Market*, COM(93) 256 final, Brussels.

—— (1993d) *Making the Most of the Internal Market – Strategic Programme*, COM(93) 632 final, Brussels.

—— (1993e) 'Stable Money – Sound Finances', *European Economy*, No. 53, Luxembourg, Office for Official Publications for the EC.

—— (1994a) *An Industrial Competitiveness Policy for the European Union*, COM(94) 319 final, Brussels.

—— (1994b) *The Europe Agreements and Beyond: A Strategy to Prepare the Countries of Central and Eastern Europe for Accession*, COM(94) 361 final, Brussels.

—— (1994c) *Strengthening the Mediterranean Policy of the EU: Establishing a Euro-Med Partnership*, COM(94) 427 final, Brussels.

—— (1994d) *Towards a New Asia Strategy*, COM(94) 314 final, Brussels.

—— (1994e) 'Annual Report for 1994', *European Economy*, No. 56, Office for Official Publications for the EC, Luxembourg.

—— (1994f) *The European Union and World Trade: A Comparison with the United States and Japan*, Office for Official Publications for the EC, Luxembourg.

—— (1994g) *Concerning the Conclusion of the Results of the Uruguay Round of Multilateral Trade Negotiations*, COM(94) 143 final, Brussels.

—— (1994h), *Integrating the Developing Countries into the International Trade System: The GSP 1995–2004*, COM(94) 212 final, Brussels.

—— (1994i) *Trade and Investment: Discussion Paper*, Office for Official Publications for the EC, Luxembourg.

—— (1994j) *Panorama of European Union Industries, 1994*, Brussels.

—— (1994k) *European Report on Science and Technology Indicators*, Office for Official Publications for the EC, Luxembourg.

—— (1994m) *The Fourth Framework Programme*, Office for Official Publications for the EC, Luxembourg.

—— (1994n) *Impact of the Framework Programme on European Industry*, Office for Official Publications for the EC, Luxembourg.

—— (1994p) *Employment in Europe, 1994*, COM(94) 381 final, Brussels.

—— (1994q) 'Europe's New Competitive Challenge', *Euro Abstracts*, vol. 32, No. 9, Office for Official Publications for the EC, Luxembourg.

—— (1994r) 'Training and Education in the European Community', *Euro Abstracts*, vol. 32, No. 4, Office for Official Publications for the EC, Luxembourg.

—— (1994s) *European Social Policy: The Way Forward for the Union*, White Paper, COM(94) 333 final, Brussels.

—— (1994t) *Interim Review of Implementation of the European Community Programme of Policy Action in Relation to the Environment and Sustainable Development – 'Towards Sustainability'*, COM(94) 453 final, Brussels.

—— (1994u) *Economic Growth and the Environment: Some Implications for Economic Policy Making*, COM(94) 465 final, Brussels.

—— (1995a) *Flexibility and Work Organisation*, Office for Official Publications for the EC, Luxembourg.

—— (1995b) *Free Trade Areas: An Appraisal*, SEC(95) 322 final, Brussels.

—— (1995c) *European Community Support for the Regional Economic Integration Efforts Among Developing Countries*, COM(95) 219 final, Brussels.

—— (1995d) *Europe and the United States: The Way Forward*, COM(95) 411 final, Brussels.

—— (1995e) *A Long-term Policy for China–Europe Relations*, COM(95) 279 final, Brussels.

—— (1995f) 'Trade Relations Between the European Union and the Developing Countries', *Development*, DE71, March, Brussels.

—— (1995g) *Preparation of the Associated Countries of Central and Eastern Europe for Integration into the Internal Market of the Union*, COM(95) 163 final, Brussels.

—— (1995h) *The European Union and Russia: The Future Relationship*, COM(95) 223 final, Brussels.

—— (1995i) *Strengthening the Mediterranean Policy of the EU: Proposals for Implementing a Euro-Med Partnership*, COM(95) 72 final, Brussels.

—— (1995j) 'Annual Report for 1995', *European Economy*, No. 56, Office for Official Publications for the EC, Luxembourg.

—— (1995k) *Twelfth Annual Report from the Commission to the European Parliament on the Community's Anti-Dumping and Anti-Subsidy Activities*, COM(95) 16 final, Brussels.

—— (1995m) *Background Report: The Lomé Convention*, 29 March, Brussels.

—— (1995n) *A Level Playing Field for Direct Investment World-Wide*, COM(95) 42 final, Brussels.

—— (1995p) 'European Patents: Untapped Potential', *Innovation and Technology Transfer*, vol. 2/95, Office for Official Publications for the EC, Luxembourg.

—— (1995q) 'Partnering Countries in Transition: EU Cooperation Programmes with Central and Eastern Europe', *Euro Abstracts*, vol. 33, No. 5, Office for Official Publications for the EC, Luxembourg.

—— (1995r) *Unemployment Report, July*, Brussels.

—— (1995s) *Social Europe 1/95: Medium-Term Social Action Programme 1995–1997*, Office for Official Publications for the EC, Luxembourg.

Corden, W.M. (1972) 'Economies of Scale and Customs Union Theory', *Journal of Political Economy*, vol. 80, pp. 465–475.

Cowling, K. and Sugden, R. (1987) *Transnational Monopoly Capitalism*, Wheatsheaf, Brighton.

Crookell, H. (1991) 'Organisation Structure for Global Operations', in P. Beamish *et al.* (eds) *International Management: Text and Cases*, Irwin, Boston.

Czinkota, M.R., Ronkainen, I.A. and Moffett, M.H. (1994) *International Business*, Dryden Press, Fort Worth, Texas.

Davenport, M. (1982) 'The Economic Impact of the EEC', in A. Boltho (ed.) *The European Economy: Growth and Crisis*, Oxford University Press, Oxford.

—— (1992) 'Africa and the Importance of Being Preferred', *Journal of Common Market Studies*, vol. 30, pp. 233–251.

Davenport, M. and Page, S. (1991) *Europe 1992 and the Developing World*, Overseas Development Institute, London.

De Grauwe, P. (1992) *The Economics of Monetary Integration*, Oxford University Press, Oxford.

Delbeke, J. (1991) 'The Prospects for the Use of Economic Instruments in EC Environmental Policy', *Royal Bank of Scotland Review*, No.172, pp. 16–29.

Dent, C.M. (1994) 'The Business Environment in Russia: An Overview', *European Business Review*, vol. 94, No. 3, pp. 15–21.

—— (1995) 'Europe and East Asia: A Trade Relationship Examined', *European Business Review*, vol. 95, No. 2, pp. 2–11.

Department of Trade and Industry (1991) *A Guide to European Community Industrial Research and Development Programmes*, DTI, London.

Deutscher Bundstag (1990) *Vorsorge zum Schutz der Erdatmosphare*, Second Report of the Enquete Commission on the subject 'Protection of Tropical Forests', Print No. 11/7220, 24 May.

Dicken, P. (1992) *Global Shift: The Internationalisation of Economic Activity*, PCP, London.

Donges, J.B. and Wieners, J. (1994) 'Foreign Investment in Eastern Europe's Transformation Process', in V.N. Balasubramanyam and D. Sapsford (eds) *Economics of International Investment*, Edward Elgar, Aldershot.

Dornbusch, R.W. (1990) 'Policy Options for Freer Trade: The Case of Bilateralism', in R. Lawrence and C. Schultze (eds) *An American Trade Strategy*, The Brookings Institute, Washington DC.

Dosi, G. (1988) 'Sources, Procedures and Microeconomic Effects of Innovation', *Journal of Economic Literature*, vol. 26, pp. 1120–1171.

Douglas, S.P. and Wind, Y. (1987) 'The Myth of Globalisation', *Columbia Journal of World Business*, winter, pp. 19–29.

Doz, Y. (1980) 'Strategic Management in Multinational Companies', *Sloan Management Review*, vol. 21, pp. 27–46.

—— (1987) 'International Industries: Fragmentation Versus Globalisation', in B.K. Guile and H. Brooks (eds) *Technology and Global Industry*, National Academic Press, Washington DC.

Drabek, Z. and Greenaway, D. (1984) 'Economic Integration and Intra-industry Trade: the CMEA and the EEC compared', *Kyklos*, vol. 37, pp. 444–469.

Dreze, J. and Bean, C.R. (eds) (1990) *Europe's Unemployment Problem*, MIT Press, Massachusetts.

Dreze, J. and Malinvaud, E. (1994) 'Growth and Employment: The Scope of a European Initiative', *European Economic Review*, vol. 38, pp. 489–504.

Drucker, P.F. (1986) 'The Changed World Economy', *The McKinsey Quarterly*, autumn, pp. 2–26.

Dudley, J. (1993) *1993 and Beyond: Strategies for the Enlarged Single Market*, Kogan Page, London.

Dunning, J.H. (1972) *The Location of International Firms in an Enlarged EEC: An Exploratory Paper*, Manchester Statistical Society, Manchester.

—— (1983) 'Changes in the Level and Structure of International Production', in M. Casson (ed.) *The Growth of International Business*, Allen and Unwin, London.

—— (1988) *Explaining International Production*, Unwin Hyman, London.

—— (1993) *The Globalisation of Business*, Routledge, London.

Dunning, J.H. and Cantwell, J.A. (1991) 'Japanese Direct Investment in Europe', in B. Burgenmeier and J.L. Mucchielli (eds) *Multinationals and Europe 1992*, Routledge, London.

Dunning, J.H. and Robson, P. (1988) 'Multinational Corporate Integration and Regional Economic Integration', in J.H. Dunning and P. Robson (eds) *Multinationals and the European Community*, Blackwell, Oxford.

EBRD (1995) *Transition Report 1994: Economic Transition in Eastern Europe and the Former Soviet Union*, EBRD, London.

Economist (1995) *Pocket World of Figures: 1995*, The Economist, London.

Economist Intelligence Unit (1995) *World Outlook 1994*, EIU, London.

ECOTEC (1995) *Sustainability, Employment and Growth – The Employment Impact of Environmental Policies*, ECOTEC, Birmingham.

EFTA Secretariat (1972) *The Trade Effects of EFTA and the EEC, 1959–1967*, EFTA, Geneva.

Eichengreen, B. (1990) 'One Money for Europe? Lessons from the US Currency Union', *Economic Policy*, April, pp. 117–189.

Ekins, P. (1994) 'World Trade and the Environment', *European Environment*, vol. 4, pp. 4–8.

El-Agraa, A. (1992) 'Japan's Reaction to the Single Internal Market', in J. Redmond (ed.) *The External Relations of the EC*, Macmillan, London.

Emerson, M. and Huhne, C. (1991) *The ECU Report*, Pan, London.

Ernst, D. and O'Connor, D. (1992) *Competing in the Electronics Industry*, OECD, Paris.

European Industrial Relations Review (1994) 'Social Policy White Paper – Part One', No. 248, September.

—— (1995a) 'The Commission's Work Programme', No. 255, April.

—— (1995b) 'Survey of International Labour Costs', No. 259, August.

Flamm, K. (1993) 'Coping with Strategic Competition in Semiconductors: The EC Model as an International Framework', in M. Hubert (ed.) *The Impact of Globalisation on Europe's Firms and Industries*, Pinter, London.

Flanagan, R.J. (1987) 'Labour Market Behaviour and European Economic Growth', in R.Z. Lawrence and C.L. Schultz (eds) *Barriers to European Growth: A Trans-Atlantic View*, Brookings Institution, Washington DC.

Fleming, D. (1992) 'Eco-labelling', *European Environment*, vol. 2, pp. 6–7.

—— (1994) 'Towards the Low-output Economy: The Future that the Delors White Paper Tries Not to Face', *European Environment*, vol. 4, pp. 11–16.

Franz, W. (1995) 'If the Labour Market is So Dynamic, Where Do All the Problems Come From?', *European Brief*, February.

Freeman, C. (1987a) 'The Challenge of New Technologies', in OECD, *Interdependence and Co-operation in Tomorrow's World*, OECD, Paris.

—— (1987b) *Technology Policy and Economic Performance: Lessons from Japan*, Pinter, London.

Freeman, C. and Hagedoorn, J. (1995) 'Convergence and Divergence in the Internationalisation of Technology', in J. Hagedoorn (ed.) *Technical Change and the World Economy*, Edward Elgar, Aldershot.

Frobel, F., Heinricks, J. and Kreye, O. (1980) *The New International Division of Labour*, Cambridge University Press, Cambridge.

GATT (1992) *International Trade Report 1990/91: Trade and the Environment*, Geneva.

Gold, M. (ed.) (1993) *The Social Dimension: Employment Policy in the European Community*, Macmillan, London.

Grabbendorff, W. (1990) 'Relations with Central and South America: A Question of Over-reach?', in G. Edwards and E. Regelberger (eds) *Europe's Global Links: The European Community and Inter-Regional Cooperation*, Pinter, London.

Grahl, J. and Teague, P. (1995) 'Employment and Competitiveness', *Jean Monnet Group Discussion Paper*, University of Hull Centre for European Union Studies, Hull.

Granell, F. (1994) 'The Enlargement of the European Union and the ACP Countries', *The Courier*, No.146, pp. 6–8.

Grant, R.J., Papadakis, M.C. and Richardson, J.D. (1993) 'Global Trade Flows: Old Structures, New Issues, Empirical Evidence', in C.F. Bergsten and M. Noland (eds) *Pacific Dynamism and the International Economic System*, Institute for International Economics, Washington DC.

Grant, W. (1992) *Economic Globalisation, Stateless Firms and International Governance*, Working Paper No. 105 (Dept of Politics and International Studies) University of Warwick.

Greenaway, D. (1987) 'Intra-industry Trade, Intra-firm Trade and European Integration: Evidence, Gains and Policy Aspects', *Journal of Common Market Studies*, vol. 26, pp. 153–172.

—— (1989) 'Regional Trading Agreements and Intra-industry Trade: Evidence and Policy Issues', in D. Greenaway, T. Hyclak and R. Thornton (eds) *Economic Aspects of Regional Trading Agreements*, Harvester Wheatsheaf, Hemel Hempstead.

—— (1991) 'GATT and Multilateral Trade Liberalisation: Knocked Out in the Eighth Round?', *Economics*, Journal of Economics Association, vol. 27, 3, 115, pp. 100–106.

—— (1993) 'Trade and Foreign Direct Investment', *European Economy*, No. 52, Office for Official Publications for the EC, Luxembourg.

Greenaway, D. and Hine, R. (1991) 'Intra-industry Specialisation, Trade Expansion and Adjustment in the European Economic Space', *Journal of Common Market Studies*, vol. 29, pp. 603–622.

Griliches, Z. (ed.) (1984) *R&D, Patents and Productivity*, NBER/Chicago University Press, Chicago.

Grilli, E.R. (1993) *The European Community and the Developing Countries*, Cambridge University Press, Cambridge.

Grubb, M. (1989) *The Greenhouse Effect: Negotiating Targets*, Royal Institute of International Affairs, London.

Grubel, H. (1967) 'Intra-industry Specialisation and the Pattern of Trade', *Canadian Journal of Economics and Political Science*, vol. 22, pp. 374–388.

Haaland, J. (1990) 'Assessing the Effects of EC Integration on the EFTA Countries: The Position of Norway and Sweden', *Journal of Common Market Studies*, vol. 28, pp. 379–400.

Haaland, J. and Norman, V. (1992) 'Global Production Effects of European Integration', in L.A. Winters (ed.) *Trade Flows and Trade Policies After 1992*, Cambridge University Press, Cambridge.

Hagedoorn, J. (1993) 'Understanding the Rationale of Strategic Technology

Partnering: Inter-organisational Modes of Cooperation and Sectoral Differences', *Strategic Management Journal*, vol. 13, pp. 371–385.

Hagedoorn, J. and Schakenraad, J. (1990) 'Leading Companies and the Structure of Strategic Alliances in Core Technologies', *MERIT Working Paper*, Maastricht.

—— (1992) 'Leading Companies and Networks of Strategic Alliances in Information Technology', *Research Policy*, vol. 21, pp. 163–190.

—— (1993) 'Strategic Technology Partnering and International Corporate Strategies', in K. Hughes (ed.) *European Competitiveness*, Cambridge University Press, Cambridge.

—— (1994) 'The Internationalisation of the Economy, Global Strategies and Strategic Technology Alliances', in U. Muldur and R. Petrella (eds) *The European Community and the Globalisation of Technology and the Economy*, CEC, Brussels.

Hager, W. (1974) 'The Mediterranean: A European Mare Nostrum?' *Orbis*, spring.

Hare, P. (1993) 'Competitiveness and Restructuring: Issues for Eastern Europe', *British Review of Economic Issues*, vol. 15, pp. 43–65.

Harrison, D. (1993) 'Who Wins and Who Loses from Economic Instruments', *OECD Observer*, No. 180, pp. 29–31.

Hayes, J.P. (1993) *Making Trade Policy in the European Community*, Macmillan, London.

Heenan, D.A. and Perlmutter, H.V. (1979) *Multinational Organisational Development: A Social Architecture Perspective*, Addison-Wesley, Massachusetts.

Heffernan, S. and Sinclair, P. (1990) *Modern International Economics*, Blackwell, Oxford.

Heitger, B. and Stehn, J. (1990) 'Japanese Direct Investment in the EC – Response to the Internal Market 1993?', *Journal of Common Market Studies*, vol. 29, pp. 1–15.

Henderson, D. (1995) 'International Economic Integration: Progress, Prospects and Implications', in J. Drew (ed.) *Readings in the International Enterprise*, Routledge, London.

Hillman, A.L. and Ursprung, H.W. (1992) 'The Influence of Environmental Concerns on the Political Determination of Trade Policy', in K. Anderson and R. Blackhurst (eds) *The Greening of World Trade Issues*, Harvester Wheatsheaf, Hemel Hempstead.

Hine, R.C. (1985) *The Political Economy of European Trade*, Wheatsheaf, Brighton.

—— (1992) 'Regionalism and the Integration of the World Economy', *Journal of Common Market Studies*, vol. 30, pp. 115–123.

Hirst, P. (1993) *Associative Democracy: New Forms of Economic and Social Governance*, Polity Press, Cambridge.

Hitiris, T. (1991) *European Community Economics*, Harvester Wheatsheaf, Hemel Hempstead.

Hoekman, B. (1993) 'New Issues in the Uruguay Round', *Economic Journal*, vol. 103, pp. 1528–1539.

Holmes, P. (1993) 'Trade, Competition and Technology Policy', in M. Hubert (ed.) *The Impact of Globalisation on Europe's Firms and Industries*, Pinter, London.

Hood, N. and Young, S. (1987) 'Inward Investment and the EC: UK Evidence on Corporate Integration Strategies', *Journal of Common Market Studies*, vol. 26, pp. 193–206.

Howells, J. and Wood, M. (1994) *The Globalisation of Production and Technology*, Belhaven, London.

Hufbauer, G.C. (ed.) (1990) *Europe 1992: An American Perspective*, Brookings Institute, Washington DC.

Huszagh, S., Fox, R. and Day, E. (1985) 'Global Marketing: An Empirical Investigation', *Columbia Journal of World Business*, twentieth anniversary issue, pp. 31–43.

Hymer, S. (1976) *The International Operations of National Firms*, MIT Press, Massachusetts.

Ishikawa, K. (1990) *Japan and the Challenge of Europe 1992*, Pinter, London.

Jackman, R., Pissarides, C. and Savouri, S. (1990) 'Labour Market Policies and Unemployment in the OECD', *Economic Policy*, vol. 5, pp. 450–490.

Jacoby, N.H. (1984) 'The Multinational Corporation', in P.D. Grub *et al.* (eds) *The Multinational Enterprise in Transition*, Darwin Press, Princeton.

Jacquemin, A. (1986) 'Exchanges Internationaux et Strategies Collusives', *Recherches Economiques de Louvain*, vol. 1.

Jacquemin, A. and Sapir, A. (1991) 'Europe post-1992: Internal and External Liberalisation', *American Economic Review*, vol. 81, pp. 166–170.

Janicke, M., Monch, H., Ranneburg, T. and Simmonis, U. (1989) 'Economic Structure and Environmental Impacts: East–West Comparisons', *The Environmentalist*, vol. 9.

Jansen, E. and De Vree, J.K. (1985) *The Ordeal of Unity, The Politics of European Integration 1945–1985*, Prime Press, Bilthoven.

Johnson, H.G. (1965) 'An Economic Theory of Protectionism, Tariff Bargaining and the Formation of Customs Unions', *Journal of Political Economy*, vol. 73, pp. 256–283.

Jorgensen, K.E. (1993) 'The European Community and Eastern Europe', in O. Norgaard *et al.* (eds) *The European Community in World Politics*, Pinter, London.

Julius, D. and Thomsen, S. (1988) *Foreign Direct Investment among the G5*, Discussion Paper No. 8, Royal Institute of International Affairs, London.

Kaikati, J. (1990) 'European Integration and Japan: Trade and Investment Issues', *Journal of European Integration*, vol. 14, pp. 31–39.

Kastrinos, N. (1994) *The EC Framework Programme and the Technological Strategies of European Firms*, Office for Official Publications for the EC, Luxembourg.

Kay, J. (1990) 'Mergers in the European Community', in London Business School, *Continental Mergers are Different*, London Business School, London.

Kemp, M. and Wan, H. (1976) 'An Elementary Proposition Concerning the Formation of Customs Unions', *Journal of International Economics*, vol. 6, pp. 95–97.

Kenen, P. (1969) 'The Theory of Optimum Currency Areas: An Eclectic View', in R.A. Mundell and A.K. Swoboda (eds) *Monetary Problems of the International Economy*, Chicago University Press, Chicago.

Kindleberger, C. (1956) 'European Integration and the International Corporation', *Columbia Journal of World Business*, vol. 1, pp. 65–73.

—— (1969) *American Business Abroad: Six Lectures on Direct Investment*, Yale University Press, New Haven.

—— (1973) *The World in Depression, 1929–39*, University of California Press, Berkley.

—— (1988) 'The New Multinationalisation of Business', *ASEAN Economic Bulletin*, No. 5, pp. 113–124.

Kogut, B., Walker, G., Shan, W. and Kim, D. (1995) 'Platform Technologies and National Industrial Networks', in J. Hagedoorn (ed.) *Technical Change and the World Economy*, Edward Elgar, Aldershot.

Kok, E. and Saint Bris, H. (1994) 'Voluntary Environmental Initiatives in Industry: What Role for EMAS?', *European Environment*, vol. 4, pp. 14–17.

Komine, T. (1993) 'The Role of Economic Planning in Japan', in J. Teranishi and Y. Kosai (eds) *The Japanese Experience of Economic Reform*, Macmillan, London.

Koutstaal, P. and Nentjes, A. (1995) 'Tradable Carbon Permits in Europe: Feasibility and Comparison with Taxes', *Journal of Common Market Studies*, vol. 33, pp. 219–233.

Kowalczyk, C. and Sjostrom, T. (1994) 'Bringing GATT into the Core', *Economica*, vol. 61, pp. 301–317.

Kramer, H. (1993) 'The European Community's Response to the New Eastern Europe', *Journal of Common Market Studies*, vol. 31, pp. 213–244.

Krasner, S.D. (1985) *Structural Conflict: The Third World Against Global Liberalism*, University of California Press, Berkeley.

Krauss, M. (1973) *The Economics of Integration*, Allen and Unwin, London.

Krugman, P. (1991) 'The International Role of the Dollar: Theory and Prospect', in J. Bilson and R. Marston (eds) *Exchange Rate Theory and Practice*, University of Chicago Press, Chicago.

Kummer, K. (1994) 'Providing Incentives to Comply with Multilateral Environmental Agreements: An Alternative to Sanctions', *European Environmental Law Review*, October, pp. 256–257.

Lam, A. (1994) 'The Integration of European Labour Markets: A Japanese Perspective', *Social Europe*, Supplement 1/94, CEC, Brussels.

Lane, S. (1994) *The Pattern of Foreign Direct Investment and Joint Ventures in Hungary*, Working Paper No. 94-04, Boston University School of Management, Boston.

Lanvin, B. (1990) 'Technology and Competitiveness', paper at OECD conference 'Technoglobalism', OECD, Paris.

Latter, R. (1989) *The Interdependent Triad: Japan, the United States and Europe*, Wilton Park Papers No.19, HMSO, London.

Lawrence, R. (1991) 'Emerging Regional Arrangements: Building Blocks or Stumbling Blocks', in R. O'Brien (ed.) *Finance and the International Economy*, The Amex Bank Review Prize Essays, Oxford University Press, Oxford.

Layard, R. and Nickell, S. (1991) 'Unemployment in the OECD Countries', Institute of Economics and Statistics, Oxford Paper No. 130, December.

Layard, R., Nickell, S. and Jackman, R. (1991) *Unemployment, Macroeconomic Performance and the Labour Market*, Oxford University Press, Oxford.

Levitt, T. (1983) 'The Globalisation of Markets', *Harvard Business Review*, May–June, pp. 92–102.

Lindbeck, A. and Snower, D. (1988) 'Cooperation, Harassment and Involuntary Unemployment: an Insider–Outsider Approach', *American Economic Review*, vol. 78, pp. 167–188.

—— (1991) *Patterns of Unemployment: An Insider–Outsider Analysis*, mimeo, Stockholm.

Lipsey, R.G. (1957) 'The Theory of Customs Unions: Trade Diversion and Welfare', *Economica*, 24.

—— (1970) *The Theory of Customs Unions: A General Equilibrium Analysis*, Weidenfeld and Nicolson, London.

Lipton, D. and Sachs, J. (1990) 'Creating a Market Economy in Eastern Europe: The Case of Poland', *Brookings Papers on Economic Activity*, vol. 1, pp. 75–133.

Lodge, J. (1992) 'New Zealand, Australia and 1992', in J. Redmond (ed.) *The External Relations of the EC*, Macmillan, London.

Lundvall, B. (1989) 'Innovation, the Organised Market and the Productivity

Slowdown', paper at OECD conference 'The Contribution of Science and Technology to Economic Growth', OECD, Paris.

Luukkonen, T., Persson, O. and Sivertsen, G. (1992) 'An Outline for Understanding Patterns of International Scientific Collaboration', *Science, Technology and Human Values*, vol. 17, pp. 101–126.

McKinnon, R.I. (1963) 'Optimum Currency Areas', *American Economic Review*, vol. 53, pp. 717–724.

McMillan, C.H. (1991) 'Foreign Direct Investment Flows in the Soviet Union and Eastern Europe: Nature, Magnitude and International Implications', *Journal of Development Planning*, No. 20.

Madeley, J. (1992) *Trade and the Poor*, Intermediate Technology Group, London.

Major, R.L. and Hayes, S. (1970) 'Another Look at the Common Market', *National Institute Economic Review*, London.

Malecki, E.J. (1991) *Technology and Economic Development: The Dynamics of Local, Regional and National Change*, Longman Scientific and Technical, Harlow.

Malerba, F., Morawetz, A. and Pasqui, G. (1994) 'International Co-operation Between Universities, Research Organisations and Industry', in U. Muldur and R. Petrella (eds) *The European Community and the Globalisation of Technology and the Economy*, CEC, Brussels.

Malthus, T. (1830) *A Summary View of the Principle of Population*, Penguin, Harmondsworth.

Marginson, P. and Sisson, K. (1994) 'The Structure of Transnational Capital in Europe: The Emerging Euro-company and its Implications for Industrial Relations', in R. Hyman and A. Ferner (eds) *New Frontiers in European Industrial Relations*, Blackwell, Oxford.

Marin, A. (1994) 'The Lomé Convention', in A.M. El-Agraa (ed.) *The Economics of the European Community*, Harvester Wheatsheaf, Hemel Hempstead.

Markheim, D. (1994) 'A Note on Predicting the Effects of Economic Integration and Other Preferential Trade Agreements: An Assessment', *Journal of Common Market Studies*, vol. 32, pp. 103–110.

Marsden, D. (1994) 'The Integration of European Labour Markets', *Social Europe*, Supplement 1/94, CEC, Brussels.

Masera, R. (1994) 'Single Market, Exchange Rates and Monetary Integration', in A. Steinherr (ed.) *Thirty Years of European Monetary Integration*, Longman, London.

Mayes, D. (1978) 'The Effects of Economic Integration on Trade', *Journal of Common Market Studies*, vol. 17, pp. 1–25.

—— (1994) 'Enlargement', in A. El-Agraa (ed.) *The Economics of the European Community*, Harvester Wheatsheaf, Hemel Hempstead.

Meade, J.E. (1955) *The Theory of Customs Unions*, North Holland, Amsterdam.

—— (1957) 'The Balance of Payments Problems of a European Free Trade Area', *Economic Journal*, vol. 67, pp. 379–396.

Merriden, T. (1994) 'How Will the EFTA Four Affect the EU Twelve?', *EIU European Trends*, second quarter, pp. 53–62

Messerlin, P. (1992) 'Trade Policies in France', in D. Salvadore (ed.) *Handbook of Comparative Economic Policies: National Trade Policies*, vol. 2, Greenwood Press, New York.

Meyer, K. (1994) *Direct Foreign Investment in Central and Eastern Europe: Understanding the Statistical Evidence*, Discussion Paper No. 12, CIS-Middle Europe Centre, London Business School, London.

Michalski, W. (1991) 'Trends and Developments in the Globalisation of

Production, Investment and Trade', in OECD, *Trade, Investment and Technology in the 1990s*, OECD, Paris.

Miege, R. (1995) 'The Future of Research and Technology Organisations in Europe', *Euro Abstracts*, vol. 33, pp. 173–178.

Milner, C. and Allen, D. (1992) 'The External Implications of 1992', in D. Swann (ed.) *The Single European Market and Beyond*, Routledge, London.

Milward, A.S. (1984) *The Reconstruction of Western Europe 1945–51*, Methuen, London.

Minford, P. (1992) 'What Price European Monetary Union?', *Economics*, autumn.

Minikin, R. (1993) *The ERM Explained*, Kogan Page, London.

Modigliani, F. (1986) 'Life Cycle, Individual Thrift and the Wealth of Nations', *American Economic Review*, vol. 76, pp. 297–313.

Molle, W. (1990) *The Economics of European Integration*, Dartmouth, Aldershot.

Molle, W. and Morsink, R. (1991) 'Intra-European Direct Investment' in B. Burgenmeier and J.L. Mucchielli (eds) *Multinationals and Europe 1992*, Routledge, London.

Mols, M. (1990) 'Co-operation with ASEAN: A Success Story', in G. Edwards and E. Regelberger (eds) *Europe's Global Links: The European Community and Inter-regional Cooperation*, Pinter, London.

Morris, J. (ed.) (1991) *Japan and the Global Economy*, Routledge, London.

Muldur, U. and Petrella, R. (eds) (1994) *The European Community and the Globalisation of Technology and the Economy*, CEC, Brussels.

Mundell, R.A. (1961) 'A Theory of Optimum Currency Areas', *American Economic Review*, vol. 53, pp. 657–664.

Murphy, J. and Gouldson, A. (1995) 'The Missing Dimension in EU Environmental Technology Policy', *European Environment*, vol. 5, pp. 20–26.

Myrdal, G. (1956) *An International Economy, Problems and Prospects*, Harper and Bros, New York.

Mytelka, L.K. (1979) *Regional Development in a Global Economy: The Multinational Corporation, Technology and Andean Integration*, Yale University Press, New Haven.

—— (1984) 'La Gestion de la Connaissance dans les Enterprises Multinationales: Vers la Formation d'Oligopoles Technologiques', *Economie, Prospective Internationale*, No. 20.

—— (1993) 'Strengthening the Relevance of European Science and Technology Programmes to Industrial Competitiveness: The Case of ESPRIT', in M. Hubert (ed.) *The Impact of Globalisation on Europe's Firms and Industries*, Pinter, London.

—— (1995) 'Dancing with Wolves: Global Oligopolies and Strategic Partnerships', in J. Hagedoorn (ed.) *Technical Change and the World Economy*, Edward Elgar, Aldershot.

Nelson, R. (1987) *Understanding Technical Change as Evolutionary Process*, North Holland, Amsterdam.

Nguyen, T., Perroni, C. and Wigle, R. (1993) 'An Evaluation of the Draft Act of the Uruguay Round', *Economic Journal*, vol. 103, pp. 1540–1549.

Nicolaides, P. and Close, A. (1994) 'The Process and Politics of Enlargement', *EIU European Trends*, first quarter, pp. 70–81.

Nicolaides, P. and Thomsen, S. (1991) 'Can Protectionism Explain Direct Investment?', *Journal of Common Market Studies*, vol. 29, pp. 635–643.

Norman, V. (1989) 'EFTA and the Integrated European Market', *Economic Policy*, vol. 9, pp. 423–466.

—— (1991) '1992 and EFTA', in L.A. Winters and A.J. Venables (eds) *European Integration: Trade and Industry*, Cambridge University Press. Cambridge.

Nugent, N. (1992) 'The Deepening and Widening of the European Community: Recent Evolution, Maastricht and Beyond', *Journal of Common Market Studies*, vol. 30, pp. 311–328.

Nuttall, S. (1990) 'The Commission: Protagonists of Inter-Regional Cooperation', in G. Edwards and E. Regelberger (eds) *Europe's Global Links: The European Community and Inter-Regional Cooperation*, Pinter, London.

O'Cleireacain, S. (1990) 'Europe 1992 and Gaps in the EC's Common Commercial Policy', *Journal of Common Market Studies*, vol. 28, pp. 201–217.

OECD (1989a) *International Direct Investment and New Economic Environment*, OECD, Paris.

—— (1989b) *Main Science and Technology Indicators*, OECD, Paris.

—— (1989c) *Economic Instruments for Environmental Protection*, OECD, Paris.

—— (1991a) *Technology in a Changing World*, OECD, Paris.

—— (1991b) *Environmental Policy: How to Apply Economic Instruments*, OECD, Paris.

—— (1992a) *Technology and the Economy*, OECD, Paris.

—— (1992b) *Integration of Developing Countries into the International Trading System*, OECD, Paris.

—— (1992c) *Globalisation of Industrial Activities*, OECD, Paris.

—— (1992d) *The Costs of Reducing CO_2 Emissions: Evidence from Green*, paper of the Working party No. 1 of the Economic Policy Committee, OECD, Paris.

—— (1993) *Employment Outlook: 1993*, OECD, Paris.

—— (1994a) *Employment Outlook: 1994*, OECD, Paris.

—— (1994b) *The Performance of Foreign Affiliates in OECD Countries*, OECD, Paris.

—— (1994c) *Jobs Study: Facts, Analysis and Strategies*, OECD, Paris.

—— (1995a) *Economic Outlook: June 1995*, OECD, Paris.

—— (1995b) *Education Indicators at a Glance*, OECD, Paris.

Office of Technology Assessment, US Congress (1993) *Multinationals and the National Interest*, US Government Printing Office, Washington DC.

Ohmae, K. (1985a) 'Becoming a Triad Power: The New Global Corporation', *The McKinsey Quarterly*, spring, pp. 2–25.

—— (1985b) *Triad Power: The Coming Shape of Global Competition*, Free Press, New York.

—— (1990) *Borderless World: Power and Strategy in the Interlinked Economy*, Collins, London.

Ostry, S. (1990) *Governments and Corporations in a Shrinking World: Trade and Innovation Policies in the US, Europe and Japan*, Council on Foreign Relations, New York.

—— (1991) 'Beyond the Border: The New International Policy Arena', in OECD *Strategic Industries in a Global Economy: Policy Issues for the 1990s*, OECD, Paris.

Owen, N. (1983) *Economies of Scale, Competitiveness and Trade Patterns within the European Community*, Claredon Press, Oxford.

Oxfam (1993) *Africa, Make or Break: Action for Recovery*, Oxfam, Oxford.

Ozawa, T. (1991) 'Japanese Multinationals and 1992', in B. Burgenmeier and J.L. Mucchielli (eds) *Multinationals and Europe 1992*, Routledge, London.

Padoa-Schioppa, F. (1991) *Mismatch and Labour Mobility*, Cambridge University Press, Cambridge.

Pardoe, G., Green, F., Fawcett, J. and White, L. (1992) *Technology and the Future of Europe*, Office for Official Publications for the EC, Luxembourg.

Patel, P. and Pavitt, K. (1991) 'Europe's Technological Performance', in C. Freeman,

M. Sharp and W. Walker (eds) *Technology and the Future of Europe: Global Competition and the Environment in the 1990s*, Pinter, London.

—— (1995) 'Divergence in Technological Development among Countries and Firms', in J. Hagedoorn (ed.) *Technical Change and the World Economy*, Edward Elgar, Aldershot.

Pearce, J. and Sutton, J. (1985) *Protection and Industrial Policy in Europe*, Routledge, London.

Pearce, R. and Singh, S. (1992) *Globalising Research and Development*, Macmillan, London.

Pedersen, T. (1994) *European Union and the EFTA Countries: Enlargement and Integration*, Pinter, London.

Pelkmans, J. (1984) *Market Integration in the European Community*, Martinus Nijhoff, The Hague.

Peterson, J. (1993) *Europe and America in the 1990s*, Edward Elgar, Aldershot.

Pinder, J. (1993) 'The European Community and Investment in Central and Eastern Europe', in P. Artisien, M. Rojec and M. Svetlicic (eds) *Foreign Investment in Central and Eastern Europe*, Macmillan, London.

Pio, A. and Vannini, A. (1992) 'European Investment in Developing Countries: Recent Trends and the Potential Impact of Project 1992', in S. Sideri and J. Sengupta (eds) *The 1992 Single European Market and the Third World*, Frank Cass, London.

Pitelis, C.N. and Sugden, R. (1991) 'On the Theory of the Transnational Firm', in C.N. Pitelis and R. Sugden (eds) *The Nature of the Transnational Firm*, Routledge, London.

Pollard, S. (1974) *European Economic Integration 1815–1970*, Thames and Hudson, London.

Pomfret, R. (1992) 'The European Community's Relations with the Mediterranean Countries', in J. Redmond (ed.) *The External Relations of the European Community: The International Response to 1992*, St. Martin's Press, London.

Porter, M. (1980) *Competitive Strategy: Techniques for Analysing Industries and Competitors*, Free Press, New York.

—— (1985) *Competitive Advantage*, Free Press, New York.

—— (1986a) 'Changing Patterns of International Competition', *California Management Review*, vol. 28, pp. 9–40.

—— (1986b) 'Competition in Global Industries', in M. Porter (ed.) *Competition in Global Industries*, Harvard Business School Press, Boston.

—— (1990) *The Competitive Advantage of Nations*, Macmillan, London.

Poynter, T.A. (1986) 'Political Risk: Managing Government Intervention', *Columbia Journal of World Business*, winter.

Preston, J. (1992) 'Education and Vocational Training Policy', in A. Griffiths (ed.) *European Community Survey*, Longman, London.

Prewo, W.E. (1974) 'Integration Effects in the EEC: An Attempt at Quantification in a General Equilibrium Framework', *European Economic Review*, vol. 3, pp. 379–405.

Pryce, R. (1973) *The Politics of the European Community*, Butterworth, London.

Psacharopoulos, G. (1993) *Returns to Investment in Education: A Global Update*, Policy Research Working Paper No. 1067, World Bank, New York.

Quelch, J. *et al.* (1992), *The Marketing Challenge of Europe 1992*, Addison Wesley, Wokingham.

Radice, H. (1995) 'The Role of Foreign Direct Investment in the Transformation of Eastern Europe', in H.J. Chang and P. Nolan (eds) *The Transformation of the Communist Economies: Against the Mainstream*, Macmillan, London.

Rainbird, H. (1993) 'Vocational Education and Training', in M. Gold (ed.) *The*

Social Dimension: Employment Policy in the European Community, Macmillan, London.

Redmond, J. (1993) *The Next Mediterranean Enlargement of the European Community: Turkey, Cyprus and Malta*, Dartmouth, Aldershot.

Regelsberger, E. (1990) 'The Dialogue of the EC/Twelve with the Other Regional Groups: A New European Identity in the International System?', in G. Edwards and E. Regelberger (eds) *Europe's Global Links: The European Community and Inter-regional Co-operation*, Pinter, London.

Reich, R. (1991) *The Work of Nations*, Knopf, New York.

Reinicke, W.H. (1996) *Deepening the Atlantic: Towards a New Trans-Atlantic Marketplace*, Bertelsmann Foundation, Gütersloh.

Ricardo, D. (1817) *The Principles of Political Economy and Taxation*, Cambridge University Press, Cambridge.

Robson, P. (1987) *The Economics of International Integration*, Allen and Unwin, London.

Robson, P. and Wooton, I. (1993) 'The Transnational Enterprise and Regional Economic Integration', *Journal of Common Market Studies*, vol. 31, pp. 71–90.

Rollo, J. (1995) 'EU Enlargement and the World Trade System', *European Economic Review*, vol. 39, pp. 467–473.

Rugman, A.M. and Verbeke, A. (1990) *Global Corporate Strategy and Trade Policy*, Routledge, London.

—— (1991) 'Competitive Strategies for Non-European Firms', in B. Burgenmeier and J.L. Mucchielli (eds) *Multinationals and Europe 1992*, Routledge, London.

Runnalls, D. and Cosbey, A. (1992) *Trade and Sustainable Development: A Survey of the Issues and a New Research Agenda*, International Institute for Sustainable Development, Winnipeg.

Rychetnik, L. (1992) *The Transition to a Market Economy in Central/Eastern Europe: Opportunities and Problems*, University of Reading Discussion Paper in European and International Social Science Research, No. 49, March.

Sachwald, F. (ed.) (1994) *European Integration and Competitiveness*, Edward Elgar, Aldershot.

Salzman, J. (1991) 'Green Labels for Consumers', *OECD Observer*, No. 169, pp. 28–30.

Sandholtz, W. and Zysman, J. (1989) '1992: Recasting the European Bargain', *World Politics*, vol. 62, pp. 95–128.

Sapir, A. (1992) 'Regional Integration in Europe', *Economic Journal*, vol. 102, pp. 1491–1506.

Saucier, P. (1991) 'New Conditions for Competition between Japanese and European Firms', in B. Burgenmeier and J.L. Mucchielli (eds) *Multinationals and Europe 1992*, Routledge, London.

Saxonhouse, G. (1983) 'The Micro- and Macro-economics of Foreign Sales to Japan', in W. Cline (ed.) *Trade Policy in the 1980s*, Institute for International Economics, Washington DC.

Schienstock, G. (1994) 'Technological Policy in the Process of Change: Changing Paradigms in Research and Technology Policy', in G. Aicholzer and G. Schienstock (eds) *Technology Policy: Towards Integration of Social and Ecological Concerns*, Walter de Gruyer, Berlin.

Schmitt, N. (1990) 'New International Trade Theories and Europe 1992: Some Relevant Results for EFTA Countries', *Journal of Common Market Studies*, vol. 29, pp. 62–73.

Schmookler, J. (1966) *Invention and Economic Growth*, Harvard University Press, Massachusetts.

Schmuck, O. (1990) 'The Lomé Convention: A Model of Partnership', in G. Edwards and E. Regelberger (eds) *Europe's Global Links: The European Community and Inter-Regional Co-operation*, Pinter, London.

Schumpeter, J.A. (1942) *Capitalism, Socialism and Democracy*, London: Allen and Unwin.

Selincourt, K. and Thussu, D.K. (1994) 'GATT and the Global Environment: The View From the South', *European Environment*, vol. 4, pp. 9–10.

Sengenberger, W. (1994) 'Protection – Participation – Promotion: The Systematic Nature and Effects of Labour Standards', in W. Sengenberger and D. Campbell (eds) *Creating Economic Opportunities: The Role of Labour Standards in Industrial Restructuring*, International Institute for Labour Studies, Geneva.

Servan-Schreiber, J.J. (1968) *The American Challenge*, Hamish Hamilton, London.

Sharp, M. and Pavitt, K. (1993) 'Technology Policy in the 1990s: Old Trends and New Realities', *Journal of Common Market Studies*, vol. 31, pp. 129–51.

Shunker, A., Salles, J-M. and Rios-Velilla, C. (1992) 'Innovative Mechanisms for Exploiting International CO_2 Emission Abatement Cost Differences', *European Economy*, special edition No. 1, Office for Official Publications for the EC, Luxembourg.

Silvestre, J.J. (1994) 'The Integration of the European Labour Market: Reflections on the Forms, Actors and Structures of Mobility', *Social Europe*, Supplement 1/94, CEC, Brussels.

Skak, M. (1993) 'The EC Policy of the Visegrad Countries', in O. Norgaard *et al.* (eds) *The European Community in World Politics*, Pinter, London.

Smith, A. (1776) *The Wealth of Nations*, Penguin, Harmondsworth.

Smith, A. (1993) *Russia and the World Economy: Problems of Integration*, Routledge, London.

Smith, M. (1993a) 'The North American Free Trade Agreement: Global Impacts', in K. Anderson and R. Blackhurst (eds) *Regional Integration and the Global Trading System*, Harvester Wheatsheaf, Hemel Hempstead.

—— (1993b) 'The US and 1992: Responses to a Changing EC', in J. Redmond (ed.) *The External Relations of the EC*, Macmillan, London.

Smith, M. and Woolcock, S. (1993) *The US and EC in a Transformed World*, Pinter, London.

Snape, R.H. (1992) 'The Environment, International Trade and Competitiveness', in K. Anderson and R. Blackhurst (eds) *The Greening of World Trade Issues*, Harvester Wheatsheaf, Hemel Hempstead.

Sodersten, B. and Reed, G. (1994) *International Economics*, Macmillan, London.

Soskice, D. (1994) 'Labour Markets in the EC in the 1990s', *Social Europe*, Supplement 1/94, CEC, Brussels.

Srinivasan, T.N., Whalley, J. and Wooton, I. (1993) 'Measuring the Effects of Regionalism on Trade and Welfare', in K. Anderson and R. Blackhurst (eds) *Regional Integration and the Global Trading System*, Harvester Wheatsheaf, London.

Stevens, B. (1991) 'Strategic Industries: What Policies for the 1990s?' *OECD Observer*, No. 172, pp. 7–11.

Stevens, B. and Andrieu, M. (1991) 'Trade, Investment and Technology in a Changing Environment', in OECD, *Trade, Investment and Technology in the 1990s*, OECD, Paris.

Stevens, C. (1994) 'The Greening of Trade', *OECD Observer*, No. 187, pp. 32–34.

Stopford, J., Strange, S. and Henley, J.S. (1991) *Rival States, Rival Firms: Competition for World Market Shares*, Cambridge University Press, Cambridge.

Stopford, J.M. and Baden-Fuller, C. (1988) 'Regional-level Competition in a Mature Industry: the Case of European Domestic Appliances', in J.H. Dunning and P. Robson (eds) *Multinationals and the European Community*, Blackwell, Oxford.

Strange, S. (1995) 'European Business in Japan: A Policy Crossroads?', *Journal of Common Market Studies*, vol. 33, pp. 1–25.

Strubel, M. (1994) 'Environmental Policy in Europe: The Greening of Europe?', in P.M. Lutzeler (ed.) *Europe after Maastricht*, Berghahn, Oxford.

Svetlicic, M., Artisien, P. and Rojec, M. (eds) (1993) *Foreign Investment in Central and Eastern Europe*, Macmillan, London.

Symes, V. (1995) *Unemployment in Europe: Problems and Policies*, Routledge, London.

Taverne, D. (1995) *The Pension Time Bomb in Europe*, Federal Trust, London.

Teague, P. (1989) *The European Community: The Social Dimension*, Kogan Page, London.

Thomas, E. (1995) 'Developing Continuing Education and Training in European Universities', *Journal of European Industrial Training*, vol. 19, pp. 11–15.

Thomsen, S. and Nicolaides, P. (1991) *The Evolution of Japanese Direct Investment in Europe*, Harvester Wheatsheaf, Hemel Hempstead.

Thomsen, S. and Woolcock, S. (1993) *Direct Investment and European Integration: Competition among Firms and Governments*, Pinter, London.

Thurow, L. (1992) *Head to Head: The Coming Economic Battle Among Japan, Europe and America*, Nicholas Brealey, London.

Thygesen, N. (1993) 'Towards Monetary Union in Europe – Reforms of the EMS in Perspective of Monetary Union', *Journal of Common Market Studies*, vol. 31, pp. 447–472.

Tinbergen, J. (1954) *International Economic Integration*, Elsevier, Amsterdam.

Toffler, A. (1990) *Power Shift: Knowledge, Wealth and Violence at the Edge of the 21st Century*, Bantam Books, New York.

Trebilcock, M. and Howse, R. (1995) *The Regulation of International Trade*, Routledge, London.

Truman, E.M. (1969) 'The European Economic Community: Trade Creation and Trade Diversion', *Yale Economic Essays*, spring.

—— (1972) 'The Production and Trade of Manufactured Products in the EEC and EFTA: A Comparison', *European Economic Review*, vol. 3, pp. 271–290.

Tsoukalis, L. (1981) *The European Community and its Mediterranean Enlargement*, Allen and Unwin, London.

—— (1993) *The New European Economy*, Oxford University Press, Oxford.

United Nations (1991) *World Investment Report: 1991*, UN, New York.

—— (1992a) *World Investment Directory 1992, Volume II: Central and Eastern Europe*, UN, New York.

—— (1992b) *World Population Prospects: The 1992 Revision*, UN, New York.

—— (1993) *World Investment Report 1993*, UN, New York.

—— (1994a) *World Investment Report 1994*, UN, New York.

—— (1994b) *Trade and Development Report: 1994*, UN, New York.

—— (1994c) *World Economic and Social Survey 1994*, UN, New York.

—— (1994d) *International Environmental Law: Emerging Trends and Implications for Transnational Corporations*, UN, New York.

US Treasury (1995) *Survey of Current Business*, August.

Van Rompuy, P., Abraham, F. and Heremans, D. (1991) 'Economic Federalism and the EMU', *European Economy*, special edition No. 1, Office for Official Publications for the EC, Luxembourg.

Vaubel, R. (1988) 'Monetary Integration Theory', in G. Zis (ed.) *International Economics*, Longman, London.

Venturini, P. (1988) *1992: The European Social Dimension*, Office for Official Publications for the EC, Luxembourg.

Verdoorn, P.J. (1960) 'The Intra-bloc Trade of Benelux', in E.A.G. Robinson (ed.) *Economic Consequences of the Size of Nations*, Macmillan, London.

Vernon, R. (1966) 'International Investment and International Trade in the Product Cycle', *Quarterly Journal of Economics*, vol. 80, pp. 190–207.

—— (1971) *Sovereignty at Bay*, Penguin, Harmondsworth.

—— (1974) 'The Location of Economic Activity', in J.H. Dunning (ed.) *Economic Analysis and the Multinational Enterprise*, Allen and Unwin, London.

Viner, J. (1950) *The Customs Union Issue*, Steven and Sons, London.

Wallace, C.D. and Kline, J.M. (1992) *EC 92 and Changing Global Investment Patterns: Implications for the US–EC Relationship*, Center for Strategic and International Studies, Washington DC.

Warrant, F. (1994) 'Transnationalisation of R&D: A Tentative Overview', in U. Muldur and R. Petrella (eds) *The European Community and the Globalisation of Technology and the Economy*, CEC, Brussels.

Weber, A. (1909) *Theory of the Location of Industries*, University of Chicago, Chicago.

Wegberg, M.V. and Witteloostuijn, A.V. (1995) 'Multicontact Collusion in Product Markets and Joint R&D Ventures: The Case of the Information Technology Industry in an Integrating Europe', in J. Hagedoorn (ed.) *Technical Change and the World Economy*, Edward Elgar, Aldershot.

Welch, L.S. and Luostarinen, R. (1988) 'Internationalisation: Evolution of a Concept', *Journal of General Management*, vol. 14, pp. 34–55.

Welford, R. (1992) 'A Guide to Eco-labelling and the EC Eco-labelling Scheme', *European Environment*, vol. 2, pp. 13–15.

Wells, L.T. (1972) *The Product Life Cycle and International Trade*, Harvard Business School, Boston.

West, J. (1993) 'Economic Integration: Three Actors on the International Stage', *OECD Observer*, No. 180, pp. 19–22.

Whalley, J. (1992) 'CUSTA and NAFTA: Can WHFTA Be Far Behind?', *Journal of Common Market Studies*, vol. 30, pp. 125–141.

Whitehead, G.M. (1993) 'Globalisation: A Multinational Corporation's Approach to Environmental Responsibility', *European Environmental Law Review*, February, pp. 41–43.

Whitehill, A. (1991) *Japanese Management: Tradition and Transition*, Routledge, London.

Wijkman, P.M. (1993) 'The Existing Bloc Expanded? The European Community, EFTA and Eastern Europe', in C.F. Bergsten and M. Noland (eds) *Pacific Dynamism and the International Economic System*, Institute for International Economics, Washington DC.

Winters, L.A. (1992a) *The European Community: A Case of Successful Integration?*, paper presented at the World Bank and CEPR Conference on New Dimensions in Regional Integration, 2–3 April, Washington DC.

—— (ed) (1992b) *Trade Flows and Trade Policy After 1992*, Cambridge University Press, Cambridge.

—— (1993) 'Expanding EC Membership and Association Accords: Recent Experience and Future Prospects', in K. Anderson and R. Blackhurst (eds) *Regional Integration and the Global Trading System*, Harvester Wheatsheaf, Hemel Hempstead.

—— (1994) 'The EC and Protection: The Political Economy', *European Economic Review*, vol. 38(3–4), pp. 596–603.

Wise, M. and Gibb, R. (1993) *Single Market to Social Europe*, Longman Scientific and Technical, Harlow.

Wolf, M. (1994) *The Resistible Appeal of Fortress Europe*, Centre for Policy Studies, London.

Woolcock, S. (1991) *Market Access Issues in EC–US Relations: Trading Partners or Trading Blows?*, Pinter, London.

—— (1993) 'The European *Acquis* and Multilateral Trade Rules: Are They Compatible?', *Journal of Common Market Studies*, vol. 31, pp. 539–558.

—— (1995) 'Trade and the EU Commercial Policy', Jean Monnet Group Discussion Paper, University of Hull Centre for European Union Studies, Hull.

Woolcock, S. and Yamane, H. (1993) *EC–Japanese Trade Relations: What are the Rules of the Game?*, Royal Institute for International Affairs, London.

World Bank (1992) *Development and the Environment*, World Bank, Washington DC.

—— (1993) *The East Asian Miracle: Economic Growth and Public Policy*, Oxford University Press, Oxford.

World Commission on Environment and Development (1987) *Our Common Future*, Oxford University Press, Oxford.

World of Information (1995a) *The Africa Review 1995*, Kogan Page, London.

—— (1995b) *The Asia Review 1995*, Kogan Page, London.

—— (1995c) *The Europe Review 1995*, Kogan Page, London.

—— (1995d) *The Middle East Review 1995*, Kogan Page, London.

World Trade Organisation (1995) *Regionalism and the World Trading System*, WTO, Geneva.

Yamawaki, H. (1991) *Locational Decisions of Japanese Multinational Firms in European Manufacturing Industries*, mimeo, Department of Economics, Catholic University of Louvain.

Yamazawa, I. (1992) 'On Pacific Economic Integration', *Economic Journal*, vol. 102, pp. 1519–1529.

Yannopoulos, G. (1990) 'Foreign Direct Investment and European Integration: The Evidence from the Formulative Years of the European Community', *Journal of Common Market Studies*, vol. 29, pp. 235–259.

Young, S. (1992) 'European Business and Environments in the 1990s', in S. Young and J. Hamill (eds) *Europe and the Multinationals*, Edward Elgar, Aldershot.

—— (1993) 'East Asia as a Regional Force for Globalism', in K. Anderson and R. Blackhurst (eds) *Regional Integration and the Global Trading System*, Harvester Wheatsheaf, Hemel Hempstead.

Young, S. and Hood, N. (1992) 'Stimulating European Competitiveness', in S. Young and J. Hamill (eds) *Europe and the Multinationals*, Edward Elgar, Aldershot.

Young, S., McDermott, M. and Dunlop, S. (1991) 'The Challenge of the Single Market', in B. Burgenmeier and J.L. Mucchielli (eds) *Multinationals and Europe 1992*, Routledge, London.

Index